VOLUME 563

S0-ADX-541

MAY 1999

THE ANNALS

of The American Academy *of* Political
and Social Science

ALAN W. HESTON, *Editor*
NEIL A. WEINER, *Assistant Editor*

THE SILENT CRISIS
IN U.S. CHILD CARE

Special Editor of this Volume

SUZANNE W. HELBURN
University of Colorado
Denver

SAGE Periodicals Press *THOUSAND OAKS LONDON NEW DELHI*

41235498

The American Academy of Political and Social Science

3937 Chestnut Street   Philadelphia, Pennsylvania 19104

Board of Directors

ELIJAH ANDERSON	RICHARD D. LAMBERT
LYNN A. CURTIS	SARA MILLER McCUNE
FREDERICK HELDRING	MARY ANN MEYERS
KATHLEEN HALL JAMIESON	HENRY W. SAWYER, III

Editors, THE ANNALS

ALAN W. HESTON, *Editor*   RICHARD D. LAMBERT, *Editor Emeritus*
ERICA GINSBURG, *Managing Editor*   NEIL A. WEINER, *Assistant Editor*

Origin and Purpose. The Academy was organized December 14, 1889, to promote the progress of political and social science, especially through publications and meetings. The Academy does not take sides in controverted questions, but seeks to gather and present reliable information to assist the public in forming an intelligent and accurate judgment.

Meetings. The Academy occasionally holds a meeting in the spring extending over two days.

Publications. THE ANNALS of the American Academy of Political and Social Science is the bimonthly publication of The Academy. Each issue contains articles on some prominent social or political problem, written at the invitation of the editors. Also, monographs are published from time to time, numbers of which are distributed to pertinent professional organizations. These volumes constitute important reference works on the topics with which they deal, and they are extensively cited by authorities throughout the United States and abroad. The papers presented at the meetings of The Academy are included in THE ANNALS.

Membership. Each member of The Academy receives THE ANNALS and may attend the meetings of The Academy. Membership is open only to individuals. Annual dues: $59.00 for the regular paperbound edition (clothbound, $86.00). Add $12.00 per year for membership outside the U.S.A. Members may also purchase single issues of THE ANNALS for $12.00 each (clothbound, $16.00). Add $2.00 for shipping and handling on all pre-paid orders.

Subscriptions. THE ANNALS of the American Academy of Political and Social Science (ISSN 0002-7162) is published six times annually—in January, March, May, July, September, and November. Institutions may subscribe to THE ANNALS at the annual rate: $281.00 (clothbound, $332.00). Add $12.00 per year for subscriptions outside the U.S.A. Institutional rates for single issues: $49.00 each (clothbound, $57.00).

Periodicals postage paid at Thousand Oaks, California, and additional offices.

Single issues of THE ANNALS may be obtained by individuals who are not members of The Academy for $19.00 each (clothbound, $29.00). Add $2.00 for shipping and handling on all pre-paid orders. Single issues of THE ANNALS have proven to be excellent supplementary texts for classroom use. Direct inquiries regarding adoptions to THE ANNALS c/o Sage Publications (address below).

All correspondence concerning membership in The Academy, dues renewals, inquiries about membership status, and/or purchase of single issues of THE ANNALS should be sent to THE ANNALS c/o Sage Publications, Inc., 2455 Teller Road, Thousand Oaks, CA 91320. Telephone: (805) 499-0721; FAX/Order line: (805) 499-0871. *Please note that orders under $30 must be prepaid.* Sage affiliates in London and India will assist institutional subscribers abroad with regard to orders, claims, and inquiries for both subscriptions and single issues.

Printed on recycled, acid-free paper

THE ANNALS

© 1999 *by* The American Academy *of* Political *and* Social Science

All rights reserved. No part of this volume may be reproduced or utilized in any form or by any means, electronic or mechanical, including photocopying, recording or by any information storage and retrieval system, without permission in writing from the publisher. All inquiries for reproduction or permission should be sent to Sage Publications, 2455 Teller Road, Thousand Oaks, CA 91320.

Editorial Office: 3937 Chestnut Street, Philadelphia, PA 19104.

For information about membership* (individuals only) and subscriptions (institutions), address:

SAGE PUBLICATIONS, INC.
2455 Teller Road
Thousand Oaks, CA 91320

From India and South Asia,	*From the UK, Europe, the Middle*
write to:	*East and Africa, write to:*
SAGE PUBLICATIONS INDIA Pvt. Ltd	SAGE PUBLICATIONS LTD
P.O. Box 4215	6 Bonhill Street
New Delhi 110 048	London EC2A 4PU
INDIA	UNITED KINGDOM

SAGE Production Staff: ERIC LAW, LISA CUEVAS, DORIS HUS, and ROSE TYLAK
*Please note that members of The Academy receive THE ANNALS with their membership.
International Standard Serial Number ISSN 0002-7162
International Standard Book Number ISBN 0-7619-2029-3 (Vol. 563, 1999 paper)
International Standard Book Number ISBN 0-7619-2028-5 (Vol. 563, 1999 cloth)
Manufactured in the United States of America. First printing, May 1999.

The articles appearing in THE ANNALS are indexed in *Academic Index, Book Review Index, Combined Retrospective Index Sets, Current Contents, General Periodicals Index, Public Affairs Information Service Bulletin, Pro-Views,* and *Social Sciences Index.* They are also abstracted and indexed in *ABC Pol Sci, America: History and Life, Automatic Subject Citation Alert, Book Review Digest, Family Resources Database, Higher Education Abstracts, Historical Abstracts, Human Resources Abstracts, International Political Science Abstracts, Journal of Economic Literature, Managing Abstracts, Periodica Islamica, Sage Urban Studies Abstracts, Social Planning / Policy & Development Abstracts, Social Sciences Citation Index, Social Work Research & Abstracts, Sociological Abstracts, United States Political Science Documents,* and/or *Work Related Abstracts, Westlaw,* and are available on microfilm from University Microfilms, Ann Arbor, Michigan.

Information about membership rates, institutional subscriptions, and back issue prices may be found on the facing page.

Advertising. Current rates and specifications may be obtained by writing to THE ANNALS Advertising and Promotion Manager at the Thousand Oaks office (address above).

Claims. Claims for undelivered copies must be made no later than twelve months following month of publication. The publisher will supply missing copies when losses have been sustained in transit and when the reserve stock will permit.

Change of Address. Six weeks' advance notice must be given when notifying of change of address to ensure proper identification. Please specify name of journal. **POSTMASTER:** Send address changes to: THE ANNALS of the American Academy of Political and Social Science, c/o Sage Publications, Inc., 2455 Teller Road, Thousand Oaks, CA 91320.

THE ANNALS

of The American Academy *of* Political
and Social Science

ALAN W. HESTON, *Editor*
NEIL A. WEINER, *Assistant Editor*

See page 2 for information on Academy membership and
purchase of single volumes of **The Annals.**

CONTENTS

HOLY SPIRIT LIBRARY

CABRINI COLLEGE, RADNOR, PA.

BOOK DEPARTMENT CONTENTS

INTERNATIONAL RELATIONS AND POLITICS

AFRICA, ASIA, AND LATIN AMERICA

EUROPE

UNITED STATES

SOCIOLOGY

ECONOMICS

PREFACE

In the twentieth century, we have witnessed the massive movement of women and young mothers into paid employment in the United States and other industrialized countries. By 1995, 64 percent of married mothers with a preschool child were in the labor force, compared to 30 percent only 25 years earlier (U.S. Bureau of the Census 1997). Commodification of goods previously produced at home and the invention of home appliances, along with declining birthrates and increasing levels of education, have made it increasingly expensive for women to stay at home. Given the reduced demands of housework, they can make a greater contribution to family income and well-being through paid work.

Other structural changes have made mothers' income from paid employment increasingly important to family finances. Rising divorce rates and the increasing percentage of female-headed households make more families dependent on the mother's earnings; 21 percent of all children lived in these families in 1988, compared to only 8 percent in 1960 (Hofferth 1996). The relative decline in manufacturing has reduced job opportunities and contributed to wage stagnation in blue-collar male occupations, while the expansion of service industries that has increased employment opportunities for women makes working-class families more dependent on the mother's earnings.

These structural shifts, along with women's growing aspirations for careers and more independence, have changed social norms. Employers have come to depend on the pool of female workers to fill jobs in low-wage female-dominated occupations and in high-skilled occupations where gender-based wage differentials make female employees a good buy. Clearly, some child-rearing responsibilities must be carried out by others than mothers, and we have come to accept children in child care as normal. In 1995, 60 percent of children aged 1 to 5 years, or 13 million children, were in nonparental child care or early education programs (Hofferth 1996). Families make less use of arrangements for the out-of-school time of school-age children, though there is increasing public interest in creating programs for them. In 1991, of the 36 million children in the United States between the ages of 5 and 14, about two-thirds lived in families with working parents, but fewer than 2 million were enrolled in formal before- or after-school programs. About a third were latchkey children (Seppanen, deVries, and Seligson 1993).

Families increasingly depend on formally provided child care. Working parents are losing their neighborhood support network as more women go to work. Geographic mobility breaks down dependence on kin. The smaller size of families limits the availability of sibling care. Transformations in residential areas have destroyed the neighborliness of neighborhoods and made them less inviting, sometimes dangerous places for children to play on their own. Furthermore, with the growing emphasis on education as the key to upward mobility, both working and nonworking mothers see the benefits of early education and enroll their children in preschools. Opportunities like Head Start and prekindergartens make these programs available to poor children.

Although most other industrialized countries have responded to these changed needs of families by establishing publicly supported affordable, and often free, early education, in the United States we rely mostly on private markets to supply services to parents who can afford to pay for them. Public subsidies finance services for some poor families, and private charitable donations help finance some nonprofit centers. Nevertheless, millions of low- and middle-income families who cannot afford or find formal child care must patch together informal and often unsatisfactory arrangements as best they can. Financial limitations of parents, and highly competitive markets, pressure child care providers into cost cutting that lowers quality, limiting children's experiences and opportunities for growth.

Several factors cause parents to purchase services of questionable quality: many do not know what to look for because of their limited experience as consumers of child care; they cannot easily monitor services; problems of accessibility and availability narrow their choices; and lack of information makes them believe they have even less choice. Policies of local government agencies that administer child care subsidies to low-income families also reduce demand for good-quality services. Since their main goal is to move parents into the labor force, they permit, even encourage, parents to use informal care arrangements of questionable quality.

The child care crisis is easily overlooked. It is a silent, voiceless crisis. Three-, 4-, and 5-year-old children cannot speak for themselves. Low- and middle-income children and mothers, those most directly affected, have little economic or political power. The mundane work of raising children is a task that every society has managed one way or another. The crisis does not present an immediate danger to our way of life or our national security. It is not dramatic enough to occupy much space in the news.

Politically, at the end of the 1990s the child care crisis is caught between conflicting forces. Progressives, child development professionals, and most of industry recognize that children are not being well served in the present system. They see that quality child care is desirable but expensive, beyond the budgets of most families. They call for major increases in public investment.

Social and economic conservatives agree that children are not well served, but they recommend incentives to encourage middle-class women to forgo employment while their children are young so as to care for them at home. Meanwhile they have been instrumental in eliminating the Aid to Families with Dependent Children (AFDC) welfare entitlement for poor mothers (and men), forcing them into the labor force in spite of inadequate provision of early child care and education.

CHILD CARE IN THE UNITED STATES:
THE VARIETY OF OPTIONS

In the United States, child care arrangements exist along a continuum that starts with parents themselves and ends with highly institutionalized settings. The most common include care by fathers; by both parents who organize their work schedules so one parent can always be home with the children; by a nanny, relative, or baby-sitter in the child's home; by a relative, neighbor, or provider in the caregiver's home; by a child care center or preschool; by community recreation center, school, church, and museum programs for school-age children; even by the children themselves.

Of the 10 million preschool children of working mothers in the United States, roughly one-third are cared for in their own home by their father, a relative, a nanny, or their mother; one-third are in family child care in the home of the provider or relative; and one-third are in child care centers, nursery schools, or preschools. Although formal child care is becoming more common, children's relatives, including their working mothers, still provide about half of the child care for working mothers. If families are poor, the mother works part-time, or the mother works other than a day shift, then they rely more on relatives. Sandra Hofferth's article in this volume gives more detail on the demand for and supply of services, public programs that subsidize child care, and the limitations of these programs for some groups of working parents.

Almost 30 percent of the children of working mothers under the age of 5 and about 15 percent of the children of nonemployed mothers are enrolled in child care centers or preschools—establishments where children are cared for in a group in a nonresidential setting for all or part of the day (Casper 1997; Hofferth et al. 1991). The center sector is a mixed industry composed of private for-profit, private nonprofit, and publicly operated organizations. Roughly 40 percent of centers are operated for profit; most of these are independently organized, but an increasing percentage are part of national or regional chains. The majority of centers in most states are nonprofit, either operated as independent entities or under the auspices of a sponsoring agency such as religious organizations, Head Start, public schools, community agencies, or employers. The prevalence of nonprofit centers reflects the merit good aspect of child care (the desire to provide the services to deserving children regardless of their parents' ability to pay) and the trust good aspect (parents' desire to use trustworthy providers motivated to provide good-quality care). A very small percentage of centers are publicly operated, usually by public hospitals, colleges, universities, school districts, or local municipalities.

Center care is used mostly by parents working full-time day shifts. All categories of parents, however, prefer formal center care for older preschoolers; about 41 percent of children are enrolled in formal programs by the age of 3, 65 percent by the time they are 4 years old, and 75 percent if they are 5 years old and not yet in school (West, Wright, and Hausken 1995). Since so many nonemployed mothers enroll their children in preschool programs by the time they are 3 or 4 years old, labor force participation of mothers is not a predictor of center use.

Types of family child care differ by legal status and the relation of the caregiver to the child. About 15 percent of the children of working mothers are cared for by nonrelated family child care providers who care for a small group of children in their own home. Family child care is an ideal form of self-employment or small business for women who want to combine remunerative work with staying at home and running their household. Usually, they are mothers, often with young children of their own at home. They may be either licensed by the state or not, depending on the state and on their own decision. Whereas center care is regulated in every state, only 22 states and territories currently require licensing of family child care providers, 13 require registration, and many states exempt providers caring for a small number of children (Children's Foundation 1997). Although the percentage of children in nonrelative family child care has been declining steadily, parents of infants and toddlers still tend to prefer family child care. Nonrelative family child care providers serve the same clientele as centers—full-time working mothers with daytime jobs—creating a competition that keeps fees (and quality) in check.

About 16 percent of the children of working mothers receive family child care from their grandparents or other relatives in the relative's home. Most states honor extended family ties by exempting relatives from regulation. In 1990, about 2.3 million children were in family child care (Kisker et al. 1991). About a quarter of this care occurs in licensed homes, a quarter is unregulated and possibly illegal care, and a half is relative care (Casper 1997).

Of the young children with working mothers cared for in their own home, 18 percent are cared for by their fathers, and grandparents or other relatives look after 9 percent of these children. Relative care in the child's home is used more often by low-income families and by mothers working part-time. Nonrelatives care for about 5 percent of children in the child's own home, and this arrangement is most common for employed mothers with infants. Nanny care fulfills parents' need for flexible child care arrangements and for more control over the child care relationship than they could get with center or family child care. While we think of the nanny arrangement as limited to the affluent, lower-income families also use in-home nonrelative care.

NAMING THE SERVICE: WHAT IS IT?

Part of the problem in creating a reasonable public response to the nation's child care needs is confusion about the basic nature of the service and who benefits from it. Child care is really two different services: a service to parents that enables them to go to work or otherwise be away from their children, and a service to their children that affects their development and general well-being. To the extent that one considers child care a service to parents, it is mainly a private good that benefits the parents and should be paid for by the family. To the extent that one focuses on child care as services to children—contributing to (or hindering) their well-being and development—how well it is provided has the potential to create benefits or costs to society as a whole or offend our moral sense of the way children should be treated. In these cases, the public must pay its share, or not enough (or not enough good) quality services will be provided. In this latter view, child care involves early education and is no different from education of older children, long considered a public responsibility. Only historical circumstance distinguishes it from elementary school, which all modern societies consider a public good.

The term "child care" implies that the services are limited to caregiving—changing diapers, feeding, caring about the child. In fact, child care involves both caregiving and early education. Because children spend much of their time in child care, the environment created for them affects their early experiences and learning opportunities. The term used by professionals, "early care and education" (ECE), incorporates these two aspects. Debby Cryer's article in this issue of *The Annals* details the ingredients of good-quality services, describes the observational instruments used to evaluate quality in different child care settings, and reviews major quality findings based on these instruments. She argues that the instruments provide valid measures of quality characteristics related to aspects of development associated with school success in mainstream American society.

In spite of the early education aspects of child care as well as the important health maintenance and safety responsibilities, many child care staff and providers have been recruited from the pool of unskilled workers and paid at or near the minimum wage. The recognition of the educational aspect of ECE suggests that providing this care involves special knowledge or skills. Should the ECE providers have professional training and experience and be paid accordingly? Should they be trained professionals, or is it satisfactory to rely, as we do to a great extent today, on women's supposedly natural nurturing instincts to ensure reasonable quality care? If we can agree that they do need training, then how should these requirements be put in place? These questions are discussed in the papers by William Gormley and Marcy Whitebook.

At least some parents have long recognized the importance of early education for their children. The history of preschool education for children from well-educated, affluent families goes back to the mid-nineteenth century. Such parents continue to use (and often organize) preschools, accounting for the widespread use of centers regardless of the mothers' work status. Day care for poor children has an even longer history, which can be traced back to the end of the eighteenth century (Michel forthcoming), when wealthy matrons began organizing charitable day nurseries for the young children of poor working mothers. They provided meals, naps, baths, clean clothing, and socialization, teaching the children manners and respect for their betters.

Poor mothers endured the often patronizing attitudes of the matrons if they had no alternative for their children's care. The distinction between early childhood education and day care persists, both institutionally and in people's minds. As out-of-home care of young children becomes the rule rather than the exception, however, there is growing recognition that child care and early education are necessarily intertwined and that children need both a loving and a stimulating environment.

WHAT IS WRONG WITH CURRENT ECE ARRANGEMENTS?

ECE in the United States is a disorganized jumble of services of varying but mostly poor to mediocre quality that families have trouble finding, affording, and evaluating. Moreover, much of it occurs out of sight, not subject to official monitoring. Experts argue that ECE suffers from the trilemma of affordability, availability, and quality.

Affordability, availability, and quality are interrelated problems. If parents cannot afford to pay for formal child care, then they have to make informal arrangements or find low-cost, low-quality care. This means that licensed centers and family child care providers will not be as available in poor neighborhoods because there is not enough business to support them. Similarly, for high-cost services like caring for infants or sick children, there is a disconnect between the incentives providers need to offer the service and what parents are prepared to pay that creates an availability problem.

There is no doubt that child care is expensive for many parents. In her article in this volume, Sandra Hofferth describes affordability in terms of budget shares—the percentage of income families spend on child care—reporting that working poor families who have to pay for child care spend about 33 percent of their income on it, compared to middle-class families, who spend only 6 percent. These poor families can spend as much on child care as on housing, which leaves only a third of their income for all other expenses. In his article, John Morris estimates that center fees (in 1998 prices) average about $5000 per year for preschool children and $6100 per year for infants or toddlers, while family child care fees average $4500 for preschoolers and $4800 for infants or toddlers. Paying these fees can wreck the budget of families with even moderate incomes.

Child care advocates argue that there are serious gaps in supply. When they refer to the "availability" problem, they are asserting that market forces do not satisfy specific needs for formal care for certain groups of parents. Most studies of the subject conclude that there is no general shortage of formal services and that supply has generally expanded to meet demand. However, high utilization rates of center slots predominate and one study found that on average it takes working parents seven weeks to find acceptable services, suggesting that parents may not have an easy time finding adequate services (Hofferth et al. 1991, 229). Moreover, there are serious shortages in poor urban neighborhoods, in rural areas, and for infants, sick children, and children needing care at night and on weekends (Kisker et al. 1991; Witte and Queralt 1997; Fuller and Liang 1996; Fuller et al. 1997).

The articles by John Morris and Debby Cryer indicate that, generally, the quality of formal, licensed center and family child care is not good by the standards set by ECE experts. All recent studies indicate that services are of mediocre or poor quality and that infants and toddlers received the lowest quality. Although not much is known about unregulated and relative care, the most recent study found it to be of much lower quality than licensed family child care (Kontos et al. 1995).

Why is quality important? Margaret Burchinal reviews the literature on the relation between the quality of child care and children's development. The statistical research indicates that, while the age at which a child enters nonparental care and the number of hours of care do not matter to the child's development, good-quality services have positive effects on children's cognitive and social development, even when the children's home environment is taken into consideration. Although family variables are most important to children's development, good-quality early childhood education has consistently been shown to be beneficial for children considered at risk of school failure.

Furthermore, recent research (not discussed by Burchinal) highlights the importance of infants' daily experiences in increasing brain capacity. Using brain imaging technology, scientists have found that experiences in the first three years of life determine how the neural circuits in the brain develop, strengthening with use, atrophying with disuse, and how toxic effects of stress hormones create hyperactivity or anxiety and reduce the child's capacity to learn (Shore 1997).

The United States lags behind the rest of the developed nations in providing minimal parental leave policies. This means that, increasingly, infants are experiencing nonparental care for at least part of the day within two or three months of birth. These services need to be provided by individuals who truly substitute for the loving and active caring of a devoted parent; unfortunately, these are the children most likely to receive poor care and little intellectual or social stimulation.

Several articles in this volume detail specifics of the child care crisis. Susan Holloway and Bruce Fuller raise concerns about the limitations of the current child care system in satisfying needs of parents from minority cultures. They critique the mainstream definition of good-quality care that emphasizes values of the majority culture, and they summarize studies showing the inequitable distribution of services. John Morris gives an economic interpretation of empirical research on the cost and quality of child care to explain why child care markets produce expensive but relatively low-quality services. William Gormley's article outlines the regulatory environment within which child care services are delivered, an environment that varies from state to state. He reviews the literature demonstrating that regulation improves quality but at the expense of availability and affordability. Marcy Whitebook, longtime activist and advocate for child care workers, reviews the dismal state of compensation for center staff and family child care workers, and she reviews current initiatives to create a more stable and professional workforce in the field. Julia Wrigley deepens the analysis of child care work in her discussion of the problems inherent in using nanny care—for the children, the nannies, and the parents. In focusing on the class differences between nannies and parents, she argues that these households come to mirror larger social inequalities. In addition, by solving individual needs for child care, these arrangements deflect concern from the broader social problems related to the conflicts between family and work responsibilities.

Perhaps the most revealing insights into the child care crisis are provided by Lorna Kellogg's description of the child care center she founded and directs. Her case study illustrates a point emphasized by both Cryer and Morris that excellent child care delivery involves a kind of gestalt—the individual ingredients have to be transformed into an effective whole. It also illustrates why there is not more excellence in the field. Kellogg asserts that her model is easily replicable; however, the dedication necessary to provide excellent care and the current low levels of compensation in the field make it unlikely to find a lot of such programs under current conditions.

CREATING A VIABLE
ECE DELIVERY SYSTEM

In their article, Paula England and Nancy Folbre argue that the time, money, and care that parents devote to raising their children create a public good—the next generation of workers and citizens who will create benefits enjoyed by people who are currently paying a small share of the costs. Child rearing involves an intergenerational exchange. For instance, this generation of parents is raising the next generation of taxpayers, who will pay social security taxes that finance social security benefits for the present generation of boomers. Child rearing, however, is a public good that people can enjoy without paying for it and without reducing other people's enjoyment of it. England and Folbre argue that the citizens who do not raise children are freeloading on parental efforts unless the government acts to pay their share. Furthermore, parents' decisions about investing in their children are based on their family's priorities and resources. If the public would benefit from a larger investment than parents choose to make, that increment must be paid for, either individually through philanthropy or collectively through government action. England and Folbre argue that we need to think of the costs of child rearing as an investment and that a new social contract needs to be negotiated to finance this investment in our future.

Many European countries already invest heavily in ECE. Wolfgang Tietze and Debby Cryer describe ECE availability, affordability, quality of services, and levels of public support for the 15 European Union countries. They conclude that although most countries have made progress in expanding publicly funded ECE services, deficits remain, particularly for children under 3 years old. Only two countries, Denmark and Sweden, have achieved the level of spending deemed appropriate by European experts, 1 percent of gross domestic product (GDP) or one-fifth of national expenditures for the education of older children (including university spending). In the United States, public investment of 1 percent of GDP would equal about $70 billion per year, almost six times current public spending.

Assuming the existence of a political consensus in the United States to work toward a more effective and equitable ECE system, there are several alternative approaches that build on current policies. We could incorporate preschool for 3- and 4-year-olds into the public school system as well as before- and after-school programs. We could extend Head Start to more families and to younger children and provide full-day and full-year programs. We could increase the current federal child care tax credit and provide benefits to low-income families who do not pay income taxes through a refundable tax credit. We could extend eligibility of the current child care voucher system that subsidizes a small percentage of the working poor to include all of the working poor as well as middle-income families and use a realistic voucher fee-reimbursement system based on program quality to encourage providers to improve the quality of their services.

In her article, Barbara Bergmann argues for the fourth alternative. Her recommendations have several advantages. Unlike the first two alternatives, they build on the existing market-oriented delivery system, allowing parents to choose their provider while eliminating the affordability constraint. Unlike the tax credit option, they require that the subsidy be spent on child care services. Through a policy of differential provider reimbursement rates based on quality of services, they create an incentive for providers to improve the quality of their services. All four alternatives would increase disposable income available to lower-income families to make it easier for them to make ends meet.

THE POLITICAL STALEMATE

Federal funding to finance a more adequate ECE system seems an unattainable goal in this period of devolution of political power to the states on social policy, and containment of federal expenditures on social programs. Major expansion of federal funding for child care appears particularly unlikely given the opposition being mounted by social and economic conservatives whose assault on public child care policy has been quite effective. Nevertheless, the fact that most economically advanced nations (other than the United States) recognize the importance of public investment in ECE suggests that there are objective economic and social considerations that can, in time, overcome conservative opposition to the creation of a coherent national child care policy.

Social conservatives in the United States use some of the same research results reported in this volume—on the low quality of nonparental child care, the primacy of family characteristics for children's cognitive and social development, the importance of infant attachment and environmental factors to infants' brain development and social competence—to argue that children should be raised by their mothers and that public policy should be designed to create incentives for women to choose to do so. Theirs is a moral argument, that there has been a "flight from parenting" encouraged by feminists and abetted by early childhood professionals, all part of a rising narcissism in our culture. Social conservatives address a specific segment of the population, middle-class mothers who, presumably, could choose to stay home with their children, and they minimize the economic realities discussed earlier in this preface. Recent comments by Karl Zinsmeister, editor in chief of the *American Enterprise*, are illustrative of this viewpoint:

The question is whether everyday middle-class Americans should produce children without the intention of nurturing them. There is a difference between compromise made in reaction to some crisis of fate, and an arrangement made simply because one wants to maximize one's own position while ignoring serious costs to others.

By transforming day care from a necessary stopgap for the unlucky few into a normal and accepted part of average lives, we are thoughtlessly taking a step of great consequence. (Zinsmeister 1998, 6)

As already documented, "the unlucky few" suffering the "crisis of fate" turn out to be a large segment of the U.S. child-rearing population. Social conservatives advocate tax incentives to induce mothers to stay home with their children, oppose public spending on child care, support more flextime, part-time jobs, and home work—employer strategies that provide more job flexibility but also further marginalize women in the labor force.

Much of the attack on national child care policy mounted by economic conservatives is similarly inconsistent with the facts. They contend that child care markets are effective in giving parents choices and responding to their needs. They minimize problems of affordability and availability, arguing that poorer parents have inexpensive options, that unregulated child care markets will provide the wide variety of services that suit the tastes and budgets of parents. Government intervention, they hold, only reduces options by increasing costs and creating the availability and affordability problems we have. They consider the quality problem a bogus issue created by ECE experts promoting their own professional interests. They believe that parents are well informed and the best judges of what their children need, and they argue that the quality of child care that children are receiving is good based on studies reporting parent satisfaction with their child care arrangements. They contend that government regulation to control quality is just another form of social planning that promotes the interests of regulated child care providers and government bureaucrats (Olsen 1997).

The massive shift in women's roles has spawned a powerful backlash among conservatives intent on preserving their version of traditional family values. To these groups, any public policy that provides incentives for mothers to go to work is morally wrong and wasteful of tax dollars that would be better spent subsidizing mothers who raise their own children. Child care public policy formation has become a battleground for resisting further public investment in ECE programs.

The fundamental question remains: must individual women personally carry all the costs of rearing their own children, and should they and their children be penalized if marital breakup or husband's employment results in inadequate support for their children? Or is our society ready to recognize the injustices and insecurities in our economic and social system as well as the public interest in both children's optimum social, emotional, intellectual development and mothers' full participation in the economic and social system?

SUZANNE W. HELBURN

References

Casper, Lynne M. 1997. *Who's Minding Our Preschoolers? Fall 1994 (Update)*. Current Population Reports, P70-62. Washington, DC: Department of Commerce, Economics and Statistics Administration.

Children's Foundation. 1997. *The 1997 Family Child Care Licensing Study*. Washington, DC: Children's Foundation.

Fuller, Bruce, Casey Coonerty, Fran Kipnis, and Yvonne Choong. 1997. *An Unfair Head Start: California Families Face Gaps in Preschool and Child Care Availability*. Berkeley: University of California, PACE Center.

Fuller, Bruce and Xiaoyan Liang. 1996. Market Failure? Estimating Inequality in Preschool Availability. *Educational Evaluation and Policy Analysis* 18:31-49.

Hofferth, Sandra. 1996. Child Care in the United States Today. *The Future of Children* 6(2):41-61.

Hofferth, Sandra, April Brayfield, Sharon Deich, and Pamela Holcomb. 1991. *National Child Care Survey, 1990*. Report 91-5. Washington, DC: Urban Institute.

Kisker, Ellen, Sandra Hofferth, Deborah Phillips, and Elizabeth Farquhar. 1991. *A Profile of Child Care Settings: Early Education and Care in 1990*. Vol 1. Washington, DC: Government Printing Office.

Kontos, Susan, Carollee Howes, Marybeth Shinn, and Ellen Galinsky. 1995. *Quality in Family Child Care and Relative Care*. New York: Teachers College Press.

Michel, Sonya. Forthcoming. *Children's Interests/Mothers' Rights: The Shaping of America's Child Care Policy*. New Haven, CT: Yale University Press.

Olsen, Darcy. 1997. *The Advancing Nanny State: Why the Government Should Stay out of Child Care*. Cato Policy Analysis, no. 285. Washington, DC: Cato Institute.

Seppanen, Patricia S., Dianne Kaplan deVries, and Michelle Seligson. 1993. National Study of Before- and After-School Programs: Executive Summary. Final report to the Office of Policy and Planning, RMC Research Corporation, Portsmouth, NH.

Shore, Rima. 1997. *Rethinking the Brain: New Insights into Early Development*. New
York: Families and Work Institute.

U.S. Bureau of the Census. 1997. *Statistical Abstract of the United States*. Washington,
DC: Government Printing Office.

West, J., W. Wright, and E. G. Hausken. 1995. *Child Care and Early Education Program Participation of Infants, Toddlers, and Preschoolers*. Washington, DC: Department of Education.

Witte, Ann Dryden and Magaly Queralt. 1997. Factors Influencing the Neighborhood
Supply of Childcare in Massachusetts. Working paper 97004, Wellesley College.

Zinsmeister, Karl. 1998. Why Encouraging Daycare Is Unwise. *American Enterprise*
9(3):4-7.

ANNALS, *AAPSS*, **563**, May 1999

Child Care, Maternal Employment, and Public Policy

By SANDRA L. HOFFERTH

ABSTRACT: Increased work requirements in new welfare reform legislation may further increase the demand for child care in the United States. Consequently, this article focuses on (1) the relationship between child care and self-sufficiency, particularly among low-income mothers; (2) factors affecting the demand for and availability, cost, and quality of child care that parents use; and (3) the part played by public subsidies in the availability, cost, and quality of child care. Low-income mothers' ability to achieve self-sufficiency depends on the availability of reliable child care, for they want the same types of care that middle-class mothers want. The federal government has played an important part in making child care available and affordable and also contributes to its quality. Much of the funding, however, has gone to middle-income or poor nonemployed parents. Child care for working poor and working-class parents is the important missing piece.

Sandra L. Hofferth is a senior research scientist at the Institute for Social Research and co-director of the Panel Study of Income Dynamics at the University of Michigan. Her current research focuses on children's time and on parental employment, child care, and child well-being. She is a member of the Council of the Family and Population sections of the American Sociological Association and chair of the Sociology of Children Section.

WHEN we refer to child care, most of us think about the arrangements mothers use when they are at work. In 1995, 64 percent of U.S. married mothers with a preschool child were in the workforce, compared with 30 percent in 1970 (U.S. Bureau of the Census 1997). Since employed mothers are more likely to use some form of nonparental arrangement than are nonemployed mothers, the increased employment of mothers outside the home has sharply raised the use of nonparental child care over the past several decades. Today, the majority of parents with preschool children depend on substitute caregivers to supplement their own time spent with their children (Hofferth et al. 1991; Casper 1996).

This article focuses upon the relationship between work and the demand for child care in the United States. I concentrate on three issues: (1) the relationship between child care and self-sufficiency, particularly among low-income mothers; (2) factors affecting the demand for and availability, cost, and quality of child care that parents use; and (3) the part played by the federal government in the availability, cost, and quality of child care.

CURRENT USE OF CHILD CARE IN THE UNITED STATES

The types of arrangements that employed mothers use have changed over the past several decades, with more children in centers and family day care, and fewer cared for by relatives. In 1993, 47 percent of the preschool children of employed mothers were cared for in a center or family day care as their primary child care arrangement, compared with 22 percent 30 years earlier (see Figure 1). Growth occurred in center care, which increased fourfold, from 6 to 30 percent, rather than in family day care, which was about the same level in 1993 as in 1965. The use of relatives declined from 33 percent in 1965 to 25 percent in 1993, and the use of sitter care declined from 15 to 5 percent.

In addition to a shift toward center-based care, children enter formal care at younger and younger ages. Not only has there been a doubling in the proportion of 3- to 4-year-olds in center-based programs since the late 1970s, but the same type of increase has affected toddlers 1 to 2 years of age and infants under age 1. In 1993, 19 percent of infants, 24 percent of toddlers, and 39 percent of older preschool children with an employed mother were enrolled in a center-based program as their primary arrangement, compared with 6 percent, 12 percent, and 27 percent, respectively, in 1982, the earliest year for which detailed data by age are available. The high use of child care for infants in the United States reflects the fact that half of mothers are back at work by 6 months after the child's birth (Hofferth 1996). Though labor force participation in developed countries such as Sweden is very high, few mothers with infants are actually working. Thus few developed countries face such a need for infant care (Hofferth and Deich 1994).

FIGURE 1
PRIMARY CARE FOR YOUNGEST PRESCHOOL CHILD, EMPLOYED MOTHERS, 1965-93

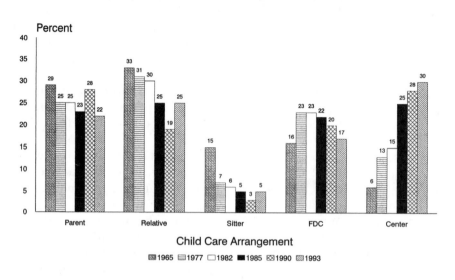

SOURCES: U.S. Bureau of the Census 1982, 1983, 1987, 1995; Hofferth et al. 1991.

Maternal employment is a key factor in the use of formal child care programs, but it cannot explain the entire shift toward the use of formal programs. Over the last 25 years, interest in preschool programs for children's development and enrichment rose. More and more mothers who were not employed outside the home began to utilize primarily part-day preschool programs for their children. In 1991, 53 percent of 4-year-old children were enrolled in a preprimary program (including kindergarten), compared with 28 percent in 1965 (U.S. Bureau of the Census 1993, tab. 236). Among older preschoolers, the enrollments of children of employed and nonemployed mothers began to converge. In 1991,

for example, 50 percent of 3- to 5-year-old children of mothers not in the workforce were enrolled in a nursery school, compared with 60 percent of children of mothers in the labor force (U.S. Bureau of the Census 1993, tab. 237).

PATTERNS OF CHILD CARE
USE BY INCOME

The national distribution of the 16.2 million families with children under age 6 in six income-employment subgroups is shown in Figure 2. Families are grouped based upon the income and employment status of parents. In 1990, of American families with children under age 6, 7 percent were what we call working

FIGURE 2
DISTRIBUTION OF FAMILIES WITH CHILDREN UNDER AGE 6 IN SIX SUBGROUPS

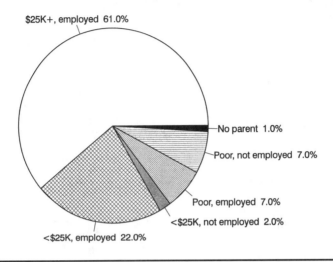

$25K+, employed 61.0%

No parent 1.0%

Poor, not employed 7.0%

Poor, employed 7.0%

<$25K, not employed 2.0%

<$25K, employed 22.0%

SOURCE: Reprinted from *Children and Youth Services Review*, 17(1-2), Sandra L. Hofferth, Caring for Children at the Poverty Line, p. 65, 1995, with permission from Elsevier Science.

poor families (annual incomes under the poverty level and at least one employed parent); another 7 percent were nonworking poor (annual incomes under the poverty level and no employed parent); 22 percent were so-called working-class families (annual incomes above poverty but below $25,000); and 61 percent were middle-class families (annual incomes $25,000 or higher). An annual income of $25,000 represented about 75 percent of the median income of families in the United States in 1989, the year in which these data were collected, and is about twice the poverty level (Hofferth et al. 1991). In 1 percent of American families, the children under age 6 were not living with parents; in another 2 percent, family income was between poverty and $25,000, but no one worked. There were too few of these latter two groups to include in our analyses.

Clear income differences in child care use are shown in Table 1, with higher proportions of children of middle-income than working-class or poor families in center care. However, income is not the only factor. Even though they are both poor, it is clear that there are substantial differences in child care use between the working poor and the nonworking poor. In particular, the children of the working poor who are 2 years old or younger are much less likely to be enrolled in centers than comparable children of the nonworking poor. This age group of children of the working poor are more likely to be cared for by relatives than comparable children of the nonworking poor.

TABLE 1

PERCENTAGE OF FAMILIES USING SPECIFIC CHILD CARE ARRANGEMENTS FOR YOUNGEST PRESCHOOL CHILD UNDER 6, BY INCOME GROUP AND AGE OF CHILD

	Children 2 and Younger		Children 3-5		All Children under 6	
	Center	Relative	Center	Relative	Center	Relative
Nonworking poor	19	44	45	35	30	40
Working poor	5	57	40	28	22	43
Working class	28	38	43	25	35	32
Middle class	25	30	52	16	38	24
Total	24	35	48	20	35	28

SOURCE: Reprinted from *Children and Youth Services Review*, 17(1-2), Sandra L. Hofferth, Caring for Children at the Poverty Line, p. 70, 1995, with permission from Elsevier Science.

FACTORS AFFECTING
DEMAND FOR CARE

What are the reasons for the differences in use between these different groups? First, they may be due to differences in availability or to differences in schedules of the working poor and nonworking poor. Second, they could be due to differences in prices resulting from differences in subsidies. Third, they could be due to differences in preferences. Fourth, they could be due to differences in quality. What do we know about how these factors constrain parental choices?

Supply of programs

Availability, as measured by spaces for children in programs, has increased greatly over the past two decades. In early 1990, there were three times as many centers as there were in the mid-1970s and four times as many children were enrolled in such programs. Enrollment in regulated family day care also increased, by 53 percent, over the same period

(Willer et al. 1991). Some studies have found geographic differences in the number of programs and/or spaces by income level of the community (Fuller and Liang 1996), and others have found none (Fronstin and Wissoker 1994). In better-off areas, the actual number of centers and family day care homes per capita is linked to the employment of parents. In low-income areas, the number of Head Start programs is associated with parental employment (Fronstin and Wissoker 1994). Specifically, the greater the number of programs, the greater the likelihood that a parent will be employed.

Perceived availability. The National Child Care Survey asked parents who were not using a type of arrangement both whether it was available to them and, if available, how far away it was located (Hofferth et al. 1991). In 1990, three-quarters of parents reported that they lived within 30 minutes of a child care center, almost 60 percent lived that close to a family day care home, and half lived that close to a relative who could provide care. Do low-income parents have the same perceived geographic access to preschool programs as do high-income parents? The answer is no. While nonworking poor parents were more likely than other parents to say that they knew of a relative who could care for their child, working poor parents were least likely to say a relative was available. Poor and working-class families reported the least availability of center care, with middle-class families reporting the most. Nonworking poor families also reported the least access to family day care.

Age differences. Even though there are few overall differences by income, there are differences by age of the child, with few centers accepting infants, and few vacancies available for them. As a result, parents who want a center-based program for an infant may have a difficult time finding a space (Willer et al. 1991). Recent research suggests that the United States has no shortage of programs for 3- to 5-year-olds but has a shortage of programs for infants and toddlers (U.S. General Accounting Office 1997).

Schedules. Income-employment groups differ in schedules. Nonemployed-parent families are unconstrained by work schedules. While there are no income differences in evening work, with 8-9 percent of mothers working during the evening or night, availability of care is limited. Thirteen percent of regulated and 20 percent of nonregulated family day care providers provided

care in the evenings, compared to only 3 percent of centers. There are income differences in weekend work and availability of care at that time. One-third of working poor and one-quarter of working-class mothers work weekends. Only 10 percent of centers and 6 percent of family day care homes reported providing care on weekends. Finally, almost half of working poor parents worked on a rotating or changing schedule, compared with one-quarter of working middle-class mothers and one-third of working middle-class fathers. This presents a greater obstacle to the stability of care than either a regular weekend or regular evening schedule.

Price and budget shares

Child care is expensive, averaging about $4000 for full-time care in 1993. In 1993, employed mothers who paid for care paid, on average, $1.67 per hour for center care, $1.35 per hour for family day care, $2.30 per hour for sitter care, and $1.11 per hour for a relative's care of a preschool child. Not everyone pays for care, however. In 1990, only 8 percent of nonworking poor families, compared with 27 percent of working poor, 32 percent of working-class, and 43 percent of middle-class households (with working and nonworking mothers) paid for child care. While they paid less in absolute terms, working poor families who paid for care spent a large proportion of their incomes on it—33 percent, compared with 13 percent for working-class and 6 percent for middle-class families (Hofferth 1995).

Numerous researchers have documented a relationship between the cost of child care and maternal employment (Connelly 1992; Kimmel 1998); labor force participation decreases as the price of care increases. Blau and Robins (1989) found that higher-cost child care was associated with a lower probability of starting and a higher probability of exiting employment among mothers of all income levels. The effects are not large. Maume (1991) found a $10 difference in weekly child care expenditures to be associated with a 1.6 percent increase in the probability of leaving employment a year later. According to Blau and Hagy (1998), full subsidization of all nonparental child care would result in a 10 percent increase in maternal employment among all mothers.

The cost of care is also linked to parental child care decisions. Several studies have documented that, controlling for indicators of quality and other factors, the higher the price, the less likely families are to use a type of care (Hofferth and Wissoker 1992; Chaplin et al. 1998; Blau and Hagy 1998). Price appears to matter primarily for the child care choices of employed mothers (Blau and Hagy 1998). Full subsidization of all nonparental child care would increase the use of paid arrangements by 19 percent. Price appears to be a modest deterrent to employment but a substantial deterrent to the use of paid arrangements (Blau and Hagy 1998).

While nonparental child care is generally necessary for mothers to work, it may be an even more critical factor for low-income mothers, who are likely to be raising children alone

(Chilman 1991). Fronstin and Wissoker (1994) and the U.S. General Accounting Office (1995) found a stronger effect of child care cost on the work decisions of low-income compared with high-income mothers. The latter found that subsidizing child care costs completely would lead to a 15 percent increase in employment of poor mothers, from 29 to 44 percent. Hofferth and Collins (1998) found a stronger effect of child care price on the job stability of moderate-income mothers ($6 to $8 per hour) than on that of the lowest-income mothers, presumably because of the differential access of low-income mothers to subsidies. A study of the Aid to Families with Dependent Children (AFDC) population in Illinois estimated that problems with child care caused 20 percent of AFDC mothers to quit school or a training program in the previous 12 months; another 20 percent were estimated to have returned to public assistance because of child care problems (Siegel and Loman 1991).

FEDERAL CHILD CARE POLICY

Child care and family policies in most developed countries were designed for one of two purposes: (1) to facilitate or promote childbearing by reducing the costs of raising children or (2) to facilitate parental employment by assisting mothers (and fathers) in balancing home and family life (Hofferth and Deich 1994). In the United States, an important additional objective is to provide parents the maximum degree of choice as to how to combine employment and care of children. The second goal is generally limited to mothers (and fathers) who have been employed; the first applies to all parents. Other goals are possible, such as increasing gender equality; however, that is not generally a goal in the United States, whereas it is in the Scandinavian countries. Promoting all children's development and education have played a part in policy formation in other countries (Sweden and France, for example), whereas U.S. efforts focus on low-income children (Bergmann 1996; Hofferth and Deich 1994). The following describes U.S. programs that fit these three social objectives.

Supporting families
raising children

There are at least four different types of federal programs in the United States that support families raising their children, regardless of the employment status of the parents. These are not explicitly pronatalist because benefits do not rise with the number of children as they do in France, for example (Hofferth and Deich 1994; Bergmann 1996). First, families can take an individual tax exemption of $2150 for each family member. Second, in 1997 a tax credit for children was implemented. This tax credit of $500 per child per year offsets taxes paid by middle-class families. It is not available to low-income or to high-income families. Third, low-income families with a working parent can take the Earned Income Tax Credit, which provides up to $2152 in refundable credits to families with one child and $3556 for families with two or more

children. Support for low-income families raising children with disabilities is available through the Supplemental Security Income program. Children must have "a medically determinable physical or mental impairment, which results in marked and severe functional limitations" (Loprest 1997, 1). Children from low-income families also have access to medical assistance through the Medicaid program. Beginning in 1997, most states have implemented a state children's health insurance program that enables states to enroll low-income children in public and private health insurance coverage or directly provide health assistance to children who are ineligible for other coverage. Eligibility is generally limited to families with incomes below 200 percent of the poverty level. Finally, 3- to 5-year-old children from low-income families are eligible for enrollment in Head Start, a preschool program providing educational enrichment and social services.

Supporting maternal employment

Until October 1990, the most extensive federal program for assisting working families with child care was the federal Child and Dependent Care Tax Credit, which reimburses one-working-parent or two-working-parent families for 20-30 percent of their child care expenses (up to $2400 for one child and $4800 for two or more children) but is not refundable. The maximum that parents can receive is $800 for one child and $1600 for two children. The Child and Adult Care Food Program, administered by the U.S.

Department of Agriculture's Food and Nutrition Service, provides federal subsidies for meals and snacks that are served in licensed nonresidential child care centers and family or group day care homes. Providers also receive training and technical assistance from monitors. In 1996, three major child care programs—AFDC/Job Opportunities and Basic Skills child care, which provided child care assistance to welfare families; At-Risk Child Care, which assisted low-income working families at risk of becoming welfare dependent; and Transitional Child Care, which provided one year of child care assistance to families leaving AFDC because of employment—were folded into the Child Care and Development Block Grant, now called the Child Care and Development Fund (CCDF). The CCDF provides federal funds to states for child care subsidies to families who are working or preparing for work and who have incomes of up to 85 percent of a state's median income. Finally, the Title XX Social Services Block Grant provides funding to states for services to help clients achieve economic self-sufficiency, child safety, or appropriate care. In 1995, approximately 15 percent of Title XX funds were used for child care (U.S. Department of Health and Human Services 1995).

Employer policies. In the United States, benefits that help parents manage work and family responsibilities are offered at the discretion of employers. A variety of policies such as flexible spending accounts, cafeteria benefit plans, vouchers, informa-tion and referral services, unpaid leave, work at home, part-time work, and flextime, as well as on-site child care, are offered by some employers. In 1990, about half of U.S. families with children under age 13 reported that they had at least one benefit available to assist them in balancing work and family life (Hofferth et al. 1991). The most common benefit was part-time work; 36 percent of families reported that part-time work was available through an employer. Unpaid leave and flextime were reported by 28 percent and 21 percent, respectively. About 10 percent reported a child care center at one parent's work site.

Parental leave. Legislation creating parental leave can be considered child care legislation since it provides an option for parents to care for children themselves while keeping their jobs and health benefits. In the most generous cases, this leave includes partial income replacement. Between 1986 and 1990, 23 states had passed laws mandating maternity or parental leave (Finn-Stevenson and Trzcinski 1990). Although one-third of employers with 100 or more employees offered unpaid maternity leave in 1989, only about 2 percent offered paid maternity leave (U.S. Bureau of Labor Statistics 1989). In 1993, parental leave became a nationwide benefit. The Family and Medical Leave Act, which mandates unpaid parental leave of employers of 50 or more employees in all states, passed both houses of Congress and was signed by President Clinton in February 1993 as one of his first acts after taking office. This legislation requires that employers offer a job-protected but unpaid leave of 12 weeks to care for a newborn or ill child.

Promoting parental choice

Many of the programs previously discussed were designed to maximize parental choice in child care arrangements. Parental leave facilitates parents' own caring for their newborn children for several months. Subsidies to parents give them more choice by reducing cost constraints. The tax credits cover all types of care, as does the CCDF. The CCDF permits states to establish their own criteria for subsidies. Previous legislation required states to offer parents an option of either enrolling their child with a provider who has a grant or contract to provide services, or to receive a child care certificate to be used as payment by the parents for child care services for any eligible provider of their choice, and this is likely to continue in most states. Eligible providers include for-profit or nonprofit center-based programs and group home or family day care providers that are licensed, regulated, or registered according to state law. Family members, such as grandparents, who provide care are also eligible. Allowing providers related to the child to be subsidized expands parents' choices.

ROLE OF PUBLIC SUBSIDIES

In this section, we focus on the part played by public subsidies in making care affordable, in improving

FIGURE 3
PERCENTAGE OF FAMILIES WITH PRESCHOOL CHILDREN WHO RECEIVED DIRECT FINANCIAL ASSISTANCE OR WHO CLAIMED TAX CREDITS

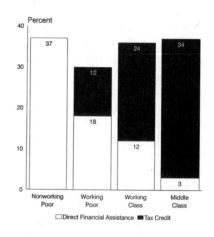

SOURCE: Reprinted from *Children and Youth Services Review*, 17(1-2), Sandra L. Hofferth, Caring for Children at the Poverty Line, pp. 77, 80, 1995, with permission from Elsevier Science.

program quality, and in promoting parental choice.

Making care affordable

Financial assistance is critical for parents to be able to afford care. In 1990, 37 percent of nonworking poor and 18 percent of working poor families with a child in child care reported receiving financial assistance (see Figure 3). Twelve percent of working-class and 3 percent of middle-class families with a child in child care received direct assistance. Percentages are higher for those using center-based care: 89, 42, 24, and 5 percent for nonworking poor, working poor, working-class, and middle-class families, respectively.

In contrast, 12 percent of working poor, 24 percent of working-class, and 34 percent of middle-class families claimed the Child and Dependent Care Tax Credit. When we add the subsidies received through the tax system, we find that working poor families are the least likely to receive subsidies (30 percent, compared with 36-37 percent of nonworking poor, working-class, and middle-class families). This is because they are less likely to be eligible for subsidies for low-income families and less likely than middle-income families to take a tax credit.

The type of care parents select is closely related to the size and form of the subsidy they receive. One study found that those using vouchers were more likely to select a formal center-based arrangement than those who paid out-of-pocket and were later reimbursed for their expenses (Siegel and Loman 1991). The type of care appears to be important to employment in several ways. Although type is not necessarily related to quality, in that there are high- and low-quality examples of each type of care (Hayes, Palmer, and Zaslow 1990), it is related to cost, with centers and family day care homes being more expensive than relatives, and licensed care more expensive than nonlicensed care (Casper 1996). This suggests that subsidies improve choice, but parents do not have equal access to subsidies.

Improving program quality

Do subsidies improve program quality? If the use of center-based programs increases but the quality of the programs is poor, then children and their families will suffer. Most federal funds go directly to parents, who purchase the care themselves. However, these funds have not brought about improved quality, first, because parents do not necessarily purchase care in higher-quality programs and, second, parents may not have access to higher-quality programs. Consequently, many believe that direct investment in programs is the only way that quality can be improved.

What is program quality? While quality generally reflects the nature of the interactions between child and provider, it is usually measured in terms of child-staff ratios, training, group size, and staff turnover. A lower ratio of children to staff, small group sizes, higher education and training of staff, and lower turnover promote children's optimal development. Health and development screening and referrals are also important (Hofferth and Kisker 1994). Research suggests that, since the mid-1970s, the education of center staff has increased; however, the ratio of children to staff and staff turnover have risen over the past decade, a consequence of increased competition, lower staff salaries, and declining direct federal support (Willer et al. 1991).

Research has shown that parents respond to low-quality care. For example, parents with poor care are more likely to leave their jobs than are parents with good care (Meyers 1993). However, there is very little evidence that increased income or subsidies lead parents to select higher-quality care in the first place. Parents often will not spend more money, even though they get some of it back at the end of the year. Even more important, research finds little relationship between measures of quality and the cost of care to families (Waite, Leibowitz, and Witsberger 1991). Recent research (Hofferth et al. 1998) finds a relationship between what parents are looking for and what they actually purchase. This suggests that an alternative approach could help parents become better consumers by teaching them what to look for in a high-quality program.

Besides whether parents seek better-quality programs, a question is whether low-income parents have access to the same quality of care as do high-income parents. What is the role of subsidies? While the question of differential quality has not been resolved, the evidence to date suggests that on structural features, the lowest-income and highest-income families have the highest-quality care, with working- and middle-class children in somewhat lower-quality care (Hofferth et al. 1994; Whitebook, Howes, and Phillips 1990; Phillips, Voran, and Kisker 1994). With respect to the interaction between provider and child, high-income children are better off (Phillips, Voran, and Kisker 1994).[1]

The stability of child care, that is, the number of arrangements for a child in a period of time, is another indicator of quality because it is considered to be an important factor affecting child development (Hayes, Palmer, and Zaslow 1990). It is also likely to be strongly related to employment stability. In work by Meyers (1994), parents who had to give up their child care arrangements when they changed activities in California's Greater Avenues to Independence program were more likely to drop out of the program than those who did not have this discontinuity in child care. Informal arrangements tend to be much less stable than formal arrangements. Parents report a greater incidence of losing time from work because the provider was not as available in in-home than in formal out-of-home arrangements (Hofferth et al. 1991). Research also shows that those parents with informal arrangements were more likely to report that child care problems prevented work than were those with formal center-based arrangements (Siegel and Loman 1991). Finally, stable care has been shown to be associated with stable employment (Hofferth and Collins 1998).

In addition to subsidizing parents, the government can provide direct funding to improve quality. This includes direct subsidies for program startup, subsidies for services such as food provision under the Child and Adult Care Food Program, and complete federal funding for Head Start programs that deliver higher-quality care than average.

Substantial funds to improve program quality are made available in the CCDF. A minimum of 4 percent of each state's CCDF funds must be used to improve the quality and availability of child care. This could amount to as much as $40 million per year, were all the available funds expended. States may provide funds to child care resource and referral agencies to help parents find care and train providers, or to state licensing offices for hiring additional staff to monitor and provide technical assistance.

A recent study of cost, quality, and outcomes in child care centers found evidence that federal and employer subsidies as well have made a difference in the quality of child care centers (not including Head Start). Publicly operated centers, work site centers, and centers that conform to higher standards in order to receive public funding provide higher-quality care than other centers. They have higher expended costs and total revenue per child hour, have more donated resources, are less dependent on parent fees, pay higher wages, provide more staff benefits, have higher staff-to-child ratios, and have teachers with more education, more training, and longer tenure in the centers (Helburn 1995, chap. 15).

Another way the federal government can ensure quality is through the regulation of health and safety conditions. A recent four-state study found that care in states with more stringent regulations was, indeed, of higher quality (Helburn 1995, chap. 15). Recent research in 37 states found evidence that inspections to enforce compliance with regulations are as important as the levels of the regulations themselves (Hofferth and Chaplin 1998). Generally, stricter regulations are associated with increased price and reduced availability to consumers. This

research, however, found that frequent inspections were not associated with increased price and that, rather than reducing use, they increased it. One explanation is that more frequent inspections provide information to consumers about unmeasured aspects of quality. Parents say that they are very concerned about the quality of child care. Therefore, any information that increases their confidence about the quality of the care available may increase use. A possible reason why regulations per se are not strongly associated with improved structural aspects of quality is that states with stringent regulations may not enforce them. This study found, in fact, a negative relationship between the stringency of the regulation and enforcement of it (Hofferth and Chaplin 1998).

Public subsidies can be used indirectly as incentives to improve quality. By providing funding for some types of programs and not others, nonregulated family day care programs have an incentive to become licensed. Funds provided by the Child and Adult Care Food Program to regulated family day care homes serve as an incentive to bring nonregulated homes into the regulated market (Kisker et al. 1991).

Promoting parental choice

As described earlier, federal policies are also designed to promote parental choice. Two concerns raised by this policy stance are whether existing policies provide incentives or indirect pressure that forces parents into a kind of care they do not want and whether the policy of parental choice results in lower-quality care than could otherwise be achieved.

Conservatives have expressed concern that public subsidy programs force low-income families into using center-based programs against their will (Family Research Council 1998). It has been argued that, while many want to use centers on a part-day schedule, those who really have a choice do not want centers (or any other arrangement) on a full-time basis. Thus a test of preferences is whether families without an income constraint are more or less likely to use centers full-time. Using data from the National Child Care Survey 1990, I found the use of full-time centers to be higher among middle- and upper-income than among lower-income families. This suggests that those using centers are not doing so because they have no other option; rather, it is their preference. Other research shows that low-income parents are particularly concerned about the children's safety and see centers as being safer than home-based settings.

The second concern is that, while public funds can help raise the quantity and reduce the price of child care, simply providing additional funds to parents to purchase care will not lead to greatly increased quality. Parents do not necessarily want those aspects of quality that are easily monitored and regulated. In their questionnaire responses, parents emphasize quality and downplay the importance of price and convenience in making their child care decisions. In their choices, however, research has found strong effects of price and convenience on choice but only weak and inconsistent evidence for the effects of structural characteristics of programs such as child-staff ratio or group size (Hofferth and Wissoker 1992; Hofferth and Chaplin 1994; Blau and Hagy 1998). One study found that when prices fell, parents tended to select either more hours or larger (rather than smaller) child-staff ratios (Blau and Hagy 1998). Structural characteristics may not affect choice as anticipated because parents do not believe that they are important aspects of programs. Alternatively, their choices of characteristics may be severely limited. Research using the 1995 National Household Education Survey found evidence that characteristics are so closely tied to the particular type of program parents select that parental ability to further select quality aspects is limited (Hofferth et al. 1998). After controlling for type of program, parents who wanted a smaller number of children in their children's program were not more likely to get it. Nor did they appear to pay more to obtain a smaller number of children. The only attributes for which parents appeared to pay more were to have a more convenient location (closer to home) and to have a provider trained or educated in child development (Hofferth et al. 1998). Our analytic models assume variation in program characteristics within program types; this may not be the case.

While low child-staff ratios do not appear to be parent-sought, increasing research evidence highlights training as desirable. Most research suggests that training not only is critical for the quality of care children receive but also is relatively inexpensive, depending on the amount of training. Parents apparently have some control over training of the provider; research found that those parents for whom this was important were more likely to report their children in a program with a trained provider. Working with parents to recognize good quality is a critical objective.

Child care preferences of low-income and high-income parents are similar. What differs is access, including convenience and the ability to afford the program. While poor families have access to substantial subsidies that help them secure child care and preschool programs for their children, more nonworking than working poor families appear to benefit from these subsidies.

SUMMARY AND CONCLUSION

Child care is an underrated success story of return on public investments. U.S. federal expenditures on early education and care for low-income families have tripled since 1980 (Hofferth 1993), and the supply of center-based care rose threefold as well (Willer et al. 1991). What was the result of these investments? Most child care programs, including Head Start, are privately run; Head Start centers and public-school-based centers make up only about 17 percent of all centers (Willer et al. 1991). Privately funded centers receive some public funding. One study found that the highest-quality center-based programs were those that received substantial public funding (Helburn 1995). Global ratings of developmentally appropriate care for three different age groups of children, by the income level of the families using the center, showed that low- and high-income children were in higher-quality care than children of the working poor (Phillips, Voran, and Kisker 1994). Another study found children from both low- and high-income families to be in centers with higher quality ratings than those just above the poverty line (NICHD 1997). While we expect children of high-income families to be in high-quality centers—their parents can afford them—we do not expect this of children from low-income families. The reason these children receive better care than children from middle-income families is their eligibility for subsidized programs such as Head Start and publicly subsidized preschool programs (Hofferth 1995), thus demonstrating the difference that such subsidies make to low-income children's lives.

Children from working poor families are still at a disadvantage because of their parents' inability to take advantage of nonrefundable tax credits such as the Child and Dependent Care Tax Credit and their ineligibility for direct subsidies. Though the federal government more than doubled its child care expenditures between 1980 and 1997 (from $6 billion to about $14 billion, in constant dollars), still, in 1997, only about 63 percent of federal expenditures for child care went to low-income families; the rest went to middle-class families, primarily through the Child and Dependent Care Tax Credit. When direct assistance and tax relief are summed, only 30 percent of working poor families receive subsidies at the present time (compared with 36-37 percent of other families) because they are least likely to take the tax credit.

While the United States has mostly chosen to give subsidies to providers and vouchers or tax refunds to parents, other countries have made different decisions. Several nations have developed systems of maternal care through maternity and parental leave during much of the first year of the child's life, transitional informal arrangements during the second and third year, and universal state-funded preschool programs for 3-year-olds up to kindergarten entrance. The United States is unlikely to change its objectives, which are to provide maximum choice and flexibility to parents and to devolve control to the states. But it continues to increase subsidies, which have been shown to meet the three objectives of supporting families raising children, supporting maternal employment, and facilitating choice, though not without some concern for program quality.

Our review suggests that public provision of services can raise the quality of children's experiences; actual increases in quality will depend upon making sure that the services provided match those that parents want and need; not all those who are currently eligible benefit from publicly subsidized programs; and there is a substantial group of parents whose transition to work might be eased and independence stabilized by child care assistance. Unfortunately, it is expensive to provide these services. Welfare, it turns out, really was cheap. Providing a small stipend to a mother costs $25 billion per year, compared with more than $50 billion for child care and related services (Bergmann 1996). Of course, simply cutting off support entirely would be the least expensive way to move low-income mothers off welfare. Federal child care funds have been important in providing a stable and high-quality source of early education and care for the low-income children fortunate enough to have qualified. Children in high-income families do not need assistance. Children of low-income nonemployed parents are eligible for a variety of high-quality preschool programs. Many low-income employed and working-class parents are not benefiting from these same programs. To improve the care of children, more attention will need to be paid to the child care needs of low-income employed parents.

Note

1. Head Start children were not included in this study, however.

References

Bergmann, Barbara R. 1996. *Saving Our Children from Poverty: What the United States Can Learn from France*. New York: Russell Sage Foundation.

Blau, David M. and Alison P. Hagy. 1998. The Demand for Quality in Child Care. *Journal of Political Economy* 106(1):104-46.

Blau, David and Philip Robins. 1989. Fertility, Employment, and Child Care Costs. *Demography* 26:287-99.

Casper, Lynne M. 1996. *Who's Minding Our Preschoolers? Fall 1993*. Current Population Reports, P70(53):1-7. Washington, DC: Bureau of the Census.

Chaplin, Duncan, Philip Robins, Sandra Hofferth, Douglas Wissoker, and Paul Fronstin. 1998. The Price Elasticity of Child Care Demand: A Sensitivity Analysis. Urban Institute. Manuscript.

Chilman, Catherine S. 1991. Working Poor Families: Trends, Causes, Effects, and Suggested Policies. *Family Relations* 40:191-98.

Connelly, Rachel. 1992. The Effect of Child Care Costs on Married Women's Labor Force Participation. *Review of Economics and Statistics* 74(1):83-90.

Family Research Council. 1998. *Americans Believe Mom Is Best Child Care Provider*. Fact sheet no. IF98B2CC. Washington, DC: Family Research Council.

Finn-Stevenson, M. and E. Trzcinski. 1990. Public Policy Issues Surrounding Parental Leave: A State-by-State Analysis of Parental Leave Legislation. Cornell University. Manuscript.

Fronstin, Paul and Doug Wissoker. 1994. The Effects of the Availability of Low-Cost Child Care on the Labor Supply of Low-Income Women. Urban Institute. Manuscript.

Fuller, Bruce and Xiaoyan Liang. 1996. Market Failure? Estimating Inequality in Preschool Availability. *Educational Evaluation and Policy Analysis* 18:31-49.

Hayes, Cheryl, John Palmer, and Martha Zaslow. 1990. *Who Cares for America's Children? Child Care Policy for the 1990s*. Washington, DC: National Academy Press.

Helburn, Suzanne, ed. 1995. *Cost, Quality and Child Outcomes in Child Care Centers*. Denver: University of Colorado, Department of Economics, Center for Research in Economic and Social Policy.

Hofferth, Sandra L. 1993. The 101st Congress: An Emerging Agenda for Children in Poverty. In *Child Poverty and Public Policy*, ed. J. Chafel. Washington, DC: Urban Institute.

———. 1995. Caring for Children at the Poverty Line. *Children and Youth Services Review* 17(1-3):61-90.

———. 1996. Child Care in the United States Today. *The Future of Children* 6(2):41-61.

Hofferth, Sandra L., April Brayfield, Sharon Deich, and Pamela Holcomb. 1991. *National Child Care Survey 1990*. Washington, DC: Urban Institute.

Hofferth, Sandra L. and Duncan Chaplin. 1994. *Child Care Quality Versus Availability: Do We Have to Trade One for the Other?* Washington, DC: Urban Institute.

———. 1998. State Regulations and Child Care Choice. *Population: Research and Policy Review* 17:111-40.

Hofferth, Sandra L. and Nancy Collins. 1998. Child Care and Employment Turnover. Revised version of paper presented at the annual meeting of the Population Association of America, 1996, New Orleans.

Hofferth, Sandra L. and Sharon Gennis Deich. 1994. Recent U.S. Child Care and Family Legislation in Comparative Perspective. *Journal of Family Issues* 15(3):424-48.

Hofferth, Sandra L. and Ellen Kisker. 1994. Comprehensive Services in Child Care Settings: Prevalence and Correlates. *Pediatrics* 94(6, pt. 2): 1088-1091.

Hofferth, Sandra L., Kimberlee A. Shauman, Robin Henke, and Jerry West. 1998. *Characteristics of Children's Early Care and Education Programs*. Washington, DC: National Center for Educational Statistics.

Hofferth, Sandra L., Jerry West, Robin Henke, and Phillip Kaufman. 1994. *Access to Early Childhood Programs for Children at Risk*. Washington, DC: National Center for Educational Statistics.

Hofferth, Sandra L. and Douglas Wissoker. 1992. Price, Quality, and Income in Child Care Choice. *Journal of Human Resources* 27(1):70-111.

Kimmel, Jean. 1998. Child Care Costs as a Barrier to Employment for Single and Married Mothers. *Review of Economics and Statistics* 80(2):287-99.

Kisker, Ellen E., Sandra L. Hofferth, Deborah A. Phillips, and Elizabeth Farquhar. 1991. *A Profile of Child Care Settings: Early Education and Care in 1990.* Washington, DC: Government Printing Office.

Loprest, Pamela. 1997. *Supplemental Security Income for Children with Disabilities, Part of the Federal Safety Net.* New Federalism: Issues and Options for States, ser. A, no. A-10. Washington, DC: Urban Institute.

Maume, David. 1991. Child-Care Expenditures and Women's Employment Turnover. *Social Forces* 70(2):494-508.

Meyers, Marcia. 1993. Child Care in JOBS Employment and Training Programs: What Difference Does Quality Make? *Journal of Marriage and the Family* 51:593-603.

———. 1994. Cracks in the Seams: Durability of Child Care in JOBS Welfare to Work Programs. Syracuse University. Manuscript.

NICHD Early Child Care Research Network. 1997. Mother-Child Interaction and Cognitive Outcomes Associated with Early Child Care. Symposium presented at the biennial meeting of the Society for Research in Child Development, Washington, DC.

Phillips, Deborah, M. Voran, and Ellen Kisker. 1994. Child Care for Children in Poverty: Opportunity or Inequity. *Child Development* 65:472-92.

Siegel, Gary L. and L. Anthony Loman. 1991. *Child Care and AFDC Recipients in Illinois: Patterns, Problems and Needs.* St. Louis, MO: Institute of Applied Research.

U.S. Bureau of Labor Statistics. 1989. *Employee Benefits in Medium and Large Firms.* 1988 Bulletin 2336. Washington, DC: Department of Labor.

U.S. Bureau of the Census. 1982. *Trends in Child Care Arrangements of Working Mothers.* Current Population Reports, P-23, no. 117. Washington, DC: Government Printing Office.

———. 1983. *Child Care Arrangements of Working Mothers.* Current Population Reports, P-23, no. 129. Washington, DC: Government Printing Office.

———. 1987. *Who's Minding the Kids? Child Care Arrangements: Winter 1984-85.* Current Population Reports, P-70, no. 9. Washington, DC: Government Printing Office.

———. 1993. *Statistical Abstract of the United States 1993.* Washington, DC: Government Printing Office.

———. 1995. *What Does It Cost to Mind Our Preschoolers?* Current Population Reports, P-70, no. 52. Washington, DC: Government Printing Office.

———. 1997. *Statistical Abstract of the United States 1997.* Washington, DC: Government Printing Office.

U.S. Department of Health and Human Services. 1995. *The Green Book (Overview of Entitlement Programs).* Washington, DC: Department of Health and Human Services.

U.S. General Accounting Office. 1995. *Child Care Subsidies Increase Likelihood That Low-Income Mothers Will Work.* GAO/HEHS report, vol. 95-20. Washington, DC: General Accounting Office.

———. 1997. *Implications of Increased Work Participation for Child Care.* GAO/HEHS report, vol. 97-75. Washington, DC: General Accounting Office.

Waite, L. J., A. Leibowitz, and C. Witsberger. 1991. What Parents Pay For: Quality of Child Care and Child Care Costs. *Journal of Social Issues* 47(2):33-48.

Whitebook, Marcy, Carollee Howes, and Deborah Phillips. 1990. *Who Cares? Child Care Teachers and the Quality of Care in America: Final Report.* Washington, DC: Center for the Child Care Workforce.

Willer, Barbara, Sandra L. Hofferth, Ellen Eliason Kisker, Patricia Divine-Hawkins, Elizabeth Farquhar, and Frederic B. Glantz. 1991. *The Demand and Supply of Child Care in 1990.* Washington, DC: National Association for the Education of Young Children.

Defining and Assessing Early Childhood Program Quality

By DEBBY CRYER

ABSTRACT: In the United States, there is a definition of quality of early care and education (ECE) programs that is widely accepted in the early childhood profession. It emphasizes a child-centered approach to raising children, with caring adults who are kind and gentle rather than restrictive and harsh and who protect children's health and safety, while providing a wealth of experiences that lead to learning through play. According to the definition, individuality and creativity are encouraged rather than conformity. This definition is often criticized by those with differing perspectives, but in general, it appears to be valid for those who value the aspects of development that are associated with success in the current mainstream American educational system and society. In this article, the content, rationale, and criticisms of that definition of quality are presented. Methods used in its assessment, and information regarding its validity, are explained.

Debby Cryer, Ph.D., is an investigator at the Frank Porter Graham Child Development Center, University of North Carolina at Chapel Hill, and director of the child care program at the center. She has studied and written about early childhood program quality during the past 20 years, combining her interests as a practitioner with those of a researcher, examining real-world issues and translating research findings into practice for early childhood staff, parents, and policymakers.

NOTE: The work reported herein was partially supported under the Educational Research and Development Centers Program, PR/Award R307A60004, as administered by the Office of Educational Research and Improvement, U.S. Department of Education. However, the contents do not necessarily represent the positions or policies of the National Institute on Early Childhood Development and Education, the Office of Educational Research and Improvement, or the U.S. Department of Education, and endorsement by the federal government should not be assumed.

I N an attempt to define the quality of almost any service, it is obvious that subjective values will come into play. Just what quality is can be controversial, depending on what aspect of the service is being considered and who is doing the defining. This is certainly true when attempts are made to define the quality of early care and education (ECE) environments, for both center-based classrooms and family child care environments. The quality of ECE settings can be defined from many perspectives and can include a variety of indicators. Any definition is likely to be challenged by those with differing priorities or perspectives. In other words, ECE quality might be viewed as being in the eye of the beholder.

Nevertheless, in the United States, there is a widely accepted definition of ECE classroom quality. This definition comes under fire quite often and is adapted to meet different emphases with the passing of time, but in general it appears to be relatively stable. In this article, I will discuss the definition of ECE program quality that is currently widely accepted in the American early childhood profession. The rationale and content of this definition, and methods used in its assessment, will be presented. In addition, attention will be given to common criticisms of the definition. This will be followed by information on the validity of the definition, including the relation between ECE quality and children's development and between ECE process and structural quality.

DEFINING ECE QUALITY

Defining the quality of ECE settings is a complex task, partly due to the complexity of the ECE system itself. The ECE classroom can be viewed as being embedded within various spheres of influence, including the center in which the classroom operates as well as the community, at the local, state, and national levels. The same can be said for family child care homes. The conditions under which a center or family child care provider operates include variables that can influence what children experience.

The actual child environment (for example, the classroom or family child care setting used for children) can be characterized by both structural and process (or dynamic) quality features (Phillips and Howes 1987). Process quality consists of those aspects of an ECE setting that children actually experience in their programs, such as teacher-child and child-child interactions; the types of space, activities, and materials available to children; and how everyday personal care routines, such as meals, toileting, or rest, are handled. Children directly experience these processes, which are thought to have an influence on their well-being and developmental outcomes (Peisner-Feinberg and Burchinal 1997; Whitebook, Howes, and Phillips 1990).

Structural quality consists of inputs to process—characteristics that create the framework for the processes that children actually experience. These characteristics are part of the setting used by children and also the environment that surrounds that setting, such as a center or community. Examples of structural quality variables include measures of group size, adult-child ratios, and the education and experience of the teachers or the director of a program. Originally, structural quality variables represented aspects of ECE that are considered amenable to regulation (Phillips and Howes 1987). However, the definition has expanded to include variables, such as staff wages, teacher turnover, or parent fees, which are not particularly regulatable in the mixed market system of child care that presently exists in the United States (Phillipsen et al. 1997).

It is possible to evaluate both the structural and process quality of an ECE system. For example, in the article by Tietze and Cryer describing quality of European ECE in this volume, much of the discussion relates to the quality of the structures available to support classroom quality, rather than to the more proximal features of classroom quality that children experience. In this article, my concern is with defining and evaluating process quality—the quality of what children experience directly, either in child care centers or in family child care homes. The quality definition discussed here does not include important, but more distal, factors that will also affect children but in a less direct way, such as the availability or affordability of programs to families, the effectiveness of regulatory standards, or the overall family policy of a nation. My discussion focuses on those aspects of ECE program quality that are

thought to most directly affect children's development in child care.

Defining early
  childhood process quality

In defining ECE process quality, early childhood professionals have depended heavily on practitioners' concepts of best practice and, whenever possible, on findings from child development research. The definition is often thought of as a best bet for positive child development in areas that are associated with traditional success in later schooling as well as in later life in the mainstream U.S. democratic and capitalist society. The definition emphasizes practices that are assumed to encourage language; intellectual and physical abilities; social competence, including a balance of independence and cooperation; as well as emotional well-being. It is characterized by a child-centered approach to raising children, emphasizing children's play and interactions with materials and peers as the primary means of attaining developmental goals. It requires a safe environment that encourages good health. In this definition, the adult's role is to act as a facilitator of children's enriched play and to provide protection, positive attention, access to information, resources, support, and guidance. In practice, this means that adults in high-quality programs are very nice to the children (but certainly not totally permissive), rather than being negative, harsh, restrictive, punitive, or uninterested. They introduce children to a wealth of safe and healthful experiences to provide vast opportunities for learning.

There are various versions of the definition of ECE quality, but in general all share the same major tenets, differing only in the details. The core elements that are recognized as being necessary for children's positive development are

— safe care, with diligent adult supervision that is appropriate for children's ages and abilities; safe toys; safe equipment; and safe furnishings;
— healthful care, where children have opportunities for activity, rest, developing self-help skills in cleanliness, and having their nutritional needs met;
— developmentally appropriate stimulation, where children have choices of opportunities for play and learning in a variety of areas such as language; creativity through art, music, and dramatic play; fine and gross motor skills; numeracy; and nature or science;
— positive interactions with adults, where children can trust, learn from, and enjoy the adults who care for and educate them;
— promoting individual emotional growth, encouraging children to operate independently, cooperatively, securely, and competently; and
— promoting positive relationships with other children, allowing children to interact with their peers, with the environmental supports and adult guidance required to help interactions go smoothly.

Whatever the setting, family child care or care in a center, the same components of quality are addressed. This is because it is believed that children need the same basics for positive development, whether they are at home, in family child care, or in center-based programs. For example, the National Association for the Education of Young Children (NAEYC) has developed quality criteria for center-based early childhood programs (NAEYC 1984, 1991a, 1998a). There are also quality criteria for family child care (Family Child Care Quality Criteria Project 1995; Modigliani and Bromer 1997). These criteria were developed with input from many constituents in the respective professions. Although the family child care home and center-based ECE settings might appear to be very different, when the two quality definitions are closely examined, there is significant overlap, and the themes of these core elements are found in both, with only some of the details differing. Whatever the setting, it is believed that children require the same kinds of basic inputs for developmental success, although there is room for some flexibility in the details.

Interestingly, the quality elements previously listed appear to cross international borders. The points represented in NAEYC's accreditation criteria (1984, 1991a, 1998a) overlap substantially with the view of quality presented in the European Union's ECE quality definition (Belageur, Mestres, and Penn 1992) as well as with the view of quality presented in the World Health

Organization's Child Care Facility Schedule (World Health Organization 1990). In addition, parents of children in U.S. ECE programs value similar aspects of quality. Mitchell, Cooperstein, and Larner (1992) report that parents' views of quality are centered around ensuring their children's health and safety and positive interactions with the teacher. Browne Miller (1990) reports that parents see staff warmth, a good educational program, social activities, and physical activities as being important aspects of quality. Cryer and Burchinal (1997) report that parents of infants, toddlers, and preschoolers indicate that issues related to health, safety, and adult-child interactions were the most important in terms of quality for their children and that curriculum aspects of care were also very important. Of course, in terms of structural quality, parents also indicate the high importance of accessibility and affordability in child care, which represents their very realistic concerns. But this does not detract from parents' desire for positive experiences for their children while in child care.

Criticisms of the mainstream quality definition are abundant. They range from arguments about the inappropriateness of one small detail in the definition to much broader complaints. A good example of the range of criticisms is seen in the responses to NAEYC's version of the widely accepted definition of quality early childhood programs. A major component of NAEYC's definition of quality known as "developmentally appropriate practice" (Bredekamp 1987) has been attacked on

many fronts. It has been viewed as being far less relevant for programs serving minority cultures than for the white middle class. Powell (1994) notes that its emphasis on a child-centered teaching approach is in contrast to the more didactic teaching that is preferred by many lower-income, ethnic-minority parents. Williams (1994) explains that the child-centered approach, where the child is encouraged to develop as an individual, would also not apply well to many Native American children, where the development of the individual is not as important as the relationship of the individual to the group and where knowledge is not seen to be individually constructed but socially constructed. Others judge the definition as inadequate in terms of meeting the needs of children with disabilities, who often require more exacting teaching strategies than do typically developing children (Atwater et al. 1994).

Despite such criticisms, when the arguments are carefully examined, they are usually found to be focused on relatively small components of the larger construct, not on the core elements. Thus the definition can sometimes be adapted to incorporate changes, but the core, as a whole, does not really change radically. In fact, the concept of developmentally appropriate practice has recently been revised (Bredekamp 1997) to incorporate input from various segments of the profession. The definition, however, still maintains its basic identity. It is likely that disagreements about the content of the definition will continue, and ongoing efforts will be required to update the definition in response to input from various critics.

In some cases, the mainstream quality definition is rejected, with no sign of a possible compromise in viewpoint. Moss (1994) argues that early childhood program quality is a relative concept, not an objective reality, and that definitions change over time, according to values, beliefs, needs, and other requirements of the various stakeholders involved. Thus quality must be continually redefined, and only through a process of definition will any result be accepted by the constituents for whom it was created. This relativistic approach questions the validity of the mainstream process quality definition and, at the extreme, whether there can ever be agreement on any one definition. Perhaps this perspective can be best understood in terms of how the religious Right in the United States seems to view the mainstream definition of ECE quality child care. Here we see values that appear to be in substantial conflict with those of the early childhood profession. The religious Right emphasizes "spare the rod, spoil the child" and ensuring that young children learn religious information rather than the more authoritative, developmental approach that is represented in the mainstream definition. An adaptation of the U.S. mainstream definition to incorporate these values would not be very possible, although it is still likely that in the end, a definition of quality developed by the religious Right might still overlap with the mainstream definition in some areas, such as health or safety.

With all the differing perspectives on what is and is not early childhood program quality, it becomes especially important to examine relationships between child outcomes and the practices that are used in raising children in out-of-home care settings. Perhaps the real question is not, What is quality? but rather, What outcomes are produced under this definition of quality? Depending on the desired outcomes, the answer to the question What is quality? will then become apparent.

For example, if the definer of ECE process quality wants to ensure that children learn to communicate well, there might be several alternatives for what a quality definition might include to encourage that outcome. From the point of view of U.S. mainstream ECE quality, children would need to be in an environment where conversations take place frequently, where children's talk is encouraged, and where there are many things to talk about. It is thought to be unlikely that children would learn to communicate well when the environment does not provide these opportunities. (This definition is supported by research findings.) However, there are other perspectives about how to bring about good child communication. For example, a more didactic approach is sometimes thought to be effective (although not supported by research findings), where children practice talking and listening under more structured conditions such as those where memory drills and recitation tasks are emphasized and where natural child conversations are restricted. Of course, it cannot be forgotten that there will be some for whom learning to communicate well is not an important consideration in raising children. But any definition of ECE process quality is only an assumption until it has been tested for validity (that is, do children learn to communicate better under these conditions?). If relationships between the definition and the desired outcomes are found, then the definition becomes valid for those who value that outcome.

ASSESSING ECE PROCESS QUALITY

In order to validate any definition of ECE process quality, the definition must first be operationalized so that the extent to which it is being implemented in practice can be measured. Various measures for the specification and evaluation of the mainstream definition of ECE process quality have been developed in the past 20 years. Each represents a version of process quality that is assumed to produce specific child outcomes. Some have been used in research, while many were designed to evaluate and improve program quality. All the procedures discussed here require direct observation of children and adults in ECE settings during times of child activity. In addition, a staff interview or review of documents to collect information on unobserved requirements may be needed to supplement observations. Global process quality assessments are used to document the overall physical and learning quality of an ECE environment, as opposed to more specific assessments of quality.

The overlap in all instruments assessing process quality is overwhelming, and demonstrates the widespread agreement on an ECE quality definition in the United States. However, the instruments vary in scope and differ in the details. The content and format of the most widely used global assessments, as well as two examples of instruments that assess the quality of far more specific aspects of process quality, will be described in this article. Some instruments evaluate ECE quality for all children in a group, while others attempt to evaluate the quality experienced by an individual child. All of the instruments discussed here have been tested to ensure statistical reliability. For example, all have acceptable interrater reliability, indicating that the measures have been designed to produce similar scores when used by different observers.

One series of environment rating scales has been highlighted in the larger child care quality studies of the decade (Helburn 1995; Galinsky et al. 1994; Scarr, Eisenberg, and Deater-Deckard 1994; Whitebook, Howes, and Phillips 1990). These scales comprehensively assess the quality of ECE experienced by preschool-age children (Early Childhood Environment Rating Scale [ECERS]) (Harms and Clifford 1980), infants and toddlers (Infant/Toddler Environment Rating Scale [ITERS]) (Harms, Cryer, and Clifford 1990), and children in family child care (Family Day Care Rating Scale [FDCRS]) (Harms and Clifford 1989). The scales measure quality as experienced by all children in a specific group. The original ECERS has recently been revised (ECERS-R) (Harms, Clifford, and Cryer 1998) to represent new findings from research and to address issues related to meeting the needs of children with disabilities and children from diverse families. The revision represents the constantly changing details in ECE quality definitions but maintains the same basic principles found in the original ECERS.

Each scale provides a score of overall global process quality and consists of about 30-40 items organized into categories that vary somewhat depending on which scale is being used. Each scale includes items on personal care routines, furnishings and display for children, language experiences, learning activities, social development, interactions, and adult needs. It should be noted that, in most research, the calculation of a process quality score does not include items in the adult needs subscale, since these are considered indicators of structural rather than process quality. In all three instruments, items are presented as a seven-point scale with quality descriptors anchoring four points: 1 (inadequate), 3 (minimal), 5 (good), and 7 (excellent). Scoring is based primarily on what is observed during a period of two or three hours when the children are most actively involved, usually during the morning.

The *Assessment Profile for Early Childhood Programs* (Abbott-Shim and Sibley 1987) has also been used in a major research study (Scarr, Eisenberg, and Deater-Deckard 1994). Like the scales by Harms and colleagues described earlier, the profile assesses quality experienced for all children in a group. There is a family day care version of the profile that has been used extensively as the observation instrument to assess accreditation requirements of the National Family Day Care Association. The profile consists of a presence-absence checklist of about 150 items, arranged in components for administration, preschool, infant, and school-age. Subscales for the preschool, infant, and school-age groups include safety and health, learning environment, scheduling, curriculum, interacting, and individualizing. These vary somewhat depending on the age group that is being evaluated. For example, a nutrition subscale is included for groups of infants but not for the older groups. Subscales for the administration component include physical facilities, food service, program management, personnel, and program development. Besides observation and an interview with the teacher, reviewing certain documents to score some items is required. Ideally, an observation should take place to include a variety of typical classroom events (such as meals, learning activities, outdoor play, and so on). A total score is calculated by summing the number of yes responses.

The NAEYC Accreditation Instruments (NAEYC 1985, 1991b, 1998b) were developed to be used in the self-study process that programs undergo when applying for accreditation. The instruments are also used by validators who confirm the information presented by a program that has completed the self-study. The instruments are based completely on the NAEYC Accreditation Criteria, which were operationalized for assessment purposes. The instruments have been revised twice to represent changes in the criteria based on input from various constituents in the profession. The complete self-study assessment includes both structural and process measures. The process quality items are found in the Early Childhood Classroom Observation section of the materials. This observation consists of 71 items grouped in the following sections: interactions between teachers and children; curriculum; physical environment; health and safety; and nutrition. Items are scored on a 3-point scale, with 3 indicating that the requirement has been fully met. Observations are meant to take place when children are actively involved, for a period of at least one hour in a classroom. Scores for each item are considered individually, so no total score is calculated. However, it is possible to sum all scores for a total classroom score.

A more recently developed measure of ECE quality, the Observational Record of the Caregiving Environment (ORCE) (NICHD 1996), was developed for use in a major study of infant care and development. The ORCE measures quality of ECE as experienced by a single child, and it can be applied in different types of settings because it focuses on the caregiver's behaviors with a specific child rather than on what happens in a classroom or other ECE setting. It was developed for use with infants.

The ORCE requires both frequency counts and qualitative ratings of caregiver behaviors from trained observers. Items requiring frequency counts of care behaviors include more positive behaviors such as sharing positive interactions with the child (such as laughing, smiling, or cooing together), providing positive physical contact, or doing activities such as reading or playing a social game. Neutral behaviors are also counted, such as providing physical care to the child. More negative interactions, such as speaking negatively to the child or restricting the child, are counted as well. Qualitative ratings are made on aspects of care such as how sensitive or responsive the caregiver is to the child or how intrusive the caregiver is.

More specific definitions of process quality have been operationalized, often to assess the nature of teacher interactions with children. The Caregiver Interaction Scale (CIS) (Arnett 1989) yields four scores: sensitivity (warm, attentive, and engaged); harshness (critical, threatens children, and punitive); detachment (low levels of interaction, interest, and supervision); and permissiveness. The Teacher Involvement Scale (TIS) (Howes and Stewart 1987) allows an observer to code the nature of a teacher's involvement with a child every 20 seconds whenever a teacher is within three feet of the target child. The six scale points range from ignore, to routine (touches the child for routine care such as feeding or toileting, without any verbal interaction), to minimal, then simple, elaborative, and finally intense (engaging a child in conversation or actively playing with the child).

RESULTS FROM RESEARCH
USING PROCESS QUALITY
ASSESSMENT MEASURES

Research during the last 20 years (for example, Helburn 1995; Galinsky et al. 1994; Roupp et al. 1979; Whitebook, Howes, and Phillips 1990) has examined variations in child care quality, according to the mainstream ECE quality definition. The focus of the research has been to determine the status of ECE program quality in the United States, to examine the relations between structural quality and process quality, and to present the implications of varying quality in terms of children's well-being. Most of the research has defined children's positive outcomes in terms of the developmental areas that are associated with future school success, with the assumption that school success will lead to greater chances for adult success in the majority society. This research has provided validity for the mainstream definition of process quality while discovering the status of children's developmental outcomes in ECE programs in the United States.

Relationship between
process quality definitions
and child outcomes

The validity of a process quality definition is best found in its relationship to the outcomes desired for children. When defining "process quality," the definition can be only an assumption about what is good for children until it has been securely tied to the outcomes one would expect it to produce. There have been many studies, both large and small, that examine the extent to which a relationship exists between the widely held ECE process quality definition and children's development outcomes. An in-depth summary of findings that relate quality to outcomes will be found in Burchinal (this volume). Here I briefly describe findings that demonstrate the validity of the process quality definition that has been discussed in this article.

The National Child Care Staffing Study (Whitebook, Howes, and Phillips 1990), in which the ECERS, ITERS, CIS, and TIS were used, indicates a relation between aspects of quality and positive child development outcomes. Results from this study linked better levels of development to higher-quality care and teachers' positive behaviors. For example, children were found to spend more time in purposeful play rather than aimless wandering when teachers were more responsive and had more intense interactions with children. In addition, children had higher language development scores when they had teachers who took part in better teacher-child interactions and provided more appropriate caregiving (102). The Cost, Quality and Child Outcomes in Child Care Centers study (Peisner-Feinberg and Burchinal 1997) found that the quality of center-based care was related to preschool children's concurrent development across all domains studied, including receptive language, pre-academic skills, classroom behaviors, attitudes toward child care, and perceptions of competence. All of these are considered important for later success in school. These analyses adjusted for family factors and included children from diverse family backgrounds. In addition, the results provided evidence that children who might be considered at risk for school failure, especially children from less advantaged backgrounds, were more susceptible to the effects of child care quality, while no children were protected from the effects of low-quality care by more advantaged family backgrounds. The NICHD Early Child Care Research Network (1996) studied children during the first three years of life and found that higher child care quality was related to better mother-child relationships, fewer reports of children's behavior problems, higher cognitive and language outcomes, and better readiness for school.

These findings are supported by numerous smaller studies, which are described in various reviews of the literature (such as Doherty 1991). Generally, the literature indicates that higher-quality child care settings result in higher scores on measures of language and social development for the children enrolled in those settings, even allowing for family characteristics. In a recent study (Burchinal et al. 1996), it was found that even when controlling for the quality of infants' home learning environments, the development of infants was significantly related to the quality of their child care as measured using the ITERS. The TIS has been found to predict child developmental outcomes (Howes and Stewart 1987; Whitebook, Howes, and Phillips 1990). Specifically, it has been found to differentiate between children who behave as if they were securely attached to their caregivers and children who behave as if they were insecurely attached (Howes and Hamilton 1992). This is considered important because it has been found that children who are securely attached to their caregivers are more likely to demonstrate social competence with peers (Howes, Matheson, and Hamilton 1994). Higher scores on the CIS have been related to more positive child care teachers' involvement with children and to better children's language development and attachment security (Whitebook, Howes, and Phillips 1990).

Results for family child care settings are similar to those found for center-based care. The Study of Children in Family Child Care and Relative Care (Galinsky et al. 1994) found that homes were positively related to various better child care outcomes where providers were more sensitive, where they were responsive to the needs of children, and where the homes were rated as good or adequate on the FDCRS.

Information on the long-term effects of child care of varying quality is more limited due to the complicating factor that children are in multiple child care settings over time. There are indications, however, that social gains in child care carry into the school years (Zaslow 1991).

Status of U.S. child care quality

Access to higher-quality child care obviously makes a significant contribution to the positive development of children. But the same studies previously reported also show that this access is rarely available to most children in child care. In attempting to determine the status of U.S. child care in terms of process quality, findings have shown that good care is rarely found. In addition, there is great variation in the quality found, with a few programs providing very good ECE while many others provide ECE of much lower quality. The Cost, Quality, and Child Outcomes study (Cost, Quality and Child Outcomes 1995), for example, used combined scores from the ECERS, ITERS, CIS, and TIS to measure global process quality in child care centers in four states (California, Connecticut, Colorado, and North Carolina) and concluded that care provided in most centers in the United States is of mediocre quality, with infant and toddler care being of the poorest quality. Mediocre care is the condition that most older preschoolers in child care experience and is defined as care in which children's basic needs for health and safety are met, some warmth and support is provided by adults, and some learning experiences are provided. Poor care, which characterized almost half of the infant and toddler rooms, included problems in basic sanitary conditions related to diapering and feeding; safety-related problems; lack of warm, supportive relationships with adults; and lack of materials required for physical and intellectual growth. These findings are similar to those found in other studies using these instruments in other states, where average quality levels were also rarely found in the good range (Scarr, Eisenberg, and Deater-Deckard 1994; Whitebook, Howes, and Phillips 1990).

One assumption in the early childhood field has been that higher process quality is more likely to be found in nonprofit, rather than for-profit, child care programs. This assumption was supported by findings from Whitebook, Howes, and Phillips 1990. However, the relationship between sector and process quality is actually more complicated than originally shown. Helburn and colleagues (1995) found no differences in process quality scores between for-profit and nonprofit programs in California, Connecticut, and Colorado, but in North Carolina, where child care regulations were less stringent, for-profit centers did provide lower quality than nonprofit programs did. Further analyses showed that nonprofit programs tended to provide higher quality than for-profit programs did, except for nonprofit centers run by churches (excluded from the Whitebook, Howes, and Phillips analyses), which provide quality similar to that found in the for-profit sector.

Family child care study results tend to be similar to those found for center-based care. The most recent major study to be completed in the context of family child care (Galinsky et al. 1994) used the FDCRS, CIS, and TIS to assess process quality. In this study, it was found that few homes (9 percent) had high scores (less than "good") on the FDCRS, the majority (56 percent) fell into the adequate or custodial range, and a substantial number were scored as being of low quality (35 percent).

The relation between structural and process quality

Research has also examined which structural features have the strongest association with process quality. The practical intent of this research has been to help policymakers and practitioners know where to focus quality improvement efforts. Results have been reasonably consistent across various studies but not overwhelmingly strong. Higher levels of teacher education, fewer children per teacher, and better teacher wages have been significant predictors of process quality (for example, Phillipsen et al. 1997; Whitebook, Howes, and Phillips 1990). Thus it comes as no surprise that centers in states where regulation is more stringent regarding ratios and teacher education have, on average, better process quality scores (Helburn 1995). The positive effect of regulation is also clear when examining its relation to family child care process quality. Galinsky and colleagues (1994) found that providers who are regulated by their states are more sensitive to children and offer more responsive care than nonregulated family child care providers or relatives of the children. In addition, while only 13 percent of regulated family child care homes were found to be inadequate when assessed using the FDCRS, 50 percent of nonregulated homes and 69 percent of relative care environments were in the inadequate range.

Although the associations between structural and process quality are still not fully understood, research continues to clarify the relationship. For example, it has been recently shown that the effects of the many structural features of ECE programs are highly interwoven and that no one structural variable strongly accounts for differences in process quality. Cryer and colleagues (1998) have shown that when examining the variance in process quality accounted for by any specific structural variable, much of its power of association is actually shared with other variables. For example, in these analyses, wages appeared to be one of the stronger predictors of process quality in the United States, but further examination of the influence of this variable showed that wages actually accounted for 4 percent of the unique and 15 percent of the common variance in ECERS scores. In other words, most of the association between wages and process quality was shared with other structural variables and was not unique only to wages. Blau (1997) also showed that results of past analyses can be questioned and that there is no strong obvious answer for policymakers when considering how to create regulation that will improve ECE quality. Thus it is most likely that to improve process quality, many structures must be considered simultaneously rather than just a few. For example, highly qualified or well-paid teachers can do only so much to provide high-quality programs for children if they do not have appropriate space, materials, equipment, and administrative support. Obviously, a broad range of structural supports must be provided if we wish to increase the availability of higher ECE process quality in the United States.

SUMMARY

It is true that the quality of ECE programs can be considered to be in the eye of the beholder. The priorities of those who define quality will determine any quality definition. However, for process quality definitions to have validity, it must be shown that they are associated with the outcomes that are desired for children. In the United States and even beyond, the early childhood profession has come to a significant consensus in establishing what is required for high-quality programs. The priorities in this definition of quality include safe and healthful care, developmentally appropriate stimulation, positive interactions with adults, encouragement of individual emotional growth, and promotion of positive relationships with other children. The various versions of this definition may differ in the details, but few would argue that these priorities are not necessary for the positive development of young children. The validity of the definition has been proven in many studies. When higher process quality is provided, all children gain in the development of skills and abilities that are associated with success in school and later life in the democratic, industrialized society of the United States.

It is distressing to note that in the United States, the quality experienced by children varies radically. High numbers of children receive poor to mediocre care and education, which is related to poorer child development outcomes, while only a few receive ECE that actively encourages success in our society. There is great diversity in the quality of programs to which families have access, providing unequal opportunity for children to have the same chances to come to school ready to learn.

For those who do not accept the current, widely accepted definition of ECE quality, either because of small differences in the details or because of their relativistic perspective, it is important that they create alternative measures of quality that are proven to be valid. Parents, practitioners, policymakers, and other interested constituents need to understand how the implementation of a definition will affect children's development, both at present and in the long term. Of course, this will require careful research, but assumptions about child-rearing practices are insufficient. Those who raise young children need to fully understand the strengths and drawbacks to any practices they use to optimize children's prospects for the future.

References

Abbott-Shim, Martha and Annette Sibley. 1987. *Assessment Profile for Early Childhood Programs*. Atlanta, GA: Quality Assist.

Arnett, J. 1989. Caregivers in Day-Care Centers: Does Training Matter? *Journal of Applied Developmental Psychology* 10:541-52.

Atwater, J. B., J. J. Carta, I. S. Schwartz, and S. R. McConnell. 1994. Blending Developmentally Appropriate Practice and Early Childhood Special Education: Redefining Best Practice to Meet the Needs of All Children. In *Diversity and Developmentally Appropriate Practices: Challenges for Early Childhood Education*, ed. B. L. Mallory and R. S. New. New York: Teachers College Press.

Belageur, I., J. Mestres, and H. Penn. 1992. Die Frage der Qualität in Kinderbetreuungseinrichtungen (Diskussionspapier) (Quality of child care centers [A discussion paper]. Kommission der Europäischen Gemeinschaften.

Blau, David M. 1997. The Production of Quality in Child Care Centers. *Journal of Human Resources* 32(2):354-87.

Bredekamp, S. 1987. *Developmentally Appropriate Practice in Early Childhood Programs Serving Children from Birth Through Age 8*. Washington, DC: National Association for the Education of Young Children.

————. 1997. *Developmentally Appropriate Practice in Early Childhood Programs Serving Children from Birth Through Age 8*. Washington, DC: National Association for the Education of Young Children.

Browne Miller, A. 1990. *The Day Care Dilemma: Critical Concerns for American Families*. New York: Plenum.

Burchinal, Margaret R., Joanne E. Roberts, Laura A. Nabors, and Donna M. Bryant. 1996. Quality of Center Care and Infant Cognitive and Language Development. *Child Development* 67:606-20.

Cost, Quality and Child Outcomes Study Team. 1995. *Cost, Quality and Child Outcomes in Child Care Centers: Public Report*. Denver: University of Colorado, Department of Economics, Center for Research in Economic and Social Policy.

Cryer, Debby and Margaret Burchinal. 1997. Parents as Child Care Consumers. *Early Childhood Research Quarterly* 12:35-58.

Cryer, Debby, Wolfgang Tietze, Margaret Burchinal, Teresa Leal, and Jesús Palacios. 1998. Predicting Process Quality from Structural Quality in Preschool Programs: A Cross-Country Comparison. University of North Carolina, Chapel Hill. Manuscript.

Doherty, Gillian. 1991. *Quality Matters in Child Care*. Huntsville, ON: Jesmond.

Family Child Care Quality Criteria Project. 1995. *Quality Criteria for Family Child Care*. Washington, DC: National Association for Family Child Care.

Galinsky, Ellen, Carollee Howes, Susan Kontos, and Marybeth Shinn. 1994. *The Study of Children in Family Child Care and Relative Care: Highlights of Findings*. New York: Families and Work Institute.

Harms, Thelma and Richard M. Clifford. 1980. *Early Childhood Environment Rating Scale*. New York: Teachers College Press.

————. 1989. *Family Day Care Rating Scale*. New York: Teachers College Press.

Harms, Thelma, Richard M. Clifford, and Debby Cryer. 1998. *Early Childhood Environment Rating Scale: Revised Edition*. New York: Teachers College Press.

Harms, Thelma, Debby Cryer, and Richard M. Clifford. 1990. *Infant / Toddler Environment Rating Scale*. New York: Teachers College Press.

Helburn, Suzanne, John R. Morris, Mary L. Culkin, Sharon Lynn Kagan, and Jean Rustici. 1995. Within Sector Comparisons and the Impact of Government Spending. In *Cost, Quality and Child Outcomes in Child Care Centers: Technical Report*, ed. S. Helburn. Denver: University of Colorado, Department of Economics, Center for Research in Economic and Social Policy.

Helburn, Suzanne W. ed. 1995. *Cost, Quality and Child Outcomes in Child Care Centers: Technical Report*. Denver: University of Colorado, Department of Economics, Center for Research in Economic and Social Policy.

Howes, Carollee and Claire Hamilton. 1992. Children's Relationships with Caregivers: Mothers and Child Care Teachers. *Child Development* 63:859-66.

Howes, Carollee, C. Matheson, and Claire Hamilton. 1994. Maternal, Teacher and Child Care History Correlates of Children's Relationships with Peers. *Child Development* 65:264-73.

Howes, Carollee and P. Stewart. 1987. Child's Play with Adults, Toys and Peers: An Examination of Family and Child Care Influences. *Developmental Psychology* 23:423-30.

Mitchell, A., E. Cooperstein, and M. Larner. 1992. *Child Care Choices, Consumer Education, and Low-Income Families*. New York: National Center for Children in Poverty.

Modigliani, Kathy and Juliet Bromer. 1997. *Quality Standards for NAFCC Accreditation: Pilot Study Draft*. Boston: Wheelock College, Family Child Care Study.

Moss, Peter. 1994. Defining Quality: Values, Stakeholders and Processes. In *Valuing Quality in Early Childhood Services: New Approaches to Defining Quality*, ed. Peter Moss and Alan Pence. London: Paul Chapman.

National Association for the Education of Young Children (NAEYC). 1984. *Accreditation Criteria and Procedures of the National Association for the Education of Young Children*. Washington, DC: National Association for the Education of Young Children.

———. 1985. *Guide to Accreditation by the National Association for the Education of Young Children*. Washington, DC: National Association for the Education of Young Children.

———. 1991a. *Accreditation Criteria and Procedures of the National Association for the Education of Young Children*. Washington, DC: National Association for the Education of Young Children.

———. 1991b. *Guide to Accreditation by the National Association for the Education of Young Children*. Washington, DC: National Association for the Education of Young Children.

———. 1998a. *Accreditation Criteria and Procedures of the National Association for the Education of Young Children*. Washington, DC: National Association for the Education of Young Children.

———. 1998b. *Guide to Accreditation by the National Association for the Education of Young Children*. Washington, DC: National Association for the Education of Young Children.

NICHD Early Child Care Research Network. 1996. Characteristics of Infant Child Care: Factors Contributing to Positive Caregiving. *Early Childhood Research Quarterly* 11:269-306.

Peisner-Feinberg, Ellen S. and Margaret R. Burchinal. 1997. Relations Between Preschool Children's Child-Care Experiences and Concurrent Development: The Cost, Quality and Outcomes Study. *Merrill-Palmer Quarterly* 43(3):451-77.

Phillips, Deborah A. and Carollee Howes. 1987. Indicators of Quality in Child Care: Review of Research. In *Quality in Child Care: What Does Research Tell Us?* ed. D. Phillips. Washington, DC: National Association for the Education of Young Children.

Phillipsen, Leslie, Margaret R. Burchinal, Carollee Howes, and Debby Cryer. 1997. The Prediction of Process Quality from Structural Features of Child Care. *Early Childhood Research Quarterly* 12:281-303.

Powell, D. R. 1994. Parents, Pluralism, and the NAEYC Statement on Developmentally Appropriate Practice. In *Diversity and Developmentally Appropriate Practices: Challenges for Early Childhood Education*, ed. B. L. Mallory and R. S. New. New York: Teachers College Press.

Roupp, R., J. Travers, F. Glantz, and C. Coelen. 1979. *Children at the Center: Final Results of the National Day Care Study*. Cambridge, MA: Abt Books.

Scarr, Sandra, M. Eisenberg, and K. Deater-Deckard. 1994. Measurement of Quality in Child Care Centers. *Early Childhood Research Quarterly* 9:131-51.

Whitebook, Marcy, Carollee Howes, and Deborah Phillips. 1990. *Who Cares? Child Care Teachers and the Quality of Care in America: Final Report*. Washington, DC: Center for the Child Care Workforce.

Williams, L. R. 1994. Developmentally Appropriate Practice and Cultural Values: A Case in Point. In *Diversity and Developmentally Appropriate Practices: Challenges for Early Childhood Education*, ed. B. L. Mallory and R. S. New. New York: Teachers College Press.

World Health Organization. Division of Mental Health. 1990. *WHO Child Care Facility Schedule with User's Manual*. Geneva: World Health Organization, Division of Mental Health.

Zaslow, M. 1991. Variation in Child Care Quality and Its Implications for Children. *Journal of Social Issues* 47:125-38.

ANNALS, *AAPSS*, **563**, May 1999

The Kellogg Child Development Center: High-Quality Child Care

By LORNA KELLOGG

ABSTRACT: After a 10-year, hands-on study of high-quality child care both in the United States and abroad, Lorna Kellogg founded a child care program intended to be a model for high standards in the field. The Kellogg Child Development Center of Boulder, Colorado, in less than four years of operation, has become renowned for its deceptively simple solutions to some of the largest problems that plague child care centers in general. This success has enabled the center to begin actively pursuing the second half of its mission, to improve the quality of care provided in child care centers everywhere. It is Lorna Kellogg's firm belief that it is absolutely possible for every child growing up outside of his or her home to have high-quality, affordable child care.

Lorna Kellogg is the founder and executive director of the Kellogg Child Development Center in Boulder, Colorado. She has worked extensively in the field of early childhood education as a teacher, nanny, director of child care centers, and consultant to families hiring in-home child care providers, as well as in programs trying to increase the quality of care provided in their center. Named for her grandparents, the Kellogg Center is both a model high-quality child development center and a quality standards advocacy group.

T WO generations ago, the typical American family had 2.6 children. Today the typical child has 2.6 parents. The problem is that while there are statistically more parents, there is significantly less parenting. This is due to a variety of forces outside the control of individual families. The trade deficit, the global economy, inflation, and corporate restructuring have created a need for the two-income family. But if parents need to work in order to support a family, who is going to raise the children?

Unfortunately, the raising of our children has fallen to a workforce that is largely ill prepared and inadequately compensated for the job. Consequently, at the most important time of their lives, our children are enduring highly inconsistent standards of caregiving. Today's children are shuttled through a succession of underpaid, randomly trained, overworked, and stressed-out child care personnel. Many highly motivated caregivers leave the field rather than remain in a situation where they are unable to provide the level of care they believe to be essential. But, of course, the children remain.

THE KELLOGG MODEL

This so-called "quiet crisis" is described, along with a call to action, in the Carnegie Corporation's 1994 report *Starting Points: Meeting the Needs of Our Youngest Children* (Carnegie Task Force 1994). The Kellogg Child Development Center (KCDC), in Boulder, Colorado, was founded in 1994 in response to this "quiet crisis." The Kellogg Center incorporates all the recommendations in *Starting Points* for quality child care (low teacher-child ratios, small group sizes, qualified caregivers, health and safety as priorities, linkage to parents and the community) and has attracted the interest of families, government, foundations, and early childhood educators. The Kellogg Center is a successful and replicable model program that utilizes simple, cost-effective solutions to address the spectrum of problems that plague child care centers.

Two goals motivate our work at the Kellogg Center—to be a replicable model of a high-quality child care program and to be part of the national and international movement to raise quality standards in the field of early childhood education (ECE). While it is unusual to house a child care center and advocacy group under the same roof, I believe it is essential to have an exemplary model program dedicated to providing high-quality care that can be easily emulated by others. In turn, we must be part of the larger movement to both benefit from and contribute to it. This article focuses on our narrower challenge of creating a model program and only briefly discusses our broader objective.[1]

Part of our long-term goal is to help diffuse good practice throughout ECE. A common complaint among early childhood educators is that, unlike the fields of science or medicine, where new information and better methodologies are implemented quickly, child care programs do not regularly utilize available knowledge to improve the quality of the care provided to families. For example, the large body of research on brain development is underutilized in this field. Professor Linda Darling-Hammond of Columbia University's Teachers College notes that "in most states, neither teachers nor administrators are required to know much about how children learn in order to be certified" (Begley 1996, 59). At the Kellogg Center, we work hard to stay abreast of new findings and incorporate them into our work.

In addition, we feel strongly that child care centers, both for-profit and nonprofit, must behave more like businesses, not just human service organizations. To be successful, they must also be financially viable. A commitment to financial stability and programmatic improvements involving ongoing self- and external evaluation continually increases the quality of care in our center.

Our center is housed in a 3000-square-foot ranch-style house that had been renovated for child care use prior to our renting it. (Our long-term goal is to raise funds to construct a new building since our current facility meets only our minimum needs.) We have five classrooms, a kitchen, a tiny administrative office, and a few small playground areas. We are licensed for 52 children aged 6 weeks to 6 years. We are open from 7:30 a.m. to 5:30 p.m., Monday through Friday. Our infant nursery has a maximum of seven infants. We encourage parents to use our center for part-time care but also offer full-time care to serve parents who do not have flexible employment situations. Figure 1 outlines our organizational structure.

We believe that the problems prevalent in child care centers are solvable. We have found practical solutions for everything from low teacher salaries and the corresponding low levels of teacher education, to high child-teacher ratios and inadequate individual attention to children, to lack of curriculum and developmentally appropriate intellectual stimulation, to lack of appreciation for diversity, to lack of affordability for low-income parents, and to general neglect of children. These are all issues that educators, parents, and government can work together to solve. We work closely with our families, businesses, community members, and the city of Boulder to jointly address these issues. Indeed, as Hillary Clinton and Marian Wright Edelman have emphasized, it does take a village to raise a child.

The motivation to create the Kellogg Center came after 10 years of international hands-on study of high-quality child care programs as well as my own childhood experience with primary care. I had the same teacher, Brucie Tucker, from kindergarten through second grade. The individual attention she gave me, along with the support in strengthening the areas that were challenging for me as a student, made a world of difference to me. I fully credit Brucie Tucker and New Canann Country School for providing the foundation I needed to have success in all areas of my adult life. My experience visiting and working in child care centers in developing countries also had a profound effect on the design of our program. In these nonindustrialized

FIGURE 1
THE ORGANIZATIONAL STRUCTURE OF THE KELLOGG CENTER

Board of Directors
Lorna Kellogg
Tamah Matejka
Diane Hagemark
Kathy Thomas
Laurence Freedom

Administrative Staff

1 FTE	Executive Director
1 FTE	Program Director
1 FTE	Administrative Coordinator

Enrollment and Teaching Staff Chart					
	Infant	Toddler I	Toddler II	Preschool	Pre-Kindergarten
FTE Children	4	4	5	8	8
PTE Children (MWF)	3	4	3	2	6
PTE Children (T and TH)	3	4	3	2	4
Maximum Daily Group Size	7	8	8	10	14
FTE Primary Caregivers	2	2	2	2	2
PTE Assistant Caregivers	2	2	2	2	2

Support Staff

1 PTE	Cook and Nutrition Director
1 PTE	Janitor
1 PTE	Maintenance Coordinator
1 PTE	Infant Massage Coordinator (On Call)
2 FTE	Interns (Substitute Teachers)

NOTE: "FTE" stands for "full-time employee(s)"; "PTE," for "part-time employee(s)"; "M," "W," "F," "T," and "TH," for the days of the week.

countries where there is strong societal support and appreciation for children, I found a high level of self-esteem among children. This was often a direct result of extended family members' living together and showering children with individual attention. I found this especially true in West Africa. Since high self-esteem is a key element for a successful life, I became determined to emulate the "It takes a village" model in the Kellogg Center. Having a familylike atmosphere in our center is therefore the first of three guiding principles that underlie our work.

The second principle is primary caregiving. In the early childhood literature, I found validation for my own experience that what often makes the difference between a child's success and failure in life is the emotional support and intellectual stimulation from just one adult who takes special interest in the child. This view has been substantiated by Ann Masten and J. D. Coatsworth's resilience research on children who succeed despite tremendous environmental and economic forces working against them (Masten and Coatsworth 1995). This suggests that one of the crucial factors for children growing up outside of the home is continuity of care and emotional attachment between the child and his or her caregiver. The centrality of the teacher-child relationship is therefore a philosophical foundation of KCDC.

Our third principle combines the benefits of long-term relationships with essential developmentally appropriate practice (Bredekamp and Copple 1997). Developmentally appropriate practice identifies developmental phases that children move through in early childhood education and the appropriate language, curriculum, and activities that early childhood educators should use with each developmental phase. Surprisingly, many teachers are not even familiar with the term, let alone developmentally appropriate practice itself.

The teachers at the Kellogg Center are all professional early childhood educators. I consider it essential that primary caregivers have a minimum of a bachelor's degree in early childhood education as well as teaching experience in an early childhood environment. If teachers lack basic knowledge of the various developmental stages that infants, toddlers, and preschoolers move through, the children are then at risk for understimulation intellectually, emotionally, socially, and physically. Since we now know that the first five years in a child's life are the most important for brain development, we place an emphasis on a high level of teacher (adult) education.

Our program director and I also network in the early childhood community, both locally and internationally via the Internet and e-mail. We have found that by participating in research projects on high-quality care, attending workshops and seminars, brainstorming with other educators, and continuing our own education in our field, the quality of care in our program continues to improve. I used this same approach to design our program. Based on years of research and interviews with other early childhood educators, I discovered that my ideas were not unique and already existed under the name of primary caregiving.

Why primary caregiving?

The design of our primary caregiving program is simple and focuses on individual care and attention for each child. Children enter the program as infants, toddlers, or preschoolers and are placed in a small cluster of two to six children of similar age and development. Each cluster stays together with one primary caregiver throughout their years at the center until the children leave for kindergarten. The children shift classrooms together with their teachers every fall when the oldest cluster graduates to kindergarten. The teachers of the graduating class are then available to start over with a new cluster of infants.

Our primary caregivers are all professional early childhood educators with a variety of backgrounds, areas of expertise, and pedagogical approaches. Teacher-to-child ratios are 1:3.5 for infants (seven infants with two teachers in the nursery), 1:4.0 for 1- and 2-year-olds, 1:5.0 for 3-year-olds, and 1:6.0 or 1:7.0 maximum for 4- and 5-year-olds. Low ratios produce beneficial results in both obvious and subtle ways. Teachers and children form close emotional bonds, and children develop levels of security and trust similar to those in familial relationships. Each teacher becomes, in essence, a surrogate parent and a very important partner in parenting with the child's family. The following describes a typical moment in our 2-year-old room. Two-and-a-half-year-old Sally (not her real name) wanted very much to play with a toy her friend was using. Normally, a 2-year-old would walk over, thump her friend on the head, and grab the toy. However, in this instance, after negotiating an agreement that her turn would be next, Sally sat down on a chair a few feet away and watched her friend for several minutes until her teacher asked her, "Sally, what are you doing sitting there so quietly on that chair?" Sally promptly replied, "I'm being patient." Her teacher later told me how happy it made her to see the results of two years of supporting and teaching the children to treat each other respectfully. These types

of camaraderie, sharing, and negotiation skills are typical among the toddlers in our program, but they are atypical in many other programs.

Over and over, we have seen how important it is for children to develop strong, long-term bonds with their teachers. In the primary caregiving model, each child receives continual one-on-one guidance and instruction and as a result has very high levels of self-esteem and communication skills. Primary caregiving is child care at its best. "Formal and informal results from this approach are very positive, with dramatic increases in children's academic attainment" (Katz and McClellan 1997, 34).

There are other benefits to primary caregiving in addition to the emotional support children receive. Teachers come to know and understand children as individual learners. As each child is unique and has his or her own strengths and weaknesses in learning, teachers are able to provide individual instruction and assist children in turning their weaknesses into strengths. The teachers track each child's growth and development in a journal filled with photographs and notes. The journals provide parents with a record of their child's early years and help parents deepen their knowledge of their child's learning processes. Our annual survey of Boulder-area kindergarten teachers indicates that the level of kindergarten readiness of children graduating from KCDC is exceptionally high.

Another benefit of primary caregiving is that it helps teachers identify possible developmental delays in children early on. Unfortunately, developmental delays often go unnoticed in traditional settings until children begin their elementary education. With primary caregiving in small groups, teachers know their children so well that delays and learning disabilities can be identified very early and families gently alerted so that evaluations and outside help can be brought in. Early identification of delays can contribute to the success of a child's lifelong learning.

The Kellogg Center is an inclusive program, and children with special needs are enrolled according to their developmental stage as opposed to their chronological age. Teachers work closely with families and often attend therapy appointments (speech therapy, occupational therapy, and so on) along with parents in order to ensure congruence between the center, home, and therapy. Parents are always grateful to have this kind of additional support.

The self-esteem levels of children receiving regular, respectful, loving, and individual attention are remarkably high. Strong self-esteem is an essential part of the development of a child's ability to think critically. Effective communication skills and the capacity for critical thought are additional benefits of receiving individual attention through primary caregiving.

Parents also benefit from primary care relationships. Teachers become valuable extended family members and provide tremendous support. They are able to draw on their years of experience and education to offer information, resources, and professional referrals for parents. This also allows parents to feel safe and secure leaving their children. In a recent anonymous survey asking how often parents worried when leaving their children at our center, over 94 percent of our families responded "never" or "almost never." This unusually high level of parental comfort translates into less parental absenteeism and tardiness at work as well as increased productivity because parents do not have to worry about their children during the workday.

Our teachers benefit from primary caregiving as well because they come to care deeply for the children in their classrooms. One of the contributing factors in teacher burnout that I heard repeatedly in interviewing over 500 applicants for our 27 teaching positions was frustration over working closely with a group of children and then having to turn them over to a new teacher every year. Consider a teacher working with a group of infants from the age of 3 months through 24 months. Preverbal communication and exercises are a huge part of developmentally appropriate practice during that time. Understandably, it is discouraging to work so closely with a group and then have them move to a new classroom just as they are beginning to construct sentences and use the two years of support, stimulation, and instruction. Teachers view five-year primary caregiving as a unique and exceptional teaching opportunity. For a committed early childhood educator, having the opportunity to guide a small group of children through every developmental stage from birth until kindergarten is a cherished and rare experience. Primary caregiving provides teachers with the opportunity to care personally about every child in their cluster. This is obviously a deeply gratifying, emotional experience.

Brain development
  and developmentally
  appropriate practice

One of the serious risks children face growing up in child care settings is understimulation. There is much "maintaining" of children in centers. Diapers are changed, snacks are given, and nap times are dictated. Understaffing puts teachers in a position of maintaining order. Commonly called "four walls and a teacher," understaffing means teachers are left with no time for the type of individual attention that is so emotionally nurturing and intellectually stimulating. Recently published research on brain development has reinforced and brought a new sense of urgency to what early childhood educators have always known: developmentally appropriate practice is crucial for healthy growth and development, especially in the first five years of a child's life. With the utilization of sophisticated brain scans, we now have proof that, after basic genetic imprinting, a child's environment is the most powerful determinant of how a child's brain becomes "wired" and that the most important years are the first five. According to the now-famous *Newsweek* article, "Your Child's Brain," there are "windows of opportunity that nature flings open, starting before birth, and then slams shut, one by one, with

every additional candle on the child's birthday cake" (Begley 1996, 56). Knowledge of these windows, or critical periods, is essential for both parents and educators. Child care centers must become child development centers that focus on each child's individual growth and development.

Thanks to educators and social philosophers like Montessori, Piaget, Vygotsky, Steiner, and Bredekamp, we have known for decades what constitutes an intellectually stimulating environment for children. The curriculum at KCDC is based on a combination of developmentally appropriate practice and the individual Kellogg faculty member's vision of its relevance to each child. While each teacher's personal educational philosophy is unique at the center, we ensure curriculum congruence by monitoring the program through director observation and feedback sessions and staff development meetings where centerwide discussion of program philosophy occurs. The curriculum draws inspiration from many sources, including Waldorf, Montessori, and *Storybook Journey* (McCord 1995). We believe there are many ways to teach and that every child learns differently. Individual children should therefore be supported in learning in ways that suit them best. This diagnostic approach helps teachers take individual and group developmental stages into consideration when planning weekly activities to ensure that every child is stimulated and learning. This avoids the rigidity in teaching and labeling that can occur when children's individual levels of development are not taken into account. It is respectful and mindful teaching that encourages children to learn.

Health and wellness

Children in child care centers are exposed to high levels of illness, so health and wellness are a priority. Our full-time pediatric nurse oversees the infant nursery. With over 40 years of experience, her presence is especially important as we learn more about the negative effect of overuse of antibiotics and how repeated exposure to illness can wear on a young child's immune system. She is available to parents for consultation, resource, and referral. She is also an invaluable resource to the other teachers who regularly ask for assistance in assessing possible illness in children. Levels of illness are significantly lower at the Kellogg Center as a result. We know this to be true based on the observations of parents who have moved their children to our center from other programs. Additionally, many of our teachers who have previously taught in programs with less emphasis on health and wellness testify to the success of our approach. By making such a conscious commitment to maintaining health and wellness awareness, our program succeeds in preventing the unnecessary spread of illness while other programs place children at constant risk.

There is pressure from parents (who are pressured by their employers) to keep ill children in their child care programs so that parents can remain at work. Oftentimes, child care personnel succumb to parental pressure and do not send sick children home; this means that every child is then repeatedly exposed to every illness that passes through. Our primary caregivers recognize when their children are in the early stages of illness, and our families agree to come within an hour of being called and told their child is ill. We do not allow children to return to the center until their symptoms have completely subsided for 24 hours. This policy cuts down on contagion and helps children's immune systems remain strong as they are exposed to less illness. It also keeps parental work absences to a minimum, as fewer children become ill. Consequently, staff have fewer absences due to illness as well.

We also have a cook on staff and offer children a hot breakfast, hot lunch, and healthy afternoon snack. Working parents appreciate not having to pack a lunch every day and are glad to know that their children are receiving nutritious meals throughout the day.

An on-call infant massage therapist rounds out our faculty. Infant massage is beneficial for everything from soothing colic to decreasing separation anxiety. Parents use these services only if they are interested. We once had an infant who was terrified of everything and would shriek if her caregiver set her down. The only other person at the center she would let near her was our massage therapist. A 10-minute massage would leave her calm, relaxed, and comfortable enough to sit and play with the other babies for extended periods of time. The extensive positive results of massage therapy have surprised even us.

Staffing policy
to promote quality

One of the most disturbing things I witnessed during my teaching career in child care centers was the gradual internal withdrawing of the children who were continually losing their caregivers due to high teacher turnover. Prior to opening the Kellogg Center, to familiarize myself with the child care available in Boulder, I spent four months substitute teaching at different centers. In many centers, the children had become accustomed to high teacher turnover rates and were invariably unaffected by the presence of a stranger in their classrooms. In some centers, the children did not respond to my reading books or playing games with them. It was as if they had given up hope of having positive adult attention and were disengaging from adults in general. Mostly what I observed was understaffed programs and classrooms where maintaining control of an overly large group of children was all that the poorly qualified and untrained staff could manage. On many days, I heard almost exclusively negative commands from the teachers I worked with. "Don't push, don't hit, don't yell" would wear any child down emotionally, not to mention the physical punishment that was sometimes resorted to. One day, a teacher of toddlers candidly confessed to washing toddlers' mouths out with soap. On another occasion, I found a weeping child locked in a pitch-dark broom closet for a time out. As a result of such experiences, I have become passionately interested in why child care centers in America have been in such a state and why the professionals that should have been staffing them have been fleeing. Turnover rates are high due to low wages, social undervaluing and underappreciation of early childhood educators as professionals, and little opportunity for professional growth and promotion. Small wonder that the average teacher turnover rates in American child care centers exceed 39 percent annually (Helburn 1995, 99).

The teachers at the Kellogg Center are all professional early childhood educators with degrees in child development or related fields such as child psychology. As teacher turnover rates in child care are so high, fostering staff retention is of paramount importance. The Kellogg Center acknowledges the inherently exhausting nature of the teachers' work and proactively addresses the issue of burnout. One simple solution is to offer professional-level compensation packages that realistically address burnout issues. Early childhood professionals in the United States typically work for low wages and minimum benefits: vacation, sick time, retirement, and health insurance. Even teachers working for the best-intentioned employers cannot help but feel undervalued and unappreciated. The most common reason given for leaving the field is better pay. The best teachers, those with healthy enough self-esteem to teach and convey high self-esteem to children, frequently leave the field because they know their work is worth much more than what they are being paid.

Teachers at the Kellogg Center commit to staying with their clusters from infancy through the age of 5 years (kindergarten). Center salaries are set significantly higher than the industry norm, anywhere from $3 to $8 an hour more and sometimes close to double the norm. Benefit packages include up to seven weeks of annual paid vacation and sick time, as well as a financial benefits package that employees can choose to utilize for health insurance or retirement plans. Employees choose how to spend their benefit money based on their individual needs. The center does not offer a set health insurance program. Instead teachers choose services for themselves. This way, center funds are not spent on unwanted programs. (For example, a teacher who has excellent health insurance through his or her spouse's company might choose to put all his or her benefit money into a retirement fund.)

Paid vacation and sick leave are crucial for people working in high-stress, caring positions in human service organizations. The Kellogg Board of Directors requires teachers to take the full amount of earned vacation every year. This is feasible for us organizationally as we close for one week each winter and spring. Full tuition is still due during school breaks as well as on other holidays when the school closes (such as the Fourth of July and Martin Luther King Day). Parents learn about the relation between paid time off for teachers and burnout prevention and agree with this policy before enrolling their children.

We also have a comprehensive staff development program. When new teachers are hired, it is with the understanding that continual growth as educators is an integral part of their job. Teachers' work experience, areas of expertise, and opportunities for growth are identified during the interview process. Individual quarterly observation and feedback sessions with our program director ensure that each teacher has a personal plan for developing new skills and pedagogical strengths. For example, a teacher who is not skilled at communicating with parents might be coached in this area by our program director or a fellow teacher. We would also pay for a class or workshop on the subject. Because teachers know that evaluation is integral to the program (even the directors are evaluated) and professional growth is the expected norm, they rarely have negative associations with it. Teachers working in an environment where constructive criticism is given regularly and with respect learn very quickly how to solve problems among themselves when faced with new challenges in their classrooms. Creating this environment of respect generates trust and camaraderie between faculty members, which translates into a high-quality environment for the children. As good communication skills are one of the social bedrocks of the foundation we lay for each child, it is especially important to have teachers who are open to learning through clear and respectful communication. If a teacher is working in a learning environment that values open-mindedness and willingness to change, then he or she cannot help but teach that to the children. Teachers also report that they find working in this kind of supportive, healthy environment a benefit in and of itself.

We provide staff development opportunities through monthly staff development meetings, occasional in-service training, and two annual teacher planning days. In addition, staff development includes annual infant and toddler cardiopulmonary resuscitation, first aid, Occupational Safety and Health Administration, and universal precautions training. Staff development can mean anything from a faculty member's sharing findings learned in a recent course in child development to professional growth workshops run by nationally recognized ECE experts. In addition, we reimburse fees for workshops, conferences, and classes on ECE. Staff also participate in professional days where they visit other programs to observe and brainstorm with other educators. Our emphasis on continued adult education is important for more subtle reasons, such as the psychological sense of support employees feel when they realize their needs are a management priority.

There are also two full-time permanent substitute teachers on the faculty. The substitutes are trained to work with children of all ages and teach wherever they are needed on any given day. By having two substitutes on staff full-time, we are able to guarantee the quality of care provided even when a primary caregiver is out sick or on vacation. This is essential, as safety issues can be a problem when substitute teachers, unfamiliar with classrooms, are brought in just for a day. There usually is not time to fully orient substitutes and provide vital information such as which children have fatal food allergies or how to operate certain pieces of equipment. Further, it is comforting for the children to have substitutes who are familiar, thereby meeting the children's emotional need for continuity of care. It is also reassuring for parents, as they worry less when a familiar face replaces the usual teacher.

Many would argue that having two extra staff members is an unaffordable luxury. We believe there are no such things as luxuries in primary caregiving. There are only essentials and nonessentials. The challenge lies in finding economically feasible ways to provide the essentials of quality child care. These staff substitute positions are made affordable by offering them to qualified interns who complete a year of student teaching with us and who earn a small stipend. They spend a year with five clusters of children, each in different developmental phases, and co-teach with 10 exceptional teachers. Our intern program has been so successful that we are planning to expand it when we complete construction of our new building, slated for the year 2003. We will then be able to provide on-site housing for them. We recruit on a national basis and find the intern program to be a simple cost-effective solution to one of the greatest problems in early care and education: finding last-minute, high-quality substitute teachers. It also increases the quality standards held by the interns, who will bring those standards to the programs where they will work on a permanent basis.

By offering professional salaries and benefit packages that reflect teachers' need for time off, we encourage staff retention and attract high-quality teachers to our program. Teachers are at the heart of our success, and we could not provide high-quality child care without them. Taking care of the caregivers is therefore a core value as well as just plain good business. Treating our faculty with the respect and professionalism they deserve creates the trust and loyalty that is essential for successful child care programs.

Financing quality child care

Tuition at the Kellogg Center is unusual in that it reflects the real cost of the care provided. This is rare in child care. Most child care centers underpay their employees and undercharge their families. The teachers essentially subsidize the cost of care to families by being willing to work for low pay. This generates understandable resentment from teachers and contributes significantly to high teacher turnover rates.

Our tuition reflects the true cost of care provided and can run as much as 20 percent higher than other programs in our community. We ensure affordability for our families by subsidizing the cost of care to our low-income families. According to the guidelines of the U.S. Department of Housing and Urban Development, approximately 40 percent of our families fall under the very-low-, low-, or middle-income categories. We have an annual fund-raiser to generate funds for financial assistance, and we keep those funds separate from our regular tuition revenues. Currently, all families falling in the very-low- to low-income categories receive assistance, as do some of our middle-income families. We receive support from the City of Boulder Housing and Human Services Division as well as from foundations and individual donors. We also receive funding from the Department of Social Services for publicly subsidized children, which helps offset the cost of their care.

The Kellogg Board of Directors considers it important to charge the true cost of care for families who can afford to pay it. Not doing so creates one of the biggest economic problems in child care, and it is one of the most common mistakes child care centers make. Providing lower-quality care at a lower cost and hiring staff at less than their worth leave programs in a state of perpetual financial crisis and teachers frustrated enough to leave their jobs. It is tempting to caregivers to take care of families financially by keeping prices low. We believe that prices must be kept very low for very-low-income families and at the higher, real rate for families who can afford it. While a long-term goal is to lower tuition for most families through our endowment program, common sense dictates that we not subsidize the cost of child care for a family with a six-figure income.

Once families understand the economic dynamics and true cost of high-quality care, they are willing to pay our tuition, especially since we offer sliding-scale fees to our lower-income families. Other programs in our community, admittedly an affluent one, are also beginning to use this strategy successfully. As a result, they, too, have been able to pay their teachers higher salaries and decrease their teacher turnover rates.

We work hard to provide sliding-scale fees to reflect family income because we believe in equal access to high-quality child care regardless of the family's ability to pay. Diversity is celebrated in every way possible at the Kellogg Center, and having children from diverse economic backgrounds is important. In this time of global integration, children need to grow up appreciating racial, ethnic, religious, and gender differences if they are going to be successful in life. Children who grow up in diverse environments are more open-minded, are less likely to have racially based prejudices, and are more likely to appreciate differences in others rather than feeling threatened by them. The racial makeup of our families and teachers matches the demographics of the city of Boulder.

There are many programs designed to ease the financial burden of both for-profit and nonprofit child care centers. Federal programs such as the Child and Adult Care Food Program provide financial support for meals served at child care centers. Every state and city offers different types of support for everything from staff development and training to tuition assistance for low-income families. Making efforts to become part of the Colorado early care and education community has helped us tremendously. The information and networking ideas our program director brings back to the center more than make up for the time spent at a Directors Support Meeting or a Health Department brainstorming session. We have found that we must be vigilant networkers with our peers, both locally and internationally, in order to keep current on what assistance is available. The importance of collaboration cannot be emphasized enough.

REPLICABILITY OF THE KELLOGG MODEL

With careful financial management and committed leadership, our program can be replicated. The following list, which applies to both for-profit and nonprofit child care centers, describes essential management practices to consider prior to implementing a program like the Kellogg Center.

1. Strong leadership. A dedicated, passionate, and skilled program director is the core of any child development program. Ongoing training and support for directors is essential, whether as board support for nonprofits or corporate support for for-profits.

2. Professionally trained teachers. An essential part of any high-quality program is professionally trained early childhood educators with degrees in ECE and a commitment to lifelong learning.

3. Familylike atmosphere. Child care centers must have cozy, familylike (not institutional) atmospheres.

4. Primary caregiving. Continuity of care is essential.

5. Curriculum. Developmentally appropriate curriculum and practice are essential.

6. Community support from local city or town officials, businesses, corporations, and individuals. Support for the center as well as financial assistance for lower-income children must be ensured.

7. Financial management. Allowances must be made in the budget for professional-level salaries and benefits. Centers serving low-income families will have to be successful fund-raisers and plan for long-term financial stability, for example, by creating endowments.

8. Fee structure. High-income families should be charged the real cost of care; low-income families should be charged a subsidized lower cost; and sliding-scale fee structures should be utilized. How subsidies will work (using federal poverty guidelines often excludes struggling middle-income families) and what sources of public and private funding are available should be determined ahead of time.

9. A high-quality budget. Higher-quality care can cost up to double the cost of average care; it requires a high-quality budget. The budget should permit substitute staff, administrative support, a separate cook, and so on, so teachers are not pulled from classrooms to cover these needs. Budget should also include staff development training, high-quality educational materials, and the like.

10. Owned facilities. Rental fees for child care facilities are often a make-or-break factor. Raising capital to purchase a facility or to build one from scratch is, therefore, essential. There is a direct positive correlation between a center's ownership of its facility and its chances for financial success, as rising rent costs often drive child care centers out of business.

COMMITMENT TO EXCELLENCE

Communities, families, and educators are attracted to high-quality programs that hold excellence, open-minded evaluation, and continued growth as goals. Centers need to ask for more support and help. Teachers and administrators need to reach out to the community and seek mentors. Centers need to use the quality standards available to them, voluntarily become accredited through the National Association for the Education of Young Children, and incorporate outside evaluations using instruments such as the Early Childhood Environment Rating Scale and Infant/Toddler Environment Rating Scale (Harms and Clifford 1980; Harms, Cryer, and Clifford 1990).

Teachers need to be encouraged to take classes, read early childhood materials, and share and implement new ideas with each other. Networking with other early childhood programs is necessary to reduce directors' isolation and increase the chances of learning about support that is available. Diversity also needs to be held as a crucial value. It must be celebrated and represented in every way possible.

The African proverb "It takes a village to raise a child" is an essential philosophy that makes the KCDC a success. Continually seeking external support, whether to raise $1.2 million for a new building or to find mentors for our directors, we have been able to create a healthy, viable early care and education program that supports the growth and development of children, parents, teachers, and community members alike. By sharing our knowledge and lessons learned, we are supporting other child development programs in raising their standards without reinventing the wheel. By being an articulate, persistent, and uncompromising voice for children and by demanding higher standards, we are slowly but surely making a difference and achieving the secondary aspect of our mission: to be successful advocates for higher standards internationally in the field of child care and early childhood education. We see engaging in such advocacy as a clear, unequivocal choice that our children need us to make.

Note

1. Advocacy takes on many forms at the center and is becoming an increasingly large part of our work. We spend an enormous amount of time educating parents, other educators, community members, businesspeople, and politicians about what defines high-quality child care and how important it is. We mentor educators who are starting new programs and provide them with pro bono support and consultation. We network internationally via the World Wide Web and in this way support educators and parents globally. We regularly make presentations on our work to Colorado companies through our collaboration with Community Shares of Colorado, a federation of 86 nonprofit organizations that engage in fund-raising together through payroll deduction. We make our literature on finding high-quality care (for parents) and creating high-quality care (for educators) available free of charge to anyone who requests it. We have had requests for assistance as close as across the street and as far away as South Africa. We write letters to editors of newspapers, have had a documentary made about our work, and write articles for academic journals. Everyone associated with the Kellogg Center becomes an advocate sooner or later, but so far most of our advocacy work is completed after hours by me and, increasingly, by our program director. Our long-term goal is to fund staff members full-time to run our advocacy program.

References

Begley, Sharon. 1996. Your Child's Brain. *Newsweek*, 19 Feb., 55-61.

Bredekamp, Sue and Carol Copple. 1997. *Developmentally Appropriate Practice in Early Childhood Programs*. Rev. ed. Washington, DC: National Association for the Education of Young Children.

Carnegie Task Force on Meeting the Needs of Young Children. 1994. *Starting Points: Meeting the Needs of Our Youngest Children*. New York: Carnegie Corporation of New York.

Harms, Thelma and Richard M. Clifford. 1980. *Early Childhood Environment Rating Scale*. New York: Teachers College Press.

Harms, Thelma, Debby Cryer, and Richard M. Clifford. 1990. *Infant/Toddler Environment Rating Scale*. New York: Teachers College Press.

Helburn, Suzanne, ed. 1995. *Cost, Quality and Child Outcomes in Child Care Centers: Technical Report*. Denver: University of Colorado, Department of Economics, Center for Research in Economic and Social Policy.

Katz, Lillian G. and Diane E. McClellan. 1997. *Fostering Children's Social Competence: The Teacher's Role.* Washington, DC: National Association for the Education of Young Children.

Masten, A. S. and J. D. Coatsworth. 1995. *Competence, Resilience and Psychopathology.* New York: John Wiley.

McCord, Sue. 1995. *Storybook Journey.* Englewood Cliffs, NJ: Merrill.

Child Care Experiences and Developmental Outcomes

By MARGARET R. BURCHINAL

ABSTRACT: Regular nonparental care during the first five years of life has become the norm, rather than the exception, during the past 30 years in the United States. Parents and professionals have expressed concerns about the impact of such care on children's development. Initially, much of the research focused on whether, when, and how much nonparental care the child received, suggesting that early and extensive care might negatively affect children's social and cognitive development. More sophisticated studies followed in which child care quality and family characteristics known to be related to both quality of care and child outcomes were also examined. Much of this literature indicates that children who experience better-quality care tend to display more optimal cognitive and social development than children who experience lower-quality care, although the associations tend to be modest. Implications for public policy are discussed.

Margaret R. Burchinal is a statistician at the Frank Porter Graham Child Development Center at the University of North Carolina. She earned her Ph.D. in quantitative psychology at the university in 1986. She has served as a statistician for a number of child care projects, including the Abecedarian Project: Project CARE; Cost, Quality, and Outcomes Study; and NICHD Study of Early Child Care.

OVER the last two decades, dramatic increases in the number of working mothers have resulted in marked increases in the number of children experiencing regular nonparental care. The majority of infants and over two-thirds of preschoolers in the United States are cared for on a regular basis by someone other than the parent (Lamb 1997). This represents a major societal change in how young children are raised in this country, and it has provoked a major controversy among professionals about the impact of early group care on very young children's development (Scarr and Eisenberg 1993). These controversies have, to some extent, shaped the empirical research to date (for a comprehensive review of these controversies and empirical results, see Lamb 1997).

The most recent estimates regarding the proportions of children in child care and the types of child care they attend can be found in the National Household Education Survey, conducted by National Center for Educational Statistics in 1995 (1996). This survey indicates that the proportion of children receiving 10 or more hours per week of regular nonparental care varies from 39 percent in the child's first year, to 42 percent in the second year, 45 percent in the third year, 55 percent in the fourth year, and 64 percent in the fifth year. Whereas the proportion of children receiving care by relatives or nonrelatives in the child's home or the caregiver's home is relatively constant across ages, the proportion attending child care centers increases dramatically between

infancy and the preschool years. The proportion of children being cared for by a relative varies from 18 percent of infants to 11 percent of 4-year-olds, and the proportion cared for by nonrelatives varies from 17 percent of 2-year-olds to 11 percent of 4-year-olds. In contrast, the proportion of children in center care increases from 6 percent in the child's first year, 9 percent in the second year, and 14 percent in the third year, to 27 percent in the fourth year and 42 percent in the fifth year.

The effects of this nonparental care on very young children's development have concerned some psychologists. For example, Belsky (1986) cautioned that "entry into [routine full-time nonmaternal] care in the first year of life is a 'risk factor' for the development of insecure-avoidant attachments in infancy and heightened aggressiveness, noncompliance, and withdrawal in preschool and early years" (7). In marked contrast, Clarke-Stewart (1989) and Phillips et al. (1987) reviewed the empirical evidence and concluded that the continuity and the quality of both the home and the alternative caregiving environments—rather than nonparental care per se—were the major influences on children's development. These controversies have focused originally on the impact of the child's age when regular nonparental care begins, the quality of care, the type of care, and the amount of care. The controversies, more recently, have focused on whether differences between families who do and do not use child care have been adequately considered in analyses. These differences on family selection factors have framed much of this debate and are presented in the next section before the sections discussing the research relating child outcomes to these child care factors.

FAMILY SELECTION OR CONTEXT

Much of the recent controversy regarding child care and its impact on child development has hinged on whether researchers appropriately controlled for differences between families that do and do not use child care. Much of the early research included few, if any, family characteristics as covariates to control for such differences. Results from these studies were questioned, especially after early research indicated that nonparental care beginning in infancy might harm children. This is because family and child characteristics known to be related to child outcomes are also related to the family choices about child care (for example, Belsky and Eggebeen 1991; Burchinal et al. 1995; Dunn 1993; Goelman and Pence 1987; Hayes, Palmer, and Zaslow 1990; Kontos and Fiene 1987; Kontos et al. 1995; Phillips, McCartney, and Scarr 1987; Phillips et al. 1994). Infants entering child care during infancy have mothers who tend to be better educated, have higher-status occupations, be single, and be of color (Burchinal et al. 1995; Hoffman 1989; NICHD 1996). Families who select higher-quality child care tend to be better educated, have more income, have more stimulating and responsive home environments, and have child rearing beliefs and practices that have been linked to

better child outcomes (Lamb 1997; NICHD 1996). Accordingly, current child care research must attend to issues of family context and include family selection variables to be credible (Scarr and Eisenberg 1993).

More recently, researchers have extended this contextual approach by asking whether associations between child care experiences and child development vary as a function of child or family characteristics. At least three sets of hypotheses regarding interactions between child care experiences and child outcomes have been generated. Some have hypothesized that differences in developmental patterns will be found when a discrepancy exists between quality of care at home and in child care, with good-quality child care enhancing development for children with less responsive home environments and poor-quality care impairing development for children with more responsive home environments (Caughy, DiPietro, and Strobino 1994). Still others have hypothesized that development will be impaired if children experience discontinuities between home and child care, arguing that what constitutes appropriate child care should vary across children depending on the values and beliefs of their home environment (Garcia-Coll 1990; Lamb 1997). Such analyses have focused on identifying child and family factors that serve as risk or protective factors for children who receive varying qualities of child care. Of particular interest has been determining whether children from stimulating and responsive home environments are buffered from the negative effects of low-quality child care and whether children from stressed families are at increased risk for experiencing negative effects of low-quality care. Finally, others have questioned whether the impact of aspects of child care, such as quantity and quality, will vary as a function of ethnicity or culture because of cultural differences in child care practices and beliefs. They argue that what constitutes high quality and quantity of care may be different for children of color and white non-Hispanic children because of differences in the history of societal discrimination and cultural practices (Garcia-Coll et al. 1996).

INFANT CHILD CARE

The most vigorous debate about child care concerns the potential influence of early nonparental care—especially in the first year of life—on later social and emotional development. This concern has, in part, been based on attachment theories that posit the importance of the primary caregiver (typically the mother) as a predictable, contingent, and responsive care provider to the infant. It was believed that the infant who experiences multiple caregivers may not be able to form as strong an attachment bond with the mother as the child who experiences a single caregiver, placing the multiple-caregiver child at risk for more problematic social development since the infant-mother attachment bond was believed to be the basis from which other relationships form. There is mixed empirical evidence for this general linkage between infant day care and poor social development (for

example, increased aggression with peers and lowered compliance with adult demands) (cf. Clarke-Stewart 1989). Both short-term and long-term correlates of infant child care have been examined in this literature.

Much of the early evidence suggested that children receiving non-maternal care in their first year were more likely to display insecure attachment to their mothers compared with children receiving exclusively maternal care bonds, as shown by the most commonly used paradigm, the strange situation. The strange situation (Ainsworth et al. 1978) is the most common method used for measuring infant-mother attachment. It involves observing the child's reaction to reunion with the mother following brief separations in an unfamiliar context. Most studies of middle-class children indicated that infants who began full-time nonmaternal care during their first year were significantly more likely than other infants to be judged as having an insecure infant-mother attachment (Barglow, Vaughn, and Moliter 1987; Belsky and Rovine 1988; Jacobson and Wille 1984), although the association between full-time care and insecure attachment was not obtained in some studies of either middle-class (Chase-Lansdale and Owen 1987; Easterbrooks and Goldberg 1985; Owen et al. 1984; Thompson, Lamb, and Estes 1982) or lower-class children (Burchinal et al. 1992; Vaughn, Gove, and Egeland 1980) or in two studies using a different method to assess attachment (Belsky and Rovine 1990; Weinraub, Jaeger, and

Hoffman 1988). A meta-analysis of the published studies of both middle-class and lower-class children assessed with the strange situation indicated that children in full-time infant care were slightly more likely to have insecure attachments (36 percent) than were infants in part-time or no nonmaternal care (29 percent) (Clarke-Stewart 1989). However, much of this research was questioned for two reasons. First, it is likely that families who do and do not use infant care differ in many ways, some of which are likely to be related to children's social development. Failure to use covariates to adjust for all substantial differences in demographic and parenting characteristics between families who do and do not use child care likely led to biased analyses (Scarr and Eisenberg 1993). Second, questions were raised about whether the assessment paradigm, the strange situation, is equally appropriate for infants who do and do not experience daily separations from their parents (Clarke-Stewart 1988, 1989; Thompson 1988).

Perhaps the most comprehensive examination of this issue was described in a recent publication from the NICHD Early Child Care Research Network (1997a). The NICHD Early Child Care Research Network is conducting a prospective study of the consequences of child care decisions on child development. Over 1300 children and families were recruited at birth in 10 sites across the country. Child care experiences, demographic characteristics, and parenting styles were collected prospectively and the infant-mother

attachment was assessed when the infant was 15 months of age. Comparisons of reactions to the strange situations for infants who did and did not experience child care indicated that the paradigm was valid for both types of children. Analyses indicated that neither the amount nor the quality of child care experience was related to the security of the infant-mother attachment for children in general. Interactions between child care experiences and maternal sensitivity indicated that insecure attachments were more likely among children with less sensitive mothers if they also experienced extensive amounts of nonmaternal care, poor-quality care, or multiple care arrangements.

Only a few studies have examined whether infant child care is linked to later social, emotional, or cognitive development. Long-term negative correlates have been detected among three samples, but inadequacies in the research design of these studies call into question the generalizability of their results. The first is a sample of children from impoverished families who were enrolled in an early-intervention project in Chapel Hill, North Carolina (Haskins 1985). Children were rated as more aggressive in kindergarten and first grade if they had been randomly assigned to the experimental group than to the control group. The experimental children attended a high-quality child care center for 30 or more hours per week beginning in the first 3 months of life. The control children received some incentives for participating in the study such as disposable diapers and formula. While these families did not receive financial assistance with child care, most enrolled their children in local child care centers. The second study involved 8-year-olds in Texas who had received extensive infant day care of dubious quality (Vandell and Corasaniti 1990). Among these children, full-time nonparental care beginning in infancy was related to poorer academic and social skills in analyses that adjusted for family selection variables but not quality of child care. Three analyses of the National Longitudinal Survey of Youth (NLSY) mother-child data also addressed this question. Caughy, DiPietro, and Strobino (1994) examined the association between day care experience in the first three years and achievement scores of 867 white, Hispanic, and African American children at 5-6 years of age. They found that initiation of day care during the first year of life was related to reading achievement at 5-6 years positively for children from less stimulating and responsive home environments and negatively for children from more optimal home environments. Baydar and Brooks-Gunn (1991) focused on 3- and 4-year-old white non-Hispanic children, reporting that children whose mothers returned to work full-time during the child's first year tended to score lower on IQ and behavioral adaptation assessments than other children. Also analyzing the NLSY mother-child data, Belsky and Eggebeen (1991) found that 4- to 6-year-old white non-Hispanic children and black children were less compliant if their mothers returned to work

during the child's first two years. Again, family selection variables were included in these analyses, but measures of child care quality were not available. Questions about the dubious quality of the care of the children in Texas and about the representativeness of the 1986 NLSY child sample (the children included in the 1986 sample were disproportionately from poor, very young, undereducated mothers) make it difficult to generalize from these studies to middle-class children.

Other studies have reported no or positive associations between children's long-term development and infant child care. A retrospective study of middle-class white and African American families in the Seattle area suggested that entering care during the child's first year was neither positively nor negatively related to measures of social, emotional, or cognitive development during middle childhood (Burchinal et al. 1995). In contrast, Fields (1991) reports better adjustment socially, behaviorally, and academically among 28 upper-middle-class children who began attending high-quality day care centers early during their first year than among comparable children who began attending the same center later.

In summary, the most comprehensive and recent studies suggest that full-time child care during infancy is not linked to insecure infant-mother attachment or impaired social or cognitive development during early or middle childhood. It appears that findings of earlier studies linking infant care to negative social outcomes were due to differences between families who did or did not elect to use infant child care or to failure to consider child care quality. Lamb (1997) comprehensively described this literature, concluding,

The empirical evidence reveals that enrollment in infant day care is problematic only when it co-occurs with other indices of risk, including poor quality care at home and unstable care arrangements. When studies have revealed significant associations between nonparental care and insecure attachment, they may have been attributable to sampling biases, as well as to the unrecognized co-occurrence of multiple adverse risk conditions. After determining that infant day care per se is not harmful, researchers now need to specify what types of care are potentially harmful and potentially beneficial for specific subgroups of infants and families, and to define with greater precision those aspects of quality likely to be of particular significance in defined circumstances. (37)

CHILD CARE QUALITY

Poor-quality child care is of concern because developmental theories are based on the assumption that infants and preschoolers need responsive and stimulating interactions with adults to enhance social, cognitive, and language development in early childhood (Sameroff 1983). In particular, it is believed that infants and young children best learn language and cognitive skills during interactions with adults that involve taking turns and focusing attention on the child (Tomasello and Farrar 1986). Such interactions also provide young children with the secure base and positive role models needed to develop social skills (Bradley et al. 1989). Accordingly, children in group care are very unlikely to experience such interactions unless there are relatively few children per adult and unless their teachers provide developmentally appropriate interactions with each child in the class. High-quality child care should provide the child with these opportunities, whereas poor-quality classrooms do not (Harms, Cryer, and Clifford 1990). Two almost distinct research literatures have examined the relations between child care experiences and children's development: the early intervention literature and the community child care literature.

A number of measures of child care quality exist (for more detail on quality measures, see Cryer, this volume). Most of these studies have employed measures of global quality such as the Early Childhood Environment Rating Scale (ECERS) by Harms and Clifford (1980) or the Infant/Toddler Environment Rating Scale by Harms, Cryer, and Clifford (1990) or measures of caregiver sensitivity such as the Caregiver Interaction Scale (CIS) developed by Arnett (1989). A few have used other measures, such as the Observational Record of Childcare Environment (ORCE) (NICHD 1996) or the Assessment Profile for Early Childhood Programs (Abbott-Shim and Sibley 1987). Fortunately, comparisons of these measures suggest that they are likely measuring the same or similar constructs (NICHD 1996).

Early intervention child care

Center-based early childhood interventions have been provided for children from families living in poverty based on the assumption that their family settings too often did not provide sufficient early learning opportunities. The assumption underlying these programs is that frequent, responsive, and stimulating interactions with caregivers and exposure to a variety of educational materials and experiences through their center-based experiences will enhance children's cognitive development over time. Most of these early intervention projects were implemented between 1964 and 1980 and provided child care at research child care centers. At least some studies randomly assigned children to either treatment (child care) or control groups. Most of these programs were operated by university-based research teams, employed well-trained staff with high levels of supervision, and were presumed to be of high quality. Program evaluations provide clear support that these child care experiences enhanced children's cognitive and language development, at least for the duration of the intervention (see Barnett 1995; Haskins 1989; Infant Health and Development Project 1990; Lazar and Darlington 1982; O'Connell and Farran 1982). The early intervention programs appeared, in part, to enhance cognitive development through increasing children's interest and responsiveness to objects and people in their environments through responsive and contingent care at the child care center (Burchinal et al. 1997).

Both short-term and long-term effects of early intervention on at-risk children's development have been documented. Lazar and colleagues conducted a comprehensive evaluation of 12 early intervention programs. Compared with those in the control groups, low-income children who attended high-quality child care centers had higher cognitive scores during the preschool years in those 12 studies conducted in the 1960s and also in later intervention programs conducted in the 1970s and 1980s (Lazar and Darlington 1982; Infant Health and Development Project 1990; Burchinal, Lee, and Ramey 1989). These short-term effects translated into some academic advantages for treated children but not always maintenance of the observed cognitive gains. Only treated children from the most intensive early intervention projects continued to show higher cognitive and academic scores than control children after the intervention programs ended and the children attended public school (Campbell and Ramey 1994; Haskins 1989; Schweinhart, Weikart, and Larner 1986). More modest gains were observed for the children who received less intense early interventions. They, when compared with control children, were more likely to be promoted in school, graduate from high school, and become productive young adults (Lazar and Darlington 1982). In contrast, control children were more likely to be retained in grade, be placed in special education, and drop out of school (Lazar and Darlington 1982). In intensive early childhood programs, benefits endured into adolescence (Campbell and Ramey 1994; Garber 1988).

Community child care

Other researchers have examined the relations between the quality of child care and children's development among families using child care available in their communities. This literature has demonstrated that factors such as parental education and beliefs about child rearing are related both to the type of care that families select for their child and to child outcomes, creating a potential bias that must be considered in analyses. Much of the current research has examined the quality of center-based child care and developmental outcomes, although a few studies have examined quality of care in other settings. Almost separate literatures have developed in which quality of care is related to either cognitive and language development or to social and emotional development.

Cognitive and language development. An extensive literature exists relating child care quality to cognitive and language development, with most studies indicating that preschool-age children display better cognitive and language development if they experience higher- rather than lower-quality care. Using standard measures of child care quality, some of these researchers have found that child care quality was related to language and cognitive development, even after controlling for family selection factors such as socioeconomic status, maternal edu-

cation, or family structure in the large multisite studies (NICHD 1997b; Peisner-Feinberg and Burchinal 1997; Whitebook, Howes, and Phillips 1989) and in smaller single-site studies (Dunn 1993; Phillips et al. 1987; Schliecker, White, and Jacobs 1991). In most of these studies, the quality of child care was modestly related to children's development, with quality of care often accounting for less than 5 percent of the variance in children's developmental outcomes in analyses that adjusted for family selection factors. However, these associations between child care quality and child outcomes have not always been observed (Clarke-Stewart, Gruber, and Fitzgerold 1994; Goelman and Pence 1987; Kontos 1991), perhaps because of relatively small samples or restricted range of observed child care quality.

The impact of quality of care on infant development has not been examined as extensively. At least two studies have related infant care quality to infant language and cognitive development. Infants experiencing higher-quality care were more likely to demonstrate better cognitive and language skills in a large multisite study that included children in a wide variety of care settings (NICHD 1997b) and in a sample of 89 African American infants who began attending a child care center during their first year (Burchinal et al. 1996). Melhuish and colleagues (1990) found that the language development was poorer among infants experiencing lower-quality care in child care centers than among infants receiving better-quality care at home, with relatives, or in family child care in a middle-class sample.

Quality of care during infancy has also been related to cognitive and language development during preschool years. Preschoolers who experienced high-quality child care beginning during infancy show better progress on tests of language and cognitive functioning than preschoolers without such child care experiences (Burchinal, Lee, and Ramey 1989; Roberts et al. 1989). Similarly, children who attended presumably poor-quality child care centers beginning during infancy scored lower on standardized academic assessments during middle childhood than did their peers without such infant child care (Vandell and Corasaniti 1990).

Based in part on the early intervention literature, it has been assumed that high-quality community-based child care can serve as a protective factor for children at risk for impaired development due to risk factors such as low parental education, minority ethnic background, single-parent homes, and poverty (Lamb 1997). Researchers have argued that family factors and child care factors interact such that positive child care experiences can serve to protect or buffer at-risk children from the negative impact of these risk factors, whereas positive family factors protect the child from the impact of negative child care factors. These investigators point to the large intervention effects for poor children and small or nonsignificant child care effects among middle-class children observed in many studies of

children attending community child care centers (see Lamb 1997). Several studies have reported differential effects of child care on cognitive or language development related to socioeconomic status or family structure (Baydar and Brooks-Gunn 1991; Bryant et al. 1994; Caughy, DiPietro, and Strobino 1994; Vandell and Corasaniti 1990), ethnicity (Bryant, Peisner-Feinberg, and Clifford 1993; Burchinal et al. 1995), gender (Baydar and Brooks-Gunn 1991; Bryant et al. 1994; Vandell and Corasaniti 1990), and mother's education (Peisner-Feinberg and Burchinal 1997). Most found that the effects of child care are stronger for preschool children from less advantaged circumstances. However, several recent studies failed to find evidence for moderating effects when examining interactions between quality of care and family and child factors such as parent education, family income, quality of home environment, or child sex (Burchinal et al. 1996; NICHD 1997b; Stipek et al. 1995).

Two large studies are among the recent studies that examined the association between child care quality and cognitive and language development and that tested whether child care effects are differentially related to child outcomes for children from varying family backgrounds. These are presented in more detail as they are likely the most comprehensive studies to date.

The Cost, Quality and Outcomes Study examined 100 child care centers in each of four states (California, Colorado, Connecticut, and North Carolina) selected to represent variation in economic and regulatory climates. Preschool-age children in observed classrooms were recruited, and cognitive, language, and social development was assessed for 757 children (Peisner-Feinberg and Burchinal 1997). A composite quality measure was created from a measure of global quality (ECERS), teacher sensitivity (CIS), teacher responsiveness, and child-centeredness. In addition, the teacher's rating of the closeness of her relationship with the target child was included as a separate measure of child care quality. Hierarchical linear models examined the association between these measures of quality and standardized measures of receptive vocabulary and academic skills and the teacher's perceptions of behavior problems and cognitive and attention skills. Analyses were adjusted for maternal education, the child's sex and ethnicity, and classroom effects related to selecting multiple children from the same classroom. Results indicated that child care quality was positively, albeit modestly, related to higher vocabulary and reading scores on standardized tests and to the teacher's ratings of the child's cognitive skills. Tests of interactions between the two child care quality measures and mother's education, ethnicity, and child sex were conducted. An interaction between maternal education and care quality indicated that the quality composite was related to children's reading skill only for children with mothers who had less education. Child care quality was correlated ($.15 < r < .30$) with these outcomes prior to adjusting for covariates, with somewhat smaller associations after adjust-

ment. Follow-up assessments indicated that this measure of child care quality was related to the child's vocabulary and math skills when longitudinal analyses were conducted on data collected through kindergarten (Peisner-Feinberg et al. 1998). These analyses indicated that children who had experienced higher-quality child care tended to perform better across time on measures of vocabulary and math skills. Results, however, did not yield the anticipated interactions between maternal education and reading skills or the interaction between rates of change over time and child care quality. Child care quality was not more strongly related to later academic skills for children whose mothers had less education rather than more education, nor was it related to faster acquisition of skills over time.

The second study examined the association between child care quality and cognitive and language assessments in the 10-site NICHD Study of Early Child Care (NICHD 1997b) for over 1100 children. Quality of care for children in a wide variety of settings (centers, child care homes, baby-sitters in child's home, and care by relative including grandparents and fathers) was measured using the ORCE when the children were 6, 15, 24, and 36 months of age. Children's cognitive development was measured with two standardized assessments, and language development was measured with parent ratings at 15 and 24 months and with a standardized assessment at 36 months. Hierarchical regressions examined each outcome as a function of selection variables, child gender, parenting variables, global child care variables (average number of hours of nonmaternal child care per week, number of child care centers attended, number of child care homes attended, and total rating of quality from the ORCE), and a specific child care variable (amount of language stimulation in child care environment from the ORCE). Blocks of variables were entered in this order into the hierarchical regressions. Analyses indicated that children experiencing higher-quality child care tended to score higher on the cognitive tests at 15, 24, and 36 months and on the language tests at 36 months and have mothers who reported more receptive and expressive vocabulary at 15 and 24 months. Comparisons of models that included and excluded the specific measure of child care quality, language stimulation, indicated that language stimulation in child care accounted for most of the association between the 15- and 24-month outcomes and overall global child care quality. Tests of interactions between child care quality and the home, income, ethnicity, and gender did not yield consistent findings that indicated that child care quality was differentially related to these cognitive or language outcomes for children with varying home environments, family income, ethnic backgrounds, or gender.

Social and emotional development. Whether child care quality is related to children's social and emotional development has been studied widely, in part due to concerns about the impact of child care on the infant-mother attachment and, consequently, on the child's social development. Many of the early studies examined amount of care, often without concern for family selection biases. In contrast, most of the more recent studies have measured child care quality and have included family and child characteristics as covariates. These studies have examined a variety of outcomes such as compliance to requests made by parents and caregivers, pro-social behaviors, behavior problems, and relationships with peers.

Whereas a relatively large number of studies have related compliance to child care experiences, only a few studies have measured quality of child care. Full-time child care, often beginning in infancy, has been shown to be related to less compliance (Belsky and Eggebeen 1991; Rubenstein, Howes, and Boyle 1981; Schwarz, Strickland, and Krolick 1974; Thornburg et al. 1990; Vandell and Corasaniti 1990). In contrast, three studies that collected quality information provided limited evidence that center care quality was related to more compliance at least in some settings (Howes and Olenick 1986) and that child care quality across multiple settings was modestly related to observations of compliance in the United States (NICHD in press) and Sweden (Steinberg et al. 1991). Quality was not related to all measures of compliance used in the studies. Howes and Olenick reported that child care quality was related to compliance in the lab but not in the home. The NICHD study found that child care quality was related to observed compliance at 36 months but not at 24 months and not at either age in analyses that adjusted for demographic selection factors, parenting, and infant-mother attachment. The Swedish study reported that child care quality was not related to either parent or teacher reports of child behavior. Furthermore, both the NICHD study and the Swedish study found that compliance was much more strongly related to family characteristics than to care quality.

Several studies demonstrated that quality of child care is related to both infant and preschool social development. The National Child Care Staffing Study found, for infants, toddlers, and preschoolers, that children in higher-quality classes were more likely to be securely attached to their caregiver and to be more socially oriented than were children in poor or minimally adequate care (Howes, Phillips, and Whitebook 1992). These relationships between quality of care and infant social development were observed for both structural and process measures of quality in analyses that included family selection factors. Similarly, studies of child care in Bermuda (Phillips, McCartney, and Scarr 1987) and the United States (Clarke-Stewart, Gruber, and Fitzgerold 1994; McCartney et al. 1997) showed that preschool-age children attending higher-quality centers were more likely to exhibit pro-social behaviors than were children in lower-quality centers after adjusting for family selection factors.

Other studies have reported that quality of child care is related to behavior problems. Most studies that measure child care quality report modest negative associations between a measure of child care quality and behavior problems at some ages or in some settings after adjusting for family selection variables. The Cost, Quality, and Outcomes Study found that teachers reported fewer behavior problems when the center teacher reported a closer relationship with the child (Peisner-Feinberg and Burchinal 1997). High-quality center care between one and three years was related to declines during the preschool years in maternal reports of externalizing problems (Brooks-Gunn et al. 1993). The NICHD Study of Early Child Care found that child care quality as measured by the ORCE was very modestly related to mother and caregiver reports of behavior problems at 24 months and to caregiver reports at 36 months in analyses that adjusted for demographic characteristics, but not in analyses that adjusted for the quality of parenting. Finally, a study of low-income families indicated that children in high-quality care tended to be less defiant than children in low-quality care (Crockenberg and Litman 1991). However, as many or more nonsignificant associations between child care quality and measures of behavior problems, compared to significant associations, were reported in almost all of these studies. In addition, a study of child care centers in three states reported no significant associations between child care quality and the parent's rating of behavior problems and security among infants, toddlers, and preschoolers (McCartney et al. 1997).

Relationships with peers have also been related to child care quality. Better peer interactions have been shown for children in higher-than lower-quality center care (Howes, Smith, and Galinsky 1995) and higher- than lower-quality family child care (Kontos et al. 1995). Better peer interactions among socially fearful children have been related to the quality of their child care (Vollig and Feagans 1994). These associations appear to be obtained when caregivers encourage group interactions (Rosenthal 1994), are more socially competent in interactions with the children (Howes, Phillips, and Whitebook 1992), or demonstrate closer relationships with the children (Pianta and Nimetz 1991).

Long-term associations have been obtained in at least three studies that adjusted for family selection factors. The Cost, Quality, and Outcomes Study found that the closeness of the preschool teacher-child relationship predicted fewer behavior problems and more pro-social behaviors between the ages of 4 and 6 (Peisner-Feinberg et al. 1998). Quality of center care during preschool years predicted peer acceptance at 8 years of age (Vandell, Henderson, and Wilson 1988). The infant-caregiver attachment at 1 year of age significantly predicted that child's relationship with the caregiver and preschool peer competence at 4 years of age (Howes, Matheson, and Hamilton 1994) and perception of his or her relationship with the teacher at 9 years of age (Howes, Hamilton, and Phillipsen 1998).

In summary, most studies have indicated that children who receive higher-quality child care have better cognitive and language development, fewer behavior problems, better social skills, and better relationships with peers. In general, these associations appear to be very modest for children who do not experience major risk factors such as poverty, with child outcomes being more strongly related to family characteristics than to child care quality.

TYPE OF CHILD CARE

A few studies have compared child outcomes for children attending different types of child care, with some studies suggesting that center care may be related to better cognitive, language, and social skills and other studies indicating center care may be related to worse social skills. Preschool or center-based child care has been linked to both positive and negative developmental outcomes, but these associations may not continue after children begin attending primary schools. In an extensive earlier review, Clarke-Stewart and Fein (1983) concluded that center-based child care related with remarkable consistency to better intellectual performance, at least when children were attending centers. Further, this relationship maintained regardless of children's gender, ethnicity, social class, or temperament. Later, Clarke-Stewart (1989) reviewed the greatly expanded literature and concluded that attendance at a high-quality center or preschool correlated positively in the early years with higher intelligence, as well as more self-confidence, independence, extroversion, and assertiveness compared with children with no or other types of child care experience. Other studies have reported no reliable differences between infants or preschoolers attending center or child care homes (Barglow, Vaughn, and Moliter 1987; Clarke-Stewart 1992; Moore, Snow, and Poteat 1988).

Such differences favoring preschool-age children with center care were reported in two comprehensive studies. In a study comparing six types of child care arrangements experienced by 150 2- to 4-year-old predominantly middle-class children, children who experienced care in a center or preschool, whether full- or part-time, demonstrated greater competence in verbal ability, cognition, social competence, cooperation with peers, and social cognition compared to those who experienced home-based care, whether with their parents, sitters, or day care providers (Clarke-Stewart 1992). The NICHD Study of Early Child Care compared cognitive, language, and social outcomes for over 1100 children experiencing child care in a variety of settings in analyses that were adjusted for family and child characteristics, amount of child care, and quality of child care. Analyses of cognitive and language outcomes indicated that children in center care scored higher on measures at 24 and 36 months than did children in other types of care after adjusting for the family and

other child care characteristics (NICHD 1997b). These advantages, however, have not always been detected in middle childhood for middle-class children in the United States (cf. Clarke-Stewart 1989). In fact, one of the NLSY studies found that center child care experience of unknown quality was negatively related to math achievement score at 5-6 years of age for children from more optimal home environments, whereas center experience was positively related for children from more impoverished home environments (Caughy, DiPietro, and Strobino 1994). In contrast, longer-term follow-up studies in Sweden (Andersson 1989, 1992) and West Germany (Tietze 1987) on large population-based cohorts reported that children who attended high-quality child care centers had significantly better academic performance and social adjustment at 8-13 years of age than children who did not.

Other studies have found that center care was related to poorer outcomes. A longitudinal study of Swedish children compared children receiving child care at centers and at home and found that children attending child care homes engaged in more positive and competent play with peers in their child care setting than did children attending centers (Lamb et al. 1994). A retrospective study of U.S. middle-class children indicated that white, but not black, children who attended centers tended to be rated slightly higher on a measure of externalizing problems (acting-out problems) in middle childhood when compared with children who experienced either no regular child care or other types of child care (Burchinal et al. 1995).

In conclusion, limited evidence exists suggesting that center care during the preschool years may be related to slightly better cognitive outcomes and that both center care and family child care homes may be related to slightly better social outcomes. Reassuringly, these findings were obtained from studies that measured both type and quality of care as well as from studies that did not measure quality of care.

QUANTITY OF CHILD CARE

Linked to concerns about infant child care have been concerns about the effects of full-time or extensive nonparental child care (Lamb 1997) on children's social development. Developmentalists expressed concerns that time away from parents may inhibit formation of the infant-mother attachment and undermine the parent's socialization efforts. They also worried that more time with peers, especially in poor-quality care, may reinforce aggression if children get what they want simply by taking it (NICHD in press). Early studies seemed to support these contentions but did not take quality of child care or family selection factors into account. More recent studies provide more equivocal support.

Somewhat different conclusions are drawn from studies that did and did not measure child care quality. Children experiencing full-time child care, compared with children experiencing no or part-time child care, have been shown to be less compliant

(Belsky and Eggebeen 1991; Rubenstein, Howes, and Boyle 1981; Rabinovich et al. 1987; Schwarz, Strickland, and Krolick 1974; Thornburg et al. 1990; Vandell and Corasaniti 1990) in analyses that did not adjust for child care quality but not in the NICHD study that included quality in the analysis (NICHD in press). Extensive child care was related to increased levels of behavior problems (Bates et al. 1994; Baydar and Brooks-Gunn 1991; Haskins 1985; Schwarz, Strickland, and Krolick 1974; Steinberg et al. 1991; Thornburg et al. 1990; Vandell and Corasaniti 1990) and lower levels of positive adjustment (Bates et al. 1994) in analyses that did not adjust for quality. It was very modestly related to extensive child care in the NICHD study that did adjust for quality (NICHD in press). In contrast, extensive care in high-quality child care centers has been related to more positive social and cognitive outcomes into middle childhood in the United States (Fields 1991) and Sweden (Andersson 1989, 1992).

In conclusion, evidence linking extensive care to negative child outcomes appears to emerge primarily from studies that did not measure quality and quantity of care. Extensive, full-time care has been linked very weakly, both positively and negatively, to social development in studies that also measured child care quality.

CONCLUSIONS AND PUBLIC POLICY IMPLICATIONS

After 30 years of research into the relations between child care experiences and child development, it appears that some aspects of child care experiences are related to some developmental outcomes for at least some children. Of the various components of child care, child care quality shows the strongest and most consistent positive associations with cognitive and social development. The associations tend to be modest at least for middle-class children, with characteristics of the family showing stronger associations with all outcomes than with characteristics of child care when hierarchical regression analyses are performed. In contrast, studies of early intervention for children from families living in poverty suggest that high-quality child care, beginning in infancy, can have large and long-term effects on cognitive development. Other aspects of the child care experience such as timing, quantity, and type of care appear to be less related to development outcomes in studies that also considered child care quality and family selection factors, although there is some evidence that extensive care may be modestly negatively related to social outcomes and that center care may be modestly positively related to cognitive outcomes.

At least some developmentalists and economists have argued that the modest effects associated with child care quality imply that quality really does not matter (Blau 1997; Scarr 1998). This view has not been widely accepted for at least two reasons. Some developmentalists argue, based on the few studies that have followed children into middle childhood, that child care quality may

have long-term effects indirectly, not directly, because of its impact on children's expectations regarding the teacher-child relationship (Howes, Hamilton, and Phillipsen 1998). Howes argues that children who experience poor relationships with teachers are likely to develop lower, more problematic expectations regarding relationships with teachers and other adults in general. These expectations make it difficult for the child to adjust and learn within the classroom environment.

Other developmentalists argue that it is unreasonable to expect large associations when analyses are conducted using regression models that include a wide array of family selection variables or are based on general systems or ecological models. These models describe a child's development as a function of interconnected systems such as the parent-child relationship, the family, child care, and the community. Overlapping systems will lead to smaller portions of variance that will be uniquely accounted for by any component of the child's life. That is, regression analyses that include family factors related to both child outcomes and to child care quality are likely to underestimate the impact of both the family and child care on children's development since a regression coefficient represents the independent contribution of that factor given all other variables in the regression model. Any variance in the child outcome that is caused by child care, but overlaps with family characteristics, will not be attributed to either child care or the family characteristic. Whereas failure to include important covariates will likely result in overestimation, extensive overlap between child care and family characteristics is likely to underestimate the impact of either set of variables on the outcome measures. With family characteristics tending to be moderately to highly correlated, it is more likely that analyses that include at least a few key family selection variables will underestimate the child care effects rather than overestimate them. This problem is exacerbated when developmentalists use hierarchical regression analyses from which they report the coefficients when blocks of variables enter the model, in sequential, not simultaneous, regression analyses. Accordingly, all of the overlapping variance is attributed to the block of variables that enter first. Indeed, comparisons of individual regression coefficients from the full regression model, not the hierarchical model, suggest that child care quality can be as strongly related to outcomes such as cognitive development as characteristics such as the mother's IQ or the quality of mother-child interactions (NICHD 1997b).

In summary, statistical analyses of observational data are unlikely to provide precise estimates of the amount of influence that child care has on children's development. Further work is clearly needed to identify and clarify the mechanisms by which these global measures of quality are related to children's cognitive and social development and to determine whether these mechanisms operate similarly or differently for children from diverse backgrounds (Lamb 1997). Identification of these mechanisms should help provide us with better tools than regression analysis for disentangling these overlapping systems of influences on children's development.

If one concludes that child care quality does matter, then there are public policy implications. Characteristics of child care such as child-adult ratios, class sizes, and caregiver education and training that can be regulated have been linked to child care quality (Arnett 1989; Berk 1985; Howes 1983; Howes and Rubenstein 1985; Kontos and Fiene 1987; McCartney et al. 1997; Phillipsen et al. 1997) and directly to child outcomes by most, but not all, researchers (Blau 1997). Whereas Blau analyzed data based on mother report of structural quality measures from the NLSY, the other researchers have based their conclusions on classroom observations. In these studies, children's cognitive and social developmental outcomes are more positive (Burchinal et al. 1996; Howes 1997; Howes and Olenick 1986; Howes et al. 1988; Ruopp et al. 1979) in classrooms with a smaller than with a larger number of children per caregiver. In classrooms with smaller group sizes, children have been found to behave more positively (Howes 1983; Howes and Rubenstein 1985; Kontos and Fiene 1987; Ruopp et al. 1979), and their language and intellectual development is enhanced when compared to children in classrooms with larger group sizes (Kontos and Fiene 1987; Ruopp et al. 1979). Children who are placed in the care of teachers with more education and training have been found to have better child development outcomes than children with less-educated teachers (Howes 1997; Howes and Olenick 1986; Ruopp et al. 1979; Vandell and Powers 1983; Whitebook, Howes, and Phillips 1989). Particularly relevant for policymakers, several studies have demonstrated that children's cognitive and social development is enhanced when classrooms meet professional recommendations regarding teacher education and caregiver-child ratios (Howes, Phillips, and Whitebook 1992; Howes, Hamilton, and Phillipsen 1998; NICHD 1997b). The NICHD study showed that children's cognitive and social outcomes at 36 months were linked linearly to the number of professional recommendations met in that child's classroom.

In conclusion, nonparental child care has become the norm, not the exception, for children in the United States. Concerns about the quality of much of the care in this country (for more details, see Cryer, this volume) raise concerns about the cognitive and social development of children because quality of care is a fairly consistent, albeit modest, correlate of these developmental outcomes. Public policies that promote fewer children per caregiver and better-educated and better-trained caregivers are likely to enhance child outcomes by increasing child care quality.

References

Abbott-Shim, Martha and Ann Sibley. 1987. *Assessment Profile for Childhood Programs*. Atlanta, GA: Quality Assistance.

Ainsworth, Mary D., Mary C. Blehar, Evert Waters, and S. Wall. 1978. *Patterns of Attachment*. Hillsdale, NJ: Lawrence Erlbaum.

Andersson, Bengt Erik. 1989. Effects of Public Day Care: A Longitudinal Study. *Child Development* 60:857-66.

———. 1992. Effects of Day-Care on Cognitive and Socio-Emotional Competence in 13-Year-Old Swedish School Children. *Child Development* 63: 20-36.

Arnett, James. 1989. Caregivers in Day-Care Centers: Does Training Matter? *Journal of Applied Psychology* 10:541-52.

Barglow, Peter, Brian E. Vaughn, and Nancy Moliter. 1987. Effects of Maternal Absence Due to Employment on the Quality of Infant-Mother Attachment in a Low-Risk Sample. *Child Development* 58:945-54.

Barnett, W. Steven. 1995. Long-Term Effects of Early Childhood Programs on Cognitive and School Outcomes. *The Future of Children* 5:25-50.

Bates, John, Denny Marvinney, Timothy Kelly, Kenneth Dodge, David Bennett, and Gregory Pettit. 1994. Child-Care History and Kindergarten Adjustment. *Developmental Psychology* 30(5):690-700.

Baydar, Nazli and Jeanne Brooks-Gunn. 1991. Effects of Maternal Employment and Child Care Arrangements on Preschoolers' Cognitive and Behavioral Outcomes: Evidence from the Children of the National Longitudinal Survey of Youth. *Developmental Psychology* 27:932-45.

Belsky, Jay. 1986. Infant Day Care: A Cause for Concern? *Zero to Three* 6:1-7.

Belsky, Jay and David Eggebeen. 1991. Early and Extensive Maternal Employment and Young Children's Socioemotional Development: Children of the National Longitudinal Survey of Youth. *Journal of Marriage and the Family* 53:1083-1110.

Belsky, Jay and Michael Rovine. 1990. Q-Set Security and First-Year Nonmaternal Care. *New Directions for Child Development* 49:7-22.

Belsky, Jay and Michael J. Rovine. 1988. Nonmaternal Care in the First Year of Life and the Security of Infant-Parent Attachment. *Child Development* 59:929-49.

Berk, Laura. 1985. Relationship of Caregiver Training to Child-Oriented Attitudes, Job Satisfaction, and Behaviors Towards Children. *Child Care Quarterly* 14:103-29.

Blau, David. 1997. The Production of Quality in Child Care Centers. University of North Carolina. Manuscript.

Bradley, Robert H., Bettye M. Caldwell, Stephen L. Rock, Craig T. Ramey, Kathryn E. Barnard, C. Gray, M. A. Hammond, S. Mitchell, A. W. Gottfried, L. Siegel, and D. L. Johnson. 1989. Home Environment and Cognitive Development in the First Three Years: A Collaborative Study Involving Six Sites and Three Ethnic Groups in North America. *Developmental Psychology* 25:217-35.

Brooks-Gunn, Jeane, Pam K. Klevanov, Fong-ruey Liaw, and Donna Spiker. 1993. Enhancing the Development of Low-Birthweight, Premature Infants: Changes in Cognition and Behavior over the First Three Years. *Child Development* 64:736-53.

Bryant, Donna M., Margaret R. Burchinal, Lisa B. Lau, and Joseph J. Sparling. 1994. Family and Classroom Correlates of Head Start Children's Developmental Outcomes. *Early Childhood Research Quarterly* 9:289-309.

Bryant, Donna M., Ellen S. Peisner-Feinberg, and Richard M. Clifford. 1993. *Evaluation of Public Preschool Programs in North Carolina: Final Report.* Chapel Hill, NC: Frank Porter Graham Child Development Center.

Burchinal, Margaret R., Donna M. Bryant, Marvin W. Lee, and Craig T. Ramey. 1992. Early Daycare, Infant-Mother Attachment, and Maternal Responsiveness in the Infant's First Year. *Early Childhood Research Quarterly* 7:383-96.

Burchinal, Margaret R., Frances A. Campbell, Donna M. Bryant, Barbara A. Wasik, and Craig T. Ramey. 1997. Early Intervention and Mediating Processes in Cognitive Performance of Children of Low-Income African-American Families. *Child Development* 68:935-54.

Burchinal, Margaret R., Marvin W. Lee, and Craig T. Ramey. 1989. Type of Day-Care and Preschool Intellectual Development in Disadvantaged Children. *Child Development* 60:128-37.

Burchinal, Margaret R., Sharon L. Ramey, Molly K. Reid, and James Jaccard. 1995. Early Child Care Experiences and Their Association with Family and Child Characteristics During Middle Childhood. *Early Childhood Research Quarterly* 10:33-61.

Burchinal, Margaret R., Joanne E. Roberts, Laura A. Nabors, and Donna Bryant. 1996. Quality of Center Child Care and Infant Cognitive and Language Development. *Child Development* 67:606-20.

Campbell, Frances and Craig T. Ramey. 1994. Effects of Early Intervention on Intellectual and Academic Achievement: A Follow-Up Study of Children from Low-Income Families. *Child Development* 65:684-98.

Caughy, Margaret O., Janet A. DiPietro, and Donna M. Strobino. 1994. Day-Care Participation as a Protective Factor in the Cognitive Development of Low-Income Children. *Child Development* 65:457-71.

Chase-Lansdale, P. Lindsay and Margaret T. Owen. 1987. Maternal Employment in Family Context: Effects on

Infant-Mother and Infant-Father Attachments. *Child Development* 58:1505-12.

Clarke-Stewart, K. Alison. 1988. "The Effects of Infant Day Care Reconsidered" Reconsidered: Risks for Parents, Children, and Researchers. *Early Childhood Research Quarterly* 3:293-318.

———. 1989. Infant Day Care: Maligned or Malignant? *American Psychologist* 44(2):266-73.

———. 1992. Consequences of Child Care for Children's Development. In *Child Care in the 1990s: Trends and Consequences*, ed. A. Booth. Hillsdale, NJ: Lawrence Erlbaum.

Clarke-Stewart, K. Alison and Greta C. Fein. 1983. Early Childhood Programs. In *Handbook of Child Psychology*. Vol. 2, *Infancy and Developmental Psychobiology*, ed. M. M. Haith and J. J. Campos. 4th ed. New York: John Wiley.

Clarke-Stewart, K. Alison, Christian P. Gruber, and Linda M. Fitzgerold. 1994. *Children at Home and in Day Care*. Hillsdale, NJ: Lawrence Erlbaum.

Crockenberg, Susan and Cindy Litman. 1991. Effects of Maternal Employment on Maternal and Two-Year-Old Child Behavior. *Child Development* 62:930-53.

Dunn, Loraine. 1993. Proximal and Distal Features of Day Care Quality and Children's Development. *Early Childhood Research Quarterly* 8:167-92.

Easterbrooks, M. Ann and Wendy A. Goldberg. 1985. Effects of Early Maternal Employment on Toddlers, Mothers, and Fathers. *Developmental Psychology* 21:774-83.

Fields, Tiffany. 1991. Quality Infant Day-Care and Grade School Behavior and Performance. *Child Development* 62:863-70.

Garber, Howard L. 1988. *The Milwaukee Project: Preventing Mental Retardation in Children at Risk*. Washington, DC: American Association on Mental Retardation.

Garcia-Coll, Cynthia T. 1990. Developmental Outcome of Minority Infants: A Process-Oriented Look into Our Beginnings. *Child Development* 61:270-89.

Garcia-Coll, Cynthia T., Gontran Lamberty, Renee Jenkins, Harriet P. McAdoo, Keith Crnic, Barbara H. Wasik, and Heidi V. Garcia. 1996. An Integrative Model for the Study of Developmental Competencies in Minority Children. *Child Development* 67:1891-1914.

Goelman, Hillel and Alan R. Pence. 1987. Effects of Child Care, Family, and Individual Characteristics on Children's Language Development: The Victoria Day Care Research Project. In *Quality in Child Care: What Does the Research Tell Us?* ed. D. Phillips. Washington, DC: National Association for the Education of Young Children.

Harms, Thelma and Richard M. Clifford. 1980. *Early Childhood Environment Rating Scale*. New York: Teachers College Press.

Harms, Thelma, Debby Cryer, and Richard M. Clifford. 1990. *Infant/Toddler Environment Rating Scale*. New York: Teachers College Press.

Haskins, Ron. 1985. Public School Aggression Among Children with Varying Day-Care Experience. *Child Development* 56:689-703.

———. 1989. Beyond Metaphor: The Efficacy of Early Childhood Education. *American Psychologist* 44:274-82.

Hayes, Cheryl D., John L. Palmer, and Martha J. Zaslow, eds. 1990. *Who Cares for America's Children? Child Care Policy for the 1990's*. Washington, DC: National Academy Press.

Hoffman, Lois W. 1989. Effects of Maternal Employment in the Two-Parent Family. *American Psychologist* 44:283-92.

Howes, Carollee. 1983. Caregiver Behavior in Center and Family Day Care. *Journal of Applied Developmental Psychology* 4:99-107.

———. 1997. Children's Experiences in Center-Based Child Care as a Function of Teacher Background and Adult:Child Ratios. *Merrill-Palmer Quarterly* 43:404-25.

Howes, Carollee, Claire E. Hamilton, and Leslie C. Phillipsen. 1998. Stability and Continuity of Child-Caregiver and Child-Peer Relationships. *Child Development* 69:418-26.

Howes, Carollee, Catherine C. Matheson, and Claire E. Hamilton. 1994. Maternal, Teacher, and Child Care History Correlates of Children's Relationships with Peers. *Child Development* 65:264-73.

Howes, Carollee and Michael Olenick. 1986. Family and Child Care Influences on Toddler Compliance. *Child Development* 57:202-16.

Howes, Carollee, Deborah A. Phillips, and Marcy Whitebook. 1992. Thresholds of Quality: Implications for the Social Development of Children in Center-Based Child Care. *Child Development* 63:449-60.

Howes, Carollee, Carol Rodning, Darlene C. Galluzzo, and Lisabeth Myers. 1988. Attachment and Child Care: Relationships with Mother and Caregiver. *Early Childhood Research Quarterly* 3:403-16.

Howes, Carollee and J. Rubenstein. 1985. Determinants of Toddlers' Experiences in Care: Age of Entry and Quality of Setting. *Child Care Quarterly* 14:140-51.

Howes, Carollee, Ellen Smith, and Ellen Galinsky. 1995. *The Florida Child Care Quality Improvement Study: Interim Report*. New York: Families and Work Institute.

Infant Health and Development Project. 1990. Enhancing the Outcomes of Low-Birth-Weight, Premature Infants: A Multisite, Randomized Trial. *Journal of the American Medical Association* 263:3035-42.

Jacobson, Joseph L. and Diane E. Wille. 1984. Influence of Attachment and Separation Experience on Separation Distress at 18 Months. *Developmental Psychology* 20:477-84.

Kontos, Susan and R. Fiene. 1987. Child Care Quality, Compliance with Regulations, and Children's Development: The Pennsylvania Study. In *Quality in Child Care: What Does Research Tell Us?* ed. D. Phillips. Washington, DC: National Association for the Education of Young Children.

Kontos, Susan, Carollee Howes, Marybeth Shinn, and Ellen Galinsky. 1995. *Quality in Family Child Care and Relative Care*. New York: Teachers College Press.

Kontos, Susan J. 1991. Child Care Quality, Family Background, and Children's Development. *Early Childhood Research Quarterly* 6:249-62.

Lamb, Michael E. 1997. Nonparental Child Care: Context, Quality, Correlates. In *Handbook of Child Psychology*. Vol. 4, *Child Psychology in Practice*, ed. W. Damon, I. E. Siegel, and K. A. Renninger. 5th ed. New York: John Wiley.

Lamb, Michael E., Kathleen J. Sternberg, N. Knuth, C.-P. Hwang, and A. G. Broberg. 1994. Peer Play and Nonparental Care Experiences. In *Children's Play in Childcare Settings*, ed. H. Goelman and E. V. Jacobs. Albany: State University of New York Press.

Lazar, Irving and Richard Darlington. 1982. Lasting Effects of Early Education: A Report from the Consortium for Longitudinal Studies. *Monographs of the Society for Research in Child Development* 47:2-3, serial no. 195.

McCartney, Kathleen, Sandra Scarr, Anne Rochleleau, Deborah Phillips, Martha Abbott-Shim, Marlene Eisenberg, Nancy Keefe, Saul Rosenthal, and Jennifer Ruh. 1997. Teacher-Child Interactions and Child Care Auspices as Predictors of Social Outcomes in Infants, Toddlers, and Preschoolers. *Merrill-Palmer Quarterly* 43:426-50.

Melhuish, Edward C., E. Lloyd, Susan Martin, and Ann Mooney. 1990. Type of Child Care at 18 Months—II. Relations with Cognitive and Language Development. *Journal of Child Psychology and Psychiatry and Allied Disciplines* 31(6):861-70.

Moore, Beverly F., Charles W. Snow, and Michael Poteat. 1988. Effects of Variant Types of Child Care Experience on the Adaptive Behavior of Kindergarten Children. *American Journal of Orthopsychiatry* 58:297-303.

National Center for Educational Statistics. 1996. *1996 National Household Education Survey.* Washington, DC: Department of Education, Office of Educational Research and Improvement.

NICHD Early Child Care Research Network. 1996. Characteristics of Infant Child Care: Factors Contributing to Positive Caregiving. *Early Childhood Research Quarterly* 11:269-306.

———. 1997a. Infant Child Care and Attachment Security: Results of the NICHD Study of Early Child Care. *Child Development* 68:860-79.

———. 1997b. The Relationship of Child Care to Cognitive and Language Development. Poster presented at the biennial meeting of the Society for Research in Child Development, Apr., Washington, DC.

———. In press. Early Child Care and Self-Control, Compliance, and Problem Behavior. *Child Development.*

O'Connell, Joanne C. and Dale C. Farran. 1982. Effects of Day Care Experience on the Use of Intentional Communicative Behaviors in a Sample of Socio-Economically Depressed Infants. *Developmental Psychology* 18:22-29.

Owen, Margaret T., M. Ann Easterbrooks, P. Lindsay Chase-Lansdale, and Wendy A. Goldberg. 1984. The Relation Between Maternal Employment Status and Stability of Attachments to Mother and to Father. *Child Development* 55:1894-1901.

Peisner-Feinberg, Ellen, Robert Clifford, Noreen Yazejian, Mary Culkin, Carollee Howes, and Sharon L. Kagan. 1998. The Longitudinal Effects of Child Care Quality: Implications for Kindergarten Success. Paper presented at the annual meeting of the American Education Research Association, Apr., Anaheim, CA.

Peisner-Feinberg, Ellen S. and Margaret R. Burchinal. 1997. Relations Between Preschool Children, Child Care Experiences, and Concurrent Development: The Cost, Quality, and Outcomes Study. *Merrill-Palmer Quarterly* 43:451-77.

Phillips, Deborah, Kathleen McCartney, Sandra Scarr, and Carollee Howes. 1987. Selective Review of Infant Day Care Research: A Cause for Concern. *Zero to Three* 7:18-21.

Phillips, Deborah A., Kathleen McCartney, and Sandra Scarr. 1987. Child Care Quality and Children's Social Development. *Developmental Psychology* 23:537-43.

Phillips, Deborah A., Miriam Voran, Ellen Kisker, Carollee Howes, and Marcy Whitebook. 1994. Child Care for Children in Poverty: Opportunity or Inequity? *Child Development* 65:472-92.

Phillipsen, Leslie C., Margaret R. Burchinal, Carollee Howes, and Debby Cryer. 1997. The Prediction of Process Quality from Structural Features of Child Care. *Early Childhood Research Quarterly* 12:281-303.

Pianta, Robert C. and Sheri L. Nimetz. 1991. Relationship Between Children and Teachers: Associations with Classroom and Home Behavior. *Jour-*

nal of Applied Developmental Psychology 12:379-93.

Rabinovich, B., Martha Zaslow, Peter Berman, and Robert Hyman. 1987. Employed and Homemaker Mothers' Perceptions of Their Toddlers Compliance Behavior in the Home. Poster presented at the meetings of the Society for Research in Child Development, Apr., Baltimore, MD.

Roberts, Joanne E., Shoshanna Rabinowitch, Donna M. Bryant, Margaret R. Burchinal, M. A. Koch, and C. T. Ramey. 1989. Language Skills of Children with Different Preschool Experiences. Journal of Speech and Hearing Research 32:773-86.

Rosenthal, M. K. 1994. An Ecological Approach to the Study of Child Care: Family Day Care in Israel. Hillsdale, NJ: Lawrence Erlbaum.

Rubenstein, Judith, Carollee Howes, and Patricia Boyle. 1981. A Two-Year Follow-Up of Infants in Community-Based Day Care. Journal of Child Psychology and Psychiatry 22:209-18.

Ruopp, R., J. Travers, F. Glantz, and G. Coelen. 1979. Children at the Center. Cambridge, MA: Abt.

Sameroff, A. J. 1983. Developmental Systems: Contexts and Evolution. In Handbook of Child Development. Vol. 1, History, Theories, and Methods, ed. W. Kesson. New York: John Wiley.

Scarr, Sandra. 1998. American Child Care Today. American Psychologist 53:95-108.

Scarr, Sandra and Marlene Eisenberg. 1993. Child Care Research: Issues, Perspectives, and Results. Annual Review of Psychology 44:613-44.

Schliecker, Earl, Donna R. White, and Ellen Jacobs. 1991. The Role of Day Care Quality in the Prediction of Children's Vocabulary. Canadian Journal of Behavioral Science 23:2-24.

Schwarz, J. Conrad, Robert Strickland, and George Krolick. 1974. Infant Day Care: Behavioral Effects at Preschool

Age. Developmental Psychology 10:502-6.

Schweinhart, Lawrence J., David P. Weikart, and Mary B. Larner. 1986. Consequences of Three Preschool Curriculum Models Through Age 15. Early Childhood Research Quarterly 1: 15-45.

Steinberg, Kathleen, Michael Lamb, Carl Phillip Hwang, A. Broberg, R. Ketterlinus, and F. Bookstein. 1991. Does Out-of-Home Care Affect Compliance in Preschoolers? International Journal of Behavioral Development 55:1340-48.

Stipek, Deborah, Rachelle Feiler, Denise Daniels, and Sharon Milburn. 1995. Effects of Different Instructional Approaches on Young Children's Achievement and Motivation. Child Development 66:209-23.

Thompson, Ross A. 1988. The Effects of Infant Day Care Through the Prism of Attachment Theory: A Critical Appraisal. Early Childhood Research Quarterly 3:273-82.

Thompson, Ross A., M. E. Lamb, and D. Estes. 1982. Stability of Infant-Mother Attachment and Its Relationship to Changing Life Circumstances in an Unselected Middle-Class Sample. Child Development 53:144-48.

Thornburg, Kathy R., Peggy Pearl, Dwayne Crompton, and Jean M. Ispa. 1990. Development of Kindergarten Children Based on Child Care Arrangements. Early Childhood Research Quarterly 5:27-42.

Tietze, Wolfgang. 1987. A Structural Model for the Evaluation of Preschool Effects. Early Childhood Research Quarterly 2:133-53.

Tomasello, Michael and Michael Farrar. 1986. Joint Attention and Early Language. Child Development 57:1454-63.

Vandell, Deborah L. and Mary A. Corasaniti. 1990. Child Care and the Family: Complex Contributors to Child Development. In *New Directions in Child Development*, ed. K. McCartney. San Francisco: Jossey-Bass.

Vandell, Deborah L., V. Kay Henderson, and Kathy S. Wilson. 1988. A Longitudinal Study of Children with Day Care Experiences of Varying Quality. *Child Development* 59:1286-92.

Vandell, Deborah L. and Carol P. Powers. 1983. Day Care Quality and Children's Free Play Activities. *American Journal of Orthopsychiatry* 53:489-500.

Vaughn, Brian, Frederick Gove, and B. Egeland. 1980. The Relationship Between Out-of-Home Care and the Quality of Infant-Mother Attachment in an Economically Disadvantaged Population. *Child Development* 51:1203-14.

Vollig, Brenda and Lynne Feagans. 1994. Infant Day Care and Children's Social Competence. *Infant Behavior and Development* 18:177-88.

Weinraub, Marsha, Elizabeth Jaeger, and Lois Hoffman. 1988. Predicting Infant Outcome in Families of Employed and Nonemployed Mothers. *Early Childhood Research Quarterly* 3:361-78.

Whitebook, Marcy, Carollee Howes, and Deborah Phillips. 1989. *Who Cares? Child Care Teachers and the Quality of Care in America: Executive Summary*. Washington, DC: Center for the Child Care Workforce.

ANNALS, *AAPSS*, **563**, May 1999

Families and Child Care: Divergent Viewpoints

By SUSAN D. HOLLOWAY and BRUCE FULLER

ABSTRACT: The authors outline two perspectives on the respective roles of families and preschools in socializing and educating young children. The family-oriented perspective emphasizes the primacy of parents as educators, moral guides, and nurturers of their children. The early childhood education perspective is more likely to view preschools as independent of the family. This perspective highlights the scientific basis of the early socialization enterprise and emphasizes research on universal developmental sequences. These two perspectives yield distinct responses to important policy questions about child care. Those with a family-oriented perspective advocate obtaining descriptive accounts of parents' goals, values, and practices and creating child care choices that reflect these considerations. Early childhood education advocates are concerned about promoting universal guidelines based upon professional expertise to ensure high quality and feel that parents will select this care if given appropriate education concerning its value to their young children. The authors argue that attempts to improve quality and increase supply must integrate the culturally based preferences of parents with knowledge about universal developmental processes gleaned from research and practice.

Susan D. Holloway is a developmental psychologist interested in the socialization and education of young children. She has taught at the University of Maryland and Harvard University and is currently at the University of California, Berkeley. With Bruce Fuller, she recently authored Through My Own Eyes: Single Mothers and the Cultures of Poverty.

Bruce Fuller is associate professor of public policy and education at the University of California, Berkeley. His work focuses on understanding how government can improve schools and families from diverse cultural backgrounds. He has worked at the World Bank and Harvard University.

NOTE: Bruce Fuller's contribution to this article was assisted by funding to the Growing Up in Poverty Project from the Child Care Bureau of the U.S. Department of Health and Human Services; the U.S. Department of Education (OERI); the Annie E. Casey Foundation; the David and Lucile Packard Foundation; the Luke Hancock Foundation; the Spencer Foundation; and the Miriam and Peter Haas Fund.

NEARLY 30 years ago, President Nixon vetoed the first child care bill passed by the United States Congress, and the country is still in turmoil as to how to address parents' need for reliable, affordable, high-quality child care. Why has the United States lagged so far behind other industrialized countries in developing a reasonable child care policy? In this article, we argue that developing a clearer consensus concerning the rights and responsibilities of parents is essential to resolving policy debates about which type of care to promote, how to define quality care, and how to ensure adequate supply. It is our contention that many disagreements on these issues result from a clash of perspectives concerning the role of the family in the lives of young children.

At a recent conference, we had an experience that illustrates the divergent ways in which academic researchers conceptualize parents and their relationships with preschool staff. We presented data from a qualitative study on 14 low-income mothers to illustrate that these mothers had definite—and varied—ideas about what sorts of early childhood programs would benefit their children. We portrayed their cultural models of child rearing—beliefs and strategies shaped through experiences and interactions within their cultural and economic contexts. We argued that one component of high-quality care is having child care staff who understand parents' values and are adept at synthesizing parents' knowledge and perspectives with the professional expertise of the staff. During the discussion period, a prominent member of the research community vigorously challenged our attempts to document the views of mothers with little or no professional training in education. By "going native," as he literally put it, we were implying that these parents' beliefs were "adaptive" for children's development. He objected to our describing parenting practices without objectively evaluating them in terms of their effects on children and did not see any implications of the mothers' beliefs for the practices used in early childhood settings. The ensuing debate did little to bridge the wide gulf between his position and ours. Each side was operating from entirely different assumptions about the role of parents in the lives of young children.

Our perspective is that many in the field of early childhood education (ECE) espouse a rather narrow view of child care quality that largely represents the socialization and educational practices—the cultural models—of the white, American middle class. This representation of quality is often characterized by its proponents as "cultureless" by virtue of being rooted in universal norms of child development rather than socially constructed models of appropriate practices. We argue that all formulations about child rearing are constructed within a cultural context, including those that incorporate research findings and professional expertise. While few early childhood educators intentionally undermine parents' authority and perception of self-efficacy, many may do so inadvertently by promoting only the cultural models embedded in the mainstream early childhood construction of quality—to the exclusion of the cultural models held by parents.

In this article, we address these issues by reviewing two separate bodies of literature, each of which embodies a distinctive orientation toward the respective roles of families and preschools. One perspective emphasizes the family as the primary, superordinate locus of socialization. This family-oriented perspective assumes the primacy of parents as educators, moral guides, and nurturers of their children. Within this framework, parents are also seen as managers who select and monitor nonfamilial settings such as the school, summer camp, or peer group. Most parents are assumed to have a coherent set of child-rearing goals and strategies for bringing up their children. Parents are seen as having a legitimate desire to ensure that institutions encountered by their children share beliefs and practices consistent with their own. Parents are also seen as capable of mediating the effects of outside institutions by evaluating their effects and reinterpreting them to their children.

The second perspective, ECE, emphasizes the importance and autonomy of formal child care as an institution for socializing and educating young children. ECE-oriented individuals are more likely to view preschools as settings independent of the family. One way they emphasize the disconnection between families and preschools is by highlighting the scientific basis of the early socialization enterprise. They advocate an approach to early education that flows from research on universal developmental sequences as well as practitioners' experience in working with young children, and they frequently differentiate their views and practices from those of parents. Traditionally, advocates of this view have seen parents as highly variable in their ability to socialize young children effectively; the early childhood setting is seen as providing significant input into children's development, either in synergy with parents or in compensation for those whose parenting is not up to par.[1]

Distinct policy implications follow from each perspective on the linkage between families and child care institutions. Each perspective yields specific answers to important questions: Who defines the parameters of high-quality care? What kind of information is made available to parents about their options? Which types of institutions are supported with government funds? How can supply gaps be identified and remedied? We focus on one illustrative example at various points throughout the article: policy debates concerning the emerging evidence that Latino parents are far less likely to select center-based care than are Anglo or African American parents. Family-oriented individuals have argued that Latino parents may avoid child care centers because they prefer caregivers who can speak Spanish and impart culturally valued behaviors like respect for adults. Policymakers taking a family-oriented perspective might advocate funding a voucher program that allows parents to use less formal care options as well as funding centers that address the cultural models of child rearing held by Latino mothers (for example, Goldenberg and Gallimore 1995). Those who see early childhood settings as operating autonomously are more likely to argue that low enrollment of Latino children in centers does not represent an informed preference but, rather, reflects parents' lack of exposure to information on the benefits of developmentally appropriate practice. Policy initiatives favored by those with this perspective might include funding centers that embody the early childhood field's more generic definition of quality and conducting parent education efforts to convince parents of the benefits these centers can have for their children.

We begin by providing a fuller characterization of these two perspectives in the academic literature. We then discuss how proponents of each side have examined parental views about child care quality. The next section analyzes how parents' child care choices are driven by culturally based preferences for certain types of care and the availability of various forms of care. The issue of child care choice is typically studied from the perspective of the individual family or child, ignoring community-level variables such as supply. Yet individual families are situated within neighborhoods that differ dramatically in their organizational environments, including the availability of different forms of child care. We review studies employing multilevel perspectives and methods that assess how supply characteristics and culturally based preferences condition family-level selection

processes. We conclude the article by discussing research and policy implications based on our conceptualization of home and child care processes that affect children's early development.

HISTORICAL ROOTS OF THE FAMILY-ORIENTED POSITION

In the psychological literature, the study of families and children's development dates from as early as 1874, when Galton documented social class differences in children's school attainment (see Hess and Holloway 1984 for a review). The notion of parents as teachers became particularly popular in the 1960s when researchers began to study parents' interactions with their children (for example, Hess and Shipman 1965). This work formed part of the philosophical basis of early intervention programs developed during President Johnson's War on Poverty. Now considered by many to stigmatize low-income parents as deficient in their child-rearing practices, it was nevertheless pathbreaking in that it highlighted the importance of micro-level family interactions in shaping children's social and cognitive development. Subsequent researchers have been more careful to examine family strengths as well as weaknesses, using such strategies as contrasting high and low achievers within the population of low socioeconomic status (SES) children (for example, Clark 1983) or examining children who exhibit resiliency in generally disadvantageous circumstances (for example, Snow et al. 1991).

Early approaches to studying family influences on children's development tended to see the parent-child dyad as operating in a vacuum, without considering the effects of other institutions on the child or on the family. This acontextual approach was challenged by Bronfenbrenner (1979), who drew attention to proximal institutions affecting children, like the school and the community, as well as those whose effects were more diffuse or indirect. As the ecological perspective became more accepted, psychologists, sociologists, and educators began studying the relations between the family and other institutions. A major contribution of this approach has been the work on family-school partnerships (for example, Epstein 1992; Powell 1989; Valdés 1996).

In the last 15 years, the study of families has been increasingly informed by conceptualizations of culture rooted in the anthropological literature. The earlier predominance of laboratory-based research has been balanced by a large number of qualitative studies; these have served the important purpose of identifying and describing emic parenting constructs that emerge from the cultural context (Heath 1983). Researchers have become less likely to identify practices common among white, middle-class families as the standard against which other families should be compared. Most important, anthropologists have argued from a cultural-ecological perspective that parents are motivated to inculcate in their children competencies essential for success in their cultural milieu (Whiting and Whiting 1975; LeVine 1974; Ogbu 1981). To understand why parents in a certain group employ the strategies that they do, according to this perspective, it is first necessary to clarify the actual and imagined opportunity structure their children will face as adults. In the wake of these persuasive arguments that communities have diverse goals and afford varying opportunities to their members, studies have become more descriptive and less evaluative of parenting practices. With increased awareness that families can legitimately take different paths to socializing their children, there has been a gradual diminishing of the notion that there is a silver bullet, a set of family practices that are universally optimal for stimulating children's development (for example, Harwood, Miller, and Irizarry 1995).

Typically, those who take a family-oriented perspective are interested in how parents conceptualize their children's learning and development (for example, Johnson, Dyanda-Marira, and Dzvimbo 1997). They are also likely to accept the likelihood that the effects of any given practice will depend on the features of the child's social, economic, and physical environment. Such individuals also stress that the meaning of a given parenting practice depends on the cultural milieu; for example, the effects of a spanking depend on the goals and intentions of the parent, the overall relationship between parent and child, the child's relationships with other authority figures, and the norms of the community concerning physical punishment. The family-oriented perspective is summarized by New and Mallory (1994) in the following statement: "[A] view of the child that embraces an attitude of inquiry rather than prescription encourages a broader, less linear view of development and, by implication, results in more inclusive strategies of care and education" (8).

In this context, it is also important to mention the perspective on families held by economists, many of whom share the general view that most parents are basically competent and typically operate in their children's best interest. Becker (1976), for example, has argued that the household should be viewed as a collective organization that seeks to maximize its economic returns through work, income from public welfare, and investment in the human capital of children, including their early development. According to this perspective, if parents have sufficient resources to invest, they will make rational choices for the development and long-term success of their children.

Those scholars taking the family-oriented perspective tend to view institutions such as the child care center as surrogate parents, extending and complementing the basic goals and strategies of parents. They are likely to anticipate that child care institutions—as well as families—reflect diverse cultural models of child rearing and education and to reject the notion that child care centers can be cultureless. Indeed, some have provided analyses of the cultural assumptions underlying supposedly universal templates of good-quality child care (New 1994).

HISTORICAL ROOTS OF THE EARLY CHILDHOOD POSITION

The origin of the early childhood position can be found in the earliest settlement houses serving poor and immigrant families in the late 1800s, where providers who cared for children of working mothers acted as parent educators as well, teaching about hygiene, nutrition, and related issues. Accounts of the time paint a picture of these well-meaning caregivers as sympathetic to the plight of poor mothers and also somewhat patronizing as they sought to overcome their "backward" views (Youcha 1995). In preschools established for affluent families, the attitude toward parents was less condescending, but a fundamental assumption was that the scientific approach to learning offered something beyond what parents could provide at home.

As preschools flourished in the years following World War II, a number of curriculum models were initiated and refined. While research failed to establish a clear advantage of one specific model over the others, many leading educators came to prefer those that promoted learning through play rather than didactic instruction. In the 1970s, the play orientation was bolstered by research and theory from the field of developmental psychology, particularly the work of Jean Piaget. According to Piaget, it is by interacting with the physical and social environment in the context of play that the child "constructs" his or her own knowledge, which undergoes continual refinement through adolescence (Flavell 1963). A distinctive feature of Piaget's theory is the notion that a child learns primarily through solitary exploration of the material world and through interactions with other children; the role of the adult—teacher or parent—is primarily to create a rich, stimulating physical environment and to create opportunities for peer interaction (Wadsworth 1996).

In the 1960s and 1970s, early childhood educators became increasingly concerned about the quality of ECE programs. Accordingly, a number of national organizations, including the National Association for the Education of Young Children (NAEYC), began a process of articulating standards for the profession. In 1987, the NAEYC published guidelines for "developmentally appropriate" practice to be used in evaluating centers that wish to be accredited by the NAEYC. The guidelines reflect a general interpretation of development according to Piagetian theory combined with practice-based suggestions concerning the role of the teacher (Bredekamp 1987). Consistent with the established orientation of the field, the guidelines' authors initially conceptualized parents primarily as the recipients or consumers of information about developmentally appropriate practice (see Powell 1994 for a complete analysis). For example, the publication containing the guidelines states that "most parents do not fully understand how young children learn" and make "negative comments about developmentally appropriate practice" due to economic pressure, their own need for self-esteem, media misrepresentation, and the proliferation of inappropriate programs (Black and Puckett 1987, 85-86).

During the same period, other leading early childhood educators began to engage in a more complete analysis of the role of parents' goals and expectations—and their implications for early childhood programs. Numerous early childhood educators sought to clarify the role that cultural values played in practices advocated by early childhood professionals (Bowman 1992; Garcia et al. 1995; New and Mallory 1994). Early childhood educators were becoming aware of the ideas of Soviet psychologist Lev Vygotsky, whose focus on interindividual communication provided a clear conceptual model for the ways in which both teachers and parents helped shape children's understandings (Rogoff 1990). Additionally, a group of early childhood educators known as reconceptualists challenged the dominance of psychological perspectives in current conceptions of appropriate practice by showing how these conceptions are guided by political, cultural, and historical factors—as well as by empirically derived facts about child development (for example, Kessler and Swadener 1992).

In 1997, reflecting this increased awareness of diversity issues, the NAEYC published a new set of guidelines for developmentally appropriate practice that was more explicit in recognizing cultural variation in child-rearing practices (Bredekamp and Copple 1997). The new manual takes quite a different approach to parent communication; in the latest edition, teachers are cautioned not to say to themselves, "These parents don't really understand development. I'll educate them about theory and research and then they'll agree with me" (49); instead they are encouraged to "probe further about their [parents'] goals for their children" (49).

The NAEYC leadership and others (for example, Charlesworth et al. 1993) have tried to acknowledge the notion of cultural variation without abandoning their conviction that a set of generic practices can be articulated that are equally applicable to all children. This position is very difficult to defend to those who see all specific child-rearing practices as cultural constructs; from this perspective, any guidelines that advocate particular caregiver practices are always embedded in a set of cultural assumptions about the nature of children, values about how human relationships should be conducted and what types of individual competencies should be nurtured. However, the authors of the NAEYC guidelines have become increasingly open in acknowledging that teachers function as decision makers responsible for synthesizing (1) parents' goals and concerns, (2) empirically demonstrated facts about universal developmental processes, and (3) teachers' own values and assumptions about desirable goals and outcomes for children. By identifying which of their own ideas and pedagogical approaches are based upon moral and philosophical assumptions, early childhood educators can participate in highly useful discussions with parents and other community members, encouraging everyone to clarify and articulate their assumptions, values, and goals for children. For example, rather than defending a no-spanking policy on scientific grounds—when in fact recent reviews suggest that mild corporal punishment has no demonstrable negative effects on child outcomes (Baumrind 1996; Larzelere 1996)—teachers can acknowledge this as a challenging matter of moral values and philosophical assumptions and then argue the merits of their own position on such grounds as values pertaining to nonviolence, respect for authority, and the like.

In this brief overview of the family-oriented and ECE-oriented perspectives, it should be apparent that each perspective is not nested in a distinct disciplinary approach. Not all family researchers have portrayed parents as devoted to their children's best interests and competent in their role as socialization agents; many have chosen to emphasize parents' limitations and have made disparaging comparisons to professionals presumed to approach child rearing from a more informed, scientific perspective. By the same token, not all early childhood educators have focused on the deficits of parents' child rearing or promoted the view that the scientific approach is inevitably superior to parents' so-called folkways. Overall, many individuals in both fields have moved in the direction of recognizing the ways in which both families and preschools operate within a cultural context, and have made a commitment to challenge theory and practice that are based primarily upon the experiences of white, middle-class American children.

HOW DO FAMILIES AND EDUCATORS CONCEPTUALIZE CHILD CARE QUALITY?

One way that those taking a family-oriented perspective have tried to tease out the cultural models embedded in early childhood settings is by analyzing the reactions of parents from varying ethnic groups and social classes to different types of programs. For example, Joffe (1977) revealed how the aims of white middle-class teachers in one cooperative nursery school conflicted sharply with low-income black parents' expectations about what their children should be learning. Cultural conflicts were also explored by Zinsser (1991) in a study of child care in a working-class Italian American community. The older women who provided family child care provided a safe, clean environment, but the younger generation of parents, as well as professional newcomers to the community, expected child care that offered cognitive stimulation and preparation for school. In our study of low-income mothers in the Boston area (Holloway et al. 1997), mothers expressed clear cultural models that often conflicted with the criteria of high-quality care articulated by the early childhood profession. Some mothers rejected child care that was too oriented toward play, or too permissive and child centered, preferring programs that provided structure and academic content. However, others—particularly the Latinas—felt that center-based care was too cold and institutional; while these women valued academic learning for older children, they felt that it was particularly important for their preschoolers to experience warmth, acceptance, and moral guidance. This view led them to search for family members or familiar family day care providers rather than enrolling their children in centers.

Investigations utilizing the ECE perspective have also assessed parent perceptions about child care, but they have tended to focus primarily on whether parents understand or appreciate practices considered beneficial by early childhood educators. One approach has been asking parents to rank or rate the importance of various aspects of nonparental care nominated by the researchers. These studies find little variation across parents, and strong agreement with the perceptions of early childhood professionals. For example, in one study, parents of infants and preschoolers gave high ratings to nearly every indicator of quality on the Early Childhood Environmental Rating Scale (Cryer and Burchinal 1997). Similarly, in a large survey of mothers and family child care providers, the authors conclude that "parents and providers agree about what is most essential" (Galinsky et al. 1994, 2). This conclusion is based upon the similarity between mothers and providers regarding their average ratings of the relative importance of certain features of child care (such as "attention children receive" and "more like home than school").

Studies whose methods encourage parents to discriminate between credible and specific practices tend to find more variation between parents regarding their views about which practices are most important, and considerable disagreement with the position of early childhood educators. These findings are convergent with those of the family-oriented researchers to the extent that middle-class parents are more in agreement with the values and practices of early childhood professionals than are low-income parents. For instance, Stipek (1993) found that less educated parents more highly valued the attainment of basic skills, knowledge, and work habits than did more highly educated parents, who gave high ratings to the goal of enhancing children's self-concept.

When parents are asked to evaluate their own children's child care arrangement, they are usually quite positive, whereas researchers estimate that most centers are of mediocre quality (see Holloway and Fuller 1992 for a review). This discrepancy has been found even when parents and teachers are given the same detailed evaluation criteria to use in rating centers (Cryer and Burchinal 1997). Cryer and Burchinal suggest that parents are "imperfectly" informed about their children's care because they do not have adequate opportunity to view what goes on and that they may assume, falsely, that their own hopes and desires are shared by center staff. Institutional forces undoubtedly play a role as well. The amount and nature of information that parents receive about child care vary across communities depending on the availability of services like resource and referral agencies (for a review, see Fuller and Kagan 1998).

CHILD CARE SELECTION IN DIVERSE COMMUNITIES

Parents make many important decisions about their children's child care arrangements. They frequently attempt to select child care programs whose policies and practices are in accordance with their own beliefs about how children should be raised. Several family-level characteristics that influence the propensity of parents to select center-based child care rather than an informal provider or a family day care home include maternal education, family size, mother's age at first birth, ethnicity, and beliefs about child learning (Fuller, Holloway, and Liang 1996). These same factors operate differently when estimating children's age at which parents first select any form of nonparental care (Singer et al. 1998), although some of the family-level factors that predict children's early development also predict the propensity of entering more formal types of child care or preschooling. Thus the act of selection complements and indirectly reinforces the contribution of parents' child-rearing practices to children's development. Studies of child care effects on children's development that neglect to account for parental selection are likely to overestimate the program effects.

Parental preferences, however, are clearly constrained by the types of care available in their communities. Recent studies illustrate the powerful effects of availability on family selection of child care. Although the availability of licensed child care organizations (centers and family day care homes) has expanded in recent years, it continues to vary based on community wealth.[2] One early study, based in five metropolitan areas, provided preliminary evidence that middle-income families face a more limited availability of good-quality center-based programs, compared to affluent or poor families (Whitebook, Howes, and Phillips 1990). A more recent national survey found a curvilinear relationship between family income and enrollment in centers for Latino and black families, but for white families the relationship was linear (Fuller, Holloway, and Liang 1996). Studies that focus directly upon distribution of child care centers—an organizational level of analysis—find sharp disparities in availability across local communities. One study of 100 counties found one center-based classroom for every 45 preschool-age children within the 25 most affluent counties. In the poorest quartile of counties, one classroom was available for every 77 children. This variation in the availability of centers was related to several characteristics of the county, including mean family income, presence of single-parent households, and population growth (Fuller and Liang 1996).[3]

Variation in availability can also be found across zip codes. In Massachusetts, per capita supply of center slots was over one-third greater in affluent zip codes, relative to poor inner-city areas (Fuller and Liang 1996), and in California per capita availability of slots in centers and licensed day care homes was three times as great in affluent areas (Fuller et al. 1997). In the California study, the availability of center-based programs was also lower in heavily Latino zip codes and higher in communities with more churches, the latter being a likely proxy for levels of community organization.

In sum, while targeted subsidies over time have helped to equalize the number of center-based programs and slots in family day care homes, the basic availability of programs still varies depending on both the income level and the ethnic makeup of particular communities. In recent years, funding for child care has greatly increased, creating a new set of policy questions about what types of care to fund and in which communities. The policy position concerning child care availability held by most early childhood–oriented individuals, from the origins of Head Start forward, has been to expand the number of child care slots in formal organizations, assuming that parents will respond by enrolling their children. However, the effectiveness of this remedy has been questioned in the case of Latino families. Those Latino children whose mothers are employed full-time participate in center-based programs at a rate 23 percent below that of African Americans and 11 percent below whites (Fuller, Holloway, and Liang 1996). Given the relatively low academic achievement of Latino youths in the United States, educators have expressed concern that Latino children may be missing important preparatory experiences by not attending preschools, and have tried to understand the reasons behind this tendency to avoid them. Studies suggest that Latino families may rely on informal care because they more frequently live with extended family who can provide care, because they have a stronger orientation toward social development rather than academic preparation when their children are of preschool age, and because they prefer caregivers who share their views about discipline and who speak Spanish (Fuller, Holloway, and Liang 1996; Fuller et al. 1996; Liang 1996). Within the Latino community, advocates demanding a fair share of center-based slots find themselves at odds with those who seek to respond to parental preferences for alternative forms of care (Healy 1998).

SUMMARY AND CONCLUSION

We have argued that the child care field would benefit from a more careful analysis of the role of the family in socializing and educating children. We have illustrated two perspectives: one that recognizes the family as the primary institution affecting young children and one that places more emphasis on the child care setting. These divergent perspectives are clearly illustrated in the different approaches taken by researchers to the issue of defining child care quality.

To understand the effects of child care on children, it is first crucial to understand how parents come to select a particular arrangement. Only recently have researchers paid sufficient attention to family characteristics related to the selection of a particular child care arrangement; earlier work examining child care effects on children's development tended to omit family variables entirely or include only a few superficial indicators. We have showed how families' child care choices are conditioned by their individual and culturally based preferences—as well as by child care availability. Multilevel studies are needed to examine how federal and state subsidies affect the availability and quality of care in communities and how those factors then combine with family-level variables to result in selection of care.

The issue of who is the most efficacious actor on behalf of children—formal organization or parents—lies at the heart of several current policy debates. In the past three years, with the devolution of welfare, funding for child care has risen precipitously. A large proportion of this funding will go out in the form of vouchers for parents to use at the child care setting of their choice, reflecting the increasingly popular idea of empowering citizens by subsidizing them directly rather than funding organizations. But debate continues about the relative amount of funds that should be directed toward building up child care institutions like Head Start. One side argues that market forces will shape the child care market to respond to parental demand. If parents want to use their vouchers to enroll their children in formal centers, the market will respond by creating more centers. According to this view, with the help of well-funded referral agencies, parents will become increasingly sophisticated consumers, skillfully able to apply pressure to the market to create child care arrangements that match their criteria of quality. Critics of this position argue that many parents may never be sufficiently informed about ECE to make the best choice for their children or to monitor whether the arrangement is meeting the child's ongoing educational needs. These critics are particularly concerned about lower-income parents, who may lack the resources of time, educational background, and funds needed to investigate, select, and monitor child care arrangements.

While the market-oriented position is often associated with a politically conservative point of view, it is also expressed by some parents from ethnic minority groups who wish to find arrangements that are culturally sensitive, as well as by liberals who are disenchanted with the one-size-fits-all approach common to public schools and other big organizations. As Americans become increasingly disillusioned with the efficacy of government-run bureaucracies, the support grows for decentralized policies that encourage diverse, grassroots enterprises (Holloway and Fuller 1992).

We suspect that research can help to resolve some of the apparently intractable problems in this debate. We recommend a moratorium on studies that compare parents to professionals with respect to their conceptual frameworks about development, parenting, and education. We suggest that it is more valuable to obtain descriptive accounts of parents' own goals and their cultural

models of parenting and educating. Because over 90 percent of the research in leading journals is conducted with white middle-class children and their parents, we have very little sense of the status of parenting among ethnic subgroups in the United States or abroad (New 1994). Until early childhood educators have a sense of the context in which children are being raised, they will be limited in their approach to integrating their professional expertise with the home experiences of the children in their care.

Second, we suggest that more research be conducted on the behavior of parents as they navigate the child care market. While some studies have documented the type of resources parents typically utilize in selecting care, this research is limited by its reliance on cursory surveys, and it predates much of the current emphasis on helping parents learn about their child care options. How do social service agencies approach the task of informing low-income parents about their subsidies? What are the cultural preferences that channel parents into certain options and away from others? When are parents most open to information, and what form is most useful to them? Recent developments in the areas of parental expectations and knowledge can be helpful in structuring these inquiries (for example, Goodnow 1995).

Whether one emphasizes the strengths and resources of parents or their vulnerabilities and lapses in carrying out this complex role, the fact remains that while other caregivers come and go (often with alarming frequency), parents alone have a lifelong connection to their children. In recent decades, the structural supports available to help parents accomplish their own goals have eroded significantly (Hewlett and West 1998). As economic, emotional, and moral support for families declines, parents are left with increasing responsibilities, and they come under increasing fire when their children experience problems. The most effective policies are likely to be those that acknowledge, support, and build from the knowledge and vision parents have gained through their experiences in raising their own children.

Notes

1. In fact, research consistently reveals that family processes are far more powerful determinants of developmental outcomes than are features of early education settings. Research examining family practices in isolation has often been able to explain in the range of 30-50 percent of the variance in cognitive and school-related outcomes (for example, Estrada et al. 1987). Early research comparing curriculum models in ECE tended to find little difference with respect to impact on children's development (Clarke-Stewart 1987; Clarke-Stewart and Gruber 1984), although some recent comparisons find that children benefit particularly from well-structured, play-oriented programs (Schweinhart and Weikart 1997). Recent studies assessing both family and child care processes tend to find significantly more variance accounted for by family variables, even for children who spend significant amounts of time in nonparental care (for example, Holloway and Reichhart-Erickson 1988, 1989; NICHD 1997, 1998). For a complete review of the effects on children of attending child care of various types and levels of quality, see Burchinal (this volume).

2. We use the term "availability," given that the word "supply" has a distinct meaning for economists. In addition, we argue that political-economy factors heavily determine the availability of centers or child care vouchers in a community, since institutions both centrally and locally mediate the flow of subsidies. In affluent suburban areas, supply may indeed be codetermined by the expressed demand of parents. But the two spheres constitute a sharply segmented market of providers, one segment highly subsidized and the other operating more under market dynamics (for further discussion, see Edwards, Fuller, and Liang 1996).

3. To disentangle availability and demand factors, we reran this analysis within a simultaneous equation framework. The aggregate number of child care hours supplied by centers was lower when prices were higher. (Note that these price effects may hold for certain segments of the market, especially more affluent suburban communities, but not for low-income families and neighborhoods.) Demand for more child care appeared to be higher in counties with more black single parents and where population growth rates were higher. Counties with larger public sectors provided more hours of center-based care. Where Head Start and school districts offered more child care hours, the availability of independent non-profit and for-profit centers was lower (Edwards, Fuller, and Liang 1996). This relationship, however, also would be observed cross-sectionally if Head Start and school districts were building availability in poor or blue-collar communities where the independent sector was failing to respond to demand.

References

Baumrind, Diana. 1996. A Blanket Injunction Against Disciplinary Use of Spanking Is Not Warranted by the Data. *Pediatrics* 98(4):828-31.

Becker, Gary. 1976. *A Treatise on the Family*. Cambridge, MA: Harvard University Press.

Black, Janet K. and Margaret B. Puckett. 1987. Informing Others About Developmentally Appropriate Practice. In *Developmentally Appropriate Practice in Early Childhood Programs Serving Children from Birth Through Age 8*, ed. Sue Bredekamp. Washington, DC: National Association for the Education of Young Children.

Bowman, Barbara T. 1992. Child Development and Its Implications for Day Care. In *Child Care in the 1990s: Trends and Consequences*, ed. Alan Booth. Hillsdale, NJ: Lawrence Erlbaum.

Bredekamp, Sue, ed. 1987. *Developmentally Appropriate Practice in Early Childhood Programs Serving Children from Birth Through Age 8.*Washington, DC: National Association for the Education of Young Children.

Bredekamp, Sue and Carol Copple, eds. 1997. *Developmentally Appropriate Practice in Early Childhood Programs*. Rev. ed. Washington, DC: National Association for the Education of Young Children.

Bronfenbrenner, Urie. 1979. *The Ecology of Human Development: Experiments by Nature and Design*. Cambridge, MA: Harvard University Press.

Charlesworth, Rosalind, Craig H. Hart, Diane C. Burts, and Michele DeWolf. 1993. The LSU Studies: Building a Research Base for Developmentally Appropriate Practice. In *Perspectives in Developmentally Appropriate Practice: Advances in Early Education and Day Care*, ed. Stuart Reifel. Vol. 5. Greenwich, CT: JAI Press.

Clark, Reginald M. 1983. *Family Life and School Achievement: Why Poor Black Children Succeed or Fail*. Chicago: University of Chicago Press.

Clarke-Stewart, K. Alison. 1987. In Search of Consistencies in Child-Care Research. In *Quality in Child Care: What Does Research Tell Us?* ed. Deborah A. Phillips. Washington, DC: National Association for the Education of Young Children.

Clarke-Stewart, K. Alison and C. P. Gruber. 1984. Day-Care Forms and Features. In *The Child and Day-Care Setting: Qualitative Variations and Development*, ed. R. Ainslie. New York: Praeger.

Cryer, Debby and Margaret Burchinal. 1997. Parents as Child Care Consumers. *Early Childhood Research Quarterly* 12:35-58.

Edwards, John, Bruce Fuller, and Xiaoyan Liang. 1996. The Mixed Preschool Market: Explaining Local Variation in Family Demand and Organized Supply. *Economics of Education Review* 15:149-61.

Epstein, Joyce L. 1992. School and Family Partnerships. In *Encyclopedia of Educational Research*, 6th ed., ed. M. Alkin. New York: Macmillan.

Estrada, Peggy, William F. Arsenio, Robert D. Hess, and Susan D. Holloway. 1987. Affective Quality of the Mother-Child Relationship: Longitudinal Consequences of Children's School-Relevant Cognitive Functioning. *Developmental Psychology* 23:210-15.

Flavell, John H. 1963. *The Developmental Psychology of Jean Piaget*. New York: D. Van Nostrand.

Fuller, Bruce, Casey Coonerty, Fran Kipnis, and Yvonne Choong. 1997. An Unfair Head Start: California Families Face Gaps in Preschool and Child-Care Availability. University of California, Berkeley. Working paper.

Fuller, Bruce, Costanza Eggers-Piérola, Susan Holloway, Xiaoyan Liang, and Marylee F. Rambaud. 1996. Rich Culture, Poor Markets: Why Do Latino Parents Forgo Preschooling? *Teachers College Record* 97(3):400-418.

Fuller, Bruce, Susan D. Holloway, and Xiaoyan Liang. 1996. Family Selection of Child-Care Centers: The Influence of Household Support, Ethnicity, and Parental Practices. *Child Development* 67:3320-37.

Fuller, Bruce and Sharon L. Kagan. 1998. How Are Children's Environments Changing Under Welfare Reform? Child-Care Selection, Family Context, and Effects on Development.

University of California, Berkeley. Manuscript.

Fuller, Bruce and Xiaoyan Liang. 1996. Market Failure? Estimating Inequality in Preschool Availability. *Educational Evaluation and Policy Analysis* 18:31-49.

Galinsky, Ellen, Carollee Howes, Susan Kontos, and Marybeth Shinn. 1994. *The Study of Children in Family Child Care and Relative Care: Highlights of Findings.* New York: Families and Work Institute.

Garcia, Eugene E., Barry McLaughlin, Bernard Spodek, and Olivia N. Saracho, eds. 1995. *Meeting the Challenge of Linguistic and Cultural Diversity in Early Childhood Education.* Yearbook in Early Childhood Education, vol. 6. New York: Teachers College Press.

Goldenberg, Claude and Ronald Gallimore. 1995. Immigrant Latino Parents' Values and Beliefs About Their Children's Education: Continuities and Discontinuities Across Cultures and Generations. *Advances in Motivation and Achievement* 9:183-228.

Goodnow, Jacqueline J. 1995. Parents' Knowledge and Expectations. In *Handbook of Parenting.* Vol. 3, *Status and Social Conditions of Parenting,* ed. Marc H. Bornstein. Hillsdale, NJ: Lawrence Erlbaum.

Harwood, Robin, Joan G. Miller, and Nydia L. Irizarry. 1995. *Culture and Attachment: Perceptions of the Child in Context.* New York: Guilford Press.

Healy, Melissa. 1998. Latinos at Center of Chicken-Egg Debate over Child-Care Funds. *Los Angeles Times,* 29 Sept.

Heath, Shirley B. 1983. *Ways with Words: Language, Life and Work in Communities and Classrooms.* New York: Cambridge University Press.

Hess, Robert D. and Susan D. Holloway. 1984. Family and School as Educational Institutions. In *Review of Child Development Research.* Vol. 7, *The Family,* ed. Ross D. Parke. Chicago: University of Chicago Press.

Hess, Robert D. and Victoria Shipman. 1965. Early Experience and the Socialization of Cognitive Modes in Children. *Child Development* 36:867-86.

Hewlett, Sylvia A. and Cornel West. 1998. *The War Against Parents: What Can We Do for America's Beleaguered Moms and Dads.* Boston: Houghton Mifflin.

Holloway, Susan D. and Bruce Fuller. 1992. The Great Child-Care Experiment: What Are the Lessons for School Improvement? *Educational Researcher* 21(7):12-19.

Holloway, Susan D., Bruce Fuller, Marylee F. Rambaud, and Costanza Eggers-Piérola. 1997. *Through My Own Eyes: Single Mothers and the Cultures of Poverty.* Cambridge, MA: Harvard University Press.

Holloway, Susan D. and Marina Reichhart-Erickson. 1988. The Relationship of Day-Care Quality to Children's Free Play Behavior and Social Problem Solving Skills. *Early Childhood Research Quarterly* 3:39-40.

———. 1989. Child-Care Quality, Family Structure, and Maternal Expectations: Relationship to Preschool Children's Peer Relations. *Journal of Applied Developmental Psychology* 10:281-98.

Joffe, Carole. 1977. *Friendly Intruders: Childcare Professionals and Family Life.* Berkeley: University of California Press.

Johnson, Deborah J., C. Dyanda-Marira, and P. K. Dzvimbo. 1997. Urban Zimbabwean Mothers' Choices and Perceptions of Care for Young Children. *Early Childhood Research Quarterly* 12:199-219.

Kessler, Shirley A. and Elizabeth B. Swadener, eds. 1992. *Reconceptualizing the Early Childhood Curriculum.* New York: Teachers College Press.

Larzelere, Robert E. 1996. Review of the Outcomes of Parental Use of Nonabusive or Customary Punishment. *Pediatrics* 98(4):824-28.

LeVine, Robert A. 1974. Cultural Values and Parental Goals. *Teachers College Record* 76:226-39.

Liang, Xiaoyan. 1996. Economic Constraints, Parental Beliefs, or Ethnicity? Explaining Preschool Enrollment in America. Ph.D. diss., Harvard University.

New, Rebecca S. 1994. Culture, Child Development, and Developmentally Appropriate Practices: Teachers as Collaborative Researchers. In *Diversity and Developmentally Appropriate Practices: Challenges for Early Childhood Education*, ed. B. Mallory and R. New. New York: Teachers College Press.

New, Rebecca S. and Bruce L. Mallory. 1994. Introduction: The Ethics of Inclusion. In *Diversity and Developmentally Appropriate Practices: Challenges for Early Childhood Education*, ed. B. Mallory and R. New. New York: Teachers College Press.

NICHD Early Child Care Research Network. 1997. The Effects of Infant Child Care on Infant-Mother Attachment Security: Results of the NICHD Study of Early Child Care. *Child Development* 68:860-79.

——. 1998. Relations Between Family Predictors and Child Outcomes: Are They Weaker for Children in Child Care? *Developmental Psychology* 34:1119-28.

Ogbu, John U. 1981. Origins of Human Competence: A Cultural-Ecological Perspective. *Child Development* 52:413-29.

Powell, Douglas R. 1989. *Families and Early Childhood Programs*. Research Monographs of the National Association for the Education of Young Children, vol. 3. Washington, DC: National Association for the Education of Young Children.

——. 1994. Parents, Pluralism, and the NAEYC Statement on Developmentally Appropriate Practice. In *Diversity and Developmentally Appropriate Practices: Challenges for Early Childhood Education*, ed. B. Mallory and R. New. New York: Teachers College Press.

Rogoff, Barbara. 1990. *Apprenticeship in Thinking: Cognitive Development in Social Context*. New York: Oxford University Press.

Schweinhart, Lawrence J. and David P. Weikart. 1997. The High/Scope Preschool Curriculum Comparison Study Through Age 23. *Early Childhood Research Quarterly* 12:117-43.

Singer, Judith D., Bruce Fuller, Margaret K. Kelley, and Anne Wolf. 1998. Early Child-Care Selection: Variation by Geographic Location, Maternal Characteristics, and Family Structure. *Developmental Psychology* 34:1129-44.

Snow, Catherine E., Wendy S. Barnes, Jean Chandler, Irene F. Goodman, and Lowry Hemphill. 1991. *Unfulfilled Expectations: Home and School Influences on Literacy*. Cambridge, MA: Harvard University Press.

Stipek, Deborah J. 1993. Is Child-Centered Early Childhood Education Really Better? In *Perspectives in Developmentally Appropriate Practice: Advances in Early Education and Day Care*, ed. Stuart Reifel. Vol. 5. Greenwich, CT: JAI Press.

Valdés, Guadalupe. 1996. *Con Respeto: Bridging the Distances Between Culturally Diverse Families and Schools: An Ethnographic Portrait*. New York: Teachers College Press.

Wadsworth, Barry J. 1996. *Piaget's Theory of Cognitive and Affective Development: Foundations of Constructivism*. New York: Longman.

Whitebook, Marcy, Carollee Howes, and Deborah Phillips. 1990. *Who Cares?*

Child Care Teachers and the Quality of Care in America: Final Report. Washington, DC: Center for the Child Care Workforce.

Whiting, Beatrice B. and John W. M. Whiting. 1975. *Children of Six Cultures: A Psycho-Cultural Analysis.* Cambridge, MA: Harvard University Press.

Youcha, Geraldine. 1995. *Minding the Children: Child Care in America from Colonial Times to the Present.* New York: Scribner.

Zinsser, Caroline. 1991. *Raised in East Urban: Child Care Changes in a Working Class Community.* New York: Teachers College Press.

Regulating Child Care Quality

By WILLIAM GORMLEY, JR.

ABSTRACT: Child care quality depends on child care regulation as plants depend on water. An insufficient amount guarantees problems, but an excessive amount may also be problematic. The principal responsibility for child care regulation in the United States resides with state government officials, who must regulate a highly diverse industry. Research shows that regulation promotes quality but that trade-offs exist. Quality improvements that undermine availability or affordability should be evaluated with care. Also, regulatory enforcement deserves as much attention as regulatory standard setting. To improve child care regulation, state policymakers should consider eliminating some local regulations, regulating more family day care homes, upgrading teacher-training requirements, allocating more resources to regulatory enforcement, and designing more effective enforcement strategies.

William Gormley, Jr., is professor of government and public policy at Georgetown University. He was formerly professor of political science and public affairs at the University of Wisconsin–Madison. Among other books, he has written Everybody's Children: Child Care as a Public Problem *(1995). His latest book, with David Weimer, is* Organizational Report Cards *(1999). His book* Taming the Bureaucracy *(1989) received the Louis Brownlow Book Award from the National Academy of Public Administration. His articles have appeared in the* American Political Science Review, *the* American Journal of Political Science, *the* Public Administration Review, *and related journals.*

C HILD care regulation is the thin blue line that protects millions of children from threats to their health, safety, and well-being. Like other forms of regulation, however, it is subject to the twin dangers of insufficient vigor and excessive severity. As a result, it is often controversial.

In this article, I analyze child care regulation from several perspectives. First, I outline the framework for regulating child care in the United States. Second, I offer a few observations on the nature of the highly diverse industry being regulated. Third, I review the results of several research studies on the relationship between regulation and child care quality. Fourth, I discuss some of the controversies surrounding child care regulation. Fifth, I explain how regulatory enforcement can support or undermine the quest for quality. Sixth, I summarize some recent trends in child care regulation. Finally, I identify some regulatory reforms that could improve child care regulation in the United States.

THE REGULATORY FRAMEWORK

In many policy domains (such as environmental policy and health policy), regulatory responsibility is shared by the federal government and the state governments. Child care policy is different. For a variety of reasons, the federal government has been reluctant to impose national regulatory standards on the child care industry (Camissa 1995, 39-66; Gormley 1996). Thus, while the federal government plays an increasingly important role in child care policy, its regulatory role remains circumscribed.

State governments have primary responsibility for adopting and enforcing child care regulations for group day care centers and family day care homes. Child care licensing bureaus are usually located within the state department of social services. Rules are formulated by state administrators, subject to guidance from the state legislature. Rules are enforced by state inspectors, known as licensers or, in some instances, consultants. State child care rules typically cover a wide range of subjects, such as child-staff ratios, staff qualifications, room dimensions, hand-washing and diapering practices, play equipment specifications, fire precautions, immunization schedules, liability insurance provisions, and emergency procedures. Requirements for family day care homes average 16.6 pages; requirements for group day care centers average 30.2 pages. The actual number of regulations is considerably higher. In Connecticut, for example, a 19-page handbook includes 133 regulations (Gormley 1990).

The federal government provides child care subsidies to middle-class parents (through the tax code) and to poor parents (through the Child Care and Development Block Grant and Head Start) but has virtually no regulatory role. However, at least 4 percent, or $80 million per year, of the Child Care and Development Block Grant (approximately $2 billion per year) must be devoted to quality improvement and related activities (supply enhancement and parental education). In this respect, the federal government helps to fund certain regulatory activities undertaken by the states but does not determine their content.

Local governments do play a regulatory role, through mandatory building inspections, fire inspections, and other mechanisms. Group day care centers are more thoroughly regulated than family day care homes, but even the latter are regulated in many jurisdictions. In 1990, I found that a family day care provider who cares for six children must obtain a business license in 31 percent of U.S. cities, an occupancy permit in 36 percent of U.S. cities, and a zoning permit in 25 percent of U.S. cities (Gormley 1990).

THE REGULATED INDUSTRY

Who exactly is being regulated? The U.S. child care industry is diverse enough to present some serious challenges to public policymakers. If most day care centers were run by the government, as in France, or by churches, as in Germany, it would be easier to design regulatory policies suitable for the industry as a whole. But that is not the case.

In 1990, 35 percent of all group day care centers were for-profit enterprises (Willer et al. 1991). That figure has probably increased to about 40 percent today. About one of every six for-profit centers is part of a chain. The biggest chain is Kinder Care, which runs approximately 1200 centers serving 141,000 children. Although for-profit centers are not unusually profitable, they present special challenges because the quality of care they provide is weaker than that provided by other day care centers (Gormley 1995).[1]

In 1990, 15 percent of all group day care centers were affiliated with churches (Willer et al. 1991). Church-affiliated centers are officially exempt or partially exempt from regulation in 13 states. In states where they are not officially exempt (such as Pennsylvania), they sometimes enjoy a de facto exemption because state officials are reluctant to enforce the law when a minister denies an inspector access to a child care facility (Gormley 1995; Carpenter 1996). According to rulings by both state and federal courts, state governments are free to regulate church-based centers like everyone else or exempt them from regulations, whichever they wish.

All states regulate family day care homes, but many states exempt small family day care homes from regulation. For example, in Wisconsin, a family day care provider who cares for fewer than four children need not be regulated. In Louisiana, a family day care provider who cares for fewer than seven children need not be regulated, unless he or she accepts federal funds for child care services. Regardless of what the legal requirements are, many family day care providers choose to remain underground, thus creating a huge black market. Analysts estimate that between 82 and 90 percent of all family day care homes in the United States are unregulated, some legally, others illegally (Willer et al. 1991).

EFFECTS OF
REGULATION ON QUALITY

A key rationale for child care regulation is the presence of information asymmetries between producers (child care providers) and consumers (parents, as agents for children). Because parents lack reliable information about the quality of care offered by different providers, they rely upon government regulators to specify and to guarantee a minimum quality floor. The assumption is that child care quality will be better in states with higher regulatory standards. But is that assumption correct?

In 1995, investigators from several universities published a landmark study assessing the quality of child care offered by group day care centers in four states: California, Colorado, Connecticut, and North Carolina (Helburn 1995). This study examined the quality of care children received in 401 group day care centers by observing interactions between children and providers and by testing the children. At the same time, investigators studied the content of each state's regulations and measured each center's structural quality by recording the child-staff ratio, the group size, staff education and experience, the square footage per child, and other widely used indicators (Helburn 1995, 351). The authors found that the state with the weakest regulatory standards (North Carolina) had the lowest structural quality. For example, North Carolina allowed 1 adult to every 6 infants or 15 3-year-olds, while the other states required 1 adult to every 4 or 5 infants or 10 or

12 3-year-olds. Also, North Carolina required far less early childhood education of its center staff than the other three states did (Helburn 1995, 321). These findings are important because a number of studies have established a positive relationship between child development and lower child-staff ratios and higher staff education levels.

In addition to documenting effects of regulations on structural quality, the authors measured actual interactions between providers and children, using established scales such as the Infant/Toddler Environment Rating Scale (ITERS) for infants and toddlers and the Early Childhood Environment Rating Scale (ECERS) for preschoolers. These indexes, which require approximately six hours of observation per center, measure such things as age-appropriate activities, access to suitable play equipment, and good hygienic practices (Harms and Clifford 1980; Harms, Cryer, and Clifford 1990). Of the four states, North Carolina had the worst ITERS scores for infants and toddlers. With regard to for-profits, North Carolina had the worst ECERS scores for preschoolers; with regard to nonprofits, North Carolina and Colorado nonprofits had the worst ECERS scores for preschoolers (Helburn 1995, tab. 6.2). These findings support the proposition that regulation has a positive impact on child care quality.

Of course, this study focused exclusively on group day care centers. Does regulation also enhance the quality of care offered by family day care providers? To answer that question, Galinsky et al. (1994)

studied the quality of care received by children in regulated and unregulated family day care homes in three states: California, North Carolina, and Texas. Using measures of teacher involvement and peer play, the authors observed provider-child pairs for two to three hours and studied both the extent of conversation and the nature of the conversation that took place (Kontos et al. 1995, 26-27). Based on observations of 235 provider-child pairs, the authors concluded that the quality of care in regulated family day care homes is superior. Specifically, the quality of care was deemed "inadequate" at 13 percent of the regulated family day care homes, 50 percent of the nonregulated family day care homes, and 69 percent of the relative care settings (Galinsky et al. 1994). While this study strongly suggests that regulation has a positive impact, it is not definitive. In particular, it is possible that better-educated or better-trained child care providers are more willing to accept government regulation, in which case quality would be determining regulation rather than vice versa.

Using a different research approach, I also studied the connection between government regulation and child care quality. Specifically, I wanted to know whether government inspections improved the quality of care that children receive. In the state of Vermont, I gathered data on the number of code violations identified during every licensing visit to every day care center during a five-year period (1989-93). This permitted me to take advantage of a natural experiment that occurred in 1991, at which time Vermont implemented a differential licensing system. Centers with good or excellent track records were given a two- or three-year license, while centers with bad or mediocre track records were given a one-year license. Of the centers that received a one-year license in 1991 ($N = 44$), 27 percent grew worse. Of the centers that received a two-year license in 1991 ($N = 71$), 62 percent grew worse. Roughly the same pattern appeared if I focused on very serious problems (such as inadequate supervision) and excluded less serious problems (for example, ipecac missing from a first aid kit). This suggests that centers perform better if they receive more frequent inspections and that centers perform worse if they receive less frequent inspections. Even good child care centers benefit from regular regulatory visits (Gormley 1995).

REGULATORY CONTROVERSIES

Regulation is a powerful tool that can correct for information asymmetries, reduce harmful externalities, and limit threats to public health and safety. Regulation has proven effective in many policy domains, including environmental protection and occupational safety. Common sense and a significant body of social science research suggest that regulation can improve the quality of care offered by child care providers, including both center-based and home-based providers. Nevertheless, numerous controversies surround child care regulation, raising questions about its effectiveness and its appropriateness.

One argument against child care regulation is that conventional measures of child care quality are flawed. For example, Blau (1997) has argued that low child-staff ratios are only weakly related to child care process quality. If so, regulations that succeed in lowering child-staff ratios do not necessarily succeed in improving the quality of care that children receive. In reviewing the literature, Scarr (1998) has reached similar conclusions.

A second argument is that child care regulation has negative effects on supply. In support of that proposition, several scholars have found that more stringent child-staff ratio requirements are associated with a lower supply of group day care centers or less utilization of nonparental child care (Rose-Ackerman 1986; Gormley 1991; Lowenberg and Tinnin 1992; Hotz and Kilburn 1994). However, effects on choices made by working parents are rather modest (Hotz and Kilburn 1994), and ratio requirements do not appear to influence the supply of family day care homes (Gormley 1991). The effects of education and training requirements on supply or choice are in greater doubt. Although Lowenberg and Tinnin (1992) found negative effects for day care center directors, I found no such effects for teachers at either group day care centers or family day care homes (Gormley 1991). Also Hotz and Kilburn (1994) found no effects of education and training requirements on the weekly hours of care at group day care centers or family day care homes. Effects of inspections on supply and parental choice are also in dispute. Pending more

definitive research, the only clear finding is that higher child-staff ratios reduce supply and utilization of group day care centers.

A third argument is that child care regulation boosts the price of child care, thus making it less affordable. Research by Chipty (1995) supports this proposition. Stronger family day care regulation is associated with higher prices at family day care homes. Stronger group day care center regulation is associated with higher prices at group day care centers. There are also spillover effects, with regulation in one sector (family day care homes) affecting prices in the other sector (group day care centers) and vice versa. All of this is important because price significantly affects the child care choices that parents make (Hofferth and Wissoker 1992).

A fourth argument is that a good deal of child care regulation is redundant or worse. Do we really need parallel systems of regulation at the state and local levels? The principal purpose of state regulation (for example, health and safety requirements) is to protect children; the principal purpose of local regulation (such as zoning laws) is to protect grouchy neighbors from children (Gormley 1990). The thrust of local regulatory requirements for family day care homes, for example, is to create obstacles to starting up a family day care home (or any other type of commercial enterprise) in a residential neighborhood. Occupancy permit requirements and conditional use permit requirements for family day care homes at the local level serve no good public purpose. On the contrary, by discouraging family day care providers from surfacing and accepting government regulation, such local requirements help to ensure that only a very small fraction of family day care homes are regulated by state governments.

Although many critics of child care regulation object to what they perceive as excessive regulation, or regulatory overkill, other critics believe that child care regulation is too weak, too decentralized, and too poorly enforced.

One of the most compelling arguments in favor of stronger child care regulation is that current rules seldom require well-trained, well-educated staff members to supervise, stimulate, and protect young children. Only 18 states require preservice training for teachers in group day care centers, and only 11 states require preservice training for family day care providers. Although a greater number of states require inservice training, two states require no training whatever for teachers at group day care centers and 11 states require no training whatever for family day care providers (Azer and Eldred 1997). Given the absence of a clear negative relationship between training requirements and supply, the weakness of staff training requirements is both puzzling and unfortunate.

A second argument from supporters of regulation is that the 50 states should not be free to regulate child care establishments as they see fit. Other countries, such as France and Sweden, have national child care standards. Why not the United States? One answer to that question is that France and Sweden are not federal systems. The United States, like Canada, Germany, and other federal systems, leaves child care regulatory rule making in the hands of the states (Gormley 1996). Beyond that, it is important to note that decentralized child care standard-setting need not result in either weak standards or sharply divergent standards. Germany, for example, leaves its child care standards in the hands of its 16 *Bundesländer*, all of which have adopted rigorous teacher training requirements (Gormley and Peters 1992). If our regulatory standards are too weak in the United States, federalism is not the culprit.

A third argument from supporters of regulation is that child care standards are poorly enforced. Evidence from a handful of states would seem to substantiate that point of view. The commonwealth of Pennsylvania, for example, revoked or refused to renew the licenses of only 6 group day care centers (of nearly 3000 centers) and the registrations of only 7 family day care homes (of over 6000 registered family day care homes) in one recent year (Gormley 1995, 110). During the same year, Pennsylvania imposed no monetary fines on any group day care centers, even though it was authorized by statute to do so. Nor is Pennsylvania unusually lax (Gormley 1997).

REGULATORY ENFORCEMENT

Poor enforcement can undermine regulatory standards and threaten the health and safety of children. At worst, it can lead to the death of a child. For example, a 4-year-old girl enrolled at the Creation Station day care center near Pittsburgh, Pennsylvania, suffocated to death after being left unattended in a hot van following a field trip. Records show that regulators had observed serious problems at the facility during previous visits but had failed to shut the center down (Kalson and Carpenter 1996).

What accounts for weak regulatory enforcement? A key factor is inadequate licensing staff. In many states, child care inspectors are expected to visit so many child care facilities each year that they lack the time to probe for serious problems, to devise sensible solutions, and, if necessary, to take vigorous enforcement measures. In Pennsylvania, the average child care inspector is responsible for 92 day care centers (Gormley 1997, 291). In some other states, caseloads are even higher. In New Jersey, each inspector is responsible for approximately 300 day care centers (O'Crowley 1997). If licensers are to conduct thorough annual inspections, allow for follow-up visits, respond to inquiries and complaints, and complete their paperwork, a caseload greater than 75 or 80 centers is probably excessive.

Another important factor is the absence of intermediate sanctions that fall somewhere between the twin extremes of a notice of violation (or warning) and facility closure (or license revocation). When the U.S. General Accounting Office (1992, 19) investigated the matter, it found that only 19 states authorize the issuance of monetary fines to deal with recalcitrant centers and only 11 states allow the mandatory posting of a public notice of violation on the premises of a center. Intermediate sanctions are important because most state licensing agencies are understandably reluctant to shut down centers, especially at a time of growing demand for child care.

Even states with intermediate sanctions in their arsenal of enforcement tools have enforcement problems, in part because state departments of justice are notoriously reluctant to prosecute child care cases. Overwhelmed by a backlog of child abuse, child neglect, and other cases, state attorneys general seldom take child care providers to court, even for serious rule infractions (Gormley 1995, 112). Knowing that, negligent providers can behave with impunity.

A more subtle enforcement problem is that child care inspectors offer limited technical support to child care providers—support that could reduce the need for inspections and enforcement sanctions. While the degree of technical support varies from state to state (Gormley 1998, 377), it is generally quite low and is not commonly regarded as an invaluable enforcement tool. As a direct consequence, relations between inspectors and providers tend to be more adversarial than they might otherwise be. Although one can imagine a situation where technical assistance became a substitute for, rather than a supplement to, meaningful regulation, that is not the case. Inspectors who offer technical assistance are actually more likely to perceive a given problem as serious and worthy of remedial action (Gormley 1998, 372). The provision of technical assistance is not a sign that regulators have been captured by regulated firms.

REGULATORY TRENDS

Child care regulation has changed for the better in some respects during the 1990s. For example, staff training requirements have gotten tougher. Between 1986 and 1997, the number of states requiring in-service training for teachers at group day care centers increased from 33 to 44, while the number of states requiring in-service training for family day care providers increased from 8 to 31 (Azer 1997-98, 5). This improvement is important, given research demonstrating positive effects of staff training on child development (Ruopp et al. 1979; Whitebook, Howes, and Phillips 1989; National Research Council 1990).

A growing number of states have begun to use financial incentives to induce family day care providers to become regulated. At least 10 states now offer regulated family day care providers higher reimbursement rates for subsidized care than they offer unregulated family day care providers (Blank and Adams 1997, 39-40). Whether such differential reimbursement rates actually induce family day care providers to become registered or licensed has not yet been studied.[2] Nevertheless, this can also be construed as a positive sign.

Other trends have been more worrisome. In particular, federal welfare legislation has fueled a sharp increase in demand for child care without a corresponding increase in the number of regulatory inspectors.

As a result, many state inspectors are struggling to cope with growing caseloads. The number of inspectors has increased in some states, such as Missouri (Smith 1997), but other states, such as Vermont (Gram 1997), have experienced no growth in their licensing staffs.

REGULATORY REFORM

In thinking about regulatory reform, it is useful to consider several possibilities. One would be jurisdictional reform or a realignment of regulatory responsibilities. A second would be to expand or contract the scope of regulation, thus bringing more or fewer child care establishments under a regulatory aegis. A third would be to alter regulatory standards, making them more or less stringent. A fourth would be to alter regulatory enforcement to emphasize either deterrence or persuasion.

Enthusiasm for a given strategy depends in part on one's value premises. Those who care primarily about quality tend to endorse national standards, a broader scope, more stringent regulations, and more vigorous regulatory enforcement. Those who care primarily about availability and affordability tend to endorse state standards, a narrower scope, less stringent regulations, and greater emphasis on technical assistance.

My own position is a bit different (Gormley 1995). Quality, availability, and affordability are all important and must be taken into account. Above all, we should focus our attention on what is best for children. Parents and providers have legitimate interests in these disputes, but the interests of children are those that tend to be lost in the shuffle. Children benefit from a regulatory regime that protects them from threats to health and safety and that nurtures their cognitive and social development. Children do not benefit from a regulatory regime so severe that it keeps providers underground or prevents them from earning a decent wage.

There is much to be said for jurisdictional reform, but a shift of responsibilities to the federal government could backfire. When the federal government sets a regulatory floor, guaranteeing minimum standards, that floor often becomes a ceiling (Heidemann 1989). The principal consequence of national standards would probably be to compress or homogenize regulatory rules, thus discouraging both high and low extremes. Such standards could also discourage innovation, which would be unfortunate. A far better approach would be to eliminate most local regulations. Because local regulations tend to treat child care establishments as public nuisances and as revenue sources, their principal impact is to dampen supply. If state governments were more clearly responsible for child care regulation, the focus of child care regulation would shift more noticeably to quality considerations, which state regulations tend to emphasize. At the same time, availability and affordability should improve, with the elimination of sclerotic local regulations.

The scope of regulation refers to the number of child care establishments that are regulated or, conversely, the number that are exempt. With family day care homes, the scope of regulation is arguably more important than regulatory content. The overwhelming majority of family day care homes in the United States (between 82 and 90 percent) are regulated by no one. That means that children are being cared for by providers who need not know first aid, who need not ensure that children are properly immunized, and who need not know how to prevent the outbreak of infectious diseases. One can argue, of course, that parents, as good consumers, should be able to demand these things (or other positive practices), allowing market forces to work. But child care is a "post-experience good" (Weimer and Vining 1989, 74) whose full consequences are not apparent until after it has been consumed. Also, without some government regulation, there is no paper trail to alert other parents that a particular provider has been negligent. The evidence clearly suggests that regulated family day care is superior to unregulated care (Galinsky et al. 1994), but it is not easy to convince family day care providers to become registered or licensed. A high priority of state governments should be to develop a family day care licensing or registration system that covers all or most children in family day care homes. Financial incentives, such as higher reimbursement rates for subsidized care, should be used to encourage providers to come forward. Also, overly stringent rules should be relaxed. It is more important to offer some protection to most children in family day care homes than it is to offer gold-plated protection to a privileged few.

The debate over regulatory standards usually focuses on a few key regulations with a demonstrated connection to child care quality: child-staff ratios, group size limits, and teacher education and training. Lower child-staff ratios allow for more interaction between the individual teacher and the individual child. This in turn accelerates cognitive development. On the other hand, lower child-staff ratios result in higher prices and a reduced supply. Thus lower child-staff ratios can improve quality but at the expense of affordability and availability. Higher teacher education and training requirements also improve quality but with little or no impact on price and supply. For example, Walker (1992, 62) found no statistically significant impact of teacher training on family day care prices. Similarly, I found no statistically significant impact of teacher training requirements on the supply of group day care centers or regulated family day care homes (Gormley 1991). In comparison to other industrialized countries, U.S. teacher education and training requirements are unusually weak, but U.S. child-staff ratio requirements are not (Gormley and Peters 1992). The European approach, which assumes that better-educated and better-trained teachers are better equipped to cope with a larger number of children, makes a great deal of sense, especially for preschoolers, who need less personal attention than infants and toddlers. Of course, it would require additional financial support from the government (presumably the federal government), because higher salaries are needed to recruit and retain qualified personnel.

Effective regulatory enforcement is discriminatory. If they are doing their jobs well, licensers should discriminate between "good" and "bad" firms (Bardach and Kagan 1982). They should also utilize a wide array of regulatory sanctions (including monetary fines) so that the punishment fits the crime (Ayres and Braithwaite 1992). Fortunately, some states have begun to experiment with child care inspection strategies that embody these principles. Examples include indicator checklists, which subject providers with bad track records to closer scrutiny at inspection time, and differential monitoring, which subjects providers with bad track records to more frequent visits (Gormley 1995). Many states are handicapped, however, by acute staff shortages, which, ironically, can result in more rigid enforcement practices (Hutter 1989). As the number of child care establishments and child care slots increases, partly as a response to federal welfare reform, the need for additional child care inspectors becomes more urgent. Without larger workforces and more reasonable caseloads, state child care licensing agencies cannot counsel and educate providers who genuinely want to do better but do not know how.

CONCLUSION

Child care regulation is of critical importance to young children in family day care homes and group day care centers. The quality of care they receive depends on choices made by state policymakers and licensers. Children are better protected when regulatory standards are high and when regulatory enforcement is vigorous, but excessive severity promotes quality at the expense of availability and affordability. In the case of family day care, it may even fail to promote quality if it discourages underground providers from surfacing. The challenge that faces regulators today is to regulate wisely by considering availability, affordability, and quality simultaneously, by choosing finely calibrated regulatory instruments, and by combining regulations with incentives. If regulators do this, political support for child care regulation is likely to grow. At its best, such regulation can correct for market failures and offer young children much-needed support at a critical time in their lives.

Notes

1. For data that both support and challenge these conclusions, see Helburn 1995.

2. I am, however, currently studying this question, with funding from the Foundation for Child Development.

References

Ayres, Ian and John Braithwaite. 1992. *Responsive Regulation: Transcending the Deregulation Debate.* New York: Oxford University Press.

Azer, Sheri, ed. 1997-98. *Linking Up.* Boston: Wheelock College, Center for Career Development in Early Care and Education.

Azer, Sheri and Darnae Eldred. 1997. *Training Requirements in Child Care Licensing Regulations.* Boston: Wheelock College, Center for Career Development in Early Care and Education.

Bardach, Eugene and Robert Kagan. 1982. *Going by the Book: The Problem of Regulatory Unreasonableness.* Philadelphia: Temple University Press.

Blank, Helen and Gina Adams. 1997. *State Developments in Child Care and Early Education.* Washington, DC: Children's Defense Fund.

Blau, David. 1997. The Production of Quality in Child Care Centers. *Journal of Human Resources* 32(2):354-87.

Camissa, Anne. 1995. *Governments as Interest Groups: Interest Group Lobbying and the Federal System.* Westport, CT: Praeger.

Carpenter, Mackenzie. 1996. Answering to a Higher Regulator. *Pittsburgh Post-Gazette*, 6 June.

Chipty, Tasneem. 1995. Economic Effects of Quality Regulations in the Day-Care Industry. *American Economic Review* 85(1):419-24.

Galinsky, Ellen, Carollee Howes, Susan Kontos, and Marybeth Shinn. 1994. *The Study of Children in Family Child Care and Relative Care.* New York: Families and Work Institute.

Gormley, William, Jr. 1990. Regulating Mister Rogers' Neighborhood: The Dilemmas of Day Care Regulation. *Brookings Review* 8(4):21-28.

———. 1991. State Regulations and the Availability of Child-Care Services. *Journal of Policy Analysis and Management* 10(1):78-95.

———. 1995. *Everybody's Children: Child Care as a Public Problem.* Washington, DC: Brookings Institution.

———. 1996. Governance: Child Care, Federalism, and Public Policy. In *Re-*

inventing Early Care and Education, ed. Sharon L. Kagan and Nancy Cohen. San Francisco: Jossey-Bass.

———. 1997. Regulatory Enforcement: Accommodation and Conflict in Four States. *Public Administration Review* 57(4):285-93.

———. 1998. Regulatory Enforcement Styles. *Political Research Quarterly* 51(2):363-83.

Gormley, William, Jr. and B. Guy Peters. 1992. National Styles of Regulation: Child Care in Three Countries. *Policy Sciences* 25(Nov.):381-99.

Gram, David. 1997. Flanagan Says State Needs Child Care Inspectors. *Rutland Daily Herald*, 19 Dec.

Harms, Thelma and Richard Clifford. 1980. *Early Childhood Environment Rating Scale*. New York: Teachers College Press.

Harms, Thelma, Debby Cryer, and Richard Clifford. 1990. *Infant/Toddler Environment Rating Scale*. New York: Teachers College Press.

Heidemann, Mary Ann. 1989. Regional Ecology and Regulatory Federalism: Wisconsin's Quandary over Toxic Contamination of Green Bay. Ph.D. diss., University of Wisconsin.

Helburn, Suzanne W., ed. 1995. *Cost, Quality and Child Outcomes in Child Care Centers: Technical Report*. Denver: University of Colorado, Department of Economics, Center for Research in Economic and Social Policy.

Hofferth, Sandra and Douglas Wissoker. 1992. Price, Quality, and Income in Child Care Choice. *Journal of Human Resources* 27(1):70-111.

Hotz, V. Joseph and M. Rebecca Kilburn. 1994. Regulating Child Care: The Effects of State Regulations on Child Care Demand and Its Cost. Harris School of Public Policy, Chicago. Manuscript.

Hutter, Bridget. 1989. Variations in Regulatory Enforcement Styles. *Law and Policy* 11:153-74.

Kalson, Sally and Mackenzie Carpenter. 1996. Quest for Quality Care. *Pittsburgh Post-Gazette*, 4 June.

Kontos, Susan, Carollee Howes, Marybeth Shinn, and Ellen Galinsky. 1995. *Quality in Family Child Care and Relative Care*. New York: Teachers College Press.

Lowenberg, Anton and Thomas Tinnin. 1992. Professional Versus Consumer Interests in Regulation: The Case of the U.S. Child Care Industry. *Applied Economics* 24:571-80.

National Research Council. 1990. *Who Cares for America's Children?* Washington, DC: National Academy Press.

O'Crowley, Peggy. 1997. N.J. Found Lax in Day-Care Oversight. *Bergen County Record*, 10 July.

Rose-Ackerman, Susan. 1986. Altruistic Nonprofit Firms in Competitive Markets: The Case of Day-Care Centers in the U.S. *Journal of Consumer Policy* 9:291-310.

Ruopp, Richard, Jeffrey Travers, Frederic Glantz, and Craig Coelen. 1979. *Children at the Center: Summary Findings and Their Implications*. Cambridge, MA: Abt.

Scarr, Sandra. 1998. American Child Care Today. *American Psychologist* 53(2):95-108.

Smith, Robert. 1997. It's Not Child's Play. *Joplin Globe*, 20 July.

U.S. General Accounting Office. 1992. *Child Care: States Face Difficulties Enforcing Standards and Promoting Quality*. Washington, DC: General Accounting Office.

Walker, James. 1992. New Evidence on the Supply of Child Care. *Journal of Human Resources* 27(1):40-69.

Weimer, David and Aidan Vining. 1989. *Policy Analysis: Concepts and Prac-*

tice. Englewood Cliffs, NJ: Prentice Hall.

Whitebook, Marcy, Carollee Howes, and Deborah Phillips. 1989. *Who Cares? Child Care Teachers and the Quality of Care in America: Executive Summary*. Washington, DC: Center for the Child Care Workforce.

Willer, Barbara, Sandra Hofferth, Ellen Kisker, Patricia Divine-Hawkins, Elizabeth Farquhar, and Frederic Glantz. 1991. *The Demand and Supply of Child Care in 1990*. Washington, DC: National Association for the Education of Young Children.

ANNALS, *AAPSS*, **563**, May 1999

Market Constraints
on Child Care Quality

By JOHN R. MORRIS

ABSTRACT: This article uses the data from *Cost, Quality and Child Outcomes in Child Care Centers, The Study of Children in Family Child Care and Relative Care*, and the Economics of Family Child Care Project to argue that most child care in the United States today is mediocre or worse and that this mediocrity is the result of supply and demand conditions in the market for child care. Imperfect knowledge on the part of suppliers and researchers about how to efficiently provide good care limits quality. More important, monopolistic competition with a broad range of modes of care, each with different cost structures, forces centers without subsidies to cut their costs in order to compete. Many parents cannot afford the cost of high-quality care, and even those who can afford it have trouble identifying it. Policy to improve quality needs to be multifaceted. Regulation, incentives, and training will help providers who either do not care about quality or do not understand how to create it. Subsidies are needed for parents who cannot afford the cost of quality care. Information and ratings of providers will help the parents who cannot identify quality or do not appreciate its importance.

John R. Morris is professor emeritus from the University of Colorado at Denver. He has conducted research on economic issues in the provision of child care over the past 10 years and was a contributor to the Economics of Family Child Care Project and Cost, Quality and Child Outcomes in Child Care Centers.

THIS article uses the data from Cost, Quality and Child Outcomes in Child Care Centers (CQO) (Helburn 1995), The Study of Children in Family Child Care and Relative Care (FCC) (Galinsky et al. 1994), and the Economics of Family Child Care Project (EFCC) (Helburn and Morris 1996) to argue that most child care in the United States today is mediocre or worse and that this mediocrity is the result of supply and demand conditions in the market for child care. That result has important implications for public policy. Better quality will come about only with some market restructuring.

The studies found most child care quality to be mediocre or worse. Only one in seven centers provided good care, a level of quality that promotes healthy development. Only 1 in 12 infant-toddler rooms provided that quality of care (Helburn 1995). In family child care, one in eight regulated child care homes provided good care, but only about 1 in 30 in nonregulated care and 1 out of 60 in care provided by relatives were rated good (Galinsky et al. 1994). Further, nearly half of all center infant care, fully half of nonregulated family child care, and two-thirds of child care by relatives were rated inadequate or failing to meet basic safety standards. These results raise several questions: Are they truly representative? If so, why doesn't the market drive centers to provide better-quality care? What public policy would improve the situation?

The article argues that quality of care is lower than is desirable and that imperfect knowledge on the part of suppliers and researchers about how to efficiently provide good care limits quality. More important, a monopolistically competitive market and a wide range of modes of care, each with different cost structures, force centers without subsidies to cut their costs in order to compete. The centers cut costs by cutting labor cost, the largest component of total cost, and this, in turn, reduces quality of care. Many parents cannot afford the cost of high-quality care, and even those who can afford it have trouble identifying it. These difficulties prevent parents from becoming a force for improvement in child care quality. Policy to improve quality must take the major market constraints on provision of good-quality services into account and try to ameliorate them. The analysis in this article relies on results from the three cited studies because they are the most recent and most comprehensive studies of provider behavior, the first in a generation to combine multiple types of quality assessment with data on the production cost of caregiving, fees for caregiving, and outcomes of children.

CQO studied a sample of 401 child care centers during the spring of 1993. The sample included 50 for-profit and 50 nonprofit centers providing full-time care, randomly selected from licensing lists in urban areas in the four states selected for geographic, demographic, economic, and regulatory diversity: Los Angeles County, California; the front range in Colorado; the Hartford–New Haven corridor in Connecticut; and the Piedmont Triad in North Carolina. The sample included Head Start and public school–sponsored preschool programs if they provided full-time care.

The FCC sample included 226 family child care providers in Los Angeles, Dallas–Fort Worth, and Charlotte, North Carolina, serving a mean of four children per home. One hundred twelve of the homes were regulated, 54 were nonregulated, and 60 were homes of relatives of the child(ren) in care (two-thirds of the providers were grandmothers). Not all the children were in care full-time. This study focused on quality of services, the characteristics of providers, their relations with their parent-customers, and parent and provider attitudes about quality. Observations occurred between September 1991 and December 1992.

EFCC is a companion study to FCC. Using a subsample of 134 providers from the FCC study, data were collected through extended telephone interviews during the spring of 1993. The topics of the interviews were the cost of producing family care, provider finances and tax reporting, provider business practices, reasons for becoming a provider, and plans for remaining in the field. Carried out in conjunction with members of the CQO research team, the study was designed to permit comparison of family child care and center production costs.

QUALITY LEVELS BASED ON FCC, EFCC, AND CQO

In CQO, on-site interviews with center directors and reviews of center records provided in-depth information on center finances, personnel, and program characteristics.

Trained observers visited 228 infant-toddler and 521 preschool classrooms for 5-6 hours (two observers per center unless the center had just one class) to observe quality characteristics. The observers used four instruments: the Early Childhood Environment Rating Scale (ECERS) (Harms and Clifford 1980), the Infant/Toddler Environment Rating Scale (ITERS) (Harms, Cryer, and Clifford 1990), the Caregiver Interaction Scale (CIS) (Arnett 1989), and the Teacher Involvement Scale (TIS) (Howes and Stewart 1987). (For description of these instruments, see Cryer, this volume.) ECERS and ITERS have been scaled to score 3 for what professionals in the child care field consider minimally adequate and 5 for developmentally appropriate care. In CQO, an overall center quality score was constructed using results from all four instruments in order to increase the weight given to items evaluating relations between staff and children. Scores for each classroom were combined based on a principal components analysis of the four total scores and rescaled to ECERS to yield scores ranging from 1 to 7. Center scores were averages of the two classroom scores, weighted by the enrollment in preschool and infant-toddler age groups.

In FCC, observers used the Family Day Care Rating Scale (FDCRS) (Harms and Clifford 1989) with similar questions and the same rating scale as ECERS and ITERS, as well as CIS and TIS.

Both FCC and CQO combined individual items within the quality instruments into factor scores based

TABLE 1
MEASURES OF QUALITY OF
CARE IN CHILD CARE SETTINGS

Setting	Instrument	Value	Scale
Centers	Early Childhood Environment Rating Scale	4.0	(1-7, 7 is best)
	Caregiving	4.4	(1-7, 7 is best)
	Developmental activities	3.8	(1-7, 7 is best)
	Infant/Toddler Environment Rating Scale	3.4	(1-7, 7 is best)
	Interaction	4.4	(1-7, 7 is best)
	Activities	3.3	(1-7, 7 is best)
	Health practices	2.5	(1-7, 7 is best)
	Caregiver Interaction Scale		
	Sensitivity	2.7	(1-4, 4 is most sensitive)
	Harshness	1.7	(1-4, 4 is harshest)
	Detachment	1.7	(1-4, 4 is most detached)
	Teacher Involvement Scale		
	Percent responsive interactions	34	(0-100, 100 is responsive)
	Center Quality Index	4.0	(1-7, 7 is best)
Family child care	Family Day Care Rating Scale	3.4	(1-7, 7 is best)
	Caregiver Interaction Scale		
	Sensitivity	2.8	(1-4, 4 is most sensitive)
	Harshness	1.5	(1-4, 4 is harshest)
	Detachment	1.6	(1-4, 4 is most detached)
	Teacher Involvement Scale		
	Percent responsive interactions	54	(0-100, 100 is responsive)

SOURCE: Computed by author from CQO and EFCC data.

on principal components analysis. Table 1 shows the factor results for the various instruments and the weighted average center index. Scores on each of the instruments show substantial room for improvement. The CIS factor scores for harshness and detachment are relatively good at 1.5-1.7 (1.0 is not harsh or not detached) in both centers and family child care, but scores on ITERS, ECERS, and TIS percent responsive are mediocre at best. The ECERS average was 4.0; ITERS, 3.4; and FDCRS, 3.4 (3.0 is minimally adequate and 5.0 is developmentally appropriate). The teacher responded more than perfunctorily only 34 percent of the time in centers and 54 percent of the time in family child care when the target child was within 3 feet. The overall weighted average center quality score was 4.0, exactly in the middle of the ECERS or ITERS mediocre range. For preschool-age children, the scores were slightly better, but, for infants and toddlers, the scores were substantially worse. Average ITERS scores for infants and toddlers were 3.4, and 40 percent of the infant and toddler rooms scored below 3.0, below minimally adequate. In FCC, the overall average FDCRS score was 3.4, toward the bottom of the mediocre range.

The CQO study covers only four states and thus might not be fully representative of child care in the United States. However, two of the states, Connecticut and California, are among those thought to have generally high-quality care (and they had modestly higher average quality scores than the overall sample). Geographically, these two states represent the northeast and the West Coast, a total of perhaps 40 percent of the country but 50 percent of the sample. North Carolina is representative of the south, about one-third of the country but one-fourth of the sample. Colorado represented the midwest, about one-fourth of both the country and the sample. A priori, each of these states would be expected to be either average or above average for their region, and the south, with its relatively low quality, is underrepresented. Further, the study required voluntary participation; one would expect that center directors who knew they had something to hide would have been more likely to refuse to participate. Although the study found little evidence of selection bias (based on zip code, ownership, size of center, or age of center), the most likely direction of such bias would be to overestimate quality within each state. Based on the sample, then, estimated quality seems more likely to overestimate quality for the country than to underestimate it. Thus CQO study results provide strong evidence that, by professional standards, the quality of child care in the United States is mediocre and for infants and toddlers, worse than mediocre.

Geographically, FCC sampling was similar to the CQO sample except that it excluded Connecticut and substituted Dallas–Ft. Worth, Texas, for the front range of Colorado. Also, because of the nature of family child care, infants and toddlers made up a larger share of the sampled children. These two differences may depress the FCC results somewhat relative to the CQO results. Hence the small differences in quality measures between centers (4.0 on ECERS) and the regulated family child care homes (3.92) may reflect sample variation. The substantially lower scores in unregulated and relative child care (3.06 and 2.64, respectively), however, appear to reflect real differences in quality of care.

Within the limits of our ability to measure, and by the standards used by educators in this field, child care in the United States really does appear to be mediocre or worse. This conclusion is confirmed by the more extensive literature review in Cryer (this volume).

Another possible explanation of the finding of mediocre quality is that the professionals' definition of quality does not accurately reflect parents' views. If that is so, then there is an issue of what really represents quality. To test for this, CQO and FCC looked at whether parents valued the same things as professionals. In CQO, a parent survey asked, for each characteristic measured on the ITERS or ECERS instrument, whether the parent considered it important and how well the parent thought the center was performing on the characteristic. On a scale of 1 to 3, with 3 meaning "very important," the average parent score for all questions was 2.8, nearly as high as was possible. Parents, however, evaluated quality in their centers far more highly than the observers did (Cryer and Burchinal 1997). Further, where the parents' importance ratings were highest, as in the case of health practices for infant care (such as washing hands after changing a child's diaper), the differences in evaluations were highest (Helburn 1995). In FCC, mothers and providers were asked to rank a list of 19 characteristics for relative importance in the provision of child care. Mothers and providers were in reasonably close agreement and, except for a low rating for licensing, the rankings appear to be consistent with the goals stated by the profession. Thus parents appear to want the same things for their children that the professional researchers do but seriously overestimate the extent to which they are getting them.

Finally, there is the question of whether good quality matters. The CQO study also examined child development outcomes for children in care, using the Peabody Picture Vocabulary Test-Revised (Dunn and Dunn 1981), the Woodcock-Johnson pre-reading and pre-math tests (Woodcock and Johnson 1990), a measure of self-perception (Stipek 1993), and teacher ratings. The concurrent results indicated that children in better-quality centers show modest but significantly greater development in some areas than children in poorer-quality centers when family characteristics were held constant (Helburn 1995). A follow-up longitudinal study suggests that these differences persist at least through kindergarten (Peisner-Feinberg et al. 1998). Better-quality family child care also appears to be related to children's social and cognitive functioning. In FCC, children in better-quality centers scored higher on security of attachment to their provider, complexity of peer play, and complexity of object play. Good quality is apparently what the children need.

THE MARKET AND CHILD CARE QUALITY

In order to explain mediocre quality in child care, one must review the economic constraints on the participants. On the supply side, these quality studies have shown wide variation in quality, and my research experience suggests that some providers do not know how to provide really good quality. Further, researchers have been unable to isolate a complete set of measurable variables to explain quality. The market structure in child care limits profitability and fails to reward quality. On the demand side, center services are costly when compared to family income so that many parents and other agencies subsidizing care cannot afford it. These buyers are very price conscious and choose less costly family child care or unregulated care. Within the center sector of the market, where the extra cost of higher quality is not terribly high, the parents do not see the differences easily and appear unwilling to pay for them.

The quality production function

In terms of what produces quality, the CQO and FCC data suggest that the conventional answers are at least partially correct. High-quality centers were generally those with higher adult-to-child ratios, better-educated teachers, higher staff wages, more experienced and more involved administrators, and lower staff turnover. Better-quality family care was associated with the same factors except for ratios, but most important for family care were licensure, professional commitment to the field, and good business practices. In the center study, all variables tested accounted for slightly less than 50 percent of the variance in quality, suggesting that there is more to the story than the study could identify. Blau (1997) has suggested that most center differences in quality are idiosyncratic to the center, and Cryer (this volume) points out that all of the structural quality factors work together to produce good quality. There is something about the way staff members work together to produce quality or not that the standard measures do not catch. Similarly, director characteristics important to quality might be hard to measure statistically, even though, in the real world, good directors can be identified and rewarded. How well the staff thought the director worked with them on curriculum was positively associated with quality in CQO.

Although there is no clear formula that always produces high-quality care, we know enough to say that hiring a good director and better-trained staff, paying them well enough to stay, and improving the adult-to-child ratio will usually produce better care. Kellogg's article (this volume) shows the design and workings of a high-quality child care center from a practitioner's point of view. At least some of her design would be difficult to quantify; nevertheless, we know much of what works. Most centers are not implementing enough of what works to get beyond mediocrity.

Market structure

The structure of the child care industry itself affects incentives to improve quality. Child care centers fit rather nicely into the market model of monopolistic competition: the industry is easy to enter, and each center serves a niche created by product differentiation. Easy entry is apparent in the large number of independent centers and high provider turnover in any large city. As can be seen in Table 2, which compares financial data for centers and family child care, costs in child care are overwhelmingly labor costs (two-thirds of total cost). Only one-sixth of total cost was accounted for by the building that houses the center (slightly more in for-profit centers). Further, as Table 3 shows, the high turnover rates among staff, especially in the for-profit centers, suggest that labor is even more a variable cost than it is in other industries. With this cost structure, there is little financial commitment to stay in business, and, indeed, other studies have found high turnover in child care center licenses (Kisker et al. 1991).

Family child care is even easier to enter than center care. In the extreme, unlicensed family child care requires only declaring oneself in the business. Even with a license, family child care requires only minor modification of an existing home and a provider willing to start the business. Exit, of course, is even easier.

With monopolistic competition, one expects to find low rates of profit. The CQO study was unable to estimate capital invested in each center and therefore unable to estimate return on capital. It did, however, estimate profit (or surplus, for nonprofit centers) as a percentage of sales. Table 2 shows that profits averaged 5 percent of sales in for-profit centers and surplus averaged 3 percent of sales in nonprofit centers, a difference that was not statistically significant. Profits as percentage of sales did not vary significantly with the quality of the center and, indeed, seem inversely related to quality. If the centers cannot profit from raising quality, then there is little incentive for them to do so, at least in the for-profit sector.

Child care is a mixed industry made up of for-profit, nonprofit, and publicly operated centers as well as family child care, each with different cost structures. Historically and at present, nonprofit and publicly operated centers receive substantial supply subsidies for facilities and other expenses and volunteer help. The subsidies reduce expended costs of centers, enabling them to provide their services for fees that do not cover the total cost of all resources used. The savings appear to go toward paying more for staff, which improves quality with only a slight reduction in fees, except in church-operated centers. Church-operated centers did not produce higher quality but passed on subsidies in the form of much lower fees, averaging about $50 per month lower than other centers.

For-profit centers compete with nonprofits (particularly the church-

TABLE 2

MONTHLY CHILD CARE COST AND PROFIT BY SECTOR AND QUALITY LEVEL PER FULL-TIME-EQUIVALENT CHILD, EXCLUDING CONNECTICUT

	Centers			Family Child Care
	Sector		All	
	For-Profit	Nonprofit		
Monthly costs				
Labor	$201	$270	$236	$218
Occupancy	77	30	53	18
Food	17	21	19	42
Other	52	32	44	65
Total cost	$348	$355	$352	$343
Monthly fees				
Preschool	$346	$318	$332	$318
Infant	448	423	436	341
Profit or surplus	19	12	16	NA

	Centers			Family Child Care
	Quality			
	Low	Medium	High	
Monthly costs				
Labor	$181	$238	$314	$218
Occupancy	51	56	48	18
Food	21	19	23	42
Other	40	44	36	65
Total cost	$293	$357	$421	$343
Monthly fees				
Preschool	$271	$340	$347	$318
Infant	320	401	473	341
Profit or surplus	$ 25	$ 15	$ 15	NA

SOURCE: Computed by author from CQO and EFCC data.

NOTES: NA is "not applicable"–profits are included in labor costs in a proprietorship. Items may not add to totals due to rounding.

TABLE 3
CENTER COSTS AND TEACHING STAFF TURNOVER, BY SECTOR, INCLUDING CONNECTICUT

Sector	For-Profit Chain	For-Profit Independent	Church Operated	Church Affiliated	Nonprofit Independent	Public
Turnover	54%	48%	26%	28%	36%	20%
Monthly cost per child	$386	$385	$301	$358	$478	$507

SOURCE: Computed by author from CQO data.

related centers) for many of the same customers and therefore must match nonprofit fees. To the extent that their markets overlap with family child care, they must also at least approach family child care fees. Table 2 also shows that for-profit centers spend more per child on occupancy costs (they have less occupancy subsidy or better facilities) than nonprofits and family child care. To offset their occupancy cost disadvantages, for-profit centers appear to skimp on the wages and qualifications of their staff. For-profit center advocates have occasionally complained about subsidized competition, but it appears that the for-profit sector is growing faster than the nonprofit sector. Helburn and Howes (1996) suggest that this is due to capital constraints in the nonprofit sector; these centers cannot access financial markets as easily as for-profits can and therefore are often dependent on some sponsor to provide a facility.

The lack of reward for quality appears also to have a basis in the history of the industry. The child care industry is relatively young, developing as a consequence of increasing labor force participation of women since World War II.

Parents as consumers do not have the experience purchasing care that is needed for a clear idea of what impact child care has on their children in the long run. Many working mothers (and working fathers) receive relatively low wages that restrict their ability to pay for higher-cost, higher-quality care.

One way to improve profits in a monopolistically competitive industry is to identify a market niche that increases differentiation from other producers. Market niches in child care can come from several sources. Low cost is one. Centers also differentiate by location. Parents tend to look for child care along their natural route to and from work. Centers can be differentiated by appearance. Some centers differentiate themselves with indicators of quality such as accreditation.

Most of the available market niches do not lead to higher average levels of quality. There is no reason to expect low cost or convenient location to have any particular relationship to higher quality. Center appearance might have such a relationship, but the CQO study found no evidence for it. The curriculum can be differentiated, by adopting Montessori, Waldorf, or some other known approach.

CQO results were inconclusive regarding the effects of particular curricula on quality. Accreditation is an indicator of quality but is no guarantor of it. A niche for high-quality care can emerge only if the center can show the quality to the customers (parents). Even if such a niche is possible, it will raise overall market quality only if the niche comes to dominate the whole market.

CQO found little evidence of a high-quality niche that would permit charging high fees. Statistically, there was little relationship between fees and quality and even less between quality and profitability. If anything, profitability declined as quality improved. The market simply does not appear to reward high quality in child care.

High cost of care

Much of what we know increases quality also increases cost, such as hiring more skilled staff. The overriding reality, however, is that the cost of mediocre child care is already high. The average cost to parents in 1992 of providing care in the entire CQO sample was $372 per child per month. At 1998 prices, that would be about $5400 per year, and the fee for mediocre infant or toddler care is still higher, at close to $6300 per year (at 1998 prices). The median income of parents who answered the CQO parent survey was $56,000 in 1992. Even the cost of mediocre care can exclude many of the children of low- and middle-income families. Without subsidy, the average cost of center care is 20 percent of the total family income for a family earning $30,000 per year.

For a single center, facing a given wage structure in the larger labor market, the extra cost for improving quality from a score of 4 to 5 was estimated at only about 10 percent of average cost. If all centers try to improve, however, then a shortage of higher-quality staff would develop and drive up wages substantially, and hence the cost of improvement. CQO found that teachers were being paid an average of $5200 per year less than other persons of the same gender, education, age, minority status, and location. If an overall improvement of quality by one point on ECERS or ITERS required paying wages equivalent to those in other industries to draw more skilled people into this industry, then the elimination of the differential might raise current costs per child by as much as 50 percent.

Parents may be even more reluctant to pay higher prices for center care because they have a cheaper alternative in family child care. FCC found average fees of $318 per month for preschool-age children, about $4600 per year in 1998 prices. Fees for care in the inadequate range were lower in both centers (about 20 percent lower) and family care (40 percent lower). Fees for infant care average about $5000 per year in 1998 prices in a family care setting. While most parents have the best interests of their child at heart, their budget constraint may lead them to buy less than the optimal care from the child's perspective. Child care must compete in the family's budget with other items that benefit the parents more directly, such as cars, recreation, or food. Not surprisingly, lower-income parents tend to use care by relatives, while middle-income and higher-income parents move toward family child care homes and centers (Casper 1998; Hofferth et al. 1991).

Third-party reimbursement also plays a role in holding down quality. States pay for some child care through their social services departments (or an equivalent agency). Each state sets maximum reimbursement rates for centers, family child care, and relatives for a child of a particular age. Within the CQO sample, the two states with higher average quality of care, California and Connecticut, paid higher reimbursement rates on average for subsidized children than parents paid in fees to the same center. In the two states with lower quality, state reimbursement rates for subsidized children were lower than parental fees. The effect of lower state fees is to reduce total revenue per child, and this evidently reduces quality. It appears that, in some states at least, the public agency is more concerned with cost than quality, reflecting the same conflicts that parents have over spending priorities.

Uninformed consumers

The competition from other forms of child care at the low end of the market might be expected to drive centers to produce high-quality care as a market niche. That, however, assumes a knowledgeable customer. Because child care is a new market and because most parents have only a small number of children, parents bring little experience as buyers to the market from either their own childhood or earlier children. They may simply not be able to judge the quality of care their children are receiving. This possibility is suggested by the substantially higher scores that CQO parents gave their centers across the board on quality than the trained observers did (Helburn 1995). The evaluation problem is exacerbated by the parents' not being present to monitor services most of the day. In order to observe what is going on, parents must take time off from work to visit the center or family child care home. Otherwise, they have to depend on the comments of their preschooler and the greeting and departure experience, both less than ideal proxies for all-day quality.

Parents can identify actual quality of service only by sitting down in the center and observing (preferably after some research into what to look for). This circumstance may be clearer by analogy to the restaurant industry, which is both similar to and different from child care. There are many restaurants with a range of quality. Most would probably be described as mediocre. However, the mediocrity results from people's choosing to patronize those restaurants either because that is the quality that the people want or because the cost of better quality is too high. Restaurants differ from child care, however, in that the purchaser has an immediate and direct experience with the meal. If the quality is inadequate, one simply does not return. In child care, the experience of the buyer is indirect. It is easy to assume that the quality is good when it is not. Hence the buyer-parent brings the child back day after day to care that is not really adequate.

Hidden action

Parents' limited information permits centers to produce lower quality on those aspects of quality that parents do not value or cannot monitor. That is, centers operated for profit have an incentive to practice hidden action. Some parts of the child care experience are more visible to the parent than others. Therefore, a center that is concerned about profit has an incentive to improve those parts of the experience (such as the building or the parental greeting) more than, or even at the expense of, parts that the parent cannot see as easily (teacher-child interactions through the day) and therefore do not demand, if this practice lowers cost. To the extent that the center acts on these incentives, there will be differentially lower quality in hard-to-observe characteristics of quality than in easy-to-observe quality characteristics. One would not expect a nonprofit center to practice hidden action if its main objective is to produce high-quality child care.

Morris and Helburn (1998) have tested the CQO data for differential quality on indices of 13 hard-to-observe and 14 easy-to-observe quality characteristics. Table 4 shows that the profit motive appears to play some role. Where all centers averaged 0.1 point higher in easy-to-observe quality in preschool rooms and 0.3 point higher in infant-toddler rooms, some groups showed larger or smaller differences. In for-profit chains, the easy-to-observe quality was 0.5 and 0.6 point higher than hard-to-observe quality in preschool and infant-toddler rooms, respectively. Church-operated centers showed a 0.3 point difference in both age groups. For-profit independent centers, church-affiliated (but not directly church-operated), and other nonprofit centers showed no significant differences, and publicly operated centers actually showed 0.4 and 0.3 point higher quality in the hard-to-observe characteristics than in the easy-to-observe ones. These differences would be possible only if parents either were not aware of the differences in hard-to-observe quality or they were unconcerned about them.

For-profit chains appear to be the most profit oriented of all the subsectors in center child care, and publicly operated centers, the least. To that extent, these results suggest that profit orientation conflicts with quality orientation. However, for-profit independent centers did not exhibit any tendency toward hidden action, and church-operated centers did. In the case of for-profit independents, the profit motive might have been secondary to some professional motive to provide good quality care. In the church-operated subsector, it is notable that these centers operated with substantially lower fees than any other and the drive to reduce costs may have led to the hidden action. Church-operated centers may also be obligated to support the church budget.

Overall quality differs somewhat similarly. For-profit chains, church-operated centers, and, this time, for-profit independents had lower overall quality than church-affiliated and other nonprofit centers. Again, publicly operated centers produced higher overall quality than any other

TABLE 4

MEAN SCORES ON OVERALL QUALITY AND EASY-TO-OBSERVE AND HARD-TO-OBSERVE QUALITY CHARACTERISTICS, BY SUBSECTOR AND AGE LEVEL

	For-Profit Chains	For-Profit Independent	Church Operated	Church Affiliated	Other Nonprofit	Public	All
Center-level quality index	3.76	3.91	3.78	4.15	4.14	4.70	4.02
Preschool rooms							
Easy-to-observe	4.28	3.95	4.21	4.47	4.46	4.92	4.27
Hard-to-observe	3.70	4.01	3.95	4.48	4.47	5.36	4.18
Infant-toddler rooms							
Easy-to-observe	3.82	3.42	3.50	3.90	3.88	4.15	3.85
Hard-to-observe	3.23	3.56	3.22	4.07	3.90	4.47	3.58

SOURCE: Morris and Helburn 1998.

group. Apparently, the differences in hard-to-observe quality explained much of the differences between ownership subsectors in overall quality.

Summary

On reviewing this evidence, it is apparent that there are multiple reasons to explain why the market does not sort out and eliminate low-quality centers. Our knowledge of how to produce high quality is imperfect and especially hard to quantify. High provider turnover may add to the variety in quality. Some customers (parents or third parties) cannot afford the extra cost of higher quality, do not care beyond some minimal level of safety, or do not know much about alternatives. Centers have to compete against other centers that may have subsidies they use to hold down fees and against noncenter providers that have lower cost structures. Parents and other buyers of care find it difficult to observe the quality of care in a center so that even if they are willing and able to pay for higher quality, they may not be able to monitor it, providing an opportunity for some producers to sell low-quality care as if it were of high quality.

POLICY IMPLICATIONS

Public policy should be oriented toward overcoming the problems enumerated in this article. Both providers and parents need more information about how to produce and identify quality in child care. Producers of high-quality care need some protection from being undersold. Families need some way to hold down costs.

The CQO study found that some public policies were at least associated with provision of higher-quality care. In CQO, public regulation via the licensing process seemed to make a difference. In Connecticut, California, and Colorado, regulations were clearly more restrictive than in North Carolina, and substantially fewer poor-quality centers were found in the former states than in North Carolina (particularly compared to for-profit centers in North Carolina). The limits to basic regulation are shown, however, by the case of Colorado, which had fewer developmentally appropriate quality centers than any other state (nearly all were in the mediocre range) despite licensing standards similar to those in Connecticut and California. In FCC, the differences between licensed and unlicensed care suggest a need to extend licensing to all states. Thus, licensing as currently practiced cannot create good care, but it can reduce the incidence of really poor-quality care.

Some states are experimenting with a variant on licensing: combining licensing with an incentive system to improve quality and provide information to parents. North Carolina and Colorado are both experimenting with differential reimbursement rates for different quality levels. North Carolina is implementing a differential licensing system based on quality level. Centers will be evaluated on ECERS, and those that score higher will be given a higher-level license, entitling them to greater reimbursement by the state for subsidized children. If this quality gradation system is well publicized, presumably it will raise fees generally for higher-quality centers.

Colorado is not as far along, but a public-private partnership is attempting to develop a rating system in addition to licensing that would become the basis of differential reimbursement to centers and family child care homes for all users regardless of income. In both states,

the rating would be performed by trained professionals and would provide parents with a simple criterion for demanding quality care. In both states, the intent is that the reimbursement differential will be enough to induce centers to increase their quality.

Both systems extend the restaurant analogy described previously one step further. In travel guides, where customers do not have market knowledge to identify good restaurants, the guide (for example, a Mobil Travel Guide) often rates restaurants with stars to identify relative quality. The rating systems in North Carolina and Colorado will function similarly. Oklahoma and New Mexico are also implementing differential rating systems.

Professional accreditation of centers and certification of individual providers and child care workers could also function as a basis for a rating system. CQO found that, on average, accredited centers had substantially higher quality than unaccredited ones and that only rarely did they provide below-average quality. A problem with relying too much on accreditation is infrequent reevaluations (currently every three years), so that quality can change long before reaccreditation takes place.

Another approach is to train parents directly to observe the quality of the care their children receive. Such training would need to include the importance of individual items in the evaluation instruments that exist and what is possible in a center. Parents would then need guidance on what things they may be able to observe in a relatively short visit to their child's classroom or potential classroom. The training and time necessary for parents to take on this task individually seem cumbersome enough to limit its usefulness. A more efficient alternative might be for parents to use a multivalued rating system as in the restaurant analogy to quickly ascertain at least an approximation of a center or home's quality.

Family child care presents somewhat different problems from those of center care for public policy. Because there are so many and such small units, it is difficult to control quality. Incentives to obtain licenses and training for providers will help reduce the incidence of low-quality care. Some combination of incentives, frequent inspections, and additional support (both financial and other) is probably necessary to encourage provision of good care.

If better care comes at the expense of the parents of the children receiving it, we do not know how many will choose certified higher quality at higher cost. If, however, the cost of the higher quality is subsidized for lower- and middle-income families and if they become informed enough to identify it, there seems little reason to believe that they would not choose it.

References

Arnett, J. 1989. Caregivers in Day-Care Centers: Does Training Matter? *Journal of Applied Developmental Psychology* 10:541-52.

Blau, David. 1997. The Production of Quality in Child Care Centers. *Journal of Human Resources* 32(2):354-87.

Casper, Lynn. 1998. *Who's Minding Our Preschoolers?* Update, P70-62, U.S. Bureau of the Census, Population Division.

Cryer, Debby and Margaret Burchinal. 1997. Parents as Child Care Consumers. *Early Childhood Research Quarterly* 12:35-58.

Dunn, L. and L. Dunn. 1981. *Peabody Picture Vocabulary Test - Revised*. Circle Pines, MN: American Guidance Service.

Galinsky, Ellen, Carollee Howes, Susan Kontos, and Marybeth Shinn. 1994. *The Study of Children in Family Child Care and Relative Care: Highlights of Findings*. New York: Families and Work Institute.

Harms, Thelma and Richard Clifford. 1980. *Early Childhood Environment Rating Scale*. New York: Teachers College Press.

———. 1989. *The Family Day Care Rating Scale*. New York: Teachers College Press.

Harms, Thelma, Debby Cryer, and Richard Clifford. 1990. *Infant / Toddler Environment Rating Scale*. New York: Teachers College Press.

Helburn, Suzanne, ed. 1995. *Cost, Quality and Child Outcomes in Child Care Centers*. Denver: University of Colorado, Department of Economics, Center for Research in Economic and Social Policy.

Helburn, Suzanne and Carollee Howes. 1996. Child Care Cost and Quality. *The Future of Children* 6(2):62-81.

Helburn, Suzanne and John Morris. 1996. Provider Costs and Income. University of Colorado at Denver. Manuscript.

Hofferth, Sandra, April Brayfield, Sharon Deich, and Pamela Holcomb. 1991. *National Child Care Survey*. Urban Institute Report 91-5. Washington, DC: Urban Institute.

Howes, Carollee and P. Stewart. 1987. Child's Play with Adults, Toys and

Peers: An Examination of Family and Child Care Influences. *Developmental Psychology* 28:961-74.

Kisker, Ellen, Sandra Hofferth, Deborah Phillips, and Elizabeth Farquhar. 1991. *A Profile of Child Care Settings: Early Education and Care in 1990.* Princeton, NJ: Mathematica Policy Research.

Morris, John and Suzanne Helburn. 1998. Hidden Action in the Child Care Industry. University of Colorado at Denver. Manuscript.

Peisner-Feinberg, E., R. Clifford, N. Yazejian, M. Culkin, C. Howes, and S. Kagan. 1998. Longitudinal Effects of Child Care Quality: Implication for Kindergarten Success. Paper presented at the American Educational Research Association, Apr.

Stipek, Deborah. 1993. Attitudes/Perceptions of Competence. University of California at Los Angeles. Rating scale.

Woodcock, R. and M. Johnson. 1990. *Woodcock-Johnson Psycho-Educational Battery - Revised.* Allen, TX: DLM Teaching Resources.

ANNALS, *AAPSS*, **563**, May 1999

Child Care Workers:
High Demand, Low Wages

By MARCY WHITEBOOK

ABSTRACT: This article provides an overview of child care employment, identifying its key characteristics and issues impeding the development of a skilled and stable workforce to meet the need for quality early care and education services. Characteristics of child care jobs are summarized, including information about poverty-level earnings, poor benefits, unequal opportunity, and high turnover. Market pressures that depress wages in this sector are explored with particular attention to the impact of welfare reform. Also reviewed are institutional barriers to improving child care jobs, such as insufficient funding, lack of organizational representation, a stark resistance to national program standards, and unsupportive reimbursement and funding policies. The article concludes with highlights of current initiatives to improve child care jobs, including the North Carolina scholarship program, the U.S. Army Child Development Services' Caregiver Personnel Pay Plan, Head Start quality improvement efforts, mentoring and apprentice programs, grant programs, and union and community organizing.

Marcy Whitebook is executive director of the Center for the Child Care Workforce (previously the National Center for the Early Childhood Work Force and the Child Care Employee Project). She was the project director for the National Child Care Staffing Study (1988, 1992, 1998), NAEYC Accreditation as a Strategy for Improving Child Care Quality (1997), and Salary Improvements in Head Start: Lessons for the Early Care and Education Field (1996). She coauthored Taking on Turnover: An Action Guide for Child Care Center Teachers and Directors and The Early Childhood Mentoring Curriculum *(1998).*

CHILD care employment is riddled with contradictions. Consider that a severe shortage of qualified staff coexists with exceedingly low wages, and that ideal candidates for jobs have completed postsecondary education, yet most states require no preservice training for employment in child care. As reflected in the comments of former California governor Pete Wilson (1998), who recently vetoed legislation aimed at addressing a severe staffing crisis by providing wage supplements to child care teachers and providers with professional training, the notion that the market will resolve these problems persists:

While recognizing the important role child care providers play in caring for our children, I do not believe it is appropriate for the State of California to provide wages subsidies or otherwise interfere in the private child care market. This bill would introduce state regulation of wages into a field that is currently controlled by the market and allow direct wage supplements to private sector employees. This may constitute a gift of public funds.

Yet the current child care market does not support the cornerstone of child care that promotes healthy development and reliable services: the presence of sensitive, consistent, well-trained, and well-compensated caregivers.[1] Children who attend higher-quality child care programs with lower staff turnover have been found to be more competent in their language and social development (Whitebook, Howes, and Phillips 1990). But, due to a general disregard for the needs of the child care

workforce—not only by government officials and policymakers but by most advocacy organizations as well—job conditions in this female-dominated occupation remain woefully inadequate (Bellm et al. 1997).

CURRENT STATUS OF
CHILD CARE WORKERS

Child care workers' low status is reflected in poverty-level earnings, poor benefits, unequal opportunity, and high turnover.

Poverty-level earnings

The average center-based child care teacher nationwide earns roughly $6.70 an hour, despite above-average levels of education (see Figure 1). Roughly one-third of teaching staff are paid the minimum wage (Whitebook, Howes, and Phillips 1990). Figure 2 shows that even those with experience earn on average less than $20,000 a year (Whitebook, Howes, and Phillips 1998). Family child care providers, who care for small groups of children in their own homes, earn even lower wages: those who are subject to licensing or other forms of regulation earn between $8500 and $10,000 per year after expenses, and nonregulated providers earn only $5132 (Helburn and Howes 1996; Burton et al. 1995). Providers can work very long hours, often 50 or more hours per week with children as well as several hours shopping, cleaning, preparing activities, and so on. Further, some also make costly renovations to their homes to make them safe and appropriate for group child care.

FIGURE 1
CHILD CARE WORKFORCE EARNINGS IN PERSPECTIVE

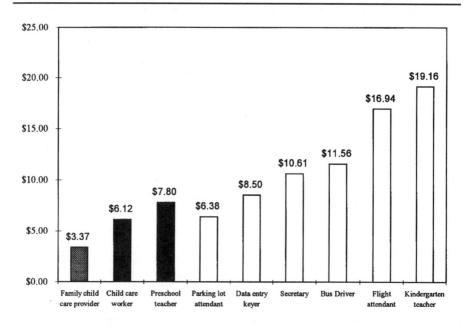

SOURCE: *Current Data on Child Care Salaries* 1998, 3. Reprinted by permission of the Center for the Child Care Workforce.

NOTE: The Bureau of Labor Statistics of the U.S. Department of Labor reports the median wage for 764 occupations, as surveyed by the Occupational Employment Statistics (OES) program. (A "median wage" indicates that 50 percent of workers in an occupation earn wages below this figure, and 50 percent earn wages above it.) The median wage for family child care providers is surveyed through the bureau's Office of Current Employment Analysis. (The Bureau of Labor Statistics collects child care workforce data through numerous surveys and uses such occupational titles for child care center employees as aides, child care assistants, day care assistants, teacher assistants, child care attendants, day care attendants, and early childhood teacher assistants. The OES definitions and data are used [for this figure] instead of [those from] other surveys because those other titles are not mutually exclusive and are not used consistently across states.) According to the most recent OES survey, based on data from 1996, only 15 occupations report having lower median wages than [those of] child care workers. Those who earn higher wages than child care workers include service station attendants, messengers, and food servers. These data are based on the OES occupation title definitions, which include the categories of managerial, professional, sales, clerical, service, agricultural, and production employment. Unfortunately, the OES categories create a misleading division of the child care workforce into preschool teachers and child care workers. A preschool teacher is defined as a person who instructs children (normally up to 5 years of age), in a preschool program, day care center, or other child development facility, in activities designed to promote social, physical, and intellectual growth in preparation for elementary school. A child care worker is defined as a person who performs such duties as dressing, feeding, bathing, and overseeing play. Employees of before- and after-school child care programs may be included in the child care worker category, or in other categories such as teachers' aides, which also include K-12 classroom assistants and aides. Only 4.8 percent of the professional occupations, among which preschool teachers are classified, earn an average wage of less than $10.00 per hour, and nearly 70 percent of professional workers earn

(Note continued)

more than $15.75 per hour. Child care workers are classified as service workers, the lowest-paid divi-
sion, in which 55 percent of workers earn less than $8.50 per hour, placing them at the low end of the
wage range for all occupations surveyed by the OES. The median weekly wage for family child care
providers is $118.00, based on the 1996 Current Population Survey (CPS) definition of usual weekly
earnings of full-time wage and salaried workers. The CPS considers "full time" to be at least 35 hours
per week. The figure of $3.37 per hour reflects a 35-hour week; most family child care providers, how-
ever, work 50 hours or more per week. The Bureau of Labor Statistics collects child care workforce
data through numerous surveys and uses such as occupational titles for child care center employees
as aides, child care assistants, day care assistants, teacher assistants, child care attendants, day
care attendants, and early childhood teacher assistants. The OES definitions and data are used [for
this figure] instead of [those from] other surveys because those other titles are not mutually exclusive
and are not used consistently across states.

FIGURE 2
AVERAGE ANNUAL EARNINGS OF CHILD CARE TEACHING STAFF, 1997

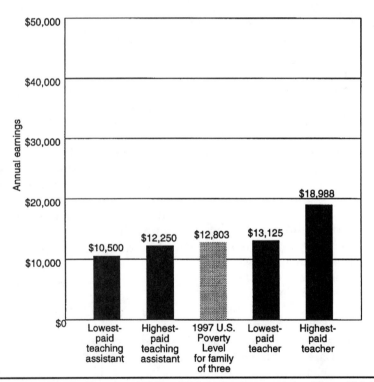

SOURCE: Whitebook, Howes, and Phillips 1998, 14. For the poverty-level figure, U.S. Bureau of
the Census. Reprinted by permission of the Center for the Child Care Workforce.

NOTE: Full-time annual earnings based on 35 hours per week, 50 weeks per year—the average
work week of teaching staff in the original sample. In the original sample, 34 percent of all teaching
staff had completed some college education and 22 percent had completed a B.A. or more. We do not
have comparable data for 1997 and thus cannot determine the extent to which the educational background of providers has changed in the last decade.

Poor benefits

Despite workers' high exposure to illness and physical strain on the job, less than one-third of child care centers provide fully paid health insurance. Many more centers provide partial coverage; however, anecdotal reports suggest that teaching staff frequently do not utilize partially paid health benefits due to their inability to afford the premium, a phenomenon that is common across industries (Ginsburg, Gabel, and Hunt 1998). Even fewer centers offer a pension plan (Whitebook and Burton 1996). In seeking access to health insurance and other benefits, family child care providers not covered by a spouse fare even worse. Many center-based child care staff are expected to work without breaks, and often for extra hours without pay. Less than 4 percent of them have a union contract (Whitebook, Howes, and Phillips 1990).

Unequal opportunity

Child care is a relatively easy field of employment for anyone to enter. But because of unequal access to training, education, and other avenues of career advancement, poor and minority women tend to remain disproportionately at the entry-level, lowest-paid child care jobs (Center for the Child Care Workforce 1995a, 1995b, 1995c; National Black Child Development Institute 1993). There are some exceptions. The San Francisco Unified School District, for example, pays the highest wages in the city, and two-thirds of the staff are people of color (Child Care Law Center 1995). Among home-based providers, there is a higher concentration of women of color among relatives and unregulated caregivers than among those who are regulated. For example, a recent study found that 71 percent of regulated providers were Caucasian, in contrast to 59 percent of nonregulated and 28 percent of relative caregivers (Kontos et al. 1995).

High turnover

More than one-third of the nation's child care workforce leave their jobs each year—most often in order to earn a better living elsewhere. At such a rate of turnover, the shortage of trained and qualified workers has created a national staffing crisis. Those who do remain on the job share the extra burden of constantly training new coworkers. Many teachers and directors report working with less trained coworkers and worry that the quality of services that children and parents receive is continuing to decline dangerously (Whitebook and Bellm 1998). See Figure 3 for a comparison of turnover in child care and other industries.

MARKET PRESSURES
THAT DEPRESS WAGES
AND THEIR CONSEQUENCES

Despite a major public investment in the U.S. child care system during the last decade, job conditions in the profession remain substandard, leading to problems of inconsistent care, understaffing, and the strong potential for unsafe conditions for children. Wages in center-based care have stagnated at near poverty level, according to a nine-year follow-up of

FIGURE 3
TURNOVER IN CHILD CARE AND OTHER OCCUPATIONS

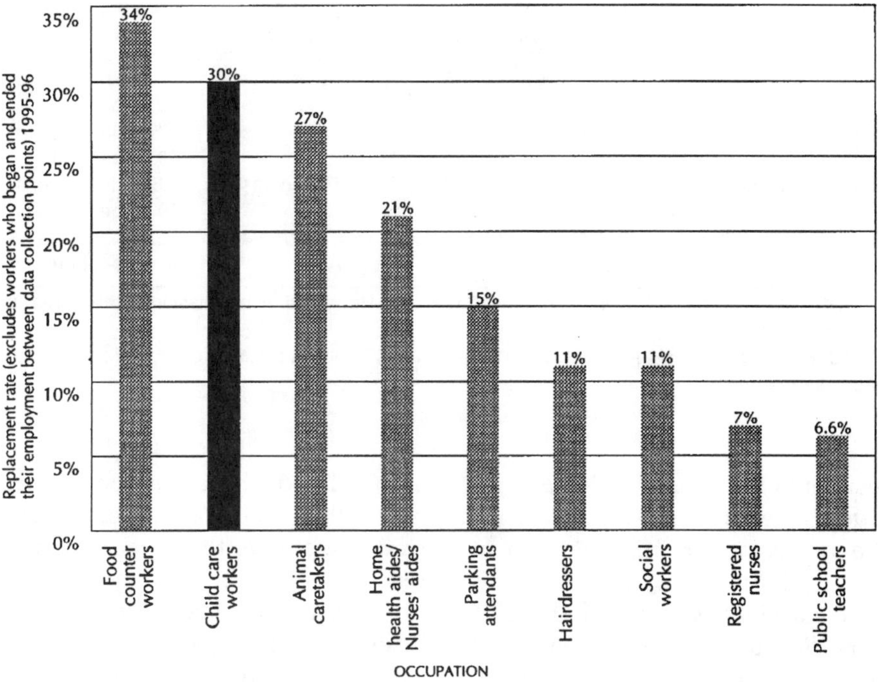

SOURCE: Whitebook and Bellm 1998, 32. Reprinted by permission of the Center for the Child Care Workforce.

the National Child Care Staffing Study, which originally examined the quality of care in 225 centers in five cities (Atlanta, Boston, Detroit, Phoenix, and Seattle) (see Table 1 and Figure 2). Public funds have had little if any effect in stabilizing the child care workforce. More child care centers receive public dollars now than in the past, allowing more of them to assist low-income families with child care costs, but programs paying the lowest wages are experiencing the greatest increase in public subsidies (Whitebook, Howes, and Phillips 1998).

The current pressures on the child care workforce are formidable—as are the pressures on parents, who cannot shoulder alone the heavy burden of child care costs. A serious teacher shortage in many elementary school districts,[2] as well as a healthy U.S. economy overall, are creating new incentives for the best-trained, most experienced child care workers to leave the field for better-paying careers. At the same time, as welfare reform rapidly increases the demand for child care services nationwide, over half of the states are encouraging former welfare

TABLE 1
TRENDS IN HOURLY WAGES FOR CENTER-BASED CHILD CARE STAFF

Staff Position	1988 Wage	1992 Wage	1997 Wage	Real Change Between 1992 and 1997	Real Change Between 1988 and 1997
Lowest-paid assistant	$5.99	$5.91	$6.00	1.50% increase	0.17% increase, or $0.01 per hour
Highest-paid assistant	$6.96	$7.03	$7.00	0.43% decrease	0.57% increase, or $0.04 per hour
Lowest-paid teacher	$7.38	$7.55	$7.50	0.66% decrease	1.60% increase, or $0.12 per hour
Highest-paid teacher	$9.53	$10.33	$10.85	5.00% increase	13.90% increase, or $1.32 per hour

SOURCE: Whitebook, Howes, and Phillips 1998, 12. Reprinted by permission of the Center for the Child Care Workforce.

NOTE: All wages and the 1988-97 trends are in 1997 dollars. Each category reflects average wages for the position.

recipients to become child care providers themselves—often without the necessary training or support that leads to quality care or decent child care jobs (Center for the Child Care Workforce 1998b). As currently designed, the majority of these programs place limited emphasis on skill training and education and are thus unlikely to prepare participants for the limited number of better-paying child care jobs, which require college course work and degrees (Bloom 1997). In most cases, child care work is a highly unlikely avenue to economic independence for poor women coming off public assistance. For more experienced and trained teachers and providers, such an influx of untrained, entry-level workers is likely to drive wages down and reduce opportunities for advancement even further (Weisbrot 1997). The nation appears to be on the brink of a dramatic shift in the overall composition of the child care workforce; on one hand, there may be a major new influx of untrained, entry-level workers, and on the other, a serious teacher shortage in many elementary school districts is creating new incentives for the best-trained, most experienced child care workers to leave the field for better-paying careers.

The pressure on low-wage female-dominated occupations such as child care to absorb an influx of former welfare recipients is also coming at a time when the low-wage labor market supply is already high. Adding this influx to such a supply will depress wages. The Washington-based Economic Policy Institute has recently estimated that

to absorb almost one million new workers, the wages of low-wage workers (defined as the bottom 30 percent of workers—about 31 million men and women who earn less than $7.19 per hour) will have to fall by 11.9 percent nationwide.

Wages for low-wage workers in states with relatively large welfare populations will have to fall by even more: in California, by 17.8 percent; in New York, by 17.1 percent. (Mishel and Schmitt 1996)

The staffing crisis reported anecdotally by directors, and currently under investigation by the Center for the Child Care Workforce, suggests a dire situation marked by little improvement. Action to improve child care compensation will never be more urgently needed than in the coming period.

To date, the limited investments in child care employment have most often been motivated by a desire to improve the quality of services for children and only secondarily to provide better opportunities for advancement for low-income teachers and providers (Bellm et al. 1997). In reality, these two goals should be closely linked, since high turnover and low compensation among caregivers have been shown to have direct and harmful effects on the quality of care that children receive and on children's ability to socialize and learn. Research has also shown that poor children are more vulnerable than others to low-quality child care, and that they benefit more than others from better-quality care (Helburn 1995; Whitebook, Howes, and Phillips 1990, 1993).

INSTITUTIONAL BARRIERS TO
IMPROVING CHILD CARE JOBS

It should perhaps go without saying that the entire U.S. child care system will need to be infused with major new sources of funding, both public and private, in order to truly meet the demand for quality services and decent worker wages. At present, the system is based heavily on parent tuition, and since many parents have a sharply limited ability to pay more, fees and wages are kept depressed at levels that are incommensurate with the actual cost of providing high-quality care (Willer 1990). Among broader social barriers, the persistence of a low U.S. minimum wage also clearly keeps child care wages depressed. With an estimated one-third of caregivers working as minimum wage earners, the recent increase in the minimum wage to $5.25 has resulted in an immediate, badly needed boost for the profession as a whole. Even this increase, however, is not likely to hold much ground against the cost of living over recent decades; it has been estimated that to match the buying power of the $2.00 minimum wage of the mid-1970s, the minimum would have to be well over $6.00 per hour now. In addition, the lack of a guaranteed national health care insurance system continues to keep health benefits out of reach for many child care workers.

Fundamentally, the direct-service, caregiving child care workforce remains unorganized. It lacks a national association or union that can amplify the voice of teachers and providers in the political arena, mobilize their activism, defend their interests, and devote itself to meeting their economic and professional needs. The largest professional association, the National Association for the Education of Young Children, composed of university professors, advocates, trainers, employees, and teachers, does not and cannot play this role given its diverse membership. Equally critical, child care teachers and providers are almost completely excluded from positions of leadership and influence in their chosen field. Most child care organizations do not address the economic concerns of teachers and providers or do so only nominally as one of many issues. Indeed, many have traditionally viewed an active call for better wages as unprofessional or inappropriately political behavior.

Unlike other fields, such as medicine, law, and even K-12 education, child care spokespersons are generally not practitioners who spend their days in direct service. When service providers are invited to take part in advocacy efforts, they are generally program directors rather than classroom staff, who cannot lobby effectively for teachers and providers. In addition, compared with the early childhood workforce as a whole, the leadership is also disproportionately Caucasian and male (National Black Child Development Institute 1993; Whitebook 1997). It is unlikely that the field will place workforce concerns high on its agenda until a significant number of teachers and providers have their own organizations and have reached positions of leadership in other organizations so that they can represent themselves.

A historical resistance to consistent national program standards or regulations also remains a severe barrier in the entire child care field. In states where licensing requirements are minimal or absent,

better-paying child care jobs are much harder to find, since the market tends to favor unregulated care. The inevitable result is wide variability between the states—and there are rising pressures to chip away at the relatively minimal standards on adult-child ratios, group size, and training that do exist. As states increasingly promote unregulated forms of child care under welfare reform, the importance of sound training and education for teachers and providers is becoming more undervalued than ever.

The failure of wages to rise can be traced to the virtually free entry into child care employment. Child care is not only a female-dominated occupation; it is derived from the gender division of labor that has existed throughout history. Any woman thinks she can do the work, and this attitude is generally shared by the public at large, including some consumers of child care services as well as many employers and policymakers. Thus, when demand for child care increases, the supply of workers can come from the large pool of untrained and inexperienced women looking for jobs. The situation is reinforced by a regulatory system that does not require individuals caring for young children to be licensed. Although there is a great deal of emphasis within the child care field on professionalism, the reality remains that a rigorous course of training to learn a specific body of knowledge, a hallmark of professionalism and a key to high-quality services, is not required of those employed in this field. Furthermore, although skilled caregivers have expert knowledge, this information is not their exclusive domain. Indeed, most child care teachers and providers are eager to share their expertise with their clients, that is, the parents who consume their services.

Commitment to child care quality varies greatly across states, often depending on the department of government that administers subsidized child care services. This commitment can be especially undependable if it is tied too closely to certain elected officials' presence in office. Further, state and federal payment guidelines for subsidized child care often act as a barrier to program quality and decent compensation—with reimbursement rates set at a percentage of the market rate, for example, or parent fees set at a percentage of the cost of care, rather than based on parents' ability to pay. A heavy or exclusive reliance on voucher payment systems, in particular, can easily prevent child care centers from being able to predict enrollments and income, which in turn tends to keep wages depressed.

Because increased public funding for child care over the last several years has rarely been targeted to quality improvements or increased compensation, these dollars have not resulted in better wages or lower staff turnover. In the National Child Care Staffing Study follow-up, for-profit chain centers that paid the lowest wages experienced a threefold increase in revenue from public subsidies over nine years, and revenue doubled for independent for-profit centers, the next lowest paying. By contrast, independent nonprofit centers, which pay the highest wages, experienced a 4 percent decrease in revenue from public subsidies, and church-sponsored programs received a modest 4 percent increase (Whitebook, Howes, and Phillips 1998).

IMPROVING CHILD CARE JOBS

The nation's challenge now is to create model programs to improve child care jobs without placing the burden of the cost solely on parents. Over the past decade, a few models have emerged as promising ways to address the problems of child care quality and workforce stability.

Teacher Education and Compensation Help (TEACH), an educational scholarship and compensation initiative begun in North Carolina and now operating in six other states, has led to better pay and lower turnover for center teaching staff and home providers. In North Carolina, participants receive scholarships to offset the cost of earning a North Carolina Child Care Credential or Child Development Associate (CDA) credential, completing course work toward an A.A. or B.A. degree in early childhood education, or becoming an early childhood model/ mentor teacher. Any teacher, director, or family child care provider in a regulated child care setting is eligible to apply for a scholarship. TEACH participants receive a salary increase or bonus for each contract period that they are in the program, so that each additional educational attainment is rewarded with additional compensation. The funding for TEACH comes from a variety of sources, including the state, corporate contributions, and foundation support. In 1995, 1,805 North Carolina child care workers received a TEACH scholarship.

The U.S. Army Child Development Services' Caregiver Personnel Pay Plan is a systemwide program for Army child care center staff and family child care providers that links training to increased compensation (Zellman and Johansen 1998).[3] The program has resulted in a dramatic reduction in staff turnover within Army Child Development Services. Major goals are to make early childhood staff salaries competitive with comparable professions within the military and to break the link between staff compensation and parent fees. Entry-level staff receive three salary increases over an 18-month period, linked to completion of specified training and demonstrated classroom competency. Staff with CDA credentials or associate's or bachelor's degrees can also increase their compensation by taking advanced training. They now receive regular cost-of-living increases commensurate with those received by all federal employees (Bellm et al. 1997). The Army has also begun to reward family child care providers with a quality care subsidy in recognition of completing a CDA credential or associate's or bachelor's degree. Training is free. Parent fees are set as a percentage of family income, with the Army providing the difference between the cost of care and the price charged to families.

The Head Start Expansion and Quality Improvement Act of 1990 (reauthorized in 1994), devoted 25 percent of all new funds to the improvement of services, with half of those funds to increasing personnel compensation. The 1998 reauthorization allocates nearly $90 million for salary improvements. From 1991 through 1994, $470 million in salary increases raised average employee salaries by about $1500 per year. Actual staff compensation plans varied widely depending on local discretion in how to distribute the funds and/or develop new salary schedules. Some programs rewarded training, tenure, a combination of both, or some other valued staff characteristic (Whitebook and Gaidurgis 1995). In 1994, after two years of salary improvements, entry-level teachers still earned only $14,350 per year on average, and those with at least six years of experience, many with college degrees, earned an average of only $17,883 per year (Bellm et al. 1997; Whitebook and Gaidurgis 1995). The pending increases could improve wages substantially in this sector, but they may also attract teachers from other child care programs.

Mentoring programs that train and reward experienced teachers are encouraging them to remain in the field by helping them learn to share their skills with others and grow in the profession. By creating a new step on the child care career ladder that is rewarded with improved compensation, by addressing a serious shortage of on-the-job child care training, and by emphasizing excellence in daily practice, mentoring programs have been instrumental in stemming staff turnover and enhancing program quality. Mentoring also offers novice caregivers (often called protégés) a practical and supportive way to learn and to overcome the hurdles of the critical first years on the job (Whitebook, Hnatiuk, and Bellm 1994). The programs described next also have made important strides in rewarding mentors financially.[4] They are all local or state-level initiatives financed by private foundations, local government, and increasingly by federal Child Care Development Block Grants.

The California Early Childhood Mentor Program has successfully been rewarding teachers' increased skills and training with higher compensation since it was cofounded as a pilot program by the Center for the Child Care Workforce and Chabot College in Hayward in 1988. Now operating at 68 community college sites statewide, it is the largest program of its type in the country. Teachers who complete a mentor-training course can apply to become mentors and then earn a stipend on a per student basis (at an average of $1000 per year) for using their classroom to train student teachers, helping students to link child development theory with on-the-job, high-quality practice. Mentors also receive an annual $500 in-service training stipend, as well as ongoing training and support to enhance their own professional development and their efforts to upgrade the quality of services in the community.

The Minnesota Child Care Apprentice/Mentor Program combines training, support services, wage subsidies, and job placement to help low-income women find decent-paying child care jobs. Apprentices work one-on-one with mentors at a child care center for two years, receive a 90 percent tuition reimbursement for 30 college credits toward a certificate in early childhood education, and become qualified as head teachers under Minnesota licensing guidelines. The college credits articulate with two-year community college degree programs and the four-year community psychology degree available from Minnesota State University. Participating centers are required to meet certain wage goals, and apprentices have averaged about $2000 in wage increases over the two years.

The Milwaukee Early Childhood Mentor Program selects qualified caregivers in child care centers and family child care homes who then enroll in a two-credit seminar to prepare for a new mentoring role. Mentors and protégés are matched and enroll in a three-credit course that structures and enhances their one-on-one work. Once center-based mentors and protégés have completed the program, their directors are required to increase their wages, and family child care providers are encouraged to raise their rates. The Wisconsin Department of Workforce Development now funds the program, which has been expanded to five counties, with priority for participation going to welfare recipients in work experience or community service programs. Retention grants and salary supplements, also piloted in Wisconsin and in selected counties of New York and North Carolina, focus on rewarding and retaining already trained teachers and providers.

The Wisconsin Quality Improvement Grants Program helps centers and family child care providers boost the quality of care through staff training and retention strategies. The initiative supports child care programs that seek to improve quality by undergoing accreditation, promoting teacher training, and raising compensation. Programs must certify to the state that they have a plan to improve compensation and reduce turnover. Between 1992 and 1996, 340 centers and 133 family child care providers participated in the program; of these, 31 percent of the centers and 43 percent of the family child care providers have become accredited. Once programs meet a certain level of quality, as measured by accreditation, they can reapply indefinitely to receive staff retention grants to augment salaries.

Legislation introduced in California (and to be reintroduced in 1999) would create Compensation and Recognition Enhances Stability (CARES). It comprises two components: the Child Development Corps and Resources for Retention. The Child Development Corps would include family child care providers and center-based staff who meet certain education and training qualifications, commit to continuing their professional development for at least 21 hours per year, and agree to provide child care services for a specified period of time. Members of the corps would receive monetary rewards ranging from $500 to $6500 per year, depending on their education, background, and bilingual skills. Resources for Retention would provide additional support to public and private child care programs by providing differential reimbursement rates and Quality Improvement Rewards to assist them in achieving accreditation, improving staff retention, and making progress toward meeting state-recommended compensation guidelines (Burton and Whitebook 1998).

Modest, new efforts at organization are under way and have stimulated many of the efforts previously described. Since 1991, the Worthy Wage Campaign, coordinated nationally by the Center for the Child Care Workforce, has raised awareness of the dilemmas facing the workforce through public education. At the local community level, the Worthy Wage Campaign serves as a fledgling organizational home for child care teachers and providers. The Center for the Child Care Workforce also conducts research and engages in public policy efforts at the federal, state, and local levels to improve child care jobs. A membership organization committed to building the voice of teachers and providers through leadership training, the capacity of the Center for the Child Care Workforce to represent child care workers continues to grow, but the organization has limited resources. Model work standards and compensation guidelines developed by the center are helping to galvanize and focus local community efforts (Burton and Whitebook 1998; Center for the Child Care Workforce 1998a).

Union-organizing drives in Seattle and Philadelphia reflect creative approaches to the challenges of organizing in high-turnover, small-shop occupations. Although nascent, these drives are attempting to create an industrywide contract and an employer association to facilitate organizing and to minimize adversarial tensions between employers and workers in settings with limited resources. Both drives recognize the need for a third-party payer to truly address the quality of child care employment and are involved in legislation initiatives to get more resources targeted to child care jobs.

CONCLUSION

The American child care system suffers basic structural failure, in which caregivers' wages are almost always based directly on what parents pay for these labor-intensive services. The result is high consumer costs combined with poverty-level earnings for a workforce that is 98 percent female and one-third women of color. In effect, our nation has adopted a child care policy that relies on an unacknowledged subsidy: the contribution that child care workers make by being paid much less than the value of their skilled and vital work. Particularly in low-income communities, where child care is a major service need and a major employment option for women, the dilemmas of low compensation and inconsistent child care quality are two of the major factors that make the cycle of poverty so persistent.

Notes

1. In this article, I focus primarily on caregivers working within a publicly regulated system, and I use the terms "child care jobs" and "child care workforce" as broadly as possible. This diverse workforce includes center-based teachers and assistants in public and private, nonprofit and for-profit, full-day and part-day programs; family child care providers, both licensed and unlicensed, who care for groups of children in their own homes; Head Start program employees; teachers and assistants in school-based prekindergarten programs; staff of before- and after-school care programs serving school-age children; and a wide range of unregulated caregivers, typically working in private homes.

2. In California, for example, recent class-size reduction in the early primary grades has greatly increased opportunities for well-trained child care teachers and family child care providers to obtain better-paying elementary teacher jobs. In the fall of 1998, Congress passed a similar size-reduction policy nationwide.

3. Each branch of the military has its own system.

4. See also Stahr-Breunig and Bellm, 1996 for an in-depth survey of 19 mentoring programs across the United States.

References

Bellm, Dan, Alice Burton, Renu Shukla, and Marcy Whitebook. 1997. *Making Work Pay in the Child Care Industry.* Washington, DC: Center for the Child Care Workforce.

Bloom, Dan. 1997. *After AFDC Welfare-to-Work Choices and Challenges for States.* New York and San Francisco: Manpower Demonstration Research.

Burton, Alice and Marcy Whitebook. 1998. *Child Care Staff Compensation Guidelines for California, 1998.* Washington, DC: Center for the Child Care Workforce.

Burton, Alice, Marcy Whitebook, Laura Sakai, Mary Babula, and Peggy Haack. 1995. *Valuable Work, Minimal Rewards: A Report on the Wisconsin Child Care Workforce.* Washington, DC: Center for the Child Care Workforce; Madison: Wisconsin Early Childhood Association.

Center for the Child Care Workforce. 1995a. *A Profile of the Alameda County, California Child Care Center Workforce*. Washington, DC: Center for the Child Care Workforce.

———. 1995b. *A Profile of the Alexandria, Virginia Child Care Workforce*. Washington, DC: Center for the Child Care Workforce.

———. 1995c. *A Profile of the Child Care Workforce in Los Angeles County, California*. Washington, DC: Center for the Child Care Workforce.

———. 1998a. *Creating Better Child Care Jobs: Model Work Standards for Teaching Staff in Center-Based Child Care*. Washington, DC: Center for the Child Care Workforce.

———. 1998b. *State Initiative to Train TANF Recipients for Child Care Employment*. Washington, DC: Center for the Child Care Workforce.

Child Care Law Center. 1995. *Seeds of Opportunity: Final Report on the San Francisco Unified School District Child Development Program*. San Francisco: Child Care Law Center.

Current Data on Child Care Salaries and Benefits in the United States. 1998. Washington, DC: Center for the Child Care Workforce.

Ginsburg, Paul B., Jan R. Gabel, and Kelly A. Hunt. 1998. Tracking Small-Firm Coverage, 1989-1996. *Health Affairs* 17(1):167-71.

Helburn, Suzanne W., ed. 1995. *Cost, Quality and Child Outcomes in Child Care Centers: Technical Report*. Denver: University of Colorado, Department of Economics, Center for Research in Economic and Social Policy.

Helburn, Suzanne W. and Carollee Howes. 1996. Child Care Cost and Quality. *The Future of Children* 6(2):62-82.

Kontos, Susan, Carollee Howes, Marybeth Shinn, and Ellen Galinsky. 1995. *Quality in Family Child Care and Relative Care*. New York: Teachers College Press.

Mishel, Laurence and John Schmitt. 1996. Cutting Wages by Cutting Welfare: The Impact of Reform on Low-Wage Labor Market. Economic Policy Institute, Washington, DC. Briefing paper.

National Black Child Development Institute. 1993. *Paths to African American Leadership Positions in Early Childhood Education: Constraints and Opportunities*. Washington, DC: National Black Child Development Institute.

Stahr-Breunig, Gretchen and Dan Bellm. 1996. *Early Childhood Mentoring Programs: A Survey of Community Initiatives*. Washington, DC: Center for the Child Care Workforce.

Weisbrot, Mark. 1997. *Welfare Reform: The Jobs Aren't There*. Washington, DC: Preamble Center for Public Policy.

Whitebook, Marcy. 1997. Who's Missing at the Table? Leadership Opportunities and Barriers for Teachers and Providers. In *Leadership in Early Care and Education*, ed. S. L. Kogan and B. T. Bowman. Washington, DC: National Association for the Education of Young Children.

Whitebook, Marcy and Dan Bellm. 1998. *Taking on Turnover: An Action Guide for Child Care Center Teachers and Directors*. Washington, DC: Center for the Child Care Workforce.

Whitebook, Marcy and Alice Burton. 1996. *California Child Care and Development Compensation Study: Toward Promising Policy and Practice*. Palo Alto, CA: American Institute for Research.

Whitebook, Marcy and Andrew Gaidurgis. 1995. *Salary Improvements in Head Start*. Washington, DC: Center for the Child Care Workforce.

Whitebook, Marcy, Patty Hnatiuk, and Dan Bellm. 1994. *Mentoring in Early Care and Education: Refining an*

Emerging Career Path. Washington, DC: Center for the Child Care Workforce.

Whitebook, Marcy, Carollee Howes, and Deborah Phillips. 1990. *Who Cares? Child Care Teachers and the Quality of Care in America: Final Report*. Washington, DC: Center for the Child Care Workforce.

———. 1993. *Four Years in the Life of Center-Based Child Care: National Child Care Staffing Study*. Washington, DC: Center for the Child Care Workforce.

———. 1998. *Worthy Work, Unlivable Wages: The National Child Care Staffing Study, 1998*. Washington, DC: Center for the Child Care Workforce.

Willer, Barbara, ed. 1990. *Reaching the Full Cost of Quality in Early Childhood Programs*. Washington, DC: National Association for the Education of Young Children.

Wilson, Pete. 1998. Veto Message to the Legislature, Sacramento, CA, 24 Sept.

Zellman, G. and A. Johansen. 1998. *Examining the Implementation and Outcomes of the Military Child Care Act of 1989*. Santa Monica, CA: Rand.

ANNALS, *AAPSS*, **563**, May 1999

Hiring a Nanny: The Limits of Private Solutions to Public Problems

By JULIA WRIGLEY

ABSTRACT: Dual-career couples in urban areas commonly rely upon nannies or housekeepers to allow them to flexibly combine work and family lives. Highly personalized services allow parents to manage competing demands. Such forms of child care also contain their own tensions and dilemmas, though, in part because they are based on profound social inequality between parents and caregivers. Based on 155 in-depth, tape-recorded interviews with parents and caregivers in the New York and Los Angeles metropolitan areas, dilemmas arising between even parents with egalitarian ideologies and caregivers are analyzed. One dilemma concerns the parents' authority over the caregiver. Parents may want to let the caregiver exercise her own authority and judgment; yet, to the extent that there are class differences between caregivers and parents, there are likely to also be different definitions of quality child care. The second dilemma arises from parents' and caregivers' efforts to maintain some social distance while still wanting commitments that transcend employment obligations. Private forms of child care solve some problems but have limits that must be considered in assessing social policy options.

Julia Wrigley is a professor in the Ph.D. Program in Sociology at the City University of New York Graduate Center, where she also serves as the program's executive officer. Her work focuses on class relationships on the political and micro levels. She is the author of Class Politics and Public Schools *and* Other People's Children, *a study of relationships between middle-class parents and the women they hire to help raise their children. She edited* Sociology of Education *from 1991 to 1994.*

NOTE: This article is based on research that is more fully reported in the author's book *Other People's Children: An Intimate Account of the Dilemmas Facing Middle-Class Parents and the Women They Hire to Raise Their Children* (New York: Basic Books, 1995).

AT first sight, hiring a nanny or housekeeper seems the ideal way to go for hard-pressed professionally employed parents with demanding careers. Housekeepers provide the only form of child care that serves both the parents and the child. When parents rely on center care or take their children to family day care providers, they must do auxiliary labor—dressing and feeding the child and driving to the center or the provider's home—while preparing themselves for the workday. The return pickup is even worse. They must scramble to the child care center or provider's house, often tangling with rush hour traffic. Then they pick up a tired child, drive home, and cook dinner. The normal routine is exhausting enough, but it can completely unravel when any type of crisis or disruption occurs, such as a child's illness, a pressing deadline, or an important late-afternoon meeting.

No wonder housekeepers seem to provide ideal solutions. They can look after the children and, in the interstices of their day, do some housecleaning. They might not cook dinner for the parents, but most will make and serve meals for children. In a pinch, most will stay late. Those who live in the parents' home usually expect to work extra hours when needed. If parents need to travel, as many professional jobs require, caregivers can often step into the breach. For the many parents who operate in unforgiving work worlds, caregivers can provide flexible and highly personalized services that allow parents to manage competing demands.

Yet caregiving arrangements contain their own tensions and dilemmas, in part because they are based on profound inequality between parents and caregivers. Middle- or upper-middle-class parents hire women, often recent immigrants from Mexico, Central America, or the Caribbean, who are struggling to get a first foothold on the American job ladder. This inequality structures relationships that inevitably are far removed from the egalitarian ideals commonly found on university campuses and among women who hold feminist views. Whatever their individual personalities or ideologies, when parents hire caregivers, they become employers, and not just any employers. They hire, supervise, and pay women who are their direct social subordinates and who work, and sometimes live, in their (the parents') homes. I will explore some of the complexities created by unequal employment relationships in the home, with the larger purpose of suggesting the limits of private solutions to child care problems.

This article is based on information collected for a larger project on cross-class socialization of children. For that project, I conducted 155 in-depth, tape-recorded interviews with parents and caregivers in the Los Angeles and New York metropolitan areas. In each city, interviews were concentrated in two neighborhoods. Because the study explored the implications of educational differences between parents and caregivers, I also interviewed a professional cluster of doctors, lawyers, and professors. Parents and caregivers were found through social networks and snowball samples. Caregivers were interviewed in parks in the relevant neighborhoods and were found through immigrant service agencies. Many of the interviews with caregivers were conducted in Spanish. In some cases, parents and caregivers in the same relationship were interviewed; in all cases, they were interviewed separately.

Those in the neighborhood samples came from a wide variety of middle- and upper-class occupations. Here I focus on those parents who operate in a specifically intellectual, cultural, or social service milieu and exclude those strongly tied to the corporate sector, such as lawyers, financial specialists, or businesspeople. Cultural specialists include parents who work as freelance writers, artists, clinical psychologists, or researchers.[1]

As with other long-standing and intimate relationships, many caregivers and parents become genuinely attached to each other. Caregivers often speak of loving the children in their charge as if they were their own, and parents speak of their children's affection for their caregivers. Despite such positive circumstances, two dilemmas often arise even when parents have egalitarian ideologies. Their ideologies, in fact, can intensify the dilemmas. One concerns the parents' authority over the caregiver. Parents may want to let the caregiver exercise her own authority and judgment; yet, to the extent that there are class differences between caregivers and parents, there are likely to also be different definitions of quality child care. The second dilemma arises from parents' and caregivers' efforts to maintain some social distance while still wanting commitments that transcend employment obligations. These dilemmas cannot easily be overcome because they arise from the structure of caregiving relationships and the personal subordination that they entail.

PARENTS AS EMPLOYERS:
THE EXERCISE OF
AUTHORITY IN THE HOME

Parents hire caregivers partly because they want control over their children's experiences and treatment. They recognize that they might not be able to influence a child care center or a family day care provider. They expect, however, to have their wishes and child-rearing values respected when they hire a caregiver. After all, the caregiver works for them. She presumably will accept the basic child-rearing framework they create.

The reality turns out to be more complex. People are not automatons, and they have their own values. This is particularly true when it comes to child rearing. Many caregivers have raised their own children. They do not just have abstract ideas about child rearing, but they have put their own ideas into practice. If they are asked to accept a radically different child-rearing style, they can only compare it with what they did. Interviews show that caregivers often invidiously compare the parents' style with that common in their own social milieu. This is true for young women who have not yet had children as well as those who have raised their own.

Parents and caregivers often come from different worlds, and many social forces reinforce initial value differences. While there is much individual variation in child-rearing styles, sociologists have observed general patterns. People's jobs and educational levels affect their child-rearing values. Those with more education and with complex and demanding jobs tend to stress children's autonomy, while those with lower levels of education and jobs where they take others' orders emphasize children's conformity to adult directives (Kohn 1977; Alwin 1989). Highly educated parents rely more on experts who generally espouse a developmental philosophy, where children are seen as unfolding beings who need to explore and express themselves.

When middle-class, highly educated parents hire caregivers from Mexico, Central America, or the Caribbean, they often set the stage for a cultural clash. Many parents do not experience it as a clash, but this is partly because caregivers do not tell them what they actually think about children's care. They suppress their own child-rearing values. They recognize that, if they are to work in private homes, they must suppress these values. Many caregivers reported that they did not agree with how the parents raised their children. Even when they were fond of the children, they often saw them as spoiled and overly free with both their parents and the caregivers.

Caregivers were seldom critical of very young children but tended to become more distressed by older children's behavior. Many caregivers take childish rudeness seriously, as they see the children gradually coming to awareness of the caregivers' subordinate status and then reflecting this in rude or commanding remarks.

Because children's care involves thousands of tiny daily interactions, parents cannot give global orders to cover all situations. They have to rely on caregivers' initiative, judgment, and motivation; that is, they need to depend on caregivers as whole human beings who are engaged with their tasks and who have an emotional investment in their charges. Caregivers need some level of authority. Yet, if the caregivers have different child-rearing values from those of the parents, they may not use their authority to act as the parents wish. When and if parents become aware of value differences, it can lead them to a more directive stance that places them in the role of dominating a personal subordinate. Parents who may value cultural differences in the abstract can find they have rather different views when those cultural differences affect the socialization and daily experiences of their own children. If they value their children's autonomy and free expression, this may lead them to limit the autonomy of the adult who looks after those children.

When parents assert their authority over caregivers, it means their children grow up witnessing their parents' domination of the women who provide their care. The social inequality in the household also means that it can be hard to discern employees' true emotions. Caregivers have no job security. Children's affection for them can be their best safeguard. Many caregivers genuinely come to love the children in their charge: instrumental objectives and genuine emotions can become entangled in ways that are hard to unravel. Caregivers cannot hide themselves behind a veneer of professionalism. They are selling their capacity to feel as well as their capacity to work. They need to retain the children's affection and the parents' trust, tasks that can involve the caregivers in much tiring and potentially stressful "emotion work," in Arlie Hochschild's phrase (1983).

The complicated situation of a Los Angeles couple who hired two caregivers from Guatemala illustrates some of the tensions that can arise over issues of authority and values, each within the framework of a basically positive relationship. The mother, a physical therapist, and the father, a film editor, live in a middle-class neighborhood where skyrocketing house prices have turned what had once been a blue-collar area into a neighborhood of half-million-dollar, expensively remodeled homes. The parents did not grow up with domestic workers and were initially uneasy about becoming employers. Interviewed when their two sons were 5 and 2 years old, they had first hired a caregiver when the older child was a baby. They chose a Guatemalan immigrant, Elena, who reached for the baby and who was "not dogmatic" about the tasks she would do in the house.

The parents remained basically happy with Elena's work for several years, although the mother did not feel she had much control over Elena's daily schedule. The situation took a turn for the worse when the parents hired a second caregiver, also a Guatemalan woman, to cover a day when Elena had other work. Elena had recommended the second caregiver and had a family connection to her but soon became hostile to her. Interviews show that this is not uncommon; caregivers often distrust others who work in the household, afraid they might speak against them or supplant them in the children's affections. Elena's situation deteriorated. The second caregiver, Lydia, became the children's favorite. She also shook the parents' trust in Elena by telling them that Elena had disciplined one of the boys by locking him in a garage and turning out the lights.

The mother confronted Elena about how she had treated the boy, and Elena did not deny the basic charge. The mother recounted the exchange:

She said that she felt that I needed help with disciplining my children. We discussed it and I told her that I never wanted that to happen again and she said it wouldn't. But it changed my feelings toward her because I never thought that she would do anything like that. And I die if I think about it. I had trusted this woman implicitly with my children, and having heard that and knowing that had happened, I could never really [trust her again].

The mother had thought the caregiver shared her child-rearing values, but the garage incident made her aware that Elena did not. She began thinking about other issues that disturbed her. Elena shamed the older boy when he cried, telling him that only girls cried. "It was a cultural thing and she would never, ever change that." With her trust in the caregiver broken, the mother also began to see Elena as trying to manipulate her sons' emotions. She commented that when Elena left the house, she often created theatrical departures where the children would end up being upset. She believed Elena did this to show how much the children loved her.

When the two caregivers continued to have conflicts, the employers fired Elena. The mother was more comfortable with Lydia, but basic issues of authority and values remained. Lydia had to struggle to understand the parents' child-rearing practices. A 43-year-old woman with a fourth-grade education, she had been impoverished in Guatemala. Married at 14, by 23 she had six children (although one died). The decision to leave her children and seek work in the United States had been very painful. She liked her employers and considered herself lucky, but she found it strange that the boys in her charge had no household obligations. She had raised her own children to pitch in from an early age, as a matter of necessity. Lydia was also sometimes disturbed by the children's tendency to order her around, but she felt it would be unwise to try to protest. She had triumphed in the battle of the caregivers partly because the children liked her better than Elena. She had seen at close hand how important it was to retain the children's affection. She took an essentially passive attitude toward the older child:

I don't try to stop him from doing things, because that's the way his parents are. Whatever he wants to do is "okay" with me. I do it, because if this is the way that they have trained him, I am not going to change it. If I tried, what could happen is that he could turn against me.

While working for this couple, Lydia had a baby with a man who was an alcoholic and sometimes beat her. Lydia's employers agreed that she and the baby could come and live with them. The employer was surprised to find that Lydia treated her own baby quite differently from how she treated the employers' children. While very attentive to them, in the way the employer wanted, Lydia trained her baby to expect less. The employer noted that Lydia did not hold the baby when she fed him.

Lydia had come from a different world, where to raise a high-demand child was to create expectations that probably could not be met. Lydia's employers, however, paid her to meet their expectations regarding their children's care, and Lydia struggled to do this. She said she watched the parents closely to see how they treated their children, and then she tried to treat them the same way. She retained reservations, even if she did not express them to the parents. She felt that because the parents let the children do as they chose, they came to believe they ruled the roost. Lydia said Latinos raised their children differently: "I have gotten used to this way because it is my job and I have to accustom myself to it. But with my own children, I do it differently."

The mother did not feel she had resolved her ambivalence about exerting her own authority as an employer. Just as Lydia knew she needed the children's affection to hold the job, so the mother's genuine liking for Lydia rested on a bedrock of self-interest. She thought if Lydia was not happy, she would not do a good job.

It's extremely difficult for me to think of myself [as an employer]. I know I'm the employer and that Elena and Lydia answer to me and that I am in charge. But for me it's extremely important to be able to get on with Lydia, for her to be happy here and for her to like it, because I don't want her to bear any grudges that ultimately she is going to take out on my children. It's important to me that she's happy and content here so that she's able to reflect that to them.

The desire to maintain Lydia's goodwill limited the employer's willingness to exert her authority, yet she had also come to believe that it was her responsibility to her children to do so. The situation was complex, because enforcing standards that were not the caregiver's own could lead to treating Lydia as a servant rather than as a person with independent judgment and ideas. The unequal authority relations could also reinforce her sons' tendency to treat Lydia as subservient. Lydia complained in my interview with her that if she tried to get the children to help her clean up, they told her it was her job. She worried that as the children in her charge got older, they would become more imperious. The mother disapproved of her sons' ordering Lydia around and felt it was another reason why she should not act as a "dictator" toward Lydia.

This mother was unusually open about the difficulties and conflicts of being an employer. Her basically egalitarian ideology made it harder for her to settle into the role than it was for some other employers, but the ambivalence she expressed and the tensions she experienced were not unique to her. She wanted to respect the caregiver yet have the children raised as she wished, a dilemma many others confront in one form or another. Some parents try to resolve this by systematically instructing caregivers how they want their children treated. Others have less sense that there is one right way to raise a child. These parents are more willing to grant the caregiver authority, but they often work hard to reinforce middle-class values in other ways. They enroll the child in preschool, with trained teachers who accept a developmental philosophy. They sign the child up for the organized, adult-directed activities that have become so pervasive for middle-class children. In today's America, the schedules of such children can be nearly as frenetic as those of their parents. The parents create a de facto division of labor in the house such that they take on the activities most infused with a specific cultural content. They read to the children or discuss issues with them, while leaving the caregiver more routine tasks. The caregiver may have authority but in a narrow sphere.

These arrangements can work out well but for a limited time. As children get older, they move more decisively into the cultural sphere of their parents and become more distant from their caregivers. This reduces the caregivers' emotional leverage. The caregivers can find this painful. They do not have the parents' satisfaction of seeing the children entering the larger world they also inhabit. Instead, they see the children leaving the private world they have shared and, often, coming to a fuller realization of the caregivers' subordinate status. Caregivers of much lower social class level than parents often have great trouble establishing authority in households, and even those who can do so anticipate that their authority will diminish over time.

THE UNCERTAIN BOUNDARIES
OF CAREGIVING ARRANGEMENTS

The inherent instability of caregiving jobs intensifies a second type of dilemma. Caregivers and parents have minimal formal obligations to each other, but caregiving arrangements can entail high levels of dependency. On the caregivers' side, this dependency can have both economic and emotional aspects. Employers can benefit from a caregiver's emotional investment in their family but can also discover the downside of having a dependent. For their part, caregivers may build their worlds around their employers, but then can find themselves without work and without accumulated resources. As with growing numbers of workers in the United States, caregivers can work full-time (in fact, usually more than full-time) and still not earn enough to support a family. Their low pay and lack of job security make them vulnerable, and it is not surprising that in crises they turn to their employers, with their greater resources and know-how.

Most employer-employee relationships are marked by a certain amount of social distance. Caregiving relationships involve greater complexity, though, because they combine daily household intimacy with enormous class differences between employers and employees. It can be hard for both parents and caregivers to adapt to the contradictory pressures for distance and for emotional investment. Parents want caregivers to invest emotionally in their children. They also want to be able to call on caregivers for special help if the employers face crises at work or if they have to travel or if children are sick. The parents expect flexibility and loyalty from caregivers. They want caregivers to transcend specific obligations and to recognize a more global obligation when circumstances require it. For their part, caregivers also hope employers will recognize an obligation to them that transcends the specific terms of their employment relation.

In re-creating a form of employment relation that was on the decline in modern societies, that between employer and employee in the private household, parents can acquire a dependent, with all that that entails. Employers can find themselves serving as informal lending agencies. Caregivers sometimes see employers' granting favors as a way of exerting psychological leverage over them. For their part, employers can come to see their employees as ungrateful. One employer, a teaching psychologist in Los Angeles, commented about a Mexican immigrant who looked after her two daughters, "She'd always had a little bit of an attitude problem in terms of her work, feeling like everything was due her. I really felt like I was very good to her. I did a lot of extra things for her . . . I was servicing her." The employer had helped her to get amnesty, had arranged a bridal shower for her, and had helped her get a Social Security card. When the employee did not manifest her gratitude by showing up for work on time, the employer felt she had been burned.

Most employers are willing to lend money, up to a point, but have more trouble responding to difficulties in caregivers' family lives. Those who become entangled in caregivers' problems sometimes see themselves entering an emotional sinkhole. Not all caregivers bring problems to employers. Many do not want to discuss their personal lives, afraid of interference or just wanting to maintain their privacy. Some do, however, and employers can then find it difficult to reestablish social distance. Employers hire caregivers to ease their own lives. Few want to deal with another person's problems. This is particularly the case when the class gulf between caregivers and parents is large and caregivers' problems can seem disturbing or even frightening. When parents hire class peers (such as au pairs, young women from Western Europe) to look after their children, they may have to hear about their problems with boyfriends, but the au pairs seldom bring the parents face to face with the hardships experienced by America's poor.

Caregivers are skilled at crossing social boundaries. If they were not, they could not do their jobs. They are often affiliated with people, however, who do not see a need to develop or display these skills. Employers may not like caregivers' husbands or boyfriends and may feel class gulfs more strikingly with them. In part, this may reflect prejudice. Lower-class men can be seen as threatening by middle-class employers. It may also reflect the reality that caregivers' lives can be very harsh, living on the economic margin as they and those close to them do, and abusive conditions may not be uncommon.

Some employers accept caregivers' social lives and the entanglements they may create. One Los Angeles professor agreed that the caregiver's boyfriend could move in with them. He was, the professor said, a "jerk, but Carmen's jerk." Another employer energetically helped her much-appreciated Barbadian caregiver when her husband remarried without divorcing her first. A Los Angeles employing couple lent their caregiver $200 when she got married and also lent the husband-to-be a suit for the wedding (despite a history of alcoholism and abuse on his part).

The United States is a modern, not a traditional, society. Caregiving arrangements reflect uneasy blends of modern and traditional characteristics. In a traditional society, servants offer employers loyalty and deference, and they often have to forgo personal lives. In exchange, they could expect a certain amount of security. In modern-day America, domestic workers such as caregivers have much more freedom and autonomy than servants of old. They also, however, work for just one employer, with the dependency this implies, and do not receive the security that servants used to be able to claim. Employers accept a certain amount of responsibility for employees, but they try to limit employee dependence upon them. If employees become too dependent, employers often fire them. Very few accept any long-term responsibility for an employee, yet the employees are outside the framework of institutional provision.

When interviewing older caregivers, those in their fifties or sixties, the full meaning of the caregivers' insecurity strikes home. Their jobs entail turnover, as most families want caregivers only while their children are young. It can be harder and harder to start over with new families as caregivers get older. Starting again can mean moving backward in pay and working conditions, and it also means caregivers once again have to learn a new family's ways and create new relationships. It is not surprising that caregivers find this daunting. Caregivers, with no pension plans (and, generally, no participation in Social Security), cannot look forward to easy retirements but, rather, to vistas of new families and new starts. While dependency is increasingly dealt with on an institutional basis in modern societies, this does not extend to private caregiving relationships. Parents can receive customized care for their children because of the growth of a low-wage labor pool (Sassen 1994).

THE LIMITS OF PRIVATE SOLUTIONS

Some employer-caregiver relationships work out well and can enable parents to combine family lives and jobs. They turn the clock back, though, to earlier forms of dependency and social subordination. Caregiving relationships can lead backward in another sense. They enable parents to accommodate to negative conditions, rather than leading parents to challenge those conditions. Specifically, caregiving arrangements allow gender relations in the employers' households to continue more or less undisturbed. They also allow the parents' workplaces to maintain unreasonable demands that are geared to male careers carried on with disregard for children or family life.

As middle-class mothers have gone to work, many have fought gender inequality. They would like to restructure both their households and their workplaces. Most have run up against a wall on both fronts (South and Spitze 1994; Presser 1994). Men have proved resistant to taking on household tasks and child care. Many husbands point to their careers as reasons for not doing more. That men's careers are still often accorded priority in two-career families emerged in interview after interview. Time and again mothers discussed how they cut back their hours when their children were born. In describing their families' daily schedules, they often said they left for work later than their husbands and returned earlier. Some essentially put their careers on hold when their children were infants. A Los Angeles law professor, married to another law professor, described how she had taken an "inferior," low-status job at a law school. There was little pressure to publish, which suited her because it allowed her time with her children. Only when her children got older did she seriously start publishing, and only then did she get a tenure-track teaching job. Her husband, although helpful with the couple's three children, never went off track as she had.

When parents hire caregivers, they often implicitly see the caregiver as substituting for the mother. Mothers sometimes describe their guilt at having caregivers do what they think they should be doing. Sometimes they feel conflicted both about leaving work and about leaving home. Because the caregiver is seen as the mother's replacement, the mother usually takes the leading role in hiring and supervising her. This can be a very time-consuming proposition. The law professor previously described said she did the hiring and firing: "It was exhausting. Yea, it was always me and that part was exhausting. A lot of mental energy goes into making a decision like that." Commonly, mothers would screen candidates and bring fathers in for the final set of interviews.

When caregivers are hired, their presence can alter family dynamics. Mothers do most of the sensitive work of making the required adjustments and communicating with the caregivers. Often, caregivers speak quite well of the employing fathers, impressed that they do more household work than the men in their own lives, but they are also often intimidated by them. Seldom do they make any demands on these men. Basically, the employing fathers can go about their lives with some reasonable confidence that, even if their wives are not doing the daily housework and child care, another woman is. If the caregiver does not work out, generally they can count on their wives to replace her with another candidate. They may have to engage in some minimal interaction, but no more than they feel comfortable with and not enough to deflect them from their work lives.

The disparity between men's and women's work lives emerged more strongly in my interviews with doctors and lawyers than in my interviews with professors and cultural workers. Many women lawyers and doctors are married to men in the same professions. It is striking that, despite this formal similarity in their lives, the women's jobs were downgraded within the family. Often the test is who stays home when the caregiver does not show up or is late. The sample included two sets of female surgeons married to male surgeons. The women used almost exactly the same words to describe what happened when the caregiver did not show up: the men said, "Oh, how terrible," and then walked out the door. Nothing, the women said, would stop them from being on time for surgery.

The women faced the same truly compelling constraints but lacked the psychic freedom simply to declare their jobs the top priority. These women tried to solve the problem by investing great energy in finding backup arrangements. Their experiences left them with no illusions about the relative status of their work lives compared to those of their husbands.

Professors and cultural workers often have more flexible schedules, and this does seem to foster greater male participation in child rearing. Inequalities remain strong and widespread, though, with women basically struggling to replace themselves on the household front. Caregivers take on a sufficient range of tasks that husbands and wives do not have to fully confront the gender inequalities that remain. Similarly, when caregivers adapt to parents' work schedules, the parents' employers do not have to face a challenge to their time-honored ways of structuring their employees' days and careers. Caregivers add enough social fluidity to households to limit pressure for gender equality and for work restructuring.

Children learn from what they see around them as well as from what they are taught. What those raised by caregivers see is a division of family labor that runs along lines of class and gender. They see who does which work, and which work is most valued. The households come to mirror larger social inequalities, as those with few employment options offer parents the customized services they have the money to buy. These relationships have their good qualities

and can be deeply meaningful to participants, but in a broader sense they reinforce rather than undermine social inequalities.

Today there is little broad pressure for group child care. Although this was one of the earliest demands of the second wave of American feminism, it has slipped into the background. Women do not stand united on this demand, in part because those with the most power and social influence often choose another form of care. Group care becomes irrelevant to them. They can accommodate even nursery schools that close their doors in the early afternoon, because caregivers pick up their children.

While caregivers are pleased to have the work, and it is of tremendous importance in their lives, they earn low wages and have no job security. Workers in child care centers also earn low wages, but they also operate with more autonomy and there is some potential for their collective organization. An adequate child care policy should, at a minimum, entail a commitment to pay workers decent wages for the socially important work they do. To the extent that families rely on in-home caregivers, pressure for such changes is reduced. More broadly, a move toward a system of good child care requires recognition that private child care solutions cannot solve social problems.

Note

1. I omit doctors and architects, on the grounds that they occupy a middle ground between those in the corporate and intellectual/cultural sectors (for discussion on this point, see Lamont 1992).

References

Alwin, Duane F. 1989. Social Stratification, Conditions of Work, and Parental Socialization Values. In *Social and Moral Values: Individual and Societal Perspectives*, ed. Nancy Eisenberg, Janusz Reykowski, and Ervin Staub. Hillsdale, NJ: Lawrence Erlbaum.

Hochschild, Arlie Russell. 1983. *The Managed Heart: Commercialization of Human Feeling*. Berkeley: University of California Press.

Kohn, Melvin. 1977. *Class and Conformity: A Study in Values*. 2d ed. Chicago: University of Chicago Press.

Lamont, Michele. 1992. *Money, Morals, and Manners: The Culture of the French and American Upper-Middle Class*. Chicago: University of Chicago Press.

Presser, Harriet B. 1994. Employment Schedules Among Dual-Earner Spouses and the Division of Household Labor by Gender. *American Sociological Review* 59:348-64.

Sassen, Saskia. 1994. *Cities in a World Economy*. Thousand Oaks, CA: Pine Forge Press.

South, Scott J. and Glenna Spitze. 1994. Housework in Marital and Nonmarital Households. *American Sociological Review* 59:327-47.

Current Trends in European Early Child Care and Education

By WOLFGANG TIETZE and DEBBY CRYER

ABSTRACT: In this article, selected quality characteristics of the early care and education (ECE) systems in 15 European Union (EU) countries are examined. To understand the systems in their respective national contexts, statistics concerning maternal employment, single-parent families, and birthrates are presented. Issues discussed for each country include the availability and affordability of ECE provisions for parents and children, the level of public support provided for in-home parental care, teacher educational requirements, and the quality of care and education experienced by children. Although several of the EU countries provide adequate services to support families with young children, there are areas that need improvement in many countries. The problems of insufficient services to meet the needs of children under 3 years of age and inadequate funding of ECE services in most of the EU countries are discussed.

Wolfgang Tietze is professor of education at the Freie Universität, Berlin. He has conducted studies on availability, costs, and quality of early care and education, family participation in child care, and children's use of television. He coordinates the European Child Care and Education Study, which examines child care in four European countries.

Debby Cryer, Ph.D., is a researcher at the Frank Porter Graham Child Development Center, University of North Carolina at Chapel Hill, and director of the child care program at the center.

NOTE: The work reported herein was partially supported under the Educational Research and Development Centers Program, PR/Award R307A60004, as administered by the Office of Educational Research and Improvement, U.S. Department of Education. However, the contents do not necessarily represent the positions or policies of the National Institute on Early Childhood Development and Education, the Office of Educational Research and Improvement, or the U.S. Department of Education. Endorsement by the U.S. federal government should not be assumed.

SYSTEMS of organized early care and education (ECE) for children have a long history in Western Europe. The social roots for these systems can be found in the nineteenth century, when child care evolved in response to conditions associated with industrialization, including urbanization, the breakup of traditional family structures, and the entrance of mothers into the industrial workforce. During this time, two types of center-based programs were developed to serve different social classes. Care-oriented, primarily full-time asylum-type programs were established to satisfy the physical and socialization needs of working-class children in difficult family situations. Part-time educationally oriented programs were established for the middle classes for whom education was regarded as an essential step toward securing social status. The focus of the part-time programs was on enriching and complementing children's experiences through planned learning activities.

Many aspects of these two types of programs can still be found in present-day Western European early care and education. Distinctions between types of programs continue, with the more custodial programs, usually offering services to children under 3 years, providing full-time care, having administrative affiliations with health and welfare agencies, offering spaces to families on a limited, prioritized basis, and charging fees. This is in contrast to the more educationally oriented programs for older preschoolers, which are more often part-time, administratively affiliated with educational

agencies, universally available to all children, and free for those who wish to use them.

Although ECE systems in the European countries still vary in many characteristics due to differing national traditions, there is a strong convergence in thinking among both professionals and the public within the European countries that is based on a more comprehensive awareness of children's and parents' current needs. It is now generally recognized that ECE programs should provide the fundamental requirements for children's personal care, health and safety, socialization, and education in an integrated manner and that those services should be available to support family life, at an affordable cost for all parents who need and want them (Council Recommendation 1992). ECE systems meeting those requirements are considered to be high-quality systems.

The purpose of this article is to examine some selected quality characteristics of the ECE systems in European countries. To better understand the systems in their respective national societal contexts, some statistics concerning maternal employment, single-parent families, and birthrates will be presented. The following issues will be addressed:

— the availability and affordability of ECE provisions for parents and children as the users of the system;
— public support for in-home parental care; and
— the quality of teachers' educational requirements and of the care and education that children experience.

The article will conclude by identifying selected areas of weakness that should be considered to improve the ECE systems in the European countries.

It should be noted here that this article concentrates on the ECE systems in the 15 European Union (EU) countries. This is due mainly to the availability of information on the EU countries, especially from the work of the European Commission Network on Childcare and Other Measures to Reconcile Employment and Family Responsibilities completed between 1986 and 1995. Since the vast majority of ECE programs in the EU countries are publicly supported, the discussion focuses on the characteristics of these programs, rather than the less commonly found private programs that receive no public support. The article does not provide information about the former socialist countries in middle and eastern Europe. There is little consistent information available about the ECE systems in these countries, and most of the ECE systems in the former socialist countries are in a state of rapid transition, which is occurring as part of the general societal changes that have been ongoing in the recent past.

SOCIETAL CONTEXT: MATERNAL
EMPLOYMENT, SINGLE
PARENTS, AND BIRTHRATES

ECE provisions are embedded in a societal context characterized by a variety of socioeconomic, cultural, and policy-related components. As was true in nineteenth-century Europe, the need for appropriate child care provisions is still very much driven by increases in maternal employment and changing family structures, especially with regard to the increase in single-parent families. In addition, low birthrates in all European countries provide for changes in the social environments for children (that is, both siblings and children from other families are becoming rarer in neighborhoods, so planned environments where extensive peer contacts can occur are required for children's socialization and play). Some basic figures relating to these issues in the 15 EU countries are depicted in Table 1.

The employment rate of mothers with children under 10 years of age averages about 50 percent in the EU. An additional 8 percent of mothers with children in that age group are seeking employment. For mothers with children under 3 years of age, the employment rate is somewhat, but not much, lower (45 percent). Two countries, Germany and the United Kingdom, appear to be an exception: the difference between the employment rate of mothers with children aged 3 to 10 years and mothers with children under 3 is greater in these two countries than in the other countries.

Maternal employment rates in the EU countries have increased considerably in the past two decades. In the 1980s, general female employment increased on average by 1.8 percent per year (Maruani 1992). Although the employment rate of mothers in the EU who have children under the age of 10 years is 50 percent, maternal employment differs considerably between countries. At the extremes, we see maternal employment rates in Denmark, Portugal, and Sweden

TABLE 1

MATERNAL EMPLOYMENT, SINGLE-PARENT FAMILIES, AND BIRTHRATES IN EU COUNTRIES

	BE	DK	DE	EL	ES	FR	IR	IT	LX	NE	OS	PO	SU	SV	UK	EU
Employment rate of mothers with children younger than 10 years old (1993)	62	78	51	44	35	59	35	43	42	46	64	70	65	75	53	50*
Part-time employment rate of mothers with children younger than 10 years old	24	25	25	3	6	19	10	6	13	41	24	7	8	40	35	20*
Hours usually worked per week by mothers employed part-time	21	26.1	19.2	24.3	18.5	23.6	18.4	23.3	19.4	16.1	—	24.4	—	—	16.5	19.2*
Unemployment rate of mothers with children younger than 10 years old	9	10	8	7	14	11	8	6	3	5	—	5	12	7	6	8
Employment rate of mothers with children younger than 3 years old (1993)	62	70	40	40	33	52	38	42	—	45	—	69	—	—	44	45*
Percentage of single-parent families of all families (1990-91) (OS and SV:1993)	15	20	15†	6	6	11	11	6	12	12	20	9	—	19	19	—
Birthrate (1993)	1.59	1.75	1.28	1.34	1.26	1.65	1.93	1.22	1.7	1.57	1.48	1.52	1.87	1.99	1.75	1.46

SOURCE: Derived from European Commission Network on Childcare 1995a, tabs. 1, 2, 3, and 4.
NOTES: The following abbreviations are used for EU member states: BE = Belgium, DK = Denmark, DE = Germany, EL = Greece, ES = Spain, FR = France, IR = Ireland, IT = Italy, LX = Luxembourg, NE = Netherlands, OS = Austria, PO = Portugal, SU = Finland, SV = Sweden, UK = United Kingdom. EU = European Union.
*Excluding Austria, Finland, and Sweden.
†Only western Germany.

at 70 percent and above, whereas in Ireland and Spain they are 35 percent. Further differences can be observed when full-time and part-time employment of mothers is distinguished. On average, the majority of the 50 percent of mothers who are employed work full-time (30 percent) rather than part-time (20 percent). Again, countries differ considerably. In the Netherlands, the United Kingdom, Sweden, and Germany, half or more of employed mothers are employed part-time, while in Greece, Italy, Portugal, Spain, and Finland, this figure drops to around 15 percent or less. With only a few exceptions, higher percentages of maternal part-time employment coincide with fewer part-time hours worked per week, whereas lower percentages of part-time employment are associated with more part-time hours worked per week (see Table 1). This reflects two different national orientations regarding maternal employment. Countries with an orientation toward full-time maternal employment tend to have a higher percentage of mothers in full-time employment and extended working hours for the relatively low percentage of part-time employees. Countries with an orientation toward maternal part-time employment tend to have a higher percentage of mothers working part-time, who work relatively few working hours per week. In other words, countries with higher maternal labor force participation rates tend to have higher participation rates of full-time work and more hours per week for mothers working part-time.

Throughout Europe, the proportion of single-parent families has increased. This is due to an increase in the number of births outside marriage or cohabitation as well as in the number of separations and divorces. The proportion of single-parent families is growing in each of the countries, although considerable differences between countries exist. In the Scandinavian countries, including Denmark and Sweden, as well as in Austria and in the United Kingdom, approximately every fifth family is headed by a single parent (usually the mother), whereas in Greece, Italy, and Spain this is true for only 6 percent of the families. This shows a clear difference in Europe between North and South regarding single-parent families. In addition, there seems to be a link to religious traditions in the sense that, in predominantly Protestant countries, the proportion of traditional families is lower.

The birthrate in EU Europe has decreased to a historical low (1.46) after more than three decades of decreasing births, resulting in a decrease of 45 percent compared to the birthrate found prior to the 1960s. Children under 10 years of age currently account for less than 12 percent of the total population. Birthrates are especially low in southern European countries (Italy, Spain, Greece) and in Germany. Birthrates have increased somewhat in the Scandinavian countries during the last decade. In Sweden, Denmark, and Finland, the highest birthrates of EU countries can be observed. (This higher rate is also true for Ireland.) However, the birthrate of 2.1 children, needed to replace the present population, is not met in any of the countries. The extremely low birthrates in most of the countries are widely associated with a need to develop efficient parental supports for child rearing and to provide organized environments where children can have access to experiences that may not be sufficiently available in their families, social networks, and neighborhood environments.

AVAILABILITY AND
AFFORDABILITY OF
ECE SERVICES

Availability

A basic quality issue of an ECE system is the availability of services for parents and children, respectively. First, availability relates to the pure existence of services, although, from the consumer's perspective, this might in itself be insufficient. Availability for any consumer might become possible only when further conditions are met, such as a convenient location, a schedule of care that matches the family needs, an educational program orientation that matches the family values, or affordability. In this article, two of these conditions are discussed in terms of European ECE services: supply rates of services for children differentiated by the age of the child being served (under 3 years of age and from 3 to 6, the beginning of compulsory schooling in most countries); and parental costs for these services.

Because of the high aggregation level (country level), figures will not be detailed. It should be noted that within many countries different kinds of provision can occur under the category "publicly funded services." These services may differ in terms of whether they are center- or family-based. They may also differ considerably by the number of hours during which the programs operate per day as well as by the program orientation toward either care or education. Considerable regional differences within countries (especially urban-rural differences) are often observed. These variations should be kept in mind when considering the summary figures of Table 2. In addition, it should be noted that Table 2 relates exclusively to publicly funded programs. However, with the exception of the United Kingdom and, to some extent, Portugal, exclusively privately funded services are rare, occurring mainly in family child care.

In the early 1990s, European countries either achieved or were moving toward comprehensive ECE coverage for children from 3 years of age to compulsory schooling (see Table 2). In 8 out of the 15 countries discussed here, publicly funded ECE places are available for about 80 percent or more of the children in this age group. Since 1970, a period of a little more than two decades, coverage rates doubled, tripled, or, in some countries, grew even faster, indicating tremendous expansion of the ECE systems for this age group. In some countries, national commitments exist to guarantee publicly funded places for children of certain age groups. For example, in Denmark the central government made a

TABLE 2

PUBLICLY FUNDED CARE AND EDUCATION SERVICES FOR CHILDREN BEFORE COMPULSORY SCHOOLING IN EU COUNTRIES

	BE	DK	DE West	DE East	EL	ES	FR	IR	IT	LX	NE	OS	PO	SU	SV	UK
Percentage of children younger than 3 served																
1988	20	48	2	56	4	5	22	2	5	2	2	—	6	—	—	2
1993	30	50	4	50	3	5	23	2	6	—	8	3	12	27	33	1-2
Percentage of children aged 3-6 served																
1970	95	20	33	65	—	42	87	—	58	—	60	—	3	—	22	16
1993	>95	79	78	100	64	84	99	52	97	68	69	75	48	43	79	53
Compulsory school age	6	7	6	6	5.5	6	6	6	6	5	5	6	6	7	7	5
Governmental system (educational or welfare) taking responsibility for ECE of majority of children under 6	E	W	W		E	E	E	E	E	E	E	W	W	W	W	E
Average percentage of ECE costs paid for by parent	17-30	27	15-30	—	—	20	23-28	—	—	—	6-20	—	—	15	<13	—
Sliding scale for parental fees	Yes	Yes	Yes		Yes	Yes	Yes	—	Yes	Yes	Yes	Yes	Yes	Yes	Yes	Yes
Tax reduction for ECE costs to families	Yes	No	No		Yes	Yes	Yes	No	No	No	Yes	—	No	No	No	No

SOURCES: Derived from European Commission Network on Childcare 1995a, 1995c; Tietze and Paterak 1993, tabs. 1 and 4.

NOTES: The term "publicly funded services" refers to a variety of nationally different services for children below compulsory school age including types such as day care centers, preschools, schools, and family child care. They may be partly or fully publicly funded. The following abbreviations are used for EU member states: BE = Belgium, DK = Denmark, DE = Germany, EL = Greece, ES = Spain, FR = France, IR = Ireland, IT = Italy, LX = Luxembourg, NE = Netherlands, OS = Austria, PO = Portugal, SU = Finland, SV = Sweden, UK = United Kingdom. EU = European Union. ECE = early care and education.

commitment to guarantee each child a publicly funded place from age 1 year to compulsory schooling. In 1995, a law with a similar purpose was passed in Sweden. In Finland, as of 1996, each child below school age became entitled to a publicly funded ECE place. The same is true for German children from 3 years of age to compulsory schooling. Spain made a policy commitment to providing schooling for all children aged 3 to 6 by 1995.

In all countries, the availability of places for children under 3 years old is considerably lower compared to that found for the older age group (see Table 2). In the five-year period between 1988 and 1993, however, several countries increased their coverage rates. The highest coverage rates for these younger children are currently found in Denmark and eastern Germany, the former German Democratic Republic, which at one time had the largest supply of center-based child care in the world (Melhuish and Moss 1991).

Among the countries with high ECE supply rates for children under 3, the Scandinavian countries provide many places in organized family child care (in Denmark and Finland, about 50 percent; Sweden, about 30 percent), whereas in Belgium and France the emphasis is more on center-based provisions. In eastern Germany, care for this age group is almost completely center-based. Unlike the supply for older preschool children, a gap between supply and parental demand can be observed in many countries. The relatively low supply rates for the under-3-year-olds, however, should be regarded in the context of extended parental leave regulations present in many of the countries.

Affordability

Another major criterion for quality of an ECE system is universal access to ECE services to parents. Services should not be exclusive or heavily limited due to income conditions of families. The principle of affordability is in line with traditional European thinking and is emphasized in the Council Recommendation on Childcare of 1992, where it is established that ECE services should be "offered at prices affordable to parents" (art. 3). Indeed, all publicly funded ECE services in the EU countries are more or less oriented to this concept insofar as they are free of charge, or parental fees for them take the family income into consideration. However, data directly focusing on affordability, such as the proportion of family income that is charged as fees, are not available. Therefore, a more indirect approach to understanding affordability is used here.

The funding of ECE provisions in European countries is complicated since, in most countries, two governmental systems for providing services are involved: the education system and the welfare system. Provisions in the education system are generally free to parents. They predominantly consist of nursery schooling, or preschool, such as the *école maternelle* in France and Belgium, *scuola materna* in Italy, *escuela infantil* (3-6) in Spain, and *jardim de infância* in Portugal. However, they may also be reception classes, as found in the United Kingdom, or early primary education schemes, as in Ireland, which serve only older children (older than 3) as an introductory period before entering elementary school. Provisions in the welfare system mainly serve younger children but also complement the provisions in the education system for older children. The relationship between the two systems varies from country to country. Provisions in the welfare system are generally partially supported by parent contributions. Contrary to the provisions in the education system, which are funded by the central or regional governments (that is, a single agency), public funding of ECE in the welfare system typically comes from more than one source, in some cases including employer-financed funds.

In general, parental fees contribute 12-28 percent of operation costs (capital and infrastructure costs excluded) for services where parental fees are required, with a range of 15-25 percent being most common (see Table 2). However, since the ECE systems operate in a decentralized welfare system in most countries, considerable within-country variation occurs. In addition, it should be noted that the figures do not necessarily indicate the share that individual parents have to pay. The variation in individual contribution may far exceed the ranges mentioned. Differences in parental fees are also found in all countries, based on family income and other factors, such as the number of children in a family or enrolled in the same service. Sliding-scale fee formulae usually apply at a regional or local level, rarely at the national level as found in France and the Netherlands. A study conducted in Germany (Tietze, Rossbach, and Roitsch 1993) indicated that the actual parental share of operating costs in publicly funded services could be as high as 52 percent for 3- to 6-year-old children and 60 percent for children under 3.

Five countries provide some kind of tax reduction related to child care fees. Four countries have implemented other forms of subsidies, including Denmark, France, Germany, and the United Kingdom, the latter two restricting the subsidies to families with low incomes.

There are indications that the principle of affordability is not always met. For instance, statistics in Germany indicate that kindergarten participation (by 3- to 6-year-olds) correlates with the income of the families (Tietze, Rossbach, and Ufermann 1989). Similarly, it was found in France and Sweden that families with higher incomes are more likely to use publicly funded services for children under age 3 than families with low incomes (Melhuish and Moss 1991). Often services may not be affordable, especially for parents who are seeking ECE services for children under 3 years of age. The services for this age group are more expensive than for 3- to 6-year-olds, who, to a large extent throughout Europe, can attend free or very inexpensive programs in the education system.

PUBLIC SUPPORT FOR PARENTAL CARE AS PART OF PUBLICLY FUNDED ECE SYSTEMS

In a discussion of ECE, it becomes easy to forget that the child's parents are the first and foremost educators and caregivers in the child's life. In many EU countries, publicly supported, out-of-home care and education for very young children are often considered secondary to the primary goal of supporting parents who wish to stay home to raise their children. Ensuring availability and affordability supports out-of-home care. In contrast, in-home parental care is supported by providing the time and financial resources that allow parents to leave the workforce in order to raise a young child.

European countries have developed a variety of policies and measures to help support parents' caring for and educating their own children. In particular, four measures can be distinguished. The purpose of each is not necessarily just to meet the needs of at-home parents, but may also meet other societal needs as well. However, all help parents to stay at home with their children for some time, especially while children are very young. The measures are maternity leave, paternity leave, parental leave, and leave for family reasons.

Maternity leave is considered a protection for the health and welfare of the mother and her new infant. It is usually provided during the last weeks of pregnancy and during the first weeks after the child's birth. Thus it supports the mother's caring for the child at home for only a short

period of time, with an emphasis on health, rather than on child care. Maternity leave is available as a general right in all EU countries, and generally a high proportion of the mother's earnings are paid (usually 75 percent or more). The leave lasts between 14 and 18 weeks in the majority of countries, with most of the leave usually given after the birth of the child. In some countries, the leave is flexible and parts of it can be taken before or after the birth.

Six countries (Belgium, Denmark, Finland, France, Spain, and Sweden) have introduced paternal leave. Its length varies between 2 days and 2 weeks. Its purpose is to enable the father to be present at the birth of the infant, to offer support to the mother, and to provide care for the home and/or other children. Like maternity leave, this type of parental support is short-term and is not focused primarily on child care.

Parental leave is for both mothers and fathers and is focused specifically on child care—it allows parents to care for their young children at home. Because of the specific goal of providing care to children, this type of leave will be discussed more fully here (see also Figure 1). It should be noted that most of the EU countries have enacted leave regulations that allow parents to care for sick children. These leave days are limited and can be paid or unpaid, depending on the country. In 12 out of 15 EU countries, parents are entitled to parental leave in which the return to work is guaranteed. In Belgium, parental leave is actually embedded

FIGURE 1

ECE SYSTEM PERFORMANCE IN EU COUNTRIES: PARENTAL LEAVE REGULATIONS AND COVERAGE RATES OF PUBLICLY FUNDED OUT-OF-HOME SERVICES

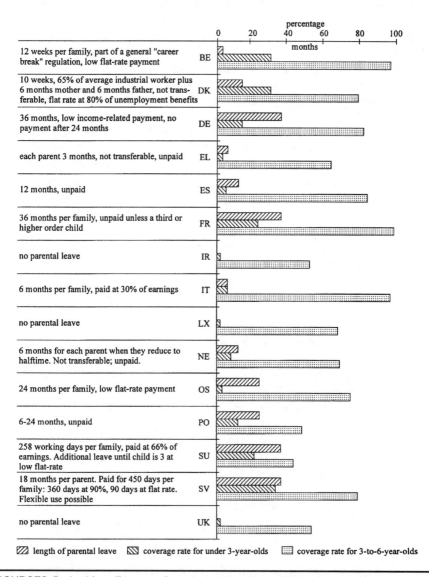

SOURCES: Derived from European Commission Network on Childcare 1994, 1995a.

NOTES: The following abbreviations are used for EU member states: BE = Belgium, DK = Denmark, DE = Germany, EL = Greece, ES = Spain, FR = France, IR = Ireland, IT = Italy, LX = Luxembourg, NE = Netherlands, OS = Austria, PO = Portugal, SU = Finland, SV = Sweden, UK = United Kingdom. EU = European Union. ECE = early care and education.

in a broader system of career breaks that are not earmarked as parental leave, but this leave is usually used for parenting responsibilities. No parental leave system exists in Ireland, Luxembourg, or the United Kingdom.

Generally, parental leave is available for at least six months, and it extends to three years in France and Germany. Usually the leave regulations apply to the family (that is, it can be taken by either the mother or father), and there is flexibility built into the system so that the leave can all be taken by one parent or the other, and they can change who is taking the leave if they wish. In Greece and the Netherlands, however, the leave is an individual right for the mother and for the father and is not transferable from one parent to the other.

Parental leave is unpaid in Greece, the Netherlands, Portugal, and Spain. In France, it is unpaid unless it is required for a third (or additional beyond the third) child. Payment to both parents and for the whole period of leave is available only in Belgium, Denmark, and Italy. Other countries provide payment for parental leave that is between these two extremes (unpaid versus fully paid). In Germany, for instance, payment is made only for the first 24 months of the possible 36 months for which leave is guaranteed, and the payment depends on the family income. With the exceptions of Denmark, Sweden, and Finland, payment is low, does not compensate for lost wages, and does not exceed the equivalent of about $300 per month.

The use of parental leave arrangements differs by country, although there is a lack of solid data needed to fully understand actual use (European Commission Network on Childcare 1994, 22). However, a clear pattern across countries can be seen. First, parental leave is widely used when it is paid. It is estimated that at least 95 percent of mothers participate under paid conditions, although they may not make use of the full period available. Second, available data prove that parental leave arrangements are used almost exclusively by mothers and that paternal leave hardly exceeds 3 percent of parental leave in most of the countries. These data indicate that leave regulations acceptable for families can add considerably to a society's commitment to support the care and education of young children, especially the youngest.

TEACHER EDUCATIONAL REQUIREMENTS AND THE CARE AND EDUCATION THAT CHILDREN EXPERIENCE

Teacher educational requirements

The importance of teacher education to the quality of ECE programs has been widely documented in research (for example, Phillipsen et al. 1997; Whitebook, Howes, and Phillips 1990). Generally, higher levels of teacher education are associated with a higher overall quality of children's classrooms. More specifically, it has also been found that teachers with higher levels of education (for example, university versus high school) provide more developmentally appropriate activities for children and show more positive behaviors with children, such as being responsive to the children's needs.

The necessity for high levels of staff education has been supported in the requirements placed upon the ECE systems in the EU countries. In a study of staff training in provisions for children under 6 years of age in the EU countries (Oberhuemer and Ulich 1997), it was found that requirements for staff training are relatively stringent in most countries. As Table 3 indicates, three or more years of university education are required of teachers in the prevalent type of ECE used in Finland, France, Greece, Ireland, Sweden, Spain, the United Kingdom, and Italy. However, this requirement has not been fully implemented in Italy, and in Greece, educational requirements vary according to whether the teacher will work in half-day kindergartens or full-day programs. EU countries that do not require education in a university have less stringent requirements, but at least 3 years of professional training, in vocational colleges or in secondary school, is required. Oberhuemer and Ulich point out, however, that there are ECE programs that operate with less highly qualified staff. For example, in the United Kingdom, Ireland, and the Netherlands, many children are enrolled in less formal playgroups or in private, for-profit programs, where teachers are not required to be so highly educated. In addition, the figures shown in Table 3 apply primarily to programs that are publicly funded for older preschoolers, since preschoolers represent the majority of children in programs. Less stringent qualifications are almost always required for programs serving children under 3 years of age, and the least training is required for family child care providers.

Global process quality of care and education

Although there is a substantial amount of information that indicates the quality of European ECE, based on the structural characteristics of the various national ECE systems, there are few studies where process quality, or the quality of children's direct experiences while in classrooms, has actually been assessed (for a definition of process quality, see Cryer, this volume). In other words, we know how country ECE systems perform in terms of some of the less direct influences on children's development, such as the availability and affordability of programs, support for in-home parental care, or teacher education requirements. However, we have little information about the quality variables that are likely to affect children more directly—what actually happens to children in the programs in terms of quality. There is a rationale for using information on the structural framework of the ECE system as a proxy for actual measures of classroom quality. Research findings show significant relationships between structural quality variables that provide the framework for the classroom environment and process quality or child outcome measures (for example, European Child Care and

TABLE 3
TEACHER EDUCATION REQUIREMENTS FOR CARE AND EDUCATION SERVICES FOR CHILDREN BEFORE COMPULSORY SCHOOLING IN EU COUNTRIES

	BE	DK	DE	EL	ES	FR	IR	IT	LX	NE	OS	PO	SU	SV	UK
Level of training required for personnel in prevalent type of publicly funded ECE	V	V	S2	U/V	U	U	U	U*/S1	V	V	S1	V	U	U	U
Number of years required	3	3.5	3	4/3.5	3	5	3	4*/5	3	3	5	3	3	3	4
Age range covered in training, by years	2.5-6	0-100†	0-27†	3, 5-6/4-6	0-6	2.5-11	4-11	3-6/0-100†	4-6	4-12	3-6	0-6	0-7	0-7	3-11

SOURCE (for first two rows): Oberhuemer and Ulich 1997, 16.

NOTES: U = university; V = vocational college; S1 = secondary school ages 15-16, initial years; S2 = secondary school ages 17-19, final years. The following abbreviations are used for EU member states: BE = Belgium, DK = Denmark, DE = Germany, EL = Greece, ES = Spain, FR = France, IR = Ireland, IT = Italy, LX = Luxembourg, NE = Netherlands, OS = Austria, PO = Portugal, SU = Finland, SV = Sweden, UK = United Kingdom, EU = European Union, ECE = early care and education.

*Required but not yet implemented.

†Training applies to work with adults as well as young children.

188

TABLE 4

OBSERVED PROCESS QUALITY IN EUROPEAN CENTER-BASED ECE SERVICES

Country	Source	Sample Size	Mean Total Score	SD	Instrument
Age: 3-6 years (preschool classrooms)					
Austria	Tietze et al. 1996	37	4.70	.49	ECERS
Germany	Tietze et al. 1996	103	4.57	.71	ECERS
Portugal	Tietze et al. 1996	88	4.27	.51	ECERS
Spain	Tietze et al. 1996	80	4.06	.90	ECERS
Spain	Lera 1996	59	3.58	.69	ECERS
Sweden	Kärrby and Giotta 1994	40	4.4*	.78*	ECERS
Age: under 3 (infant-toddler classrooms)					
England	Mooney, Munton, and Rowland 1996	60	3.00	.7	ITERS
Germany	Beller et al. 1996	30	3.91*	.47	ECERS
Greece	Petrogannis and Melhuish 1996	25		.7	ITERS
Netherlands	van IJzendoorn et al. in press	43		.67	ITERS/ECERS

NOTE: ECE = early care and education, ECERS = Early Childhood Environment Rating Scale, ITERS = Infant/Toddler Environment Rating Scale.

*Based on subscale scores.

Education Study Group 1997; Phillipsen et al. 1997; Whitebook, Howes, and Phillips 1990). However, structural quality measures are only a proxy for process quality and cannot replace its direct assessment.

The one major study to date that has assessed process quality in European ECE classrooms is the European Child Care and Education study (ECCE), carried out in Austria, Germany, Portugal, and Spain (European Child Care and Education Study Group 1997; Tietze et al. 1996). In this study, one of the measures of process quality used was the Early Childhood Environment Rating Scale (ECERS) (Harms and Clifford 1980), which was translated and adapted, with shared training to ensure consistent use across countries. The ECERS provides a

measure of the global quality that children experience throughout the day. Scores can range from 1 (inadequate) to 7 (excellent). Higher scores on the ECERS have been associated with a variety of positive child development outcomes, across a range of developmental areas, including language, social-emotional, and cognitive (for more information, see Cryer, this volume).

Results of classroom observations showed that ECERS mean total scores ranged from 4.06 in Spain to 4.70 in Austria (see Table 4, rows 1-4). The differences in scores are not great, and all are within the range that has been classified by the authors as mediocre care. However, Spain has lower ECERS scores than do the other three countries (see Table 4, rows 1-4), and Portugal has lower scores than those observed in Austria. Spain and Germany tend to have greater variability in their ECE programs, as seen in the higher standard deviations found in those two countries. In Germany, this variability is probably accounted for by the two different systems of child care that were present before German reunification. These two systems were characterized by completely different philosophical approaches to caring for and educating young children, and practices in the new unified system have not yet become consistent. In Spain, the higher variability is likely due to the diversity in child care sponsorship as well as the gap between the formation of new ECE policy and its actual implementation in all programs. Some programs in Spain are meeting recent policy goals, while others are still moving toward the goals.

This study also shows that a combination of process and structural measures representing ECE program quality were found to explain a substantial amount of children's developmental outcomes (European Child Care and Education Study Group 1997). The results generally show that an ECE program's better quality is related to more social competence in children's behavior with peers and with adults, better mastery of daily living skills, and better language development. These effects are seen in addition to the large effects of the children's home environments.

There have also been some smaller studies in European ECE, completed within individual countries where the ECERS, the infant and toddler version of the scale (the Infant/Toddler Environment Rating Scale) (Harms, Cryer, and Clifford 1990), or a combination of both were used (see Table 4, rows 5-10). Although it is unknown whether data were collected reliably in terms of cross-country comparisons, and it is unlikely that the limited samples represent the actual national conditions, the scores give us a hint of what the quality of ECE might be like for the children in the various countries. Ranges in mean scores are similar to those found in the European Child Care and Education study, with all mean scores falling into the mediocre range. In addition, similar to findings in the United States, we see an indication that process quality is lower in groups of children under 3 years of age, when compared to the scores of classrooms for older preschoolers (Cost, Quality and Child Outcomes 1995).

CONCLUSION

Throughout the European countries, it appears to be broadly acknowledged that publicly funded ECE services are an increasingly important part of the educational, social, and economic infrastructure in the countries. Most countries have made considerable progress in expanding their publicly funded out-of-home ECE services and in setting up parental leave schemes for supporting care of especially young children in the family setting. However, identifiable deficits clearly remain observable in many of the countries. These deficits are centered around the following issues.

There is insufficient availability of ECE services especially for young children under 3 years of age in most of the countries. In addition, parental leave for supporting care of very young children by the family at home is underfunded. Related to this, in most countries, with few exceptions, there is often a lack of continuity for the provision of care and education during the child's early years. Coherence of ECE services is sorely lacking since most of the countries, through historical tradition, operate ECE services within two different systems: education and welfare. This creates barriers to establishing ECE services that provide both high-quality education and high-quality care in an integrated manner.

A general theme seems to be the public underfunding of most national ECE systems. There appears to be a consensus among experts that not less than 1 percent of the gross domestic product of the countries should be spent on the ECE system. This proportion would equal about one-fifth of the national expenditures for education of older children, including primary, secondary, and university levels. Such a proportion, which is currently found only in Denmark and possibly in Sweden, may be a prerequisite to the establishment of a coherent high-quality ECE system that includes an appropriate infrastructure for planning and monitoring the system as well as providing training and research and development of services. The EU has established a frame for such a perspective (Council Recommendation 1992) as part of the Third Action Programme for Equal Opportunity for Women and Men. In addition, there are proposals for a 10-year action plan developed by the Childcare Network (European Commission Network on Childcare 1995b). However, based on their national traditions, it is up to the individual member countries to focus their national policies on developing their ECE systems with an orientation toward a coherent system that provides flexible high-quality services, choices for parents, and equal access for all families.

References

Beller, E. K., Marita Stahnke, P. Butz, W. Stahl, and Holger Wessels. 1996. Two Measures of the Quality of Group Care for Infants and Toddlers. *European Journal of Psychology of Education* 11(2):151-67.

Cost, Quality and Child Outcomes Study Team. 1995. Cost, Quality and Child Outcomes in Child Care Centers: Public Report. University of Colorado, Denver.

Council Recommendation (92/241/EEC) on Childcare. 1992. OJ L 123, 8.5.1992. 31 Mar.

European Child Care and Education Study Group. 1997. European Child Care and Education Study: Cross National Analyses of the Quality and Effects of Early Childhood Programmes on Children's Development. Freie Universität Berlin. Final report.

European Commission Network on Childcare and Other Measures to Reconcile Employment and Family Responsibilities. 1994. *Leave Arrangements for Workers with Children.* Brussels: European Commission.

———. 1995a. *A Review of Services for Young Children in the European Union.* Brussels: European Commission.

————. 1995b. *Quality Targets in Services for Young Children: Proposals for a Ten Year Action Programme*. Brussels: European Commission.

————. 1995c. *The Costs of Funding of Services for Young Children*. Brussels: European Commission.

Harms, Thelma and Richard M. Clifford. 1980. *Early Childhood Environment Rating Scale*. New York: Teachers College Press.

Harms, Thelma, Debby Cryer, and Richard M. Clifford. 1990. *Infant / Toddler Environment Rating Scale*. New York: Teachers College Press.

Kärrby, G. and J. Giotta. 1994. Dimensions of Quality in Swedish Day Care Centers—An Analysis of the Early Childhood Environment Rating Scale. *Early Child Development and Care* 104:1-22.

Lera, María-José. 1996. Education Under Five in Spain: A Study of Preschool Classes in Seville. *European Journal of Psychology of Education* 11(2):139-50.

Maruani, M. 1992. *The Position of Women in the Labour Market*. Women's Information Services, Report no. 36. Brussels: European Communities.

Melhuish, Edward and Peter Moss, eds. 1991. *Daycare for Young Children: International Perspectives*. London: Routledge.

Mooney, A., A. G. Munton, and L. Rowland. 1996. Quality in Group Care: Self-Assessment as Agent of Change. Paper presented at the meeting of the International Society for the Study of Behavioral Development, Quebec City, Quebec, Canada.

Oberhuemer, Pamela and Michaela Ulich. 1997. *Working with Young Children in Europe: Provision and Staff Training*. London: Paul Chapman.

Petrogannis, K. and Edward C. Melhuish. 1996. Aspects of Quality in Greek Day Care Centers. *European Journal of Psychology of Education* 11(2):177-91.

Phillipsen, Leslie C., Margaret R. Burchinal, Carollee Howes, and Debby Cryer. 1997. The Prediction of Process Quality from Structural Features of Child Care. *Early Childhood Research Quarterly* 12:281-303.

Tietze, Wolfgang, Debby Cryer, Joachim Bairrão, Jesús Palacios, and Gottfried Wetzel. 1996. Comparisons of Observed Quality in Early Child Care and Education Programs in Five Countries. *Early Childhood Research Quarterly* 11:447-75.

Tietze, Wolfgang and H. Paterak. 1993. Hilfen für die Betreuung und Erziehung von Kindern im Vorschulalter in den Ländern der Europäischen Gemeinschaft. (Measures of support for child care education in the countries of the European Union.) In *Erfahrungsfelder in der frühen Kindheit. Bestandsaufnahme, Perspektiven* (Early childhood environments: The current state and perspectives), ed. W. Tietze and H.-G. Rossbach. Freiburg: Lambertus.

Tietze, Wolfgang, Hans-Gunther Rossbach, and K. Roitsch. 1993. *Betrenungsangebate für Kinder im Vorschulischen Alter* (Care and education services for children before school age). Stuttgart: Kohlhammer.

Tietze, Wolfgang, Hans-Gunther Rossbach, and K. Ufermann. 1989. Child Care and Early Education in the Federal Republic of Germany. In *How Nations Serve Young Children: Profiles of Child Care and Education in 14 Countries*, ed. P. Olmsted and D. Weikart. Ypsilanti, MI: High/Scope Press.

van IJzendoorn, M. H., L. W. Tavecchio, G.-J. J. Stams, M. J. Verhoeven, and E. J. Reiling. In press. Quality of Center Day Care and Attunement Between Parents and Caregivers: Center

Day Care in Cross-National Perspective. *Journal of Genetic Psychology*.

Whitebook, Marcy, Carollee Howes, and Deborah Phillips. 1990. *Who Cares? Child Care Teachers and the Quality of Care in America: Final Report.* Washington, DC: Center for the Child Care Workforce.

ANNALS, *AAPSS*, **563**, May 1999

Who Should Pay for the Kids?

By PAULA ENGLAND and NANCY FOLBRE

ABSTRACT: This article emphasizes collective struggles over the distribution of the costs of children. Because the production of children's capabilities creates a public good that cannot be priced in the market, individuals can free ride on the efforts of parents in general and mothers in particular. We need to redesign the social contract in ways that encourage more sustainable forms of intergenerational altruism and reciprocity.

Paula England is professor of sociology at the University of Arizona and author of Comparable Worth: Theories and Evidence *(1992) as well as many articles on gender and labor markets. From 1993 to 1996, she served as editor of the* American Sociological Review.

Nancy Folbre is professor of economics at the University of Massachusetts–Amherst and author of Who Pays for the Kids? *(1994). An associate editor of* Feminist Economics, *she is also cochair of a research network on the family and the economy, funded by the MacArthur Foundation.*

NOTE: We gratefully acknowledge the support of the John D. and Catherine T. MacArthur Foundation's Research Network on the Family and the Economy.

Power never concedes anything without a struggle. It never has and it never will.

—Frederick Douglass

The debate over family policy in the United States is dominated by rhetorical concern over children's welfare. However noble and sincere, this rhetoric tends to conceal some underlying distributional conflicts. Increased public support for child rearing—such as subsidized child care, universal health insurance, and more generous assistance to poor families with young children—would redistribute income from men to women, from adults and the elderly to the young, and, most likely, from the rich to the poor. In the short run, it would benefit the least powerful groups in our society at the expense of the more powerful. In the long run, however, a more equitable distribution of developing children's capabilities could help equalize opportunities and enhance economic efficiency.

These important issues are largely obscured by the lack of a coherent picture of the costs and benefits of children. In this article, we argue that the time, money, and care that parents devote to the development of children's capabilities create an important public good whose economic benefits are enjoyed by individuals and institutions who pay, at best, a small share of the costs. Economists define a public good as one that is difficult to put a price on because it is nonexcludable (someone can enjoy it without paying for it) and nonrival (one person can enjoy it without diminishing someone else's enjoyment of it). Individuals who do not contribute to the production of a public good are likely to ride free on other people's efforts unless their responsibilities are enforced through explicit laws and rules, including taxes.

In the first section of this article, we explain why the conventional economic analysis of child-rearing decisions needs to be augmented by consideration of social institutions that affect the distribution of the costs of children between men and women, parents and nonparents, and old and young. An implicit social contract governing the relationship between parents, children, men, and women is now being renegotiated as the structure of family and work life is changing. Yet economists and policymakers have remarkably little to say about who should pay for the costs of rearing the next generation. Some seem to hold an implicit children-as-pets assumption—those who want them should pay for them. Our own view is just the opposite: We believe that all members of society have a moral responsibility to help develop children's capabilities. Even those who disagree with this claim, however, should agree that individuals and institutions enjoying the economic benefits of human capabilities should help pay the costs of developing them.

In the second section, we review the literature on the net costs of children (the difference between the economic costs and benefits). Most researchers have focused on the cost side; closer attention to the benefits leads toward more explicit consideration of what economists call positive externalities, or benefits that are not captured by the actual producers of children's capabilities, especially parents.[1] Both the taxation of the working-age population and less direct amenities enjoyed by friends, spouses, and employers mean that individuals who devote time and money to developing their children's capabilities generate important but unremunerated benefits for other people. As a concrete illustration, consider two individuals who have the same marriage and employment history—they will receive exactly the same retirement benefits from Social Security, even if one of them raised three children who grew up to become productive members of society and to pay taxes on the income they earned, while the other raised none and simply enjoyed higher levels of personal consumption. Current policies in the United States socialize many of the economic benefits of children while requiring parents, mothers in particular, to pay most of the costs. Children themselves suffer from a high risk of poverty.

In the final section, we discuss some of the implications of this emphasis on externalities, showing that both individuals and groups have an economic interest in free riding on parents' efforts. Yet state policies can be an important vehicle for more equitable distribution of the costs of children across lines of gender, race, age, and class. Several European countries, including France and Sweden, impose higher taxes on the entire working-age population to defray the costs of child care (Bergmann 1996b; Kamerman and Kahn 1991). These policies are sometimes construed as spending more on children, but they can also be construed as lending more to children, asking them to repay their loans through taxes paid as adults. We do not have to present adults with a bill for what we have collectively spent on them, nor do we have to schedule explicit interest and loan repayments in order to make this point (though it might be interesting to do so!). We can develop the loan metaphor as a way of demonstrating the point that greater public expenditures on children may be economically productive as well as morally desirable.

WHO SHOULD PAY
THE COSTS OF CHILDREN?

There is something risky, perhaps even unpleasant, about applying the vocabulary of costs and benefits to children. Family life is one of the few areas of human endeavor that enjoy some protection from the cold logic of self-interest. But consideration of economic factors does not imply that these dominate family decisions. It simply calls attention to the economic consequences of the organization of family life, which has become increasingly costly for women in the United States over time. Women generally devote more time and money to children than men do. Over the last 25 years, they have substantially increased their overall hours of market work to help provide family income. Men, however, have only slightly increased their hours of child care and domestic labor. The percentage of families maintained by women alone is increasing, and enforcement of paternal child support responsibilities remains poor (Folbre 1994b, 1997; Bittman and Pixley 1997).

Over the same time period, the costs of raising children have increased. Education has a heightened impact on the probability of economic success, and the price of college and university services has gone up much faster than the general rate of inflation. As women's earnings have improved, the opportunity cost (or forgone earnings) of time devoted to family has increased. That many other traditional obstacles to gender inequality have been overturned means that parental responsibilities loom large as a current cause of lower earnings and restrictions on career advancement for women. Parents in general and mothers in particular remain highly susceptible to poverty in the United States (Wolff 1996; McLanahan and Kelly forthcoming). Furthermore, poverty rates among children in this country are among the highest in the industrialized world, largely as a result of public policies such as poor enforcement of paternal child support obligations and reluctance to extend public education to children under the age of 5 (Smeeding, Torrey, and Rein 1988; Garfinkel 1996; Bergmann 1996a).

How do economists interpret these trends? Mainstream neoclassical economists focus on adult decisions to maximize utility. By their account, individuals choose to have children and to continue caring for them, only if they get utility (or pleasure) from doing so. By definition, they must be better off as a result (Becker 1960).

Applying this reasoning, Victor Fuchs (1988) suggests that single mothers are poor largely because they have stronger preferences for children than fathers do. The implication is that their utility gains must counterbalance their economic losses. Single mothers may have less money than fathers, but they also get more pleasure from their children.

This is consistent with what we call the children-as-pets approach. If people spend a lot of money on their golden retriever, it must be because it makes them happy to do so. In utility terms, they are no worse off than those who simply put an equivalent amount of money in the bank. From this point of view, people who acquire pets but cannot maintain them at a decent level of health and well-being are irresponsible and should be punished. The innocent pets may suffer in the meantime, but if all else fails they can be removed to the animal shelter (also known as the orphanage or foster care).

One can challenge this approach on moral and philosophical grounds. Amartya Sen (1993) argues persuasively that we should aim not to maximize utility but to promote the development of human capabilities. But one can also challenge the children-as-pets approach on its own terms by pointing out that children create far more significant positive externalities than pets do. This may sound obvious, but, as many feminist scholars have pointed out, the legacy of Western political theory from Thomas Hobbes to John Rawls dwells on relations between adult men, relegating mothers and children to the world of nature outside the social contract (Hartsock 1983; Pateman 1988; DiStefano 1991; Okin 1989). Neoclassical economic theory cannot take all the blame—the classical economic theories of Ricardo and Marx treat children as a nonproduced commodity.

Sociologists point out that children pay back their parents by raising children of their own, fulfilling an implicit contract that is obviously crucial to social reproduction (Davis 1937; Ryder 1973). But despite a widespread realization that fertility decline and modernization have transformed the nature of intergenerational relations, the terms of the payback have never been closely interrogated. We lack any systematic theory of what we collectively owe children and what they owe us. It is hardly surprising, therefore, that we lack a coherent vision of what we collectively owe those who take care of children.

HOW DO THE PUBLIC COSTS
OF CHILDREN COMPARE TO
THE PUBLIC BENEFITS?

Our understanding of who actually pays the net costs of rearing children (costs minus benefits) is equally underdeveloped. Microeconomists' efforts at quantification have evolved from rather narrow estimates of private monetary expenditures on individuals under the age of 18 to more sophisticated statistical analysis of the opportunity cost of parents' time. Very little attention has been devoted to analysis of the value of the transfers of time, money, and care from children to parents, or to calculation of the net costs. However, macroeconomists have noted that the working-age population as a whole transfers significant benefits to the elderly through taxation. This literature strongly suggests that investments in children's capabilities (which conventional human capital theorists term "child quality") create important externalities for society as a whole.

Since direct parental expenditures cannot be directly observed, they must be indirectly inferred from comparison of the overall expenditures of families with varying numbers of children through the use of equivalence scales. Despite some theoretical problems with the interpretation of such scales (Nelson 1993), this approach yields useful estimates of what families actually spend on children. The U.S. Department of Agriculture, using data from the Expenditure Survey, provides such estimates on an annual basis. The results, not surprisingly, differ by the age of the child and the income of families. For instance, in 1997, the estimated annual expenditure was about $6000 for husband-wife families with an income of less than $35,000, but about twice as high for families with an income of more than $59,700 (U.S. Department of Agriculture 1997, 15).

This summation of direct expenditures omits the cost of nonmarket time devoted to child care, which often results in lower labor force participation and reduced earnings for mothers. These indirect costs can be estimated by asking how much a mother would have earned had she not reduced her labor force participation, an exercise that yields varying estimates depending on the assumptions made regarding the opportunity cost of women's time. Examining the effect of fertility on transitions in employment status, Calhoun and Espenshade find that the mothers' forgone earnings amounted to about 20 percent of the total cost of raising children (1988, 29).

Missing from most such calculations, however, is a full consideration of the effects of interrupted labor force participation on mothers' future earnings, what might be construed as an indirect opportunity cost. Recent research by Heather Joshi (1990, 1991) and Jane Waldfogel (1997) suggests that this cost is quite substantial, especially in careers where there is a high rate of return to on-the-job experience and tenure. Mothers who lack or lose a secure claim on the earnings of a man face, at best, a significant reduction in their market income. Those with lower levels of education and labor market experience are likely to fall into poverty.

Women who put time and energy into children are investing in what is essentially a "family public good." They pay most of the costs, but other family members, including children and fathers, claim an equal share of the benefits (Lommerud 1997). This investment is far less fungible or transferable outside the family than investment in a career (England and Farkas 1986). The resulting loss of bargaining power may lead to a reduction of women's consumption and/or leisure time even if they remain married and enjoy a share of

their husband's market income (McElroy 1990).

Individuals who devote time and energy to parenting often enjoy some economic as well as psychological benefits. Adult children seldom transfer much income to their parents, but they often provide care and assistance to those who are elderly. Partly as a result, elderly individuals with living children are less likely than others to require publicly subsidized nursing home care (Wolf in press). However, these private benefits are small compared to the transfers provided through taxation of the working-age population, as well as the less tangible benefits enjoyed by friends, spouses, and employers (Lee 1990; Folbre 1994a). Development economists have long emphasized that economic development is accompanied by a reversal in intergenerational income flows. In simple agrarian societies, children defray many of their economic costs by beginning work at an early age and continuing to contribute to family income as young adults. The more modern and technologically developed the society, however, the less likely parents are to capture the economic benefits of their child-rearing labor (Caldwell 1982). This process promotes fertility decline, which offers important economic and environmental benefits.[2] However, the public payoff to investments in children's capabilities, or what neoclassical economists call child quality, tends to increase. Parental altruism may be a driving force of economic development (Willis 1982), but parents (mothers in particular) and children in poor families are penalized in the process.

Furthermore, failure to fully develop the capabilities of children living in poverty reduces overall economic efficiency.

The fiscal externalities created by children in advanced industrialized countries have been widely acknowledged. Members of the working-age population are taxed to help pay the debts accumulated by the previous generation, as well as the direct costs of old age provision through Social Security. As Kotlikoff (1992) emphasizes, differences in the relative size of cohorts (particularly the large bulge of the baby-boom generation in the United States) can lead to significant redistribution across age groups. But the complete list of positive externalities created by parental and social investments in children's capabilities is quite large, and includes both returns to education and noncognitive skills such as "emotional intelligence" (Goleman 1994). These contribute directly to the stock of human capital and also to the network of relationships and climate of trust and reciprocity that is sometimes termed "social capital" (Gustafsson and Stafford 1997; Kennedy and Welling 1997).

Public expenditures on children are modest compared to those made by parents. Haveman and Wolfe estimate that the sum of public expenditures on children in the United States, composed mostly of education, housing, and income transfers, accounted for about 38 percent of the total cost, and their estimate of total cost is probably low (1995, 1829). Public expenditures on children in the United States are far lower per child than those in countries that,

like France, provide subsidized child care for all children at age 3 and beyond (Bergmann 1996b). Over the last 30 years, the elderly in this country have received far greater transfers per capita than the young have (Preston 1984; Fuchs and Reklis 1992).

The distributional effects of child-rearing externalities deserve especially careful consideration. Children raised in low-income families are disadvantaged in terms of health, cognitive development, school achievement, and emotional well-being (Duncan and Brooks-Gunn 1997). Furthermore, the structure of public school finance in the United States leads to marked differences in expenditures per student, reinforcing significant class and race inequalities. Recent innovations such as school choice and voucher programs are unlikely to solve this problem—and could make it worse. Parents are constrained by low income and imperfect capital markets (restricted capacity to borrow money to help pay for educational investments).

High-quality day care programs such as Head Start remain underfunded despite the evidence that they can significantly improve educational outcomes for poor children (Leibowitz 1996). More serious attention to the larger organization of the production of human capabilities could inform a number of important policy debates (England and Folbre 1997). In particular, we should develop better measures of economic success than measures of market output such as the gross domestic product. We should also emphasize that the overall structure in children in this country is inconsistent with principles of equal opportunity.

REDISTRIBUTING THE COSTS OF CHILDREN

The public-good aspect of child rearing helps explain why both groups and individuals engage in forms of strategic behavior designed to help them enjoy the benefits without paying the costs. As Frederick Douglass put it long ago, power concedes nothing without a struggle. A rich historical record demonstrates many complex forms of collective conflict based on gender, race, class, age, and nation (Folbre 1994b). Examples of gender-based conflict range from men's opposition to strict specification and enforcement of child support responsibilities to the cultural claim that women naturally feel greater love and responsibility for children than men do. The relevance to current policy debates is obvious. Publicly subsidized child care tends to increase mother's labor force participation and reduce gender inequalities in both the workplace and the home (Juster and Stafford 1991). Many more single women than single men take responsibility for the care of young children, and they would therefore benefit more from child care subsidies.

Other forms of collective conflict are evident in struggles over taxation and public spending. Affluent families who purchase high-quality services in the private market are particularly likely to oppose tax increases to finance public provision of child care and education. Age-based conflict also comes into play. Elderly families, especially those who believe that they have already paid for the public benefits they are receiving, are not enthusiastic about paying taxes to care for other people's children.

The emergence of welfare states represented an explicit effort to socialize many of the transfers of income and labor once located within the family, such as the education of the young and the support of the elderly. Many welfare state policies, influenced by women's increased political power, can be described as a victory for "maternalist" values (Skocpol 1993; Koven and Michel 1993). But race and class differences, as well as perceptions of national self-interest, have significantly shaped policy outcomes. In general, ethnically and religiously homogeneous countries that have lost population through out-migration or war have been particularly likely to provide public support for child rearing. In the United States, on the other hand, white apprehensions about the growth of the black and Hispanic population discouraged policies that could be construed as pronatalist, even when it became apparent that fertility rates were steadily declining (Folbre 1994b; Quadagno 1994).

To illustrate how the public-good aspect of human capabilities creates temptations to free ride on parental and other forms of caring labor, consider the similarities between a mother who devotes considerable time and energy to child rearing and a country that devotes a large portion of its national budget to family welfare. In the short run, both are at a competitive disadvantage, because they are devoting fewer resources to directly productive activities. In the long run, their position depends on their ability to claim some share of the economic benefits produced by the next generation, which is quite limited.

Consider the following scenario. A multinational corporation, tired of the frustrations of negotiating over taxation and regulation with host governments, buys a small island, writes a constitution, and announces the formation of a new country. Its name is Corporation Nation. Anyone who is a citizen of the new country will automatically receive a highly paid job. However, the following restrictions apply to citizenship: individuals must have advanced educational credentials, be physically and emotionally healthy, have no children, and be under the age of 60. They do not have to physically emigrate but can work from home over the Internet. They immediately lose their new citizenship and their job, however, if they become seriously ill, acquire children, or reach the age of 60.

Corporation Nation can completely free ride on the human capabilities of its citizen-workers without paying either for their production or their maintenance when ill or old. It can offer high wages to attract the very best childless workers in the world, without threatening its own profitability. As a result, it is likely to enjoy unprecedented success in global competition. This disturbing fantasy is not as far-fetched as it might initially seem, because it combines policies already in effect in a number of countries. Canada has largely credential-based immigration policies; the state of California refuses to provide any social services for illegal immigrants; Germany deports immigrant workers when its unemployment rate rises. The Asian economic crisis has led to deportation of nonnative workers from Malaysia and other countries.

Out-migration is not a serious problem for the United States, but the ability to attract highly skilled immigrants (or to directly employ foreign citizens in multinational enterprises in their own country) reduces incentives to invest in the national labor force. Competition also comes into play within states. Children raised and educated in a state with relatively good income support, child care, and educational facilities may, when they grow up, go to work in a state with a lower tax rate and inferior public services that is able to capture the higher taxes they pay as a result of their higher productivity. National standards and minimum requirements for income support, child care, and education would raise costs for states that are currently spending less than the average.

One can acknowledge these political conflicts without treating them as inevitable. Even proposals that offer important long-term benefits are likely to be resisted by those most likely to pay the short-run costs. On the other hand, if the costs are not paid, the benefits will not be realized. As with many public-good scenarios, the outcome is rather similar to that of the Prisoner's Dilemma. In this central parable of game theory, the best outcome for two individuals caught at the scene of a crime is to remain loyal to each other and refuse to confess, because the police do not have enough evidence to convict them. If the two are separated, however, and cannot make or enforce a binding commitment to each other, the temptation to rat on each other becomes overwhelming. Each prisoner hopes to gain immunity from prosecution by providing evidence incriminating the other. The outcome is usually not what either had hoped for: because both confess, neither gains immunity and they both go to prison for a long time.

Similarly, the best outcome for any player in the Reproduction Game is to free ride on the child rearing and other caring efforts of others. However, if everybody tries to free ride, this strategy obviously does not work. What is needed is a clear and consistent solution to the coordination problem.[3] This requires explicit debate over the question of how the costs of developing human capabilities should be distributed.

In this debate, much depends on how public spending on children is conceptualized. Taking the term "human capital" seriously implies that expenditures on it should be treated as bona fide investment, rather than consumption. Some macroeconomists suggest that educational spending should be treated as investment rather than consumption in the national income accounts (Jorgenson and Fraumeni 1990). We believe that all expenditures on the development of human capabilities—including paid and unpaid child care—should be treated as investments. This may seem like a small conceptual change, but it would have very large implications for the debate over levels of provision for children.

Investment may, of course, be private as well as public. Several scholars suggest that greater privatization of the economic benefits of children would provide a solution to the externality problem. James Coleman (1988) argues that parents should be awarded support based on the "value added"—their success in raising productive children. Paul Demeny (1987) and Shirley Burggraf (1993) propose that parents should be given a percentage of their own children's earnings as support in old age, rather than or in addition to a share of the earnings of the working-age generation as a whole. Greater privatization of the benefits of children, however, has several disadvantages, including greater vulnerability to risk. What would happen to parents whose children were killed in an auto accident? What about parents raising children with physical or mental disabilities?

Moral problems also arise. Do we really want to encourage parents to think of their children as individual investments, part of their larger portfolio? Would it not be preferable to provide support and recognition for parental labor without assuming that we can measure the "value added"? Privatization would reinforce class and race inequalities, since poor families would not have the same means as affluent families to invest in their children. Moreover, underinvestment in the children of poor families leads to underdevelopment and underutilization of their capabilities, with losses for society as a whole.

Rather than privatizing the benefits of children, we could socialize more of the costs in ways that create positive incentives for overall improvements in human capabilities. In a classic public finance text, Musgrave and Musgrave (1989) point out that incentives facing the elderly would change if their retirement benefits comprised a constant share of what the younger generation earned rather than a Social Security stipend based on their own historical earnings. Under this arrangement, they would collectively benefit from public investments enhancing the productivity of the younger generation and be more willing to vote in favor of greater expenditures on them.

Such intergenerational income-sharing is an interesting idea. We think that it might be easier to gain public support for an intergenerational contract in which the working-age generation lends the younger generation enough to offer equal opportunities to develop their most important capabilities, with some specification of a minimum payback required. Public spending on children could be conceptualized as a form of public lending. Respect for moral and political obligations to others could be combined with an emphasis on the long-run benefits of a contract based on fairness and reciprocity.

This proposal, of course, requires a great deal more careful thought and specification. It would be interesting to calculate the actual size of the implicit loan and interest rate. If, as we argued earlier in this article, the positive externalities of developing children's capabilities are high, the loans already made may have been more than repaid. The distributional implications also require consideration. What does equal opportunity for children to develop their capabilities mean in a world in which parental capabilities vary greatly?

Some scholars and journalists argue that greater public investments in children's capabilities would not pay off for those who live in dysfunctional families (Samuelson 1998; Mayer 1997). However, we believe that more creative public policies, as well as more sustained research efforts, could yield substantial evidence of a very high public payoff. Efforts to rethink the production of human capabilities in the broader terms we have outlined here could help us specify the terms of a new social contract and build support for more equitable—and more efficient—public policies toward children and families.

Notes

1. Parents are not the only producers of children's capabilities. We argue elsewhere that many individuals who engage in caring labor, such as teaching or child care, do so as well (England and Folbre 1999). Furthermore, children help produce their own capabilities. A full consideration of this issue is beyond the scope of this article.

2. Julian Simon (1981) insists that population growth itself contributes to economic growth. We disagree. The quantity of children is far less important than their standards of living, upbringing, and education, and, while it is difficult to specify the optimal rate of

growth of population, we doubt that a case can be made for a rate above replacement levels.

3. For more discussion of the game-theoretic aspects of this problem, see Folbre and Weisskopf 1998.

References

Becker, Gary. 1960. An Economic Analysis of Fertility. In *Demographic and Economic Change in Developed Countries*. Princeton, NJ: Princeton University Press.

Bergmann, Barbara. 1996a. Child Care: The Key to Ending Child Poverty. In *Social Policies for Children*, ed. Irwin Garfinkel, Jennifer L. Hochschild, and Sara McLanahan. Washington, DC: Brookings Institution.

———. 1996b. *Saving Our Children from Poverty: What the United States Can Learn from France*. New York: Russell Sage Foundation.

Bittman, Michael and Jocelyn Pixley. 1997. *The Double Life of the Family: Myth, Hope, and Experience*. Sydney: Allen & Unwin.

Burggraf, Shirley. 1993. How Should the Cost of Child Rearing Be Distributed? *Challenge* 37(5):48-55.

Caldwell, John. 1982. *The Theory of Fertility Decline*. New York: Academic Press.

Calhoun, Charles A. and Thomas J. Espenshade. 1988. Childbearing and Wives' Foregone Earnings. *Population Studies* 42:5-37.

Coleman, James S. 1988. Social Capital in the Creation of Human Capital. *American Journal of Sociology* 94(supp.):S95-120.

Davis, Kingsley. 1937. Reproductive Institutions and the Pressure for Population. *Sociological Review* 29:289-306.

Demeny, Paul. 1987. Re-Linking Fertility Behavior and Economic Security in Old Age: A Pronatalist Reform. *Population and Development Review* 13(1):128-32.

DiStefano, Christine. 1991. *Configurations of Masculinity: A Feminist Perspective on Modern Political Theory*. Ithaca, NY: Cornell University Press.

Duncan, Greg and Jeanne Brooks-Gunn, eds. 1997. *Consequences of Growing Up Poor*. New York: Russell Sage Foundation.

England, Paula and George Farkas. 1986. *Households, Employment, and Gender: A Social, Economic, and Demographic View*. Hawthorne, NY: Aldine de Gruyter.

England, Paula and Nancy Folbre. 1997. Reconceptualizing Human Capital. Paper presented at the annual meeting of the American Sociological Association.

———. 1999. The Cost of Caring. *The Annals* of the American Academy of Political and Social Science. 561 (Jan.):39-51.

Folbre, Nancy. 1994a. Children as Public Goods. *American Economic Review* 84(2):86-90.

———. 1994b. *Who Pays for the Kids? Gender and the Structures of Constraint*. New York: Routledge.

———. 1997. The Future of the Elephant Bird. *Population and Development Review* 23(3):647-54.

Folbre, Nancy and Thomas Weisskopf. 1998. Did Father Know Best? Families, Markets and the Supply of Caring Labor. In *Economics, Values and Organization*, ed. Avner Ben-Ner and Louis Putterman. New York: Cambridge University Press.

Fuchs, Victor. 1988. *Women's Quest for Economic Equality*. Cambridge, MA: Harvard University Press.

Fuchs, Victor and Diane Reklis. 1992. America's Children: Economic Perspectives and Policy Options. *Science*, 3 Jan., 41-46.

Garfinkel, Irwin. 1996. Economic Security for Children: From Means Testing and Bifurcation to Universality. In *Social Policies for Children*, ed. Irwin Garfinkel, Jennifer L. Hochschild, and Sara McLanahan. Washington, DC: Brookings Institution.

Goleman, Daniel. 1994. *Emotional Intelligence*. New York: Bantam Books.

Gustafsson, Siv and Frank P. Stafford. 1997. Childcare, Human Capital, and Economic Efficiency. In *Economics of the Family and Family Policies*, ed. Inga Persson and Christina Jonung. New York: Routledge.

Hartsock, Nancy. 1983. *Money, Sex, and Power: Toward a Feminist Historical Materialism*. New York: Longman.

Haveman, Robert and Barbara Wolfe. 1995. The Determinants of Children's Attainments: A Review of Methods and Findings. *Journal of Economic Literature* 33(Dec.):1829-78.

Jorgenson, Dale W. and Barbara M. Fraumeni. 1990. Investment in Education and U.S. Economic Growth. In *The U.S. Savings Challenge*, ed. Charles E. Walker, Mark A. Bloomfield, and Margo Thorning. Boulder, CO: Westview Press.

Joshi, Heather. 1990. The Cash Opportunity Cost of Childbearing: An Approach to Estimation Using British Evidence. *Population Studies* 44:41-60.

———. 1991. Sex and Motherhood as Sources of Women's Economic Disadvantage. In *Women's Issues in Social Policy*, ed. D. Groves and M. McClean. New York: Routledge.

Juster, F. Thomas and Frank Stafford. 1991. The Allocation of Time: Empirical Findings, Behavioral Models, and Problems of Measurement. *Journal of Economic Literature* 24(June):471-522.

Kamerman, Sheila B. and Alfred J. Kahn, eds. 1991. *Child Care, Parental Leave, and the Under 3s: Policy Innovation in Europe*. New York: Auburn House.

Kennedy, Peter W. and Linda Welling. 1997. Parental Externalities and the Private Provision of Childcare. *Canadian Journal of Economics* 30:822-34.

Kotlikoff, Laurence J. 1992. *Generational Accounting: Knowing Who Pays, and When, for What We Spend*. New York: Free Press.

Koven, Seth and Sonya Michel, eds. 1993. *Mothers of a New World: Maternalist Politics and the Origins of Welfare States*. New York: Routledge.

Lee, Ronald with the assistance of Tim Miller. 1990. Population Policy and Externalities to Childbearing. *The Annals* of the American Academy of Political and Social Science 510(July):17-32.

Leibowitz, Arleen. 1996. Child Care: Private Cost or Public Responsibility. In *Individual and Social Responsibility: Child Care, Education, Medical Care, and Long-Term Care in America*, ed. Victor R. Fuchs. Chicago: University of Chicago Press.

Lommerud, Kjell Erik. 1997. Battles of the Sexes: Non-Cooperative Games in the Theory of the Family. In *Economics of the Family and Family Policies*, ed. Inga Persson and Christina Jonung. New York: Routledge.

Mayer, Susan. 1997. *What Money Can't Buy: Family Income and Children's Life Chances*. Cambridge, MA: Harvard University Press.

McElroy, Marjorie. 1990. The Empirical Content of Nash-Bargained Household Behavior. *Journal of Human Resources* 25(4):559-83.

McLanahan, Sara and Erin L. Kelly. Forthcoming. The Feminization of Poverty: Past and Future. In *Handbook of Gender Sociology*, ed. Janet Chafetz. New York: Plenum.

Musgrave, Richard A. and Peggy B. Musgrave. 1989. *Public Finance in Theory and Practice*. New York: McGraw-Hill.

Nelson, Julie A. 1993. Household Equivalence Scales: Theory Versus Policy? *Journal of Labor Economics* 11(3):471-93.

Okin, Susan Moller. 1989. *Justice, Gender and the Family*. New York: Basic Books.

Pateman, Carol. 1988. *The Sexual Contract*. Stanford, CA: Stanford University Press.

Preston, Samuel. 1984. Children and the Elderly: Divergent Paths for America's Dependents. *Demography* 21:435-57.

Quadagno, Jill. 1994. *The Color of Welfare: How Racism Undermined the War on Poverty*. New York: Oxford University Press.

Ryder, Norman. 1973. A New Approach to the Economic Theory of Fertility Behavior: A Comment. *Journal of Political Economy* 81(2):S65-69.

Samuelson, Robert J. 1998. Investing in Our Children. *Newsweek*, 23 Feb., 45.

Sen, Amartya. 1993. Capability and Well-Being. In *The Quality of Life*, ed. Martha Nussbaum and Amartya Sen. Oxford: Clarendon Press.

Simon, Julian L. 1981. *The Ultimate Resource*. Princeton, NJ: Princeton University Press.

Skocpol, Theda. 1993. *Protecting Soldiers and Mothers: The Politics of Social Provision in the United States, 1870s-1920s*. Cambridge, MA: Harvard University Press.

Smeeding, Timothy M., Barbara Boyle Torrey, and Martin Rein. 1988. Patterns of Income and Poverty: The Economic Status of Children and the Elderly in Eight Countries. In *The Vulnerable*, ed. John L. Palmer, Timothy Smeeding, and Barbara Boyle Torrey. Washington, DC: Urban Institute.

U.S. Department of Agriculture. 1997. Expenditures on Children by Families, 1997 Annual Report. Washington, DC: Department of Agriculture. Available from http://www.huduser. org/publications/publicassist/ welreform.html.

Waldfogel, Jane. 1997. The Effects of Children on Women's Wages. *American Sociological Review* 62:209-17.

Willis, Robert. 1982. The Direction of Intergenerational Transfers and Demographic Transition: The Caldwell Hypothesis Reexamined. In *Income Distribution in the Family*, ed. Yoram Ben Porath, supp. to *Population and Development Review* 8:207-34.

Wolf, Douglas A. In press. Efficiency in the Allocation and Targeting of Community-Based Long-Term Care Resources. *Journal of Aging and Health*.

Wolff, Edward N. 1996. The Economic Status of Parents in Postwar America. Paper prepared for the meeting of the National Parenting Association, 20 Sept.

Making Child Care
"Affordable" in the United States

By BARBARA R. BERGMANN

ABSTRACT: Two alternative federally financed plans are presented as models for a program that would make child care of acceptable quality "affordable" for millions of American families. Taking a cue from currently operating state programs, care is defined as "affordable" if it costs parents no more than 30 percent of the amount by which their income exceeds the poverty line. The first plan would cost the government $25 billion per year and would concentrate help on families with incomes up to twice the poverty line. The second would cost $39 billion per year, would provide higher-quality care, and would allow all U.S. families to have access to care that was "affordable" by the definition. Costs of these magnitudes preclude financing of any significant part by employers or philanthropies.

Barbara R. Bergmann is the author of Saving Our Children from Poverty: What the United States Can Learn from France *(1996),* In Defense of Affirmative Action *(1996), and* The Economic Emergence of Women *(1986). She is professor emerita of economics at American University and the University of Maryland.*

NOTE: This article is based on material from the forthcoming book *What Child Care System for America?* by Suzanne W. Helburn and Barbara R. Bergmann (St. Martin's Press). Financial support was provided for this work by the Foundation for Child Development.

A realistic approach to the problem of child care in America requires recognition of the need for a reliable flow of funds that would finance on a continuing basis, year after year, the provision of high-quality services to millions of children, while at the same time allowing hard-pressed parents to reduce what they currently pay for care out of their own pockets. As we shall see, the new funds that would be needed are in the tens of billions of dollars per year. The federal and state governments currently spend about $5 billion subsidizing care for low-income families and about $3 billion a year on tax credits to higher-income taxpayers with child care expenses.[1] What is needed is a new national plan that would build on and go beyond our present system.

Making that new money available would do three things. First, the subsidies, together with the copayments that would be made by the parents, would give to providers the flow of financial resources that would enable them to offer an adequate supply of high-quality services. Second, subsidies would relieve parents of the pressure to put their children into hole-in-corner care of dubious quality and safety. Third, by reducing the amounts that lower-income parents would have to take out of their own pockets to secure care for their children, it would raise parents' and children's living standards to a significant degree. "Affordable child care" is, after all, care at a price to parents that does not cripple a family's budget and leave it with insufficient resources to buy food and shelter.

Child care proponents have been quite reticent about pushing such an overall federal financial plan, although few of them, if any, could entertain the hope that state, local, and voluntary efforts, together with those of employers, could in time fill the need. The reluctance to put forth a well-worked-out national plan may be due to fear that the magnitude of the funds needed to implement it would be so large as to make it an easy target for attack by those opposed to "big government," by those who would like mothers to stay home, and by those with other priorities for government spending. They may fear that pushing for a large national program with a low chance of enactment might make them look foolishly unrealistic and might get in the way of obtaining the more modest advances in child care funding they have some hope of attaining.

Despite these hopes and fears, there are good reasons for formulating such plans, estimating their cost, and trying to get them discussed. First, most discussions on "affordable care" are lacking in concreteness. Specifying the characteristics of a plan and costing it out forces us to define what is meant by "affordable care," to realize what is meant by its lack, and to come to an understanding of what would constitute an acceptable and prudent solution. Second, it is worthwhile to get an estimate of the financial magnitude of the task because the strategy that is adopted for dealing with the problem depends crucially on that magnitude. The kinds of voluntary efforts to increase the supply of affordable child care that are frequently called for might suffice if the financial magnitude of the effort needed were found to be relatively modest. Considerably larger magnitudes would require a sizable program financed by the federal government in order for serious progress to be made on a uniform basis throughout the country. Third, the discussion of a significant new national program in child care is necessary if such a program is to have any chance of eventual enactment. Even if that discussion takes place in a period when public opinion (and politicians' opinion of what the public might be thought to favor) is unsupportive of its enactment, the discussion itself may help to nudge opinion in its favor.

Would increased funding guarantee that an adequate quantity of care would be provided and that the services would be of high quality? On the matter of quantity, we can, based on past performance, put our confidence in the responsiveness of the American economy. If sufficient funding were available, the child care industry, like any other industry, could be expected to respond with a supply of its product that would meet the demand. While anxiety over the quantity of care supplied would not be justified, anxiety would certainly be warranted concerning the quality of the child care that would result from an enlarged subsidy program. Quality provided would depend on the level of the subsidies, the standards set, and the extent and efficacy of enforcement of those standards. If effective regulation of the providers were absent, a considerable portion of public sub-

sidies would be likely to flow to care that is mediocre or outright poor, just as some parent fees do now. A subsidy level that did not cover the costs of high-quality care would not produce it, regardless of the nature of the regulations or the effort put into enforcing them. High quality depends on a combination of generous subsidies and effective regulation.

TWO ALTERNATIVE COMPREHENSIVE FEDERAL PLANS AND THEIR COST

Rather than formulate a single plan, we show two basic federal plans, so that their virtues, defects, coverage, and costs can be compared. The two plans differ in terms of how many families receive help, the extent of the help they would receive, the quality of the care that each plan would offer, and, of course, what the plans would cost. I would anticipate that, as now, they would be mostly federally financed but administered by the states.

The first plan is based on the type of rules that currently govern the state plans, financed by federal block grant and state money. We use Iowa's rules as a model, because its plan is typical of what the states have adopted and, moreover, comes from a state that can be classed as politically conservative. The Iowa plan requires families in the program to make copayments for the care they receive equal to about 30 percent of the amount by which their income exceeds the poverty line.[2] Since this represents a conservative state's view of what parents should have to pay for child care, one might perhaps be somewhat protected against accusations of being overly generous if one defines care provided at that level of payment as "affordable." I shall use that definition for the purposes of cost calculations on the second plan, discussed later. Obviously, a definition of "affordability" is a matter of judgment and ethical feelings rather than a matter of scientific determination. Other definitions might certainly be chosen.

The child care subsidy programs that actually operate currently in most of the states, Iowa included, have three major weaknesses: (1) they cover only a minor fraction of the eligible population; (2) help is cut off abruptly as a family's income rises, leaving many families with moderate incomes without access to "affordable" care, as we have defined such care; and (3) the reimbursement rates to providers that the programs allow are not based on quality considerations. The first national program presented here, which is based on the rules currently operating in Iowa, cures only the first of these weaknesses—it provides enough funds so that all eligible children in the country could participate in the program. The second plan I present—which I call the "sufficient" plan—also covers all children who would be eligible for it nationwide. It differs from the plan based on Iowa rules in giving benefits to a wider range of families and in offering reimbursement rates to providers that would pay the cost of providing all children with care at a level of quality equal to the current national average. It would also incorporate a system of giving providers a bonus payment if they achieved higher quality.

A national plan using Iowa rules

This first plan builds a national entitlement to child care subsidies based on the reimbursement rates and copayment schedule set by the state of Iowa. The subsidies for child care available in Iowa to a family consisting of a single working mother, an infant, and a preschool child (with both of the latter needing full-time care) are shown in Table 1. The state maximum reimbursement for care for a 50-week year in a day care center would be $5750 for the infant and $4750 for the preschooler, for a total of $10,500.[3] Families with income equal to or below $12,672 (a few dollars above the official U.S. poverty level for this family in 1997) would owe no copayments. Families with income above this would make payments as indicated in the column headed "family's copayment for child care." The subsidy for a given family is equal to the reimbursement allowed for the children's care (the first figure in the second column), less the required copayment. Those included in the program would have to pay about 30 percent of the amount by which their income exceeds the poverty level, regardless of the number of children in care. However, under the Iowa rules, parents whose income exceeds the program limits would have to pay as much as 82 percent of their income over the poverty line for this kind of child care.

We have simulated the cost of a national program based on the

TABLE 1

**SUBSIDIES PAYABLE FOR FULL-TIME CARE IN A CENTER UNDER IOWA RULES, FOR
A FAMILY CONSISTING OF A MOTHER, AN INFANT, AND A PRESCHOOL CHILD, 1998**

Maximum Income for Receiving State Subsidy at Right	State Subsidy from Block Grant	Federal and State Child Care Tax Credits*	Family's Copayment for Child Care	Family's Copayment as a Percentage of Income Above Poverty Line
$12,672	$10,500		$0	—
13,344	10,240		260	37
14,088	9,980		520	36
14,880	9,720		780	35
15,708	9,460		1,040	34
16,596	9,200		1,300	33
17,520	8,940		1,560	32
18,504	8,680		1,820	31
19,536	8,420		2,080	30
20,640	8,160		2,340	29
21,792	7,900		2,600	28
23,016	7,640		2,860	28
24,300	7,380		3,120	27
24,301	0	$1,392	9,528	82
30,000	0	1,680	9,240	53
40,000	0	1,536	9,384	34

SOURCE: Computed by the author on the basis of state documents.

NOTE: All dollar amounts are at annual rates.

*A small amount of state income tax credits may be available also on parents' copayments under the state subsidy system, which are given in the column to the right, for families with income of $24,300 or below.

reimbursement rates and copayment rules contained in the Iowa plan, using information on family incomes, parental hours of work, and ages of children in a large sample of American families taken from the 1997 Current Population Survey. This information was used to assign a child care subsidy to (or to withhold one from) each family with children under age 13 in the sample. If all of the adults of a family were in the labor force (at a job or looking for work), the family was assigned a subsidy if they met the income requirements of the Iowa plan. Mothers who, on account of welfare reform, might be expected to make the transition from welfare to work were also assigned a subsidy.[4] Sixty percent of mothers receiving welfare were assumed to be making the transition and needing child care. For families with at least one adult at home out of the labor force and who had not been welfare recipients, the initial simulation was made on the assumption that their children would continue to be cared for at home at no cost to the government.[5] Children currently being cared for by others than their parents at no charge, as well as those in paid-for care in centers, in licensed family day care, or in "informal care," were assumed in the simulation to continue in those arrangements.[6] The information on mothers' hours of work was used to assign some

TABLE 2

**ESTIMATES OF COST AND COVERAGE OF NATIONAL PLAN
FOR SUBSIDIZING CHILD CARE BASED ON 1998 IOWA RULES**

Age at Last Birthday	Program Serving Children Currently Needing Care		Program Enlarged by a Quarter of the Children Not Currently in Care	
	Cost	Children served	Cost	Children served
Total	$19.6	10.3	$24.7	12.4
0-1	6.4	1.7	7.9	2.0
2-4	9.0	2.6	11.2	3.1
5	1.2	0.8	1.5	1.0
6-12	6.7	5.1	8.5	6.3
Parent copayments	(3.7)		(4.4)	

SOURCE: Estimated by the author.
NOTE: Annual public cost in billions of dollars; number of children served in millions.

children to part-day care. Five-year-olds with mothers in full-time work were assumed to get part of their care through kindergarten classes.[7] Children in grades 1-6 whose mothers worked full-time were assumed to need after-school care for 10 months and full-time care for 1.5 summer months.

Providing Iowa-level benefits to all income-eligible families nationally who currently have their children in paid care, and allotting child care subsidies as well to 60 percent of welfare recipients, is estimated to cost $20 billion a year.[8] Reimbursements to providers would total $24 billion, of which $4 billion, or 16 percent, would be covered by parents' copayments (see Table 2).

This program would give benefits to an estimated 10 million children, as compared with the 2 million currently estimated to be getting benefits under the federal block grants and associated state funds.[9] Of the $20 billion, an estimated $3 billion would be needed to take care of

children whose mothers were shifting from welfare to work.[10] The remainder would be devoted to the children already receiving paid care.

If there is a substantial expansion in subsidies for child care, some parents who currently do not hold jobs will decide to enter the paid labor force. Furthermore, some children whose parents are already working but who are now in unpaid care will be switched to paid-for care. The potential costs of these increases in the demand for paid-for care need to be considered. We have calculated the cost of the program on the assumption that one-quarter of the children currently cared for on an unpaid basis (whether by parents or others) would move into paid-for care. As shown in the right-hand side of Table 2, we estimate the cost of the program in that case to be $25 billion per year. If, instead, half of the non-welfare children not now in paid care moved into paid care, the program of Iowa-level benefits would cost $30 billion. Costs might rise still further on account of per child cost increases that might occur as the number of children cared for increased. For example, increased wage levels for child care workers might prove necessary to attract additional workers.

Current state programs are in many cases poorly publicized, with very little outreach on the part of the agencies running them. Our cost estimates are based on the assumption that the national program would be well publicized, so that a high proportion of eligible children who need paid care could benefit.

The calculations described so far have not taken account of the current federal tax credit for dependent care. Almost all of the money spent under the Iowa-level subsidy program would go to families not earning enough to owe federal income tax and thus not able to take advantage of the tax credit. In the case of some families, the subsidies envisioned by an Iowa-level program would be larger than the amounts they would receive under the federal tax credit and would presumably replace the latter.

It would be administratively simplest to integrate the benefit from the tax credit with the benefit from the Iowa-type subsidy program by repealing the tax credit but allowing families to receive subsidies that are no less than they are now entitled to as a federal tax credit. To do this would add about $2.5 billion a year to the cost of the program. However, none of this would be new spending.

*A "sufficient" plan of
national child care subsidies*

In this section, we describe and present estimates of the cost of a national program that would overcome the major faults of the program based on Iowa rules described in the previous section. We will call it the "sufficient" plan. It is far from the most generous program that might be proposed, since it is not universal and free to all parents. However, it would provide sufficiency in three important respects. Like the plan based on the Iowa rules, it would provide services to all families who meet its income-eligibility test. It would also allow all families, not just those with the lowest incomes, access to "affordable" care, as we have defined it, by requiring families to pay no more for care than 30 percent of the excess of the family's income over the poverty line. It would thus avoid the abrupt cutoff of aid to families in the mid-ranges of income that the Iowa rules mandate (following current federal guidelines).

What reimbursement rates should be selected for this "sufficient" plan? Data from the study Cost, Quality, and Child Outcomes in Child Care Centers (CQO) allow us to relate the quality of the service provided to its cost (see Helburn 1995). Using standard techniques, the study rated the quality of centers, giving scores from 1 to 7. Centers scoring 3 were designated in this system as "minimally adequate"; centers that used what child care professionals call "developmentally appropriate practices" were rated 5 and were given the designation "good." The average grade given centers in the study was 4. Average annual cost per child for centers rated 4 was found to be $6914 and for those rated 5, $7979.[11]

If we established "good" as the standard of quality for the "sufficient" plan, we would be choosing a standard of quality that only a distinct minority of the nation's child care providers currently meet. Only 24 percent of the care provided to preschoolers by centers observed by the CQO study was given a rating of good or better. Centers providing care of that quality for infants and toddlers were even rarer: only 8 percent of the care they received in centers observed was rated good or better (Cost, Quality and Child Outcomes 1995, 26-27). The care in family day care homes and that given by friends and relatives is likely to be poorer still on average.

It would seem sensible to set a basic quality standard for the "sufficient" plan that the average provider currently meets (a grade of 4), which would entail paying centers $5971 for preschool children and $10,166 for the care of infants. We have set the reimbursement for family day care at $5000 and $8000, respectively. In estimating the cost of the program, we have included funds to allow extra payments ($1100 annually per child) to providers whose quality reaches the "good" level.[12] These extra funds would be available to finance better pay for child care workers.

In setting copayment schedules, we again set zero copayment for families below the poverty line, and for those above we set a copayment equal to 30 percent of any income over the poverty line. The subsidies and copayments for a family consisting of a mother, an infant, and a preschool child at various income levels are shown in Table 3, which is set up analogously to Table 1, which displayed these magnitudes for Iowa rules.

The "sufficient" plan does not cut off subsidies abruptly, as the Iowa plan does. There is no sudden rise in out-of-pocket expenditure for care as families pass a particular point in the income scale. The subsidies shown in Table 3 drop off gradually and go to zero at an income of about $66,000. Beyond that income, the percentage of income above the poverty line that the family spends for child care drops below 30 percent. For families with only one preschooler, subsidies go to zero at an income of $32,500 (not shown in table).

Finally, Table 4 shows estimated annual costs for the "sufficient" plan. To serve children currently needing care, plus those children of mothers expected to transit from welfare to work, would cost $31 billion. This program would raise the number of children younger than 6 receiving benefits by about 35 percent over the number served by the plan based on Iowa rules, and the costs for this group would almost double. Moving from the Iowa-based plan to the "sufficient" plan would have relatively little effect on the number of children in grades K-6 who are served, because the costs for their care are smaller and, in the case of most families, will not exceed 30 percent of the family's above-poverty income. Copayments would almost triple, however, as some moderate-income families received benefits not available under Iowa rules.

If a quarter of the children not currently in paid care had to be taken

TABLE 3

**SUBSIDIES PAYABLE FOR FULL-TIME CARE IN A CENTER
UNDER THE "SUFFICIENT" PLAN FOR A FAMILY CONSISTING
OF A MOTHER, AN INFANT, AND A PRESCHOOL CHILD, 1998**

Income at Which Subsidy at Right Is Received	Subsidy	Family's Copayment	Family's Copayment as a Percentage of Income Above Poverty Level
$12,641	$16,136	$0	—
12,672	16,127	9	30
13,344	15,925	211	30
14,088	15,702	434	30
14,880	15,464	672	30
15,708	15,216	920	30
16,596	14,950	1,187	30
17,520	14,672	1,464	30
18,504	14,377	1,759	30
19,536	14,068	2,069	30
20,640	13,736	2,400	30
21,792	13,391	2,745	30
23,016	13,024	3,113	30
24,300	12,638	3,498	30
24,301	12,638	3,498	30
30,000	10,928	5,208	30
40,000	7,928	8,208	30
50,000	4,928	11,208	30
60,000	1,928	14,208	30
70,000	0	16,136	28
80,000	0	16,136	24
90,000	0	16,136	21

SOURCE: Computed by the author.
NOTE: All dollar amounts are at annual rates.

TABLE 4

**ESTIMATES OF COST AND COVERAGE OF THE "SUFFICIENT"
NATIONAL PLAN FOR SUBSIDIZING CHILD CARE**

Age at Last Birthday	Program Serving Children Currently Needing Care		Program Enlarged by a Quarter of the Children Not Currently in Care	
	Cost	Children served	Cost	Children served
Total	$31.2	11.7	$38.7	14.9
0-1	18.1	2.4	22.3	3.0
2-4	16.6	3.4	20.6	4.3
5	1.4	0.9	1.7	1.1
6-12	7.0	5.0	8.5	6.4
Parent copayments	(12.0)		(14.4)	

SOURCE: Estimated by the author.
NOTE: Annual public cost in billions of dollars; number of children served in millions.

care of in addition, the cost of the "sufficient" plan would rise to $39 billion per year. This includes the cost of the quality bonus, estimated to be about 3 percent of expenditures under the program. However, if, as would be hoped, providers responded by upgrading their program quality, the cost of the quality bonus would grow.

Again, these estimates do not include possible rises in per child costs due to the expansion of the number of children cared for. They also do not include the costs of evaluating providers for quality or the costs of enforcement.

WHERE WOULD THE
MONEY COME FROM?

The national plans that have been outlined would not need to be financed entirely by new money. We are already spending $2.8 billion of federal funds and $2.0 billion of state funds for child care subsidies based on vouchers and contracted care spaces.[13] The amount of new money required for either type of national program would depend to some degree on the future direction of the Head Start and kindergarten programs. If all Head Start providers were enabled to become full-day providers as part of the program, then the $4 billion now being expended on Head Start could be used for the program, and less new money would be needed. If, on the other hand, Head Start continued to provide mainly part-day services and to concentrate on the children of non-jobholding parents (children who certainly need such services), then its current

appropriation could not help to defray the costs of the child care subsidy program serving working parents.

Cities and states have for some time financed with their own funds an expansion of the number of children accommodated without charge in full-day kindergartens, and some are starting to provide kindergarten services to younger children. To the extent that this occurs, it would reduce the need for additional federal funds. We may conjecture that a new large-scale federal child care program would, however, reduce the ardor of states and localities for expanding kindergartens with their own tax money.

As the foregoing discussion should have made clear, for the definition of "affordable care" we have adopted and, for that matter, for any plausible one we might adopt, the expenditure that would be necessary to achieve it year after year throughout the United States would be far too large to be raised from nongovernmental sources. Business and charitable groups currently contribute about 1 percent of the costs of child care (see Mitchell, Stoney, and Dichter 1997, 3). Even if they tripled or quadrupled their contributions, they would not make even a small dent in the need for funds.

While states and localities could, in principle, fund child care as they currently fund public education, it is unlikely that they will do so. (It has been remarked that if the United States had failed to establish universal free public education previously, it would be difficult—perhaps impossible—to establish it now.) The competition that forces states to keep taxes in line with those of other states makes it difficult even for those favorably inclined to undertake big new initiatives.

The federal government is surely the only promising source of large-scale amounts of funds. While the current political situation makes a big federal program unlikely in the near future, a change in strategy on the part of activists might change the odds. The activists might try to collaborate in lobbying with the for-profit providers and the business community more generally, both of whom would benefit from government-supported child care. The energy and resources of activists for child care are limited; concentrating that energy on the federal level might have a better payoff than attempting to run 50 state-level campaigns.

Notes

1. This does not include the $4 billion appropriation for Head Start, which, being mostly part-time, has not been organized to help working parents with their child care needs. Nor does it include the Child and Adult Care Food Program, which spends $2.5 billion for meals and snacks for children in care. State and local spending for preschools amounted to $0.7 billion in 1990 but probably has grown considerably since. Information on federal spending is from U.S. House 1998, 679. Information on expenditure-based state outlays comes from National Governors' Association 1998, 20. Other state spending estimates are from Stoney and Greenberg 1996.

2. See Table 1 for copayments required by Iowa for a family of three. Larger families have smaller copayments, and smaller families, larger ones. When costing out the second plan, we have adopted 30 percent of an "affordable" copayment for all sizes of family. Information on Iowa rules comes from an untitled docu-ment used internally by the Iowa Department of Human Services.

3. Reimbursement rates for family day care run about 25 percent lower.

4. In order to calculate the size of the copayment such a family would owe, a wage was calculated for the mother. It was based on wage data for that part of the sample that consisted of mothers who had been on welfare but were currently employed, using number of children, education, and age as explanatory variables. This estimation process probably gives a result that is biased upward, as the mothers in the labor force are likely to have better earning power than the mothers who have refrained.

5. Many families that include adults who are not in the labor force do send their children at least part-time to out-of-home caregivers, particularly preschools. Current rules prevent a married couple from receiving tax credits on account of such expenses if both are not in the labor force. Subsidizing the child care expenditures of such families would add to the cost of the program but might well result in an improvement in cognitive functioning for many children.

6. The distribution of children by type of care is given in U.S. Bureau of the Census 1997. "Informal care" is defined as nonlicensed family day care, care by a relative, or care by a nanny.

7. About half of 5-year-olds attend full-time kindergarten, and their needs for care were treated similarly to those of children in the elementary grades. Those attending kindergarten part-time, whose mothers worked full-time, were assumed to need other care half-time for 10.0 months and full-time care for 1.5 summer months. Children attending kindergarten whose mothers worked part-time were assumed to need care half-time for 1.5 months.

8. These estimates do not take into account large differences in child care costs from one area to another within the United States. These differences are due at least in part to differences in average quality and in the cost of living. Such differences would considerably complicate the design of a national program.

9. Estimated by the author on the basis of Green Book (U.S. House 1998). It is estimated that about 1 million families are covered by various child care programs, as of 1997.

10. Sixty percent of mothers who were out of the labor force in March 1997 and whose family received welfare payments in the previous year were assumed to be moving from welfare to full-time paid work and to require paid-for child care. No information is available in the Current Population Survey about March 1997 welfare recipiency.

11. These figures were derived from the data generated by the CQO study, increased by the change in child care prices, as measured by the child care index of the Consumer Price Index, between 1992 and 1998.

12. This amount is the estimated difference in costs between centers graded 4 and 5 by the CQO study, taking account of 1998 child care prices.

13. For federal spending, see U.S. House 1998, 679; for state spending, see National Governors' Association 1998, 20; Stoney and Greenberg 1996.

References

Cost, Quality and Child Outcomes Study Team. 1995. *Cost, Quality and Child Outcomes in Child Care Centers: Public Report*. Denver: University of Colorado, Department of Economics, Center for Research in Economic and Social Policy.

Helburn, Suzanne W., ed. 1995. *Cost, Quality and Child Outcomes in Child Care Centers, Technical Report*. Denver: University of Colorado, Department of Economics, Center for Research in Economic and Social Policy.

Mitchell, Anne, Louise Stoney, and Harriet Dichter. 1997. *Financing Child Care in the United States*. Kansas City, MO: Ewing Marion Kauffman Foundation and Pew Charitable Trusts.

National Governors' Association and National Association of State Budget Officers. 1998. *The Fiscal Survey of States, 1998*. Washington, DC: National Governors' Association and National Association of State Budget Officers.

Stoney, Louise and Mark Greenberg. 1996. The Financing of Child Care: Current and Emerging Trends. *The Future of Children* 6(2):83-102.

U.S. Bureau of the Census. 1997. *Who's Minding Our Preschoolers? Fall 1994*. P70-62. Washington, DC: Government Printing Office.

U.S. House. Committee on Ways and Means. 1998. *1998 Green Book*. Washington, DC: Government Printing Office.

Book Department

INTERNATIONAL RELATIONS AND POLITICS

GUTH, JAMES L., JOHN C. GREEN, CORWIN E. SMIDT, LYMAN A. KELLSTEDT, and MARGARET M. POLOMA. 1997. *The Bully Pulpit: The Politics of Protestant Clergy.* Pp. xi, 221. Lawrence: University Press of Kansas. $35.00. Paperbound, $19.95.

This book is another solid research effort from a group of political scientists who have added significantly to our knowledge about contemporary American relationships between religion and politics. The scope here is broadened beyond their customary attention to religious conservatives, examining Protestant clergy across the spectrum. The authors use survey data to study religious beliefs and commitments, and relate them to elements of conventional politics such as voting, partisan identification, and issue attitudes.

The primary conclusion is that, among Protestant clergy, there are two basic constellations of values, beliefs, and attitudes, running from religious theology to political participation. It supports a limited version of the two-party thesis in American Protestantism and lends credence to the idea that our major political cleavage currently is a cultural divide. In the authors' model, those who hold "orthodox" theologies are likely to endorse "individualist" social theologies, support "moral reform" political agendas, be ideologically conservative, and vote Republican. In contrast, those with "modernist" theologies more strongly support "communitarian" social theologies, support "social justice" political agendas, are ideologically liberal, and vote and identify as Democratic. This alignment makes sense logically, and the authors use their considerable data to demonstrate the polarization and clustering at each step. They emphasize that this logical coherence is an aspect of studying religious elites—people whose stock-in-trade is ideas and values and to whom this type of consistency is important (a consistency often not found in surveys of mass publics).

It is difficult to make meticulous analyses of survey data into scintillating reading, and often this book is not. While the findings are well articulated for those who are not statistically minded, there are nonetheless a plethora of tables, qualifying comments, and tentative conclusions. This is careful social science; flamboyant overstatement, so common in work on religion and politics, is absent here.

I was generally convinced by the findings. Further, one wonders if we need any more survey analysis of these issues; this book feels complete. But I also felt that we learned all we were going to from this method. Survey research produces some artificial clarity from the forced choices in many of the answers. Voting patterns are easily discerned this way, but less conventional political involvement is more difficult to capture, and salience is more elusive still. Finally, limiting the subject to white Protestant clergy gives the work a nicely bounded field of study, but the politics of the next century may leave the Protestant conflict that divided evangelicals and mainliners early in this century well behind.

In sum, this book will be a constant reference on my bookshelves and a requirement for my graduate students. It answers the conventional questions about religion and politics among Protestant clergy. New research should ask different questions with different methods.

RHYS H. WILLIAMS

Southern Illinois University
Carbondale

MAIR, PETER. 1997. *Party System Change: Approaches and Interpretations*. Pp. xvi, 244. New York: Oxford University Press. $69.00.

Peter Mair is a world authority on political parties. In this volume, he collects a number of important writings on the subject, concentrating on Western European party systems. While seven of the nine chapters have been published previously, Mair adds a theoretical introduction and a new essay on the emerging post-Communist democracies of the Continent.

Mair's principal thesis is the stability of patterns of party competition. A generation ago, prominent scholars presented the "freezing" hypothesis: that the major alignments among democratic parties had been frozen in the mold of the ideological cleavages evident in the early twentieth century. Since then, we have witnessed great massive changes in class structure and personal values, the rise of new issues, and great volatility in voting patterns. Nevertheless, Mair effectively argues, the original hypothesis remains valid, "with the evidence of long-term continuities in party systems far out-weighing the ostensibly more striking and more immediate evidence of change."

Mair, a professor at the University of Leiden, uses a number of techniques to support his argument. One strand is quantitative analysis. It reveals, for example, that the vaunted voter volatility in contemporary elections is actually less than in either the early postwar or even the allegedly stable interwar years. Another approach is methodological, making precise and relevant distinctions. He demonstrates, illustratively, that electoral volatility is largely a matter of the shifting of votes between parties within the same ideological camps, rather than a significant change of votes across the continuing cleavages between Right and Left.

The major contribution of this volume, and Mair's work generally, is theoretical. He insists on the autonomy of politics, on the ability of parties to affect, not only reflect, the social and institutional environment. The persistence of past cleavages is seen as the result of deliberate party adaptation to new forces, and planned efforts to control the character of social and political change. These efforts have created a new kind of political party, the "cartel party." It lacks the popular grounding of older party forms, but it has new strengths in professional management, state financial support, and access to government.

This book evidences Mair's deep knowledge of European politics. It gives only limited attention, however, to the United States and to some major American authors, particularly Leon Epstein. I would argue against its outdated interpretation of American parties as decentralized and nonideological. Such peripheral concerns aside, Mair has given us a central contribution to the theory of political parties.

GERALD M. POMPER

Rutgers University
New Brunswick
New Jersey

TONG, YANQI. 1997. *Transitions from State Socialism: Economic and Political Change in Hungary and China.* Pp. xi, 264. Lanham, MD: Rowman & Littlefield. $66.50. Paperbound, $26.95.

Yanqi Tong has written an excellent book on similarities and differences in "uncommunization" in Hungary and China. Her approach provides four critical analytical themes:

1. In both Hungary and China, the Soviet model of extreme state control of the economy led to inefficiencies and stagnation. Leaders in both countries introduced market mechanisms. Economic reforms led to greater social independence, the preliminary development of civil society, and independent political organization.

2. If moderates in the regime can cooperate with moderates in the opposition and if both can control extremists in the regime and in society, then democratic change is possible (Hungary). However, if conservatives are very strong, then economic reform is possible but democratic political reform is unlikely (China).

3. Historical influences shape this process. In Hungary, the conservative forces were inherently weak and were propped up by the Soviet Union. Hungarians in and outside the regime cooperated in making cautious reforms that the Soviet Union would tolerate. In contrast, in China the conservatives still had military, political, and popular support. They have been able to repress democratic tendencies. Anti-regime forces were poorly organized and unable to control their own extremist elements.

4. After the changes in 1989-91, Hungary weakened its state sharply. The results were inflation, unemployment, loss of welfare programs, and so on. So upsetting were the results that a reformed Communist party won elections. China

retained a strong state that could regulate its economy, and the country has seen vigorous growth and not too much economic instability. A coherent state seems helpful for stable transformation.

These four themes are developed very clearly in Tong's book and are important to convey to students. This is why I find the book so good.

That said, two other themes merit sharper attention. Hungary is a small country in Europe while China is the huge center of Asian civilization. Democracy is very powerful in Europe, attracting Spain, Portugal, and Turkey in recent decades. In contrast, in China the age-old Confucian values of statecraft and personal relations bring autocratic government of men, not laws.

Second, for decades scholars assumed that Communist leaders would resist reform that would undermine the bases of their power. However, cadres eagerly traded political capital for economic assets. New social-political elites are being created that fuse old political elites (and their children and other relatives) with new entrepreneurs. Widespread anger at this corruption is fueling the next stage of development.

BENEDICT STAVIS

Temple University
Philadelphia
Pennsylvania

YOUNG, IRIS MARION. 1997. *Intersecting Voices: Dilemmas of Gender, Political Philosophy, and Policy.* Pp. ix, 195. Princeton, NJ: Princeton University Press. $49.50. Paperbound, $12.95.

In her introduction, Iris Marion Young refers to the essays in this collection as having a "practical intent," insofar as they all aim to "solve a conceptual or normative problem that arises from a practical context." Young calls for "pragmatic" feminist theorizing that is concerned with "developing accounts and arguments that are tied to specific practical and political problems," rather than with "providing a systematic account and explanation of social relations as a whole." At the same time, however, she sees "theoretical" and practical or "pragmatic" concerns as mutually informing and shaping one another.

Young simultaneously invokes and critiques the traditional distinction between the theoretical and the practical, and she reconceptualizes these terms to some degree. Her opening remarks manifest themselves in an overarching concern with how to articulate (practical, pragmatic) feminist politics that is not merely reformist. While these essays address various specific feminist issues (families, motherhood, citizenship, democracy), they all in some sense raise and, more important, engage the question of how it might be possible to deal with immediate, practical issues in ways that do not reinscribe the status quo of women's oppression.

The difficulty of such a project is apparent in Young's work. On one hand, she argues that social, political, and economic justice cannot be attained in a structurally unjust society; a thorough critique of state institutions must occur. Yet, at the same time, Young turns to state institutions in order to accomplish a "revaluation" of women's traditional sociopolitical and economic position. A strength of Young's work is that she actively tries to work through this apparent paradox, employing both normative and what might be thought of as "transformative" (rather than "revaluative") strategies. Within the context of Young's project, "transformation" can be understood in terms of a politics in which claims for justice are not tied to state institutions.

Indeed, Young implicitly recognizes the limits of a state-centered politics in chapters 2 and 3, where she argues that "communication" and "respect" are possible in a politics characterized by asymmetry and irreducible difference. (In fact, she suggests that they are possible only in such a context.) That the spirit of these chapters does not transfer easily to Young's more "practical" essays demonstrates both the complexity of the political project she has undertaken and the significance of her work for feminist political thought.

DIANNA TAYLOR

Binghamton University
New York

AFRICA, ASIA, AND LATIN AMERICA

WEYLAND, KURT. 1996. *Democracy Without Equity: Failures of Reform in Brazil*. Pp. xii, 293. Pittsburgh, PA: University of Pittsburgh Press. $49.95. Paperbound, $22.95.

In this fine book, Kurt Weyland analyzes why democratic governments in Brazil failed to achieve redistribution between 1985, when the military government relinquished power, and 1995. Weyland places the Brazilian case within a broad theoretical and comparative framework and in so doing raises a question of scholarly and practical importance: under what conditions can democracy promote redistribution? This issue is particularly salient in the world's many new democracies that are plagued by egregious inequalities.

Weyland marshals substantial empirical evidence to show that democratic governments in Brazil failed to achieve redistribution in three key policy areas: tax policy, social security, and health care. In all three areas, governments attempted to undertake redistributive measures, but these initiatives were consistently watered down, blocked, or offset by other policies that undermined their impact. The empirical evidence on all three policy areas is thorough and compelling.

Why did democratic governments fail to achieve redistribution? Weyland lays out competing theoretical explanations for the failure to reform, including rational choice approaches and structural factors (external dependency and class). His own explanation emphasizes institutional factors; he focuses on how Brazil's political institutions have constructed barriers to effective coalitions on behalf of progressive redistribution. Social fragmentation, corporatism, clientelism, and weak parties account for the inability of actors in civil society to put together an effective pro-redistribution coalition. These features weaken popular unity and organization, and, since the popular classes are the major beneficiaries of redistributive policies, this weakness strikes a blow against reformist initiatives from below. Prospects for reform from above (that is, led by state actors) are dampened by clientelism and the balkanization of the state. The final chapter assesses the generalizability of the argument on institutional obstacles to equity-enhancing reforms in other new democracies.

The book provides a careful examination of the state in Brazil, with implications for understanding the state throughout Latin America. As is well known, in late-developing countries the state has played a preponderant role. Much of the key to understanding why development policies succeed or fail lies within the state. Yet surprisingly little quality work has been done on the state. This book constitutes one of the best treatments of politics within the state in Latin America.

Weyland's book evinces theoretical acumen and comparative breadth in addition to quality empirical research. It is a welcome contribution to the understanding of democracy and development in Latin America.

SCOTT MAINWARING

University of Notre Dame
Indiana

EUROPE

MERRITT, RICHARD L. 1997. *Democracy Imposed: U.S. Occupation Policy and the German Public, 1945-1949.* Pp. xxi, 452. New Haven, CT: Yale University Press. $40.00.

Richard Merritt should have chosen a more effective title. He does not limit his discussion to the immediate postwar years—as the title implies—but instead explores issues relating to the development of democracy in western Germany from the end of World War II to the mid-1990s. He finds both continuity and discontinuity. On one hand, under Allied tutelage the postwar Germans successfully built democracy and thus broke with the recent past. On the other hand, after 1945 the Germans were unable to disconnect completely from their country's troubled history, and the experience of the Nazi dictatorship in particular continues to haunt them to this day.

The literature on the Allied occupation of Germany and U.S. efforts to democratize the Germans is extensive. An expert on public opinion surveys in occupied Germany, Merritt makes a significant contribution by examining the response of the German public to specific U.S. policies, and in the process he debunks several myths. Unlike Germany's elite, Merritt argues, the general public responded positively to U.S. efforts to impose democracy. Even programs that specialists have long viewed as highly unpopular with postwar Germans—such as war crimes trials and denazification—enjoyed considerable public support. In some areas, especially education, the occupiers initially encountered indifference only to find appreciation for their reform efforts decades later. On the whole, postwar Germans not only did not resist but accepted the occupation, believing that democratization might improve the quality of life in Germany.

However, Merritt's study also has weaknesses. It largely ignores the British and French contributions to the democratization of western Germany. This is unfortunate because democracy triumphed in all three western zones of occupation. Considering their evolution during the past 50 years, it can in fact be argued that the provinces formerly occupied by Britain and France have developed more positively than some of those in the American zone. Further, Merritt tends to exaggerate some elements of continuity. His book appears to have been written during the height of the xenophobia that swept Germany after reunification in 1990 and led to numerous violent attacks against foreigners living in Germany. As a consequence, he pays more attention to the German Right than it deserves. Democracies will never be able to clean up to everyone's satisfaction the mess left by dictatorships. The Germans had to put their house in order twice within the past 50 years, and they appear to have done no worse than others.

FRANK BUSCHER

Christian Brothers University
Memphis
Tennessee

WYN REES, G. 1998. *The Western European Union at the Crossroads: Between Trans-Atlantic Solidarity and European Integration.* Pp. x, 158. Boulder, CO: Westview Press. $55.00.

If you stand in the middle of Bad Godesberg and gaze upward across the Rhine, you will focus upon the Petersberg, a mountain redoubt that today serves as a conference center for the German government. If you focus upon the subject of this book, the Western European Union (WEU), you also cannot avoid the Petersberg, for it was a conference held there in 1992 that has endowed this star-crossed European institution with its current defense and security rationale. And therein hangs a tale, one that Wyn Rees skillfully tells, about an organization that has for decades remained suspended between two aspirations: to contribute to the defense of Western Europeans and to help build Europe.

One would think the two aspirations would be complementary. Not so. This concise book explains better than any other work I have read why it has been so difficult for the Western Europeans to make of the WEU, whose origin predates that of the North Atlantic Treaty Organization (NATO) itself, the long-awaited European "pillar" of defense (now known as the European Security and Defense Identity).

In a word, what has kept the WEU from attaining the potential some have seen it to have is NATO (aided and abetted by the United States and the United Kingdom). Not that the two organizations are sworn (or even undeclared) rivals, for Wyn Rees demonstrates not only that tension between the two was always more apparent than real during the past but that they are actually working closely together at the moment. The WEU, Wyn Rees correctly judges, has "emerged as the junior partner of the [a]lliance." It has become one of those "interlocking institutions" that NATO officials like to argue shore up today's European "security architecture."

But the WEU's effectiveness is limited by its having been unable to carve out a military niche for itself. If it served useful functions in getting NATO built in the first place, and assisting the integration of Germany into the alliance, it has never been given core collective-defense roles; these have belonged to NATO, and few Western Europeans have been bold enough to wish them devolved to the WEU. Instead, the WEU has been entrusted with the "Petersberg tasks" of humanitarian intervention, peacekeeping, and crisis management. The problem is that NATO has increasingly moved into these areas, leading many to wonder what role exists for the WEU.

I suspect Wyn Rees is premature in concluding that the problem of the European Security and Defense Identity has been "resolved" as a result of the NATO-WEU partnership, for, as he hints himself, the junior organization may yet find its niche as the vehicle for the construction of the European defense industrial base. If poorly managed, this initiative may prove to be more divisive for transatlantic security relations than any other role the WEU has been asked to play.

DAVID G. HAGLUND

Queen's University
Kingston
Ontario
Canada

UNITED STATES

APPIAH, K. ANTHONY and AMY GUTMAN. 1996. *Color Conscious: The Political Morality of Race.* Pp. 191. Princeton, NJ: Princeton University Press. Paperbound, $14.95.

K. Anthony Appiah and Amy Gutman work with the growing understanding that, as a biological or moral foundation of human difference, race does not exist. Their efforts are both reasonable and confusing given two conflicts: American egalitarian ideals versus racist social practices; the oppressive origins of racial identities versus their apparent use in resisting oppression.

In the section Race, Culture, Identity: Misunderstood Connections, Appiah explores ideas of race held by Thomas Jefferson and Mathew Arnold that included hereditary traits of individual character and group culture. These metaphysical notions eventually became attached to speculations about biological essences that have never been found (as W.E.B. Du Bois himself was aware). There are no general genes for race, no stable empirical basis for racial divisions, no sets of traits shared by all members of any so-called race. Nonetheless, nonwhites value and need racial identities, for group cohesion and resistance against oppression. Appiah's solution is that racial identities be retained in ways that do not make new oppressions out of identity politics.

In the section Responding to Racial Injustice, Gutman begins by summarizing the arguments against the reality of race that Appiah and others have recently made famous. Attending to the persistence of racism in American life, she proposes that color consciousness, an awareness of those differences that people (falsely) think are racial, be used as a basis for public policy intended to create a more just society for blacks. Given historical inequality, fairness precludes judging present policies according to ideal color-blind standards. Gutman argues that preferential treatment is necessary to create equal opportunities for employment and admission; political representation by race is democratic because elected blacks are more likely to promote racial justice than are whites; color-conscious policies are as important as class-based ones because if class is held constant, blacks are still always worse off than whites. Gutman concludes by claiming that all are morally obligated to correct racial injustice, but whites more so than blacks because they have benefited from it more.

David B. Wilkins introduces this book as the millennial answer of two prominent public intellectuals to "the problem of the color line." But he misses the fact that race itself has no scientific foundation in the way the public thinks it does. This does not help the reader to understand how it is logically possible to promote racial identification and color consciousness—without race.

NAOMI ZACK

University at Albany
State University of New York

BUSCH, ANDREW E. 1997. *Outsiders and Openness in the Presidential Nominating System.* Pp. vii, 248. Pittsburgh, PA: University of Pittsburgh Press. $45.00. Paperbound, $19.95.

This rich analysis of outsider candidacies and openness in presidential nominating systems belongs on the shelf of every expert in the field. Many readers will recognize Andrew Busch's openly acknowledged debt to James Ceaser as they work through a book that in many ways is an extension of Ceaser's 1979 classic, *Presidential Selection.*

Like his mentor and coauthor of 1992 and 1996 election books, Busch finds important connections between the institutions of presidential nominating politics and the kinds of candidates encouraged to run or discouraged from it. This subtext informs Busch's view of outsider candidacies, the role of political movements, and the access granted or denied connected and unconnected outsiders. He is at his best when revisiting the presidential bids of Estes Kefauver, Barry Goldwater, and George McGovern. Numerous others, like those of Jesse Jackson and Pat Robertson, are also well covered. The book also nicely supplements Ceaser's earlier history of how presidential nominating politics developed.

My one quarrel with this otherwise strong offering is that the definition of "outsider" is too broad and multidimensional to distinguish also-rans, serious challengers, and advocates of particular causes from plausible outsiders. Some aspirants like Jesse Jackson and Steve Forbes are deemed outsiders because they have never held elective office. Others like Jackson also qualify for leading movements "outside the corridors of power" that somehow challenge "the dominant element in the party." Still others like Pat Buchanan and the scarcely mentioned Lamar Alexander make attacking the party "establishment" or "mainstream" the centerpiece of their campaigns. Still another meaning carries over from Ceaser's 1979 account of the "mixed system" of 1912-68, when primaries supplemented but did not dominate national conventions: the "outside" strategy called for so impressing party bosses with primary victories that they would give way at the convention.

One consequence of casting the net so widely is that it snares Barry Goldwater, Ronald Reagan, and Paul Tsongas as well as George Wallace, Pat Robertson, David Duke, and others more plausibly cast as outsiders. Busch himself concedes that the Goldwater and Reagan designations are tenuous owing to the historic importance of conservatism to the GOP. What, one might ask, made Goldwater an outsider and Bob Taft an insider? Why cast Paul Tsongas as an outsider but not Tom Harkin or Bob Kerrey? A narrower definition of "outsider"—perhaps based on the candidate's explicit self-definition as such—might have avoided such difficulties.

EMMETT H. BUELL, JR.
Denison University
Granville
Ohio

CONTOSTA, DAVID R. 1997. *Philadelphia's Progressive Orphanage: The Carson Valley School*. Pp. x, 262. University Park: Pennsylvania State University Press. $34.95.

The Carson Valley School, located just outside the legal boundaries of Philadelphia, opened in 1918 as the Carson College for Orphan Girls, the product of the estate of Robert N. Carson, a local traction magnate. On the surface, a monograph on so narrow an institution would seem an exercise in antiquarianism, but David R. Contosta has used his exclusive access to people and archives to good effect. A much-published historian on the histories of education and of the Philadelphia area, he has provided the profession with an exceptionally useful monograph that touches firmly on topics of much larger interest.

As the book title indicates, the original college was something of a laboratory for progressivism in education. Familiar with the writings of John Dewey, Maria Montessori, and others in the experimental field of applying pragmatic and reformist notions to the nurturing of the young, Elsa Ueland also had personal experience in Richmond Hill House, a New York settlement, when she became the school's first president. In classic progressive fashion, she also visited the Gary school system, perhaps the best-publicized effort at radical reform along a John Dewey–style platform. Very much aware of the work of Lawrence Cremin and Patricia A. Graham, Contosta provides a fresh example of progressivism at work within an institution that goes way beyond the work on Gary currently available. All educational historians and students of progressivism need to take note.

At the same time, Contosta takes up two related ideas of importance to cultural history. Architect Albert Kelsey was very much involved with the aesthetic currents of the late nineteenth century in both England and America, and he made extensive and expensive efforts to replicate such ideas in the lovely setting opened up to his ministrations. In a wry summary, which is complemented nicely with photographs, Contosta notes that "it was all very romantic, all very Ruskinian, and all awash with Victorian neomedievalism, with its partly pagan and partly Christian idealization of woman as fertility goddess and Virgin Mother." Ralph Adams Cram and James Gamble Rogers are not the only names to conjure under the rubric of collegiate Gothic.

Simultaneously and contrastingly, Contosta is at great pains to take feminist contexts into account. In Greenwich Village before World War I, Ueland had contact with John Reed, Big Bill Haywood, Max Eastman, and Emma Goldman and developed strong views on gendering in the process. The college became something of a gynecocracy, single women living and working together, helping orphaned girls achieve self-sufficiency. Subsequent contacts with Lucy Sprague Mitchell, Jessie Taft, and other feminists reinforced liberal democratic views that supported the New Deal and the Great Society while opposing entry into World War II and Vietnam.

The writing is clear and to the point, only rarely sinking to the dutiful chronicle level; the archives are useful if not copious; the bibliography lengthy and pointed. All around, a worthy effort.

ROBERT M. CRUNDEN

University of Texas
Austin

GUSTERSON, HUGH. 1996. *Nuclear Rites: A Weapons Laboratory at the End of the Cold War*. Pp. xxviii, 351. Berkeley: University of California Press. $39.95. Paperbound, $19.95.

The cover of this book includes a surreal photograph that signals the argument found inside. In this image, ritual Indian clowns "dance" before a display of missiles. This juxtaposition suggests primitive and tribal influences operating among nuclear weapons professionals. Gusterson pursues this theme by advocating a cultural perspective on meaning and power within this community. This perspective, he argues, transcends the constraints of international relations theory and Lifton's nuclearism. The volume reports the findings of Gusterson's fieldwork conducted between 1987 and 1990 at the Lawrence Livermore National Laboratory (a premier U.S. nuclear weapons design facility) and the surrounding community of Livermore, California. The data produce four arguments.

First, Gusterson examines the socialization of nuclear weapons scientists. He argues that this process involves several turning points (for example, in questions asked during selection interviews) that incrementally normalize the axiomatic belief system of deterrence. Second, Gusterson focuses on the practices of secrecy that isolate scientists from reflective ethical dialogue with colleagues, friends, and family members. The required security-clearance investigation, he argues, is a "bureaucratic variant of classic initiation rituals" in secret societies. Third, Gusterson reviews the paradoxical status of the body for nuclear weapons professionals. They require injured and dead bodies of nuclear victims as real evidence of the usually symbolic nuclear threat. Yet these bodies are also unstable, because they potentially implicate American policymakers as the villains of Hiroshima and as potential victims of a thermonuclear war. Finally, Gusterson examines the centrality of nuclear testing, which serves a number of scientific and cultural functions. It verifies nuclear weapons designs, provides an important rite of passage for junior designers, and reassures various audiences that nuclear explosions can be successfully contained.

Surprisingly, Gusterson extends this analysis to include the opponents of Livermore science. Here, he relativizes the "different reality" of local antinuclear groups, noting their opposition to the cult of expertise, privatized ethics, and repressed emotion. These groups also possess ritual practices, such as the use of images to create a "culture of terror" in which members are encouraged to "confess" their recovery of repressed nuclear dread and outrage.

What is to be gained from this analysis? Not easy answers. A cultural perspective can demystify the excess and distortion practiced by both pro- and antinuclear groups. Comments included in the volume's postscript, however, suggest that this outcome is not welcomed by true believers. With the passing of the Cold War, a new generation of readers can use volumes such as this to interrogate the conventional wisdom that surrounds nuclear weapons like a thick, choking fog.

BRYAN C. TAYLOR

University of Colorado
Boulder

PFIFFNER, JAMES P. 1998. *The Modern Presidency*. 2d ed. Pp. x, 246. New York: St. Martin's Press. $35.00.

The Modern Presidency is a historically informed, up-to-date, and nuanced treatment of the development of the United States' most notable institutional innovation. Each chapter treats an important facet of the presidency, including its origins, the presidential selection process, the institution of the White House and Executive Office of the President, the presidency's relations with the bureaucracy and with Congress, its role in national security policy, and issues of ethics and presidential reputations.

The strength of this book, and what makes it so engaging, is Pfiffner's extensive use of concrete examples and events to illustrate his analytical points. Pfiffner begins each chapter with a general discussion of the broad contours of its topic and then fleshes out the meaning and implications of his arguments with well-written and insightful case studies drawn from a wide range of presidencies. A lot of work went into the case studies, with many so current that one feels as if they were pulled from yesterday's headlines. This approach draws the reader into the text and demonstrates the importance of the concepts and theories discussed in the opening and concluding sections of each chapter. Readers who are already well versed in the presidency will find that most of the case studies cover familiar territory, but Pfiffner's focused use of the case studies to illustrate and document his arguments makes them valuable even to these readers. And those

who are looking to build up their base of knowledge on the presidency will find the case studies interesting and informative in their own right, as well as insightful in terms of bringing the underlying theories to light.

To some extent, the emphasis on the topics covered reflects Pfiffner's own interests. For example, some readers may find the treatment of presidential chiefs of staff in particular, and the extensive discussion of the presidential institution more generally (chapters 3, 4, and part of 5), somewhat overwhelming. In contrast, other readers may wonder why greater attention is not given to the role of interest groups or the media or why a chapter is devoted to national security matters but not to an equally pressing presidential role in economic policy. These, however, are minor issues that could be raised with most books. In the final analysis, Pfiffner has provided us with a well-balanced, informative, and interesting overview of the presidency. Scholars and students alike will benefit from reading it.

CARY R. COVINGTON

University of Iowa
Iowa City

RUBIN, JEFFREY W. 1997. *Decentering the Regime: Ethnicity, Radicalism, and Democracy in Juchitán, Mexico*. Pp. xii, 316. $54.95. Paperbound, $17.95.

Juchitán (pronounced hoo-chee-*tahn*), an ethnically Zapotec Indian town in southern Mexico, has long been remarkable for its political radicalism in defense of local autonomy. In a most stimulating and challenging way, Jeffrey Rubin traces the historical trajectory of such intransigence and reaches several illuminating conclusions: (1) the "resistance" of the Juchitecos has incorporated enormous dosages of negotiation and compromise to create a balance with threatening outsiders; (2) the Zapotec villagers have always been (and still are) severely factionalized over what approaches to problems and issues best suit themselves and their community; (3) the swirl of ambiguities and contradictions that characterize Juchitán's local culture have energized the brand of democracy that characterizes the place.

Such findings generally support much of the current scholarship on village life in Mexico, especially that proffered by proponents of the so-called subaltern approach to understanding the nature of state hegemony. In this view, the power of the state is delimited and proscribed by an unrelenting dynamic process of contestations that radiate from family to village, testing and sparing, opposing and accommodating, on to regional, national, and even global levels. As these struggles are naturally shaped by the context of place and time, outcomes differ and often in surprising ways.

Rubin is acute in tracing these developments for Juchitán. Because those directing the country's modernization program at the turn of the century saw Indians as obstacles to progress, interventions by the regime forced the Juchitecos into outright rebellion. However, after the Revolution of 1910, when the glorification of Mexico's Indian past became the hallmark of officially promoted nationalism, the Juchitecos established a kind of détente with the government—one in which they traded peace for limited autonomy. By the 1960s, Zapotec leaders from the region had become quite cozy with the ruling powers, too cozy for students and others radicalized by the worldwide political and social upheaval of the period. Their outcries for meaningful change—the end of corruption, relief for the poor, fair elections—gave birth to a political movement called the Coalition of Workers, Peasants, and Students of the Isthmus (COCEI), which suffered military repression in the 1970s but has governed Juchitán since 1989. Bolstered by assistance negotiated with the federal government, Juchitecos now enjoy relative economic well-being, cultural autonomy, and political democracy.

Rubin, a political scientist, focuses much of his attention on the COCEI, an organization marked by vagueness and controversy in such important arenas as gender relations, attitudes toward the use of violence, historical representations, and the value of their work, matters that members openly debate in the course of their daily activities. Such open-ended, free-wheeling practices have created opportunities for the Zapotecs to elaborate on their cultural traditions and has given them the wherewithal to resist the encroachments of national urban culture, even as they borrow from that culture. It is this concentration on culture that distinguishes Rubin's work. One might wish that he had treated religion and faith more thoroughly, and some will argue that his attempt to generalize his findings at Juchitán to other localities in Mexico runs rather thinly, but with this fine book, Jeffrey Rubin has certainly proved himself to be a keen participant-observer and a thoughtful, original analyst who can clearly state his case.

PAUL J. VANDERWOOD

San Diego State University
California

TOLCHIN, SUSAN J. 1996. *The Angry American: How Voter Rage Is Changing the Nation*. Pp. xvi, 170. Boulder, CO: Westview Press. $45.00. Paperbound, $13.95.

Poor Susan Tolchin. By the time her book on the angry American reached my desk, Americans seemed to be over their anger. Both Bill Clinton and the Gingrich Congress had been reelected, and, despite allegations of sleaze, Clinton was enjoying unprecedentedly high ratings. By the time this review is published, who knows what adjective will best describe the American citizenry!

After an opening chapter that focuses on the 1994 elections and their aftermath, Tolchin discusses the roots and nature of political anger; how the stagnant economic position of the middle classes feeds that anger; cultural cleavages of the 1990s, including battles over sexual permissiveness, the media, intolerance, and "gangsta rap"; and the difficulties that moderate politicians have in responding to political anger. A brief summary chapter ends with a call for "creative" political leadership to convert anger into a "force for justice." The operative assumption is that despite short-term fluctuations in the public mood, demands on politics and the underlying economic and cultural discontents will be with us for a long time.

Evaluating this short book in a journal devoted to social science requires understanding that, although Tolchin teaches public administration at George Washington University, her target audience is not the social science community. Most of the jacket blurbs are from journalists, and indeed the book might well have been written by one of them. The reader is treated to numerous illustrations of the mid-1990s political mood but searches in vain for a comprehensive theory that ties together the various elements of Tolchin's analysis. Near the end of her final chapter, she seems to endorse former Senator James Sasser's comment that it is corporations, not government, that are "screwing" Americans, but her closing exhortation for creative leadership does not focus on economic power.

Nor is Tolchin's methodology informed by social science. Hers is the anecdotal method. Seldom, in a book devoted

to analyzing the American mood, are there references to survey data, and nowhere is there close analysis of particular surveys. At one point she refers to an "anger scale" but without describing it. One need not be a conservative to notice that most of her favorable references are to liberal politicians, while most of her examples of political chicanery are of conservatives; she even includes in her list of "hate language" the use of "liberal" as a label for one's opponent.

With vigorous style, Tolchin provides the reader with an inventory of the preoccupations of many Americans in our own fin de siècle. Those who are seeking an interpretation informed by rigorous social scientific analysis will need to look elsewhere.

HOWARD L. REITER

University of Connecticut
Storrs

SOCIOLOGY

ALBROW, MARTIN. 1996. *The Global Age: State and Society Beyond Modernity*. Pp. ix, 246. Stanford, CA: Stanford University Press. $45.00. Paperbound, $17.95.

Although linkages between different parts of the world have existed for millennia, it is only in recent years that quantitative and qualitative increases in global networks, global activities, and global flows (of capital, information, and peoples) have begun to enter our vocabulary and our conceptual frameworks. Thus, one will be hard-pressed to find publications before 1985 that discussed globalization, while the World Wide Web became a reality only in the present decade. British sociologist Martin Albrow has been a promoter of extending sociological inquiry beyond national frontiers, and *The Global Age* represents the capstone of his efforts to date.

Albrow is persuaded and seeks to persuade the reader that even new approaches emphasizing globalization provide an inadequate conceptual framework for the emergent epochal change. What has to be grasped, he posits, is nothing short of a new age replacing the Age of Modernity, the latter having various characteristics that have shaped our experiencing the world in the past two or three centuries. The "Global Age" will have new configurations, new forms of social relationships, new forms of leadership, new forms of citizenship. To grasp these emergent configurations, the social sciences will need a new conceptual framework, which Albrow seeks to sketch out. "Globalization" itself contains ambiguities in its usage: if taken as an appendage to "modernization," it falls short of catching the important set of transformations taking place in the current transition from a nation-state–centered world to a decentered "globality."

A central part of his argument is the emergent decoupling of the nation-state and all that that entails given that the social sciences have anchored their basic unit of analysis in the nation-state. The nation-state provided the basic territorial frame for the analysis of society, and the basic standard for that which is modern. The new playing field of world society lacks the directionality and expansionism of nation-state societies in their prime but has "the dynamism of an untrammeled sociality." This suggests that Albrow's discussion of the end of "the Modern Project," begun in the eighteenth century, is not mired in pessimism (as are some of the secular apocalypses warning of global warming, population explosions, and so forth), late-modernity nihilism (post-modernism), or undue optimism (as the modernization analyses of Kahn, Parsons, and Inkeles might be viewed). More positive than negative in his outlook, he views unfolding possibilities for the global state, global citizenship (such as Doctors Without Borders), and global social movements (already in place with environmentalism and the women's movement); basic features of this "Global Age" are shifting boundaries and the "contemporaneity of the past and the copresence of different cultures."

Like Fukuyama and Huntington seeking to provide new global paradigms at a closing phase of modernity, Albrow covers a wide range of materials in bold brush strokes. Some may extol *The Global Age* in the prophetic tradition of Nietzsche's *Thus Spoke Zarathustra* but, at the same time, wish it contained greater and more detailed empirical evidence.

EDWARD A. TIRYAKIAN

Center for Advanced Study
   in the Behavioral Sciences
Stanford
California

Duke University
Durham
North Carolina

EARLE, TIMOTHY K. 1997. *How Chiefs Come to Power: The Political Economy in Prehistory.* Pp. xv, 250. Stanford, CA: Stanford University Press. $45.00. Paperbound, $17.95.

This concise and elegantly written book examines how chiefs develop and maintain political power in prestate complex societies, or what anthropologists commonly refer to as chiefdoms. While chiefdoms are regional polities of significantly smaller scale and complexity than states, and they retain strongly kin-based social and political relations, Earle emphasizes that the dynamics of chiefly power are similar to those of state rulership. Therefore, historians, political scientists, and other social theorists studying more complex states will find much of interest in Earle's anthropological discussion of how institutions of governance and strategies of political coercion emerge and evolve.

In his analysis, Earle distills the fundamental elements from the political process in chiefdoms, showing how leaders manipulate economic, military, and ideological sources of power to reinforce and expand their political spheres of influence. However, he demonstrates through historical and archaeological analysis that the long-term evolutionary trajectories of chiefdoms vary dramatically, depending on how these economic, military, and ideological sources of power are combined into integrated power strategies. These differing power strategies—in some cases, culminating in the evolution of more strongly centralized states and, in other instances, resulting in the perpetuation of fragmented and unstable polities—are seen as arising out of differing historical circumstances, ecological conditions, and cultural milieus. Earle empirically documents this multilinear nature of chiefdom evolution by focusing on three divergent cases known through archaeological and historical investigation: Denmark during the Late Neolithic and Early Bronze Ages (2300-1300 B.C.), Hawai'i from its early colonization phase to European domination (A.D. 800-1824), and Andean chiefdoms of Peru in the thousand years prior to Inca conquest (A.D. 500-1534). Adding weight to Earle's comparative analysis is the fact that he has carried out extensive archaeological field research programs in each of these far-flung locales, and he is well versed in the historical literature relevant to the contact-period culmination of chiefdom development in Polynesia and Europe.

While he provides a synopsis of what is known about the cultural history of each of these regions of chiefdom emergence in the introductory chapters, the main chapters are organized around theoretical issues of economic, military, and ideological power. He examines how these sources of power are materialized in the political economy, how they were differently used by chiefs in prehistoric Denmark, Hawai'i, and Peru to create unique power strategies, and the evolutionary implications of these contrasting paths to power. Nonanthropologists who are less interested in the archaeological details of these cases than in how anthropologists think about political evolution will find Earle's book more accessible than any previous anthropological studies of prestate complex societies. For anthropologists, this book is path-breaking in its sophisticated dissection of the relationship between ideology and other sources of power that narrows the gap between cultural evolutionary, Marxist, symbolic, and human agency theories of complex society development.

LAURA JUNKER

Vanderbilt University
Nashville
Tennessee

HOWE, MICHAEL J. A. 1997. *IQ in Question: The Truth About Intelligence.* Pp. x, 173. Thousand Oaks, CA: Sage. $69.95. Paperbound, $23.95.

This relentlessly tendentious and narrowly selective book strives to overturn accepted views of intelligence, its strongly genetic basis, and the importance of its effects, as recently supported, for example, by 52 experts in the journal *Intelligence* (Jan.-Feb. 1997). A few diagnostic illustrations follow.

IQ approximates the interval scale level of measurement. Howe describes real measurement as though it consisted only of ratio scales and so misleadingly denies that IQ, which lacks a ratio scale's meaningful zero point, represents measurement at all.

Howe never mentions that IQ correlations between unrelated adults reared together are zero, whereas IQ correlations between identical twins reared apart are about .72, well above that of fraternal twins reared together. These findings indicate that sociological correlates of IQ are causally weak and that Howe's efforts to discredit heritability and mainstream science on intelligence are suspect.

A 1946 study by Bernardine Schmidt is cited as evidence for the great malleability of IQ. Howe reports only that her "investigation was criticized on a number of counts" and blithely insists, "but the main findings appear to be genuine." Criticism of Schmidt's unreplicated claims for massive IQ gains stopped just short, however, of declaring them fraudulent.

Howe reports the average black-white difference in IQ as 10 points, when, in fact, it is typically close to 18. Without alerting readers to its aberrant nature, he has apparently chosen to report only the inexplicably low value observed for the middle age group (7-11) from the 1986 standardization of the Stanford-Binet.

The Nazi genocide is distractingly injected and the Pioneer Fund, which has supported much IQ research, is consequently maligned in a familiar manner. Howe reports, "Its treasurer, John B. Trevor, worked for a group that was named in a . . . Justice Department sedition indictment for pro-Nazi activities." Unsuspecting readers might conclude that Trevor's group had been indicted; gullible ones might assume further that this somehow invalidated certain findings about IQ that conflict with Howe's views.

Trevor's father, who was never a Pioneer officer, had been president in 1942 of the American Coalition of Patriotic Socie-ties, for which his son, the Pioneer treasurer, later worked. Both Trevors bear the same name. A "Coalition of Patriotic Societies" was merely listed in 1942 as one of many organizations targeted by the persons who actually were indicted, and the name John Trevor, to the senior Trevor's distress, was identified with the organization in a handout at a Justice Department press conference. Neither the senior Trevor nor other members of the organization were among those indicted, Howe's misleading reference to "named" notwithstanding.

Eventually, a charge against Trevor senior similar to Howe's was published in 1954 by Ralph McGill, of the *Atlanta Constitution*, and Trevor sued for libel. Armed with an affidavit from the U.S. assistant attorney general who had conducted the grand jury investigation resulting in the sedition indictment, Trevor's executors were able to prove after his death that both Trevor and the American Coalition were completely exculpated, and thus could secure a retraction from McGill in 1957. Perhaps Sage Publications will prove as gracious.

ROBERT A. GORDON

Johns Hopkins University
Baltimore
Maryland

JENSEN, ARTHUR R. 1998. *The g Factor: The Science of Mental Ability*. Pp. xiv, 648. Westport, CT: Praeger. $39.95.

In 1969, Arthur Jensen published an article in *Harvard Educational Review* titled "How Much Can We Boost IQ and Scholastic Achievement?" The answer, according to Jensen, was essentially "not much." Jensen argued two basic points: (1) most attempts to raise IQ had achieved, at best, modest effects; and (2) partly based on the failure of attempts to raise IQ, the preponderance of evidence indicated that IQ was primarily the outcome of inherited, rather than environmental, influences. The controversy over such assertions (both ones made in his article and others not made but misinterpreted by critics) was like no other before or since in modern psychology. Jensen's latest book finds him still answering these critics. Jensen has devoted his career to refining and bolstering his initial arguments about general intelligence (called g by Spearman in 1904) and to demonstrating the genetic basis for g in explaining racial differences.

During this period, Jensen has not been in the eye of the hurricane of controversy but, rather, at the leading edge. He has published widely on intelligence, including experimental studies and theoretical treatises. He has attempted in previous books to answer critics but also to explain the issues to the informed lay audience. This most recent book falls somewhere between these two endpoints; the book is full of highly technical information, but it is presented so that a scientifically minded lay audience can understand. He also presents a wealth of citations to original research and extensive technical notes.

This book presents the most rigorous arguments for the existence of g and a description of the consequences of individual differences in g, for example, in terms of education, social, and economic success. Jensen describes the psychological, genetic, and biological determinants of g in excruciating detail. If a reader starts with the notion that general intelligence is a fictional concept, this work will easily dispel such a belief.

What this book does not do, though, is present a balanced treatment of the literature. Jensen is best at slaying extreme critics (for example, those who hold that there is no genetic component of intelligence or that Howard Gardner's theory of multiple intelligences falsifies a theory of general intelligence), but he is an advocate for a particular view. Far too few troublesome facts (of which many exist) from the extant literature are included for discussion. Jensen's book is clearly a testimony to the insights of Spearman. However, in some ways, the book suffers from the same flaw as in Spearman's unique use of factor analysis (a critical tool for deriving g). When data were found that did not fit Spearman's "hierarchical order," investigators were instructed to "purify" the measures (that is, throw out the offending data) so that the data fit the theory.

In the final analysis, general intelligence or g is important in the same way that Newton's theory of gravity is important. It makes many important and useful predictions (and these are pointed out quite cogently in Jensen's book). However, Newton's theory was but one step in the endless search for a reductionistic truth, rather than truth itself. Jensen's theory can be no greater and still remain scientific (that is, falsifiable)—a fundamental truth that does not receive much attention in this work.

PHILLIP L. ACKERMAN

Georgia Institute of Technology
Atlanta

ECONOMICS

REDMAN, DEBORAH A. 1997. *The Rise of Political Economy as a Science: Methodology and the Classical Economists.* Pp. xviii, 471. Cambridge: MIT Press. $55.00.

This is a study of both the methodology of the English classical political economists and the philosophical sources upon which they presumably relied. The principal sources on which Redman concentrates are, not surprisingly, Francis Bacon, René Descartes, John Herschel,

Thomas Hobbes, David Hume, John Locke, Isaac Newton, Dugald Stewart, and William Whewell. They are examined in a chapter on the philosophical background and influences, followed by chapters on science in eighteenth- and nineteenth-century Britain and on a "short history of induction." Then follow three chapters on Adam Smith, Malthus and Ricardo, and John Stuart Mill, respectively.

Redman claims only to have produced a survey and not to have broken any new ground. She has succeeded admirably in producing a comprehensive work studying both the methodological heritage and methodologies of the classical economists, bringing to bear a substantial intellect and a wide mastery of primary and secondary sources.

While an important new single survey, the book has its limitations. Some have to do with coverage: Whewell is a contemporary and rival, not part of the heritage, of the four economists. Not enough attention is given to Richard Jones. Nor is sufficient attention given to other classical economists, such as Nassau William Senior, although the later ideas of William Stanley Jevons and of Karl Popper are taken up. Too much is made of deduction versus induction, or of rationalism versus empiricism, and of in-

dividuals' self-perception, in comparison with their practice, and not enough of how much in practice all work is some combination of each—and that all writers, notwithstanding their specific methodological theorizing, are practitioners of multiple methodologies. This was particularly true of Smith, Mill, and Jevons but applies to all the classical economists. Political economy was not a homogeneous "science." Also the question arises as to how much earlier philosophical thought actually channeled practice and how much it served only to selectively legitimize the practices actually followed because Smith et al. were comfortable with them. In these respects, the conventionality of Redman's survey is both its strength and its weakness. Among the other strengths of the work, on the other hand, are her sensitive treatments of eighteenth- and nineteenth-century science, the importance of Smith's essay "The History of Astronomy," and, indeed, Smith in general.

Redman's book is almost certain to become a standard reference work for historians of economic thought, no mean accomplishment.

WARREN J. SAMUELS

Michigan State University
East Lansing

OTHER BOOKS

ALAGAPPA, MUTHIAH, ed. 1998. *Asian Security Practice: Material and Ideational Influences*. Pp. xvii, 851. Stanford, CA: Stanford University Press. $75.00. Paperbound, $29.95.

ALEXANDER, RUTH M. 1995. *The "Girl Problem": Female Sexual Delinquency in New York, 1900-1930*. Pp. x, 200. Ithaca, NY: Cornell University Press. No price.

ALLEN, R. T. 1998. *Beyond Liberalism: The Political Thought of F. A. Hayek and Michael Polanyi*. Pp. x, 266. New Brunswick, NJ: Transaction. $39.95.

BARBERA, HENRY. 1998. *The Military Factor in Social Change*. Vol. 2. Pp. x, 338. New Brunswick, NJ: Transaction. $49.95.

BARILLEAUX, RYAN J., ed. 1998. *Presidential Frontiers: Underexplored Issues in White House Politics*. Pp. xiii, 237. Westport, CT: Praeger. $59.95.

BLUM, GEORGE P. 1998. *The Rise of Fascism in Europe*. Pp. xx, 196. Westport, CT: Greenwood Press. $39.95.

CALLON, MICHEL. 1998. *The Laws of the Markets*. Pp. 278. Cambridge, MA: Basil Blackwell. Paperbound, $31.95.

CHATTERJEE, PARTHA. 1998. *A Possible India: Essays in Political Criticism*. Pp. xii, 301. New York: Oxford University Press. $29.95.

CLINGMAN, STEPHEN. 1998. *Bram Fischer: Afrikaner Revolutionary*. Pp. xi, 500. Amherst: University of Massachusetts Press. $29.95.

COLL, BLANCE D. 1995. *Safety Net: Welfare and Social Security, 1929-1979*. Pp. xiii, 347. New Brunswick, NJ: Rutgers University Press. $47.00.

ELAZAR, DANIEL J. 1998. *Constitutionalizing Globalization: The Postmodern Revival of Confederal Arrangements*. Pp. vii, 250. Lanham, MD: Rowman & Littlefield. $63.00. Paperbound, $23.95.

EMERY, CARLA. 1997. *Secret, Don't Tell: The Encyclopedia of Hypnotism*. Pp. xxxi, 511. Hornbrook, CA: Acorn Hill. $39.95. Paperbound, $27.95.

FERGUSON, THOMAS. 1995. *Golden Rule: The Investment Theory of Party Competition and the Logic of Money-Driven Political Systems*. Pp. v, 432. Chicago: University of Chicago Press. $55.00. Paperbound, $17.95.

GENOSKO, GARY. 1998. *Undisciplined Theory*. Pp. viii, 206. Thousand Oaks, CA: Sage. Paperbound, $22.95.

GLADNEY, DRU C., ed. 1998. *Making Majorities: Constituting the Nation in Japan, Korea, China, Malaysia, Fiji, Turkey, and the United States*. Pp. xv, 350. Stanford, CA: Stanford University Press. $55.00. Paperbound, $19.95.

GOUX, JEAN-JOSEPH and PHILIP R. WOOD, eds. 1998. *Terror and Consensus: Vicissitudes of French Thought*. Pp. xi, 22. Stanford, CA: Stanford University Press. $45.00. Paperbound, $18.95.

HAAS, ERNST B. 1997. *Nationalism, Liberalism, and Progress*. Vol. 1, *The Rise and Decline of Nationalism*. Pp. ix, 362. Ithaca, NY: Cornell University Press. $39.95.

HANSEN, BIRTHE and BERTEL HEURLIN, eds. 1998. *The Baltic States in World Politics*. Pp. ix, 164. New York: St. Martin's Press. $59.95. Paperbound, $19.95.

HARRIS, MAXINE. 1998. *Trauma Recovery and Empowerment: A Clinician's Guide for Working with Women in Groups*. Pp. xvi, 405. New York: Free Press. Paperbound, $27.95.

HEFNER, ROBERT W., ed. 1998. *Democratic Civility: The History and Cross-Cultural Possibility of a Modern Political Ideal*. Pp. ix, 330. New Brunswick, NJ: Transaction. No price.

HENRY, RYAN and C. EDWARD PEARTREE, eds. 1998. *The Information Revolution and International Se-*

curity. Pp. xx, 194. Washington, DC: Center for Strategic and International Studies. Paperbound, $21.95.

HUBAN, MARK. 1998. *Warriors of the Prophet: The Struggle for Islam.* Pp. xix, 196. Boulder, CO: Westview Press. $25.00.

JANDT, FRED E. 1998. *Intercultural Communication.* Pp. xiii, 488. Thousand Oaks, CA: Sage. Paperbound, $36.50.

KING, CHARLES and NEIL J. MELVIN, eds. 1998. *Nations Abroad: Diaspora Politics and International Relations in the Former Soviet Union.* Pp. 240. Boulder, CO: Westview Press. $59.00.

KNIGHT, AMY. 1996. *Spies Without Cloaks: The KGB's Successors.* Pp. xiii, 318. Princeton, NJ: Princeton University Press. $24.95.

KORN, JESSICA. 1998. *The Power of Separation: American Constitutionalism and the Myth of the Legislative Veto.* Pp. 178. Princeton, NJ: Princeton University Press. Paperbound, $16.95.

KURTZ, HOWARD. 1998. *Spin Cycle: How the White House and the Media Manipulate the News.* Pp. xxii, 346. New York: Touchstone. Paperbound, $14.00.

LANDES, JOAN B. 1998. *Feminism, the Public and the Private.* Pp. x, 507. New York: Oxford University Press. $75.00. Paperbound, $19.95.

LERNER, ROBERT, ALTHEA K. NAGAI, and STANLEY ROTHMAN. 1995. *Molding the Good Citizen: The Politics of High School History Texts.* Pp. x, 187. Westport, CT: Praeger. $55.00. Paperbound, $17.95.

LEWIS, PETER, ed. 1998. *Africa: Dilemmas of Development and Change.* Pp. vii, 456. Boulder, CO: Westview Press. $79.00. Paperbound, $30.00.

LUHMANN, NIKLAS. 1998. *Observations on Modernity.* Pp. x, 147. Stanford, CA: Stanford University Press. $45.00. Paperbound, $17.95.

LUPTON, DEBORAH. 1998. *The Emotional Self.* Pp. vii, 195. Thousand Oaks, CA: Sage. Paperbound, $22.95.

MacNAGHTEN, PHIL and JOHN URRY. 1998. *Contested Natures.* Pp. viii, 307. Thousand Oaks, CA: Sage. Paperbound, $26.50.

MALLICK, ROSS. 1998. *Development, Ethnicity and Human Rights in South Asia.* Pp. 375. Thousand Oaks, CA: Sage. $44.00.

MALTESE, JOHN ANTHONY. 1995. *The Selling of Supreme Court Nominees.* Pp. xii, 193. Baltimore, MD: Johns Hopkins University Press. No price.

MANN, JIM. 1998. *Tomorrow's Global Community: How the Information Deluge Is Transforming Business and Government.* Pp. 472. Philadelphia: Trans-Atlantic. Paperbound, no price.

MATHEW, E. T. 1997. *Employment and Unemployment in Kerala: Some Neglected Aspects.* Pp. 190. New Delhi, India: Sage. $32.00.

McCRILLIS, NEAL R. 1998. *The British Conservative Party in the Age of Universal Suffrage Popular Conservatism, 1918-1929.* Pp. x, 314. Columbus: Ohio State University Press. $41.95.

McDANIEL, TIM. 1998. *The Agony of the Russian Idea.* Pp. x, 201. Princeton, NJ: Princeton University Press. Paperbound, $14.95.

McDONAGH, BOBBY. 1998. *Original Sin in a Brave New World: An Account of the Negotiation of the Treaty of Amsterdam.* Pp. xiv, 249. Dublin: Institute of European Affairs. Paperbound, no price.

McSWEENEY, DEAN and JOHN E. OWENS, eds. 1998. *The Republican Takeover of Congress.* Pp. xii, 202. New York: St. Martin's Press. $59.95.

MELANSON, RICHARD A. 1996. *American Foreign Policy Since the Vietnam*

War: The Search for Consensus from Nixon to Clinton. Pp. x, 323. Armonk, NY: M. E. Sharpe. $62.95. Paperbound, $21.95.

O'BRIEN, MARTIN and SUE PENNA. 1998. *Theorising Welfare: Enlightenment and Modern Society.* Pp. viii, 248. Thousand Oaks, CA: Sage. $74.50. Paperbound, $24.95.

PAN, ZHONGDANG, STEVEN H. CHAFFEE, GODWIN C. CHU, and YANAN JU. 1994. *To See Ourselves: Comparing Traditional Chinese and American Cultural Values.* Pp. xiv, 258. Boulder, CO: Westview Press. $49.95.

PARKER, IAN, ed. 1998. *Social Constructionism, Discourse and Realism.* Pp. xii, 159. Thousand Oaks, CA: Sage. Paperbound, $22.95.

PAYNE, RICHARD J. 1995. *The Clash with Distant Cultures: Values, Interests, and Force in American Foreign Policy.* Pp. xvii, 285. Albany: State University of New York Press. $24.50.

PECORA, DAVID V. 1998. *Between the Raindrops.* Pp. v, 248. New York: Vantage Press. $21.95.

PILKINGTON, COLIN. 1998. *Issues in British Politics.* Pp. x, 278. New York: St. Martin's Press. $55.00. Paperbound, $19.95.

RUBIN, BARNETT R. and JACK SNYDER. 1998. *Post-Soviet Political Order: Conflict and State Building.* Pp. xi, 201. New York: Routledge. $80.00. Paperbound, $25.99.

RUESCHEMEYER, DIETRICH, MARILYN RUESCHEMEYER, and BJORN WITTROCK, eds. 1998. *Participation and Democracy East and West: Comparisons and Interpretations.* Pp. xi, 290. Armonk, NY: M. E. Sharpe. $70.00. Paperbound, $29.95.

SHOGAN, ROBERT. 1998. *The Fate of the Union: America's Rocky Road to Political Stalemate.* Pp. xi, 332. Boulder, CO: Westview Press. $27.95.

SIGEL, ROBERTA S. 1996. *Ambition and Accommodation: How Women View Gender Relations.* Pp. x, 240. Chicago: University of Chicago Press. $48.00. Paperbound, $16.95.

SOFER, SASSON. 1998. *Zionism and the Foundations of Israeli Diplomacy.* Pp. xiii, 449. New York: Cambridge University Press. $59.95.

STONE, CLARENCE N., ed. 1998. *Changing Urban Education.* Pp. xv, 316. Lawrence: University Press of Kansas. $45.00. Paperbound, $17.95.

VICKERS, BRIAN. 1998. *Bacon: The History of the Reign of King Henry VII.* Pp. xlv, 284. New York: Cambridge University Press. $59.95. Paperbound, $19.95.

———, ed. 1998. *The History of the Reign of King Henry VII.* Pp. xlv, 284. New York: Cambridge University Press. $59.95. Paperbound, $19.95.

WAAL, FRANS DE. 1998. *Chimpanzee Politics: Power and Sex Among Apes.* Pp. xv, 235. Baltimore, MD: Johns Hopkins University Press. $29.95.

WALLERSTEIN, IMMANUEL. 1998. *Utopistics: Or, Historical Choices of the Twenty-First Century.* Pp. ix, 93. New York: New Press. Paperbound, $12.95.

WHETTEN, DAVID A. and PAUL C. GODFREY, eds. 1998. *Identity in Organizations: Building Theory Through Conversations.* Pp. xi, 308. Thousand Oaks, CA: Sage. $61.50. Paperbound, $31.95.

WHITCOMB, ROGER S. 1998. *The American Approach to Foreign Affairs: An Uncertain Tradition.* Pp. x, 149. Westport, CT: Praeger. $59.95.

INDEX

A Special Issue of
Journal of Adolescent Research

AT-RISK ADOLESCENTS:
Variations and Contexts, Part I and II

Editor
Gerald R. Adams, *University of Guelph*

Organizers
Brian Barber, *Brigham Young University* and
James Youniss, *Catholic University of America*

Part I

Introduction: At-Risk Adolescents

Student Council, Volunteering, Basketball, or Marching Band: What Kind of Extracurricular Involvement Matters?

Predictors of Competence Among Offspring of Depressed Mothers

Early Environmental Support and Elementary School Adjustment as Predictors of School Adjustment in Middle Adolescence

The Long Branch of Phase-Environment Fit: Concurrent and Longitudinal Implications of Match and Mismatch Among Diabetic and Nondiabetic Youth

Part II

At-Risk Adolescents: A Broader View of Context

Academic Functioning and Mental Health in Adolescence: Patterns, Progressions, and Routes From Childhood

Middle Childhood Antecedents to Progressions in Male Adolescent Substance Use: An Ecological Analysis of Risk and Protection

Political Violence, Family Relations, and Palestinian Youth Functioning

Adaptive Behavior in Adopted Children: Predictors From Early Risk, Collaboration in Relationships Within the Adoptive Kinship Network, and Openness Arrangements

The Role of Community Service in Identity Development: Normative, Unconventional, and Deviant Orientations

Journal of Adolescent Research
Volume 14, Numbers 1 & 2
Single issue rates:
Individual $17 / Institution $52

Subscribe Today!
Phone: 805-499-9774 • Fax: 805-499-0871
E-mail: order@sagepub.com

SAGE PUBLICATIONS, INC.
2455 Teller Road
Thousand Oaks, CA 91320

SAGE PUBLICATIONS LTD
6 Bonhill Street
London EC2A 4PU, England

SAGE PUBLICATIONS INDIA PVT. LTD
M-32 Market, Greater Kailash I
New Delhi 110 048, India

A Special Issue of
Family and Conciliation Courts Review

WORLD CONGRESS

Papers and Presentations From the Second World Congress on Family Law and the Rights of Children & Youth

Editor: Andrew Schepard
Hofstra University Law Department

Even if you missed the 1997 Second World Congress, you won't want to miss this Special Issue of **Family and Conciliation Courts Review** featuring papers presented at the conference. Explore important topics on children's rights at an international level. For attorneys, judges, parent educators, mediators, and professionals in mental health and social services, **Family and Conciliation Courts Review** is the primary source for the latest discussions on family court issues.

Contents: The Long-Term Impact of Divorce on Children / Child Abuse Allegations in Custody and Access Disputes in Family Court of Australia / Personality Disorder and the Measure of Dangerousness / The Care and Protection of Children and Youth / Stepparents, the Forgotten Family Member / Early Identification of Parents at Risk for Custody Violations and Prevention of Child Abductions / Children of War

Family and Conciliation Courts Review
Volume 36, Number 3 / July 1998
Single issue: Individual $17 / Institution $48

Order Today!
Phone: 805-499-9774 • Fax: 805-499-0871
E-mail: order@sagepub.com

SAGE PUBLICATIONS, INC.
2455 Teller Road
Thousand Oaks, CA 91320

SAGE PUBLICATIONS LTD
6 Bonhill Street
London EC2A 4PU, England

SAGE PUBLICATIONS INDIA PVT. LTD
M-32 Market, Greater Kailash I
New Delhi 110 048, India

Journal of Early Adolescence

Editor
E. Ellen Thornburg
Tucson, Arizona

The **Journal of Early Adolescence** is the premier forum for research with adolescents ten to fifteen. Each issue provides you with the latest, highest quality information on the care, education, and development of young adolescents. Bringing together leading researchers, scholars, and professionals, the **Journal of Early Adolescence** bridges theory, research, and practice to explore issues facing today's young adolescents.

Recent Article Highlights

Maureen E. Kenny, Richard Lomax, Mary Brabeck, and Jennifer Fife
Longitudinal Pathways Linking Adolescent Reports of Maternal and Paternal Attachments to Psychological Well-Being

Mara Brendgen, Frank Vitaro, and William M. Bukowski
Affiliation With Delinquent Friends:
Contributions of Parents, Self-Esteem, Delinquent Behavior, and Rejection by Peers

Gustavo Carlo, Scott C. Roesch, and Jeff Melby
The Multiplicative Relations of Parenting and Temperament to Prosocial and Antisocial Behaviors in Adolescence

Nancy A. Hanna
Predictors of Friendship Quality and Peer Group Acceptance at Summer Camp

Quarterly: February, May, August, November
Yearly rates: Individual $60 / Institution $198

The **Journal of Early Adolescence** is abstracted or indexed in *AGRICOLA, Chicorel Abstracts to Reading and Learning Disabilities, Child Development Abstracts and Bibliography, Current Contents/Social & Behavioral Sciences, ERIC/ CASS, Family Resources Database, Mental Health Abstracts, Psychological Abstracts, PsycINFO, Sage Family Studies Abstracts, Social Planning/Policy and Social Development, Social Welfare, Social Work Abstracts,* and *Sociological Abstracts.*

Subscribe Today!
Sage Customer Service: 805-499-9774 • **Sage FaxLine:** 805-499-0871
Visit us at http://www.sagepub.com

SAGE PUBLICATIONS, INC.
2455 Teller Road
Thousand Oaks, CA 91320

SAGE PUBLICATIONS LTD
6 Bonhill Street
London EC2A 4PU, England

SAGE PUBLICATIONS INDIA PVT. LTD
M-32 Market, Greater Kailash I
New Delhi 110 048, India

"Family historians have shown us that views of children and childhood, and of parental responsibilities, have changed over the centuries. In some segments of American society today, there is a belief that parents alone can – and should–meet all of their children's needs. But in other eras and in other places, people have recognized that parents need assistance in raising their children to adulthood; that entire communities–indeed, entire societies– must invest in all children." –*Editors*

A Special Issue of
Journal of Family Issues

The Changing Circumstances of Children's Lives

Editor: Constance L. Shehan and Karen Seccombe

In this collection of articles, prominent family scholars examine the ways in which the social circumstances of children's lives change in response to major demographic trends.

CONTENTS

The Changing Circumstances of Children's Lives

Children in Single-Father Families in Demographic Perspective

Will Johnny See Daddy This Week? *An Empirical Test of Three Theoretical Perspectives of Postdivorce Contact*

Mental Health Outcomes Following Recent Parental Divorce: *The Case of Young Adult Offspring*

Will the Children Ever Leave? *Parent-Child Coresidence History and Plans*

Staying in School: *Maternal Employment and the Timing of Black and White Daughter's School Exit*

Market Child Care Versus Care by Relatives: *Choices Made by Employed and Nonemployed Mothers*

ORDER TODAY!
Phone: 805-499-9774 • Fax: 805-499-0871
E-mail: order@sagepub.com

Journal of Family Issues
Volume 17, Number 4 / July 1996 / 151 pages
Individual $15 / Institution $54

SAGE PUBLICATIONS, INC.
2455 Teller Road
Thousand Oaks, CA 91320

SAGE PUBLICATIONS LTD
6 Bonhill Street
London EC2A 4PU, England

SAGE PUBLICATIONS INDIA PVT. LTD
M-32 Market, Greater Kailash I
New Delhi 110 048, India

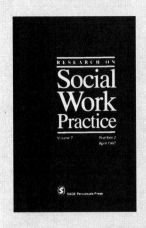

A Special Issue of
Research on Social Work Practice

Assessment and Treatment of Youth and Families

Editor
Bruce A. Thyer,
University of Georgia

Contents

*Research on
Social Work Practice*
Volume 8, Number 3 / May 1998
*Single issue: Individual $16 /
Institution $41*

Order Today!
Phone: 805-499-9774 • **Fax:** 805-499-0871
E-mail: order@sagepub.com

SAGE PUBLICATIONS, INC.
2455 Teller Road
Thousand Oaks, CA 91320

SAGE PUBLICATIONS LTD
6 Bonhill Street
London EC2A 4PU, England

SAGE PUBLICATIONS INDIA PVT. LTD
M-32 Market, Greater Kailash I
New Delhi 110 048, India

W9-DBY-351

THE LIBRARY

COLBY JUNIOR COLLEGE

COLBY JUNIOR COLLEGE FOR WOMEN
PARATI
MENS
ANIMUS
CORPUS
SERVIRE
1837

POLAND

WHITE EAGLE
ON A
RED FIELD

POLAND

WHITE EAGLE

ON A

RED FIELD

Samuel L. Sharp

HARVARD UNIVERSITY PRESS
Cambridge, Massachusetts
1953

DK
414
S45

Copyright, 1953, by the President and Fellows of Harvard College

Distributed in Great Britain by

Geoffrey Cumberlege, Oxford University Press, London

Library of Congress Catalog Card Number 53-6034

Printed in the United States of America

34097

Preface

"History-writing is not a visit of condolence."—SIR LEWIS NAMIER

This volume is not "all about Poland." It attempts to present selectively, and primarily for the benefit of the intelligent non-specialist, those aspects of the Polish problem which, in my opinion, are relevant to an understanding of the issue in its historical and contemporary setting. This necessarily means the omission, or only cursory mention, of many an episode of a heroic and heart-warming quality for Poles, yet without discernible influence on the attitudes of others. The fascinating features of Poland's vigorous cultural development are particularly neglected, not because of a lack of appreciation, but because on the record they weighed little or nothing in determining the relations between Poland and the outside world.

Some readers may find the book parsimonious in the use of so-called nice words about Poland and the Poles. I must confess to a deliberate attempt to compensate for the traditional way of discussing the problem, especially by sympathetic foreigners. The remarkable thing about evaluations of the Poles is that while many foreigners have lavished on them praise for real or imaginary virtues, their own political and spiritual leaders have had very harsh things to say, even if mostly for "internal consumption" only. It was, after all, Jozef Pilsudski who repeatedly called the Poles "a nation of idiots." Was he less concerned over Poland than the peddlers of sentimental phrases? It seems to me that the essentially tragic quality of the Polish problem requires a different approach from that fit for a mere melodrama.

Original research for this book was limited to the field of my primary interest, recent political and diplomatic history. A search in the National Archives has turned up some material pertaining

to the history of American-Polish diplomatic relations which to
my knowledge has not yet been used in published sources. I have
perused much of the underground press published in Poland during World War II, as well as materials relating to the history of
the tragic Warsaw Uprising of 1944, not fully available in English. I hope that the results of this research will arouse the curios-
ity of others, and stimulate them to study in more detail problems
frequently discussed with much heat but little documentation.

For other parts of the book, I have leaned heavily on printed
material. An attempt has been made to give credit wherever it is
due, but there may be some involuntary omissions. I wish to acknowledge here the use I have made particularly of the following
works: *Poland between Two Wars* by Ferdynand Zweig (London, 1944, by permission of the publishers, Messrs. Secker & War-
burg) ; Leon Noël's *L'Aggression allemande contre la Pologne*
(Paris; Flammarion, 1946), Stanislaw Mackiewicz's *Colonel Beck
and His Policy* (London, 1944), Beck's own posthumously published *Dernier Rapport* (Neuchâtel, n.d.), and the writings of
L. B. (now Sir Lewis) Namier—invaluable guides to the history
of Poland's crisis diplomacy of the late thirties; Robert E.
Sherwood, *Roosevelt and Hopkins* (Harper, 1948), Stanislaw
Mikolajczyk, *The Rape of Poland,* the accounts of Generals Bor-
Komorowski and Anders, and Langer and Gleason, *The Challenge to Isolation* (1952). For the history of American-Polish
relations I have used material from the monographs of the late
Miecislas Haiman and from H. H. Fisher, *America and the New
Poland* (Macmillan, 1928, by permission). It is a particular pleasure to acknowledge the permission given me by former ambassador Jan Ciechanowski to summarize details of Poland's wartime diplomacy from his *Defeat in Victory* (Doubleday, 1947) ;
by Jerzy Giedroyc, to quote from the monthly *Kultura* (Paris) ;
by the General Sikorski Historical Institute in London, to quote
from the official history of the Polish army in World War II;
by the Royal Institute of International Affairs, to quote from
R. R. Betts (ed.), *Central and South East Europe 1945–1948;*
and by the publishers of *The Reporter,* to quote from my own
article on Gomulka and other material. The publications of the
National Committee for a Free Europe were a welcome, though

necessarily imperfect, substitute for material from Poland, which has not been available as regularly and as promptly as in earlier years.

Many individuals and institutions—none in the least responsible for the conclusions of this book, for which I am solely responsible—have helped in making the volume possible. A travel grant from Harvard Russian Research Center, which made it possible for me to revisit Poland in 1948, is hereby gratefully acknowledged. I was fortunate enough to make my trip before the temperature of the cold war had dropped to the zero point of absurdity. I have therefore enjoyed, and still feel obliged to acknowledge, the customary courtesies of the Polish authorities in Warsaw, including the supreme courtesy of being left alone to study, travel, and meet people of various shades of political opinion. For valuable advice which, if followed fully, might have made this a better book, I wish to thank Professor Donald C. McKay and my good friend Barrington J. Moore, Jr., both of Harvard University. My colleagues, in particular Dean Pitman B. Potter and Professor Arthur A. Ekirch, Jr., offered useful criticism. For various forms of technical assistance I wish to thank the administration and the library staff of The American University, Benjamin and Marguerite Murdzek, Diane K. Rottenberg, Barbara Plegge, and Kitty Calvert. My wife, Laure Metzger Sharp, collaborated on the chapters dealing with economic and demographic problems, in addition to serving as captive audience. Some of those who have been of assistance will, by their expressed preference, remain unnamed. It is sad to find that not all of those who prefer not to see their names mentioned are behind the so-called Iron Curtain.

The omission of diacritical accents in the spelling of Polish names is due to a technical decision over which the author had no control.

S. L. S.

Takoma Park, Maryland
June 1953

CONTENTS

CONTENTS

POLAND

WHITE EAGLE
ON A
RED FIELD

Introduction

THE NATURE OF THE POLISH PROBLEM

It is extremely difficult to apply to the Polish problem the admirable formula suggested by Spinoza for the study of politics: Not to laugh, not to groan, not to be angry, but to understand. An emotionally charged atmosphere persists around the issue. In the thirties of the last century Richard Cobden was driven by the style of the Polish debate then raging in England to state, no doubt with exaggeration, that the problem was one "upon which has been lavished more false sentiment, deluded sympathy, and amiable ignorance than on any other subject." Three decades later Lord Salisbury called the situation of dispassionate students of the problem embarrassing. They were, he wrote in 1863, "equally obnoxious to the partisans whom they have left behind, and to the partisans of whose extravagance they fall short." In our own days a severe critic has concluded that too many works on Poland were "unhelpful, unenlightening, and unconvincing." Professor L. B. (now Sir Lewis) Namier, who wrote these words, in particular stressed the inability of many authors to muster the dispassionate aloofness considered necessary if the inexorable conclusions were to be drawn from the record. But he was aware that it was perhaps too much to expect aloofness "in days of pain, sorrow and anger."

Pain, sorrow, and anger have been the lot of Poland, of the Poles, or of certain Polish groups for some time now. In the more than one hundred and fifty years since the last Partition of Poland in the eighteenth century there have been only short, almost freakish, moments when Poland reappeared as an independent political unit. These short moments were invariably followed by long periods of political abeyance or by some sort of dependence. Not until the first World War did the occasion arise to put Poland back on the agenda as a *political* problem, to be discussed in political terms and to be offered a political solution. Prior to that, the solidarity of the partitioning Powers in keeping Poland off the map, and the lack of more than passing interest of other Powers in the nuisance value of the problem, frustrated the dogged, at times fantastic, efforts of Polish diplomacy in exile to have the issue of Poland's independence inscribed on the agenda of the major international conferences of the nineteenth century.

Banned from the sphere of practical politics, the Polish problem found refuge with individuals and movements which, for one reason or another, were opposed to the existing order of things. Romantic poets, apostles of the creed of modern nationalism, advocates of the "natural" right to self-determination, liberals of various degrees, kind-hearted socialites and radical socialists adopted the Polish problem or one or another of its aspects.[1] Almost inevitably the Polish problem, transformed into a Cause, came to be discussed in ethical and quasi-legal terms, not in the language germane to politics. The partitions of Poland were not only a mistake; they were a crime. Poland should be independent not because this is important for the balance of power in Europe, but because the Poles have a "right" to be independent. An initial contribution to the development of the language in which Poland has been discussed was made by the host of Polish political exiles who spread over Europe in the first half of the nineteenth century. Professor Waclaw Lednicki describes the phraseology used by many of these exiles as "often insupportable because of its grandiloquence and its buffoonery, lack of education and of political preparation, an irritating Polonocentricity, exaggerated opinions of Poland's role . . ."

Nor was this language limited to the sphere of appeals and anniversary speeches. It pervaded the writings of scholars on the subject. Polish historians early thought of their work as a form of national duty, not only to help the Cause on the international scene but to provide the Polish nation itself with a beautified past, to endow its sufferings with some superior sense, and to paint visions of a bright future and so help maintain faith in liberation against the odds of reality. German and Russian his-

---

[1] The First International was created on the occasion of a gathering called to protest against the suppression of the Polish uprising of 1863.

torians, no less conscious of their own national missions, also discussed Poland in terms of "good" and "bad." The partitions, they tried to prove, were not only inevitable, they were "good." The arguments and counterarguments were thus presented as if an impartial manager of the affairs of history were known to grant his favors to some nations and to deny them to others strictly on the basis of measurable merits or demerits.

The emergence of the Polish state in 1918 did not put an end to the controversy over Poland. On the contrary, the Polish state was reborn with a set of complicated problems which made its affairs the real or imaginary concern of others—Germans, Russians, Ukrainians, Jews, and various sincere or insincere embracers of causes. Poland lived the twenty years of her new independence in the glare of international publicity. There was systematic anti-Polish propaganda by German revisionists and their friends everywhere, by Ukrainian nationalists, by the Comintern, and by fellow-travelers echoing its line. This was countered by the output of official Polish propaganda agencies, the pseudo-scholarly production of apologists, and the sentimental testimony of a new generation of Poland-lovers. The affairs of Poland were again debated from the angle of "good" and "bad."

This approach was given new momentum during and immediately after World War II, especially when the fate of Poland became enmeshed in Soviet postwar designs. The communists, always given to self-righteousness and quite adroit in exploiting the propaganda value of time-honored arguments in the Polish controversy, intensified the debate over Poland in terms of "right" and "wrong." The Curzon Line thus came to be looked upon not only as a logical or inevitable frontier under the existing configuration of power; it was a "just" frontier. To this, Polish propaganda in exile answered in kind. The frontier was bad, wrong. Poland was being betrayed, raped, crucified.

The fact that those pleading for Poland—or for some specific kind of Poland, as against another Poland using or usurping the name—cling to a moralistic terminology is in itself revealing. The issue of Poland is a political one par excellence. In political terms it is easy to draw obvious conclusions about the fate of Poland, but such conclusions are rarely of a kind to generate hope for

maximal Polish aspirations. They may not even satisfy a reasonable minimum of hopes. Poland, once vast and powerful, has
become, by comparison with its two neighbors, Russia and Germany, a relatively small and weak state, and the textbook definition of a small state as a power vacuum inviting aggression applies to Poland no less than it would to any other similarly
endowed and equally unfortunately located political unit.

A small state [wrote the late John Nicholas Spykman] does not live
because of its strength but because nobody wants its territory or because its preservation as a buffer state or as a weight in the balance of
power is of interest to a stronger nation. When the balance disappears,
the small states usually disappear with it.

Yet the partisan of a Cause is not really interested in lessons in the
logic of history. He rejects conclusions based on political considerations as immoral, especially when they are applied to the object of his own passionate interest. The Polish patriot knows
that those engaged in the practical pursuit of politics rarely, if
ever, had much to offer to Poland. Isn't Talleyrand supposed to
have said that as a good European he detested the Poles? Didn't
Briand, another good European, call Poland "le rheumatisme de
l'Europe"? Hasn't Franklin D. Roosevelt allegedly "betrayed"
Poland for reasons of political expediency? As a result of sad
experiences with practical politics, advocates of the Polish Cause
at times conclude that there is no hope for a Poland worthy of the
name unless the very basis of international life is changed. *"Poland can only wait for a complete change in human relations,"* in
the opinion of an eminent Polish historian.[2] This is, in political
terms, a postponement of a "just" solution for Poland almost
sine die.

Of course, advocates of the Polish Cause do not place their
calculations entirely in the realm of millennial solutions. Appeals
to moral considerations are somehow combined, often with little
regard for consistency or for the harmony of the moral appeal,
with very earthy arguments. Yet there is a definite wariness of a
strictly political approach to matters concerning Poland. Many
Poles and their friends reject not only *Realpolitik* but all real

[2] Oscar Halecki, "The Sixth Partition of Poland," *Review of Politics*
(April 1945), p. 155.

politics because its results have never been satisfactory and have often proved fatal to their expectations.

Yet the Polish problem is and must be looked upon as a political issue. In the most general terms it is the issue of existence and survival of states unable to defend themselves by their own means in an essentially anarchic international community, a world where the rule of a supranational authority is a postulate, not a reality. In more specific terms, the problem of Poland has been that of a country without natural frontiers, most awkwardly situated between two strong and dynamic neighbors who tended to meet or to clash over the prostrate form of Poland. "Any Russian government which intends to operate in the West must control Poland," writes David J. Dallin, no friend of Stalinist Russia and no enemy of Poland. "Stalin's strength in Europe hinges on his dominance over Poland, and he would risk a war rather than restore Polish independence." [3] The problem in political terms is whether those who view Russia's schemes in Europe with apprehension will or will not undertake steps to wrest the "highway" from her control. In the past, such attempts have been, at best, halfhearted.

The "importance" of Poland to the West is a result of the strategic location of the country between Russia and Germany. Sir Halford J. Mackinder has expressed the idea most vividly, but many others before and after him have shared the view that Russia and Germany should not be permitted to combine either under German or under Russian leadership, because this would result—so it was thought—in the domination of the world by the combination. In the string of "Middle Zone" nations separating Russia from Germany the country most important in size, population, and tradition of independence is Poland. Hence its importance. Yet Poland has recurrently come to be considered unimportant because those who are or should be interested in preventing the merger of the Eurasian land mass under one sovereignty have failed to enforce this policy. To many it appears axiomatic that without an independent Poland as part of an independent Middle Zone (independent, that is, of Russia or Germany) there can be no lasting peace or stability in Europe and in the world. But this view has been challenged by those

[3] *The New Soviet Empire* (New Haven: Yale University Press, 1951), p. 6.

who argue that, Mackinder's famous aphorism notwithstanding, the rulers of the Heartland are not necessarily in a position to rule the world; that, in addition, it is more important—and feasible—to defend the still free "rimlands" of western Europe and thus, through a policy of containment, frustrate the expansionist ambitions of the rulers of the Heartland, possibly even bring about a contraction of the area under their control. This view leaves Poland and the entire Middle Zone for the time being exactly where they are: in the Soviet orbit. A mere change in terminology, from "containment" to the more dynamic sounding "liberation without war," does not necessarily alter the situation.

Whatever side one takes in this debate, the nature of the problem—and its meaning for Poland—is such that one can and must discuss it in terms divorced from extra-political considerations. Solutions concerning Poland had and will continue to have nothing to do with recognition of the contributions of Copernicus or Chopin, Kosciuszko or Madame Sklodowska-Curie; nor will they reward the Poles for attachment to Christianity; nor liberate the Polish peasant because he appears to prefer private ownership to other forms of land tenure. Practical solutions concerning Poland will necessarily move within the limits imposed by the very nature of what is by definition the art of the feasible. While those emotionally involved in the vicissitudes of the Polish problem are quite understandably inclined to seek refuge outside the framework of realities, others must try to remain within it.

THE LIMITS OF OUR POLISH PROBLEM

To individual Americans or to groups of American citizens the Polish problem may be a matter of moral convictions or of sympathies based on bonds of extraction. It may be, and has been, taken up as a political fad or used as a tool of domestic politics. Finally, the attitude of individuals and groups may be based on informed or uninformed beliefs that certain solutions concerning Poland are good for the United States while others are actually or potentially injurious to American interests.

The attitude of the United States as a country toward Poland

and the Polish problem has been influenced to some degree by all factors that shape the views of individuals and groups. However, practical manifestations of *the* American attitude, although not always reducible to a unicausal explanation, can be validly interpreted only in terms of the national interest. The hopes and calculations on which those in charge of American policies based moves and decisions affecting Poland may have been mistaken at times, but the moves were made and the decisions were taken with America, not Poland, in mind. Advantages gained by Poland and harm caused to Poland were of a derivative, if not wholly accidental, nature.

In political terms the attitude of the United States toward Poland can be understood primarily as being the by-product of American views on larger European issues and of relations with major Powers commensurable with this country. In his last interview with Stalin, Harry Hopkins, acting as the special envoy of the President of the United States, pointed out more than once that "the question of Poland *per se* was not so important as the fact that it had become a symbol of our ability to work out problems with the Soviet Union." Whether in aloofness or in action, the United States has quite naturally subordinated "feelings" about Poland to considerations of the national interest.

Official American attitudes toward Poland and the Polish problem run the full gamut from complete inaction (accompanied at times by what has become known as the figurative shedding of tears over the grave of Poland) to active intervention. George Washington offered Kosciuszko the sympathies and prayers of this country coupled with philosophical advice to accept the ways of Providence. Abraham Lincoln rejected the idea of a *démarche* in favor of the Polish uprising of 1863. Woodrow Wilson advocated the creation of an independent Poland. Franklin D. Roosevelt is said to have "betrayed" Poland at Teheran and Yalta. The Truman administration missed no opportunity to undertake whatever formal interventions it could make on behalf of Poland; it listed the withdrawal of Russian control from Poland (and from other eastern European countries) as a precondition for a settlement of differences between the United States and the Soviet Union. Yet in all these attitudes and policies, relations with other

Big Powers rather than primary preoccupation with, or interest in, Poland were the essential factor. The political motive behind Wilson's Fourteen Points was to bring about the "disestablishment" of a Prussian-dominated Middle Europe. Poland seemed important after World War I when she was considered a reliable and lasting barrier against Bolshevism; Poland became unimportant in World War II after serving for a while as "inspiration of the world," when interest in military coöperation with Russia outweighed the considerations of what is known as traditional friendship. When it appeared desirable to bring about the unconditional surrender of Nazi Germany it also seemed natural to encourage—or, at least, acquiesce in—the acquisition of German lands by Poland. But when the postwar competition for German allegiance began between East and West, it appeared equally logical to question the extent and the finality of that acquisition, if not the principle.

It has been the task of Polish propaganda and statesmanship to try to convince American leaders that the problems of Poland—and of the entire Middle Zone—are of a primary and direct interest to the United States. How successful have the Poles and their friends been in convincing the leaders of this country that there is a substantial identity between the interests of the United States and the cause of Poland? The record to date shows that in crucial moments American leaders have failed to share this view and to act on it; that, acting on another set of premises, considered valid, they have at times sacrificed Poland for what appeared to be more important considerations. The attitude toward Poland has been, politically speaking, a function of the attitude of this country toward Russia and Germany, including situations when the good will of either Russia or Germany was considered more important to American interests than the defense of Polish claims.

Of course, the nature of American interest in Poland is usually explained in different terms from those suggested here. The motive most frequently invoked is historical or traditional friendship and other allegedly constant elements in the history of Polish-American relations. Yet friendship is a very loose if not meaningless term in the sphere of international relations, unless it is defined as the lack of opportunity for being unfriendly or as the temporary sharing of a common enemy. American friendship toward Poland was possible mainly because of a lack of genuine points of political contact. After all, throughout one hundred and forty years of American independence no state existed bearing the name of Poland, only a Cause and a Problem with occasional flare-ups and long periods of latency. Most of the time the United States viewed the affairs of Europe with complete indifference or else with obvious satisfaction over the quarrels of European Powers which kept the latter from intervening in the affairs of the Union. During this period, when the Polish problem was reduced internationally to a situation where "promises became its only patrimony," the United States—as distinguished from small groups of citizens—was certainly not showering political promises on the Poles. On the contrary, in official pronouncements tribute to friendship was as a rule kept within very strict bonds by considerations of interest.

References to Polish-American friendship are sometimes narrowed down to the debt of gratitude allegedly contracted by the United States, seemingly forever, by "the sacrifice of Pulaski, Kosciuszko and scores of other noble Poles who during our Revolutionary War offered their lives in the cause of liberty, asking nothing in return." The quoted passage is from a speech made by an American ambassador to Poland on a festive occasion. It is representative of countless similar speeches offered on equally solemn occasions; it is usually the keynote of the "extended remarks" inserted in the *Congressional Record* by members with Polish constituencies.[4] In political terms, statements of this kind have a vague symbolic value; anyone checking the record might find them to be not quite accurate. The United States acquired

[4] "Encomiums of Count Pulaski . . . are the approved political approach to the favor of the Polish section of the American population." (J. H. Wallis, *The Politician, His Habits, Outcries and Protective Coloring*, New York, 1935, p. 80.) Under the circumstances it was quite courageous of Franklin D. Roosevelt to veto, on April 15, 1935, a bill which would have proclaimed October 11 a Pulaski Memorial Day. In his veto message the President stated in part: "Our tribute to the memory of the officers who served on the staff of General Washington will be the more fitting and appropriate if we do not seek to legislate separate memorial days for each of them, however illustrious they may be." (Quoted in Wallis, p. 82.)

no "debt of gratitude" towards Poland because some of those who joined its fledgling forces happened to be Poles (by the same token the contribution of Baron von Steuben should have been the source of undying friendship for Prussia.) Oratorical references are constantly being made to Tadeusz Kosciuszko and Kazimierz Pulaski, the first of whom is frequently referred to as father of American artillery and the other as father of the cavalry. Kosciuszko rendered very useful services as a military engineer; the value of Pulaski's gallant but often thoughtless acts is more debatable. Yet on what basis are these purely personal contributions to be termed "Polish" and charged as an eternal debt against this country? Even the phrase "they asked nothing in return" is, on the record, not true. Kosciuszko, for instance, was involved in long proceedings arising from his claim to a considerable sum in long overdue pay for his military services. Were utterances of this kind limited to the sphere of oratory on festive occasions it would be petty and pointless to harp on the inaccuracies they contain. Unfortunately the situations when promises are "the only patrimony" of the Poles are of a recurrent nature and what was meant to be a little oratorical bouquet is frequently seized upon as if it were a check made out in good political currency.

A more down-to-earth explanation for the interest of the United States in Poland is the presence and the political pressure in this country of a numerous group of Polish descent. Polish Americans have been described as the best national investment Poland has ever made; it was even found that the "investment" continues to pay "handsome dividends." [5] The problem of the pressure of what are known as hyphenated groups on American foreign policy is no doubt of great interest; many big words and some minor acts of American statesmen were unquestionably produced with an eye on the vote of the so-called foreign-language groups. However, there is no evidence that considerations of this kind have influenced in a *decisive* manner the steps of American leaders in situations involving basic American interests. Otherwise America would have continued forever to be a sum of hyphenates, not a unified nation. In the view of some experts most hyphenated citi-

[5] Bernadotte E. Schmitt, ed., *Poland* (Berkeley: University of California Press, 1945), p. 348.

zens of America actually vote with little regard to issues other than those which determine the attitudes of other, "real" Americans. They vote as Democrats, Republicans, or as followers of third parties and presidential cranks; they vote as farmers, workers, not as Poles or Italians.[6] The politicians seem nevertheless very eager to placate the hyphenated groups with statements if with nothing else. Why? They are simply playing safe. "The hyphenated voter has made cowards out of our political leaders," says Thomas A. Bailey in *The Man in the Street*. Those in charge of various organizations of foreign-language groups manage on occasions to scare the campaigning politicians with their "political potency." More often than not what is obtained by the pressure groups amounts merely to verbal catering and promises which are, by tacit agreement, not to be mentioned after the elections and certainly are discarded when they conflict with what are considered higher national interests.[7]

Traditional friendship and gratitude are not empty symbols. They have their valid and well-deserved place. Yet the importance of such symbols may be overrated by many who show a defensive attitude against the facts of political life which apply to this country as to any other. Opposition to German or to Russian territorial expansion and the feeling that it was important to accommodate Germany or Russia have in the past alternated in determining the direction and extent of what is called the American interest in Poland. Here was the source of the recurrent im-

[6] See, however, Samuel Lubell, *The Future of American Politics* (New York: Harper and Brothers, 1952). Lubell claims that the elections of 1940 showed a sharp break from "economic" voting. Roosevelt's heaviest losses came in German-American and Italo-American wards, while in areas where "low income status coincided with the nationality background of a country invaded by Germany," the vote for Roosevelt was "prodigious." He cites the example of Polish-American wards in Buffalo which went Democratic nine to one (p. 52).

[7] The numerical strength of the Polish Americans is often given, somewhat loosely, as six million. The United States census of 1940 listed 2,905,859 persons of Polish stock, i.e., born in Poland (993,000), and native Americans of Polish-born or mixed parents. Some estimates speak of 4.5 million inhabitants of Polish descent in this country. The figure obviously includes third generation Poles, children of American-born parents, whose continued active identification with "Polishness" may be expected to be rather vague, in spite of the surprisingly high number of those who still speak or understand some Polish.

portance of the Polish issue to America, but also the source of a serious limitation which necessarily circumscribed the solutions this country could offer the Poles. Admiral William D. Leahy, who sat at President Roosevelt's side during the reading of the final text of the Yalta agreement on Poland, tells in his memoirs that he said to the President: "This is so elastic that the Russians can stretch it all the way from Yalta to Washington without ever technically breaking it." To which the President, according to Leahy, replied: "I know, Bill—I know it. But it's the best I can do for Poland at this time." [8]

The President was thus showing awareness of the fact that, whatever the reason for American friendship to Poland, the United States had only limited possibilities of influencing the fate of that country. The decisions of American presidents could never satisfy all expectations of all Poles. It is not surprising to find that some of them felt let down not only by Franklin D. Roosevelt, but, at times, also by Woodrow Wilson, who is otherwise recognized as "the greatest friend of Poland."

Whatever the future moves of those in charge of American policies may be—whether this country can offer Poland a new liberation and guaranteed survival or, as some believe, merely a choice of evils resulting from an unfortunate geopolitical position, or even a new "betrayal" which a global settlement with the Soviet Union would almost inevitably entail, at least from the point of view of some Poles—it may be useful to realize the limits of this country's Polish problem. Those active in the field of international politics are no magicians and are therefore forced to take into account the scarcity of means available for the achievement of their aims. This basic fact has frequently been obscured by the habit of making pronouncements much broader in scope than the policies that were to follow them. The growth of American global responsibilities makes a selective approach and a judicious formulation of policies doubly imperative. Now more than ever it is being assumed all over the world that, as Professor Peffer put it, "we know the meaning of what we say and that we really intend to do as we say." If in the past Americans in official

---

[8] William D. Leahy, *I Was There* (New York: McGraw-Hill, 1950), pp. 315–316.

position have felt that they could indulge in "throwing verbal sweeps in the air," that time is gone.

Within the framework of this country's global policy, decisions may be taken one day that would include an active attempt to eradicate the results of the arrangement made at Yalta. This would necessarily mean yet another, and very dramatic, intervention of the United States in the fate of Poland. Such a development might be welcome to some, to many, or even all Poles. But with all respect due to the most abused clichés, the "rights" and the virtues of the Polish people will again have very little to do with the decisions reached. A witty Pole in exile has said that it would be fortunate for Poland if she were "the world's business rather than the world's inspiration," an object, that is, of tangible concern rather than of lofty phrases followed by only halfhearted exertions. Whatever the West may have felt in its righteousness, it has thus far managed only to put the Polish problem on the agenda, but never to persist in pressing for a lasting solution satisfactory from a traditional Polish point of view. Will the United States break this pattern? That is the question.

I. *Poland: Ten Centuries*

Where Is Poland? The political unit now known as Poland lies between the Union of Soviet Socialist Republics and the German Democratic Republic or, in other terms, the Soviet occupation zone in Germany. The eastern border line of Poland runs along a rough approximation of the Curzon Line of 1920 fame. An international agreement reached without Poland's participation—at the Yalta Conference of the Big Three—and a convention signed between the present Polish regime and the Soviet Union have made that frontier in the east "permanent." [1] In the west, the area between Poland's prewar border with Germany and the so-called Potsdam Line on the Oder and (Western) Neisse rivers is, according to the letter of the Potsdam agreement, under "Polish administration."

It is the current official view of the West that the line of administration was not necessarily meant to be identical with a permanent frontier which only a peace treaty with Germany can determine. Neither Poland nor the Soviet Union share this interpretation. The Polish regime has from the very beginning administered the "recovered" lands in the west as part of the Polish national territory. The Soviet Union, for reasons of its own, has consistently supported the view that the Polish-German frontier was "immutable." This view has also been accepted by or imposed on the East Germans, whose government has signed with Poland an agreement on the final delimitation of the border line. The territorial acquisitions in the west are quite pleasing also to those Poles, or most of them, who would otherwise like to see the present regime of their fatherland overthrown and the eastern frontier of Poland moved back at least to where it was in 1939. This includes organizations of Polish Americans whose leaders

[1] A slight modification of this "permanent" frontier, involving the exchange of two small strips of territory, apparently to facilitate transportation, was negotiated and ratified in the spring of 1951.

do not tire of calling for a repudiation of Yalta, but not of Potsdam.

The present "People's Republic" of Poland, formally considered the heir of the interwar state, is nevertheless strikingly different from its predecessor. Not only has it a different political regime and social order, and a smaller population of a more homogeneous ethnic composition; it was bodily moved some 125 miles westward, lost more than 46 per cent of the interwar territory, and has acquired—or as official terminology insists, "recovered"—more than 38,600 square miles of former German lands which for the most part had been separated from Poland anywhere between the eleventh and the fourteenth centuries.

This remarkable shift in the borders of what is political Poland brings the state back roughly to where it was almost a thousand years ago. It completes, for the time being at least, a stormy history of growth and decay, of expansion and contraction, symbolized in fluctuations in the extent and location of Poland. The eastern border of the Polish-Lithuanian commonwealth (usually referred to simply as "Poland") that existed until the partitions of the eighteenth century was for centuries quite close to the gates of Moscow. The "provisional" western frontier line of present-day Poland runs as close to Berlin as it did almost ten centuries ago. There were periods in history when the very name of Poland had disappeared from the political map of Europe, as, for instance, between the last of the three partitions in 1795 and the Congress of Vienna in 1815. The Kingdom of Poland created at that gathering revived the name banned "forever" two decades earlier, but it was to apply only to part of what formerly was Poland, while the other provinces of the old commonwealth were referred to as Prussian or Austrian Poland only colloquially, not officially. The Kingdom later became simply the Vistula Land in Russian terminology; its name re-emerged, this time under German-Austrian auspices, during World War I. Between the wars there was a Republic of Poland, partitioned in 1939 between Germany and the Soviet Union and again obliterated "forever": its component parts were incorporated into German provinces, others formed a unit called merely "the General Government," without any additional name, still others were joined to the Ukrainian, Byelorussian, or Lithuanian republics of the Soviet Union. Now the Republic of Poland (since July 22, 1952 People's Republic of Poland) is again on the map, although not exactly where it used to be.

In spite of these changes, the historian has no trouble pointing out the Poland of any given time on the map. The problem of defining what is Poland and where it is becomes much more complicated when approached from the geographer's point of view. Many impartial scholars have expressed the opinion that Poland cannot be defined geographically even with an approximate degree of accuracy, especially with reference to its eastern and western borders (in the south the Carpathian Mountains, in the north the Baltic Sea offer natural frontiers). This view is denied by Polish scholars who insist that there is such a thing as the "natural" location of Poland. Unfortunately definitions have varied in accordance with political claims which geography was called in to support or refute. Time was when the limits of the Polish commonwealth as constituted in 1772, the year of the First Partition, were considered "natural," and geography bore testimony to that effect, based on the analysis of river systems and other natural features. During and after World War II the same argument of "natural" unity was used to defend the idea that Poland is and must be where the treaties of Versailles and Riga had put her. Following the westward shift of Poland's frontier after World War II new appraisals by Polish geographers appeared which pointed out the "natural" character of the country's present location.[2]

Arguments concerning the "value" of Poland's present geographic position—essentially rationalizations of the political *fait accompli*—are for the most part the continuation of a line of approach used in the interwar period by some Polish scholars. The indefensibility of Poland's long frontier with Germany was a standard feature in arguments for the elimination of East Prussia as a German province; the shortening of that frontier as a result of the new arrangement is therefore presented as a great achieve-

[2] See, for instance, Stanislaw Leszczycki, "The Geographical Bases of Contemporary Poland," *Journal of Central European Affairs* (January 1948), pp. 357–373.

ment from the point of view of strategic geography. The Polish-German frontier has indeed been shortened from 1195 to a mere 266 miles. On the other hand, Poland's seacoast is now five times longer than in the interwar period, thus finally offering the long-coveted "real" access to the sea instead of a narrow corridor flanked on both sides by German territory. Ironically, these gains come at a time when technological progress in the methods of war-making and other factors have greatly reduced the value of this type of consideration. The Poles can hardly sit down to enjoy quietly their shorter frontier with Germany, their longer sea-coast, or the more "compact" appearance of their country on the map—a slightly distorted circle instead of the jagged pentagon of interwar years.

It is a fact that Poland's frontiers were at all times political, not "natural." From the geographer's point of view Poland is part of the open European plain which stretches all the way to the Urals. The cradle of the Polish nation was between the rivers Vistula and Oder, but soon after its appearance on the historical stage the Polish state broke out of these limits. If it returns now to lands abandoned quite early and relinquishes territories held for centuries, this has even less to do with "nature" than the original expansion. It seems advisable not to attempt to define the location of Poland in other than political terms; efforts to determine "indisputably Polish territory" by experts, on a geographic or ethnographic basis, proved quite hopeless, as Woodrow Wilson found out soon after he pledged the restoration of the Polish state within boundaries so defined.

The Beginnings. The nucleus of a Polish state was formed, at a time impossible to determine because of the lack of records, by the submission of several scattered Slav tribes, living in the forests and marshlands between the Vistula and the upper Oder, to the rule of the Polanie (meaning "inhabitants of the plain") under the Piast dynasty. By the middle of the tenth century the lands of the Polanie became the object of aggressive attention by the German margraves who were putting into effect the policy of expansion of Otto I, head of the revived Roman Empire. Until then the tribes between the Vistula and the Oder had been cut off from the blessings of civilization and from the dangers of aggression by the inaccessibility of the lands they inhabited. They were also sheltered by other Slav tribes settled more to the west, between the Oder and the Elbe.

The first recorded mention of Poland, in addition to the vague account of Ibrahim, a Jewish traveler from Arabia, is to be found in the Saxon history (*Res Gestae Saxonicae*) by Widukind of Corvey who noted the defeat suffered by "King Misica"—Mieszko, first historical duke of Poland—in a clash with Count Wichman in the year 963. This first military encounter between Germans and Poles—its symbolism was more than fully exploited by historians—apparently resulted from the simultaneous drives by Mieszko and his German adversaries to obtain control of the mouth of the Oder, near what is now the harbor of Stettin (or, in Polish, Szczecin).

Once "discovered" by the Germans, the Polish tribes could not continue to seek protection in their forests. They were forced onto the stage of history. Accordingly Duke Mieszko undertook to secure his position by military action and the kind of diplomacy known to his times. He entered into a tribute-paying relationship with the German Empire, thus obtaining some protection against the pressure of the margraves of the eastern march. Another result of the opening of Mieszko's lands to the influence of the outside world was the adoption of Christianity by the Polish ruler and, in accordance with the habits of the time, wholesale adoption by his subjects. By this conversion Mieszko no doubt hoped to blunt the edge of the evangelizing weapon used by the Germans in their expansion drive. As a result of the conversion, Poland was drawn into the orbit of the Roman Church and western civilization. At about the same time Vladimir of Kiev, the ruler of what was the nucleus of a Russian state, brought his land and people into the Eastern Church and opened the way for Byzantine cultural influence. The foundations were thus laid for a spiritual estrangement between the two leading Slav nations which was to weigh heavily on their relations in later centuries. The stage was also set at this early time for rival claims for the possession of border territory. Early chronicles note that Mieszko was deprived by Vladimir of the possession of Przemysl and other fortified places around the river San. Many centuries later the famous Curzon Line was to run roughly along the line of the easternmost extension of Mieszko's possessions.

An interesting manifestation of Mieszko's endeavors to secure a better standing for his country was the "offer" of the Polish state to the Holy See. A habit was thus inaugurated by which minor rulers sought papal protection against imperial encroachments. These symbolic gifts, described by a historian of the period as the best and cheapest insurance for the preservation of national independence, were not always an absolute guarantee.

The standing of the new Polish state was considerably improved by the conquests and diplomacy of Mieszko's son, Boleslaw the Brave, who clashed with the forces of the Empire, ruled Bohemia for a short time, and seems to have contemplated the creation of a Slav empire. It is, of course, dangerous to translate the strictly dynastic undertakings of medieval princes into modern political terms. However, Polish historians find it difficult to resist the temptation to indicate that Boleslaw almost succeeded in creating, under Polish leadership, a "third force" between east and west. This is one source of the view that it is Poland's historical mission to be the natural organizer of the region, a view not necessarily shared by other nations, regardless of its merits.

Boleslaw the Brave displayed military prowess and political influence also in the east. He recaptured territory lost by his father; in 1018 he entered Kiev, in support of the claim of his son-in-law to the throne of Rus. These eastern expeditions, writes the historian Bobrzynski, "unnecessarily distracted the attention of the nation from the banks of the Elbe and the shores of the Baltic sea, to which all energies should have been devoted." The same historian admits that the conquests in the east opened up commercial routes to the Black Sea thus securing Poland's prosperity through the Middle Ages. Yet one may say that already at the time of Boleslaw the Brave the dilemma appeared that was to plague Poland's international relations throughout the centuries. Too weak to hold its own both against East and West, Poland usually had to choose between objectives to be pursued either in the east or in the west. For a number of reasons the choice usually meant the abandonment of objectives and retreat in the west, coupled with expansion in the east.

The successful manifestations of Poland's strength and independence under her first historical rulers were followed by a period of chaos and disintegration. It is fairly easy to establish the fact that Poland's weakness and strength were intimately connected and related in time with periods of weakness and strength of the Empire which manifested themselves in increased or decreased pressure on the latter's eastern marches. A factor contributing to disintegration was the appanage system of inheritance which resulted in the division of the land, treated as the property of the ruler, among his sons. Attempts to establish a system of seniority which would be binding on the heirs were made, but without success. Competing brothers and cousins would frequently invoke German intervention and in the process more exposed provinces would slip away from Poland. The quarrels of the dukes also strengthened the internal position of the high clergy and of the incipient class of magnates who offered their support in exchange for privileges and power. Thus, says Professor Halecki, "there appears on the stage of Poland's history the prototype of the magnate with the inordinate ambitions, solicitous beyond all else for his private interest."

Tartars and Teutons. In the midst of the quarrels of competitors for the senior throne of Krakow and sporadic attempts to unite the provinces of Poland under one rule, the country underwent, in 1241, an invasion by one arm of the Tartar force which had caused the disintegration of the early Russian state and now sought its way into western Europe, primarily through the Hungarian plain. It is generally admitted by historians that the Tartar wave that went through southern Poland and was stopped at Lignica in Silesia was a secondary force, not the main body of the Mongol armies. This would tend to diminish the importance of the claim that Europe and Christendom were saved primarily by the self-sacrificing exploits of Polish knights. The honor must at least be shared with those who stemmed the Tartar advance in Hungary and Bohemia. At any rate, the Tartar invasion had no such lasting results on developments in Poland as it had, for instance, on the course of Russian history.

In the thirteenth century an attempt was made by rulers of neighboring Bohemia to bring about a union of their country with all or most of what was vaguely known as Poland. The repetition of the policy of Boleslaw the Brave—this time under Czech aegis—was no more successful than the earlier attempt. Poland and Bohemia soon began to drift apart and an occasion never again arose to bring about the "federation" which might have preserved the independence of western Slavdom.

Of lasting importance for the history of Poland and of the area as a whole was the decision of a Polish duke, Konrad of Mazowsze, to enlist the help of the German Teutonic Order of the Cross in pacifying and converting the pagan Prussians who raided his possessions. Konrad rather lightheartedly signed away to the Order all the lands that they might conquer from the Prussians and so made possible the establishment of a German military state in an area of vital importance to Poland, Lithuania, and northern Rus. The Knights, animated by motives that had nothing to do with missionary zeal, engaged in an energetic policy of territorial expansion and compact German colonization, facilitated by the all but complete extermination of the original Prussians (whose name the German settlers took over). In the fourteenth century the Knights obtained control of the mouth of the Vistula. Once established in Danzig and Marienburg,[3] they could not be dislodged by direct negotiations or even by the mediation of the Pope. It took the Poles 150 years to regain access to the sea but they never managed to eliminate the danger created by the German colonization and by the evolution of the Order into the secular state of Prussia, a future contributor to the partitions of Poland.

The growing menace of the Order eventually became the main motive for the dynastic union between Poland and Lithuania under the Jagellonians. The united forces of Poland and Lithuania defeated the Order in the Battle of Grunwald (known also as the Battle of Tannenberg, from the name of a village close to Grunwald) in the year 1410. The memory of this event survived for centuries; it was no doubt a source of satisfaction to Hindenburg to beat the Russians in the first World War on the very

---

[3] Malbork in Polish; the castle of the Knights, or, rather, a hideous reconstruction thereof made under the auspices of the late Kaiser, is now a Polish museum.

same fields where the Teutonic Order was humiliated in the fifteenth century. "Grunwald" was turned into a rallying battle cry by Soviet propaganda during World War II in appeals to Poles which, at the time, were based on slogans of Slav solidarity rather than class consciousness. The Grunwald Cross became one of the highest decorations created by the present Polish regime in the immediate postwar period when it was riding on the crest of a wave of pent up anti-German feelings.

As was to happen so often in Polish history, the victory of Grunwald was not followed up politically; the Order was permitted to rally and retain its possessions. A little over a century later, during the reign of King Zygmunt I (1506–1548), the Grand Master of the Order, Albert von Hohenzollern, abandoned the pretense of religious activity, adhered to Lutheranism, and became the first secular duke of Prussia. At the time it seemed a fortunate solution, as the duke, banned from the Empire, submitted to Polish protection. However, this secularization of Prussia was to prove fatal to Poland. The last Jagellonian king, Zygmunt August, involved in a contest with Moscow, paid for the benevolent neutrality of the elector of Brandenburg by granting the extension of succession rights in East Prussia to the elder, Brandenburg line of the Hohenzollern. In the second half of the seventeenth century East Prussia slipped away from Polish sovereignty; a few decades later the Kingdom of Prussia came into existence. It soon became a menace to Poland's very existence.

Facing East. The change in the direction of Polish territorial and political ambitions—the birth of an Eastern Orientation—was a result of increasing German pressure in the west and north. The re-unification of the Polish state, achieved early in the fourteenth century by Wladyslaw Lokietek, was possible only at the price of renouncing territorial claims in the west. Lokietek's son and heir, Kazimierz the Great, was forced to recognize the rights of Germanized Bohemia to the territory of Silesia (which was thus detached from Poland, to be returned in part after the first World War and in its entirety after the second). He also recognized, after unsuccessful mediation attempts, the right of the Teutonic Order to the province of Pomorze. Thus for a long time Poland lost access to the sea. The Polish historian Halecki, a recognized authority on the period, calls the decisions of the Polish king "unavoidable appeasement" and points out that Kazimierz "tried to find in the East a compensation for the high price which his father had paid in the West . . ." [4] Poland directed her attention and expansion toward the east—a decision which became for a while the basis of Poland's greatness but was bound eventually to cause a clash with the territorial and political aims of a unified and growing Russia.

Following the habits of the time, Kazimierz established his claim to the westernmost Russian dukedoms of Halicz and Volhynia on the basis of family ties with the last ruler of these provinces who had no direct heirs. With the support of Hungarian arms and after defeating the rival claims of Lithuania, Kazimierz established his rule in what later became known as Eastern Galicia, and in part of Volhynia. This event marked the beginning of a process of transformation: The hitherto homogeneously Polish state began to absorb non-Polish elements. Some Polish historians have seen in this development proof of Poland's "mission in the East," while others have stressed the weakening of the cohesion of the state by territorial expansion and by the change from a national to a multi-national structure.

A decisive turn in the direction of Polish policies came when a union was achieved with Lithuania, and a Lithuanian dynasty, the Jagellonians, began to rule Poland. Lithuania was, in the fourteenth century, one of the last pagan states in Europe. Its territory was three times the size of Poland. Around the original nucleus of what may be called Lithuania proper (of which Wilno—Vilnius in Lithuanian—was the ancient capital) the enterprising rulers managed to gather vast territories including most of what is now known as Byelorussia and the Ukraine. The disintegration of the authority of the early, Kievan-Russian state was a factor favoring the extension of Lithuanian control, but also a latent source of conflict. The union between Poland and Lithuania, first on a dynastic basis and later—in 1569—on a closer political foundation, created a new Polish-Lithuanian state, originally directed against the pressure of the Teutonic Order, but it eventually saddled the Polish state with the cumbersome

[4] *The Cambridge History of Poland to 1696*, p. 171.

defense problems of Lithuania and the Ukraine, areas exposed to the pressure of Moscow, the Tartars, and the Turks.

In its original, dynastic form, the union was brought about by the marriage of young queen Jadwiga to Jagello, Grand Duke of Lithuania who adopted Christianity and became king of Poland under the name Wladyslaw (1386). The achievement of the union, no doubt a most interesting and in some respects unique development for the times, was not entirely smooth, and the identity of interests between Poland and Lithuania were far from complete. The Teutonic Order saw in the union a menace to its plans of expansion along the Baltic shore and it played on the ambitions of rival Lithuanian princes to destroy the union. It took much time and effort to satisfy the restless Witold, a cousin and rival of Jagello, who repeatedly allied himself with the Order, competed with the principality of Moscow, and entertained ambitious dreams about ruling all or most of eastern Europe. A compromise ratified in 1401 recognized Witold as Grand Duke of Lithuania and endowed the Grand Duchy with a larger degree of autonomy than that originally envisaged in the union of Krewo in 1386.

The principles of the union were spelled out in more detail in the charter adopted at Horodlo in 1413, which opened the way to the spread of Polish ideas and institutions to Lithuania. This adoption of Polish ways was particularly desirable from the point of view of the Lithuanian lower gentry because of the relative democratization of privileges enjoyed by the gentry in Poland. It was frowned upon by powerful families of the higher nobility whose opposition became a source of difficulties for centuries; behind the façade of the union there was at all times a latent tendency to break the bonds between the two states, in favor of Lithuanian independence or of a combination with another neighbor. Even if no such break actually occurred until the partitions of the eighteenth century, coördination of political and military aims between Poland and Lithuania was a very delicate task for successive Polish kings. In spite of the cultural assimilation of the upper classes of Lithuania and the spread of Catholicism in an area where the mass of the population remained under the influence of the Orthodox Church, the divergence of political interests between Poland and Lithuania prevented a true consolidation of the two parts of what was one of the largest and, for some time, one of the most important areas of Europe under one sovereignty.

The "Golden Period" and "Golden Liberty." Under the system of elective monarchy and, to a large extent, because of that system, Poland developed in the fifteenth and sixteenth centuries the peculiar political and social order which distinguished the Polish-Lithuanian state from other political units and which eventually became one of the sources of disintegration of Old Poland. The system came into existence as a result of the "democratization" of privileges granted by the kings dependent on the good will of the gentry for their election, for appropriations, and for support of various political and military schemes. Like other medieval states, Poland was originally based on the principle of absolute rule by the monarch, tempered by the privileges of the magnates (and, of course, the clergy). However, the extinction of the Piast dynasty with the death of Kazimierz the Great (1370) and the succession to the throne of Louis, king of Hungary, marked an important change in the position of the mass of the *szlachta* (gentry), the tax-paying and arm-bearing landowners. In order to secure the throne for one of his daughters, against the customs of succession prevailing in Poland, Louis offered the gentry a number of privileges known as the Charter of Koszyce (1374). The Jagellonian dynasty, whose access to the throne of Poland also required general agreement, not only confirmed the privileges of the gentry but continued to broaden them whenever the need arose for mass support with arms or money. The regional and general assemblies of the gentry convoked for the purpose of obtaining agreement to new taxation eventually developed into the lower chamber of the *Sejm,* whose upper chamber, the senate, was composed of the highest officials and church dignitaries presided over by the king.

In the sixteenth century the political position of the gentry began to assume the nature of an exclusive monopoly of power, accompanied by a corresponding deterioration of the status of other social groups. Economic developments, in particular increased opportunities for the export of grain to the west, brought about a gradual attachment of the peasants to the soil and their dependence on the whim and mercy of the landowners. The position of the cities was also affected; legislation enacted in the sixteenth century in the selfish interests of the gentry undermined the position of the once flourishing cities and prevented the emergence of a prosperous and enlightened middle class as a new element of balance in the structure of the state.

The system of government which emerged in Poland as a result of the granting of privileges to the gentry is sometimes described as "democracy." It also forms the basis of a frequently advanced claim that Poland was ahead of the remaining world, and certainly ahead of its neighbors, in the spread of democratic rights. With some qualifications this is true. It is true, for instance, that the system prevailing in Poland was considered quite attractive by the middle gentry of Muscovy, which was engaged in a struggle against the unfettered power of the throne. The Russian historian Kluchevsky describes the "acquaintance with the freedom-loving manners and ideas of the Poles" as widening the political horizon of some Russian groups. What is overlooked by those who in apologetic fervor speak of the system of government of the old Commonwealth as the "most advanced democracy in the world" is that "democracy" was limited to the gentry only, a relatively numerous group but still no more than 10 per cent of the total population. And what is more important: the system of liberties eventually degenerated into irresponsible license which undermined the very foundations of the Polish-Lithuanian state.

The concept of a Republic of Noblemen enjoying broad privileges and curbing the power of elective and as a rule foreign kings was at best geared to the level of a society of patricians with a high moral standard and a high notion of civic duties. The mass of the gentry was very far from this ideal level. Nominally every *szlachcic,* every well-born Polish gentleman, was equal to every other, but this nominal equality was largely nullified by striking differences in the economic position of various strata of the gentry. The powerful magnates at the top could easily control the allegiance of a mob of noblemen who were completely destitute, lived not much better than the peasant, but had a vote and a sword to offer in return for crumbs from the table of this or that magnate. It was largely in the hire of competing clans of magnates that obscure creatures elected to regional or national assemblies would use the *liberum veto,* the right of a single member to "explode" a *Sejm* and nullify all legislative efforts. When, at the end of the eighteenth century, an attempt was made to improve matters and give the threatened Polish-Lithuanian state a stable and orderly government, too many influential clans had acquired a vested interest in the "golden liberty" of anarchy. It was also the interest of neighboring states to perpetuate the lopsided political order which kept Poland weak.

The deplorable results of the peculiar social and political development of Poland were not immediately noticeable. Before decay set in, the Polish-Lithuanian state enjoyed moments of greatness, even of what could be called, with some reservations, imperial expansion. Entirely too much is made at times of the fact that for a while Jagellonian kings occupied, in addition to the thrones of Poland-Lithuania, those of Hungary and Bohemia. This was not, as is sometimes claimed, the result of a conscious policy of "federation," but the short-lived result of dynastic and matrimonial connections. It may have been important for the morale of later generations of Poles to bask in idealized glories of the past, but there is a large element of truth in the statement that these were glories "of a bygone dawn which never blossomed into day." [5] The Polish-Lithuanian Kingdom of the Jagellonians indeed had great potentialities, but these potentialities were not always wisely used. Too much energy was frittered away in a belated pursuit of medieval ideals and of purely dynastic aims which served no visible purpose from the point of view of Poland and merely contributed to the growth of the privileges of the gentry —the price paid by the monarchy for frequent appeals to arms.

Attempts at reforming the structure of the Polish state were undertaken by the last Jagellonians and by some of the more responsible elective kings, but they were doomed to failure. Jealous of its privileges, the gentry refused to coöperate with the monarchy in providing funds for the regular armed forces called for by the changing times and techniques of warfare.

Humanism and Reformation. Before the pernicious results of

[5] Harold Butler, *Peace or Power* (London, 1947), p. 118.

Poland's political structure began to tell in terms of internal decay, loss of international prestige, and conversion of the country into the "inn of Europe," there were, as we said, flashes of greatness in the sixteenth century. Relative stability was achieved during the reign of Zygmunt I ("The Old") who occupied the throne for almost half a century, 1506–1548. This was also the period of impressive development of Polish national culture, under the influence of the Renaissance which spread with a delay due to remoteness from the center of European cultural revival. Bona Sforza, the Italian wife of King Zygmunt, successfully established in her adopted country the influence of Italian art and humanist letters; she was less successful in transplanting the methods of statesmanship of the Italian princely courts which were rejected as foreign ideas by the gentry.

In the middle of the sixteenth century another potent influence coming from the west seemed to have established itself firmly in Poland: the Reformation. The first wave, of Lutheranism, spread primarily to the German-speaking urban elements of Danzig, Torun, and other cities of northwest Poland, but it also found many adherents among the powerful aristocratic families of Poland and Lithuania. Somewhat later, Calvinism was adopted by many leading families. The Polish ecclesiastical hierarchy, at first inclined to advise moderation in dealing with the heretics, was driven by the views of the Vatican and by the threat which the Reformation presented to its social and political position, to insist on stringent measures against converts to heresy. But neither royal decrees, nor exhortations of the synods, nor even a series of spectacular trials and executions of heretics could stem the reform movement. When Zygmunt the Old was succeeded, in 1548, by his son, Zygmunt August, it seemed that the triumph of the Reformation in Poland was complete. The *Sejm* convoked in 1552 was clearly dominated by a Protestant majority in both chambers. Three years later the king—strongly influenced by Protestants among his closest advisers—put before the *Sejm* the problem of working out a set of rules for the peaceful coexistence of Catholicism and Protestantism. In spite of the opposition of the Church, which frustrated the compromise sought by the king, tolerance and freedom of worship were officially accorded to the

Protestants. For the gentry the problem was not only one of religion; it was a matter of their treasured privileges. The right of the Church to obtain the support of the secular authority for the execution of its edicts and, in particular, for the collection of the tithes, was openly repudiated.

Rapid and impressive as the spread of the Reformation movement was, it soon lost momentum and became insignificant in the last quarter of the sixteenth century. Among the causes given for the decline of the Reformation the determined counteroffensive of the Church, spearheaded by the influx of Jesuits into Poland and Lithuania, ranks first. It must be pointed out, however, that the counteroffensive was greatly facilitated by the fact that the Reformation in Poland, widespread as it was, took no roots among the population, whose bulk, the peasantry, lived in a state of dumb subjection to the landlords. The gentry had seized upon the Reformation as an instrument of asserting its class position; the movement lacked depth and a truly Protestant zeal. Finally, the weaknes of the Reformation was in the simultaneous emergence of separate sects instead of a united movement which would have made resistance to the counter-Reformation much easier. As it was, the Reformation, after making its contribution to the development of a national literature in the Polish language, lost ground rapidly. In 1598 a papal nuncio was able to report from Poland that "Catholicism is bearing heresy to its grave." Poland remained predominantly Catholic. Unfortunately for Poland the period of Catholic reaction lasted longer there than elsewhere, far into the eighteenth century, thus exposing the country to one more weapon of hostile propaganda as a nest of intolerance in an age of enlightenment.[6]

The Elective Monarchy. The death of the last Jagellonian, Zygmunt August (1572), brought into full operation the system of electing the kings of Poland by a vote of the gentry ("the

[6] The comeback of Catholicism manifested itself at times in peculiar ways. During the reign of King Stefan Batory, the papal nuncio Cardinal Bolognetto reported to the Vatican that he had successfully defeated plans for a commercial treaty between Poland and England by persuading the king to refuse the demand of the English merchants that they be given guarantees against molestation on grounds of religious difference while staying in Poland. (Ranke, *History of the Popes*, London, 1840, II, 251.)

Nation"). Formally, the throne had been elective also under the Jagellonians, but in practice father was succeeded by son or brother by brother. Now the succession was wide open to the intrigues of competing European courts and candidates supported by them. The moral standards of the nobility, including at times the highest dignitaries of the land, were undermined by foreign bribes. The quarrels and, at times, armed clashes of the partisans of competing candidates weakened the foundations of the state. This development was the more unfortunate because in the immediate vicinity of Poland the trend was in an opposite direction. The Principality of Moscow, for one, whose existence and affairs had not so long ago been a matter of tales and rumors in Europe rather than a political fact to reckon with, was growing in territory and importance under rulers determined to curb the ambitions of the boyars.

The last Jagellonian, a contemporary of Ivan IV ("The Terrible"), perceived the danger to the Polish-Lithuanian state growing in the east. He engineered the closer union between Poland and Lithuania—the Union of Lublin—and made war on Ivan in order to frustrate his designs to gain access to the Baltic Sea through the province of Livonia. Although successful militarily, Zygmunt August was not quite sure that the Polish-Lithuanian state would continue to be able to resist both Moscow's pressure and Sweden's competition in the vital Baltic area. He is said to have told his advisers to support the candidacy of the Tsar to the crown of Poland. But this deathbed advice (which, if heeded, might have changed the history of Europe in the most unpredictable way) was not followed. When "the nation," represented by some fifty thousand well-born Poles, gathered on the fields of Wola, a suburb of Warsaw, to elect a king, the issue of the succession was narrowed down in practice to the choice between a Habsburg archduke and a French prince, with the latter, Henri de Valois, finally elected. Completely lost in the quarrels between the Polish factions and inclined to consider his access to the throne of Poland as a form of exile, Henri secretly left the country upon receiving word of the death of his brother, Charles IX, which made the more alluring throne of France vacant. He became Henri III of France, tried feebly to enforce from a distance his claims to the Polish throne, but lost. His contribution to the history of Poland consists mainly in establishing the precedent of signing a detailed set of commitments, the *pacta conventa,* henceforth negotiated with each candidate to the throne and sworn to by the elect.

With the throne of Poland declared vacant, a host of foreign candidates, including once more Ivan IV of Moscow, competed in the election. The exclusion of the Tsar almost resulted in a partition of Poland between Moscow and Austria, but the latter was so certain of success in the election that she rejected Ivan's overtures. At one point Poland had two kings: the Emperor Maximilian II, "elected" by the senate, and the "popular" candidate, Stefan Batory, prince of Transylvania. The latter eventually enforced his claim and was crowned King of Poland.

Stefan Batory (1575–1586), an energetic and ambitious ruler, tried to improve the relations between Poland and Moscow by an aggressive policy. He not only reoccupied the Livonian territory seized by Ivan IV in the turmoil of the Polish interregnum but frankly thought of conquering all of Russia. Usually described by historians as a willing tool of the Catholic Church and of Jesuit diplomacy (represented at the time in eastern Europe by the brilliant Father Antonio Possevino), Batory actually seems to have played a shrewd diplomatic game. The Vatican was attracted by the prospects of a reunion of the churches held out by Ivan IV of Moscow and it looked as if Poland would have to bear the cost of this rapprochement (as was to be frequently the case when east and west got together). But Ivan's hesitations and Batory's adroitness in creating the impression that he was prepared to lead a crusade against the Turks caused a change in the policy of the Vatican in favor of Polish claims. For quite a number of reasons, including the interests of his native Transylvania, Batory was not really in favor of fighting the Turks and, in fact, he never undertook any steps against them, although he used the idea of a crusade to neutralize Vatican support for Moscow and for the Habsburgs. If this interpretation of Batory's diplomacy is correct, he may be said to have been a rare exception among

Polish kings and policy makers. As a rule it was fairly easy to obtain Polish support for political and military schemes which were directly opposed to Poland's *raison d'état*.

Relations with Moscow determined the choice of a successor to Batory, in the person of Zygmunt III of the Swedish ruling house of Vasa. There was, in the minds of some Polish leaders, the vision of a union between Poland and Sweden which would consolidate the hold of the two countries on the Baltic coast and thwart the efforts of Moscow to break through to the sea. But Zygmunt, a devout Catholic and a disciple of the Jesuits, was repudiated by Protestant Sweden. Instead of profiting from the combination, Poland became involved in its king's hopeless claims to the throne of Sweden; she acquired an enemy instead of an ally.

The Poles in the Kremlin. The reign of Zygmunt III (1587–1632) coincided with one of the most difficult periods in Russian history, known as the Time of Troubles. In the upheaval which followed the "foreclosure" of the Rurik dynasty great possibilities were opened for Poland to influence decisively the fate of Russia (and of Europe), but these opportunities were wasted by the lack of political vision on the part of the gentry, the king's undue preoccupation with the advancement of Catholicism, and his narrow-minded selfishness which prevented the accession of his own son to the throne of Moscow (just as he had frustrated his elevation to the throne of Sweden).

The Polish intervention in the troubled affairs of Russia started out as the private venture of a group of noblemen led by Jerzy Mniszech. This enterprising Polish magnate offered military assistance and the hand of his daughter, Maryna, to a pretender claiming to be Dimitri, the son of Ivan the Terrible. At this stage the expedition had no official support from the king and was strongly opposed by the aged chancellor Jan Zamoyski. Nevertheless, largely under Jesuit influence, the king negotiated with the pretender and even made him sign a "treaty" promising the cession of two border provinces to Poland, the admission of Jesuits to Moscow, and military support for the king's efforts to regain the throne of Sweden. The false Dimitri, accompanied by his Polish wife and by "a throng of unattached, peripatetic Poles," was installed at the Kremlin but very shortly thereafter was murdered by the boyars. ("His remains," writes Sir Bernard Pares, "were burned and the ashes fired from a cannon in the direction of Poland from which he came.") But a new pretender, the second false Dimitri, was to appear soon after the boyar Basil Shuiski was proclaimed tsar. "Dimitri" established himself, with the help of Polish and Cossack supporters, at Tushino; Maryna Mniszech promptly "recognized" him as her husband, although there was not the slightest resemblance between the two "Dimitris."

Looking for support against the new pretender, the Shuiskis negotiated an agreement with Sweden and an expeditionary force of five thousand appeared in Russia. At this stage an open Polish intervention followed, with the king proclaiming himself as candidate to the throne of Moscow. Some elements of the Muscovite gentry found it expedient to recognize Zygmunt's claim. From their point of view the Polish system of government was no doubt more attractive than Muscovite autocracy, and Zygmunt was understandably generous in granting a veritable Bill of Rights in the Treaty of Smolensk concluded with Russian representatives. Meanwhile Shuiski was overthrown and the boyars, threatened by the outbreak of social violence and the growing support of the lower classes for the second false Dimitri, also decided to turn to the Poles, insisting only that not Zygmunt, but his son, Wladyslaw, should become tsar. The Polish military commander, Zolkiewski, who was also a wise statesman, favored this solution, but once the road to Moscow seemed open, Zygmunt began obdurately to claim the throne for himself rather than for his son. The Russian negotiators were arrested and dragged off to Polish prisons.[7] A puppet government controlled by the Poles was established in Moscow and a heavy Polish garrison was sent in. The scandalous behavior of that garrison, and especially the disrespect shown for Orthodox places of worship and holy images, became an important factor in turning the direction of the struggle raging all over Russia against the foreign invaders. With the violent death of the second pretender the way was

[7] More than three centuries later, Stalin used exactly the same technique against the Poles. In 1945 a group of Polish Underground leaders, invited allegedly to negotiate, was imprisoned in Moscow.

opened to the efforts of the boyars and the Orthodox Church to unite the people of Russia in the name of defending Orthodoxy and the integrity of the Russian land against the Polish intruders. Very soon the Polish garrison found itself besieged in the Kremlin; its remnants, reduced to cannibalism, capitulated on October 22, 1612. The way was cleared for a new Russian dynasty, the Romanovs, who in later centuries had ample opportunities to repay the Poles for their intervention in Russia's time of weakness and upheaval. The memory of 1612 (along with that of 1812, when the Poles were by Napoleon's side when he invaded Russia) was drawn upon by militant Russian nationalists of the nineteenth century, as witnessed by Katkov's flaming articles during the Polish Uprising of 1863. Immediately after the liquidation of Zygmunt's futile expedition to Russia a Lithuanian magnate expressed in the Polish *Sejm* the fear that the Russians one day would "pay us back all that our people have done to them." In 1920, our Department of State was obviously drawing in the lesson of the Time of Troubles when it warned the Poles not to drive too far into Russia lest the Bolsheviks obtain the undeserved support of the Russian people in the struggle against the hated foreigners.[8]

Before Moscow recovered from the setback suffered in the Time of Troubles, one more attempt was made by the Poles, led by the "Tsar of Moscow," Prince Wladyslaw, to occupy the Kremlin. This expedition of 1618, only halfheartedly supported by the gentry, ended in a treaty which temporarily left the fortress of Smolensk and some hitherto disputed territory with Poland. But the strength of Poland was gone and subsequent clashes were to reveal the growing weakness of the Polish-Lithuanian state as well as the slowly increasing strength of Moscow.

The Deluge. The defense of the vast Polish-Lithuanian territory against increasing pressure from Moscow and from the Turks was the main problem facing the Commonwealth in the seventeenth century, but efforts in this direction were frustrated by the limited powers of the elective kings and the selfish and narrow-minded attitude of the magnates and the gentry. There was, on the southeastern confines of Poland-Lithuania, a force well

[8] See p. 274.

suited for the defense of distant outposts against Tartar and Turkish incursions: the Cossacks. They roamed the depopulated areas of the Ukraine and engaged in hunting and warfare rather than in agriculture. Attempts to convert this group of experienced warriors into a semi-regular defense force for the Commonwealth were started in the sixteenth century, but the *Sejm* frequently refused to vote appropriations for that purpose. In the second half of the century, a small force was engaged as "registered Cossacks," thus giving birth to a privileged group within the Cossack community. Meanwhile the ranks of the Cossacks were increased by peasants and by adventurous individuals of noble origin who, for one reason or another, took refuge in the free steppes. Many peasants from central Poland had been persuaded to colonize the steppes and they flocked there, attracted by the idea that they would be free settlers, not subject to the increasingly oppressive conditions of serfdom prevailing in Poland. They soon found that their ambitions clashed with the schemes of the magnates who obtained grants of large estates in the Ukraine. The increasing demand for Polish grain in western Europe made the agricultural lands of the Ukraine attractive and the magnates insisted on exacting from the settlers the same services and payments with which the Polish peasantry was burdened. As the Cossacks, who considered themselves free men and expected to be compensated rather than persecuted for the armed services they rendered, opposed this encroachment on their rights, the foundation was laid for a serious social conflict. Religious differences and a developing consciousness of national differences added to the economic foundations of the conflict. In 1596 King Zygmunt III, under Jesuit influence, had engineered the Union of Brest which was supposed to bring the Orthodox Church into union with Rome. The move reflected the king's Catholic zeal but it also seemed to serve a good political purpose, by creating a counterweight to the influence of the Patriarchate of Moscow which was claiming jurisdiction over all "Russian" lands. Yet the Union of Brest and Greek Catholicism was only a partial success. The higher clergy and the majority of the Russian gentry were attracted by it, but urban elements, the mass of the peasant population, and the lower clergy remained Orthodox. The line of social cleavage was thus paralleled, although not completely, by the religious split. The Cossacks, in their majority rather indifferent to religion, found themselves suddenly cast in the unexpected role of defenders of Orthodoxy.

The Polish *Sejm* and the gentry tried to meet the first signs of Cossack violence with repressive countermeasures designed to tighten the control of crown officials over them. When King Wladyslaw IV, interested in war against Turkey and seeking Cossack support, was secretly negotiating with Cossack representatives, the magnates frustrated these negotiations. Under the leadership of Bohdan Chmielnicki the Cossacks started in 1648 an uprising which the Polish magnates in the beginning treated as a minor affair to be liquidated by limited "police action." Yet before long the entire Ukraine was under Chmielnicki's control and the aroused masses of Cossacks and peasants took bloody revenge on Polish landlords, Catholic priests, and Jewish innkeepers who acted as business agents of the magnates.

For a number of year the Ukraine was in a state of turmoil. The Poles managed to curb the Cossack forces which at one time seemed to threaten Warsaw itself, but the conflict between the crown and various clans of influential magnates made a lasting solution of the problem impossible. In 1653 the Cossack leaders decided to submit to the protection of the tsar of Moscow who promised to respect their freedoms and privileges. It has been a source of bitter satisfaction to Poles to point out that Russia eventually treated the Cossacks worse than Poland ever did. Moscow indeed very soon began to curtail Cossack autonomy. In 1658 the Cossack leader Wyhowski negotiated with the Poles the so-called Union of Hadziacz which was a belated attempt to retain the Ukraine within the Commonwealth by adding to the Polish-Lithuanian state a third component, the Duchy of Ruthenia. This attempt failed because of the opposition of Moscow and the distrust of the Ukrainian masses toward Poland. Moscow and Poland clashed militarily in 1663 in a war for the possession of the Ukraine, but in spite of military successes the Poles were unable to regain all of the Ukraine while Moscow was as yet unable to "gather" the entire Ukrainian portion of the weakened Polish state. Exhausted by war and upset over Cossack attempts to double-cross both Poland and Moscow by submitting to Turkish protection, the competing neighbors concluded peace. The treaty of Andrussov (1667) sanctioned a partition of the Ukraine along the Dnieper, returned Smolensk to Russia, and provided for a temporary occupation by Russian forces of Kiev, the political and spiritual capital of the Ukraine. This arrangement, made for two years only, actually resulted in the permanent detachment of Kiev from the Polish-Lithuanian state. In 1686 the hard-pressed Polish king Jan Sobieski was forced to confirm the arrangement. The Polish-Lithuanian state was henceforth on the defensive and it could at best only retard the further shrinking of its territory.

During the war between Poland and Moscow over the Ukraine, Charles X of Sweden, apparently believing that the end of Poland was near and determined to assert his claim to the spoils (and, of course, prevent an excessive increase of Russian power by access to the Baltic coast), invaded Poland. He met no real opposition from the weakened and demoralized Polish forces. In Lithuania some magnates advocated the replacement of the Polish-Lithuanian combination by a new union between Lithuania and Sweden. In Poland proper, many influential noblemen welcomed the invader. The Swedish king negotiated for a partition of Poland with the Cossacks and with Transylvania. That he could not obtain the adherence of Moscow to this scheme was mainly because of the influence of Ordin-Naschokin, the "foreign minister" of Tsar Alexis who considered Sweden as *the* enemy of Russia and advocated moderation in dealing with Poland which, he argued, was not dangerous any more.

The "deluge" of Swedish occupation engulfed almost all of Poland, but the Poles somehow rallied to the defense of their country (apparently moved more by Catholic zeal against the Swedish "heretics" than by patriotism). The miraculous defense of the monastery of Jasna Gora shook the gentry out of its apathy. The king, Jan Kazimierz, who had fled the country, returned. The country was gradually cleared of Swedish forces. An alliance was negotiated with Austria and Denmark, but Poland had to pay a price for the benevolent attitude of Prussia in the conflict with Sweden. In 1657 it recognized the rights of the Hohenzollerns of Brandenburg to East Prussia, hitherto formally in a tribute relationship to Poland. The "corridor" was born.

Jan Sobieski. Exhausted by constant fights with the *Sejm* which vigorously opposed constitutional reforms and the strengthening of the throne, Jan Kazimierz, the last and the weakest of the Vasas on the Polish throne, abdicated in 1668. In his farewell address he prophesied the impending doom of the state. The field was again wide open for the intrigues of various foreign candidates to the throne of Poland but the gentry for once decided to elect a native king. After the short and insignificant rule of Michal Wisniowiecki, the Poles turned to a successful military leader, Jan Sobieski.

Sobieski (1674–1696) lives in the memory of Poles as their last great ruler mostly because of his brilliant action in relieving the siege of Vienna and defeating the Turks. Since this was the most spectacular instance of the defense of Christendom by the Poles, some historians "hesitate to reckon up in cold blood the advantages that Poland reaped from this campaign" (Halecki). There are good reasons for this hesitation: the advantages were none. It was by no means in the interest of Poland to weaken Turkey and thereby strengthen Austria and relieve possible pressure on Russia. Almost two hundred years after the splendid victory of Vienna the Russian tsar, Nicholas I, when visiting Warsaw in his capacity as king of Poland, exclaimed in front of Sobieski's statute: "That's the first of the fools who worked for the Habsburgs. And I was the second." Sobieski was not a fool, but he felt that it was impossible to rally the apathetic gentry to anything less spectacular than the fight against the infidel. More pedestrian but practically much more important plans which the king and worked out—for instance, for the restoration of East Prussia to Polish sovereignty—left the gentry indifferent and cold. Sobieski's attempts to improve Poland's deplorable internal situation were unsuccessful. His endeavors to make the throne hereditary failed and his sons were excluded from the contest for the succession. Sobieski died an unhappy, disillusioned man, whose military exploits—incidentally, much less successful in the second half of his life—could not restore the strength of the Polish-Lithuanian state. It was still territorially one of the vastest realms in Europe, but it was disorderly, depopulated, and in a state of economic decay. The export of grain, for instance, fell to one eighth of what it had been half a century before. On his death-bed Sobieski predicted "irreparable ruin and damnation." There were good grounds for his pessimism. This period of Poland's history is described in R. H. Lord's remarkable study, *The Second Partition of Poland,* as the "age of materialism, selfishness, apathy and stagnation." [9] The impotence of Poland, says Lord, "was now well known to all the world, her anarchy proverbial, and her complete downfall a matter of common discussion."

The Saxons. Eighteen foreign candidates, supported by intrigues, threats, and the money purses of their representatives, competed for the throne of Poland in 1697. A French candidate, Prince François de Conti, obtained the majority vote, but he was forced to yield to a minority candidate, Augustus (The Strong) of Saxony, who enjoyed the support of Peter the Great and of Austria. Augustus involved Poland in an armed conflict with Sweden which resulted in the occupation, in 1702, of the major part of Polish territory by the Swedes. The victors declared the throne of Poland vacant and forced through the election of Stanislaw Leszczynski as king. But Charles XII of Sweden became involved in the hopeless attempt to defeat Russia which ended with the battle of Poltava (1709). Augustus, restored to the throne by Peter, who began to treat Polish territory as his own domain, attempted to salvage vestigial independence for Poland by suggesting territorial concessions to Russia and Prussia for the price of guarantees for the curtailed borders. Peter the Great rejected these advances. He had more ambitious plans of submitting the entire territory of Poland to Russian control and was therefore opposed to partition schemes, whether advanced by Augustus or, later, by Prussia. In the same way Catherine the Great was to oppose at first the idea of partitioning Poland advanced by the king of Prussia. Yet the plan to liquidate the big but defenseless commonwealth had taken deep roots and it was only a matter of time and propitious circumstances until it would be put into effect.

[9] Robert Howard Lord, *The Second Partition of Poland: A Study in Diplomatic History* (Harvard University Press, 1915).

An important factor contributing to the isolation and helplessness of Poland was the growing awareness in the west that a new power, Russia, had appeared on the European scene as an active and dynamic force. French policy, which for a long time included Poland in its combinations for the creation of an Eastern Barrier, was beginning to be impressed by the change in power relations between Poland and Russia. The French ambassador at the Russian imperial court suggested to Louis XV that he jettison some old traditions of French diplomacy and replace them by an alliance with Russia. He specifically recommended that Poland be dropped without hesitation: "Weak allies are a nuisance." Consequently the French gave only lukewarm support to their candidate, the able and enlightened Pole Stanislaw Leszczynski, who had for a short while replaced Augustus on the throne as puppet of the victorious Swedes but was later elected in his own right after the death of the Saxon. Under the protection of Russian guns a counter-candidate, Augustus III of Saxony, became king of Poland, while the "French" candidate Leszczynski, after entrenching himself in Danzig to wait for reinforcements from his son-in-law, Louis XV, was forced to capitulate and leave the country.

Completely at the mercy of Russia, Poland could henceforth have no foreign policy of her own. Although the Commonwealth remained formally neutral in the various wars involving northeastern Europe, Russian troops enjoyed free passage through Polish territory. Moscow's policy consisted in guaranteeing the "liberties" of the gentry and thus preventing constitutional reforms which could have restored the strength and cohesion of the visibly decaying state. The few patriotically minded statesmen whom Poland had in the first half of the eighteenth century actually had no choice of an orientation in foreign policy that could have changed the situation. Some sought a rapprochement with Prussia (which was already plotting the partitions of Poland), others hoped to obtain Russian agreement to constitutional changes and planned a veritable revolution supported by Russian bayonets. This became unnecessary, because the death of the second Saxon king made possible the election to the Polish throne of a relative of the pro-Russian Czartoryskis, Stanislaw August Poniatowski. His election, however, was due less to the connection with the influential family (known in Poland simply as The Family) than to the approval of the empress of Russia, Catherine the Great. In a letter to Frederick the Great, Catherine described the last Polish king as "the candidate most suitable for our purposes." She opposed suggestions made by the king and The Family for a constitutional reform, insisting on a previous solution of the problem of the religious "Dissidents" by granting equal rights to the Orthodox elements of Poland. Catherine, a newcomer to Russia and to Orthodoxy and empress of Russia as a result of a *coup d'état* directed against her own husband, was obviously in need of a prestige victory that would make her popular in Russia. However, the way the issue of the "Dissidents" was put merely provoked Catholic opposition in Poland. The *Sejm* of 1768 was forced by the Russian ambassador to repeal all limitations on the "Dissidents"; it also voted to retain the *liberum veto* and all traditional features of Poland's constitution. Poland was not really independent any more.

The End of Old Poland. Before the end came, Poland managed to save her reputation, although not her existence, by an effort at cultural and political reform which for a while appeared to offer hopes of staving off the catastrophe. The influence of the Enlightenment was slowly breaking the intellectual bondage imposed on the gentry mainly by the virtual monopoly of the Jesuits in education which, to quote the British historian, W. J. Rose, had caused the nation to lapse "into an unwholesome kind of trust in Providence, a devotionalism that had in it little of enlightenment, and an apathy in regard even to vital problems of national survival." Although the belief that the best way of saving Poland was to stick to the "old liberties" and oppose every reform was still strongly entrenched, the voices calling for a change became ever louder. The rule of Poland's last king, Stanislaw August Poniatowski, was propitious for a reform movement. The king himself had absorbed the spirit of western education and was a devoted patron of the arts. Yet the belated effort of the nation could not succeed mainly because whatever faction wanted to put its ideas into effect had to rely on the support of either Russia, or Prussia, the Powers in actual control of the country's destinies. The tendency to call in foreign support and even invite direct intervention was strengthened by the bitterness with which the competing clans of magnates conducted their struggle for power. Of decisive importance was the fact that neither Russia nor Prussia wanted to see a reform carried out in Poland; the weakness of the structure of government and the spirit of anarchy were most helpful to the designs of the neighboring monarchies. Both Powers played a double game: Russia at first supported the king and his relatives, the Czartoryski clan, advocates of cultural and economic progress, but she also used the defenders of "golden liberty" as tools for perpetuating anarchy and breaking up the state. Prussia exploited the Poles by pretentions of friendship designed to push Russia into coming to an understanding, at the expense of Poland. Neither of the competing orientations of Polish foreign policy could prevent the eventual dismemberment of the state. The clumsiness of some diplomatic efforts—such as, for instance, the short-lived alliance with Prussia—merely hastened the denouement.

The first partition of Poland was preceded by an outbreak of armed resistance to Russian control in the form of the "confederation"—a term used to describe *ad hoc* associations of the gentry—organized in the town of Bar, on the southeast confines of the Commonwealth, in 1768. Its leader was Jozef Pulaski and one of its military chiefs was Jozef's son, the fiery Kazimierz (Casimir) who later fought in America and was killed in the Battle of Savannah. The "confederation" maintained armed resistance to Russia for almost four years, at the same time making frantic efforts to obtain foreign assistance. Neither Austria nor Prussia would move; France offered halfhearted assistance and only Turkey—at war with Russia—gave the uprising military aid and, after its defeat, shelter for its leaders. The aims of the uprising were obscured, in part by clever Russian propaganda, and represented as an attempt to preserve the privileges of Catholicism; the "papism" of the Pulaskis was no doubt very strong, but the uprising was above all a protest against the constant interventions of the Russian ambassador who at one time arrested and deported to Russia leading senators and dignitaries of the Church. The abortive confederation carried on widespread activities in Poland and abroad; it had an "ambassador" in Paris, Wielhorski, who commissioned Rousseau to write his *Considérations sur le gouvernement de la Pologne*, a set of not too fortunate suggestions for the improvement of Poland's institutions.

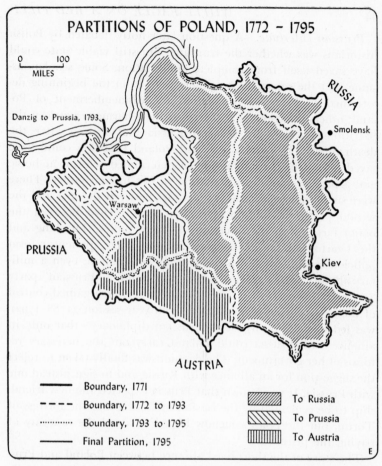

PARTITIONS OF POLAND, 1772 – 1795

0   100
MILES

Danzig to Prussia, 1793

RUSSIA

• Smolensk

PRUSSIA

Warsaw

• Kiev

AUSTRIA

——— Boundary, 1771

- - - Boundary, 1772 to 1793

·········· Boundary, 1793 to 1795

——— Final Partition, 1795

▨ To Russia

▧ To Prussia

▥ To Austria

The uprising no doubt precipitated the first partition of Poland. Catherine the Great, who had rejected earlier overtures by a special envoy of the king of Prussia, now changed her mind. Invoking somewhat distant historical claims, the three neighbors of Poland signed the first partition treaty of August 5, 1772. The pious Empress of Austria reportedly wept but, as Frederick the Great remarked, "she took nevertheless." Prussia annexed the province of Warmia (Ermeland), Pomerania, and the mouth of the Vistula; Austria occupied most of Galicia; Russia took the outlying eastern provinces of the Commonwealth, those of Polotsk, Vitebsk, and Mohylev.

Prussian Interlude.   A question later hotly debated by Polish historians was whether the truncated but still viable state could have saved itself from complete annihilation. Some scholars assume that the rapacious neighbors were from the beginning determined to bring to completion the dismemberment of Poland; others point out that there was little harmony between the partitioners, especially between Russia and Prussia after the death of Frederick the Great, and Poland probably could have saved herself by a combination of determined reforms at home and a proper choice of orientation in her foreign policy. There were such attempts in the two decades between the first and the second partition, but no agreement was reached between the major factions on the direction of Polish policy. The king and the Czartoryski family believed in long-range, patient reform policies, combined with a pro-Russian orientation, even a military alliance with Russia. On the other hand, a "Prussian" party (or the Patriots, as they called themselves) which gained control of the *Sejm* during its memorable four-year session (1788–1792) was led to believe—by clever Prussian diplomacy—that only in alliance with Prussia could Poland carry out the necessary reforms of her government. The decision was finally taken to reject the suggestion for an alliance with Russia and to sign instead one with Prussia. It was known that Prussia expected the new friendship to be cemented by the cession of Danzig and the fortress of Torun, but the Poles somehow hoped to avoid the necessity of paying the price.

The story of the short-lived alliance between Poland and Prussia is enlightening in many respects. It demonstrates the tragically limited range of choices offered to the Poles once their state became incapable of defending itself by its own strength. A similar problem confronted Poland much later, in the years preceding the outbreak of World War II. There are points of striking analogy between the decision of the Polish *Sejm* to enter the Prussian alliance in 1790 and the rapprochement with Hitler tried by Pilsudski in 1934 (even if this time it was no alliance). Above all, one is struck, in both instances, by the unduly optimistic evaluation of short-range possibilities opened by temporary estrangement between Prussia (in 1934—Germany) and Russia; the ease with which Prussian (or Hitlerian) diplomacy succeeded in lulling the Poles into a false feeling of security is also striking. One must, in all objectivity, admit that in the twentieth as in the eighteenth century, the choice was neither simple nor easy. Some historians, and especially Bobrzynski, pointed out that "an alliance with Russia looked much more advantageous than that with Prussia, because only Russia was interested in preventing the aggrandizement of Prussia and Austria at the expense of Poland." The advantage consisted in gaining guaranteed frontiers and the possibility of carrying out internal reforms. Bobrzynski's reasoning on the subject is of more than just historical interest. "Russia," he said, "would not have opposed the strengthening of a Poland dependent on her; she was interested in a strong advanced post in the West at a moment when she was making strenuous efforts to solve the great Eastern Question." Of course, the price of the alliance with Russia was abandonment of an independent foreign policy by Poland. Yet generations of Poles have been unwilling to pay the price. The unattractive prospect of complete dependence on Russia, combined with party jealousies and distrust of the king's motives in advocating the Russian alliance,[10] caused the *Sejm* to reject the plan of a military and political alliance with Russia and to plunge into the alternative scheme: the Prussian alliance. Untrained in the subtleties of eighteenth-century diplomacy, shallow and enthusiastic rather than prudent in their political thinking, the Poles were taken in by the prospect of an alliance which seemed to be part of a grand scheme, of an English-Prussian-Austrian-Polish combination directed against Moscow—a combination that failed to materialize because neither the younger Pitt nor the Prussian cabinet was determined to press for its realization.

Of course, the aim of Prussian policy was to use the Poles as pawns in the diplomatic effort to come to an eventual agreement with Russia. A Prussian minister later admitted quite frankly that the alliance had been merely *une affaire momentannée*. Almost on the same day when the alliance was signed, the Prussian envoy in Warsaw reported to his king that "we now have these people in our hand and the future of Poland depends only on our combinations." The problem, as the sly ambassador,

---

[10] The king's past love affair with Catherine the Great was general knowledge; so was the fact of financial support given him by the Russian treasury.

Count Lucchesini, put it, was "to see to it that these people should suspect nothing." Much later, another German diplomat, Ribbentrop, was to instruct his agents in almost the same words to take care that the true intentions of his master, Adolf Hitler, should not be grasped by the Poles too early.

Considering themselves sheltered by the Prussian alliance, the Poles undertook, with more enthusiasm than prudence, a constitutional reform. The Constitution of May 3, 1791 offered the right of representation and access to public office to the urban middle class, established a hereditary monarchy, and abolished the nefarious *liberum veto*. It did not abolish the serfdom of the peasants and merely put them "under the law" in a rather vague way. Its adoption was the occasion for endless patriotic demonstrations. But the direct result of this patriotic outburst was the treasonable Confederation of Targowica, organized by influential magnates with the help of Russia, a guarantor of the old constitutional order by virtue of earlier treaties. In the spring of 1792 Russian armies entered Poland to help the defenders of "golden liberty." Of course, Prussia offered no assistance to her "ally." After a short campaign the king joined the confederation himself and agreed to the abolition of the Constitution adopted a year earlier and never really put into effect. The Russian occupation of Poland caused new Prussian overtures for a partition, eventually agreed upon in 1793 and this time justified by the need to suppress "Jacobin intrigues." From a European point of view, the new partition was an attempt to restore the much coveted balance which Russian acquisitions at the expense of Turkey seemed to have upset.

The second partition was followed, in 1794, by an uprising under the leadership of Tadeusz Kosciuszko. Many of the spiritual fathers of the Constitution of May 3, 1791 had left the country after its abolition and gathered in Dresden. Taken in by the universalist phraseology of the French Revolution, the Polish exiles dispatched Kosciuszko to Paris, but he found there only indifference or outright hostility. In spite of the lack of foreign assistance, Kosciuszko was forced by the impending dissolution of the remnants of the Polish army to precipitate the outbreak of the insurrection. An ardent believer in the emancipation of serfs (just as he was in that of American slaves), he enlisted the support of peasant battalions by promising them freedom; under the pressure of the gentry, he later formulated the rights to be offered to the peasants in a more restricted way, as a reduction rather than abolition of their obligation to work for the squires. This solution was too radical in the eyes of the gentry, yet not attractive enough to the peasantry. It was to remain one. of the tragedies of the Polish uprisings that the leadership of the *szlachta* made their insurrections appear a restricted affair from which the peasant masses expected nothing. The partitioners of Poland were thus able to neutralize the peasantry and, on occasions, even to enlist its support in tracking down the insurgents.

Kosciuszko's uprising scored initial military successes but was finally crushed when the Prussian army invaded Poland while the Russians, disorganized at first, were counterattacking the dwindling forces of the insurgents. Kosciuszko was wounded and taken prisoner; Warsaw fell after a heroic resistance put up by the simple people of the city. The memory of the massacre organized in the suburb of Praga by the troops of General Suvorov became a further burden on Polish-Russian relations, although the leading members of the nobility, distrustful of Kosciuszko's radicalism, were at the time relieved to see the Russian "liberators." A month after the blood bath of Praga, General Suvorov received, from "the people of Warsaw," an expensive snuffbox with a diamond-studded inscription: *Au sauveur de Varsovie.*

In the final partition of Poland, which took place in 1795, the very heart of the former Polish lands, including Warsaw, fell to the Prussians, while Russia took the remaining eastern provinces up to the Bug, and Austria added to her Galician acquisitions. In 1797, the partitioning Powers agreed to refrain "forever" from using the very name of Poland in any of their titles. Distrustful of one another, the partitioners wanted to prevent the use of the respective Polish provinces as centers of attraction for Poles across the border. In fact, such attempts were started almost immediately after the partitions. Catherine the Great was thinking of releasing Kosciuszko from prison (her son and successor soon actually did) ; Prussian dignitaries were speaking of the necessity of "reviving the still warm corpse of Poland." Yet in later decades the "corpse of Poland" and the common interest in preventing its revival were to become, for a long time, an element of solidarity rather than a bone of contention among the partitioning Powers. Bismarck, for one, understood perfectly the joint interest of Russia and Prussia in keeping the Poles down.

The last partition intensified the emigration of political leaders and of many former officers who went into exile to seek opportunities of employing their talents in the cause of Poland, of liberty, or just to fight. At home the more settled elements were rather quick in adapting themselves to the new conditions of captivity. The Prussian representative in Warsaw, Hoym, reported to his king that many members of the nobility actually enjoyed the fact that the end of the Polish state had relieved them of the burden of contributing to the cost of elections, *Sejm* meetings, and sessions of the tribunals (although, he added, the ladies regretted the passing of the splendid social occasions connected with the functioning of the state). The Poles, Hoym concluded, were *ein frivoles Volk,* not difficult to manage if one catered to some of their vanities and sensitivities.

While at home the gentry was accommodating itself to the new situation, the leading magnates were transferring their allegiance to the splendid courts of the partitioning Powers, and the peasants hardly noticed the change, "Poland in exile" was being born, amidst the turmoil caused by the French Revolution. With the disappearance of Poland, the Polish problem was called into existence.

Napoleon and Poland.   Polish efforts to enlist the support of revolutionary France were rather unsuccessful. Kosciuszko was given no military assistance and he soon became lastingly disillusioned in the possibilities of obtaining the support of France for the cause of his fatherland. However, other Poles continued their efforts. General Jan Henryk Dombrowski, what first tried to "offer" the crown of Poland to a Prussian prince, later presented to the French Directory a memorandum advocating the creation of a Polish Legion to fight against Austria. The plan was approved by General Bonaparte. It had great advantages for France. A Polish Legion, formally created under the flag of the puppet Republic of Lombardy, would be more reliable than the local population and easier to disregard should peace with Austria be concluded. Dombrowski was not unaware of the insincere motives of the French in offering him "indirect means of fighting for his fatherland," but his gullible Legions soon began to sing about "crossing the Vistula and the Warta" in a speedy march from Italy. Their song later became the Polish national anthem, but the way to the banks of the Vistula proved long and devious. Employed in subduing, in the name of *liberté,* local uprisings against the French, forgotten in the peace settlements with Austria, the Legion became restless; parts of it were later forced to embark for San Domingo to fight the local Negroes and to perish from yellow fever. Yet after Napoleon's successful campaigns against Prussia in subsequent years it seemed to the Poles that the emperor, although extremely reluctant to make definite promises, would restore the independence of their country.

In the short period separating the zenith of Napoleon's power from his final defeat, the Polish issue acquired great importance, especially in the relations between Napoleon and Tsar Alexander I. The Duchy of Warsaw, carved out by Napoleon from the former share of Prussia in the partitions of Poland, was a caricature of a state, not viable, exploited by the French military and civil administration. A considerable part of the army of the Duchy was forced to fight in distant Spain, and for a dubious cause. The territory of the Duchy was later enlarged by the addition of the former Austrian possessions in Galicia. At Tilsit the tsar agreed to the creation of the Duchy, but the existence of a nucleus of a Polish state constituted a danger to Russian possession of former Polish territory, even if Napoleon met with evasion demands from the Poles that all of the old Commonwealth be recovered. Alexander I was still in his liberal period and under the influence of his Polish friend and one time foreign minister, Prince Adam Czartoryski, who in 1806 drew up a memorandum under the significant title: *On the necessity of restoring Poland to forestall Bonaparte.* For a while, during the period of rapprochement with Napoleon, the tsar evaded the issue, although he assured his Polish friend that his own sentiments had not changed but that he was "bound by the duty of his position, and that every Russian Emperor would have done the same."

But as conflict with Napoleon became inevitable, the tsar showed more active interest in the feelings of the Poles of the Duchy and assured Czartoryski (in the hope that the news would reach the leading Poles in Warsaw) that he intended to reunite everything that formerly constituted Poland, up to the Dvina, Berezina, and Dnieper. Of course, Napoleon began to hold out similar hopes to the Poles, although insisting that they must first, by their military and financial contribution, earn their "right" to a new independence. Actually, the Polish historian Marian Kukiel concludes, neither side was interested in more than using the Poles for its own purposes. "Such is the eternal difficulty of a barrier race . . . Its ostensible 'benefactors' view the future chiefly from the military standpoint." On the whole Napoleon was more successful in this scramble for Polish loyalties, although Polish support in the war of 1812 was by no means as overwhelming as one might think from idealized accounts. It is true that the Poles were fascinated by the personality of Napoleon and taken in by the mixture of "festivities and phrases" which he showered upon the leading groups. But many were those who must have been aware that, as General de Caulaincourt put it, Napoleon wanted "to stimulate their hopes, but not to make any undertakings so definite as to inconvenience his further plans or prevent him from adapting his course of action to future events." Napoleon had spoken "with levity" about the Poles, called them a trivial people "and a state difficult to shape to any useful purpose." Only when he became obsessed with the idea of making war did he begin to claim that he could not "prevent the Poles from wanting me." In defeat he reasoned that he could not have made peace with Russia early in the campaign because a restored Poland, to be of any value from the point of view of French and European security, must be extensive and powerful enough to serve as a barrier to Russian expansion rather than to require constant help from the West against Russia.[11]

In spite of his reserved attitude toward Polish aspirations, many Poles, and in particular the army, showed an amazing loyalty

---

[11] All quoted passages are from *With Napoleon in Russia,* the Memoirs of General de Caulaincourt, Duke of Vicenza (New York: Morrow and Company, 1935) .

to Napoleon. Hypnotized by his military successes, they saw in him an incarnation of their dreams of escaping the cadre of hard realities of geography and politics. Although the dreams were shattered, the Poles retained a tender spot for Napoleon in their memories.

Congress of Vienna. At the Congress convened to rearrange the map of Europe after Napoleon's defeat, Tsar Alexander's plans for the settlement of the Polish issue were vigorously opposed by England (and, behind the scenes, by Austria). Castlereagh's suggestion that a completely independent Poland, "more or less considerable in extent" be created was never vigorously pressed. In a statement on the subject, on January 12, 1815, the British representative admitted that he "has not been directed to press such a measure," because of "disinclination to excite, under all the apparent obstacles to such an arrangement, expectations which might prove an unavailing source of discontent among the Poles."[12] At one point during the difficult negotiations at Vienna, Lord Liverpool, although convinced that the question of Poland "cannot be settled either creditably or satisfactorily," reminded Castlereagh that, in view of the state of public opinion in England, "it would be very desirable that there should be, if possible, some record of our having expressed our opinion how desirable it would be to restore Poland . . . and of our having made some effort (for) the independence of the Duchy of Warsaw."[13] The aim of Western diplomacy was to induce the tsar to agree to a return to the arrangement of the third partition which would have kept Russia on the Bug, and thus partly restore the balance of power shaken by Russian victory. Alexander had different plans. He wanted a united Polish state controlled by Russia and suggested that Prussia be compensated for the cession of the Polish lands by the absorption of Saxony. At Alexander's side was Prince Adam Czartoryski. Kosciuszko, who had refused to have any dealings with Napoleon, wrote a letter to the tsar encouraging the "protector of humanity" to proclaim himself King of Poland "with a free

[12] Quoted from C. K. Webster, *British Diplomacy 1813–1815* (London: Bell & Sons, 1921), p. 281.

[13] Webster, *British Diplomacy*, p. 210.

constitution approaching that of England." Kosciuszko was ready
to "throw myself at your majesty's feet," but the Poland he envisaged was to spread as far as in 1772.

The compromise worked out at the Congress created a small
Kingdom of Poland, thus preventing the unification of all Polish lands. An "independent" Republic of Cracow was formed
of the old Polish city and its immediate surroundings. It survived until 1846, when the partitioning Powers liquidated it
as a hotbed of conspiracies and revolutionary propaganda. A
technically important achievement of the Congress of Vienna was
the international recognition of the Poles' right to their own
nationality, which the Powers agreed to respect. This was a sop
to western public opinion and, diplomatically, a wedge for future interventions whenever it would seem convenient and profitable to do so. The actual terms of the guarantee which allowed
every government to take the measures "it deemed useful and
proper to apply" were of little help to the Poles.

The Kingdom. The provisions of the Congress of Vienna
were in many respects a departure from the situation created
by the partitions of the eighteenth century. They reflected the
important military and political part played by Russia in the
defeat of Napoleon. With the establishment of the Kingdom
of Poland, Russia moved westward her sphere of influence, beyond the Vistula. Russia indirectly controlled more than 70 per
cent of the territory of the defunct Polish-Lithuania state. This
latter circumstance directed most of the attention of Poles and
non-Poles alike primarily to what was happening in the Russian-
held part of Poland, while events in the two parts controlled by
German powers received comparatively little attention. While
Prussia and Austria embarked almost immediately on a policy
of national oppression and economic discrimination, the Russian
part, the "Congress Kingdom," was the only one to keep the name
of Poland alive, with a liberal constitution, a separate administration, and a Polish army. This situation reflected the split
personality of Alexander I, who attempted to combine his autocratic rule of Russia with a liberal treatment of Poland and
Finland. Did he consider his Polish kingdom a testing laboratory of liberalism, hoping to apply the findings gradually to

Russia? This is, at any rate, what the Russian bureaucracy and military clique feared; they tried to check the tsar's liberal impulses and talked him out of the scheme of adding some or all of the pre-partition lands to the Kingdom or of reviving the Grand Duchy of Lithuania. On the other hand, Polish maximalism insisted on the recovery of all territories lost since 1772. This rendered impossible the development of normal relations in what was the only nucleus of Polish statehood. Nevertheless, the period of 1815–1830 was one of progress in the Russian part of Poland, which made greater strides toward modernization than ever before.

The peaceful development of the Kingdom was disrupted as a result of the double obstacle: the anti-Polish attitude of the Russian bureaucracy and Polish extremism. Various secret societies sprang up in Poland and spread from there to Lithuania. Alexander, whose early liberalism had given way to a religious stupor, fell under the influence of advisers who constantly provoked the Poles and disregarded many provisions of the liberal constitution of the Kingdom. His successor, Nicholas I, was a convinced reactionary. In 1830 the army of the Kingdom was alerted and rumors spread that it was to be used to crush the revolutionary movements in France and Belgium. An uprising broke out in Warsaw on the night of November 29, 1830, started by young cadets. Grand Duke Constantine, commander-in-chief of the army of the Kingdom, fled in haste. The uprising soon engulfed all of the Kingdom and Lithuania; it turned into a regular war against Russia.

A national government, headed by Alexander's former adviser, Czartoryski, was organized by the insurgent Poles. It proclaimed the tsar dethroned, thus frustrating attempts at a compromise. Eagerness to engage in spectacular gestures was not matched by determination on the part of the revolutionary government. The military leaders were outright defeatists. Their sickening indecision spoiled the military chances of this last regular war fought by the Poles. Meanwhile the *Sejm,* split into violently opposed factions of extremists and moderates, engaged in endless debates with no results. Attempts to pass legislation in favor of the peasants and thus to rally them to the cause of the uprising were unsuccessful; the *Sejm* spent its energies in such symbolic acts as the seating of delegates from the provinces incorporated by Russia. This gesture, meaningless as a practical move, alienated the pro-Polish sympathies of many young Russian officers, who became convinced that the Polish fight for independence had turned into an attempt "to grab Russian lands." It caused Russian poets with liberal leanings to come out against the "slanderers of Russia." [14]

Revolt and Diplomacy. An important element in Polish hopes during the uprising of 1830 was the support of the West. Diplomatic representatives were sent to Paris and London, but no assistance was obtained. It was somehow difficult for the Poles to grasp the difference between their situation and that of the Greeks and of the Belgians who had only recently been backed by Great Britain in their fight for independence. The final appeal of the Polish national government on the eve of its capitulation is a stirring document, but also an alarmingly unsophisticated one. This last appeal is directed to the western courts which "could have saved us but would not do it." Poland's services to the West, by preventing the Russian armies from marching against the revolutions there, are listed; various "promises" made by the West are hinted at, and finally the question is posed: "Haven't England and France made use of (Poland) as a proper tool for their current interests?" In despair, the Polish document states that

if France and England abandon us today and do not fulfill the hopes which they have kindled, our ruin will not have been caused by Russia's onslaught, nor by the enmity of Prussia, nor by the indifference of Austria, but by the alleged sympathy shown us by France and England.

And the document ends with the dire prediction that if Poland should by some miracle salvage her existence, she would retain the memory of the letdown by the West and align herself against the interests of the western governments. Needless to say, this appeal was not heeded. A month later, in September 1831, the French foreign minister Sebastiani was able to announce to par-

---

[14] Pushkin's poem, under that title, directed against Western expressions of sympathy for Poland, was conspicuously reprinted in 1950 on the front page of *Pravda*.

liament: *L'ordre regne à Varsovie.* Warsaw indeed was as quiet and orderly as a cemetery.

The liquidation of the uprising was followed by stern Russian measures, including the abolition of the constitution and liquidation of the separate army and *Sejm.* The eastern provinces of former Poland were now subjected to a policy of ruthless Russification. The property of the Polish gentry was confiscated and many Poles were exiled to Siberia. Thousands left the country and thus started the Grand Emigration which played an important part in maintaining alive the Polish national spirit, in cultivating Polish romantic literature, and in keeping the issue of Poland on the international agenda against most unfavorable odds.

The function performed by Polish romantic literature in the nineteenth century, and particularly between the Polish uprisings of 1830–31 and 1863, deserves mention even in a predominantly political account. While the bulk of the nation adapted itself in various ways to the conditions of political captivity, the elite, gathered in Paris and elsewhere in the west, took it upon itself to continue, in the spiritual realm, the existence of that Poland which political decisions had removed from the map. This was, from the point of view of survival of the idea of Polish nationality among a people subjected to three different political and cultural patterns and exposed to persecution for attempts to cultivate their national tradition, an extremely important function. The collapse of the uprising of 1830–31 tended to generate a feeling that continued sacrifices for the sake of reviving Poland were pointless. To counteract this feeling, Polish poets and historians in exile—imbued with the romantic spirit of the time—produced a set of ideas and theories about Poland and its fate that inspired the wavering with renewed hope or, at least, with the belief that their tribulations made sense and had active merit. Thus the concepts of Polish "Messianism" were born. As expounded by the poet Adam Mickiewicz and others, this concept presented Poland as "the Christ of the nations" redeeming by suffering the guilt of corrupt humanity. Of course, this may have appeared to outsiders "unhistoric, fantastically absurd, blasphemously and immorally proud," as Professor Dyboski points out, but this rationalization of an essentially unpromising situation performed—when put into fiery words by the poets and historians—the function of a tonic which contributed to the maintenance of the moral strength of the nation for decades to come. It was, indeed, to quote Dyboski again, "manna in the desert when there was no other food for hope to be found throughout the wide world." It certainly raised the spirits of the miserable exiles who to the eye of an observer like Heinrich Heine were ridiculous "Krapulinskis and Waschlapskis" but who, in their own opinion, were the apostles of a lofty mission. In the field of history, this period resulted in an idealization of the past of the Polish nation, in claims that Poland had been liquidated because she was just too noble to exist in a world of wickedness. The romantic poet Zygmunt Krasinski proclaimed the "immortality" of Poland, and Juliusz Slowacki, in a poetic interpretation of Poland's history, gave a remarkable twist to the Hegelian concept of historical development, with Poland triumphantly enthroned as the most perfect incarnation of The Spirit. In this atmosphere it was natural for many Poles to "bless the ancestors' fault" and to idealize the past to the point of distortion. Many romantic souls in France and elsewhere were taken in by this protective image of their own past and current position produced by a group of patriotic Polish poets who, in addition, were unquestionable masters of the word to a degree comparable with Chopin's mastery of music (another source of pro-Polish sentiments in many European salons).

While the poets were praising the merits of suffering and the historians were patriotically twisting the record, the Grand Emigration also engaged in political and quasi-political activities, with easily kindled hopes but with meager results. Yet it is impossible to deny that these activities have contributed to the survival of the name and concept of an independent Poland when there was no Poland in physical existence. Outsiders exposed to manifestations of Polish patriotism knew little of the often ugly and petty internal struggles between the various cliques and factions of the Grand Emigration.

The conservative elements of the Emigration gathered around Prince Adam Czartoryski who was considered Poland's "king" and whose Paris mansion became the center of Polish diplomacy in exile. The Prince and his followers concentrated their efforts on lobbying in the chancelleries of Europe and in the aristocratic salons, in the hope that one Power or another would consent to back Poland, especially in the case of a conflict with Russia. These diplomatic efforts were one long chain of disappointments, occasionally broken by all too optimistic flare-ups of hope. No project seemed too wild, as long as it appeared to open prospects of reviving Poland. Czartoryski and his associates were given many a lesson in power politics. Lord Brougham, who as a young man had written a flaming appeal on behalf of Poland, was quite reserved on the issue some years later when he was a member of the cabinet.

Your Highness will understand [he said to Czartoryski] the difference between the feelings of a private individual and the duties of a Minister . . . The fate of Poland will always interest us but unfortunately the Polish cause is opposed to the wishes of all the other Powers. They all want peace, while to take up the cause of Poland means war.

Nor was Palmerston more encouraging: "Russia is quite wrong . . . but how can we force her to accept our view? We cannot send an army to Poland . . ." It is not surprising that Czartoryski's representative in London, the writer Julian Ursyn Niemcewicz, noted: "Palmerston found me too hot, and I found him colder than ice."

In spite of these discouraging statements, Czartoryski's diplomacy in exile continued to make representations to the courts of Europe. On the eve of the Crimean War, Czartoryski suggested to Napoleon III and to the British diversionary landings somewhere on the Baltic coast, assuring them that this would cause an uprising in Poland. Apparently disappointed in the reaction to these suggestions, he wrote to friends in Poland, praising their "conspiracy of calmness and wisdom," advising them to "receive offers from whatever side they may come, but before taking action insist upon substantial guarantees for your future." [15]

[15] Prince Adam Czartoryski, *Memoirs* (London, 1888), II, 354. Palmerston made a vague suggestion that the Polish problem be put on the agenda of the Paris Conference called after the Crimean War, in order, as he wrote, to

Czartoryski's exhortations to "calmness and wisdom," repeated in 1861 in a letter to Count Andrzej Zamoyski, a leader of the gentry in Poland, were not only a result of his disappointment in earlier promises made to the Poles; they also expressed fear of radical currents in Polish thought and political action which tried to combine the issue of national independence with the achievement of social aims viewed with suspicion by conservatives. At no time during the hectic years of the Grand Emigration were the Poles united. The more radical elements of the Emigration, influenced by revolutionary stirrings in the west, were opposed to the policy of seeking support from the courts. They believed in the solidarity of the peoples of Europe. In 1836 a manifesto published by the Polish Democratic Society put the blame for Poland's misfortunes and downfall squarely on the shoulders of the nobility, accusing it of being "prepared to witness the destruction of their own country's cause rather than part from their usurpations." An uprising broke out in Cracow in 1846—the Poles were this time ahead of the general wave of revolutions—and spread to the Galician part of former Poland. Although it proclaimed the emancipation of the peasants, the gentry adhered to it (possibly to neutralize the social aims of the uprising), but the Austrian government managed to put down the uprising by inciting the illiterate peasants to violence and paying for every severed head of a nobleman. At the same time, Metternich justified the cruel suppression of the uprising by calling the insurgents "communists." His thesis was later indirectly confirmed by Karl Marx. "In Poland they (i.e. the communists) support the party that insists on an agrarian revolution, as the prime condition for national emancipation, that party which fomented the insurrection of Cracow in 1846"—these are the words of the Communist Manifesto. Poles were prominently involved in the revolutionary wave which "the spring of the nations" brought throughout Europe. They later gave two leaders, Wroblewski and Dombrowski, to the Paris Commune.

The series of ill-fated uprisings in Poland came to an end with

---

satisfy "Parliament, the press, public opinion and old Czartoryski." Neither the British nor the French governments were really prepared to have the problem discussed.

the revolution of 1863–64 (the January Uprising). It broke out at a time when Russia was, for many reasons, inclined to liberalize the treatment of the Polish province. In part, the new course was due to the influence of Alexander Wielopolski, a well-intentioned and misunderstood "collaborationist" who believed in gradual reform and in a "Russian" rather than a western orientation of Polish policies. Wielopolski was appointed head of the civil administration in Poland, but his patient efforts were frustrated by Russian and Polish extremists. Started by the "Reds" or radical elements but gradually taken over by the "White" or moderate groups, the January Uprising relied on guerrilla tactics. It took the Russians a long time to subdue the uprising completely, but the hoped-for mass revolt of the Polish peasants never materialized; they once more remained largely indifferent and, on many occasions, hostile. From abroad came the usual expressions of sympathy, discreet encouragement by the British,[16] and the misleading saber-rattling of Napoleon III, but no tangible support. Bismarck used the occasion to offer the help of the Prusisan army in tracking down the guerrillas, thus demonstrating solidarity with Russia in the Polish problem. Having spent a number of years prior to the uprising of 1863 at the court of St. Petersburg as Prussian ambassador, Bismarck was disturbed by what he called the "Polonismus" of high Russian officials who had apparently won the ear of Tsar Alexander II. The tsar was inclined to undo some of the more harmful things done in Poland under his father's rule. His appeal to the Poles to give up fantastic schemes (*Ainsi, messieurs, et avant tout, point de rêveries*) could be interpreted as a menace to a people who had cultivated romanticism longer and more assiduously than others, but it could also be an overture to a friendly, but reasonable understanding. Bismarck noted in his memoirs that the tsar had at one point considered the idea of restoring a modicum of independence to at least part of the Polish territory held by

---

[16] The British government employed Polish agents as "observers" on the peripheries of the rival Russian empire. The most prominent of them was General Wojciech Chrzanowski who from 1834 to 1855 reported to London from the Middle East on Russia's plans and moves. His memoranda were later collected under the title *On the Aims and Policies of Moscow and the Need for the Definite Containment of Her Actions* (Cracow, 1866).

Russia. The prospect of a "Panslavistic, anti-German brotherly association between Russia and Poland" was frightening to Bismarck and he used all his diplomatic skill to prevent the emergence of such a solidarity. The untimely Polish uprising played into his hands. He could with satisfaction describe the Alvensleben convention, on the face of it a purely military arrangement, as an important political act, as *ein Sieg der preussischen Politik ueber die polnische.*[17]

The insistence of Polish groups on the restoration of the old lands of the Commonwealth provoked a violent nationalist reaction in Russia which made Bismarck's victory over the "Polonismus" of influential personalities at the top much easier to achieve. Some Russians in exile, and especially Alexander Herzen, welcomed the Polish uprising and expected it to spread to Russia proper; the unpredictable Bakunin embarked on a romantic sea voyage which was supposed to bring him, together with a group of Polish volunteers collected in England, to the Baltic shores. There were no doubt strong sympathies among Russian groups for the Poles when their fight was interpreted as a struggle for constitutional rights. Unfortunately, the tsarist government could claim with a considerable dose of plausibility that the Poles were again out to "grab Russian lands." As a result "westernizers" and Slavophils alike were suspicious of the Poles and their motives. It was felt by many Russian writers of the period that the Poles must be effectively curbed, either because Poland "wants to separate Russia from Europe," as some "westernizers" argued, or because "Poland is the vanguard of the civilization of a decaying West (and) it is Russia's sacred duty to defend her native elements from which her radiant future would develop," as the Slavophil Samarin put it.

"Organic" Work and Socialism. Disappointment with the re-

[17] Quoted from *Gedanken und Erinnerungen von Otto Fuerst von Bismarck*, popular edition (Stuttgart-Berlin, 1905), I, 336. It has been argued by some French historians with anti-Polish leanings that the encouragement given by the French government to the Polish uprising of 1863 retarded the evolution of Russia in the direction of closer relations with France, with disastrous results for France, for Russia, and for the world. In 1916 the Russian foreign minister warned Maurice Paléologue that the Polish problem was "un terrain dangereux" for a French ambassador and reminded him of the price which France had to pay for its "sympathies pour les Polonais."

sults of the uprisings combined with economic considerations to produce a new attitude in the three parts of former Poland. The emancipation of the peasants—the partitioning Powers accomplished what the Polish gentry could never bring itself to do— was changing the social and economic structure of the country. Many estates could not be maintained economically, especially in view of the growing competition of overseas grain; others were confiscated by the Russian authorities in reprisal for their owners' patriotic activities. The sons of the gentry were compelled to look for new opportunities in the towns, for careers in the professions, in banking, in trade. The "positivist" philosophy of getting rich and serving the community through "organic work" provided the necessary rationalization for what was essentially the belated advent of capitalism to Poland. In literature the new hero was a good merchant, not a romantic poet or fighter. Closer integration with the rest of the Russian empire, undertaken as a political measure, was of great economic importance for the former Kingdom now renamed Vistula Land: it opened the huge Russian market to its industries which began to attract foreign capital. The first wave of Poles to move eastward consisted of prisoners and exiles to Siberia, but others were to follow of their free will, attracted by growing economic opportunities.

In Galicia, the new policies of the central government, initiated after the defeat suffered by the Austrians from Prussian hands, opened to Poles careers in the administration, thus compensating in part for the lack of economic opportunities in this neglected province. It is in Galicia that a new historical school developed which aimed at replacing romantic interpretations of Poland's past by realistic scholarly studies.

Under the Prussians, economic progress and coöperative organization soon became a means of opposing Bismarck's avowed schemes of weakening the Polish element, just as support of the Church was a mainstay of resistance against Germanization efforts. With impressive determination the "Prussian" Poles withstood the pressures of the *Kulturkampf* and the efforts, initiated in the 1880's, to create a protective belt of German settlements in the eastern marches of the Reich. The Poles there multiplied

faster than the Germans and threatened to "re-Polonize" groups
of Polish origin, long subjected to German influence and yet
preserving a vestigial consciousness of their separate nationality
and a diluted form of the Polish language ("Wasser-Polnisch,"
as the Germans called it). The efforts of the German government remained rather unsucessful because of the resistance of
the Poles—based on a combination of national, religious, and
economic motives—but also because it attempted, for political
and "racial" reasons, to reverse the trend of population movement in Germany, characterized by a westward direction, away
from the poor land and the harsh labor conditions of East Prussia and other border provinces to the rapidly industrializing regions of the Reich. The contempt of the Germans for the Poles
was an additional, and important, factor in preserving the apart-
ness of the Polish group under German control.

The development of a native urban middle class and of capitalist enterprise caused a social and economic differentiation of
the hitherto almost exclusively agricultural population of all
Polish provinces. An urban proletariat began to appear on the
Polish scene; it absorbed part of the surplus of peasant population (with emigration overseas forming another outlet) and was
taking in many independent artisans dislodged from their economic positions by the development of mechanical production.
Between 1870 and 1910 the number of industrial workers in
Russian Poland more than tripled (although even then it
amounted only to some 3 per cent of the population).

The growth of the proletariat and of a middle-class intelligentsia brought the socialist movement to the Polish lands.
Almost from the beginning of the movement in the last two
decades of the nineteenth century—by the creation of a clandestine organization, *Proletariat* (1882)—two tendencies, nationalism and internationalism, became noticeable in Polish
socialism.[18] The cleavage is of more than historical interest:

<hr/>

[18] Ludwik Warynski, one of the creators of *Proletariat*, wrote: "Such or
other frontiers of a Polish state, the aim of our patriots, are a matter of indifference to us. Our fatherland is the whole world . . . We are compatriots,
members of that great nation that is more unhappy than Poland: the nation
of proletarians." (Quoted in W. Feldman, *Geschichte der politischen Ideen in
Polen seit dessen Teilung*, Berlin, 1917, p. 316.) At a meeting in Geneva,

in the name of internationalism, at present harnessed to the interests of the Soviet Union, a fight is going on in Poland to stamp out the surviving nationalist trend in Polish socialism. In this ideological campaign the history of the Polish socialist movement, in an interpretation enjoying official blessing, is an important weapon. It is therefore essential for an understanding of what might otherwise look like an academic debate in contemporary Poland to trace the development of the two opposing tendencies in Polish socialism.

Poland's peculiar circumstances and, in particular, the oppression by tsarist Russia, gave a strong national slant to socialist thought and groups there. Liberation from foreign oppression was viewed as a necessary precondition of social change. While the Russian secret police felt, as is apparent from reports written in the 1870's, that Poland was the "most favorable ground for the International," the orthodox and internationalist trend won a much smaller following than the other, nationalist tendency which had a clearer appeal to many Poles and attracted to the movement elements that cared little or nothing for Marx. The Polish Socialist Party (PPS), organized in 1892 at a conference of a few dozen political leaders abroad, became the embodiment of this nationalist tendency in Polish socialism; the other, orthodox and internationalist group, created the Social Democracy of the Kingdom of Poland and Lithuania (known as SDKPL). From this group, joined by the split-off left wing of the PPS, sprang in 1918 the Polish Communist Party (KPP). Its leadership later became identified with radical socialism outside Poland: it gave Rosa Luxemburg to the German socialist movement, Karl Radek first to Germany and then to Russia, Feliks Dzierzynski to Bolshevism and the Cheka, forerunner of the GPU. The dogmatic internationalism of the SDKPL made it deny the usefulness of fighting for an independent Poland; socialism was to be the aim and its achievement was to be sought together with the workers of the entire Russian empire and within its framework. This attitude was opposed by

---

where a letter from Marx and Engels was read which ended with the words "Vive la Pologne," the Pole Kazimierz Dluski exclaimed, "Down with patriotism." Dluski later became an ardent patriot.

Jozef Pilsudski who, although connected in his youth with the revolutionary movement in Russia (he was involved in the attempt on the life of the tsar, for which Lenin's brother was hanged), wrote in 1892, "Even in the ranks of Russian revolutionaries we have no sincere friends as yet." The dogmatic rigidity of "Luxemburgism" was criticized also by Lenin who stressed the tactical importance of national liberation movements for the cause of socialism.[19] A young Georgian revolutionary, devoted to Lenin's ideas, wrote in 1901 about the Poles "injured in their most sacred feelings" because "autocracy has brutally trampled over their rights and freedom . . . granted to them by history." The writer was "Koba" who later became better known as J. V. Stalin.

While socialism was making its appearance in Poland, the middle class and a considerable part of the gentry came under the influence of the National Democrats. That party grew out of the secret Polish League organized abroad by a group animated by out-dated romantic notions. Under the leadership of Roman Dmowski it became the party of Polish social conservatism, clericalism, anti-Semitism. The growing estrangement between Russia and Austria in the beginning of this century seemed to guarantee the revival of the international aspects of the long dormant Polish problem and the choice of an "orientation" became the major issue confronting politically active Polish factions. The National Democrats were the leading exponents of the pro-Russian trend; in Galicia the Polish aristocracy, for decades admitted to high positions in the Austro-Hungarian empire, was behind an "Austrian" solution; Prussian Poland, well-entrenched economically, but politically handicapped by the lack of a plausible "orientation," adopted a cautious wait-and-see attitude.

The Peasant Movement. In the first half of the nineteenth century there were sporadic and foredoomed attempts to organize the peasantry. Economic emancipation and the slow but steady progress of education eventually directed the attention of all political factions active in partitioned Poland to the role of the peasantry; its sheer numerical weight assumed increasing

---

[19] Cf. E. H. Carr, *The Bolshevik Revolution* (New York: The Macmillan Company, 1951), I, 422.

importance with the gradual democratization of electoral franchise. Leadership of the peasant movement was provided at first from the outside, by the gentry, the Catholic clergy, the intelligentsia. Soon, however, educated or ambitious peasants appeared in the forefront of the movement to organize political parties identified exclusively with the peasantry. The paternalistic approach of the gentry, the ostentatious peasant-loving exhibitions of some elements of the intelligentsia, the idea of a "wedding" between the former serfs and their former oppressors in the name of national solidarity, became obsolete. Peasant leaders developed a consciousness of their political power. The Polish Peasant (or Populist) Party, created in 1895 in Galicia, later added the name "Piast," of the first Polish kings (allegedly of peasant origin), to its name. It was able to send an increasing number of elected representatives to the parliament in Vienna, thus breaking the monopoly of the conservatives. A leading figure in the peasant movement became, in the years preceding the outbreak of World War I, the self-educated peasant Wincenty Witos, a shrewd politician with a flair for intrigue and deals, and with rather conservative social ideas.

The peasant movement in the Russian part of Poland was socially more radical and militantly anticlerical, but the National Democrats obtained a lasting hold on the political allegiance of the more conservative elements of the peasantry.

"Young Poland." On the eve of World War I a new generation of Poles, reacting to the excessive realism of their elders, began to revolt against the "quietism" of the Polish scene. This revolution was limited mainly to the field of art and literature (it produced the Young Poland movement with an impressive number of talented and original artists and writers), but it also revived notions of active struggle for Polish independence—notions which were to animate Pilsudski's Legions. This was an understandable reaction to a period of excessive reasonableness. However, the way to independence led not through spectacular military exploits, but through correct utilization of favorable currents in the changing international situation.

When the outbreak of World War I returned the Polish problem to the international agenda, the Poles, divided in their political allegiance and social outlook, were seeking an optimum solution of their problem mostly with the support of one or another of their former partitioners and oppressors. Complete independence was a surprise result of the freak outcome of the war.

II. Between Two Wars: "Inevitable" and "Impossible"

The system of independent states created in East-Central Europe at the end of World War I meant, on the surface, a triumph of the idea that a state of its own was the "natural" and therefore supreme form of existence for any mature national group. The seemingly universal principle was applied only to groups which had been controlled by the defeated enemy or, as in the case of Russia, by an ally gone astray; and the guardians of the order created at Versailles made no provisions for its enforcement. They were neither generous enough to the defeated nor sufficiently determined to keep them down for any length of time.

The survival of the small and medium states which were called into existence or confirmed by Versailles depended either on the creation of an effective organization for the maintenance of peace or on concerted and sustained efforts of their sponsors and allies to defend the *status quo*. Some attempts were made in both directions, but they were ineffective. Another flaw in the system was one-sided concentration on the political trappings of sovereignty and all but complete disregard of the economic basis of true independence. Woodrow Wilson frankly admitted that he was "not interested in economic matters." Yet the survival of the national organisms carved out of defeated or prostrate empires was possible only under conditions of a serious and global approach to the problems of production and consumption of goods or—in the absence of such an approach—a sustained and generous effort of the victorious Powers to prop up the nominal independence of their political protegés with economic assistance. This was to be perfectly understood in 1950, but it was not so in 1918.

If the principal architects of the peace were so easily carried

away by their pseudo-realism or so easily satisfied by their idealistic cravings, the lesser beneficiaries of Versailles certainly could
not be expected to show restraint, foresight, or healthy scepti-
cism. For a nation in bondage the attainment of independence
is obviously a supreme achievement in itself. Independence may
turn out to be the beginning rather than the end of troubles,
but this becomes evident only later, and even then it does not
affect the basic conviction of a nation that it had been right in
striving for freedom. Sovereignty is the right of a nation to make
its own mistakes, and no nationally conscious group has ever
declined to avail itself of the opportunity.

The Poles, whose nationalism, kept for more than a century
under high pressure, was released under seemingly ideal conditions—the simultaneous eclipse of all partitioning Powers—obviously accepted their independence as a perfectly deserved reward
for their sufferings and endurance. For non-Poles, too, the vision
of the resurrected nation tended to overshadow doubts concerning its viability. To idealists it seemed important that what they
called the wrongs of the partitions should be righted in an age
of reason and justice. To others, who thought of themselves as
hard-boiled realists, an independent Poland was valuable, either
as the most important link of a *cordon sanitaire* or as a buffer
state between a revolutionary Russia and an unscrupulous Germany bent on destroying the system of Versailles. True, there
were in some quarters serious misgivings concerning the wisdom
of certain solutions, but the statesmen and the politicians as a
rule easily dismissed their doubts. Others voiced excessive reliance in the indomitable spirit of the Polish nation, as if this
were not only an important factor—which it is—but an absolute weapon—which it is not.

To say that it was a mistake to rebuild a Polish state in 1918
would be largely meaningless because actually no one "created"
the new Poland; she *happened*. The collapse of Germany and
Austria and the eclipse of Russia had created a void which some
kind of a Polish state was bound to fill. As Count Aleksander
Skrzynski, one of Poland's interwar foreign ministers, put it:
"Poland became inevitable." Yet the same statesman wrote, in
Poland and Peace, that his country's future was "dark and fore-

boding." He knew and, unlike many of his countrymen, admitted that the partitions of the eighteenth century were "the logical result . . . of historical developments," not just a product of the perversity of three emperors. He feared that conditions similar to those which had caused Poland's disappearance from the map might bring about a repetition of the catastrophe once again. We know that his fears were justified.

The survival of the Republic of Poland was contingent upon many "ifs," none of which materialized. Within the boundaries determined by the Treaty of Versailles and the Peace of Riga, Poland could survive politically only if an effective international organization were created to maintain peace or if the revival of German and Russian strength were prevented for an unlimited period.

The solution of Poland's economic problems again depended on a set of "ifs" which did not materialize. No matter how indomitable the spirit of the Poles and how brave their efforts, they could not successfully attack the basic problem: pressure of a population increasing faster than the developed resources of the country. *If* the flow of foreign investments had continued (preferably on more generous terms) , *if* Poland had been granted the time and the opportunity to build up her production, to capture and maintain markets in a world of free trade; *if* in addition, military expenditures—a result of the non-fulfillment of the political "ifs"—could have been cut; *if,* furthermore, the outlets for surplus population provided by emigration had not all but dried up—Poland might have been able to work out a solution of her economic problems.

A time came when the Polish state, "inevitable" in 1918, became "impossible" in 1939. To quote Skrzynski again, Poland passed from view in the eighteenth century "as a factor which could not find a place in the new political circumstances of Europe." She was overpowered again after twenty-one years of independence because she was unable to withstand the pressure of a new set of political circumstances: Hitler's Germany on the march, the West paralyzed into inaction, and the Soviet Union determined, as Stalin said, not to pull anyone's chestnuts out of the fire, but to make the best out of the conflagration.

This interpretation of Poland's rise and fall may appear fatal-
istic. Actually, all the "miracles" necessary for the survival of an
independent Poland depended on human action and foresight,
not on supernatural interventions. For instance, participation in
the European security system by the United States, the only
country that had come out of the first World War richer and
more powerful than ever, could have given real strength to what
turned out to be a caricature of collective security. Without it,
the peace of Europe was in the hands of so-called rather than real
Great Powers who, according to Winston Churchill's description,
"lived from hand to mouth and from day to day," leaving the
smaller states under the protection of principles which no one
made a serious attempt to enforce.

It is often said that the Poles have contributed to their misfortunes by an unwise and "imperialistic" policy, by insisting on
extensive frontiers and the inclusion of large national minorities
which were bound to exercise a disruptive influence. Some Poles
indeed believe that their country can only be great (and they
mean big) or not at all; it is, in their view, "doomed to greatness." They apparently think that the nation should go on trying to be great, even at the risk of periodically coming close to
being not at all.

It is possible to argue that Poland made no more mistakes than
other states; that she was let down by the West, deceived by Hitler, and stabbed in the back by Stalin. In view of the concrete
conditions prevailing in Europe between the wars, the life expectancy of a state sandwiched in between Germany and Russia
was bound to be limited. Attempts of Polish leaders to change
the fate of their country were heroic at times, pathetic and foolish on many occasions; they may have hastened the denouement
but they could not radically influence the inexorable finale.
Here, too, a number of "ifs" could be introduced. What if Hitler
had been stopped in time? What if the Poles had sided fully
with Hitler instead of playing a hopeless game of "balance"?
What if they had accepted Soviet military assistance instead of
objecting to it? In the Europe that was, Hitler could not be
stopped in time. There was neither the strength nor the will to

stop him. Neither a full alliance with Hitler nor Russian military aid against him was acceptable to the Polish regime.

In the basically impossible situation of the Polish state the excesses of nationalism, the limited talents of some leaders, their prejudices, and what Franz Werfel called their "perfect fifteenth century minds," their credulity and overconfidence, even the poor quality of citizenship—of the solid, pedestrian kind—which Poles manage to combine with a high voltage patriotism, were only secondary factors in a drama directed by others. Poland had limited possibilities of influencing her fate; even used more wisely than they were, they would have been utterly inadequate.

INTERNAL POLITICS

Prelude to Independence. The political and military activities of various groups during the years of World War I produced a rich prehistory of Poland's new statehood. Conflicting evaluations of the merits of "orientations" chosen at that time complicated later the political life of the reborn state by perpetuating lines of division that had lost any but historical significance.

All Polish political parties, groupings, combinations, and cliques—with the exception of some super-loyalists, unconditionally attached to the thrones of one or another of the partitioning monarchies—could later claim that the ultimate goal of their actions had been Poland's independence. However, this final goal could not be openly proclaimed in the early stages of the first World War; the Polish factions had to settle for the choice of "orientations" which amounted to siding with one or another of the partitioning Powers—more specifically; Austria or Russia. (Germany had nothing to offer to any Polish political orientation.) No one could, in 1914, think of the outcome of the war as resulting in the elimination of *all* partitioning Powers. The problem confronting Polish political leaders was how to make the most of the conflict between the erstwhile despoilers of their fatherland. In Russian Poland the National Democrats, led by Roman Dmowski, built their hopes on a victory of the Russian sword which would result in the gathering of all Polish lands under one sovereignty; the next step would then be to obtain either complete freedom or a tolerable arrangement with Russia. In the Austrian part of Poland—Galicia—where the Poles enjoyed considerable autonomy, the most advantageous solution seemed to be a victory of the Central Powers, detachment of the "Kingdom" and possibly other Polish lands from Russian control and their unification, either as an independent country or as a full-fledged partner of the dual Austro-Hungarian monarchy. The practical efforts of Polish leaders were concentrated on the task of overcoming the reluctance of their chosen protectors to make binding promises. In the process, the Polish groups found themselves forced to accept much less than they had hoped for.

In Galicia para-military groups were organized with the encouragement of the Austrian government and the blessing of the General Staff which considered them a potentially useful element in attracting Poles from across the border in case of an armed conflict with Russia. In 1912, the so-called "activist" parties in Galicia published a manifesto stating that their aim would be to fight side by side with Austria, "our natural ally so long as she fights Russia." In the preparation of military cadres the leading role was assumed by Jozef Pilsudski who abandoned clandestine activity within the Polish Socialist Party in the Russian provinces of Poland for the organization of a Union of Riflemen blessed by the Austrian General Staff.

When war came, Pilsudski made an attempt to proclaim himself "commander in chief of the Polish army," a nonexisting force, in the name of an equally fictitious "national government" allegedly functioning in Warsaw. He was compelled, by the Austrian military command, to abandon schemes of independent raids against Russian-held territory. His Riflemen formed the nucleus of the Polish Legions organized under official Austrian tutelage and with the support of the Polish National Committee (NKN), a body uniting all groups active in Galicia, from conservative supporters of the Austrian monarchy to socialists, peasants, and anti-Russian revolutionaries. While young Poles joining the Legions were animated by visions of an independent Poland, they were looked upon cynically as cannon-fodder by

Austrian military leaders. The same idea, of obtaining Polish cannon-fodder and labor, was in the minds of the military leaders of the Central Powers when, after chasing the Russians out of the "Kingdom," they proclaimed, on November 5, 1916, a new Kingdom of Poland under their auspices. The creation of an army for that kingdom, which for the time being was to have no sovereign and no sovereignty, was the main concern of the Germans, while the Poles coöperating with them were naturally interested in obtaining more than shadow independence. Conflicts over the use of the Legions eventually led to their dissolution; Pilsudski, identified as leader of the conspirational Polish Military Organization (POW), was interned in the fortress of Magdeburg. The provisional Council of State, and then a Regency of three prominent Poles, became the nucleus of a Polish government.

With the change in the fortunes of war to the disadvantage of the Central Powers, the Poles became more and more outspoken in demands for real independence presented to German Governor General von Beseler in Warsaw, actual ruler of the "Kingdom." Beseler's answers to Polish political leaders were a strange mixture of Prussian insolence and occasional acute observations concerning the possibilities and limitations of Poland. He made it clear that Germany could under no circumstances be a passive observer of what was going to happen in Poland; agreement to creation of a Polish "state" was based on the expectation that Germany would direct its formation and functioning in accordance with her interest in preventing the use of Polish territories by Russia as a threat to Germany. Poland, said Beseler on one occasion, could never oppose the neighboring Powers with her own force and "she must therefore lean on one of them." He admitted that the maximal Polish program, envisaging the incorporation of Galicia and Prussia in a Polish state, "was imaginable only with Russian support." As conceived by Germany and Austria, the Kingdom was to be "possibly enlarged by acquisitions in the East."

There was no clear agreement between the Central Powers on the Polish issue, with the Germans frowning upon an "Austrian" solution. With the growing misfortunes of Austria in the military field, the German command acquired the decisive voice in the matter and the disposition of Polish territory was subordinated to military considerations. The treaty of Brest-Litovsk, concluded early in 1918 between the Central Powers and the Bolsheviks, was a death blow to Polish orientations based on coöperation with Germany and Austria. The puppet government functioning in the Kingdom was not even permitted to participate in the negotiations. The German-sponsored "independent" Ukraine created by the treaty was to include a slice of territory—the region of Chelm—considered by the Poles indisputably Polish. Public manifestations of discontent broke out in a number of cities; the "cabinet" resigned in protest. On the eastern front some Polish detachments broke away from the Austrian army and crossed the line into Russia.

The "sham independence" granted to Poland by the emperors of Germany and Austria was denounced by the Allies, declared illegal by Russia, and decried by Poles active in Russia who had based their orientation on the benevolence of the tsar rather than on that of the German courts. Russia, too, was wooing the Poles. The leader of the National Democrats, Roman Dmowski, had long before the outbreak of the war advocated a pro-Russian "orientation" based on the assumption that Germany, and not Russia, was the "hereditary enemy" of Poland. When war came, the Russian army command in a proclamation directed to the Poles promised the resurrection of a Polish state. But Russia was interested only in the psychological effect of such promises on the morale of the Poles, especially those in the German and Austrian armies, not in the establishment of a Polish state. The Polish National Committee, formed in Warsaw under Dmowski's leadership, engaged in hopeless efforts to obtain more precise promises from the Russians. It was later revealed that the tsarist government thought of forming a "Polish" state consisting only of territories conquered from Germany and Austria.

Even when Russian armies were pushed out of the Kingdom, the tsarist government could not bring itself to offer the Poles more than a vague promise of autonomy. It appeared to the Russian statesmen that their country's position as an ally of the

West—and, of course, a series of secret agreements—made concessions unnecessary. But Russia's importance as a fighting ally was rapidly declining. Under these circumstances Dmowski decided to transfer the center of his political activities from Russia to the west. His Polish National Committee, at first evacuated to St. Petersburg, later established itself in Paris and branched out to London and Washington. The "Russian" orientation became the "Western" orientation. The outbreak of the revolution eventually changed the views of the French government on Russia and brought to the fore Poland as the major prop of the new Eastern Barrier.

Until the end of the war it was, however, in German-occupied Poland that the nucleus of a Polish government functioned, in the form of the Regency. Made possible by the victory of the Allies, the government of independent Poland nevertheless issued from the body established under the authority of the Central Powers.

Interwar Poland later adopted November 11 as official Independence Day. The choice of this date relegates into prehistory earlier attempts to create a central government for Poland in the weeks of turmoil preceding the final collapse of the Central Powers. On October 7, 1918, the Regency, basing itself on "the peace proposals proclaimed by the President of the United States and now accepted by the whole world," took over supreme power in what amounted to a coup, since the occupation, although disintegrating, was still in force. On November 3, 1918, the cabinet appointed by the Regency proclaimed, without consulting the Regents, a republic, upon which the cabinet was dismissed.

The Lublin Government. A few days later, in the town of Lublin, another attempt was made to proclaim a People's Republic, under the leadership of Ignacy Daszynski, a socialist from Galicia. The manifesto directed by that "Lublin government" on November 7, 1918 to "the Polish worker and peasant" declared the unpopular Regency dissolved and promised far-reaching social reforms, including compulsory expropriation of large and medium landholdings, nationalization of mines and various industries, universal, free, and secular education. The manifesto reserved for Pilsudski, then still a prisoner at Magde-

burg, the position of commander in chief. But when Pilsudski
was released a few days later and given a triumphant welcome
in Warsaw, he preferred to accept power from the Regency which
proclaimed itself dissolved as of November 14. Thus vested with
dictatorial powers, Pilsudski called upon Daszynski, head of the
ephemeral Lublin government, to form a cabinet. Personally
loyal to ex-comrade Pilsudski and apparently happy to find an
honorable way out for the "Lublin government" which was bitterly opposed by the middle class, the socialist leader accepted
the mission to form a cabinet, but failed. Pilsudski found it
necessary to justify the choice of a socialist by stating in a decree
that he was "taking into account the powerful currents at present gaining victory in the West and East of Europe." This was
obviously a reference to the revolutionary stirrings caused by the
impact of the upheaval in Russia. But Pilsudski made it clear
that he contemplated no revolutionary changes. "The nature of
Poland's situation . . . does not permit the carrying out of deep
social changes, which can be voted only by the Constituent Diet."

Polish socialists and radical populist leaders celebrated,
througout the interwar period, the anniversary of "Lublin"; they
were actually commemorating a failure.

In spite of its unquestionable "respectability," the government
finally formed by the socialist Moraczewski was suspected in the
west of "Bolshevism." Of course, the influence of Pilsudski's
competitor, Roman Dmowski, who had secured official recognition for his Polish National Committee by the victorious West,
was of decisive importance. H. H. Fisher remarks that "damaging
. . . to Pilsudski's standing in the West were his socialist opinions and his long revolutionary career. Bolshevism had succeeded
Teutonism as the great bogey of Western opinion, and Bolshevism was an inclusive term making socialists of all complexions
suspect." [1] Actually Pilsudski, far from being a "Bolshevik," as
Dmowski would have the Allies believe, was not even an evolutionary socialist. He made it quite clear to the leaders of the
Polish Socialist Party that he had "left the 'red vehicle' at the
station called Independence." His subsequent actions made it

[1] H. H. Fisher, *America and the New Poland* (New York: The Macmillan
Company, 1928) , p. 120.

more than obvious. At the time, however, Pilsudski enjoyed the
support of the socialists and the radical peasant groups. On the
other hand, the nationalist groups were bitterly opposed to him.
In the former Prussian province of Poland a regional National
Council proclaimed its allegiance to Dmowski's Committee in
Paris rather than to the central government in Warsaw. The
breach was healed by Paderewski's arrival in Poland.

Against the background of a theatrical coup staged by a
group of rightist officers to overthrow the socialist and populist
cabinet headed by Moraczewski, Pilsudski started negotiations
with the famous pianist turned statesman. "There were unmistakable intimations," states H. H. Fisher, "that the Allies would
do nothing for Poland in the way of military supplies or financial
support unless a more representative government was established
which included the conservative as well as the socialist party . . .
Paderewski had the confidence of the American government."
Only with the appointment of Paderewski as premier was the
new Poland officially recognized by the United States and the
other victorious powers. Herbert Hoover's food shipments no
doubt helped the establishment of "national unity" and the suppression of radical tendencies.[2]

American diplomacy considered it a vital task to "do everything . . . to strengthen Paderewski's hands" because it was
"important for the future of Poland" to have "a strong and
moderate government this winter," the winter of 1919, a time of
suffering and discontent "so acute as to render any relaxing
of government authority dangerous."[3] Support for Paderewski
was considered essential in spite of his growing unpopularity in
Parliament where, as the American envoy to Warsaw reported,
Paderewski was considered "subservient to the Allies" and even

---

[2] Dr. Kellogg, Hoover's representative in Poland, suggested that "Pilsudski
. . . should be put on a pedestal . . . (and) Paderewski, the favorite of all
Poles, should be placed at the head of a stronger cabinet as Prime Minister
. . . Dr. Kellogg asked that he be authorized to inform Pilsudski that unless
this was done American coöperation and aid were futile . . . I did so and got
the hint reinforced from President Wilson. As a result . . . Paderewski became Prime Minister . . ." (*The Memoirs of Herbert Hoover*, New York:
The Macmillan Company, 1951, I, 356–357.)

[3] Secretary of State Lansing to American Embassy, London (National
Archives, 86oc.01/289).

as having "sacrificed best [interests] of Poland in order to secure for himself [the] approval of Allied governments." [4]

The pressure of the victorious Allies, their sympathies for the parties "of law and order" and distrust of social radicalism even of the mild Polish variety, the irresolute stand of the Polish Socialist Party, whose leaders were bound by personal attachment to ex-socialist Jozef Pilsudski, and the withdrawal of support by the peasant leader Wincenty Witos combined to frustrate the social revolution which seemed to accompany the birth of the new Polish state. Above all, however, the need for "national unity" in the face of international difficulties was the decisive factor in determining the character of government. Pilsudski himself, although looked upon as a "Bolshevik" in the misinformed west, had little liking for a leftist government. As he stated later, in an essay written in 1930, he wanted in 1918 a "government without adjectives, for all of Poland." The adjective "ludowy" (meaning "popular," "of the people") with which the Lublin government had started out, was for Pilsudski "a ridiculous imitation of experiments coming from the East." Pilsudski continued to believe that Poland had no right to engage in radical social reforms because of the need to devote all attention to external dangers. After his return to power in 1926, he told a correspondent of *Le Matin* that "the moment has not come to solve social problems. We are the neighbors of Russia . . . I realized [in 1918] that Poland must be careful, that she was young and poor, and must avoid risky experiments . . ."

After the short socialist interlude, Poland was launched on the way of parliamentary democracy, with fairly free elections which brought into the legislature a multitude of political groups unable to produce a stable majority. Pilsudski resigned as Chief of State and withdrew to his estate at Sulejowek, to return in 1926 as leader of a coup directed against parliamentary government or, as he said, against the abuses thereof. Pilsudski then forced the President, Stanislaw Wojciechowski, to resign, had himself elected President by the cowed parliament, refused to take office because the Constitution then in power put too many

[4] Hugh Gibson to Secretary of State (National Archives, 860c.01/290, 860c.01/303) .

restrictions on the Executive, and recommended as candidate Professor Ignacy Moscicki, a chemist of international standing.[5]

Democracy and Dictatorship. The somewhat more than twenty years of Poland's internal political development between the two World Wars can be roughly divided in two parts of unequal length. A relatively short period of experimenting with democracy, or at least with the external trappings of parliamentary government, came to an end in May 1926, with the military coup staged by Marshal Jozef Pilsudski. Thirteen years of authoritarian government followed, first in the form of a personal dictatorship of the Marshal and later, after his death in 1935, and until the debacle of 1939, as rule by a clique of his political associates and sycophants.

The line of development, from what looked like the adoption of western democracy to the establishment of a local variety of "fascism," was not limited to Poland alone. It was, in fact, repeated almost everywhere in the area, mainly as a result of the passing of political, economic, and spiritual influence over eastern and central Europe from the principal victors of Versailles to Mussolini's Italy and, somewhat later and more forcefully, to Hitler's Germany. A potent factor contributing to the change, in addition to the lack of roots for democratic rule, was the increasing pressure of economic difficulties for which the dynamism and determination of the authoritarian systems appeared to offer more radical solutions than democracy.

On the Polish scene, as elsewhere in the area, neither democracy nor authoritarian rule developed fully the characteristics of the models which inspired them. Some students of interwar Poland speak of the "pseudo-democracy" of the first period, others of the "pseudo-dictatorship" of the second period. Both evaluations are correct. Unless one accepts as sufficient test of democracy the existence of the opportunity to cast a ballot at

[5] None of Poland's interwar presidents was permitted to complete his term in office. The first president, Gabriel Narutowicz, was assassinated a few days after his election by the nationalist fanatic Eligiusz Niewiadomski because he had been elected with "Jewish votes." Wojciechowski was forced to resign in May 1926. Moscicki held the presidency for one term and was reëlected for another term, which was interrupted by the German invasion of Poland in 1939.

more or less regular intervals in more or less free elections, democratic government implies an intimate contact between the citizenry and those in charge of its destinies, a constant preoccupation with the welfare of the people, and a high degree of civic responsibility resulting from a close identification of the population with its government. For many reasons most of these elements were absent in Poland.

The system of parliamentary government was transplanted, in 1919, to a Poland which had missed a century of independent political development. Whatever training Polish politicians had received in parliamentary methods was limited to the legislatures of the partitioning Powers, where they were as a rule in opposition or were engaged in a game of political intrigue. Other political leaders, especially those from the former Russian provinces, had more understanding of conspiracy than of open political activity. The average citizen was traditionally skeptical about the benefits he could expect from government—for over a hundred years alien and almost invariably hostile. Independence released a great craving of a numerous and not too prosperous intelligentsia and semi-intelligentsia for positions in the new administration; its members, recruited from among the gentry or from middle-class groups which had adopted the mentality of the gentry, had a deeply ingrained lack of respect and concern for the "mob."

The democratic process became an instrument of struggle for power and patronage by competing groups of politicians who identified themselves with one social stratum of the population or another, but devoted most of their energy to the game of parliamentary bickering in an atmosphere of petty jealousies, mutual recriminations, and demagogy. Polish politics was full of personal quarrels, clashes of ambitions and opportunistic shifts, cutting across the "class" line of division, blurring the picture of "right" and "left." There was, above all, a frightening degree of almost anarchic irresponsibility which only in extreme situations would be checked, and then only temporarily. It seemed, wrote the historian Bobrzynski, as if the old anarchy of the gentry had become democratized and spread to bourgeois, peasant, and socialist politicians.

The authoritarian system of government which in 1926 replaced what Pilsudski called "sterile, jabbering, howling" parliamentarism, managed to combine the objectionable features of totalitarian rule with a lack of clear purpose and the absence of a broad basis of support of the kind which a Mussolini or a Hitler was able to secure by kindling enthusiasm for spurious but at least attractive ideas. Here again Poland fitted into the pattern of the east-central European twilight zone which developed, in the 1930's, the non-ideological ideology of supporting The Government or The Strong Man and even produced parties identified merely as the "government party"—in the case of Poland the "Non-partisan bloc for coöperation with the government" (BBWR, better known as BB).

During the time of Pilsudski's personal rule, his will and whim were substitutes for ideas and programs. After Pilsudski's death the successors, by no means a homogeneous group, maintained themselves in power by sheer force, by making inroads in opposition ranks, and by capitalizing on the strained international situation of the later thirties which forced the opposition to attenuate its pressure for the return of a democratic system of government. Neither Pilsudski nor his heirs banned the political parties, although the Marshal spent much time calling the politicians unprintable names and insulting the very institution of parliament.[6] Aiming, rather clumsily, at uniting the nation behind their regime, Pilsudski's successors continued to tolerate the existence of various political parties, but banned them from the surface of political life by excluding them from parliamentary

[6] Immediately after the coup of May 1926 Pilsudski declared to a foreign correspondent: "The country and I are tired of party labels and programs . . . I am a strong man and I like to make my own decisions." But he added, "I don't like the whip . . . I am not in favor of dictatorship in Poland." (*Le Matin*, Paris, May 25, 1926.) Pilsudski's philosophy of government was expressed in an ominous newspaper interview which appeared a few days before the coup: "Two functions of the state, in the fields of military and foreign policy, must not be subject to the fluctuations of the party game. Such a system leads to the inevitable doom of the state." (*Kurjer Poranny*, Warsaw, May 10, 1926.) In the years that followed, foreign policy and military affairs were on an enforced "nonpartisan" basis and the government never made more than occasional and very vague pronouncements on these subjects, rarely followed by genuine debate.

elections. Poland's dictatorship was indeed as incomplete as Poland's democracy had been.

If democracy failed because its roots were not deep enough or because leadership was of a deplorably low caliber, authoritarian government of the "dictatorship without a dictator" did not have the genuine support which only an attractive central idea could have secured. The corruption of the system which had started out by presenting itself as the champion of a higher morality in Polish politics, and its inability to tackle successfully the basic issues of Poland's internal and external situation undermined popular support for the heirs of Marshal Pilsudski. Intimidation and bribery were substituted for genuine support. The regime worked to perpetuate itself. It rushed through the *Sejm,* in a rather irregular fashion, a new constitution replete with muddleheaded elite ideas, making the president responsible only "before God and History." An extra-constitutional position, that of "Second Citizen of the Republic," was assumed on the basis of a decree to that effect by Edward Rydz-Smigly, who was created Marshal of Poland (probably the only Marshal to obtain the baton without having won, or even fought, a major battle). A new electoral law banned the political parties from participation; the *Sejm* was packed with nominees of the administration. Attempts to give a popular basis to the regime by the creation, in the last interwar years, of a "Camp of National Unity" met with little response, just as the officially sponsored youth organization could not compete with the radical groups of the extreme Right which appeared on the political scene in the thirties. The program of the Camp of National Unity was an amazing concoction, full of national jingoism, anti-Semitism, a domestic variety of authoritarian rule, and a sprinkling of social ideas borrowed from Mussolini. The program provided no basis for a truly national movement which would back the government in the difficult international situation of the late thirties.[7] In the moment of peril the regime had to resort to the the "blackmail of patriotism"

---

[7] A Polish writer in exile later described the ideology of the Pilsudski-ite camp as capable only of "hatching anniversary slogans" and likened it to leaves falling off the wreath of a withering legend, good only for "cooking the soup of personal careers." (Jozef Lobodowski, "Przeciw upiorom przeszlosci," in *Kultura,* Paris, Nos. 2–3, 1052, p. 28.)

while showing little intention of relaxing its monopolistic hold
on the affairs of the state. The assertions of some writers that
the regime was just about ready to become more democratic are
not supported by the record. The regime collapsed in defeat in
the lightning war of 1939 which in a few days destroyed the last
remaining illusion of the Poles that their government had at least
adequately prepared the country's defense.

Peasants and Peasant Parties. In the Poland of 1921 the percentage of people dependent on agriculture was the same as in
the England of the late seventeenth century: about seventy out
of every hundred inhabitants. Poland, like most countries of the
area, was a predominantly peasant country. This led superficial
observers to the conclusion that peasants either would rule
Poland or, as a matter of elementary justice, they should do so.
Yet the record of interwar Polish politics shows that at no time
was the country ruled by the peasants. The political activities of
parties claiming to represent the interests of the peasantry were
by no means negligible. On the contrary; in the first, parliamentary, period of interwar development the peasant Center played
an important role because of the division between Right and
Left. In the second, authoritarian, period, the peasant parties
were able to stir their followers into manifestations of discontent and anger. But at no time were the peasant leaders in a
position to use their political strength and their claim of enjoying the support of three quarters of the nation in order to impose on Poland a peasant government or to carry out a "green
revolution" of the type staged by Alexander Stamboliiski in Bul-
garia. The reason for this failure must be sought in certain specific conditions of Polish social and political life, but also in the
general characteristics of the leading peasant parties of eastern
Europe, in their essentially conservative stand which played into
the hands of the Right and of the local variations on the fascist
theme.

In pre-partition Poland "the nation" had meant exclusively
the gentry. During the nineteenth century that class lost its monopolistic hold but it retained leadership by virtue of educational and economic advantages. The slowly rising middle class
identified itself with the traditions and habits of the gentry.

The ranks of the professions, the intelligentsia, the groups which were to provide the leadership of various political parties and, in re-established Poland, the core of the army officers' corps and the top echelons of the administration, came from the gentry.

This circumstance had a significant influence on the behavior of the political groups identified with the interests of "the masses," and especially on the attitudes of peasant leaders. Because of the survival, even after the abolition of serfdom, of what has been described as "the sentiment that the peasant belonged to an inferior class, an inferior race, destined to serfdom by divine and by human laws,"[8] the energies of peasant leaders were directed mainly at securing for the peasant bulk of the nation a political position commensurate with its numerical strength. This right of the peasants to profit from the advantages conferred upon them by universal franchise and to enter, on fair terms, the ruling fraternity, was by no means graciously conceded in Poland, or, for that matter, elsewhere. Yet there came into existence an educated and ambitious peasant intelligentsia conscious of the value of the "electoral currency" and determined to break the hold of the gentry and urban elements on the political scene. The class pride which animated some of the peasant leaders was, however, tempered by the residual inferiority complex of the newly emancipated that made them attach undue importance to the mere fact of admission to the councils of government. Once in, peasant leaders were often content to impress their followers with external manifestations of their assertiveness: the popularity of Wincenty Witos in Poland was bolstered by his habit of not wearing a necktie and by tales of his propensity for using the shiny floors of government palaces as spittoons. The leaders of the peasant parties cared little about the price of admission to share in the government of their countries. Their social, economic, political aims became rather vague wherever they extended beyond immediate advantages for the property-owning and relatively "wealthy" peasant groups. The moral level of the newcomers to the political scene was not higher than that of the old-timers. As a matter of fact, the interwar history of eastern

---

[8] Waclaw Lednicki, *Life and Culture of Poland* (New York: Roy Publishers, 1944), p. 153.

Europe shows that a considerable portion of demagogues, turn-coats, and corrupt politicians came from the ranks of the peasant parties. This was certainly true in Poland and, in a way, still is. Neither the Pilsudski regime nor the communists have found it difficult to "neutralize" a number of authentic peasant politicians.

It has been said that the inability or unwillingness of the eastern European peasant parties to establish lasting coöperation with the socialists of the area was a major misfortune which helped to bring about the advent of authoritarian government. This view is no doubt correct but it overlooks the difficulties of such coöperation. Because the peasant parties were, for obvious reasons, in favor of free elections and universal suffrage, and often used terminology which sounded revolutionary, they were thought of as socially radical. Actually, they were nothing of the kind. On the contrary, they were conservative, if not outright reactionary in their outlook, and profoundly distrustful of socialism as being alien to their ideas about property and smacking of a typically urban ideology. It is a pity that the division of the rural population into wealthy, middling, and poor peasants has become so closely identified with a communist approach to the problem and so abused by the communists in their attempts to fan class struggle in the countryside. There is no doubt a real divergence of interests between the peasant who owns a good sized farm and produces for the market, his neighbor who ekes out a living on a subsistence level, and the rural proletarian with no land or with a dwarf holding insufficient to feed a family. In their appeal to peasant solidarity the leading peasant parties of eastern Europe glossed over these differences; they served largely the interests of the well-entrenched elements of the village and catered to their conservatism.

The record of Wincenty Witos, the most influential peasant leader of interwar Poland, is illuminating. Witos refused to participate in the first Lublin government headed by Daszynski; he preferred "national unity" with the Right rather than partnership with the socialists.[9] In the parliamentary combinations which

[9] One reads with genuine surprise in *I Saw Poland Betrayed* (Indianapolis: The Bobbs-Merrill Company, 1948), by Arthur Bliss Lane, that "in 1919 Witos had been considered by the Pilsudski group a revolutionary firebrand

brought him three times the premiership, Witos once agreed to serve as an attractive symbol of "national unity" at the time of the Red Army's advance on Warsaw in 1920, and twice as an ally of the Right. Described by Pilsudski as "cynical and dishonest," and generally considered unprincipled, equally amenable to combinations with the Right and with the Left, Witos actually favored the Right, even if he had to agree to drop the issue of land reform as price of the alliance. In 1923 the leading publication of his party wrote of the necessity of forming a parliamentary majority embracing "all those who possess something and have something to lose." His last cabinet was ousted, in May 1926, by a coup in which Pilsudski enjoyed the support not only of his military followers but also of the socialists and even, for a short while, the communists. A few years later, Witos and his party were in a new political combination, this time with the socialists (known as the *Centrolew* or Left-Center bloc), in their joint struggle against the Pilsudski regime. At that time, however, the opposition could achieve very little. Witos was arrested, maltreated by his jailers on express orders from Pilsudski, and convicted for plotting against the government; forced to flee the country, he continued to exercise great, although by no means exclusive, influence on the peasants. But neither his courageous stand at the trial nor the new tactical ties with the socialists could erase the earlier record which another peasant leader, the more radical Stanislaw Thugutt, once summed up as follows: "Witos could have become a great peasant; he preferred to be an adjunct of the gentry."

In spite of his great popularity with the peasant masses, due more to political skill than to advocacy of their interests, Witos never approached the 75 per cent support immodestly claimed by his successor to the leadership of the Peasant Party, Stanislaw Mikolajczyk. There were many groups active in the countryside and coveting the vote of the peasants. Some peasant elements joined the more radical parties, such as Thugutt's *Wyzwolenie* and various ephemeral groups. The peasants also voted for non-

---

because of his liberal and progressive views" (p. 91). It was just the other way around. It was rather Witos who considered Pilsudski "a revolutionary firebrand" and refused to enter a coalition with the socialists.

rural parties, for the rightist National Democrats, for the socialists, or, in some instances, even for the communists or crypto-communist candidates. In the years preceding the outbreak of World War II the main peasant groups, persecuted by the Pilsudski regime, united; yet divergent tendencies within the "united" party continued to operate, causing frequent splits and defections.

The difficulties in the way of lasting alliance between the leading peasant parties and the socialists were not merely a matter of mistaken tactics or of the doctrinaire blindness of the socialists, as David Mitrany believes.[10] They stemmed from the essentially anti-socialist convictions of the peasant leaders. Some of them were outright conservatives. Others came to accept a conservative stand in a roundabout way, through an "agrarianist" interpretation of the problems of the peasant as representing something almost mystical, based on a biological bond with the land, and impossible of classification and solution within the range of approaches offered by urban and industrial civilization.

Witos, like so many other eastern European peasant leaders, was no doubt a "champion of democracy." Drawing support from the strongest group numerically of the population, he quite naturally was for free elections, freedom of speech, and "the proper place for the peasant." But it was not always clear for what purposes he would use the tools of democracy and the implements of political power. In the opinion of the conservative Polish scholar, Roman Dyboski, "Witos gloriously performed the difficult task of stirring up the peasant force of the country into resistance against the Bolshevik invasion, which held out to the peasant the most alluring bait of gratuitous distribution of land. But the later stages of his government were marred by political corruption and favoritism." Someone has also said that Witos

[10] Professor Mitrany claims that the hostility of socialists everywhere to the peasants resulted from "the rise of Marxist socialism, which on dogmatic grounds decreed that the peasants were an anachronism and had to be rooted out as ruthlessly as the capitalists." ("Evolution of the Middle Zone," in *Annals*, September 1950, p. 9.) Mitrany developed his favorite thesis more fully in a book, *Marx Against the Peasant*. His description of the Witos regime of 1926 as a "democratic and progressive" government overthrown by a combination of colonels and landlords, with the support of the socialists, is an amazing misstatement of the facts.

contributed more witty remarks than ideas to the history of government in interwar Poland.

The National Minorities. Within the boundaries allowed her by the treaties of Versailles and Riga, Poland was an entirely different sort of political unit from the "indisputably Polish" state advocated by Woodrow Wilson. The victorious Allies abandoned the principle of self-determination for strategic considerations. In some instances, as in the case of the seizure of Wilno and in Eastern Galicia, Poland forced the West to accept solutions imposed by force. The peace treaty with the Soviet Union actually amounted to a partition of the Ukraine and Byelorussia between Poland and Russia, without consulting the native population that was neither Polish nor Russian and, on the whole, was hostile to both the Poles and the Russians.

As a result of these developments, Poland found herself with about a third of her total population of non-Polish stock. There were some 14 per cent Ukrainians (which official Polish statistics broke down into two groups: Ukrainians and Ruthenians) ; more than 3 per cent Byelorussians; about 10 per cent Jews (according to statistics of religious distribution; some 400,000 Jews gave their mother tongue as Polish rather than Yiddish or Hebrew and were therefore classed as Poles) ; 2.3 per cent Germans, and roughly 3 per cent various other nationalities, including Lithuanians, Russians, and Czechs. The quoted figures naturally do not tell the full story; official Polish sources tended to play down the number of people who did not consider themselves Poles, while on the other hand various committees representing the minorities both in Poland and abroad claimed that the actual figures were much higher. The Ukrainians, for instance, put their number closer to 6 or even 7 million than to the figure of 4.8 million given by Polish scholars as an estimate for 1931.

The acquisition of such a large number of people of foreign nationalities would have been a source of weakness and trouble for any state. It was particularly so for Poland, surrounded by hostile and potentially strong neighbors.

Interwar Poland was unable to work out an intelligent solution or even to maintain a consistent approach to the problem of minorities. The way chosen by most interwar cabinets was to buy the support of a certain segment of the minorities and to suppress the activities of more radical groups by force. With respect to the Ukrainians, for instance, after a series of terrorist attacks organized by a militant nationalist group against Polish officials, "some brutal reprisals were inflicted pretty indiscriminately on the Ukrainian population by Polish troops and police, especially in the autumn of 1930. Libraries and coöperatives were destroyed, Boy Scout organizations with Ukrainian membership were dissolved, and Ukrainian high schools were closed." [11]

The political dilemma of the Ukrainians was tragic. Many of them were anti-Russian as well as anti-Bolshevik and could not therefore lean on the Soviet Union which was luring them with the promise of a united Ukraine. But they were also in their majority anti-Polish; the attempts of Polish governments to colonize the eastern confines of the Republic with ex-servicemen of Polish nationality helped to fan Ukrainian resistance and kept alive old feuds, going back to the time of Austrian rule in Galicia and strengthened by still older historical memories.

It was natural for more restless Ukrainians to seek refuge and political support abroad, especially in Czechoslovakia and Germany. The hesitant Polish policies, combining concessions that were not attractive enough with sporadic displays of brutal yet not determined force, kept the Ukrainian issue alive throughout the interwar years. While some elements were won for collaboration, others adhered to extremist nationalist groups or came under the spell of communist propaganda and became involved in the activities of the illegal Communist Party of the Western Ukraine. It was generally assumed in Polish government circles that the suppression of Ukrainian nationalism by the Soviets weakened considerably communist sympathies among the Ukrainian population of eastern Poland. On the other hand, the misery of the peasant population in that underprivileged part of Poland no doubt made the people receptive to subversive propaganda; the lack of outlets for the young Ukrainian intelligentsia strengthened nationalist and terrorist activities.

The less numerous and culturally less developed Byelorussian

[11] William Henry Chamberlin, *The Ukraine, a Submerged Nation* (New York: The Macmillan Company, 1944).

minority also had its collaborationists and its communist followers. The existence of a large group of Byelorussians who belonged
to the Catholic Church tended to confuse the issue of nationality
and to render attempts at obtaining statistical data quite hopeless. Many peasants considered themselves simply as being "local"
or "Christians"; they were not quite sure what they were being
asked to answer when presented with a census questionnaire.

The German minority, concentrated mostly along the border,
was not affected by the mixture of social and national grievances
which characterized the position of the Slav minorities. The Germans nevertheless voiced constant complaints about mistreatment
by the Poles, especially in the field of education. They proved
on the whole a docile instrument of revisionist propaganda from
across the "bleeding frontier" and many of them were discovered
to be Nazi agents and spies.

The problem of the Jewish population was quite different from
that of the other groups. The Jews had no irredentist connections
with foreign countries and their problem could, in theory, have
been solved by a systematic program of assimilation with the Polish majority. However, this solution was rejected both by the
Poles who refused to accept an "alien element" into the body
of the Polish nation, and by the majority of the Jews who, either
on grounds of religious orthodoxy, because of Zionist leanings,
or as followers of socialist groups advocating cultural autonomy,
insisted on preserving a separate national and cultural status. A
considerable part of the Jewish group was distinguished in dress,
language, and food habits from the surrounding Polish population. The social composition of the Jewish population differed from that of the population as a whole; the Jews were
a predominantly urban element, engaged mostly in commerce
and crafts. This peculiar occupational distribution of the Jews
was, of course, mainly the result of historical development.
The gentry of Old Poland had consciously left the towns to the
Germans and the Jews. Treated with tolerant contempt, the Jews
lived in a cultural and occupational ghetto, even though the wall
was invisible. The development of a native Polish middle class
added a new, economic motive—or, rather, rationalization—to
the "zoological" anti-Semitism involving religious and racial differences.

In the hopeless attempts of the Polish state to cope with its economic problems, the idea of squeezing out the Jews from their positions in commerce, in the crafts, and in the professions was the solution that occurred to Polish political leaders. The last decade of Poland's interwar history was one of increasing economic difficulties for the bulk of the Jewish community. The edge of taxation policies was used in discriminatory fashion against the Jews. Statism, the tendency of the government to take over and operate various branches of industry, resulted in the elimination of Jews from certain occupations. Because of their social stratification, the Jews were also the *objective* victims of certain changes, such as the organization of coöperatives which eliminated the Jewish middleman. Political representatives of the Jews did not—and probably could not—always distinguish between such objective causes operating against their constituents and deliberate anti-Semitic measures.

In the last prewar years, under the influence of the ephemeral friendship with Nazi Germany and under the pressure of local radically anti-Semitic groups, the government of Poland began quite openly to tolerate outbreaks of violence against Jews which spread from the universities to small towns and villages. From this attitude of "neutrality" the government shifted to one of advocating economic warfare against the Jews and legal limitations on the number of Jews in the universities and in certain professions. Anti-Semitism, says James Parkes in his study on the Jewish problem, was a "safety valve for general unrest." The Jews "bore the brunt of the increasing economic distress and political disorder" in the years immediately preceding the outbreak of the war. In the last year of its existence, the regime made extensive use of the safety valve to keep the population from realizing the full extent of the approaching disaster. At the League of Nations, Poland demanded international measures for the removal of Jews from Poland at the rate of 100,000 a year, of course without their money, which Poland could ill afford to lose.[12] So-called ghetto benches were officially introduced at the universities, and Jewish law graduates found it practically impossible to gain admission to the Bar. The Poles were not per-

[12] Cf. James Parkes, *The Emergence of the Jewish Problem* (London and New York: Oxford University Press, 1946).

mitted to reap the fruits of their "victory" over the Jewish population. The tragedy of the Jew in Poland was, for a while,
submerged in the general tragedy of the country under German
invasion. Hitler offered the Poles a more radical solution for the
problem than they had ever dreamed of: complete annihilation,
in gas chambers, of millions of Polish Jews.

The standard "explanations" offered for anti-Semitism in Poland are an attempt to give the appearance of rationality to what
is an essentially irrational phenomenon. Poland's last interwar
foreign minister, Colonel Beck, who could be described as the
type of anti-Semite who readily asserts that some of his best
friends are Jews, argued in his posthumously published memoirs
that the Poles simply loved their native Jews but objected to the
"Litvaks" who spoke with a Russian accent. Yet other Poles objected precisely to those Jews who were "worming their way into
Polish culture" and were speaking and writing Polish too well.
Group prejudice has little to do with the virtues or shortcomings
of the hated. It is almost entirely a problem of the haters. The
Polish approach to the issue lacked the cruel determination of the
Nazi laws and actions, but its long-range implications meant slow
economic strangulation of the Jewish community. A cold pogrom
is still a pogrom. It would be futile to enter into a discussion of
responsibilities for the turn which the Jewish problem took in
interwar Poland. Under the conditions of the Poland of 1919–
1939, the problem could not be solved in a humane way. It merely
added to the list of impossible issues with which the interwar
Polish state clumsily grappled. Extermination of the bulk of the
Jewish population by the Nazis and emigration of most survivors
deprived the Jewish problem of practical importance in the Poland that emerged from World War II.

The problem of national minorities offered Polish statesmen
ample opportunities for making silly sallies on the international
arena, in their quest for prestige victories. Such a step was the
declaration made by Beck in 1934 to the effect that Poland would
not recognize the so-called Minorities Treaty signed at Versailles.
This flashy exhibition changed nothing in the nature of the problem of minorities for which the framework of the Polish state in
its interwar setting simply provided no satisfactory solution.

ECONOMIC AND SOCIAL PROBLEMS

Holding action. The endowment of small countries with political sovereignty not supported by effective economic measures for their survival and development has been more than once compared to the situation of a slave freed with nothing but the rags on his back. Difficulties of adjustment resulting from emancipation are well-known in the lives of individuals and groups. This does not necessarily decrease the craving for independence; freedom is expected to release hidden sources of energy and to open new possibilities. It is no doubt an important, although not easily measurable, factor in mobilizing the human component of economic progress. Yet its limits are obvious. There are certain tasks which doggedness alone cannot accomplish.

In the case of interwar Poland the task of adjustment and development was enormous. The effort made by the nation was in many respects impressive, but the results on the whole were unsatisfactory, because the material basis—in simpler terms, available capital—was too limited in comparison to the country's needs and ambitions. There was also not enough time; only twenty years separated the beginning of Poland's new statehood from its actual, if not formal, end.

"Versailles," wrote the Polish economist Ferdynand Zweig, "freed [the nations of east-central Europe] from foreign domination, but left them to face all their miseries, their economic backwardness, and the utter disruption of their national economy, alone." Poland had to face all issues common to the area—predominantly agricultural, poor, underindustrialized and overpopulated eastern Europe—but she also had to cope with a set of specific problems resulting from more than a century of division between three partitioning Powers and three different economic systems. Wartime destruction was larger in Poland than elsewhere in Europe. The "battle of the frontiers" retarded reconstruction. In addition, Poland assumed larger political and military responsibilities than other countries with a similar socioeconomic structure; the defense of extensive, threatened, and "impossible" frontiers was a heavy drain on the modest resources

of the country. The sums actually spent were not high in absolute terms, and they certainly could not buy military security,
but they represented a considerable part of the state budget—
some 35 per cent in direct appropriations only, actually at least
45 per cent—and a big slice of the "ludicrously low" national income of the interwar years.

In evaluating the achievements of the twenty years of Poland's
interwar existence, it is necessary to separate sentimental considerations from statistical realities, recognition of the effort of the
nation from judgment of the results achieved. The conclusion is
inescapable that in terms of the standard of living of the population as a whole the interwar period brought little or no change.
Colin Clark's calculations of real income per head of working
population—a reliable index of progress—show that income in
Poland in the last four years before World War II (1935–1939)
was identical with what it had been in 1909–1913 for the comparable area. This means that in terms of living standard the
entire period amounted to no more than a holding battle against
deterioration. It must be remembered that the population of
Poland increased considerably during the twenty-year period and
it required a tremendous effort to keep the pace of economic development geared to that increase—an average of almost 400,000
a year. But success in a holding battle is not progress which can
be meaningfully measured only in terms of visible upward
changes in the standard of living. In 1935, General Roman
Gorecki, at the time director of the country's leading investment
bank, said: "If Poland is to raise the level of consumption by
her population to that of Western European countries, she has far
to go before the saturation point of elementary needs is reached."
This was, in Gorecki's interpretation, evidence of the immense
field of economic activities open in Poland, but it also was an
indication of how little progress had been made on the road to
actual, not pretended, "westernization."

Traditionally disinclined to bother with figures and equipped
with somewhat primitive economic notions, many Poles tended
to mistake their latent possibilities for present wealth. In 1931
American Ambassador Willys reported from Warsaw: "Poland
takes pride in the fact that the national economy has been stabi-

lized on such a low level that the country is practically immune
from financial pressure from abroad. *La faiblesse fait la force!"*
They considered their dense, growing, and unemployable population—a potential asset in a country able to develop its industries
—as a real asset in Poland's actual conditions, even as "the basis
of Poland's status as a Great Power." Actually, the growth of
population, not matched by sufficient economic expansion, was
the main source of maladjustment; it was the country's problem
Number One.

The nineteenth century had witnessed growth of population in
all European countries. In the West this unprecedented growth
was accompanied by the opening up of new possibilities for mass
employment in industry and urban occupations. In England, for
instance, the population increased, between 1850 and 1930 by 130
per cent, of which 80 per cent was absorbed by the cities. In the
area identical with the interwar Polish state the increase for
the same period was 230 per cent, but only 17 per cent shifted
to the towns. The others added to the overcrowding of the countryside. Industrialization and urbanization in Poland were slow
for a variety of reasons, not the least because of the limited interest of the partitioning Powers in developing the economy of
their Polish provinces. These provinces were on the fringes of
the partitioning empires; Germany considered her slice of Poland as the food-growing hinterland of an industrializing country,
with the exception, of course, of the mining area in Silesia; Austria kept down the industrial development of Galicia, perpetuating its proverbial misery; Russia at first encouraged the development of industries in the Kingdom of Poland, but hampered its
economic life by primitive strategic notions which discouraged
the building of a modern network of railroads and highways. The
area of Poland ceased to be an economic entity; its production
and its trade became oriented towards the markets of the partitioning empires. More than 80 per cent of the exports of the
Polish provinces were absorbed by Russia, Austria, and Prussia,
while trade between the former component parts of Old Poland
was insignificant. The reborn Polish state had to cope with the
disruption of the avenues of trade developed in the nineteenth
century, and particularly with the loss of the huge and unsatu-

rated Russian market. The job of reorientation was to a large degree accomplished, but at the price of enormous efforts and with only limited prospects of stability in holding conquered markets. The interwar Polish economy lived on a series of windfalls and "miracles," like the protracted coal strike in England in 1926.

Slow urbanization and rapid growth of the population in the nineteenth century forced millions of peasant sons to seek employment abroad. Export of manpower became one of Poland's main "industries," but only half of the natural increase was absorbed in this way. The other half added to the misery of the peasant population; only a few found employment in the slowly growing towns.

Thus independent Poland inherited an unbalanced social and economic structure. In 1921 more than 72 per cent of the gainfully employed population made their living in agriculture, 10.3 in mining and industry, 3.7 in commerce and insurance, 1.8 in communications, and 11.9 in "other occupations" (including the army, civil administration, and liberal professions). Ten years later 64.9 per cent of the professionally active population and 60.9 of the whole population still derived their living from agriculture, while the corresponding figures for industry were 15.1 and 17.7 respectively, and for commerce 4.8 and 5.5 per cent. There was no doubt a change, but in Poland's conditions the rate of change was not fast enough. In addition, progress in some fields was illusory rather than actual, owing to the use of different statistical methods. At the end of the twenty-year period the occupational composition differed little from what it had been at the end of the first decade, because the years of the depression checked whatever growth there was before. Meanwhile the population of Poland had increased from 27 million in 1921 to more than 35 million in 1939. Only one-fourth of the increase was absorbed by the cities; the pressure on the land was thus further intensified.

Too Many People? Overpopulation is a vague and relative term. Some prefer to call it underindustrialization, thus stressing the point that a change in the social and economic structure would eliminate all or at least a considerable part of the surplus of population uneconomically crowded and incapable of feeding itself in agriculture.

The number of people who could not be rationally employed in Poland's agricultural economy has been estimated in various ways; the conclusions differ with the criteria applied. Some Polish scholars maintained, rather optimistically, that only two to three million people were redundant on the land. This estimate was obviously too low. The German Theodor Oberlaender put the figure at close to five million. The Polish specialist Poniatowski came to the conclusion that "the number of people which could be removed from agriculture without any loss to the farms was 8 to 9 million." W. E. Moore, in his remarkable League of Nations study, *Economic Demography of Eastern and Southern Europe,* published in 1945, found that, with the average European level of productivity as standard (not a very high standard), Poland had a "surplus" rural population of almost ten million, or 51.3 per cent of the total. This estimate was based on the number of people required, at the chosen standard per capita level, to produce the actual agricultural output of interwar Poland. Moore also offered another approach to the problem, trying to determine what population could be "reasonably" supported if the yield per hectare were increased. Taking French productivity as standard—it was higher than the European average but lower than elsewhere in western Europe and based on low capitalization and mechanization—Moore found that there would still be in Polish agriculture a population of 5.6 million which could not be supported at the average European level. It must be remembered that this last method of calculating the surplus was based not on actual conditions but on the assumption of an increase in yield to about 150 per cent of what it was in interwar Poland. The most optimistic Polish estimates show that the total increase of the volume of agricultural production was about 30 per cent for the interwar period, only slightly more than the increase of population. The yield per hectare of arable land increased by 27 per cent, but only 6 per cent per head of rural population. Therefore Moore's original figure of close to ten million redundant people in the Polish countryside appears quite realistic.

A backward and stagnant colonial country takes its overpopulation problem for granted; starvation and epidemics are expected to act as checks. Poland was a backward country but one with awakened ambitions and awareness of needs. It was therefore inevitable that the realization of what Poland's basic difficulty was should eventually come even to the least economically minded people who reluctantly abandoned their thoughtless boast of the population "asset." But even then some of the solutions proposed to cope with the problem were fantastic. In the thirties a movement developed, inside and outside the government, to force the emigration of all or most Jews from Poland in order to make room for a few million peasants in the petty commerce of the small towns. Politically this was no doubt an attempt to dissuade the restive peasants from trying other solutions; economically it was sheer nonsense. The misery of the great mass of Jewish hucksters, whose *stragan* (stand) was presented to the peasant as a position worth conquering, was no less appalling than that of the peasants and in many respects even more hopeless; the number of redundant peasants was higher than the total number of Jews in Poland, not all of whom had *stragany* to yield; and no one was willing to open emigration outlets for millions of Jews.

Emigration, once an important regulator of the population pressure in Polish provinces, could not play the same role in the interwar period, mainly because of the introduction of immigration quotas by the United States. Until the depression of 1929 there was still a stream of emigration from Poland. While the United States admitted almost exclusively the relatives of residents and citizens, South America absorbed some of the new economic emigration. A considerable number of Poles went to work in the French coal mines, and many were employed as seasonal laborers in Germany and, to a limited extent, in other countries. This movement came to a stop with the depression, and Poland even had to accept many of her citizens squeezed out by other countries. In the thirties, Jewish emigration to Palestine continued on a limited scale, but other channels all but dried up. The excess of repatriates over new emigrants totaled between 75,000 and 80,000 in the years 1932–1936. Even continued emigration at the pre-depression interwar level—an annual average of 50,000—would have meant little in terms of alleviating the population pressure. Emigration was fostered by the government, partly because of the importance of emigrants' remittances in the balance of payments. Special banks were organized in centers of Polish emigration to facilitate the transfer of funds.

Land Reform. One of the measures advocated as a possible solution of the rural population problem was land reform. The term has various meanings but is most frequently used to describe the breaking up of large estates and the distribution of land to landless or dwarf-holding peasants. In this form the issue lent itself almost ideally to demagogy and misinterpretation. The system of land tenure in Poland was an important and potentially explosive social issue. Centuries of peasant serfdom were followed, in the nineteenth century, by formal emancipation, granted the peasants not by a national Polish government, but by the three partitioning Powers. The Polish nobility was obstinate and awkward in its approach to the peasant problem; it could not bring itself to make a magnanimous gesture, not even in times of stress. Consequently, the peasant masses remained largely indifferent to the patriotic stirrings and uprisings of the nineteenth century. There were at all times, ever since the Kosciuszko uprising of 1794, individual peasant participants, whose acts were played up to give the appearance of a show of national unity. No one seriously claims that the peasant really stirred.

The behavior of the gentry gave the partitioning Powers the opportunity to pose as the benefactors of the Polish peasant. The emancipation of the peasants, first in the Prussian and Austrian provinces, and later in the Russian part of Poland, deepened the cleavage between the manor and the village. Enacted mainly for political reasons, to weaken the economic and political influence of the gentry, the abolition of serfdom provided no basis for a healthy development of the peasant economy. In the second half of the nineteenth century a slow breakup of large estates began, but its pace was in no proportion to the land-hunger of the peasants, who were unable to find outlets outside agriculture. Peasant holdings were subjected to constant shrinking because inheritance laws permitted almost endless subdivisions of the land among usually numerous heirs.

The social aspect of the land problem determined the content of political programs in interwar Poland. These ranged from demands for expropriation without compensation to suggestions that the breakup of large estates be permitted to continue its "natural" course, thus bringing about by evolution a change in the structure of land tenure. The measures put on the book reflected the ebb and flow of radical and conservative ideas, but also the degree of external danger facing the country.

In 1919 a fairly radical land reform was voted, in response to the moods of the time and the propaganda coming from the East. In a conversation with Hugh Gibson, newly appointed American minister to Warsaw, Pilsudski stressed the importance of land reform:

> You must remember [the Marshal said, according to Gibson's report] that the peasantry has a genuine grievance in the question of the land, and the Bolsheviki offer to remedy that immediately by handing out to each man his share of the land. If the despair of the people reaches a certain pitch they will grasp at these very doctrines just as a man will take a quack remedy to allay physical suffering . . .

While assuring the envoy that he was "no Bolshevik" and declaring himself in favor of orderly and gradual change, Pilsudski nevertheless insisted that:

> Feudalism has been the curse of Poland and must be rooted out—and I say this as a large landowner descended from a long line of landowners . . . Every day that a just solution is deferred means just that much longer period of difficulties and trouble.[13]

This vigorous endorsement of land reform by Pilsudski is the more interesting because the Marshal, absorbed by military plans, never came out publicly in favor of the measure. In later years, after 1926, he quite definitely flirted with the large landowners.

In spite of the radical currents, reflected in the law of 1919, no serious effort was made to put the measure into effect. At the height of the Red army advance in Poland, in July 1920, measures for the execution of the reform, providing for a partial

---

[13] Gibson to the Secretary of State, May 13, 1919, National Archives, 86oc.01/248; also 86oc.01/264.

breakup of large estates, were rushed through the *Sejm* to arouse the interest of the sluggish peasant masses. In 1925, when the country seemed to face no external danger and the government was controlled by a combination of well-to-do peasant representatives and right-wing nationalists, the stress was shifted from forcible to voluntary parceling of the land, and the pace was slowed down. At no time did land reform in interwar Poland assume the radical character it had in some of the neighboring countries (where the demands of the peasants were satisfied at the expense of landowners of alien ethnical stock, Germans in the Baltic countries, Hungarians in Rumania, etc., whereas in Poland it was a matter of attacking the positions of the "backbone of the nation," as the gentry liked to call itself). This national argument determined the higher minimum exempted from the reform in the eastern provinces of the country, where the peasants were mostly non-Poles. The snail-pace of land reform in interwar Poland was a result of the social reluctance of the bureaucracy, the lack of a clear overall plan, and the shortage of financial means necessary to carry out a thorough reform.[14] Economically speaking, even a fuller and more radical reform could not have *per se* provided a solution to the problem of rural unemployment and land hunger. There were too many peasants, not enough land.

In the period between 1918 and 1938 roughly 2.6 million hectares were parceled, mostly on a voluntary basis. Only 160 thousand new holdings were thus created, and an average of two

[14] Poland's last interwar premier, General Slawoj-Skladkowski, writes in his memoirs: "Because of the heavy expenditures for armaments, land reform did not proceed as quickly as Poland's situation required . . . The problem of improving the life of the countryside which was burdened with overpopulation, unemployment, poverty of the smallholder,—this urgent problem could not be solved quickly and radically . . ." Faced with growing peasant unrest, the general tried to do what could be done without money. His measures included orders to the effect that dignitaries should, on official occasions, kiss the hands not only of ladies wearing hats (*panie kapeluszowe*) but also of peasant women. The general himself engaged in such exhibitions and he noted the "great impression" they made on the peasants. Skladkowski also ordered a more profuse distribution of bronze medals of merit to peasants, at a minimum ratio of two bronze medals per rural commune. (Cf. Felicjan Slawoj-Skladkowski, "Opowiesci administracyjne czyli Pamietnik Niebohaterski," in *Kultura*, Paris, Nos. 7 and 8, 1951.)

hectares added to about half a million existing holdings. This was not enough to solve or appreciably alleviate the problem. At the end of the twenty-year period two million farms—more than 50 per cent of all peasant holdings—were of a size insufficient to maintain the cultivators and their families at subsistence level. On the other hand, estates (over fifty hectares) represented some 24 per cent of the total area. The fact that these 24 per cent were owned by less than thirty thousand landlords, while millions of peasant families were landless or crowded on tiny holdings, remained a source of social grievance.

Some thought was given in interwar Poland to the problem of raising the productivity of agriculture, if possible by measures requiring a limited outlay of capital. Elementary calculations show that mere improvement in the yield through limited measures was no answer to the problem. Although it is true that the rapid growth of population was beginning to level off in Poland (its net reproduction rate, Notestein found, had fallen to little more than replacement), the impetus of past growth would have continued to be felt for at least another generation. Under these conditions the race between population growth and increase in agricultural output would have been hopeless. Assuming the possibility of a 50 per cent increase in agricultural production between the middle thirties and 1960, Moore found that per capita production in Poland would rise only from 49 to 57 per cent of the European average of the thirties. "Without the shifting of productive resources (including labor) to other economic spheres and the correlative reduction of the persons directly dependent on the products of agriculture," Moore concluded, "no substantial gains will be made in the level of production . . . Marked improvement in levels of production and consumption . . . cannot be expected from those measures that would place first and most emphasis on agricultural production." This argument retains a considerable degree of validity at present, when some people envisage for Poland and other countries of the area the role of predominantly agricultural producers within an "integrated" European economy. Many Poles detect in such plans an echo of interwar German attempts to control the area by discouraging its "unnecessary" industrialization.

Industrialization. The perpetuation of a predominantly agrarian economy was no answer to Poland's problems, given the density of the population, the awakened ambitions, and the limitations inherent in agricultural improvements. Only industrialization could relieve the population pressure, increase productivity, and raise the standard of living. But here, too, the final results, although impressive in terms of the number of establishments rebuilt or created and new industries started, were rather modest in terms of per capita value of production. Poland was in this respect in a more favorable position than Rumania, but below Spain, Hungary, and Italy, three poor countries by Western standards.

Industrial production no doubt made progress in Poland, if one considers its low point of departure after years of wartime destruction, which stripped the factories of their equipment, and the first chaotic postwar years of financial disorganization which wiped out capital resources. Measured in comparison with what the industrial output of the area was in 1913, manufacturing activities (exclusive of mining) achieved the same level only in 1938 when the results of a new dynamic investment policy, adopted under the pressure of defense necessities, began to show. According to League of Nations figures, the index of manufacturing in Poland (with 1913 = 100) presented the following picture in the interwar period: [15]

1920	35.1
1921–25	62.4
1926–29	76.8
1930	75.8
1931–35	63.8
1936–38	95.4 (it was 105.2 in 1938)

It is obvious that the index of manufacturing activities is in itself no indication of the possibilities which were created for the further development of industry as a result of the efforts made in the interwar period. Once the basis for a dynamic development was laid, growth could be impressively accelerated. However, if one looks at the twenty years of Poland's interwar history as a closed period, it is clear that the actual possibilities offered by industry were limited in comparison with the pressure

---

[15] *Industrialization and Foreign Trade* (League of Nations, 1945).

of idle labor forces on the market. The yearly intake of new
workers into mining and manufacturing (estimated for 1935–
1937) was some 75,000 in Poland, while the yearly increase of
employable population was 215,000. In other words, there was no
possibility of absorbing the new labor force, much less of attacking the problem of "invisible" unemployment in the countryside
(where, according to the calculations of J. Piekalkiewicz, the demand for agricultural labor was on the average only 48.7 per cent
of the available supply) .

The pace of industrialization could be quickened only by a
considerable investment of capital, obtained either by the ac-
cumulation of internal savings or by the import of foreign funds.
Neither source furnished anything approximating the needs of
the country.

Because of the low national income and the disproportionate
share of agriculture, capital formation in Poland was very slow.
Any increase of the rate of capital investment would have had
to be at the expense of an already inadequate level of current
consumption. Considering themselves in the field of economic
policies, as in other respects, an outpost of the West, the interwar
leaders of Poland tried to adapt to the needs of their country
criteria which could at best be considered valid for western
Europe, and at that in the nineteenth century, not in the twentieth. "Rejecting communist methods," states the Polish author
Adam Rose, "Poland had to choose the western way of industrialization." This means that reliance was based primarily on spontaneous investments which in Poland's circumstances were no
answer to the pressing needs of the country. The Western way, no
less than the communist way, necessitated the mobilization of
capital resources for investment. Throughout the interwar period,
Poland sought the necessary capital abroad, but with limited success.

While the Poles sometimes viewed themselves as a Big Power,
their country was considered a poor risk by foreign investors.
Hostile, mostly German, propaganda is usually blamed by the
Poles for the bad reputation of the country. Whatever the reason,
loans were difficult to raise; they were obtained on humiliating
conditions and at excessive rates of interest. They were used to

stabilize the currency and to cover current budget deficits. A study made by the British PEP (Political and Economic Planning) research group pointed out that foreign loans were mostly "wasted" in the area covered by the study, which includes Poland. The actual burden of interest paid on foreign loans amounted to anywhere between 8 and 12 per cent, if one takes into consideration the low price of issue and high charges. The Polish stabilization loan of 1927 was floated at a rate of 7 per cent, at a price of issue 92 and redemption price 103. Only part of the proceeds of this loan was put into new investment; other loans were used entirely to keep the currency "sound."

Direct foreign investments and short-term credits played a relatively important part in Polish industrial development, but the flow of foreign capital was limited, sporadic, and subjected to sudden withdrawals and stoppages, caused by a tendency to maintain liquidity in view of the uncertain political and financial situation. At times the withdrawal of current earnings balanced and even exceeded the influx of new capital. Nevertheless, important sectors of the national economy were controlled by foreign capital (85 per cent of the oil industry, 83 per cent of all electric works, 57 per cent of the mines, etc.). In terms of countries of origin 27 per cent of all foreign capital was French, 19 per cent American, 14 per cent German, and a little over 12 per cent Belgian. Nine-tenths of all foreign investments were concentrated in the form of controlling majority shares in 314 joint-stock companies. The divergence between the aims of the foreign investors and the requirements of national policy created clashes of the "investment friction" type. In Poland, as in most debtor countries with relatively awakened ambitions, there was an ambivalent attitude towards foreign capital: it was constantly solicited and wanted, but intangibles of "national pride" and other more tangible considerations forced the government from time to time to curb the activities of foreign investors. This was particularly true under the Pilsudski regime, which, like all authoritarian governments, was in constant need of prestige victories. Notions of honor suitable among cavalry officers were often transferred (together with the cavalry officers who were put in charge of various economic agencies) to the field of economic and financial policies. On the whole, however, the attitude of successive Polish governments was rather accommodating towards foreign industrial and financial interests, "perhaps more than some of them deserved" (Zweig). The level of industrial prices was permitted to stay unreasonably high in comparison with the low income of the agricultural population. In spite of noisy debates, some spectacular legislation, and even one or two court actions, the system of cartels and price-fixing monopolies was largely tolerated; the methods of restricting production to keep prices high led to a particularly pronounced disequilibrium between industrial and agricultural prices during the depression years. The famous price "scissors" which restricted peasant consumption widened still further. The British author W. J. Rose quotes the following example: the price of a plough expressed in terms of rye was 221 lbs. in 1927 and 595 in 1934. It is not surprising that unrest spread even among the most conservative peasant elements.

Consumption. Peasant poverty led to substandard levels of consumption of agricultural as well as industrial products. Considered a typical exporter of agricultural products, Poland owed a considerable percentage of her "surplus" to the low level of internal consumption. Compared with the daily dietary standard of 4500 calories for men in the "very active" group (according to the National Research Council, U. S. A.) or even with the League of Nations estimate of 3500 to 4000 calories, the intake of the average Polish working peasant was estimated at 2200 to 3000 calories. A comparison of yearly per capita consumption of certain commodities (in 1934–1937) between Poland and Germany—not a very well-nourished country—shows some striking differences.

	Poland	Germany
	(lbs. per head)	
Cereals	508	349
Potatoes	715	418
Meat	43	114
Sugar	21.1	48.4

These figures show the role of bread and potatoes in the diet of the Polish population and the low consumption of other essential foods. Because of the differences between town and country, consumption of meat and sugar in the villages was below the national average, especially in the case of landless rural workers.

The poverty of the peasant masses prevented the development of an internal market also for industrial goods. In 1929, the 64 per cent of the population then dependent on agriculture consumed only 47 per cent of the national income, mostly in the form of their own retained production and only 12 per cent in the form of goods purchased on the market. Consequently per capita consumption of manufactured articles was very low by Western standards. The accompanying table illustrates the situa-

	Poland	Western Europe
	(lbs. per head)	
Cotton Goods	5.0	17.6
Paper	11.2	66.0
Soap	3.3	13.2

tion in 1937. There were in Poland 25 radio sets per 1000 inhabitants, less than one automobile (in the United States at that time it was 225 cars per 1000 inhabitants), 8 telephones (53 in Germany).

The standard of living of the urban population was incomparably better than that of the peasants, but the income of urban wage-earners was still low, as can be seen from the composition of expenditures. In 1929 food took 57.2 per cent of the total consumption expenditure of urban wage-earners (and 27 per cent of the food expenditure was on bread and cereals). In the case of workers' families, 66.2 per cent of all expenditure was spent on food, alcohol, and tobacco (in 1938).

As a result of the occupational composition of the population, with a considerable portion of the peasantry having little or no cash income, a relatively insignificant part of the industrial output reached the countryside. The situation in this respect underwent no improvement in the interwar period; during the depression it further deteriorated.

Toward a Planned Economy? The devotion of Poland's interwar rulers to orthodox economic ideas was great in theory. It was in part geared to what were believed to be the tastes and views of potential foreign lenders and investors. But Poland was a "capital-

ist" country without capital. The government was therefore
forced to act as the principal pump-primer of a sluggish national
economy. There were reconstruction and new construction tasks
—often politically conditioned, as, for instance, the building of
the harbor of Gdynia a few miles from Danzig—which private
capital was unable to undertake. Government monopolies were
a tradition in the area; the Polish state took them over from the
partitioning Powers and added some new ones. There were state
monopolies of salt, tobacco, alcohol, matches, and a state lottery.
Public transportation (93 per cent of all railways, all commercial
aviation, and most merchant marine) was organized in the form
of state-owned enterprises. Defense requirements forced the government to build factories which, because of the lack of credits
and equipment for the production of armaments, were temporarily engaged in producing wringers and bicycle parts. Government credits were extended to privately owned establishments
which failed (for instance, a number of large textile factories),
and the state took them over. The intervention of the state in
later years spread to trade: stringent controls regulated production and exports. Centralization and bureaucratic management
became the basic feature of Poland's economic life; statism, not
capitalism, was the prevailing system, although the government
did not have the courage to embrace it officially, as the Turkish
Republic did in its Constitution.

In the last years before the outbreak of World War II the
Polish government, frustrated in its expectation of rewards from
dogged adherence to orthodox economic and financial policies,
and moved by the needs of national defense, embarked on what
looked like the beginning of planned efforts to change the economic structure of the country.

When plans were drawn up for the development of the Central
Industrial Region (known as COP, from the initials of its name
in Polish), priority was given to the building of war industries,
but the overall needs of the country also received attention. The
shocking disproportions between the industrialized and the agricultural parts of the country (usually referred to as Poland "A"
and Poland "B") were to be eliminated by industrialization and
a planned distribution of public works. The location of the COP

was chosen not only for its relative—very relative, as the war soon showed—safety in the "security triangle" of central and southern Poland, but also because it had the largest congestion of idle rural manpower. The first, preparatory period of three years was to be followed, according to the ideas of Eugeniusz Kwiatkowski,[16] chief author of the COP plan, by a series of three five-year plans which were expected to change the face of the country and lift it from its misery. To start the program, all financial resources of the state, various public funds, and accumulated private savings, were mobilized. The Polish government was finally breaking with the obstinate policy of deflation, artificial defense of the currency, and restrictions on public and private spending which had had disastrous results for the country's economy. A much higher percentage of the national income was to be invested. In earlier years no more than 5 per cent of the national income went into investment; now the percentage was to go up to 20. Foreign capital was to play a limited part in this effort. A major loan for defense purposes was negotiated with France in 1936 but its proceeds were slow in being transferred to Poland; a military loan granted by Great Britain had not materialized when the war came. The index of public investment, with 1936 taken as 100, was 162 for 1937, 173 for 1938, and was to be 204, according to plan, in 1939. Production and employment soon increased; the production index regained its 1928 level in 1938. Growth was relatively faster in the production of capital goods than in consumer goods.

It is difficult to say whether the efforts made in the last prewar years could have brought about a lasting change in the social and economic structure of Poland. The first effort to switch from spontaneous to planned investment was connected with immediate needs of national defense and was put into effect in an atmosphere of aroused patriotism and willingness to bring sacrifices. Whatever the long-term possibilities and merits of the new policy were, the outbreak of the war destroyed everything. Ironically

---

[16] Kwiatkowski, whose name was connected with bold economic planning and with the creation of the harbor at Gdynia, was one of the few high-ranking members of the prewar regime who returned to Poland in 1945. The new government was at the time interested in the services of technicians without regard to their party affiliation. Kwiatkowski was put in charge of the rehabilitation of Poland's seacoast, but was soon removed from his post.

enough, some of the industrial plants erected in the COP to produce for Poland's war needs, were put into action by the German occupation authorities and contributed to the German war effort.

Although prevented from bearing fruit, the new approach at least showed an effort to think about the needs of the country in concrete rather than nebulous terms. Statistical figures, so neglected in Poland or tossed around rather irresponsibly, acquired a new importance. Many Poles for the first time became aware of the poverty and backwardness of their country. They were probably still too optimistic about their possibilities, but they at least began to see some of the disproportions between Poland's claims and ambitions and the actual situation of the country.

Looking back on the twenty years of the interwar period, one cannot help feeling that, in the concrete conditions of the country, Poland was engaged in political efforts which were wholly unsupported by material foundations. Defense expenditures were a burden on the economy, yet they could not really assure the defense of the country. Certain problems were, for practical purposes, impossible of solution. Others required a different approach. Even if one should adopt the most charitable view of the social predilections of the interwar ruling groups, there were objective obstacles to progress.

Social Progress. In the social field—which we have not discussed in detail—progress was made in public health, working conditions, various types of social insurance. Propagandists and well-wishers simplify the picture considerably by drawing attention primarily to the impressive number of laws put on the books. They seem to forget not only the legislation of the thirties which tended to trim the social benefits of the twenties, but also the disparity between proclaimed aims and actual performance. In view of the limited resources of the country, it may be said that an impressive effort at betterment was made in many fields. But here again, the pace was not adapted to the growth of the population.

Let us take, for instance, the essential field of elementary education and trace the developments of the twenty-year period on the basis of official Polish statistics. The principle of compulsory schooling was proclaimed in the Constitution, but its realization was slow and incomplete. In 1922 more than 31 per cent of all children of school age received no education. This percentage dropped to 3.6 in 1928–29, but then increased again and was more than 11 per cent in 1936–37. The mere change in the number of children statistically listed as receiving education does not tell the whole story. It is important to see what percentage of the existing schools offered substandard elementary education which often resulted in recurrent illiteracy. In 1922–23 the number of schools which had one classroom instead of the prescribed seven was 63.5 per cent of the total; only 7 per cent of all schools had the full complement of classrooms and teachers. Ten years later the percentages were still 44.9 and 10.8 respectively, although measured in numbers of pupils the ratio of those receiving substandard education to those enjoying the full benefits of the elementary school system progress decreased: there were 34 per cent substandard pupils in 1922 and only 19 after ten years, while the percentage of those receiving full elementary education increased from 27.8 to 36.3. The second decade again slowed down the process of improvement.

Throughout the entire period there were glaring disproportions between the level of urban and rural education. In 1922 less than 2 per cent of the rural schools were of the full seven-grade type, while 68.8 per cent were of the one-classroom type. Ten years later there were still only 4.4 per cent full elementary schools in the countryside and 48.4 of the one-class type. The ratio of pupils per teacher was much higher in the rural schools than in urban schools; it tended to increase in both urban and rural areas, thus presenting a picture of deterioration rather than progress. In 1936–37 there was one teacher for 56.1 children in urban areas, one for 63.9 in the countryside. Not only was the cultural gap between the town and village not narrowed to any impressive extent, but the entire structure of education seemed threatened in the long run, unless the trend were reversed. Probably the saddest element in this situation was the almost total unawareness on the part of the cultivated class of this danger facing the nation.

Progress and the "National Character." The influence of psychological factors on the social and economic development of interwar Poland cannot be overlooked. It manifested itself in a number of ways. The descendants of the gentry and others who had learned to behave like "psychological gentry" [17] had their own scale of values where economic foundations of greatness weighed little. Elected representatives of the peasantry were interested in claiming—without success, on the whole—the share of political power due them, rather than in working out economic solutions, apart from a vague agrarianism and advocacy of emergency measures. Most peasant leaders had no overall conception of the kind of Poland they wanted, although they never tired of stressing the point that they were the legitimate masters of the country, because of sheer numbers. Responsibility for economic endeavor was most of the time with the government, but the government was handicapped by the lack of funds, the inexperience and limitations of the bureaucracy, and the basic unwillingness of the population to coöperate. For more than a century, Poles had learned to look upon government as alien and hostile; for centuries before, they had cultivated active disrespect for government. A considerable part of the population had almost no cash income and was therefore practically excluded from contributing to public revenue; but the anti-taxpaying mentality, of which Poland's most energetic minister of finance, Wladyslaw Grabski, complained so bitterly in his memoirs, was common also among those able to pay. The fatherland, said a Polish economist, was too often looked upon as a source of privileges, not as a responsibility. Polish patriotism was of the high-tension variety; it manifested itself willingly on big occasions, but was lacking in everyday qualities.[18] Many efforts were thwarted by the politico-

17 "On becoming intellectuals, all the newcomers, no matter what their original social milieu . . . adopted . . . the outlook, the mores, and, in general, the whole cultural pattern which characterized the intellectual circles which had descended from the gentry. In other words, they became not only absorbed by the gentry intelligentsia but they assimilated its basic traditions." (Alexander Hertz, "The Case of an Eastern European Intelligentsia," *Journal of Central European Affairs*, XI, 1, January-April 1951, p. 19.)

18 A Polish economist described it as "more blood than sweat." A generation earlier, the Polish geographer Waclaw Nalkowski spoke of his compatriots as having acquired "a certain carelessness of the morrow, a hand-to-mouth existence, frivolity, disinclination for systematic work." (*Poland as a Geographical Entity*, London, 1917.)

psychological need of catering to the moods and apprehensions of a diffident, undisciplined population, suspicious of government action to the point of not coöperating on any but extreme occasions. Training in applied citizenship was very deficient in Poland, and the level on which government operated helped little in generating respect.

But even a better, more solid kind of Polish patriotism, a greater respect for the concrete needs of living people as against the abstract welfare of the "country," better economic talent in the government machine, could not have solved problems which were of a nature requiring external assistance. Since no grand, international approach was made to the needs of the area, the only remaining possibility was financial and technological aid by the West for the purpose of maintaining its eager and willing outpost. However, such ideas would have appeared strange. In 1918 it was not as obvious as it was to be in 1950 that the United States has to offer economic support, possibly for a very long time, to its political associates. No effort was made to prop up Poland's nominal independence with more than emergency assistance in the first postwar years.

Thus Poland was bound to drift, carrying forward her structural disabilities, engaged in a hopeless struggle to defend an indefensible political arrangement, led and misled by too timid or too arrogant politicians, torn between the extremes of hope and despair, between paralyzing automatism and bureaucratically inspired economic activity of a kind which evoked sneering comments from a diffident population. After twenty years the gap between needs and achievements was not sufficiently narrowed in terms of many things that matter.

INTERNATIONAL RELATIONS

Frontiers and Security. The end of World War I gave Poland independence, but no determined frontiers. Consequently the first period of Poland's new existence as a state was devoted to the "battle of the frontiers." The struggle was carried on figuratively, in the diplomatic cabinets and at the conference table in Paris, with words, maps, and statistics used as weapons. It was also fought on real battlefields, in a series of clashes of varying intensity with almost all neighbors of the reborn state. It determined the climate in which the Polish state was to function for over twenty years.

The dualism which marked Poland's leadership and political orientation in this period resulted in a division of tasks. At the peace conference in Paris, the Polish delegation was led by Ignacy Paderewski and Roman Dmowski. Their mandate had grown out of their wartime position as leaders of the Polish National Committee, recognized at one time as the official spokesman for nascent Poland. At home, executive power was in the hands of Jozef Pilsudski, whom the West viewed with suspicion because of his socialist past. What was to the Poles their legitimate government was called in early dispatches to the Department of State "the committee of Mr. Pilsudski," while the largely self-appointed Committee in Paris enjoyed official status. This split was patched up with Paderewski's appointment—under Herbert Hoover's pressure—as prime minister.[19] The stand taken by the Polish delegation at the Peace Conference continued to be determined by Dmowski's views, while inside the country policies were molded by Pilsudski's ideas.

The direction in which the efforts of these two leaders went were an outgrowth of their past political orientations. Roman Dmowski was the leader of a Polish faction which had adopted the view that Germany was *the* enemy of Poland; he had based his early calculations on coöperation with Russia. Only when the fortunes of war began to turn against the tottering empire of the tsars did he shift the scene of action from St. Petersburg to Paris, London, and Washington. He was a keen observer and realized that the victorious Powers were unwilling to make more than minimum decisions on the subject of Poland's eastern frontiers; they still hoped that Bolshevism was just a passing episode and that an acceptable Russian regime would be established and invited to participate in international negotiations. The Treaty of Versailles indeed left the matter of Poland's eastern border open,

[19] See p. 77. For some strange reason many American authors have insisted for the last thirty years that Paderewski was "President of Poland." Paderewski's active connection with the government of Poland was limited to a short tenure of the premiership in 1919.

reserving in Article 87 the right of the Powers to decide it at some later date. The main issue, as Dmowski saw it, was to secure an advantageous settlement in the West. He had to fight Lloyd George's opposition ("hostility," as he thought) and to cope with Wilson's hesitations between the principles of self-determination for the defeated Germans and the pressures of American Poles and Poland-lovers. Even France, still hopeful of collecting the tsarist debt from a new Russian government, hesitated to support maximal Polish claims. Eventually, however, Clemenceau proclaimed the policy of "barbed wire" against the Bolsheviks and swung over to an energetic support of Polish claims in his effort to make Poland the eastern bulwark of the French security system.

Dmowski argued for extensive acquisitions of German territory, in order to satisfy Polish historical claims and, whenever history provided too shaky a basis, economic and strategic needs. Particularly determined was Dmowski's fight to secure a really free access to the sea and not just a narrow "corridor." He asked for the annexation of East Prussia, a "dagger pointed at the heart of Poland" as long as it was in German hands. He wanted all or most of Silesia.

Meanwhile inside Poland the problem of the eastern frontier was assuming paramount importance. Pilsudski had for many years opposed Dmowski's "Russian" orientation. While Dmowski was leaning on Russia, Pilsudski based his calculations on an early defeat of Russia by Germany and Austria, to be followed by a defeat of the Central Powers by the West.[20]

Dmowski believed in diplomacy; Pilsudski in the importance of an active military performance by Polish forces. When Po-

[20] When asked later what would have happened if Germany and Austria and not the Entente had won the war, Pilsudski replied, according to an account in *Le Petit Parisien* (March 16, 1919): "Poland would have had more freedom under the Germans and the Austrians than under Russian rule." In the same interview Pilsudski spoke of his "deep hatred of Russia," and expressed the conviction that "no matter what her government, Russia is imperialistic . . . Poland is a barrier against Slav (*sic*) imperialism, whether tsarist or Bolshevik." (The editors of Pilsudski's collected works, from which the above excerpt is taken, seem to doubt the authenticity of the statement as reported by the French newspaperman. Yet there is no trace of disavowal of the contents of the interview.)

land's independence was proclaimed, Pilsudski's primary preoccupation became a settlement of the frontiers in the east. In this respect, too, there was an essential difference of views between him and the National Democrats, Dmowski's followers.

The National Democrats represented the view that a return to the historical concept of the old Commonwealth and the frontier of 1772 was impossible. The border nations, separating Poland from Russia proper—the Ukrainians, Byelorussians, and Lithuanians—had either come under strong Russian and Orthodox influence, or had developed a national consciousness of their own. Poland could not afford to secure their allegiance or to alienate Russia forever. The Nationalists therefore advocated a policy of relatively limited territorial acquisitions and complete cultural and national assimilation of the incorporated regions.

Pilsudski was animated by a curious mixture of romantic notions and a realistic appraisal of the necessity—though not of the possibility—of pushing Russia back or even reducing her to "natural" ethnographic limits. He wanted to gather the border nations, including his native Lithuania, in a federation under Polish leadership. The Polish writer Mackiewicz sums up Pilsudski's plan in the following words: "He visualized Poland, as strong as possible, associated with a Ukraine governed from Kiev and supported in turn by a free Caucasus. Poland would thus be at the head of a long chain of anti-Russian nations, spreading from the Gulf of Finland, from Tallinn, to the Caspian, Tiflis and Baku." [21] This idea of "federalism" found support from a motley combination of Pilsudski's personal adherents, leaders of the Polish Socialist Party, and former owners of latifundia and estates in the Ukraine whom the revolution had dispossessed. Pil-

[21] Stanislaw Mackiewicz, *Colonel Beck and His Policy* (London, 1944). See also M. K. Dziewanowski, "Pilsudski's Federal Policy, 1919–1921," *Journal of Central European Affairs*, X, 2, 3, July and October, 1950. Mr. Dziewanowski's thesis, that Pilsudski wanted to organize eastern Europe on a basis of complete equality rather than under Polish hegemony, is very interesting but not quite convincing. His otherwise valuable and well-documented article overlooks the fact that ". . . proponents of leagues, federations, or unitary world states either have a vested interest in the *status quo* or envisage a hegemony within such a structure." (Gerard J. Mangone, *The Idea and Practice of World Government*, New York, Columbia University Press, 1951, p. 10.)

sudski's entourage was full of hot-headed enthusiasts who as adolescents had thrown themselves into the adventures of conspiracy and war-making and were unable to convert to more peaceful activities. The socialists were attracted by the idea of offering the border nations the slogan of self-determination; they were, at least in part, interested in outmaneuvering the Bolshevik appeal to the nationalism of oppressed peoples. What the dispossessed landlords were after, requires no explanation.

A state of undeclared war existed between Poland and Russia; no diplomatic relations were established with the Bolsheviks (although the latter tried to approach Pilsudski through the Polish communist Julian Marchlewski), and there were constant armed clashes. In December 1919 the Supreme Council of the Allied and Associated Powers made an attempt to define a provisional Polish frontier in the east. It later became known as the Curzon Line although Lord Curzon had nothing to do with its origins. The association with Curzon's name is due to the fact that a similar line was later offered under his signature, in the summer of 1920, as truce line in a British mediation offer directed to the Bolsheviks. When it was traced in December 1919, the main purpose was to regularize Poland's situation to the west of the line, without prejudice to rights *que la Pologne pourrait avoir à faire valoir sur les territoires situés à l'Est de ladite ligne.* Nevertheless, this line was seen by the Poles as a fairly accurate indication of what the victorious Powers considered "indisputably Polish territory." It was ominously identical with suggestions made to the Peace Conference by a committee of Russian "white" refugees in Paris. The Poles were repeatedly warned in official Allied statements that military advance beyond the line would not meet with approval (although at the same time unofficial French and other agents goaded the Poles into starting a "crusade").

Pilsudski decided that the attempt to enforce a "federalist" solution should be made by Poland before the situation in Russia jelled. He snubbed peace offers by the Bolsheviks who were then being attacked by various "white" generals, but he also was careful not to synchronize his offensive with the actions of various counterrevolutionary forces (despite the efforts of Mackinder and

others active in and around Russia at the time). He wanted to
curb Russia, not Bolshevism. The prospect of a nationalist,
"white" Russia was just as unattractive as that of a Bolshevik
Russia. Actually a revolutionary Russia appeared to Pilsudski
less dangerous. His judgment was colored by contempt and he
believed that the revolution would keep Russia in a state of weakness and chaos for a long time. "All my experiences with the
Bolsheviks," Pilsudski told a French newspaperman, "show that
. . . their soldiers are badly led and without endurance . . .
Small advanced guards fight well. The bulk of the forces behind
them hardly deserves to be called an army." Pilsudski was no
doubt more realistic than the statesmen of the West who, according to his description, used Denikin, Kolchak, and others as "an
ostrich's wing under which European diplomacy was for months
hiding its head." Pilsudski's negotiations with Denikin, under
Western pressure, were a failure. There was no use trying to revive old Russia. "One has to have the courage to admit that in
the East of Europe a tremendous change had taken place." Pilsudski thought that it was important to take advantage of the
tremendous change to carve out a vast area which would either
join Poland in a federation or serve as a security belt separating
Poland from Russia. Important it certainly was, but was it feasible? Pilsudski liked to think of himself as a realist, but his notion of realism was of a peculiar kind, strongly influenced by the
view of his idol Napoleon whom he frequently quoted to the
effect that "the art of breaking obstacles is the art of not considering this or that an obstacle."

Pilsudski's mood at the time is well reflected in a speech which
he made in Lublin on January 11, 1920:

Poland is faced by the great problem: Is she to be a state on a level of
equality with the great Powers of the world, or a small state in need
of the protection of the mighty? We have to make a great effort . . . if
we want to turn the wheel of history so far that Poland should become
the greatest military and cultural Power in the entire East.[22]

The "great effort" on which Pilsudski decided was the idea of
pushing back Russia and creating a string of buffer states closely

[22] Quoted in Pilsudski, *Collected Works* (in Polish; Warsaw, 1937), V, 138.

allied with Poland. In this mood Pilsudski rejected Soviet peace overtures that continued to reach Warsaw. One such offer, made in January 1920, was left without answer for two months and then, too, the Polish government stalled, using various excuses to delay negotiations. Pilsudski clearly wanted no peace at the time. French military intelligence played its part in bolstering Pilsudski's determination to make war by letting him in on evidence that the Bolsheviks were planning a major push into Europe.

In the spring of 1920 Pilsudski undertook to "liberate the Ukraine" and the other nations on the fringes of the former Russian empire.

The War of 1920.   In his drive to "liberate the Ukraine from foreign invaders," which started on April 26, 1920, Pilsudski found an ally in the person of the Ukrainian leader Semyon Petlura who had fought both the Bolsheviks and the Poles in an effort to secure from the chaos of the collapse of Russia and Austria an independent state for his "forgotten nation." But now his forces had been reduced by typhus and pushed out of the Ukraine by the Bolsheviks. He retired to Eastern Galicia, and the Poles, who had been secretly negotiating with him, decided to build him up politically—for a price, of course. Petlura, in the name of the "Ukrainian Government," declared his "disinterest" in Eastern Galicia. This was attractive to the Poles in view of the reluctance of the Western Powers to recognize simple annexation of the province by Poland. Pilsudski agreed to install Petlura in the Eastern Ukraine after its liberation from the Bolsheviks. It was rumored that Petlura's government, according to the secret agreement, was to include two Polish members.[23] Article 6 of the

---

[23] H. H. Fisher, in *America and the New Poland*, p. 248, lists this provision as part of the secret agreement. The text of the agreement signed in Warsaw on April 21, 1920 contains no such provision (at least in the apparently authentic version published by Oleksander Dotsenko, *Materialy i dokumenty do istorii Ukrainskoj Revolutsii, 1917–1923,* Lviv, 1924, II, 5; the same text, in a French translation, may be found in René Martel, *La Pologne et Nous,* Paris: Delpeuch, 1928). However, in a circular letter of March 18, 1920, to the heads of missions of the Ukrainian "government," Livitsky, Petlura's chief negotiator in Warsaw, mentions the possibility that "the Government will include a Minister for Polish Affairs and one more member of Polish nationality chosen by us." (Dotsenko, p. 387.) For a recent treatment of the subject, see John S. Reshetar, Jr., *The Ukrainian Revolution 1917–1920* (Princeton University Press, 1952).

treaty provided for a settlement of the status of "landowners of Polish nationality" in the Ukraine on a provisional basis until a duly constituted Ukrainian national assembly voted on the agrarian problem. This was an attempt to undo, in the interests of Polish landowners, the work of the Russian Revolution which had resulted in the expropriation of large estates. It is not surprising that this part of the agreement was to be kept secret. From the account of the negotiations by Dotsenko it appears that the Polish side justified its insistence on the restoration of Polish-owned estates mainly because "this would make a good impression in the West" and gain recognition for Petlura's "government."

Pilsudski's expedition was marked by initial military success, but was a political failure from the very beginning. Much as the peasant masses of the Ukraine may have been opposed to Russians in general and to the Bolsheviks in particular, they hated the Poles, whom they had learned for centuries to identify with landlordism, oppression, and forcible conversion to Catholicism. Petlura's exhortations yielded no results; very few volunteers joined his forces which distinguished themselves by ruthless pogroms against the Jews. On May 8, 1920, Pilsudski entered a hostile and silent Kiev. Carried away by the notion that what matters is a big idea—the means will somehow be found—Pilsudski had started his campaign with relatively limited military resources. He apparently had based great hopes in Petlura's ability to stir the Ukrainian masses into an uprising against the Bolsheviks. Yet the masses refused to stir. In June a retreat began in face of a determined Soviet counteroffensive.

The time came now for the Bolsheviks to make their mistakes. Military success revived in Moscow the notion that it was possible to carry the revolution over the crumbling Polish bridge to a Germany which, according to expectations, was ready to go communist. The decision of the Politburo was influenced mainly by Lenin's views. Trotsky did not have a high opinion of Pilsudski ("a third-rate Bonaparte") but he opposed the march on Warsaw and suggested that peace be made with the Poles. There is a certain historical piquancy in the fact that he was initially supported by another Politburo member, J. V. Stalin, who argued that, by carrying the war into Polish territory, the Red army would expose itself to the resistance of a patriotic nation. He described attempts to dictate peace in "Red Soviet Warsaw" as "bragging and harmful complacence"; yet when the vote was taken, he loyally sided with Lenin. In the military action against Poland Stalin took part as political commissar of the southern front. Official Soviet history, written under Stalin's supervision, later blamed Trotsky and Tukhatchevsky for poor planning of the offensive and overextension of the lines. *The History of the Communist Party of the Soviet Union* is particularly critical of Trotsky's orders to rush part of the southern army into the breech created in the center by the developing Polish counteroffensive: "The best . . . way of helping the Western Front was to capture Lwow." This is Stalin's version of the story. In Trotsky's account of the episode Stalin was blamed for sabotaging the order to shift the southern army to the threatened central front; Trotsky thus implied that Stalin had in a way contributed to the success of the Polish counteroffensive.[24] Actually, the entire Bolshevik leadership, from Lenin down, was to blame. The thrust into Poland was just as ill-conceived and badly executed as the Polish offensive in the Ukraine a few months earlier.

For a while, however, Poland was in serious danger in the summer of 1920. On July 10, Polish Premier Wladyslaw Grabski appeared at Spa, where the Supreme Council of the Allied Powers was gathered in session. He made an urgent appeal for assistance to Poland. Lloyd George treated him to a lecture on Polish "imperialism," but agreed to undertake a mediation effort if the Poles accepted certain preliminary conditions. One of the conditions was agreement to what was now to become the Curzon Line as a truce line. Soviet troops were to halt, according to the British proposal, fifty kilometers east of the line. A conference of the Soviet government, Poland, and the Baltic succession states, but also including representatives of the "white" general Wrangel, who was holding the Crimea, would be called in London. The Polish delegate was also forced to accept what he considered an

[24] The same interpretation is suggested by Isaac Deutscher (*Stalin,* Oxford University Press, 1949, p. 216) . Other sources put the blame on Egorov, commander of the Southwestern Front.

unjust settlement of the border conflict with Czechoslovakia, which is described later (see page 126). For many days no one in Warsaw had the courage to reveal to the people the actual extent of the concessions which Poland was forced to make.

To the British mediation offer Foreign Commissar Chicherin replied in a defiant and, as Lloyd George said, impertinent manner. Riding on the crest of victory, the Soviets questioned the right of outsiders and interventionists to meddle in their relations with Poland. They offered the Poles "a more advantageous frontier than that accorded them by the Supreme Council," but they had their own ideas about the kind of Poland they wanted. The Poles were asked to sue directly for an armistice, which they promptly did. This time, however, Lenin repeated Pilsudski's tricks. Negotiations were delayed under various excuses, obviously in the expectation of a speedy and dramatic military solution. In the van of the advancing Red army there was a communist "government" for Poland—the Revolutionary Committee, led by Julian Marchlewski, Feliks Dzierzynski, and Feliks Kon.

Meanwhile the Poles made a supreme effort to rally to a last-ditch stand. Until then the war had been a rather limited affair; some people enjoyed Pilsudski's failures; enlistment of volunteers was sluggish; the peasants were largely indifferent. Now a government of National Unity was formed with the peasant leader, Wincenty Witos, as prime minister; a land reform bill was rushed through the *Sejm;* the Church made a glowing appeal to the Catholic flock. On the diplomatic front the attitude of the West was slowly changing from one of blaming Poland for her misfortune to a realization that the Red army might soon reach the borders of Germany. Lloyd George told the House of Commons that "there are millions of trained men in Germany" and if they should have the Bolsheviks as immediate neighbors, the Allies would soon find themselves deprived of the fruits of hard-won victory. Once more the attitude of the West toward Russia and Germany revived solicitude for Poland. The Russians were warned to respect Polish independence; military missions were rushed to Warsaw, and supplies began to flow by land and sea.

On August 15, 1920 the Soviet offensive collapsed at the very gates of Warsaw. The "miracle on the Vistula" was ascribed by some to divine intervention; by others, to Pilsudski's military genius; by those who denied his merits, to the strategic plan worked out with the help of French general Weygand. It was no doubt mainly the result of gross military mistakes of the Soviet military leaders who had overextended their lines in a drive to cut off Poland from Danzig (and Allied supplies).

While this dramatic turn was taking place on the battlefield, Polish negotiators, not aware of the most recent developments, finally made contact with a Russian delegation at Minsk and were presented with harsh conditions. Although the treaty finally negotiated at Riga was based on an entirely different basis, it is useful to quote some of the initial Bolshevik conditions. They sound familiar; in 1944 they were in part revived when a victorious Soviet Union was in a position to impose her conditions on Poland. The Soviet proposals of August 19, 1920 insisted on a slightly modified Curzon Line as permanent frontier; drastic reduction of the Polish army and creation of a workers' militia; ban on the production of armaments by Poland; complete Russian control of a strategic railroad, etc. In view of the changed military situation these conditions were, of course, rejected as "incompatible with national dignity."

When negotiations were resumed, at Riga, both sides were tired of the war and dreaded the prospect of a winter campaign. The West had given a trickle of help to Poland, but was again unwilling to support a new Polish offensive. The near-disaster had a sobering effect on the "federation" schemes. On the other hand, the Bolsheviks began to look more realistically at their chances of carrying the revolution across Poland to Germany. They had, in the words of W. H. Chamberlin, learned "the folly and futility of trying to force communism on an unwilling country by using the Red Army for crusading purposes."

The compromise reached on the frontier amounted to a partition of predominantly Ukrainian and Byelorussian territories between Russia and Poland. The Peace of Riga had little to do with justice or magnanimity on either side; it was the expression of a certain relation of forces. Two decades later it collapsed, when the balance was upset.

The Acquisition of Wilno.   Before the "battle of the frontiers" came to a close, the Poles made one more effort to trace their frontier with the sword, this time against Lithuania. The controversy with the tiny state centered mainly around the possession of the city and region of Wilno. The Lithuanians looked upon Wilno as their ancient capital; to the Poles it was a cherished monument of their cultural and political mission in the East. Wilno changed hands several times following the withdrawal of the German occupation troops in January 1919. First the Bolsheviks had it, then the Poles, then the Bolsheviks again. The Bolsheviks turned it over to the Lithuanians during their successful advance in 1920, but very soon afterward the collapse of the Russian offensive reopened the issue. The Western Powers stepped in and worked out a temporary frontier agreement (accepted "quite unnecessarily" by the Polish plenipotentiaries, according to Professor Halecki) which left Wilno in the hands of the Lithuanians. Two days before the agreement was to become effective, Polish troops commanded by General Lucjan Zeligowski occupied Wilno. The affair was thinly disguised at the time as an act of rebellion of the general and his troops, but Pilsudski later openly admitted that he had ordered Zeligowski to take the city and, if necessary, to take the blame. Pilsudski was apparently not interested merely in wresting Wilno from the Lithuanians. Frustrated in his big federation schemes, he tried to salvage something from the wreckage. He apparently thought of coaxing the Lithuanians into reviving the Polish-Lithuanian Union of pre-partition times. Political opponents maliciously oversimplified the matter by saying that Pilsudski wanted to be crowned as Grand Duke of his native Lithuania. At any rate, his attempt to turn back the wheels of history was doomed to failure. The Lithuanians, too, had developed a vigorous nationalism of their own. They were not going to be bullied into accepting Polish political hegemony. Pilsudski had shown some understanding for their feelings when he explained, in May 1919, to Hugh Gibson, American minister to Warsaw, that the Lithuanians "have yet to learn whether Poland will be strong enough and stable enough to be a helpful friend." He understood that "the Lithuanians cannot stand alone and they must form a close relationship with some strong state. With many of them the choice lies between Germany and Russia." He felt, of course, that the real choice which the Lithuanians would one day make was Poland. Since the Lithuanians were slow in adopting the correct attitude, Pilsudski apparently decided to force it on them, for their own good. Unable to talk the Lithuanians into a new union with Poland, the marshal settled for the occupation of Wilno.

Wilno finally was joined to Poland in 1922, after an interlude of quasi-independence of the region under the name of Central Lithuania, which fooled no one and delighted stamp collectors. A referendum was staged, under the supervision of the Polish occupation troops. The vote was boycotted by the Lithuanians, the Jews declared their neutrality, the Byelorussians offered their votes for sale. "Central Lithuania" decided to ask for incorporation by Poland. The *fait accompli* was eventually accepted by everyone, including a tired League of Nations, but not by the Lithuanians. The frontier between Poland and Lithuania remained hermetically sealed throughout most of the interwar period.

Shortly before the outbreak of World War II the Polish government, in its quest for prestige victories, profited from the confusion created by Hitler's *Anschluss* of Austria to send an ultimatum to Lithuania, forcing the tiny neighbor to establish diplomatic relations. The ultimatum, it was later revealed, was delayed for a few days by Foreign Minister Beck "for sentimental reasons," to coincide with Saint Joseph's day, in honor of Marshal Pilsudski. The proper war mood was generated by "spontaneous" mobs of government employees given time off for that purpose; they chanted in front of Marshal Rydz-Smigly's residence "Lead us to Kowno" (Kaunas, the capital of Lithuania). The manner in which the operation was carried out was later described by an official Polish source as marked by "great brutality." [25] A little over a year after the "victory" over Lithuania thousands of Poles were seeking refuge from their deluged fatherland in the city of

[25] *Polskie Sily Zbrojne w II Wojnie Swiatowej* (Polish Armed Forces in World War II), an account published by the Historical Commission of the Polish army in exile, London (1951), I, 41.

Vilnius—the Lithuanian name for Wilno—which the Bolsheviks once more handed over to the Lithuanians.[26]

Slav "Sisters."   Some bloodshed and much bad blood marked the settlement of Poland's frontier with Czechoslovakia. References to the two nations as "Slav sisters," when meant to be more than banquet room expressions, are quite meaningless. An old saying describes the Czechs as *Polonorum infestissimi inimici.* In the distant past the Poles and the Czechs had much in common, including occasional common rulers. But their paths separated quite early and different historical experiences have produced striking dissimilarities in their "national characters." More westernized than the Poles, but more remote from Russia and exposed to German pressure only, the Czechs were early attracted by Panslavism which to the Poles appeared to be merely an instrument of Russian imperialism. Under the Austro-Hungarian monarchy Polish aristocrats frequently occupied high cabinet posts in Vienna, while the Czechs—a peasant nation ever since they lost their aristocracy in the Battle of the White Mountain—were known to be eligible for the jobs of gendarmes and postal clerks. While Poles loved to bask in the sun of greatness, the Czechs liked to make a virtue of their littleness. Military heroes were revered in Poland; the Czechs took pride in Schwejk, a typical "sad sack," supreme incarnation of unmilitary bearing.

In the first weeks of their independence, Poles and Czechs clashed over the possession of the Olza basin and its center, the town of Teschen (Cieszyn to the Poles, Tesin to the Czechs). Polish claims were based on population statistics, Czech claims on economic arguments. There was also a minor dispute over a small mountain region in the Carpathians.

In 1920, Poland was forced to accept an Allied decision on the Teschen dispute handed down at a critical moment, when the

---

[26] Even then some Poles seem to have forgotten nothing and learned nothing. The American minister to Kaunas, Owen J. C. Norem, wrote in a dispatch dated October 21, 1939: "I have had several visits paid me by a certain Polish Count Tyszkiewicz who very frankly tells me that Poland when reconstituted will oblige the Lithuanians by replacing the Russian garrisons. He speaks the mind of the Polish nobility and landowning class . . . One need only listen to several hours of such conversation to develop an intense dislike for the Polish upper crust." (*Foreign Relations of the United States; The Soviet Union, 1933–1939,* p. 973.)

Russians were nearing Warsaw. The decision of the Supreme Council split the disputed Teschen region, giving the Poles most of the town and its agricultural hinterland and allotting to the Czechs the mining district of Karwina. Bitterness engendered by the conflict contributed to the inability of the Poles and Czechs to get together—an inability considered to have been one of the main reasons for the collapse of East-Central Europe.

At the height of the Munich crisis, in 1938, Poland demanded from the Czechs the cession of the Olza region. The machinery of frontier incidents and "spontaneous enthusiasm" was put into motion. "Lead us across the Olza," chanted mobs of government employees in front of Marshal Rydz-Smigly's residence; the government press chimed in, while the more thoughtful newspapers voiced their objections as loudly as censorship permitted.

This "stab in the back" was to earn Poland, ten years later, one of Winston Churchill's angriest outbursts. He called Poland "a beast of prey" and made the observation that Poles were "glorious in revolt and ruin; squalid and shameful in triumph." [27]

Poland emerged from the battle with "better" frontiers than had been envisaged for her by others. Yet this identification of security with more extensive frontiers produced solutions which carried in themselves the seeds of constant tension and future dangers. In the West, Poland obtained less than she had wanted but much more than the Germans were willing to be reconciled to. In the East, all seemed quiet on the surface, yet the incorporation of millions of Ukrainians and Byelorussians within Poland was a standing invitation to irredentist activities and claims from across the border. The Peace of Riga had turned the wheel back, but—for how long? Relations with Czechoslovakia were never more than lukewarm and often openly unpleasant. Only with Rumania did Poland have an alliance directed against Russia (it was never tested and was not invoked in 1939). The border with Latvia was an insignificant narrow strip. The border with Lithuania was a dead end. Poland's "seventh neighbor," the Free City

---

[27] I am quoting from the American edition of Churchill's *The Gathering Storm* (Boston: Houghton Mifflin, 1948), p. 323. I understand that the passage was deleted from the British edition after energetic protests by the Poles in England.

of Danzig, was inhabited by Germans who made no secret of their readiness to rejoin the *Reich* at the first opportunity; the issue of Danzig became the technical reason for the invasion of Poland in 1939.

All these dangers were obvious from the start. However, in evaluating the results of the battle of the frontiers, many Poles at that time felt rather pleased with the results and with themselves. In the East the "federation" dreams had collapsed, but the Peace of Riga gave Poland a better deal than the West had been willing to endorse. Lloyd George had called some Polish claims "extravagant and inadmissible," but the final results looked fairly satisfactory. The uprisings in Upper Silesia, led by the nationalist Korfanty, had contributed their part in determining the final decisions on the fate of that province. Zeligowski's "rebellion" had shocked some noble souls, but Wilno was Polish, seemingly forever. Eastern Galicia had been saved from the Ukrainians by the heroic exploits of young Polish volunteers.

In spite of these early successes, Polish leaders were on the whole not inclined to view the situation as static. They knew better. History had taught them that Polish independence was merely the reverse side of German and Russian weakness. If the means chosen by Polish diplomacy appear in retrospect pathetically insufficient, or, at times, preposterously pretentious, they were probably not more so than the steps taken by others, endowed with greater possibilities and burdened with wider responsibilities. If Polish diplomatic efforts failed, this was not always the fault of the diplomats. They were unsuccessful, because they attempted to achieve what in the concrete conditions of interwar Europe was impossible, but this cannot be held against the Poles, at least not exclusively. "The only hope for Poland," a thoughtful Pole once said, "would be to move the country elsewhere." This was not meant as a joke. Yet even the best foreign minister could not take Poland out of her geographic position; the worst could only hasten the tragic end.

The French Alliance. In the period following the battle of the frontiers the so-called cornerstone of Poland's foreign policy was the military and political alliance with France. Frustrated in expectations of an Anglo-American commitment to guarantee her against Germany, France sought security in the time-honored idea of continental alliances. The "French System" included Poland and the countries of the Little Entente. It looked well on paper. Here was a solid front against Germany and, incidentally, a barrier against Bolshevism. Yet very little was done to implement the French security system by a sustained military and economic effort. France was a Big Power by default only; she had neither the strength, nor the will to exercise effective leadership. This reluctance was ascribed by the French diplomat Leon Noël to "an excess of *délicatesse*" which kept France from displaying more determination in influencing the moves of her allies and satellites. Yet good manners are no substitute for strength and determination in international affairs.

The political and military alliance between France and Poland was concluded in February 1921. Many years later it was revealed that Marshal Foch had voiced objections to French involvement in a country which had neither defensible frontiers nor a stable government. Doubts concerning the wisdom of French commitments in the east were shared by many military leaders throughout the interwar period, but the politicians for a while played a game completely divorced from realistic evaluations. To the Poles the French alliance appeared, in the beginning, a solid guarantee against a revival of German aggression. In addition to practical motives, there were sentimental considerations and general acceptance of the cliché that France was "traditionally friendly" to Poland. Nothing in the record justified this judgment, especially when actual policies, not just words and gestures, are considered. One of Poland's leading historians, Szymon Askenazy, summed up the record as follows: "The France of the Bourbons closed her eyes to the first partition of Poland; revolutionary France—to the second and third; the Restoration opposed the creation of the Kingdom of Poland; the Orleans monarchy exploited and betrayed the Polish November Uprising (1830); the Second Empire provoked the January Uprising (1863) and left it in the lurch." He significantly omitted from this listing Napoleon, for whom the Poles had a particularly warm spot in their hearts: the Great Egoist reopened the Polish issue after it had been settled "forever" by the Partitions. Napoleon's memory was also dear to the Poles because he had offered their ancestors opportunities to die gloriously, even if on distant battlefields—from Lombardy and Spain to San Domingo —and for causes that were not theirs.

Based on common interest in "containing" Germany, the alliance never developed into full and harmonious coöperation. French economic and military assistance to Poland was spotty, unplanned, ungenerous. Very early—and this was not the fault of the French only—a tendency developed to divorce security in the west from that of the countries on Germany's eastern borders. The political atmosphere in which the Locarno treaties were concluded (October 1925) appeared ominous to the Poles. Germany was being invited to rejoin the European family and to take a seat at the table of honor—the Council of the League of Nations—and at the same time encouraged to press for "peaceful change" in the east. The "spirit of Locarno," which evoked such great hopes among French leaders who wanted to be "good Europeans" and believed they had found a suitable partner in Gustav Stresemann, caused nothing but gloom in Poland where it appeared that the Poles would have to foot the bill for the new European honeymoon. The best that Polish diplomatic maneuvers could obtain was a consolation prize in the form of a semi-permanent seat in the Council of the League. This substitution of prestige victories for actual gains was to become, in subsequent years, typical of the achievements of Polish diplomacy.

When, after Hitler's seizure of power and the failure of the Four Power Pact, French diplomacy initiated attempts to draw the Soviet Union into the orbit of international coöperation, this was just as unacceptable to Poland as earlier French flirtation with the Weimar Republic.[28] The Eastern Pact, which Barthou tried to negotiate, was described by Pilsudski-ite writers as a "cordon of gendarmes" meant to hem in Hitler's Germany.

---

[28] Seeking closer relations with the Soviet Union, the French quite logically tried to bring about a revision of their alliance with Poland and to cancel their commitment to come to the assistance of the Poles in the case of hostilities with Russia. Pilsudski frustrated these attempts by simply refusing to discuss the matter with Ambassador Laroche and with special envoys of the French General Staff (Cf. *Polskie Sily Zbrojne*, I, 27) .

Formally, the alliance of 1921 survived the most difficult crises in Polish-French relations—and they were many in the last years of Poland's interwar existence. When Hitler attacked Poland the French, although reluctantly and without conviction, honored their commitments by declaring war. They later gave refuge to the Polish Government-in-Exile. However, throughout most of the interwar period France failed to provide the leadership which would have justified her pretensions as a Great Power, and the assistance the Poles expected from their senior ally. Of course, Beck and some people of his entourage had the impression that France was meddling too much rather than too little in Polish affairs. Beck once said that France was behaving toward Poland "like an elderly aunt who refuses to recognize the fact that her nephew has grown up." It is revealing to find that he made this comparison after the collapse of Poland when, isolated and abandoned in Rumanian exile, he could be expected to have finally understood that under his guidance the nephew had behaved in an adolescent rather than in a grown-up manner.

Poland and the League.   The Poles, interested in the preservation of the system of Versailles, were quite active in the League of Nations and ardently participated in international conferences. At times they seemed to base excessive hopes in the possibility of international solutions to problems of interest to their country (for instance, emigration) ; on other occasions, it appeared to be incompatible with their national dignity to accept the assistance of the League, as, for instance, when the suggestion was made that Poland be given a loan guaranteed by the League. Poland was a frequent customer of the League, especially in connection with problems arising from the treatment of minorities and the affairs of Danzig. After the Pilsudski coup of May 1926 no immediate change occurred in Poland's attitude. The first Pilsudski-ite foreign minister, August Zaleski, busied himself in Geneva where he offered a resolution condemning aggression, one of those precious products of the interwar period which were expected to exorcise the devil with words. In later years, after Zaleski was replaced by artillery colonel Jozef Beck, the League was occasionally used by the new foreign minister as arena for diplomatic pranks. Although representing a country belonging to the *status quo* camp, Beck actively opposed the idea of collective security which was the very foundation of the League. Beck represented a new era and a new style in Polish diplomacy: the swaggering, big-mouthed style which the Pilsudski-ite regime had adopted also in its domestic policies after curbing the parliamentary opposition.

"Independence" and "Balance." Pilsudski's regime had achieved by 1932, when Beck became foreign minister, a degree of stability unprecedented in Poland. Whatever reservations the people may have had about certain features of the semi-dictatorship, the stability of the regime and Pilsudski's known solicitude for the army generated a feeling of confidence: the security of the country seemed in good hands. Foreign observers, too, commented favorably on the change which had taken place in Poland. Extremely receptive to flattery, the men around Pilsudski tended to be overimpressed with their own importance.

What Pilsudski's own views were, one can only surmise. The marshal made no public pronouncements and spoke even to his closest associates in riddles. He was probably more concerned than impressed with Poland's position and with the international situation in general. In Germany the Nazis were gathering strength. The disarmament conference was lost in empty palaver. The French were hiding behind parliamentary procedure when approached for a loan. A time seemed to be coming when every country would have to look after its own interests as best it could. Under the circumstances the marshal decided that Poland must embark on an independent, "Polish" policy if she was to remain an active factor in international life rather than an object of bargains by others. To stress her independent policy, Poland must above all strive to maintain a balance between her two big and dangerous neighbors, Germany and Russia.

Independence and balance are certainly laudable aims, but they are attainable only under very favorable conditions. Pilsudski was considered by his admirers (and by himself) a realist, yet one cannot help feeling that he had romantic illusions about Poland's actual possibilities. Independence requires strength;

balance—benevolence or tolerance on the part of strong neighbors. Pilsudski's fellow countryman, the romantic poet Adam Mickiewicz, had said a century earlier that forces should be fitted to the task ahead, not the task trimmed to fit available forces. It is questionable if this beautiful exhortation is fully applicable in the field of foreign policy which, it would seem, is above all the art of doing the feasible. Yet Polish foreign policy in the last prewar years seemed animated by the spirit of spectacular Action (*Czyn*, Polish for "Action," invariably spelled with a capital C, was one of the most frequently used words in the government press).

Polish foreign policy [wrote Vaclav Fiala in his *La Pologne d'aujourd-hui*], cannot be explained from the point of view of rational thought . . . It is the Polish nature to assume a great task without worrying about the possibility of realizing it and without weighing to the last ounce the means available . . . One is more satisfied with a grandiose though useless effort than with a series of mediocre successes . . .

The assumptions underlying Polish foreign policy under the leadership of Marshal Pilsudski and, later, under his favorite aide, Colonel Jozef Beck, are revealed in the posthumously published papers of the colonel (who died in 1944 a forgotten man, in Rumanian exile). The "philosophy" of Pilsudski-ite foreign policy was based on the idea that since the end of World War I a new category of states had come into existence, states that were neither Great Powers nor mere "clients" of Great Powers. Such states were destined to play an important role, possibly not on a global scale but certainly in a circumscribed region. Similar views were, of course, expressed also by others, especially in the early twenties, when the weakness of Germany and Russia had made the medium states of East and Central Europe appear important. But Beck seems to have clung to this view until the very end of the interwar period, long after the reëmergence of German and Soviet power had made it obsolete.

In his memoirs Beck denied having considered Poland a Great Power; he dissociated himself from "puerile" tendencies, such as the clamor for colonies by a country which could hardly take care of its pressing current problems. Yet people who were very close to him seem to have been convinced that Poland either already was or was just about to become a first-rate Power. Such views were harbored until quite late in the tragic game.

Rapprochement with Nazi Germany. The most spectacular result of Pilsudski's decision to play a lone hand was the rapprochement with Hitler. The Polish-German Declaration of nonaggression of January 26, 1934 was no alliance. It contained no secret clauses directed against the Soviet Union or any other state, persistent rumors to that effect notwithstanding. It was, in the opinion of Jozef Pilsudski and his advisers, a move dictated by hard-boiled *Realpolitik,* which gave Polish policy an "independent" look and served best the interests of the state. Some of the assumptions which prompted Pilsudski's decision were later revealed (in the introduction to the official *White Book,* published after the outbreak of the war). The operating hypotheses which formed the basis of Polish foreign policy in the decisive years before World War II were the result of a study undertaken by Colonel Beck on Pilsudski's order. Wishful thinking, the basic ingredient of so much "intelligence" all over the world, combined with the attraction which Naziism had for some people in Pilsudski's entourage, to produce the following set of assumptions:

1. The Hitler regime had brought into power "new ideas and new men." Hitler had shown that his domestic policies were a radical departure from the habits of the Weimar Republic. He might try a new approach also in foreign policy. The Weimar Republic was consistently unfriendly to Poland, partly because its leaders were too weak to impose on German public opinion the idea of better relations with Poland. But Hitler was a strong man. A dictatorial regime can afford to put over even unpopular policies.

2. The leading Nazis were not Prussians. This produced, in the minds of some Polish analysts, the so-called "Bavarian theory." The White Book outlines it as follows: "Prussia (was) the land of traditional hatred for Poland . . . Hitler is an Austrian, Goering is a Bavarian, Hess is from a German family settled in Egypt, Goebbels is a Rhinelander. There was some justification for expecting that these men would be able to rise above the Prussian hostile attitude to Poland." The men around Pilsudski suddenly discovered in their history text books that not all German states had been in the past hostile to Poland. Saxony, for instance, had even provided Poland with two kings in the eighteenth century!

3. Hitler was violently anti-communist and anti-Russian. Any return

to the Rapallo policy of German-Soviet coöperation was out of the question, "as it would have meant the end of Nazi ideology and would have been a serious blow to the Fuehrer's honor."

This last assumption was quite strongly planted in the minds of some Poles. As late as 1938 a Polish author assured the British reading public that

in the case of Poland history cannot repeat itself . . . any aggression . . . undertaken against Poland by Germany and Russia jointly . . . is out of the question in view of the acute conflict between the interests and tendencies of these two neighbors of Poland.[29]

There were other assumptions, too. Pilsudski apparently did not share all the illusions of some of his advisers; he may even have considered war between Poland and Germany inevitable, but he was wrong in his evaluation of the time Hitler needed to rearm, which he put at twelve to fifteen years. By signing the nonaggression pact with Hitler, Poland appeared to be winning at least ten precious years of peace which, at least in theory, could be used to strengthen her defenses.

Even when they admitted that Hitler would eventually start on the way of military conquests, some men around Pilsudski were convinced that Germany would move toward the southeast. Hitler was "no Prussian." No matter what countries he might occupy, he would always leave Poland untouched, to guard Germany and the world against Bolshevism!

Mystery or Myth? Admirers of Pilsudski's memory insisted later, when the working hypotheses of Polish diplomacy proved to have been so frightfully wrong, that the marshal had expected the Polish-German Declaration to be mainly a drastic way of shaking the West out of its complacency. After Hitler's seizure of power, the West, unconcerned over the implications, continued to seek a formula for coöperation with Germany. France and Britain were quite receptive to Mussolini's idea of a Four Power Pact which would have placed the affairs of Europe in the hands of an unofficial directorate. Pilsudski was not worried about this attempt to violate the principles of international democracy; he thought little of democratic procedure.

[29] Leopold Wellisz, *Foreign Capital in Poland* (London, 1938), p. 161.

But Poland had been left out, and Pilsudski tried to frustrate the combination, in accordance with the principle *Nic o nas bez nas* (freely translated as: "No decisions about us without us.")

The idea that Pilsudski tried to warn the West or even to get some action against Hitler persists among some admirers of his memory. They point out that shortly after Hitler's advent to power, the Poles staged a military demonstration by landing a small detachment on Westerplatte, the base guarding Danzig. This was not merely a reaffirmation of Poland's rights in the face of Hitler's known sentiments about the Free City. In his oblique manner, Pilsudski was testing the reactions of the West, the readiness of the French and the British to intervene in Germany. All that came from the West was advice to the Poles not to engage in unwise demonstrations. Some time between the military gesture, made on March 6, 1933, and the first overtures made by the Polish ambassador in Berlin to Hitler, on May 2, Pilsudski allegedly approached France and Great Britain with the suggestion that concerted "police action" be taken against Germany. There is admittedly no trace in known Polish, French, or British diplomatic papers of such a *démarche* by Poland. Only journalistic sources are quoted in support of the thesis that it actually took place. The explanation offered by Pilsudski-ite apologists is that the suggestion was made orally, in greatest secrecy, and not through diplomatic but through military channels, presumably to the French General Staff. From that quarter, too, confirmation is lacking. On the other hand, sources unfriendly to Pilsudski assume that the *démarche* actually took place, but claim that the marshal had by that time already decided to negotiate with Hitler and was merely trying to obtain, in order to overcome the scruples of some groups in Poland, proof that the "rotten West" was unwilling to act. If such were the case, the Polish Government would no doubt have given the entire matter, including the negative reaction of the West, wide publicity. This leaves the matter of the alleged Polish suggestion of preventive action against Hitler a mystery to some, a myth to others.[30]

---

[30] The story that Poland approached France and England with the suggestion of action against Germany in 1933 seems finally laid to rest in Beck's memoirs: "The Marshal (Pilsudski) told me that he had examined with care

Beck and Hitler. The most dangerous aspect of the German-Polish rapprochement was its psychological effect on the leaders of Poland's foreign policy. Beck apparently liked Hitler and trusted him. In September 1935 he described the German dictator as a man endowed with the "simplicity of common sense." He repeated to an American diplomat, and apparently in all seriousness, Hitler's assertion that there was no issue between Poland and Germany that called for war. Hitler—according to Beck—was a thoughtful, simple-minded, direct man, full of common sense when it came to the question of foreign relations. Two years later he again pointed out, in a conversation with Ambassador Bullitt, that Poland expected no trouble from Hitler because the Fuehrer had given "the most absolute assurance that he cared too much about Germany's relations with Poland to permit the Germans in Danzig to do anything which would be totally inacceptable to Poland."

Sheltered by a preposterous set of assumptions and attracted by the flattery heaped on him by Hitler's official and unofficial agents, Beck considered the problem of Poland's security well taken care of and devoted his energies to spectacular romps in the meadows of international diplomacy which he believed to be the best way of raising Poland's prestige. Bluff and bluster seemed to him adequate substitutes for strength; nuisance value, for influence. Beck never noticed that while he pretended to play his own game, he was actually running errands for Hitler. His opposition to any but bilateral agreements, his interference with French and British attempts to reëstablish some semblance of collective action with the participation of the Soviet Union, his undermining the prestige of the League of Nations—earned the Polish foreign minister big headlines in the European press (and he easily mistook notoriety for fame), but profited only Hitler. Colonel Beck frequently acted as Hitler's auxiliary, but always in the name of Polish *Realpolitik*. He was never consciously Hit-

---

the pros and cons of a preventive war before taking the decision to negotiate with Germany . . . The weakness of our potential allies made us abandon the idea of a preventive war." (Beck, *Dernier Rapport, Politique Polonaise 1926–1939*, 1951, p. 66). See also Henry L. Roberts, "The Diplomacy of Col. Beck," in *The Diplomats 1919–1939* (Princeton, 1953), edited by Gordan A. Craig and Felix Gilbert.

ler's stooge, nor his ally. When Germany violated the demilitari-
zation clauses of the Treaty of Versailles, Beck made a solemn
statement that Poland was ready to stand by her alliance with
France if the latter should decide to act. The theory was later
advanced that Beck, who had neither love nor respect for the
French, was merely trying to embarrass them because he knew
that France would not budge. Beck was not incapable of such
tricks, but he also may have been sincere. He at all times considered himself independent of Hitler and capable of demonstrating his independence. He continued to do it even when the
last semblance of a balance of power between Poland and Germany had completely disappeared.

Beck's self-confidence and false feeling of security were particularly strengthened by the suggestions of Hitler's spokesmen
about joint action against the Soviet Union. For a while Hitler
indeed toyed with the idea of putting Russia high on his time
table of conquest. Poland was never seriously considered in this
connection as more than an auxiliary, certainly not as a full partner. The main purpose of German diplomacy was to flatter the
Poles into feeling needed and important; to build up their feeling of security by stressing the basic opposition of the Nazi leaders to communism and Russia. Already on May 2, 1933, when the
Polish envoy to Berlin was making the first overtures to Hitler
on instructions from Marshal Pilsudski, Hitler said that he "recently examined statistical tables showing the number of births
in Russia. The astonishing fertility of that nation caused him to
reflect seriously on the dangers to Europe and, therefore, to
Poland which might arise from this fact." In November of the
same year he said that "Poland was an outpost against Asia.
The destruction of Poland would be a misfortune for the states
which would consequently become neighbors of Asia." He once
intimated that he had liquidated General Schleicher in the bloody
purge of 1934 mainly for advocating collaboration with Russia
against Poland. In 1935 Goering, on one of his famous hunting
trips to Poland, invited the Poles to contemplate the great opportunities open to them in the Ukraine.

All this seemed to confirm the wisdom of Beck's policy of "independence." Obviously Hitler was thinking highly of Poland

if he so consistently offered what looked like equal partnership in a drive against Russia. But Poland was not to be drawn into a combination against Russia; she was to keep the "balance" between her neighbors. Soviet accusations that "the Polish Government intended to enter the war on the side of Hitlerite Germany" are not supported by evidence. Of course, ideas of "greatness" and expansion lingered on at all times; there were exotic little groups in Poland with high connections and strange publications which advanced fantastic schemes (directed mainly, but not exclusively against Russia). Yet the record of official Polish foreign policy was one of "balance." [31] Beck's neutrality was, of course, particularly useful to Hitler and it fed the darkest suspicions both in the Soviet Union and in the West. Only Hitler was not fooled; he mistrusted Beck and quite early concluded that, in the case of an armed conflict with the West, Poland would turn against Germany. On November 5, 1937 Hitler made it clear to a conference of military leaders that the eventuality of war with Poland must be reckoned with. The thing to do was to increase Poland's isolation; this, as Hitler said later, was "a matter of skillful politics." Germany's position was sufficiently strengthened at the time and Poland was rapidly losing her usefulness. While Beck continued to believe that "Hitler needed Poland," the Fuehrer was already beginning to think of an expedition against Poland, as a precautionary measure, to liberate the divisions tied down in East Prussia and elsewhere on the German-

---

[31] The "balance" was not perfect. In the minds of many Pilsudski-ites there was a distinction between the nature of the problems presented by Germany and the Soviet Union respectively. In a "scholarly" analysis of Polish foreign policy, Casimir Smogorzewski wrote in 1938: "German National Socialism is trying to carry on propaganda among the German minority in Poland, but it never thinks of attacking the national character of the State." On the other hand, "not a day passes . . . that the Polish police do not arrest a few Communists sent out and supported by Moscow, whose chief mission is to destroy the national character of Poland, to proclaim a Soviet republic, and to incorporate it in the Soviet Union." The quoted article contains the statement that "Poland . . . cannot be considered a small country and . . . may be on the way to taking its place as a Great Power." ("Poland's Foreign Relations," in *The Slavonic and East European Review*, London, July 1938.) While willing to admit that Poland could do little against the united forces of Germany and Russia, Mr. Smogorzewski was convinced that "we might measure our strength with either of these neighbors and the battle would not be hopeless."

Polish frontier. In Hitler's eyes Poland was less and less of a menace, but still enough of a nuisance to require elimination.[32]

The conviction that Poland was not on Hitler's list and the belief that a German-Russian understanding was out of the question constantly pushed the Polish foreign minister to overstep the limits of mere neutrality. Even assuming that Poland's neighbors would forever be interested in the existence of the Polish barrier between them, the essence of neutrality is discretion and restraint. Beck observed neither. He constantly stepped on Stalin's toes, but he also irritated Hitler. Beck developed, in the countries between the Baltic and the Black Sea, feverish activities apparently striving to organize what was called a Helsinki-Bucharest axis, amounting to a bloc of small countries in the Middle Zone between Germany and Russia. The idea of such a bloc appeared very attractive to many people in interwar Europe; it is still alive. Examined superficially it seems perfectly "natural" and logical; historically threatened by Germany and Russia, the nations of the Middle Zone had only to get together and erect a barrier between the two giants. Population figures of the Zone added to an impressive total; other factors which determine the difference between a sum of deficits and a combination of power were as a rule overlooked. Yet in the specific situation of the late thirties everything militated against Beck's conception. Assertion of Polish "leadership," revival of a historical mission weighed more with him than actual considerations of security; yet no one was eager to lend himself to the satisfaction of Beck's urges. The small neighbors of Poland were by no means as impressed with Poland's status as a great Power as Beck was. They considered Poland to be "the sick man of Europe," with high priority on Hitler's list. Beck himself had been instrumental in destroying collective or regional security; he had been among the earliest and most ardent preachers of bilateralism and had preceded others in the parade of European

[32] "The German General Staff did not consider Poland by itself a serious military problem, for it did not share either Colonel Beck's high opinion of Polish strength and valor or the wildly exaggerated estimates of some British circles." (W. L. Langer and S. E. Gleason, *The Challenge to Isolation, 1937–1940*, New York, Published for the Council on Foreign Relations by Harper, 1952, pp. 101–102.)

nations to make separate deals with Hitler. Beck's list of prospective members of the bloc significantly omitted Czechoslovakia at a time when that country was beginning to come under Hitler's pressure. Beck had no use for Czechoslovakia and expected to profit from her disintegration. In a letter to Professor Namier, written in April 1944, Edward Benes stated: "Germany and Poland smashed the whole plan (of an Eastern Pact) . . . Poland did so by a note the chief argument of which was directed against the Czechoslovak Republic; she declared that Poland could not sign the Pact because she would not submit to any obligations relating to the Danube Basin. This, she said, was not in her interests." [33]

By 1937 Beck was certain that Hitler was about to move against Czechoslovakia and enjoyed the idea. He told Ambassador Bullitt (who visited Warsaw in November 1937) that if France should go to war in defense of Czechoslovakia—which he considered unlikely—Poland would not move. "Under no circumstances," Bullitt reported him as having stated, "would Poland become involved in protecting *French satellites in Central Europe,* especially Czechoslovakia . . ." When one realizes that Poland was, even if Beck did not think so, one of France's satellites in Central Europe, the quoted statement confirms the suicidal tendencies of Beck's policies to undermine the very system that had made the existence of Poland possible. In practical terms, Beck's diplomatic maneuvers, while designed to assert Poland's position as an important Power and leader of nations, amounted to an attempt at isolating Czechoslovakia in the face of increasing German pressure. Beck was playing Hitler's game. There was no alliance between them, but the appearance of a perfect *Arbeitsgemeinschaft* (the German term was deliberately used by Leon Noël, French ambassador to Warsaw, to describe the relationship). As to the exact extent of that coöperation there were at least fragmentary indications that on the eve of the Munich crisis there was "an intimate understanding between the German and the Polish armies." This led the American military attaché in Berlin to speculate on the possibility that the

[33] L. B. Namier, *Europe in Decay* (London: Macmillan & Co., Ltd., 1950), p. 284.

coöperation was not "for this episode only" but a prelude to "a greater degree of intimacy." Polish officials, when approached by Ambassador Biddle, denied the existence of such bonds but information from other sources seems to indicate that the Polish General Staff had at least tried to work out with the German military authorities an understanding on "a line of demarcation" in the case of a concerted move of both armies against Czechoslovakia.[34]

Immediately after Munich, Beck made a statement about dismembered Czechoslovakia which even many of his followers considered ill-conceived and in very bad taste. And then Poland's turn came. On October 24, 1938, less than a month after Munich, Ribbentrop called in the Polish ambassador and put forward proposals for a general settlement of the issues pending between Germany and Poland by a return of the Free City to the Reich and the granting of extraterritorial roads through the "corridor" to East Prussia. This first approach was still couched in friendly terms, with suggestions for joint action in colonial matters and a renewed offer of a joint policy toward Russia thrown in for camouflage. Ribbentrop was aware that the dismemberment of Czechoslovakia was bound to make public opinion in Poland, if not the Polish foreign minister, "sit up," and assume that Poland was next, but, as one of his underlings wrote in a memorandum, "the later this assumption sinks in, the better." Even in the last period before the tragic denouement of September 1939, Beck helped Hitler's diplomacy by letting himself be ma-

---

[34] Charles C. Tansill, *Back Door to War* (Chicago: Henry Regnery Co., 1952), pp. 431-432. In his memoirs Beck solemnly denied the existence of an understanding between Germany and Poland concerning Czechoslovakia. His conviction that Czechoslovakia was "artificial and contrary to the principle of self-determination" survived the fall of both Czechoslovakia and Poland. His views were influenced by what Pilsudski had said on the subject. The marshal had prophesied as early as 1921 that "there were two states which could not possibly survive: Austria and Czechoslovakia . . . In his opinion the only important question was which would disappear first." Beck's "authentic biography" (English version by T. H. Harley, London, 1939) records his prophetic statement in June 1937: "Czechoslovakia, as a caricature of the Austro-Hungarian Monarchy . . . will not last longer than eighteen months." It is interesting that neither Beck's nor his master's prophetic glimpses into the future included speculation on whose turn would come after the disappearance of Czechoslovakia.

neuvered into an awkward tactical position and accepting the concentration of attention on Danzig as technical pretext for the conflict.

On the issue of Danzig Beck had helped Hitler all along. When the local government of the Free City was taken over by Nazis, Beck stated that it was a "natural" development, of no interest to Poland as long as her rights were safeguarded. He had helped to remove the problem of Danzig from the forum of the League of Nations and made it a matter for direct negotiations with the local Nazis and with Hitler. This attitude was not without influence on the mood which developed in the West, that the affairs of the Free City could be settled one way or another in negotiations, without asking Frenchmen or Englishmen to "die for Danzig." Yet for months Jozef Beck helped to maintain the impression that the limited problem of Danzig and the technical issue of extraterritorial roads were actual and important points in the controversy, while Hitler was about to tell his generals: "Danzig is not the subject of the dispute at all; it is a question of expanding our living space." A few months later, in Rumanian exile, Beck told a friend that "no one in his right mind can claim that Danzig was the cause of the war." But he certainly had behaved in the critical months of 1939 as if Danzig were really the issue.

What, if any, plan of action Beck had in mind when he rejected in strong terms the German demands, renewed without niceties or camouflage after the complete annihilation of the Czech state in March 1939, is not quite clear. If he was thinking secretly of bargaining with Hitler and making concessions—as some unfriendly sources claimed—he would have been prevented from doing so by an aroused public opinion in Poland. The Polish man in the street could not help noticing that, after the elimination of Czechoslovakia, Germany looked on the map like a wolf holding Poland between his long jaws. On the other hand, the bluster of the regime had lulled the people into believing that Poland was perfectly prepared to meet aggression. Beck may have known better—although not necessarily—but he could ill afford to oppose the rising tide. His reputation had dropped to an all-time low; there had been earlier attempts, by

President Moscicki and Marshal Rydz-Smigly, to dislodge Beck from the government. He could make a come-back only as champion of Poland's will to resist.

The unexpected decision of the British government to create a united front against German aggression came as a windfall to Beck. The diplomatic activities of the tragic months following the occupation of Prague by the Nazis (March 15, 1939) permitted Beck to regain his confidence and, on occasions, to indulge his taste for intrigue.

The British Guarantee. The circumstances which led to the surprising offer of a British guarantee to Poland are worth recalling. Chamberlain suddenly realized that his attempt to teach Hitler the habit of asking British permission for each new bite he was about to take had failed. On March 17 the British envoys in a number of European capitals, including Warsaw, were instructed to sound out the attitude of governments which might consider further German aggression a threat to their interests. The immediate cause of the sudden British decision to swing into diplomatic action was not the appearance of a threat to Poland—which seemed to be of a chronic rather than acute nature—but indications that Hitler was planning to move against Rumania if the latter rejected his economic demands presented in a way that sounded very much like an ultimatum. To this first British approach the Polish answer was rather evasive. Beck stated that he would consult directly with the Rumanian government.[35] Actually, the only positive answer to the British overture came from the Russians who suggested that a six-Power conference, including in addition to Britain, France, and Russia, also Poland, Rumania, and Turkey, be called to discuss the problems of concerted action. However, this proposal was dismissed by the British as "premature." Two days later, and quite unexpectedly, the British government proposed to France, Russia, and Poland a joint declaration voicing the determination of

[35] Beck felt that the British government had given "rather lightheartedly" a guarantee to Rumania, "without quite knowing how they could keep their promise." He suspected the British of trying to shift to Poland the responsibility for carrying out the guarantee. He refused, in the name of "Poland's own Danubian policy," to extend to Rumania a guarantee of her frontiers against Hungary. (*Dernier Rapport,* p. 195.)

the signatory powers to resist further aggression against any European country. This suggestion was torpedoed by Beck who rejected the idea of bringing in the Soviet Union, because such a step would be "as unpleasant as it would be dangerous" and possibly provoke Germany into going to war. No doubt pleased with the British suggestion which aroused his easily tumescent sense of importance, Beck expressed preference for a bilateral British-Polish agreement. From a British point of view the immediate need for the agreement apparently consisted in its value as an addition to the defense of Rumania, considered the most threatened eastern European country in March 1939. Beck, however, had other reasons for wanting to obtain a British guarantee. He had received, on March 21, 1939, new German demands for the settlement of the Danzig issue, this time formulated in a tone which the Polish ambassador to Berlin, Lipski, described as "distinctly coercive," although it was sweetened by Ribbentrop's hints about the possibility of letting Poland participate in the protectorate over Slovakia. Beck was about to reject these demands in a way that made further negotiations rather improbable. But he did not immediately inform the British or the French of the latest German demands or of the Polish decision to reject them. There is considerable plausibility in the interpretation suggested by Langer and Gleason in *The Challenge to Isolation* that when the British government on March 27 decided to make a firm offer of assistance to Poland, it had in mind primarily the enlistment of Polish aid to Rumania. The Polish-Rumanian alliance was so phrased as to be directed only against the case of Soviet aggression; the British sought to enlarge the Polish commitment to cover the case of German and, presumably, Hungarian aggression. By not divulging the new German demands Beck got the British to offer Poland a "blank check" which, as he thought, they might have been reluctant to sign had they known that the rather unpopular issue of Danzig had flared up again.

On March 31, 1939 the Polish government had the publicly announced promise of the British to lend the Poles support ("all support in their power") in the case of "any action which clearly threatened Polish independence and which the Polish government accordingly considered it vital to resist with their national forces." This was, from a short-range point of view, quite an achievement for Beck. He also was no doubt satisfied with what looked like the definite exclusion of the Soviet Union from the combination which the British were building, a decision based on Chamberlain's undisguised aversion to the Soviets and also on the view apparently held by some high British officials that "Poland was a more formidable military power than the Soviet Union." Beck never ceased to be pleased with himself. After the collapse of Poland, he told a friend in Rumanian exile that he had deliberately maneuvered so as to secure for Poland the support of the West: "Had the war broken out earlier, no one would have budged in our defense and we would have had to fight alone." This sounds like an attempt to give an *ex post facto* semblance of sense to his foreign policy.

Poland and Russia. On the surface, relations between Poland and the Soviet Union were cool but correct. There would be little advantage in listing the various diplomatic instruments negotiated between the two countries as a reliable indication of mutual feelings. This was part of what someone has called the "polite mummery" of interwar Europe. In the conviction of many Poles, Russia remained a danger to Poland's independence. The preaching of communism added to the traditional distrust. Pilsudski once said that relations with Russia were bound to remain on the basis of a "provisorium." On the other hand, the Bolsheviks never really changed their mind about Poland's role as an advanced guard of aggressive capitalism, first bourgeois, later—fascist.[36]

---

[36] In spite of the Treaty of Riga, in which Soviet Russia and the Soviet Ukraine renounced their rights to territories lying to the west of the frontier with Poland agreed upon in the treaty, the Soviet government on several occasions reminded the world of its interest in the area. "It is impossible to believe that the Ukrainian people will remain indifferent to the fate of those of their own race inhabiting Eastern Galicia," Foreign Commissar Chicherin stated in a note dated March 13, 1923. When the Polish government protested against Soviet objections to the final recognition of Poland's sovereignty over Eastern Galicia, Chicherin, in a note dated September 22, 1924, again pointed out that "the Government of the Soviet Union cannot under any circumstances consider the Eastern Galician question as an internal affair of the Polish Government and continues to look upon it as an international problem *not finally settled.*" (Italics supplied. Quoted from: **Jane Degras** (ed.), *Soviet Documents on Foreign Policy*, I, 378, 458.)

In retrospect, it is fairly easy to point out that the leaders of the Soviet Union were not really interested in helping Poland against Hitler; that they were going to negotiate with both sides, trying to figure out whose offer served Soviet schemes best. At the time when Beck first opposed Soviet participation, these arguments were not available. He was simply not inclined to consider any combination which would smack of collective security. In the clumsy and ill-fated negotiations which were started with Moscow, the British and French negotiators were hampered by the knowledge that Poland was opposed to Soviet assistance. During his visit to London, early in April 1939, Beck made his view on the subject quite clear, to the apparent satisfaction of Neville Chamberlain, who wrote to his sister: "I confess I very much agree with him, for I regard Russia as a very unstable friend."

Something more basic than concrete Soviet demands determined Beck's attitude, which was merely a repetition of the stand taken by him a few years earlier when the French had tried to negotiate an Eastern Pact. The Polish ambassador to Moscow told Molotov, who had replaced Litvinov as Foreign Commissar:

We could not accept a one-sided Soviet guarantee. Nor could we accept a mutual guarantee . . . Also we could not accept collective negotiations, and make our adoption of a definite attitude conditional on the result of the Anglo-Franco-Soviet negotiations. We rejected all discussions of matters affecting us other than by the bilateral method . . . In the event of conflict we by no means rejected specified forms of Soviet aid, but considered it premature to determine them definitely. We considered it premature to open bilateral negotiations with the Soviets before the Anglo-Franco-Soviet negotiations had achieved a result . . .[37]

This negative attitude of the Polish government underwent no change, even in the face of mounting pressure from Germany. From the British and the French, who conducted their negotiations with only limited enthusiasm, there was little insistence that Poland change her attitude. We know what Chamberlain's feelings were; others shared his apprehension and his reluctance to see the Russian bear move westward. Only in the last phase of the military negotiations in Moscow did the French cabinet

[37] *Polish White Book,* p. 208.

undertake to suggest to the Poles that they consider the Soviet proposals (which, on August 13, had been specified by Voroshilov as permission for the Red army to enter the Wilno region and Eastern Galicia). According to Noël, Beck replied:

> We are asked to endorse a new partition of Poland; if we are to be partitioned, we will at least defend ourselves. There is no guarantee that, once installed in our country, the Russians would effectively participate in the war.

And Marshal Rydz-Smigly has summed up the Polish attitude by saying (according to Paul Reynaud): "With the Germans we risk the loss of our liberty; with the Russians—of our soul." No one could offer a better description of the lack of alternatives which made Poland's situation impossible, not only in the last weeks of the interwar period but from the moment when her neighbors had again become active factors on the international scene.

Conceit and wishful thinking determined Poland's choice of a policy of "balance" which, to be successful, had to assume that Germany and Russia would forever need Poland. This assumption overlooked much of the record of Russian-German relations, the recurrence of situations in which both countries had decided that, rather than use the nuisance value of the Polish problem against one another, they might temporarily get together at the expense of Poland. This is how the Partitions of the eighteenth century had happened. This is how Bismarck maintained good relations with Russia. And even in the period since Versailles there had been a strong trend both in Russia and in Germany towards a rapprochement at the expense of Poland. This was the idea underlying the Treaty of Rapallo concluded in 1922. It is true that neither of the contracting parties was in a position at the time to put into effect its implications, but the idea survived the collapse of the Weimar Republic in spite of Hitler's rantings against communism. In 1922 General von Seeckt wrote in a secret memorandum: "Poland is the heart of the eastern problem. Poland's existence is intolerable, incompatible with the essential conditions of Germany's life. Poland must go and will go . . . For Russia, Poland is even more intolerable than she is for us; no Russian government can abide the existence of Poland." The Germany military mind certainly was not thinking in terms of the "need" for the existence of an independent Poland.[38]

A time came when Hitler decided that Poland was of doubtful value as a barrier against Russia and a nuisance in the case of war against the West. No matter where he was turning first, Poland had to be eliminated. The decision to make war was announced by Hitler at a conference of military chiefs on May 23, 1939. The tentative date for "Fall Weiss," code name of the attack on Poland, was given earlier in an order by Keitel, dated April 3, 1939. From the fragmentary evidence available it seems that Stalin was rather slow in making up his mind and that his evaluation of impending events was not quite correct. He apparently believed that England and France would *not* honor their commitments and that a new Munich would be staged.[39] The Soviet Union was determined not to be excluded from the spoils this time. On the alternative assumption that war was coming, Stalin might have seen substantial immediate advantages in signing the pact with Hitler rather than making commitments on behalf of a reluctant and doomed Poland. Hitler offered Stalin an opportunity to stay out of the war for some time, to gain territory, and to hope to derive advantages from the mutual weakening of both fighting sides. Not everything in Stalin's calculations proved correct, but, as Winston Churchill

[38] From the Soviet side there was no avowed acceptance of the need to eliminate Poland throughout most of the interwar period. But a few days after Munich the Soviet diplomat Potemkin told French Ambassador Coulondre: "For us I see now no other way except a Fourth Partition of Poland." In recording this conversation in his memoirs, M. Coulondre remarks that "it is singular that after this the Chancelleries should have dropped from the clouds when, ten months later, the German-Soviet agreement supervened." (Robert Coulondre, *De Staline à Hitler. Souvenirs de deux ambassades, 1936–1939,* quoted in Sir Lewis Namier, *In the Nazi Era,* London: Macmillan & Co., Ltd., 1952, p. 176.)

[39] Until late in March 1939 the Germans, too, appear to have thought that Beck was actually willing to agree to the occupation of Danzig by Hitler. In a directive dated March 25 Hitler explained to the army commanders that a military occupation of Danzig might have to be undertaken if the Polish government hinted that, because of public opinion, "the solution would be made easier for them by a *fait accompli.*"

was to say later, it was not only a cold-blooded policy but also a highly realistic one, at the time when it was chosen.

Did the leaders of interwar Poland have a way out? Could they have prevented the destruction of their state? The answer depends on whether one approaches the question theoretically, as a classroom problem in diplomacy or as a concrete situation, taking into account the ballast of history, prejudices, and psychological blocks which weighed heavily on Poland's interwar ruling groups. The theoretical answer is simple: at one point Poland should have thrown in her lot with *one or the other* of her neighbors. Since this answer refers to a theoretical country between two theoretical neighbors—not to the Poland of Versailles between Germany and the Soviet Union—there is no need to engage in further speculations on what would have happened if the choice had been made. In the concrete Poland of the interwar years such a choice was long considered unnecessary; later it was seen as a choice between the loss of liberty and loss of the "soul"—it was therefore impossible.[40]

Within the tragically determined limits of her existence in the interwar period, Poland probably had only the choice of not contributing actively to her own destruction. Her leaders did not avail themselves of this opportunity. Their judgment was impaired by the use of a rather unconventional scale of values, by their limited talents and their immodesty. The ardent Polish nationalist Stanislaw Mackiewicz wrote in his critical study of Beck's foreign policy: "Poles, like certain beautiful birds, are apt to lose sight of their surroundings, enraptured by their own song." Ornithological comparisons seem traditional with reference to Poland. The romantic poet Juliusz Slowacki once called Poland "the peacock and the parrot of nations." The British writer John W. Wheeler-Bennett described Poland's policy as

[40] Professor Tansill points out in his *Back Door to War* that "Hitler offered Poland the role of chief satellite . . . Beck . . . preferred to nurse the hope of continued Polish independence . . . At the greatest crossroads in all history he rejected a ride in the German war machine along a path that promised Poland power and plunder as a satellite state" (p. 510). I doubt that Hitler really thought of Poland as "chief satellite" or was really prepared to share "power and plunder" with Beck. However, it would have been theoretically correct for Beck to act on that assumption. His "independent" policy was indeed "a design for disaster."

that of "a canary who has persistently but unsuccessfully endeavored to swallow two cats."

The Consequences of "Impossibility." The Poland of Versailles was on many counts not a viable state. In the field of international relations, its survival was contingent upon the realization of a number of conditions necessary to neutralize or mitigate the inconveniences of Poland's geographic position. Wilson's Thirteenth Point spoke of an "international covenant" as the basic guarantee of Poland's political and economic independence and territorial integrity. But the "international covenant" did not become effectively operative. Other conditions for the survival of Poland were outside the realm of the practical conduct of international affairs; hence Poland was doomed. Needless to say, the congenital afflictions of a weak state do not justify its destruction; the mandate to carry out euthanasia is rather dubious under all circumstances, even if it is the practice in international life for strong states to arrogate to themselves the "right" to engage in the not so merciful liquidation of their weaker neighbors. Yet it is useless to deny that weakness, while it does not justify aggression in moral terms, certainly invites it.

What happened to Poland in 1939 was by no means surprising. The outcome had, as a matter of fact, been predicted quite early in the twenties by thoughtful analysts and a handful of statesmen. Yet these early predictions were easily forgotten. The superficial stabilization of conditions in Poland, propaganda, wishful thinking, emotional judgment, and an erroneous evaluation of the real strength behind the saber-rattling of the Pilsudski-ite regime, combined to create, in the thirties, the false picture of a Poland which had seemingly come to stay, even if under somewhat difficult conditions. The annihilation of the Polish state must have come as a shock to many who had been exposed to the optimistic picture (including the bulk of the Polish population, misled into interpreting its government's bluster as strength). To the well informed it was hardly a surprise; however, the pretense of being shocked by what was perfectly predictable is a standard form of behavior in international relations.

How much sense does it make to try to establish at this late date the responsibilities for the destruction of interwar Poland?

In particular, what is the point of attempting to determine the exact degree of contributory negligence of Poland's political leaders in bringing about or hastening the catastrophe? The fate of Poland was not unique. Other states, which treated their national minorities in a better or more intelligent way, were also crushed. Countries with a healthier economic structure were also enslaved. The wisdom of rushing to side with a strong protector rather than trying to play a hopeless policy of balance did not save other states from the consequences of the upheaval that resulted from World War II. One can simply argue that the fate of Poland was merely a particularly striking manifestation of a deep process sometimes described as the inevitable decline of "parochial sovereignty" in our days. If this is the case, it matters little to what degree the Poles or their leaders contributed to the timing or to the peculiarly tragic consequences of their national catastrophe. Unless, of course, one believes that the leaders of a nation are duty bound to attempt to delay the inevitable or mitigate the results of what cannot be reasonably averted, rather than accelerate the denouement of the tragedy.

III. *World War II: Occupation and Resistance*

War, Partition, Occupation. Of the military side of the war thrust upon Poland in September 1939 little can be said that is still of interest. Poland was utterly unprepared; her defenses were aptly compared to a thin egg-shell containing a soft yolk which presented almost no problem to the German war machine. The disproportion of forces between the Poles and the Germans, especially in the fields of aviation and armored and motorized equipment, was in itself enough to render the situation of the Poles hopeless. The Germans had more than ten to one superiority in the air, they had seventeen armored divisions against two incomplete brigades on the Polish side; but, there were eleven Polish cavalry brigades against one German. The lack of a clear plan of action, the irresponsibility of the leadership—the higher the officer, the quicker the run toward the Rumanian border—the early disruption of communications, limited the use that could have been made of the Polish soldier's unquestionable heroism and doggedness. The inactivity of Poland's western allies—British planes "bombarded" Germany with leaflets and France settled down to the phony war—permitted the full use of Germany's superior forces. And then there was the attitude of the Soviet Union.

Some accounts of the short war fought by the Poles in 1939 list as a major contribution to Poland's defeat the "stab in the back" delivered to the retreating Polish forces by the Soviet Union. Indeed, on September 17, 1939, more than a hundred Soviet divisions began to move across what was then Poland's frontier. This move was a result of the treaty of nonaggression signed between Nazi Germany and the Soviet Union on August 23, 1939 after the failure of the half-hearted attempts to create an anti-German military alliance including Russia. The treaty contained a secret protocol of the same date which "in the event of a territorial and political rearrangement of the areas belonging to the Polish state" established a Soviet sphere of influence—in other words, authorized Soviet occupation of territories up to a line determined in advance by this new partition of Poland. Militarily speaking, the Russian move had little influence on the outcome of the September campaign. No one can seriously claim that the Polish forces could have successfully re-formed their "front line"; there was no front line from the moment of the break-through effected by the Germans in the first few days of September.[1] The most that the Soviet intervention caused, in military terms, was interference with the evacuation of more Polish troops across the border to Rumania and Hungary. When Mr. Molotov declared that "the Polish state has ceased to exist" he was, technically speaking, wrong. On the day of his statement there was still in existence, in a frontier village in the extreme south of the country, the legitimate though powerless Polish government (awaiting clearance to cross into Rumania); there were isolated pockets of military resistance— such as Warsaw, or the army of General Kleeberg which did not surrender until early in October. Yet for all practical purposes the Soviet troops were moving into a political and military vacuum.

The record of events of September 1939, as revealed in the documents on *Nazi-Soviet Relations, 1939–1941,* shows that in spite of the pact with Hitler and the establishment of spheres of influence cutting across Polish territory, the Russians were rather slow and hesitant in claiming their portion of the loot. They were surprised by the speed of the German advance. On September 5, Molotov refused to reveal to the German ambassador the date of military occupation of the Soviet "sphere." The Soviet government was at that time still encouraging the Poles to ask for Russian supplies. This suggestion reveals indecision

---

[1] The statement that "efforts were made to organize a counter-attack and to stabilize the front" (while the Russians marched in) can be found in *Stalin and the Poles* (London: Hollis & Carter, 1949), an indictment of the Soviet leaders drawn up by Dr. Bronislaw Kusnierz, a Polish lawyer in exile. No serious evidence corroborates this statement. Instances of stabilizing pierced fronts were generally rare in World War II, a war of movement.

as much as duplicity. Only when the collapse of Polish resistance became obvious, did the Russians decide to intervene militarily, not before the Germans indirectly threatened to conclude an armistice with the disintegrating Polish forces, thus putting the Soviet Union in a situation where she would have had to start "a new war" to occupy her part of the former Polish state.[2] Molotov cynically suggested to the Germans that the Soviet Union be permitted to state that Russian intervention aimed at protecting the Ukrainians and Byelorussians of eastern Poland against the Nazis. He stressed in a conversation with the German ambassador that "it was of the greatest importance not to take action until the governmental center of Poland, the city of Warsaw, had fallen." Once the Soviet troops were on the march, the Russians suddenly changed their mind about the possibility of creating a residual Polish state (which the secret protocol of August 23 had left open). They insisted on immediate negotiations to dispose of the territory of Poland by a clear partition. Stalin surprised the Germans by offering them more of Poland than the secret protocol envisaged. The Russians apparently preferred not to be identified with the occupation of territory recognized as ethnographically Polish. The Ribbentrop-Molotov line (in its final version) was not strikingly different from the Curzon Line.[3]

With the end of the lightning war, "Poland in exile" came into existence. On French soil, and later in England, under the leadership of General Wladyslaw Sikorski, a long-time opponent of the Pilsudski regime, a government-in-exile was formed. Its political façade consisted of four parties (or, to be exact, of those representatives of the four parties who were available abroad) which had kept out of parliamentary activities in the last prewar years but were enjoying a considerable following:

[2] See the telegram from Schulenburg to Ribbentrop, September 10, 1939, (*Nazi-Soviet Relations*, p. 91).

[3] When Stalin stated, at Teheran, that the Soviet Union adhered to the frontiers of 1939, Eden, according to Winston Churchill's account, "asked if this meant the Ribbentrop-Molotov line," to which Stalin replied dryly: "Call it whatever you like." Molotov then remarked that "it was generally called the Curzon Line" and denied Eden's claim that "there were important differences." For a treatment of the problem of the Curzon Line from a Polish point of view, see Adam Zoltowski, *Border of Europe—A Study of the Polish Eastern Provinces* (London, 1950).

Nationalists, Social Democrats, Peasant Party, and Christian Labor. However, the presidency devolved on Wladyslaw Raczkiewicz, a former high official of the Pilsudski regime. This strange combination was the result of attempts to preserve the "legal continuity" of the Polish government. According to the authoritarian Constitution of 1935, the President of the Republic had the right to appoint his own successor in extraordinary situations making the normal functioning of government impossible. Professor Moscicki, who resigned as president before crossing the border into Rumania, transferred his powers to Mr. Raczkiewicz, and the Sikorski government had to accept this state of affairs. Of course, the "legal continuity" of a government-in-exile is a political, not a legal problem; not the providential paragraph of Poland's Constitution kept the Polish government alive and recognized, but the political good will of the western Allies and sympathetic neutrals. When the time came to de-recognize the Polish government-in-exile, its legal title proved to be of little avail.

From the point of view of the new partitioners of Poland, that country had ceased to exist, once more "forever." They went about the reorganization and absorption of the territories of what according to them was a defunct state.

The Nazis incorporated into the *Reich* a considerable part of their portion of Poland and organized a *General Gouvernement* in the remainder. Hans Frank, appointed Governor General, made no secret of the German intentions toward Poland: "Poland shall be treated like a colony; the Poles will become the slaves of the Greater German World Empire." Terror marked the German occupation from the very beginning. It is related in the judgment rendered by the Nürnberg Tribunal, which sentenced Frank to death, that the Governor General, in a comment on an announcement about the shooting of a few Czech students posted by Neurath, said to a journalist: "If I wished to order that one should hang up posters about every seven Poles shot, there would not be enough forests in Poland with which to make the paper for these posters." Extermination of the Polish intelligentsia became a special aim of the Nazis and the concentration camps were filled with representatives of the liberal professions.

The economic demands made on the General Government [the Nürnberg Tribunal found] were far in excess of the needs of the army of occupation, and were all out of proportion to the resources of the country . . . The rations of the population of the occupied territories were reduced to the starvation level, and epidemics were widespread . . .

The persecution of the Jews took on inhuman forms almost from the start; it culminated in the mass extermination of almost the entire Jewish population of Poland—some three million people. The country also served as dumping ground for Jews deported from other occupied countries who were put to death in the gas chambers of Oswiecim, Tremblinka, and Majdanek. "A thousand years will pass and this guilt of Germany will still not be erased," the conscience-stricken Hans Frank was to exclaim at Nürnberg in what was a most unpolitical estimate of the permanence of guilt in international relations.

There have been various computations of the losses suffered by Poland as a result of the German invasion and occupation. One set of figures, published by a special Reparations Commission of the postwar Polish government, estimated the "biological loss" caused by the war and by extermination at more than six million, including about three million Jews, together some 22 per cent of the total Polish and Jewish population of prewar Poland. Some 2.4 million Polish citizens went through forced labor, deportation to Germany and other occupied countries; 863,000 were detained in prisons and concentration camps; more than 2.4 million were forced to leave their homes. The same account also presents an impressive picture of material damage done to Poland's national wealth. It does not, of course, embrace biological or other losses caused as a result of the Soviet participation in the events of 1939–1945. These are presented in claims and figures prepared by Poles in exile. The major Soviet offense, according to these accounts, included the mass deportation of "anti-Soviet and socially unadapted elements" from eastern Poland in 1939–1941. The total had been estimated by some Polish sources at 1.5 million, including about 250,000 arrested, approximately a million deported and the others recruited into the Red army or sent to work, inside Russia. Of these, some were Ukrainians and Byelorussians whom the Soviet Union ceased to recognize as Polish citizens; some were released and left Russia between 1941 and 1943; others returned to Poland after the war; an unspecified number perished.

Before and After June 1941. In the political sphere, the arrangement made by the Soviet Union and Nazi Germany on the eve of World War II lasted until Hitler invaded Russia. The "spheres of influence" agreed upon a few days before the war were somewhat modified in a secret protocol signed on September 28, 1939; Lithuania was placed in the Soviet sphere and the Germans enlarged their share of Polish territory by taking the eastern part of the province of Warsaw and the province of Lublin. The partitioners agreed to suppress in their respective territories all Polish agitation which might affect the territories of the other party. Germany and the Soviet Union declared that the problems arising from the liquidation of the Polish state were "definitively settled," and appealed to the world to recognize this situation and "put an end to the state of war." The "friendship" between the two partitioners of Poland—a bilateral attempt to buy time for the inevitable clash—lasted until June 22, 1941, when Hitler attacked Russia.

This event no doubt simplified the war situation from the point of view of Great Britain, at the time lone major resister to Hitler. There was no question in Mr. Churchill's mind as to what England's course should be. He knew that Hitler's invasion of Russia was "no more than a prelude to an attempted invasion of the British isles . . . The Russian danger is, therefore, our danger, and the danger of the United States." For Mr. Churchill the invasion of Russia "altered the values and relationships of the war," just as for Mr. Stalin the hitherto imperialist war had overnight become a just and worthy one. The situation of the Poles was much more complicated. Some hopes were raised by Russia's entrance in the war on the side of the Allies, but there were also serious misgivings. Although technically Poland was at no time at war with the Soviet Union, most politically active Poles had been geared by the events of 1939 to speak and think of *two enemies*. Because of the use made by communist propaganda of this "theory of two enemies" to discredit the Polish government-in-exile as a trouble-maker between the Allies, official Polish statements hotly denied its existence or its acceptance by General Sikorski's government. On the surface, the Polish government-in-exile followed obediently the advice of its British host in renewing relations with the Soviet Union in July 1941 and in keeping relatively quiet over the territorial issue which the Soviet side refused to discuss. This caused a crisis in the government-in-exile and a widening split between Sikorski and the more militantly anti-Russian elements grouped around Raczkiewicz, the president-in-exile, former foreign minister August Zaleski, General Sosnkowski, and other military leaders.[4] Yet, in spite of all denials, Polish political thinking and writing not unnaturally continued to consider the Soviet Union as a hostile rather than friendly Power. Consequently, those Poles who were thinking in terms of restitution of the pre-1939 situation, tied their hopes to an outcome of the war that would eliminate Nazi Germany but also weaken the Soviet Union. This line was reflected in the Underground press published in German-occupied Poland.

The "Secret State." The Polish Underground received more publicity during the war than any other similar organization in occupied Europe. Impressive charts presented the setup of the "secret state" which, in defiance of the German occupants, functioned almost openly, carrying out regular administrative duties through neatly organized departments ("ministries"), educating children, and meting out punishment to some unpatriotic individuals. The cliché of Poland as the country that produced no Quisling is still in use. Of course, the reason why Poland produced no Quisling has as yet not been fully investigated. In view of what the avowed German intentions were towards Poland, it is questionable whether the Nazis really were looking for a Polish Quisling. There was no room for a Polish unit in

[4] Some dramatic details of the negotiations leading to the so-called Sikorski-Maisky agreement and the subsequent crisis in the Polish government were revealed in 1950 and 1951 by Polish writers in exile. (Cf. Kazimierz Okulicz, "Umowa Sikorski-Majskij z 30. VII 1941," in *Niepodleglosc*, London, 1950, II, 71–89; also the reviews and additions to the account by Okulicz, written by Professor Stanislaw Stronski, a former member of the Sikorski government, and by Wladyslaw Pobog-Malinowski, former chief of historical research in the Polish Ministry of Foreign Affairs. *Kultura*, Paris, April 1951, pp. 100–133.)

Hitler's Europe. With all due respect to Polish patriotism, the Germans could have unearthed enough scoundrels or weaklings if they had really tried. Some overtures were made to a few personalities, but there is no trace of a concerted German effort to achieve more than the "neutral benevolence" of the Poles in the war against Russia. Collaborationism on a very low level and for very ugly motives was as widespread in Poland as elsewhere in occupied Europe.[5]

The Underground, or that part of it which received the most publicity, was a political and military organization connected with the Polish government-in-exile. Its political composition reflected the pattern of the four-party coalition in the "London" government. Its military arm was engaged in limited acts of anti-German sabotage and concentrated its energies primarily on what Jan Karski, a former courier of the Underground, described as "preparation for a single, powerful blow in the distant future." Considering themselves a part of the fighting coalition led by London and Washington, the leaders of the Polish Underground subscribed to the theory of "waiting in preparedness" for the time when the Supreme Allied Command would consider the moment ripe and the situation propitious for a general uprising in Poland. They quite understandably refused to reckon with the possibility that a split of military responsibilities might put the Soviet armies in sole control of the theater of operations embracing the territory of Poland. Since there was little hope for them in such an eventuality, Polish Underground leaders simply preferred to ban it from their calculations and to operate on a set of unrealistic concepts.

Echoes of the ideas worked out in the Underground may be found in the pamphlets, newspapers, and press bulletins published illegally in occupied Poland. There were hundreds of such publications with a circulation ranging from one hundred to many thousands of copies, distributed through an ingenious network of volunteers. It may seem somewhat unfair to blame

[5] As George F. Kennan put it so wisely, though in another connection: "If individual life is to go on at all within the totalitarian framework it must go on by arrangement with the regime, and to some extent in connivance with its purposes." (*American Diplomacy, 1900–1950*, University of Chicago Press, 1951), p. 140.

Underground publications, produced under extremely difficult conditions by people cut off from reliable information and exposed to poisonous Nazi propaganda, for being inaccurate in their evaluations. However, what was said and written in the Underground was of importance because of the ties which that organization maintained with the government-in-exile. The "London" government very often used the "will of the Underground" to justify its own stand on certain matters, especially its unwillingness to yield to Russian demands. Yet on the other hand the Underground was largely dependent on information provided through secret channels from London. If the output of the Underground press was not just the product of wishful thinking or political blindness, it must have been influenced by information and evaluations transmitted from London by people who were either deliberately keeping their associates inside Poland in a state of optimistic ignorance or were themselves grossly misinformed.

In the beginning, the Underground press expressed the conviction that Germany would be defeated by the West and the Soviet Union somehow punished for acting in collusion with Hitler.[6] In 1940 an Underground pamphlet, *The Form and Content of Future Poland*, predicted that Germany and Russia would soon be at war. Such a development was considered by the author as conducive to "more propitious conditions" for the nations opposed to both Germany and Russia. The expected outcome of the war would be the creation of a federation including not only the Poles, Czechs, and Slovaks, but also the Ukrainians and Byelorussians. This theme, or dream, of a federation embracing the nations located between Germany and the Soviet Union to be joined by Russia's fringe nations in order to shield Poland from direct contact with Russia proper, was to recur quite often in Polish political thought during the war.

The initial phase of the Nazi-Soviet war was greeted with mixed feelings by the Poles. They could derive little comfort from German victories but could not help enjoying Russian defeats. From a Polish point of view the best solution seemed to

---

[6] All quotations from Underground publications are from the collection of photostatic copies available at the Library of Congress.

be the defeat or considerable weakening of the Russians by the Germans who would then in turn be smashed by Poland's gallant and benevolent western Allies. Even in 1943, when the tide of the war had turned to the advantage of the Russians, the Polish Underground was trying to find consolation in what it interpreted as signs of exhaustion in the East. Moscow's political offensive against the Polish government-in-exile, its insistence on a settlement of the territorial issue, were dismissed as "unilateral acts that need not create undue anxiety among the Poles." The official publication of the Chief Delegate of the Government, *Rzeczpospolita Polska,* explained, in the issue of March 11, 1943:

The war is not yet finished. It will still bring changes in the relation of forces . . . Russia will not have the last word . . . An important role in determining the map of this part of Europe will be played by Poland and her Anglo-Saxon allies . . . Note the statement made by General Sikorski after his return from Washington where he coördinated the principles of our foreign policy with the views of President Roosevelt . . .

The war is not yet finished—this slogan became the keynote of political writing and thinking in the Underground. It expressed the hopes connected by the Poles with the opening of a second front. The "Anglo-Saxons" were expected, much earlier than they actually did, to appear on the continent of Europe and deliver the decisive blow to Nazi Germany while the eastern front remained relatively stabilized. When it became clear that the second front would be delayed and that the attitude of the West was disquietingly friendly to the Soviet enemy-ally, *WRN,* a publication of the socialists connected with the London-controlled Underground, offered the following optimistic interpretation on January 14, 1944:

Officially, the United States and Great Britain cannot do anything that would jeopardize their relations with Russia . . . Actually, there are indications that the overwhelming majority of the people and official circles in both countries support Poland. This stand will be made public when the military situation at last would permit them to inaugurate an open diplomatic showdown . . .

The publication adhered faithfully to this line and stated on February 11, 1944 that the war would be decided by the "third factor"—the first two being Germany's defeat and Russia's momentary ascendancy:

> The Polish problem will not be settled now when Russia is at the zenith of success. Moscow's brutal moves against Poland will be of as little consequence for the future settlement, as the impertinence of the Germans . . . The allied armies which are reaching the continent will bring the renaissance of Europe on the basis of principles guaranteeing the full independence and integrity of the Republic of Poland.

A fortnight later the same publication played up an exchange of courtesies between Generals Anders of Poland and Patton of the United States who had expressed the hope of entering Warsaw together. ("This is, no doubt, also everybody's wish here in Poland.") Finally, in March 1944, the Socialist publication stated:

> We know that the Soviets want to extort the realization of their annexationist war aims before the last phase of the war, a phase which will be less advantageous for the Soviets than the present one.

The idea that the West would intervene successfully on behalf of Poland was expressed also in publications connected with Mikolajczyk's Peasant Party. *Orka*, a "peasant" paper for the urban intelligentsia (according to Karski's competent description), assured its readers in March 1943 that if the Polish government-in-exile had decided to bring to a head the matter of the frontier dispute with Russia, "this was done, needless to say, not without consulting the proper factors in America and England." In June 1943 *Orka* explained that England and America were supporting Poland although nothing was being said about it in the papers. The publication drew attention to the "great tension in relations between the western democracies and the Soviets. Our problem is only one of many on the agenda and we must wait patiently for the general showdown."

The full meaning and purpose of these utterances of the "pro-London" Underground press become clear when one realizes the ensemble of conditions under which they were made. Poland was still under German occupation, and defeat in the East did not make the Germans any more reasonable or friendly in their attitude towards the Poles, but Nazi propaganda kept stressing the theme of "betrayal" of Poland by her western Allies.

Some bitterness must have taken root in occupied Poland; it tended to weaken the faith of the Poles in the West and in the wisdom of the government-in-exile. Hence the constant assurances that the West had a trump card which would be brought out against Stalin at the most propitious moment.

The "official" press of the Underground sponsored and financed by the West no doubt acquitted itself loyally of its assignment to present the sponsors in the best possible light, in spite of poisonous German propaganda and the activities of the rival, pro-Moscow Underground. Insignificant in the beginning and for obvious reasons largely inactive until June 1941, the pro-Soviet Underground, although numerically weaker, in the later stages of the war enjoyed the advantage of its connection with an army that was actually, not in the imagination of analysts, to enter Poland. The propaganda spread by the Polish Workers' Party (the name under which the communists resumed their activities) was seconded by the output of the so-called *Kosciuszko Radio* broadcasting from Russian territory in the name of the *Union of Polish Patriots,* the nucleus of a counter-government created by the Russians when they decided to break relations with the London Poles.

When the events of 1944 made it clear that the advancing Red army had no intention of respecting the rights of the "secret state," the "London" Underground, while continuing to build up the prestige of the western Allies, openly returned to the terminology of "two enemies." [7] Misinformed as it was and distorted as some of its ideas may appear, the Underground press nevertheless reflected a genuinely Polish desire to escape the cadre of realities.

The "official" Underground was no doubt an impressive organization, in a way even too impressive as a form of institutionalized opposition to the occupant. For the purpose of keeping up the spirit of the Poles under German occupation a more modest organization would have been sufficient. As to the value of the Underground army in actual military operations against the Germans, it was much less than some sources in the West seemed to think. In any case, the *Armia Krajowa* (AK) was,

---

[7] Socialist *Robotnik,* July 2, 1944.

tactically and emotionally, geared for coöperation with the West only; once Poland found itself outside the theater of operations commanded by General Eisenhower, it was not exactly clear what military contribution the Underground could make, especially since the attempts to convince Stalin that the AK could be valuable in the Soviet advance through Poland were unsuccessful. Whatever military advantages the Soviet army could derive from the participation of the AK, would be, in Stalin's opinion, outweighed by the political obstacles to Soviet postwar schemes for the area resulting from that contribution. The main value of the Polish Underground consisted in providing a political background for the government-in-exile; serving the cause of the western Allies by keeping up their prestige in the face of serious doubts and corroding German and communist propaganda; contributing to the store of intelligence gathered by the West through maintaining a constant flow of information, some of first-rate importance, as, for instance, the reports on the location of sites for the launching of the V–1 rockets.[8] The mission of the Underground was not to fight the Germans in the sense of maintaining constant and large-scale military operations. Neither the nature of the terrain nor the military possibilities of the AK permitted it; in addition, its operating theory was to "wait in preparedness" for the signal from the West which failed to come. Part of the effort of maintaining the impressive and costly organization was based on the hope of preparing the nucleus of an administration and, above all, preventing the seizure of political power in the post-liberation chaos by groups standing outside the "official" Underground (extreme rightists of the National Radical

[8] It appears, from fragmentary evidence in the Department of State files, that a similar task in the field of intelligence was undertaken by the Polish National Committee in the first World War. In 1917 the Committee was promised certain funds, to be paid on a fifty-fifty basis by the United States and Great Britain, "provided we were able to work out a scheme for securing intelligence through the Committee." The intelligence was to come, of course, from Germany and Austria or from countries occupied by them. On behalf of the United States the arrangement was made by a person identified only as "C.–H." (Colonel House?). The correspondence in the files of the Department of State resulted from the fact that in 1919 the Committee was still unable to collect the sum promised by the American government, although the British side had paid its share. It was found that no budget provisions had been made for the purpose. (National Archives, 86oc.01/274.)

ilk; some Pilsudski-ites; communists; left-wing socialists, etc.).
Since the hoped-for military situation failed to materialize and
the liberation of Poland came from an uncomfortable quarter,
the Underground was being pushed into an increasingly embarrassing and untenable situation. Its tragi-comic communiqués
"authorizing" the temporary occupation of Poland by the Soviet
army in pursuit of the retreating Germans were simply disregarded by the Russian commanders who were liquidating the
AK groups wherever the latter ventured out of the forests. In
the wake of the Soviet advance a new *de facto* government, the
so-called "Lublin Committee" or Polish Committee of National
Liberation, was being installed.

Because of the lack of a political basis for coöperation with the
Russians, the legitimate Underground was bound to be dissolved
or to degenerate almost imperceptibly into a diversion directed
against the Russian "liberators" and the new Polish regime installed by them. Nothing illustrates more dramatically the lack
of a plausible political basis for the functioning of the pro-London Underground in the decisive phase of the war than the story
of the Warsaw Uprising.

The Warsaw Uprising: Background. The uprising which
broke out in Warsaw in the afternoon of August 1, 1944 amidst
expectations of an impending withdrawal of the Germans from
the city is an episode that lends itself perfectly to an emotional
evaluation. It led to the almost complete destruction by the
Nazis of the sorely tried Polish capital; it added tens of thousands of civilian victims to the long list of Polish casualties. It
broke out and was subdued under circumstances that further
aggravated the already hostile relations between the Soviet Union
and the "London" Polish government.

According to the version of the story which was worked out
during the tragic days of the uprising and has become more
or less fully accepted in the West, the Russians first provoked
the outbreak of the uprising and then deliberately slowed down
their offensive, refused to take the city, and watched "from the
suburbs" while the Germans liquidated the uprising. Moreover,
the Soviet government and military command interfered with
Western attempts to supply Warsaw by air, and groups of

Poles rushing to join the fighters in Warsaw were stopped and disarmed. The Soviet and pro-Soviet side of the story is that the uprising was premature, that it was not coördinated with the Red Army command, and that the Soviet forces advancing on Warsaw were checked by the Germans and prevented from taking the city.

The standard version of the story of the uprising as presented to the world by the "London" Poles invariably links the uprising with appeals from the Soviet-sponsored *Radio Kosciuszko* directed to the people of Warsaw and urging them to rise against the Germans and help the approaching Soviet army. These frequently cited broadcasts of *Radio Kosciuszko,* made on July 29 and 30, 1944, called upon the citizens of Warsaw "to stand as one man around the *National Council of the Homeland* and to join the ranks of the *People's Army."* The italicized terms had a perfectly clear meaning to the people of Warsaw and especially to the leaders of the "legitimate" Underground. *Radio Kosciuszko* was known to be the "clandestine" station operating on Soviet soil on behalf of the Union of Polish Patriots, a body created in Russia as the nucleus of pro-Soviet counter-government for Poland. The Council of the *Homeland (Krajowa Rada Narodowa* or KRN) was known to be the quasi-parliament created by the communists in German-occupied Poland in competition with the "legitimate" Underground. With the establishment of the "Lublin Committee" on what the Soviets considered Polish territory, the Council was acting openly in the portions of the country wrested from the Germans. It is obvious that the "legitimate" Underground was not taking orders from *Radio Kosciuszko* or from the Soviet command or from the KRN. General Bor-Komorowski, former commander in chief of the Polish Underground and leader of the Warsaw uprising, puts the exhortations of *Radio Kosciuszko* in the proper perspective:

In principle, these calls were nothing new. Soviet propaganda had continually appealed to the Polish nation for a general uprising against the Germans. They had been addressed to the Poles even when the Red Army was not on the bank of the Vistula, but on the Dnieper . . .[9]

[9] T. Bor-Komorowski, *The Secret Army* (London, Victor Gollancz, Ltd., 1950), p. 212.

The Warsaw uprising was not a spontaneous act provoked by irresponsible exhortations of the Soviet radio, but the result of a deliberate decision of the leaders of the Polish Underground. The circumstances of its outbreak can be understood only against the background of the activities of the Underground throughout the war years. The Warsaw uprising was the culmination of a long series of actions and an even longer series of stillborn plans directed against the realities of Poland's unfortunate situation.

Under modern conditions of warfare, an open uprising of ill-armed and of necessity scattered forces of civilians and semi-civilians against a regular army is possible only as a harassing action against the rear guard of a retreating enemy, carried out preferably in coöperation with an advancing allied army. Essentially, the Warsaw uprising was conceived as just that: a short action against the Germans who were believed to be in full retreat. Even if successful, the uprising would have been a negligible contribution to the war effort against the Germans. Its motivation was not military, it was political. In this sense it was not at all directed against the Germans, but against the Russians. During the war it was awkward to admit this obvious fact and the "London" Poles denied harboring schemes directed against the Soviet Union. From the perspective of 1952 there seems to be retroactive merit in an early anti-Soviet attitude. Polish sources are not reluctant any more to reveal the fact that the Underground was less concerned with the Germans, who were believed doomed, than with the Russians whose emergence as victors in eastern Europe was viewed as a catastrophe for Poland.

An official history of the Polish Underground and its military-political activities has by now become available, in the form of a volume of almost a thousand pages published by a historical commission of the Polish army in exile.[10] Because of serious internal conflicts among the Poles in exile about the responsibility for the ill-fated uprising there is a tendency to reveal many hitherto unknown or underplayed details of the dramatic story.

[10] *Polskie sily Zbrojne w II Wojnie Swiatowej. Tom III. Armia Krajowa (Polish Armed Forces in World War II. Volume III. The Home Army)*, London, 1950. All quotations by permission of the General Sikorski Historical Institute, London.

It thus becomes clear how and under what circumstances the decision to stage the Warsaw uprising was reached. The following summary is based primarily on the official Polish record.

Early Plans. As early as November 1939, when the first nucleus of an Underground organization was being formed, the idea was accepted that at the proper time, in the last phase of the war, a general uprising would be staged in Poland in coördination with Poland's western Allies and with support from abroad. However, the Polish Underground was never permitted to work out its plans along these relatively simple lines. Very soon a complicating element appeared—the problem of Russia.

A 1940 version of the plan for a general uprising included quite prophetically the assumption that Germany and Russia would go to war. The likelihood of a Russian victory over the Germans was not seriously considered, but on the hypothetical assumption that the unlikely would happen, it was concluded that "it would be folly to oppose with arms an enemy who had proved so powerful as to defeat the German army." At best, it seemed possible to hold the line of the Vistula against a Soviet army moving westward.

After the German attack on Russia and the re-establishment of diplomatic relations, General Sikorski revised earlier instructions to the Underground and, in a message dated March 8, 1942, warned the leaders in occupied Poland that "any anti-Russian moves would be misunderstood in the West and considered as helping Hitler . . ." Sikorski at the time seems to have been quite optimistic about his newly established contacts with Stalin and he expected a Polish army, then in the process of formation in Russia, to appear in liberated Poland together with the Soviet troops. The task of the Underground was now defined as "proving organizational efficiency in taking over." In other words, the advancing Russians were to be impressed with the way the Poles could speedily take over administrative functions abandoned by the retreating Germans.

General Rowecki ("Grot"), then commanding officer of the military Underground, expressed dissatisfaction with the instructions from London. In his "Report No. 132," dated June 22, 1942, he voiced the conviction that in the case of a spectacular

Russian victory over the Germans there was "no possibility and no point" in bringing the military organization into the open. This, the general insisted, should be done only after "effective guarantees" had been obtained for Poland's independence and her prewar frontiers. As an example of "effective guarantees" the report suggested "a temporary military occupation of Poland by Anglo-American forces," an understandable and interesting but rather fantastic suggestion.[11]

Under certain conditions, General Rowecki argued, it might be possible to establish on part of Polish territory a "defensive redoubt" against the Russians, where local Polish forces would hold out while waiting for the Poles in exile and their western allies to rush to their assistance. "This," wrote the author of the report, "would help to reveal the ideological face of the western world. Either the West would offer us aid in our defense of freedom and then our chances of success are considerable, or it will side with Russia and then the prospects for the immediate future are negligible." Nevertheless, even if the struggle were hopeless, it could not be abandoned "because of our responsibility to future generations."

Impressed by the intensity of the anti-Russian feelings voiced by the leader of the Underground, General Sikorski held out in his reply the hope that during his forthcoming visit to Washington he would "pose the problem as forcefully as in London" where the British, while favoring "in principle" the idea of an Anglo-American occupation of Poland, considered the entire issue "premature." While aware that "everything depends on the configuration of forces at the proper moment," Sikorski nevertheless expressed the hope of "convincing Roosevelt of the necessity of solidarity and determination vis-à-vis Russia if the latter should aim at violating the sovereignty of Poland." He rejected the idea of Underground resistance to the Russians as "folly" and recommended the open use of the Underground detachments as a manifestation of Poland's sovereign rights. Wrote the general:

---

[11] In October 1943 the same idea was suggested to Cordell Hull by the Polish ambassador to Washington, Jan Ciechanowski. The Secretary of State expressed his "understanding" and there the matter rested. (Jan Ciechanowski, *Defeat in Victory*, Garden City, L.I.: Doubleday & Co., 1947, p. 217.)

One of the purposes of my trip [to Washington] is to win Roosevelt
for the fight against anarchy and communism in Europe by throwing
vast amounts of food, medical supplies and clothing on the (liberated)
continent. I have reasons to believe that this idea will be accepted . . .

It is difficult to judge whether General Sikorski was trying to
placate the Underground by holding out optimistic prospects of
an energetic Western intervention on behalf of Poland, or was
really convinced that such assistance could be obtained by threatening Roosevelt with the prospect of "communism and anarchy."
The President at that time concentrated on fighting Naziism, not
communism. There is no indication in the available documentation that during his visit to Washington Sikorski actually approached the issue in the way described in his dispatch.

The concept of a general uprising in Poland, based on a German collapse not matched by a quick Soviet advance, had to be
completely abandoned after Stalingrad. A substitute plan of several regional uprisings was then suggested to London on February 28, 1943. This action was to receive the code name "Burza"
(Tempest). The basic assumptions underlying the plan were
expressed earlier, on January 12, 1943, in a telegram to London in which it was stated that "almost the entire nation is convinced that Russia is our Enemy Number Two . . ." The actions
to be undertaken by the Underground against the Germans were
viewed as a political maneuver against the Russians. The report
of February 28, 1943 leaves no doubt on the score: "Should the
Russians enter Polish territory, an uprising against the Germans
will be carried out under any circumstances even if the Germans
are not ripe for it (i.e., not sufficiently weakened). I will start
the struggle sufficiently early to forestall the entry of the Russians . . ."

The success of the undertaking depended, in the opinion of
the commander of the Underground, on immediate support by
Polish troops from England and by "Anglo-Saxon detachments"
to be parachuted "mainly in the eastern part of the country . . .
as a visible symbol of coöperation of the Anglo-Saxon peoples
with us . . ." This was to come as a surprise to the Russians. The
exact purpose of the planned uprising is again revealed when the
leader of the Underground writes that "the outbreak of the up-

rising would be timed with the entrance of the Russians, not [geared to] the degree of decomposition of the Germans."

Under British pressure, the Polish government in London insisted that unfriendly acts against the Russians should be avoided at all cost. Meanwhile the Soviet Union broke off relations with the London government and in view of the new situation the Underground commander suggested (in June 1943) the rejection of the fiction that the Russians were entering Poland as allies. A few days after drafting his new plan, the commander, General Rowecki, was arrested by the Gestapo. He did not live to fight the Russians, as was his desire. A change occurred also in London, where Mikolajczyk succeeded General Sikorski as premier.

In view of the changes in the international situation caused by spectacular Russian victories and the delays in the opening of the second front, the new leader of the Underground army, General Bor-Komorowski, came to the conclusion (voiced in a message dated October 27, 1943) that "the Polish sword is a weak instrument and it will not be a decisive factor." It could be used only as a "demonstration." He pressed London for instructions. These instructions belatedly and quite unrealistically discussed the possibility of the eastern front being stabilized (by the resistance of the Germans to Russian advance) somewhere east of the borders of Poland while the Anglo-Americans, after having advanced deep into the European continent, would be in a position to offer air cover and direct aid to a Polish general uprising against the Germans. Of course, the actual march of events made the application of these instructions utterly impossible. General Bor-Komorowski admits in his memoirs that it was difficult (and he implies that it was impossible) for the Underground to make a wise decision; the best it could do was to fall back on a military-political demonstration of the will of the Polish people to remain independent of Russia.

Within the leadership of the Underground there was considerable dissatisfaction with the temporizing and unrealistic instructions from London. It was felt that the Polish Underground could not limit itself to "a few shots and a few diplomatic gestures." In particular, there was opposition to the idea that if no agreement were reached with the Soviets prior to their entry into Poland, the Underground army should remain underground. Soviet and communist propaganda were beginning to make serious inroads in the ranks of the Underground and it was deemed impossible to continue to hold 300,000 people under cover and without any clear purpose. Against the latest instructions from London, General Bor-Komorowski ordered the commanders of local and regional units to come into the open when the Russians appeared on the scene and thus "document the existence of Poland." At the same time, steps were taken to prepare a skeleton organization and a secret command which would continue to function clandestinely under the Soviet occupation.

The Abandoned Barrier. The trend of thinking of the Polish Underground in this period is further revealed by an abortive plan, known under the code name "Barrier." This was an attempt to coördinate Polish Underground action with the expected Anglo-American landing on the coast of France. The gist of the plan was to interfere, by sabotage and diversionary action, with German attempts to transfer a substantial number of troops from the eastern front to the west in the case of an allied invasion. The tragi-comic element of this plan is obvious: the official purpose of the second front was exactly the opposite of what the Poles planned to do; it was to *alleviate* German pressure on the Russian front! Of course, the Poles, once more trying to swim against the current, were interested in helping the advance of their eagerly expected allies, not that of the Russians. The official Polish account quotes a letter from the British Chiefs of Staff, dated March 26, 1943, in which "considerable interest" is expressed in the Polish plan. And again in the spring of 1944 some vague encouragement was offered to the Poles both by the British and by Eisenhower's headquarters, although when the time for the invasion approached, SHAEF insisted that Polish actions be postponed until "a critical stage" in the invasion were reached. In July 1944 the Poles in London were officially informed by the British that no action was being taken on the inter-allied level to carry out the "Barrier" plan. The entire scheme was, from a western point of view, just too obviously embarrassing. It had to be abandoned.

As the fateful year 1944 rolled on, the British developed renewed interest in the activities of the Underground, apparently
because Churchill believed that the Russians could be impressed
with the value of the Polish contribution in fighting the Germans. Within the Polish government-in-exile two tendencies appeared. Mikolajczyk and others decided to base their hopes on
the diplomatic support which they expected from the West; General Sosnkowski and his followers, on the other hand, argued
that there was no point in showing good will toward the Russians
unless they were prepared first to renew relations with the London government and recognize Poland's prewar frontiers. Very
soon the Underground would be receiving contradictory orders
and information. General Bor-Komorowski, as we know, accepted
the view that all that remained for the Polish Underground to do
was to stress its willingness to fight the Germans and thus
demonstrate to the world "Poland's right to be independent."
The *Burza* actions, undertaken regionally as the Germans retreated through Polish territory, were to serve this purpose. The
records show that, with the exception of fragmentary coöperation on the lower level, the Soviets ignored the Polish attempt to
impress Stalin with their fighting contribution. Almost all groups
participating in the *Burza* were sooner or later rounded up, disarmed, and dispersed or arrested and frequently deported by the
Russians.

The Problem of Warsaw: To Fight or Not to Fight? In the
summer of 1944 the front was moving westward through Polish
territory and it soon became apparent that a decision would have
to be taken in regard to Warsaw, whose capture by the Russians
seemed imminent. What General Bor-Komorowski feared most
was the possibility (discussed in a message to London, July 14,
1944) that the Russians were preparing an uprising under the
ostensible leadership of the Polish Workers' (Communist) Party.
They expected, he wrote, that

The Polish people, tired of the German occupation and desirous of
revenge, will fly to arms . . . Soviet aims may thus succeed unless we
oppose to their plan our own action . . . Should the Soviet plan succeed, Poland will have created the appearance of being willing to cooperate with the Soviets and submit to them . . .

Did the Soviet command want an uprising in Warsaw? The nature of the appeals made by *Radio Kosciuszko* shows what kind of uprising the Russians wanted: one that could be credited to the forces of the People's Army (*Armia Ludowa,* the pro-Soviet counterpart of the AK) and to the political influence of the pro-Soviet KRN. General Anders, in his book *An Army in Exile,* published in London in 1949, evaluates quite correctly this political objective of the Russians:

> to bring about a rising that would be directed by Communist elements, so that, taking advantage of the hatred felt by all Poles toward the Germans, they could create the impression that the population of the capital welcomed the Russians as liberators and accepted the Lublin Committee as their own Government authorities.

The Russian exhortations were interpreted in the same way by the leaders of the "legitimate" Underground. Their situation was extremely difficult. One of the strongest weapons used by communist and Soviet propaganda against the "legitimate" Underground was the accusation of inactivity. Committed to wait for the "sign from the West" the Underground indeed preached the doctrine of "watchful preparedness" for the big decisive event. Now the big event was there; the Germans were being pushed out of Poland, but under circumstances that made large-scale action by the "legitimate" Underground impossible. Scattered units that went into action against the Germans in eastern Poland were rounded up by the Soviet army and disarmed or forcibly incorporated into the Polish units of General Berling accompanying the advancing Red Army. What remained under the circumstances was the possibility of a military demonstration in Warsaw, limited to a few days' fighting against the rear guards of the retreating Germans, and directed politically against the Russians. Had the forces of the *Armia Krajowa* been able to wrest Warsaw from the Germans and hold it long enough to hoist the Polish flag over the capital (or long enough for some or all members of the government-in-exile to arrive by plane from London and install themselves), this would have put the Russians—in the opinion of the political strategists of the Underground—in an embarrassing situation. *"By offering the Soviets a minimum of military assistance, we create political difficulties for them,"* General Bor-Komorowski wrote in a secret report to London. They would then have either to recognize the situation, drop their own counter-government and renew relations with the "London" government, or liquidate by force the "legitimate" Polish government in liberated Warsaw, a step that would no doubt—again in the hopes of the Underground—cause a determined reaction in the West.

That such was indeed the line of thinking of the Underground is confirmed most authentically by the memoirs of the commander-in-chief of the AK. "We hoped," writes General Bor-Komorowski, "that in our precarious situation, the Home Army battle for Warsaw would raise an echo all over the world."

"Twelve Hours." How the exact time was chosen for the Warsaw uprising is clear from the official Polish record and from Bor-Komorowski's memoirs. A combination of many factors contributed to the decision. The Soviet offensive was making rapid strides and covered some 300 miles in three weeks. There was the likelihood that "the front would bypass Warsaw earlier than expected." On July 20 the world learned of an attempt on Hitler's life and the possibility of total German collapse was seriously entertained by the Polish Underground. The Underground command decided that it was important that the Russian armies entering Warsaw should find the capital in Polish hands, controlled and administered by the "legitimate" groups who would graciously act as hosts. The problem was put to the Underground "parliament" which agreed that it was "absolutely necessary that Warsaw should be liberated by the Home Army before the Russians should capture the city." Asked what period of time they thought should elapse between "our gaining control of the city" and the entry of Soviet troops, the "parliament" replied that "at least twelve hours would be desirable in order to enable the administrative organs to get together and come out in their full part of host to receive the entering Soviet armies." [12]

In London, Premier Mikolajczyk was then preparing to go to

12 Bor-Komorowski, *The Secret Army*, p. 205. Zbigniew Stypulkowski, author of *Invitation to Moscow* (London, 1951) and a former Underground leader, claims that the "parliament" was not consulted. It seems that there

Moscow. Before his departure, according to the official account published by the Poles, he told the Minister of the Interior to transmit to Bor-Komorowski in Warsaw a decision taken by the Polish government-in-exile to authorize the leader of the Underground to order an uprising at the time chosen by him. The official Polish historian comments: "The Premier, who was about to leave for Moscow, saw in the military effort of the country directed against the Germans a strong argument in support of his talks with the Soviet government." This was also Churchill's stated position.

Mikolajczyk himself considered it necessary to state in his book that as he flew en route to Moscow he "knew nothing of these developments." There is one weak point in this alibi. While Mikolajczyk was flying to Moscow there were no "developments" he could have knowledge of. He arrived in Moscow, as he states, late on July 30, but the uprising broke out two days *later,* on the afternoon of August 1. According to some accounts he informed Stalin and Molotov of the impending uprising; according to others, he had told the British about it before leaving London.

The evaluation by the Underground of the actual situation on the front was of decisive importance because of the need to gauge correctly the "twelve hours" which were necessary for the action against German rear guards to be utilized politically against the Russians. General Bor-Komorowski seems to have concluded somewhat prematurely that the Germans had neither sufficient strength nor reserves to stem the Soviet advance. It is true that in the last days of July 1944 there were signs of panic and collapse among the Germans, but efforts were made to stop the Soviet advance across the Vistula. At one point the leaders

---

is only a slight contradiction between both versions. The full Council was indeed not consulted, only a smaller body, its presidium (*Komisja Glowna*), which was authorized to take emergency decisions. However, Stypulkowski insists that the full Council had decided two days earlier that "the time was not ripe and that premature action would prove fatal." In the same sense, General Sosnkowski, then in Italy, urged President Raczkiewicz to countermand the orders for the "senseless" uprising and to return to the old idea of continuing to keep the army underground.

of the Underground noticed that German armor—at least two well-equipped armored divisions—began to move east, toward the front, rather than west, the direction of the retreat. But apparently it was too late to call off the uprising because Warsaw was seething with excitement and was, in the words of General Bor-Komorowski, like a powder magazine where any spark could provoke an explosion. The "official" Underground could not afford to let pro-Soviet elements claim credit for the explosion, although it was known, from the observation of the German moves, that instead of undertaking a token action against a demoralized German army, Warsaw would become engaged in a heavy battle. The exhortations of the Soviet radio, the official Polish account states, "had no decisive influence"; however, the command of the Underground was interpreting the growing urgency of the Russian appeals as a sign that Warsaw was to be stormed soon. The "twelve hours" deemed necessary to hoist the Polish flag had to be timed correctly.

The "twelve hours" were to last sixty-three days.

It is impossible to recount here in detail the military history of the ill-fated uprising. After initial successes against isolated German positions, the Polish attack lost momentum and on the fourth day of the uprising the command ordered a shift from offensive to defensive action. Against heavy odds, sections of the city were held because of the hope that somehow it would be possible to outlast the Germans and thus still have five minutes, if not twelve hours, in which to hoist the Polish flag over the battered city and embarrass the incoming Russians. The possibility of capitulation was discussed early in September, but then the ominously silent Soviet front across the river from Warsaw suddenly flared up and an all-out Soviet offensive was expected at any moment. Having staged an uprising directed politically against the plans of the Russians, the defenders of Warsaw, plagued by hunger and disease, now pinned their hopes on the imminent capture of the city by the Russians as the only way of delivery from their incredible sufferings. The complete hopelessness of this infuriating prospect, and the wrath which it generated in many of those engaged in the uprising are best expressed in a poem written in dying Warsaw. It begins:

> We are waiting for thee, red pest,
> to deliver us from black death . . .

and it goes on:

> . . .
>
> If you could only know, O, hated savior,
> the kind of death we wish on you,
> while helplessly we wring our hands,
> begging your assistance—red hangman! . . .[13]

If this be considered an authentic expression of the frame of mind of the Warsaw insurgents—and it seems to be—then the entire undertaking was indeed what one of the Underground leaders, Stypulkowski, believes it to have been: a manifestation of the determination of Poles "to commit any folly in defense of their freedom and independence," a return to the tradition of the futile Polish uprisings of the nineteenth century.

The Warsaw Uprising has been described as "a glorious failure" and likened to another uprising in the Polish capital— the Ghetto Uprising of April 1943, staged by the doomed remnants of the Jewish population in the face of Nazi orders to liquidate the Ghetto completely. American readers are by now familiar with the Ghetto uprising through a remarkable fictionalized account by John Hersey, in *The Wall*. Politically speaking, it is probably a dubious compliment for the uprising of August 1944 to be likened to that of April 1943. The latter was a desperate gesture of some fifty thousand people whose fate was sealed and who could only obtain the satisfaction of dying in combat rather than undergoing the process of "scientific" extermination in gas chambers applied by the Germans to the bulk of Poland's Jewish population. The leaders of the Warsaw Ghetto were not thinking in political terms; they were under no obligation to make sense, except for the heroic sense of an honorable death. It is questionable whether the representatives of a nation of over twenty million people—and the leaders of the Warsaw Uprising no doubt believed that they were acting in

---

[13] The poem was written by "Ensign Ziutek" (pseudonym). The quoted excerpts are translated by the author of this book from a Polish text broadcast on September 29, 1950 by the *Voice of America*.

the name of Poland—have the "right" to think in such terms. It is the duty of a nation to try to live, to survive; it is under no obligation to attempt suicide periodically.

The fact that the Poles engaged in a militarily hopeless and politically provocative uprising does not, of course, change the human side of the Warsaw story. It was generally felt that whether or not the Russian army was stopped at the very gates of Warsaw, as the official Soviet version claims, the refusal of the Russians to come to the assistance of the uprising or even to permit Western planes to use Soviet shuttle bases, demonstrated what Stalin's biographer, Isaac Deutscher, described as "unscrupulous rancor and insensible spite," combined with "cynical calculations showing extreme callousness and disregard of the opinion of the civilized world."

The "civilized world" of necessity measured its exertions on behalf of the Polish insurgents very carefully against the availability of planes and pilots; the needs of Warsaw were apparently low in the hierarchy of priorities. Nor is it quite correct that no aid at all was given to the uprising by the Russians, no matter how they felt about it and what their ulterior motives were.

Western and Eastern Aid. The official Polish account offers detailed statistical figures as well as some revealing background information on the subject of Western aid for the Polish Underground in general and the Warsaw Uprising in particular. The British insisted that all acquisitions of material abroad should be channeled through them and intervened energetically whenever a special Polish mission attempted to make direct purchases or otherwise obtain material in the United States. The British were informed in advance about the plans for the Warsaw Uprising. Mikolajczyk told Churchill that the Underground army had been alerted as of July 25. On July 27 the government-in-exile notified Foreign Secretary Eden of the impending outbreak and officially requested the dispatching of a parachute brigade to Warsaw and the bombardment, by the R.A.F., of German airfields near the Polish capital. Eden expressed doubts that it could be done and thought that the Americans, who had long-range super-bombers, should be approached. The negative answer of the British government was officially communicated to the Poles on July 28. Allied

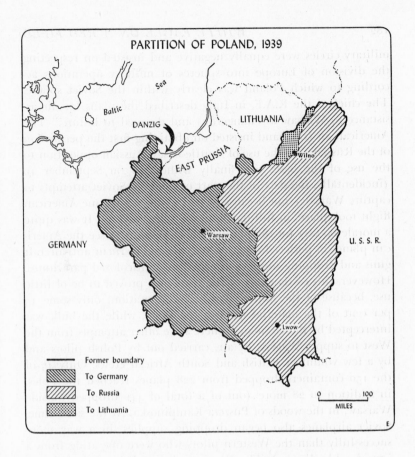

PARTITION OF POLAND, 1939

POLAND: BASIC FIGURES

	1939	*1950*
Area	150,052 sq. m.	121,131 sq. m.
Population	35,339,000 (est.)	24,976,926 (census Dec. 1950)

Population of Major Cities

Warsaw	1,289,000 (est.)	650,000 (census 1950)
Lodz	672,000	619,914
Lwow	318,000	(ceded to USSR)
Poznan	272,000	320,000
Krakow	259,000	330,046
Wroclaw [Breslau]	(belonged to Germany)	289,734

military circles were equally negative and insisted on respecting the division of Europe into spheres of military operations according to which Poland was clearly within the Soviet sphere. The chief of the R.A.F. in Italy described the plans for air assistance to Warsaw as "dangerous and doomed to failure." The American air command insisted on obtaining first the permission of the Russians for the use of shuttle bases. Russian opposition to the use of the bases was finally withdrawn on September 10 (incidentally, the date of the start of renewed Soviet attempts to capture Warsaw) but because of bad weather only one American flight took place, in full daylight, on September 18. It was quite a morale booster for the population of Warsaw to see the American planes in perfect formation defying the German anti-aircraft guns and dropping supplies attached to multicolored parachutes. However, this costly effort of the Air Force proved to be of little use, because of the imprecision of the operation; only some 15 per cent of the material reached the Poles, while the bulk was intercepted by the Germans. There were other attempts from the West to supply Warsaw by air, carried out by Polish pilots and by a few volunteer British and South African crews. Only 45 of the 150 containers dropped from 228 planes reached the Poles, in addition to 28 more (out of a total of 44) dropped outside Warsaw, in the woods of Puszcza Kampinoska. At the same time, Soviet airplanes also began dropping supplies, in a way more successfully than the Western pilots who were operating from a considerable distance. The Russians dropped, in twelve nightly operations, a total of 50 to 55 tons of supplies, as against some 104 tons from the West. Most of the material dropped by the Russians reached the Poles but, since the Red air force used no parachutes, the supplies were often either damaged or completely destroyed.

What the Russian plans were is not quite clear. They seem to have hesitated between attempts to take the city and other calculations, military as well as political. Stalin at first tried to deny that an uprising was taking place in Warsaw, then began to berate the leaders of the uprising as "provocateurs," and finally promised aid which, however, materialized only when the Soviet offensive flared up again for a few days. It is a fact that at the time the

Russian advance was stopped all along the huge front line—with the exception of the Rumanian sector—and not only at the gates of Warsaw. On several occasions attempts were made by isolated Russian units (and also units of the so-called Berling Army of Poles from Russia commanded by Russian officers) to cross the Vistula, but no large-scale action was taken. According to an official account, published in Warsaw, the Berling army suffered 2500 casualties in dead and wounded while trying to cross the Vistula. Warsaw, or the ruins of what had been Warsaw, was not captured until January 1945, in the course of the final winter offensive undertaken by the Russians.[14]

After the liquidation of the Uprising, the bitterness of the Poles, especially among the soldiers of the Anders army in Italy, was directed mainly against the West. An order of the day issued by General Sosnkowski even before the capitulation of Warsaw put the blame squarely on the British, mentioned the losses suffered by Polish airmen in the Battle of Britain, and even considered it necessary to point out that the Poles had been "encouraged by the British government" to take up their resistance to the Germans in 1939. The behavior of the West was described as "a tragic and ghastly riddle" in Sosnkowski's order of the day.

[14] In an estimate of the military situation written after the collapse of the Warsaw Uprising, General Okulicki, Bor-Komorowski's successor to the Underground command, concluded that an all-out Soviet offensive aiming at Berlin was unlikely before the elimination of German resistance on the flanks, in East Prussia and Hungary. The same conclusion, it may be said, could have been reached before the uprising. Chester Wilmot writes in *The Struggle for Europe* (New York: Harper, 1952): "There were cogent reasons of Soviet grand strategy which made it necessary for the Russians to pause on the Vistula . . . The time had come for the Red Army to make the masterstroke of its summer campaign in the extreme south . . ." (p. 437). To say that "the Red Army *by-passed Warsaw*," as Philip Selznick claims (*The Organizational Weapon*, A Study of Bolshevik Strategy and Tactics, New York: McGraw-Hill, 1952, p. 233), is, in the light of the record, inaccurate. Selznick uses the Soviet attitude toward the Warsaw Uprising as an example of "cynical willingness to annihilate organizational rivals" (p. 232). Arthur Bliss Lane records a statement made by an unidentified Polish communist to a "prominent American visitor" in 1946 to the effect that if Bor-Komorowski and his army had succeeded in liberating Warsaw, they would have "formed the nucleus of the government within Poland" and "it would have been most difficult under such circumstances for the Soviet Government to maintain in power the Lublin Committee." (*I Saw Poland Betrayed*, p. 304.) Difficult, perhaps, but certainly not impossible.

The order was frowned upon by the British and it was disavowed by the government-in-exile.

End of the Underground State. After the collapse of the Warsaw Uprising the Polish Underground entered a period of protracted liquidation. German propaganda attempted to capitalize on the emotions of the Poles who felt deceived by the Russians and betrayed by the West, but it achieved only moderate success. A relatively small group of the Underground connected with the extreme right wing, the so-called Brygada Swietokrzyska, more or less officially joined the Germans in order to fight jointly the Bolsheviks. The official Polish account estimates that the group consisted of no more than a few hundred soldiers.[15] The new military commander of the Underground, General Okulicki, who replaced General Bor-Komorowski, now taken prisoner by the Germans, revised the basic concepts of the Polish military effort. His analysis of the situation, transmitted to London, reflected the feeling of frustration which gripped the Poles, a mood similar to the recurrent post-insurrection blues of the nineteenth century. In a report, dated October 26, 1944, General Okulicki stated that the political aim of the Warsaw Uprising—to show to the world "the will of the nation to live independently and not under Soviet tutelage"—was by now clear to the "Anglo-Saxons" who alone were capable of undertaking anything against the Soviet menace. There was no need for further spectacular exertions of the Poles against the beaten Germans; the fighting should be directed so as to *make the maximum of noise on the international scene* while suffering a minimum of losses.[16] This line of thinking was known among Poles in exile as a "Czech" line. Throughout the war years, many Poles envied the Czechs who had managed to wring a maximum of propaganda advantages out of the limited incident of elimination by the Germans of the male population of

---

[15] Apologists for the "Brygada" state that it never fought together with the Germans and was merely trying to break through to the West. It was pointed out by one member of the Brygada that the American military authorities in Germany, after investigating thoroughly the case in the second half of 1945, decided to hire detachments of the Brygada to be used as semi-military guards. (W. Zbik-Kaniewski, in a letter to the editor, *Kultura*, Paris, No. 6/44, June 1951.)

[16] Polskie Sily Zbrojne, III, 912.

the village of Lidice, while the Poles, with hundreds of "Lidices" and hundreds of thousands of victims never quite succeeded in stirring the sympathies of the world.

General Okulicki's frame of mind is revealed in a letter which was found among his papers when he was arrested early in 1945 by the Russians after having been tricked into "negotiations":

Until Japan is defeated [wrote the General in a circular letter to his subordinates], we cannot expect any improvement in our political situation. The Western world will try to obtain Russia's help in the struggle for the Far East, and will be inclined to make further concessions for this. Later they will see how much Soviet greed and power will become a menace . . . The Anglo-Saxons will have to mobilize all their forces in Europe to enable them to halt the Soviets. We shall then come to the front in the defense line, and we shall probably even see some Germans there who will be under Anglo-Saxon command . . .[17]

This letter was used by the Soviet prosecutor as evidence of the general's alleged collaboration with the Germans. Of course, Okulicki was merely engaged in prophecies, and quite correct prophecies, too. However, one might argue that the business of an Underground commander is not to be right about the future, but to do something that makes sense in the immediate situation. Apart from recommending "a maximum of noise," he quite understandably had nothing to suggest.

In this last period of the Underground State, and for no clear purpose, the British government suddenly dispatched, late in 1944, a military mission commanded by one Colonel Hudson, to what remained of the Polish Underground army. The mission soon found itself in territory occupied by the Russians and was discreetly returned to England via Moscow. With the capture of Warsaw by the Russians, on orders from London the Underground army was to be officially dissolved while all weapons were to be hidden. Some detachments refused to obey the order and continued to operate from the forests, this time openly against the Russians and the new Russian-backed Polish government. In the chaos of the early postwar situation the Underground developed, as all illegal movements are likely to, a lunatic and criminal fringe. Determined police action, amnesty, an urge to return to

[17] Quoted in Stypulkowski, *Invitation to Moscow*, p. 317.

normal life, lack of an immediate political goal, and, last but not least, interruption of the flow of money and supplies from the West as a result of the de-recognition of the government-in-exile, reduced the activities of the Underground. It began to wither away, after a series of terroristic acts directed against the functionaries of the new ruling group and, incidentally, including violence against the small number of surviving Jews.[18] Early in 1947 a *New York Times* correspondent reported from Poland that "only a nucleus of diehards will remain in the hills to the end, prepared to die violently, rather than have anything to do with rebuilding the country under its present regime." Some recrudescence of isolated activities directed against the present government has been reported since 1949, but it does not add, on the evidence available, to an organized resistance movement.

[18] Some acts of violence against surviving Jews were apparently spontaneous reactions of people who had acquired, in one way or another, the property of their former Jewish neighbors and were loath to lose it. The feeling that Jews were outside the law became universal as a result of the behavior of the Germans during the war.

IV. From National Unity to "People's Republic"

In the Soviet Orbit. What has happened to Poland as a result of the way World War II was fought and won amounts to a revolution. This fact was to some extent obscured, not only by expectations that the end of the war would bring a restitution of the prewar situation or only a slight change, but also because of the relatively smooth course of the revolution, its institutionalized character, its occurrence "from above," and, in the initial stages, largely within the framework of international agreement.

As a result of World War II the Polish state has, one might say, traveled far. It has "traveled" literally, with the remarkable shift in its frontiers. It has moved a long distance from the position of an extensive buffer between Germany and Russia, endowed with the mission of holding the balance between these two Powers and keeping them apart. Its present political, social, and economic order is rapidly losing every resemblance to the conditions of the interwar period. What made this striking development possible? The main cause must be sought in the changed balance of forces in Europe, a result of the military victory of the Soviet Union.

The accommodating attitude of Russia's western Allies did not, as is sometimes claimed, create the present situation. It merely made it "legal." This aspect of the problem, the diplomatic game in which the fate of Poland was decided as a by-product of larger issues, is discussed elsewhere in the volume, mainly from the point of view of American participation.[1] The present chapter deals primarily with developments inside Poland.

The Postwar Regime. Prehistory. The postwar regime of Poland was built essentially around an organizational nucleus which the Polish communists, no doubt under Soviet guidance, began to form quite early in the war, both in German-occupied Poland and

[1] See pp. 285–307.

among Poles who took refuge in or were deported to Russia. One is tempted to describe this early organization as a potential "counter-government" created by the Soviet Union as part of a deliberate plan for the postwar period. Some students of the problem feel that this would be giving Stalin too much credit for advance planning. However, one thing is certain: the availability of a "counter-government" became a useful element in the bargaining position of the Soviet Union and, on occasions, a convenient vehicle for *faits accomplis.*

In Soviet-occupied Lwow, in 1940, a group of communist and fellow-traveling writers and scholars began to publish a Polish-language monthly, *Nowe Widnokregi* (New Horizons). It was preaching, in Polish, Soviet patriotism. With the outbreak of German-Soviet hostilities the group had the advantage of being eligible for collective and relatively comfortable eastward evacuation, although because of the weird ways of NKVD bureaucracy some of the communist and pro-communist writers found themselves, at least temporarily, in various Soviet jails.

The publication of *Nowe Widnokregi* was resumed in the winter of 1941–42, after the first military successes of the Soviet army over the Germans made political planning for the postwar period appear both possible and necessary, from the Soviet point of view. The editor of the monthly was Wanda Wasilewska, a fairly well-known writer in prewar Poland, formally a socialist but with strong pro-communist sympathies, and, incidentally, the daughter of the late Leon Wasilewski, a Polish socialist who took a prominent part in negotiating the Riga treaty with the Bolsheviks. Officially, the Soviet government had resumed relations with the Polish government-in-exile and it had even permitted the recruitment, under General Wladyslaw Anders, of a Polish military force among prisoners of war and deportees in the USSR. At the same time, however, the writers grouped around Wasilewska began a systematic propaganda campaign against the "fascist and reactionary" elements in the London government.

In March 1943, when the break between the Soviet government and the Poles in exile was about to take place, a new political group, called *Union of Polish Patriots,* came into existence and a new publication, *Wolna Polska,* (Free Poland), was started. It preached Polish-Soviet friendship, and advocated the creation of Polish military units to fight for the liberation of the homeland side by side with the Soviet army (the Anders army was evacuated to the Middle East after it became clear that Stalin was determined not to allow it to become a strong and autonomous force and when the Poles refused to agree to a plan of sending their forces in separate units to the front). When relations with the London Poles were broken, ostensibly over the issue of the Katyn massacre,[2] in April 1943, the Soviet government had in the *Union of Polish Patriots* a body ready and willing to endorse Soviet moves against the "reactionaries of London," including the demands for recognition of the Soviet acquisition of what had been, in the interwar period, eastern Poland. Two Polish divisions were created by enlisting volunteers who had refused to join the Anders army or were refused by it, and by conscription of Polish deportees in Russia. These divisions, known as the "Berling army," from the name of Zygmunt Berling, a career officer of the Polish army who broke with Anders, could claim that by fighting alongside the Soviet army they were taking the shortest route to a liberated Poland. Because of the shortage of Polish officers, a considerable part of the officers' corps was made up of Russians, although some attempt apparently was made to appoint Soviet officers who claimed Polish origin or had (or assumed?) Polish-sounding names.

Even before the Red army began its westward advance, efforts were initiated to create, in addition to the nucleus of counter-government operating on Russian soil, an Underground organization in Poland competing for the allegiance of the Poles with the "legitimate" or London-controlled Underground. The Polish Communist Party, rent by police infiltration and Trotsky-ite deviations, had been officially dissolved since 1938. During the period of Nazi-Soviet "friendship" the field for communist activities was not very propitious in occupied Poland. This situation changed radically with the outbreak of the German-Soviet war in June 1941. In accordance with the strategy which eventually crystallized in the concept of People's or New Democracy, the communists organized, in late 1941, a new party under the name

[2] See pp. 291–293.

of *Polish Workers' Party* (PPR). The party attempted to duplicate the propaganda effort of the "legitimate" Underground and engaged in, or claimed credit for, sabotage acts against the Germans. Its slogans, in accordance with the tactical requirements of the time, were of a broadly national and vaguely democratic nature. A considerable part of the propaganda effort went into stressing Slav solidarity against the hereditary Teutonic enemy, preaching the acquisition of German territory (presented as "return" to the Poland of the Piasts), and, at least implicitly, justifying the cession of the eastern half of interwar Poland to the Soviet Union, as the price of security and lasting friendship. Together with other small groups, which for a variety of reasons were opposed to the London-controlled "legitimate" Underground, the Polish Workers' Party created, on January 1, 1944, a political body called *National Council of the Homeland* (*Krajowa Rada Narodowa*), a shadow parliament presided over by Boleslaw Bierut ("Comrade Tomasz"), who was reputedly a Comintern agent with a record of imprisonment in interwar Poland for communist activities. This body, known as KRN, was to compete with a similar institution, the Council of National Unity (RJN), set up by the "legitimate" Underground as its clandestine "Parliament" in German-occupied Poland. None of the Underground bodies were based on anything approximating popular elections and it is therefore largely pointless to figure out what percentage of the population this or that organization represented. The popular basis of the pro-Soviet Underground was admittedly narrower than that of its "legitimate" counterpart. Wladyslaw Gomulka, wartime secretary general of the Polish Workers' Party, later accused of deviationism, admitted in one of his apologias that in spite of the impressive-sounding list of names of organizations under the first manifesto of the KRN, few authentic groups outside the Communist Party under its new guise had joined the pro-Soviet body. However, that organization had the advantage of ties with the army that eventually entered Poland. Therefore the problem of its "authenticity" became irrelevant; it was a revolutionary organization and, like all revolutionary bodies, derived its mandate from the ability to seize power (or to be installed in power by the Red army) and to convert its own decisions into the law of the land. Thus the KRN later became the governing body of postwar Poland; foreign ambassadors were accredited to the "obscure Mr. Bierut" functioning as president *pro tempore* of Poland, until his formal election in 1947.

When the Soviet army was about to cross into what, in Stalin's view, was indisputably Polish territory, the KRN established contact with the Union of Polish Patriots functioning in Russia. The two organizations jointly formed the *Polish Committee of National Liberation* (known as PKWN, initials of its name in Polish). On July 22, 1944 the new Committee, gathered in the town of Chelm, issued a statement of policy, known in the terminology of postwar Poland as the July Manifesto. Shortly thereafter the Committee moved to Lublin, and became known as the "Lublin Committee." Formally, the Committee was created by a decree of the KRN which assumed legislative power. A few days after the establishment of the Committee, the Soviet government signed an agreement, transferring to the Committee the civil administration of liberated Polish territories. All these moves were made on the eve of negotiations with Churchill and of the expected visit in Moscow of Stanislaw Mikolajczyk, then still premier of the government-in-exile. The same technique, of creating a *fait accompli*, was used by the Russians a few months later, on the eve of the Yalta conference: On December 31, 1944 the KRN decreed the transformation of the "Lublin Committee" into a Provisional Government. With the capture of Warsaw in January 1945 the new Provisional Government was able to establish itself in the ruins of the capital. It formed, after Yalta, the basis for the creation of the "new" government of National Unity which, by the adherence of Stanislaw Mikolajczyk, was to become acceptable to the West.

Mikolajczyk and "National Unity." The role played by Stanislaw Mikolajczyk in precipitating a crisis among the Poles in exile by acting as "a reasonable Pole" and thus facilitating the erection of the façade of "national unity" deserves some detailed attention. Mikolajczyk was one of the youngest and no doubt one of the most ambitious Polish politicians in exile. He was known in the last decade of the interwar period, first as a regional and then as a national leader of the Peasant Party, representing the more conservative wing of that party, in accordance with the general mood of the province of Poznan, his political bailiwick (he was born in western Germany, the son of an emigrant who later returned to his native Poland). In the government-in-exile he first served as Minister of the Interior under General Sikorski. His ministry was on occasions accused by Poles in exile of maintaining a virtual monopoly of contacts and information with the Underground which, it was charged, was used to the advantage of Mikolajczyk's own party and for the building up of his personal prestige. When Sikorski died in a plane accident in 1943 (foul play was rumored among the Poles in exile, but it was never made sufficiently clear who was interested in removing Sikorski: the British, the Russians, or irreconcilable Poles), Mikolajczyk became prime minister.

The appointment "made a bad impression among the Poles in Great Britain," the die-hard General Anders relates in his book. However, it made a good impression with the governments of the United States and Great Britain, especially with the latter. Quite adroit in maneuvering within the limited field of Polish politics in exile, Mikolajczyk was always impressed by the leaders of the West and invariably followed what they told him to do. He apparently maintained for a long time optimistic illusions based on the friendly, though vague, assurances given by President Roosevelt. He was exposed, according to his own account, to Churchill's rantings and almost indecent pressure for agreement to the Russian demands. The British prime minister at the time claimed to operate on the assumption that the independence of Poland could be salvaged if only the Poles would agree to the Curzon Line as frontier with the Soviet Union. At any rate, this was the view he expounded in public utterances and in private discussions with the Polish premier-in-exile. Another favorite argument with which he tried to impress Mikolajczyk was constant reference to the fact that the British ambassador and the ambassador from the United States would always be at Mikolajczyk's side to support him if he should go to Poland. Mr. Churchill went even so far as to "promise" Mikolajczyk a big American loan, "possibly without interest." [3]

[3] Stanislaw Mikolajczyk, *The Rape of Poland: Pattern of Soviet Aggression* (New York: Whittlesey House, 1948), p. 98.

Some of the harsher epithets used by Mr. Churchill in a conversation with Mikolajczyk, and related by the latter, are worth noting, not only as an expression of what the prime minister felt about his London protegés, but also as an indication of how much the Polish premier was able to take from his host:

You're no government . . . You're a callous people who want to wreck Europe. I shall leave you to your own troubles . . . You have only miserable, petty, selfish interests in mind . . . If you want to conquer Russia, we shall let you go your own way. . . . You ought to be in a lunatic asylum . . .[4]

The result of this dramatic encounter was Mikolajczyk's decision to suggest to his government the acceptance of the Curzon Line, after half-hearted efforts to secure American good offices in obtaining Soviet agreement to leave Lwow and the oil fields of Galicia within Poland. Mikolajczyk understood the situation quite well. In a message to the Underground he said: "In the matter of our eastern frontier we have against us *a united Anglo-Soviet front with the United States adopting a passive attitude.*" However, he believed in the importance of accepting the Soviet frontier demands before the entire territory of Poland was liberated and the "Lublin Committee" recognized by all allied Powers as government *de facto* of Poland.

The Polish government-in-exile refused to share this point of view. It considered it more advisable to stand on the principle of inviolability of Poland's prewar frontiers. In view of the attitude taken by the British (and the tacit concurrence of the American government in Churchill's views), the Polish government in London was becoming a serious handicap in relations with Russia. At this point Mikolajczyk agreed to serve as the instrument for splitting the Poles in exile. He resigned the premiership, and his party (with the exception of a group of rebels) accepted the Curzon Line as the basis for a territorial settlement with Russia. Although now a private citizen, Mikolajczyk had ready access to Churchill and Eden while the government-in-exile, reorganized under the leadership of the elderly socialist Arciszewski, was being increasingly ignored and left to wait for the inevitable de-recognition. Mikolajczyk's resignation certainly made the position

[4] *Ibid.*

of the Poles in exile more difficult, but it helped the British who, in the words of General Anders, obtained "Mikolajczyk's connivance" in the decisions made at Teheran. The General is rather blunt about it: "The departure of Mr. Mikolajczyk had, in fact, opened a way by which Britain and the United States could betray the lawful Government of Poland." [5]

This first occasion on which Mikolajczyk agreed to act in accordance with the wishes of the British and in opposition to the Polish group with which he had been connected throughout the war increased the hostility of certain Poles in exile toward the peasant leader but endeared him to Mr. Churchill who lavished on Mikolajczyk the compliment that he was "the only light that burns for Poland."

During and after the Yalta negotiations the representatives of the Western Powers were able to use the name of Stanislaw Mikolajczyk as that of a "reasonable" Pole who should be invited to participate in a government of "national unity." Although Mikolajczyk's own account of the post-Yalta period makes it appear that he was pessimistic about the Yalta agreement and reluctant to join the new government, this is not quite borne out by the record. His party's publication, *Jutro Polski,* issued with the blessing of the British in London, was enthusiastic about Yalta. The ex-premier was waiting impatiently in London for an invitation to join the negotiations in Moscow for the creation of a "new" Polish government. When warned by General Anders that his stand was tantamount to an endorsement of a new partition of Poland for which "our generation and those to come will curse you," Mikolajczyk echoed faithfully Churchill's views by explaining to the General that: (a) in exchange for the concessions in the East, Poland would be compensated by territory reaching to the Oder; (b) Stalin was interested in a strong Poland. He expressed the opinion that free elections, carried out under Allied supervision, "will prove the great support I have in Poland." In his own opinion he, Mikolajczyk, had more to offer to Stalin than the puppets of the Lublin Committee, something that the realist in the Kremlin would not fail to recognize. Dur-

[5] Wladyslaw Anders, *An Army in Exile* (London: Macmillan & Co., 1949), p. 244.

ing his short tenure in Poland, Mikolajczyk tried to present the same view in a memorandum to Stalin, without ever receiving an answer.

According to Mikolajczyk's own testimony, his decision to join the government created as a result of the Yalta agreement was "prompted by two meetings with Churchill." The prime minister once more combined persuasion with threats of "washing his hands" of the Polish case. There is, in Mikolajczyk's book, a passage which, if authentic, is certainly most revealing. After assuring the "reasonable Pole" of the support and influence of both the British and Americans, Churchill is reported to have said that the West was now in a better position to deal with Stalin: "We don't care whether he comes into the war against the Japanese or not. We don't need him now." Mikolajczyk's rationalizations of his final decision included also the feeling that it was his "duty . . . to share the fate of my own people." In a speech made at Chatham House before his departure Mikolajczyk gave different motives for his decision. He was going to Poland to test Stalin's good will or, if necessary, to demonstrate to the world his bad faith. This, too, was an echo of "Western" rather than Polish attitudes; for most Poles in London there was no need to demonstrate Stalin's bad faith. For them it was an established fact.

There was thus a deep cleavage between the prevailing view of Poles in exile and the stand taken by Mikolajczyk. The die-hards were described as "unreasonable," but was Mikolajczyk more reasonable in his expectation that he could force Stalin to permit the holding of free elections, respect their result, and be satisfied with the "friendship" which non-communists were offering him? In human terms his behavior was understandable. He was young and ambitious and there was something musty and hopeless in the atmosphere of Poland in exile. And there would always be "the British ambassador and the ambassador from the United States" at his side. What if some Poles in exile called him a traitor? Mikolajczyk showed on that occasion and also on subsequent ones that he cared little for what Poles of all political persuasions had to say. When his tenure in Poland and his role as "primadonna for one season" (to use an epithet coined by a writer connected with the present communist regime) came to an abrupt end and Mikolajczyk, this time called a traitor by the "other Poles," found himself once more thrown back upon Western hospitality,[6] he tried to establish himself independently of the existing organizations and activities of the Poles abroad. Believing himself assured of Western aid, as "the only light that burns for Poland," he played a lone hand, organized and dismissed his own committees, and carried on his own policies in second exile. His attitude has earned him so far a double condemnation as "traitor." Such double epithets, no matter how unjust, do not automatically cancel themselves out. It is hard to say whether future Polish generations will curse him, as General Anders thought, or bless him, as Mikolajczyk no doubt hopes, or simply fail to remember his name because, by choice or of necessity, he became a permanent exile, a situation he tried to avoid when he decided, in 1945, to lend his name to the Polish Government of National Unity.

In all fairness to Mikolajczyk, it must be noted that by comparison with many other ex-dignitaries from eastern Europe he impresses one with his dignified demeanor. His stature has grown in second exile, possibly along with some doubts concerning the prospects of the cause which he still represents with impressive vigor.

People's Democracy: Two Phases. The creation of the "new" government of National Unity as a result of implementing the decisions of the Yalta agreement boiled down in practice to the inclusion of Stanislaw Mikolajczyk, two members of his party, and the trade union leader Jan Stanczyk, another "London" Pole

---

[6] Mikolajczyk's colorful account of the details of his escape from Poland, allegedly through the Soviet zone of Germany, was later flatly contradicted by a statement in the memoirs of Stanton Griffis, U. S. Ambassador in Warsaw at the time of Mikolajczyk's flight. According to Griffis, the Polish leader was driven by an embassy agent to Gdynia where he boarded a British vessel. "Mikolajczyk asked for our advice and help. He was our man, our duty was clear . . . We had arranged and fostered his return to Poland, he was the hope of the great democratic nations . . ." The ex-ambassador believed that the story of Mikolajczyk's escape could now be told because "all of the American actors in this drama had long since left Poland." Mr. Griffis' words were fully exploited by the Polish government; they were incorporated in a collection, *Documents on the Hostile Policy of the United States Government towards People's Poland* (Warsaw, 1953).

who decided to leave the sinking ship of the government-in-exile, in an enlarged cabinet where the majority of seats was firmly held by communists and other "Lublin" elements. Thus postwar Poland was launched on the path of People's Democracy. Developments there followed the pattern of consolidation of power in the hands of the communists applied everywhere in eastern Europe, with some modifications in timing and some allowances for specific local circumstances. The emergence of the "new" government was noted "with pleasure" by the Potsdam conference and the West could finally, and with an almost clear conscience, withdraw recognition from the London government. The main political issue now became, on the surface, the fight for early and free elections; below the surface—the struggle for controlling positions in the administration. Mikolajczyk soon found that the "Lublin" group refused to put into effect an agreement which had defined in much detail the distribution of top positions in the government, nationalized banking, and state-owned industry. He complains in his memoirs that his party never received the third of the "plums" due it under the terms of the agreement with the "Lublin" group.

Determined not to hold really free elections, the "Lublin" majority of the government began negotiations with Mikolajczyk for a "front" type joint list of candidates to be presented in the elections, with the number of seats to be allotted to each party determined in advance. The Polish communists used various arguments in their negotiations with Mikolajczyk, including even the threat that unless a single list were drawn up, an occupation of Poland by Soviet troops might become inevitable. The negotiations were accompanied by interference of the police and judicial authorities with the activities of Mikolajczyk's Polish Peasant Party. Mikolajczyk kept the diplomatic representatives of the United States and Britain informed of the acts of violence committed against his party and some of its field workers. Very soon a voluminous literature of protest notes was produced by the Western representatives, only to be rejected by the Polish government as unwarranted interference in Poland's internal affairs.

During the fall and winter of 1945–46 the government concentrated its efforts on liquidating the remnants of the Underground functioning in the forests. This was accomplished through a combination of drastic police action and an amnesty. Resistance was becoming difficult and politically hopeless in view of the severance of external contacts. In the spring of 1946 the government, constantly reminded by the West of the pledge of free elections, decided to test the relative influence of the "Lublin" group and of Mikolajczyk's party. The device chosen for the test was a referendum in which the people of Poland were asked to answer with "Yes" or "No" the following three questions: Are you in favor of abolishing the senate? Are you in favor of economic reforms: nationalization of industry and land reform? Do you want the western frontier (with Germany) to be made permanent?

In order to demonstrate his strength, Mikolajczyk called upon the people to answer the first question in the negative (although his party had been traditionally opposed to the "aristocratic" institution of the senate) and to declare themselves affirmatively on the remaining two questions. According to official figures, the outcome of the referendum was as follows:

	Yes	No
Abolition of senate	7,844,522	3,686,029
Economic reforms	8,896,105	2,634,446
Western frontier	10,534,697	995,854

Mikolajczyk questioned the official returns and claimed to have unmistakable proof that a substantial majority of the people had voted "No" on the first question, thus demonstrating their opposition to the "Lublin" majority in the government. After the referendum, Western insistence on "free and unfettered elections" was increased. No one could reasonably entertain any hope that the government would hold free elections and graciously fade away once Mikolajczyk had won the contest. As early as March 1946, Ambassador Lane informed the Department of State that "Mikolajczyk's chances of winning the elections are virtually nil." Yet he recommended an increase of American representations on the subject because of the need of long-range "education of the (American) public" to bring about a change in attitude toward the Soviet Union.[7] This is a very honest description of the nature of American interest in Poland's elections as seen by the then ambassador to Warsaw. With the exception of financial pressure (which was indeed applied, but not very consistently), the American government had no way of putting Mr. Mikolajczyk in power and of effectively undermining the position of a group sponsored by the Soviet Union.

What were Mikolajczyk's expectations and why did he persist in the clearly hopeless struggle for "free and unfettered" elections? It would be unfair to assume that he merely helped build up the educational *dossier* which Mr. Lane considered important. He apparently entertained in the beginning some hope that Western pressure could actually force the government majority to hold reasonably free elections which he expected to win. In view of the elimination of the National Democrats and other prewar mass parties—only six parties were recognized as democratic and licensed for legal operations—Mikolajczyk's party indeed could have expected to receive most of the "homeless" vote in addition to that of its traditional supporters. Even if the total might not have been the 75 per cent claimed by Mikolajczyk, he could have obtained a majority in a free contest with the combination of communists, left-wing socialists, and two or three smaller groups of questionable origin operating as peasant or "democratic" parties. At one point Mikolajczyk even thought that Stalin could be impressed with the argument that it was to Russia's interest to do business with a man and a party enjoying the genuine support of the Polish people rather than with unpopular puppets.

Of course, such expectations were completely unjustified. Mikolajczyk's party, subjected to increasing police pressure, was driven into a negative and hopeless opposition; in the process it could not help establishing, at least on the local level, some fringe contact with outlawed political groups and the remnants of the Underground. This, in turn, opened the party to still more violent accusations of "harboring reactionaries." The communists, too, were building up a *dossier* for the inevitable final reckoning with Mikolajczyk.

In the elections that were finally held on January 19, 1947,

[7] Arthur Bliss Lane, *I Saw Poland Betrayed*, pp. 194–195.

Mikolajczyk's party put forward its own list of candidates, opposing the Democratic Bloc of the government majority built around the alliance of the communists and the socialists. Mikolajczyk's lists were invalidated regionally and he was not permitted to obtain more than 28 seats of a total of 444 (against 392 for the Bloc, with various splinter groups accounting for the rest). The elections were not exactly "free and unfettered." Afterward, the small group led by Mikolajczyk engaged for a few months in sterile opposition to the determined majority of the new government (appointed in February, under the premiership of the socialist Jozef Cyrankiewicz). Mikolajczyk's disappearance from Poland in October 1947 occasioned little surprise. His party, deprived of the militant top leader, underwent a process of quick streamlining. It was later forced to merge with another peasant party controlled by the communists. At present this United Peasant Party (ZSL) functions avowedly as a "transmission belt" of the will of the Communist Party to the masses.

"*Merger.*" The process of liquidating non-communist political groups was accomplished in 1948 by the merger of the Polish Workers' (Communist) Party with what remained of the Polish Socialist Party (PPS). The chewing up of the rival workers' party by the communists was more dramatic and in many respects more complicated than the streamlining of the peasant party. Essentially, however, the resistance put up by some elements of the Polish Socialist Party was as hopeless and foredoomed as were Mikolajczyk's efforts. The socialists were first maneuvered into a common front with the communists against Mikolajczyk who was plausibly presented to them as anti-Marxist. But the common front could end logically only in "organic unity." Before this unity was achieved, the PPS had to undergo a process of purging its leadership and ranks of right-wing elements. It was not particularly difficult for the police to make out a case against some of the prewar PPS leaders whose violently anti-communist record was well known and whose wartime Underground activities (in the WRN group) had a strong anti-Soviet slant. (WRN stands for the first letters in Polish of "Freedom, Equality, and Independence.") The next step was the undermining of socialist influence in the trade unions and in the coöperatives, where it was traditionally strong. Elections to the first postwar Trade Union Congress gave the socialists a misleading feeling of strength. The socialist press began to voice very openly dissatisfaction with the attempts of the communists to monopolize the allegiance of the working class. This show of strength at first forced the communists to give in to their fellow Marxists on a number of issues, especially those of patronage, but it also increased their determination to put an end to the separate existence of the PPS. Friction arose between the two parties on the ideological level, with the socialists being accused of harboring petty bourgeois ideas about such things as civil liberties, a subject on which even the left-wingers among them showed a lack of class consciousness shocking to the communists. The attempts of the socialists to continue their international connections with Social Democratic groups in western Europe in what looked like a revival of the Second International, were also criticized, to the dismay of those who liked to view themselves as a link between East and West. At the congress of the PPS, held in December 1947, there was noticeable strong opposition by the rank and file to the idea of a merger with the communists. However, only three months later Premier Cyrankiewicz suddenly came out for the merger, only to find that this time the communists were not too eager to accept the offer without having the PPS first undergo a radical purge of its right wing and a thorough indoctrination of the remaining membership in the principles of Marxism-Leninism.[8] What the communists were after was not a mechanical sum of the membership of both parties, but a new party which would openly state that it was a Leninist organization, modeling itself after the Bolshevik party of the Soviet Union. This was, in Polish conditions, an entirely new departure. In order to qualify for the merger under the new circumstances resulting from the establishment of the Cominform

---

[8] "The Fate of Polish Socialism," by "R," *Foreign Affairs* (October 1949), pp. 125-142. The extremely well-informed author of the article makes the point that right-wing socialists were eager for a quick merger once it became clear that the independent existence of the PPS would not be long tolerated: "The Socialist right hoped that if the merger could take place without delay they would be able to move into the united party with all their old ideological baggage and that they could exert an influence on it . . . The Communists, of course, knew of this hope" (p. 140).

(its founding conference was held in Poland, in the fall of 1947) and the break with Tito, the PPS had not only to drop a considerable part of its membership, but also to engage in a very drastic revision of its own past and a condemnation of what so many followers of the party had considered its most glorious traditions, especially the intensely nationalist and anti-Russian record of the PPS. In December 1948 the merger took place and the "new" United Polish Workers' Party (PZPR) was created. The former Socialists were a minority in the new party.

Those Polish socialist leaders who worked for the united front and for the merger with the communists have been condemned, somewhat too summarily, as crypto-communists or simple stooges. The behavior of Premier Cyrankiewicz in facilitating the liquidation of his own party, the PPS, is explained in Mikolajczyk's memoirs in rather sinister terms. The communists allegedly have a firm hold on Cyrankiewicz because they know some shocking facts about his record as an inmate of a German concentration camp during World War II. Other unfriendly sources stress the features of Cyrankiewicz's character—he is supposed to be "a typical opportunist, conceited and egoistic, interested in comfort, automobiles, women and wine," according to one description— which made him a pliable instrument in the hands of the communists. Even his marriage to one of Poland's best looking, if not most talented, actresses, is offered as a key to Cyrankiewicz's "liquidationism." No doubt the opportunism of some socialist leaders played into the hands of the communists and facilitated their task, but to base on it the full explanation of the merger of the PPS with the Polish Workers' Party would be to overlook some deeper elements of the situation. There had been at all times a vigorous, though small, left wing within the PPS which was, even before the war, in favor of close coöperation with the communists. There were genuine "fusionists" among those leaders of the PPS who worked in the Underground together with the communists. It was, of course, naive on their part to assume that they could really be admitted to an equal partnership with the communists. A Social Democratic party is by definition a greater danger to the consolidation of power in the hands of the communists than other groups, against which the class argument

can be used. In the present situation there is litle room, on either
side of the Iron Curtain, for "third force" policies.

The liquidation of the PPS and the fusion between Mikolajczyk's former party and the other, pro-communist peasant group,
marked the end of the first phase in the history of political developments of postwar Poland. It may be presumed that the existence of a separate peasant party, even a very tame one, will be
found one day to be superfluous, and a new act of "organic unity"
will be accomplished. People's Democracy is now defined, in Poland and elsewhere within the Orbit, as a form of the dictatorship of the proletariat, in "alliance" with the peasants. In this
new phase the issue is no more that of a struggle between the communists and the non-communists. With the reduction of the political spectrum, the process of adaptation to the new tasks of "building the foundations of Socialism" could not remain without effect
on the communist party itself.

KPP to PPR. The Communist Party of Poland (KPP) was
born in the turmoil of 1918 with a disability which made its
functioning on the surface of political life in the period between
the two world wars impossible. It issued directly from Rosa
Luxemburg's SDKPL, a group opposed on principle to an independent Poland. This heritage was to weigh heavily on the
KPP; it justified the condemnation of the party as a "foreign
agency" and its de-legalization in the early twenties. In the upheaval of the first weeks of Poland's independence, the communists attempted to organize workers' councils (soviets) or to
infiltrate similar councils controlled by the socialists. The Polish-
Soviet war found the communists on the side of the advancing
Red Army, in opposition to what was viewed by the majority of
the people as a struggle against foreign invasion. In 1921 the KPP
became a section of the Comintern. It engaged in an erratic policy
of illegal activities, mostly through provoking strikes in some
industries where the trade unions came under communist influence. Poland's first parliamentary elections were boycotted by
the KPP. When the party, following Comintern instructions, took
to the path of parliamentary action, its activities were interfered
with by the police. The communists could rarely put up electoral
lists under their own flag. As a Union of the Proletariat of Town

and Countryside they obtained some 132,000 votes (about 1.5 per cent of the total) in the election of 1922. Communist representatives in parliament as a rule were deprived of their immunity for one reason or another and found themselves in jail. In the intervals between ejections they could only engage in obstructionist speeches and in provocative interruptions of other speakers. Meanwhile the authorities of the Polish state developed a standard procedure for dealing with communist activities. Youngsters caught distributing communist handbills or painting subversive slogans on the walls would be sentenced to unduly harsh prison terms. As political prisoners were kept together, apart from common criminals, these raw "subversives" would receive from imprisoned veterans a thorough Marxist education in what became known as "prison universities." It was claimed that many of them, after coming out of prison, were better indoctrinated and more determined communists than before. On the other hand, it seemed inconceivable that a party considered a "foreign agency" by definition and occasionally linked with espionage and terroristic acts should be permitted to function openly in a country so close to the headquarters of international revolution. Isolated suggestions by lawyers and educators that the government stop "making communists" were not heeded.

Because of its disabilities the KPP never developed into a mass organization. It had, according to official admissions by communist sources, at most twenty thousand members (fewer, according to others). The membership included some workers in certain branches of heavy industry, agricultural workers, and landless peasants, especially among poor Byelorussian and Ukrainian peasants; the bulk of the membership, however, came from the intelligentsia and semi-intelligentsia. These elements either were attracted by the theoretical appeal of Marxism or, as in the case of some Jewish intellectuals, were driven into the arms of the party by the bitterness with which they viewed the narrowing outlets for their talents and work in Polish society.

While the governments of interwar Poland continued to persecute the illegal KPP and to publicize, with some exaggeration, the subversive activities of the party, the KPP enjoyed little favor with the Communist International and its Soviet bosses.

The party was rent by internal conflicts and frequent deviations in the direction of Trotskyism and anarchism. Many of the top leaders were "invited" to Russia and there liquidated in the big purge of the thirties. The Comintern leadership also claimed that because of organizational deficiencies and the lack of vigilance the party was full of police agents and other "plants." The KPP was blamed for cultivating the heritage of "Luxemburgism" because of which the party could not make proper tactical use of slogans attractive to non-proletarian groups, especially the peasant masses. "The KPP found no common language with the peasant," Franciszek Fiedler, an old hand in the communist movement, wrote in 1948. This was no doubt true, but one can also say that the nature of the assignments given the KPP by the Communist International and its entire position in the specific conditions of interwar Poland were such that the party could find no common language either with the peasants or with the mass of Polish workers. It just could not become a *Polish* party; it certainly could not be considered as such by others. This was one of the reasons why the united front period of the thirties produced such meager results in Poland (other reasons being, of course, the monopolistic hold of the Pilsudski-ites on the government and the opposition of the top socialist leadership to pressure from below for a united front with the communists). Mieczyslaw Niedzialkowski, leader of the socialists (later executed by the Germans), is supposed to have stated in the early twenties in answer to a communist invitation to work out joint tactics: "With you, gentlemen, one never knows where the ideological fighter ends and where the Russian agent begins."

Early in 1938, the Comintern ordered the dissolution of its Polish section.

The purpose of the dissolution [it was explained ten years later in the official organ of the revived party, *Nowe Drogi*] was to eliminate planted *agents provocateurs*, to separate them from the healthy basic mass of the party. On this basis a new party was to be created, Marxist-Leninist in outlook, purged of Pilsudski-ite agents, able to perform the enormous task created by the international situation of the time.

In 1939 attempts were allegedly made to revive the party organization, but the sudden rapprochement between Stalin and Hitler and the initial period of the second World War were anything but propitious for the reactivation of a communist organization on Polish territory.

Yet an opportunity soon arose not only for a revival of the party, but also for a striking change in its "line" which for the first time made it possible for Polish communism to speak the kind of language that had meaning and attraction to many Poles. After the outbreak of the war between Nazi Germany and the Soviet Union a new party came into existence in the Underground. It called itself Polish Workers Party (PPR). Its nucleus was formed by the old communist guard or, at least, by those among Polish communists who had not sought refuge in Russia or who were sent back from there. Its first organizers, Marceli Nowotko and Pawel Finder, were caught and shot by the Germans; the job was then taken over by Wladyslaw Gomulka ("Wieslaw"), an energetic regional organizer with an impressive prewar record of illegal trade union activities, clashes with the police, and repeated imprisonment.

Needless to say, the revived communist party was easily identifiable as such, in spite of its new name, the protective coloring, and the brand new set of patriotic slogans which replaced the language of Marxism-Leninism. Yet it would be a mistake to underestimate completely the attraction of the PPR to some elements in occupied Poland. There was much to criticize and question in the "legitimate" Underground. German oppression created among young people an atmosphere of impatience, in which the call for immediate action against the occupant had a stronger appeal than the logical but uninspiring thesis of "waiting in preparedness." It is politically unimportant that the exhortations of the PPR were not sincere; they achieved to some extent the tactical purpose of identifying the "legitimate" Underground with inactivity and the PPR with an active and daring attitude directed against the Nazis. The PPR also managed to establish its record as ardent advocate of the "recovery" of territory at the expense of Germany. While the connection between this acquisition and the loss of the eastern half of the prewar territory of Poland to Russia was clear to everyone, there was enough accumulated anti-Nazi feeling to lend almost irresistible appeal to the prospect of hitting back at the Germans.

With the liberation of Poland, PPR became the controlling group in the postwar government. Of course, it was not put into this position by a vote of the Polish people; it was supported by Russian bayonets. However, in the initial post-liberation period the PPR continued to claim the allegiance of the masses of Poland on the basis of its patriotic record, of its moderation in social and economic matters (land reform and nationalization of key industries were combined with deliberate insistence on the importance of private enterprise), of its determination to find a "Polish way to Socialism."

"Deviationism." This tactical line was later condemned as "rightist deviationism" and Wladyslaw Gomulka, most prominently identified with the "nationalist" trend in postwar Polish communism, was purged and jailed, (but never brought to public trial). A denounced "deviationist" is subject to multiple jeopardy.[9] Gomulka's expulsion from the leadership after a dramatic debate in the plenum of the Central Committee of the PPR—of which there exists a printed report, a unique document in the annals of communism—was primarily an echo of the break with Tito. Acting through the Cominform, the Soviet leaders gave the signal for a violent campaign of self-criticism in all communist parties. Some of the purged leaders may not have been guilty of any particular acts, not only within the scope of the criminal code, but also according to principles of party discipline. There was an "objective" need for the unmasking of deviations similar to that which had brought about the Tito episode and some leaders "objectively" fitted the need for scapegoats. In Gomulka's case, the wartime leader of the PPR, who had organized the party and developed it against heavy odds, was also made the scapegoat for the earlier "line" of the party that, in the opinion of the Soviet leaders, had outlived its usefulness

[9] For an excellent treatment of the Gomulka "deviation" within the framework of postwar relations between the USSR and the "satellite" countries, see Adam B. Ulam, *Titoism and the Cominform* (Harvard University Press, 1952).

by 1948 and was considered an obstacle in a world believed irrevocably bi-polarized. It could easily be argued—and Gomulka tried to do so in his unsuccessful apologia—that what the former leader was being accused of had been the official line of the party in the initial postwar period. But such arguments would only draw upon Gomulka the wrath of his accusers, the more so since they knew that he was right. The party as such could not be wrong; therefore the blame for what turned out to be a "deviation" had to be put on one person or group. In the case of Gomulka the person of the culprit was not picked entirely arbitrarily. There was enough in Gomulka's personal make-up and in the style of Polish postwar communism to justify the suspicion of "deviationism."

PPR to PZPR. In May 1945, at the first openly convened plenum of the Central Committee of the PPR, secretary general Gomulka branded as nonsense "reactionary rumors" about the impending sovietization of Poland.

There are two reasons [he said], why Poland cannot be a Soviet republic. First, the Polish people do not want it. Second, the Soviet Union does not want it . . . PPR draws its model for the organization of Poland's national life from the democratic spirit of the Polish people . . . Poland is not going on the way of "sovietization," but on the way of democratization . . .

In the same vein rumors about the impending organization of *kolkhozi* were rejected by Gomulka as mere reactionary gossip. In the political resolution presented to the plenum—and adopted by it— some members of the party were criticized for "leftist sectarianism," for an attempt to "simplify the tempo of historical processes and . . . overlook [the peculiarities] of the spirit of the Polish people." The coalition with Mikolajczyk and other noncommunist elements was praised and the resolution called for the application of the principle of equality between the member groups of the government coalition, for encouragement of criticism and "even opposition, as long as it does not endanger the very foundations of the coalition and its cohesion."

That Gomulka was preaching these things and that this was the official line of Polish communism in the immediate post-liberation period is not surprising. The entire phraseology fitted perfectly into the pattern adopted, no doubt as a result of centrally agreed upon tactics, by all communist parties. Nor is it astonishing that Gomulka insisted that the Polish people believe the sincerity of the democratic slogans of the PPR. Communists have an inexhaustible capacity for self-righteousness and for insisting that whatever they say at any particular stage of historical development be accepted, even if the record leaves no doubt as to the tactically dictated nature of the "correct" slogans of every historical situation. Early in 1947 the Warsaw daily *Zycie Warszawy* appealed to the people to have confidence in the sincerity of the change in communism:

People argue that the PPR is communist and one cannot trust Communists . . . Before our eyes a tremendously important historical event has taken place. The communist parties, having achieved in a number of countries the possibility of shaping directly the destinies of their respective nations, have voluntarily given up the way of violent social revolution and the dictatorship of the proletariat. In every one of these countries the Communists, together with all sincerely democratic and progressive parties, chose the way of peaceful evolution, of an evolution that is "different" and national, i.e. in accordance with the psychological and other characteristics of each nation concerned, in harmony with the traditions and specific conditions of existence of each nation. The road of the Great October Revolution remains the exclusive experience of the peoples of the Soviet Union, imposed on them by the concrete historical conditions of 1917 and by hostile encirclement by capitalist governments . . . That the extreme Left has abandoned the methods of revolutionary struggle, that it has joined other progressive parties in peaceful and creative work for the reconstruction of an independent national state—should have pleased every reasonable person in Poland. And yet . . . many people, no doubt honest and progressive people, are disturbed . . . Long standing, deeply inculcated distrust and deliberately intensified prejudices are still active. They have not been dispelled by the fact that the social reforms in Poland have not introduced communism, nor even socialism, but were merely a long postponed necessity for Poland.

. . . Well, some people may say that this is only a transition period, a kind of NEP. As soon as they (i.e. the Communists) are in the saddle, they will "show" us. Show what? They could have "shown" immediately. Why should the Polish Left leave the chosen path, after it has taken with determination a specific, Polish, evolutionary path of loyal coöperation with the entire camp of progress? Why should they do it? Maybe in order to render more difficult the task of rebuilding the country? Where is logic? . . .

The daily *Zycie Warszawy* was not officially a party organ, but an allegedly nonpartisan, popular newspaper. Moreover, the cited article was written on the eve of the January 1947 elections, when the communist-led Democratic Bloc competed with Mikolajczyk's independent list and was determined to obtain a majority, by persuasion if possible, by other means if necessary. The communists could later say—and they did—that this type of appeal was a necessary tactical maneuver justified by the conditions of the moment, a form of "not showing the cards prematurely," as the Hungarian communist leader Revai was to describe similar tactics in an article written in 1949. On the surface, there was nothing to indicate that Gomulka was doing more than a tactical chore. For an advocate of "sincere coöperation" he certainly was rather ferocious in fighting Mikolajczyk and rather insistent on a merger with the socialists. Yet it seems that, while determined to establish the PPR in an uncontested monopoly of power in postwar Poland, Gomulka felt that the party ought to go towards the goal of socialism in a way that would not necessarily be a copy of developments in Russia. Even when he faced his accusers as a deviationist and was expected to produce a satisfactory recantation, Gomulka still argued: "Is there only one pattern? . . . There must be some specific elements of a Polish way to socialism."

Nor was Gomulka alone in this line of argument. Unlike the prewar KPP, the PPR was a legally operating party, one appealing for mass support and attracting peripheral elements. There were many opportunists among them, eager to obtain the protection which a party card seemed to afford in those turbulent days. But there were also many who thought that in postwar Poland the PPR had a legitimate role to play, and one connected with the best interests of Poland, the only Poland possible under the circumstances. There were also many authentic prewar communists who, like Gomulka, had spent the war years in German-occupied Poland, trying to obtain acceptance for a party heavily burdened with the past record of the KPP. They may have found that they were most successful when they spoke to prospective followers an authentically Polish language that appealed to the possibly irrational yet genuine feelings of the people to a larger extent than the subtle abstractions of Marxism. Why throw away these advantages in the post-liberation period?

The picture of uniform opposition of the "entire nation" to the postwar regime, which some Polish political exiles paint and so many others accept, is too simple to be correct. We have it on the authority of a Polish expert on communism, Ryszard Wraga (between the wars an important figure in military intelligence, now a writer in exile), that the relative attractiveness of the idea of a "Polish way to socialism" helped to bring about an effective atomization of the will to resist the encroachments of communism. Various peripheral elements, especially youth groups, then joined the party "in the hope of building a Poland that was red yet different from the Soviet Union, with the idea of shaping conditions in Poland not on principles imposed by Moscow, but according to specific, Polish possibilities." There was, the writer admits, much "infantilism" in this attitude. The ideas of these people were frequently a strange combination of "persistent Polish Big Power tendencies (*mocarstwowosc*) with revolutionary and cosmopolitan ambitions." Consequently, according to Wraga, Poland was becoming "increasingly red" yet at the same time "increasingly anti-Russian," determined to work out its own ways.[10]

All this does not mean that Gomulka was the leader of an organized "nationalist" group within the Communist Party. Not even his most determined accusers claimed more than an "objective" connection between Gomulka's views and the danger of the emergence of an organized opposition. It is not even certain that he was in basic sympathy with anti-Russian tendencies in Polish communism. Up to a certain point he had worked loyally along lines pleasing to Moscow. But he definitely fell out of line with the majority of the Polish Politburo when it became clear that the concept of a separate Polish way to socialism was about to be condemned as a heresy because of the deplorable results which, in the view of the Kremlin, the overstressing of nationalism and of the local achievements of the communists in the war period had produced in the case of Tito. Gomulka also had at least tactical doubts about the wisdom of alienating the peasants by proclaiming a new program in agriculture which, in spite of all the soph-

[10] *Kultura,* Paris, No. 9/26, December 1949.

istry used, meant the beginning of collectivization. Finally, there was the issue of relations between Poland, Germany, and Russia. Gomulka's name was intimately connected with the administration of the territories "recovered" from Germany in the post war period. Together with many other Poles he seems to have entertained a fear that is very Polish indeed: the fear of yet another understanding between Russia and Germany, this time a red Germany, at the expense of Poland.

At the historical session of the Central Committee which debated Gomulka's heresies, Hilary Minc stated that Gomulka had "distrusted the Soviet Union" in the matter of Germany and in particular doubted the determination of the Soviet Union to impose on German communists the acceptance of the Oder-Neisse border line with Poland. Events have since shown that Gomulka's fears were unjustified. The Soviet Union has so far chosen to stand by Poland in the matter of the border with Germany. The German Democratic Republic operating in the Soviet occupation zone, has accepted as "immutable" the frontier between Germany and Poland, no doubt under Soviet pressure and at the possible cost of a loss of support for communism in Germany. Whatever Russia's long-range plans may be, on the record the Soviet leaders have chosen not only to do violence to Polish national feelings (in the matter of the eastern frontier) but also to ask, in the name of "internationalism" and for the purpose of integration, similar sacrifices from the German communists in favor of Poland. But in 1948, before Soviet policy in Germany crystallized, the uncertainty and the fears ascribed to Gomulka were genuine. Poland and the other "satellite" countries had been made to advocate, through resolutions passed by a conference of their foreign ministers, the unification of Germany. From a traditional Polish point of view the existence of a strong, unified Germany is undesirable. But for a communist to adopt this traditional point of view is indeed to be guilty of "nationalist deviationism." A good communist is supposed to subscribe to the view that a strong and unified Germany is not *per se* good or bad. It depends on who controls it. Rational as such an approach may be, many Poles find it difficult to see things that way, just as many Frenchmen cannot bring themselves to feel comfortable about a "good" Germany.

Unless one assumes that Gomulka willingly accepted the role of an "objective" scapegoat for various heretical lines of thought actually or potentially entertained by some Polish communists—and his highly egotistic and "Bonapartist" personality would seem to preclude submission to such a role—he must have indeed entertained some or all of the ideas described above which gave Polish postwar communism a specific flavor. Even the most casual foreign observer, unless he was completely blinded by a set of prefabricated prejudices, must have noticed, at least up to mid-1948, that under almost complete communist rule Poland was still preserving on the surface much of the traditional Polish style, so charming to some, so irritating to others. The phraseology of the government press was, with some exceptions, strikingly similar to that of the Pilsudski-ite period. Nor was the personnel, especially on the middle and lower levels of the administration, much different in thinking, behavior, and bureaucratic haughtiness. At the same time the foreign observer was struck by the relatively easy-going atmosphere of Poland, including Warsaw—horribly disfigured, yet insistent on living its superficially carefree life, including the long hours spent in pleasant little cafés over poor coffee and juicy gossip. Many members of the new ruling élite were visibly elated by their social promotion and tried hard, at times with pathetic results, to adopt the style of the gentry which seemed to hold Poland in spiritual bondage long after the political power of that class had evaporated. Some of the new rulers showed a curious inferiority complex which drove them to angle for the support of elements of the prewar élite. True, there was a shortage of people and it was tactically important to create the atmosphere of "national unity." Yet there was something of the pride of the *parvenu* in the satisfaction with which the new rulers pointed out the adherence of aristocrats to the regime. Prince Czetwertynski, who decided to run a first-class restaurant in Warsaw, another prince who joined the foreign service, became standard items in the "line" peddled to foreign journalists by the regime. In the craving for acceptance and for "national unity," theories developed about a general moral amnesty for everyone willing to join. In a best-selling novel, *Popioly i diament* (Embers and Diamond), the communist writer, Andrzejewski, puts the following statement in the mouth of a former judge who has a record of abominable behavior in a German concentration camp:

I have indeed made many mistakes. Does this mean that . . . I cannot be a useful and respectable person any more? . . . I shall be condemned. What good will this do? There will be one man less at a time when there is such a shortage of people . . . Yesterday's enemy can be today's friend . . . He counts who at this moment, under today's conditions is socially useful. That's all.

What is significant is not the rationalization of his wartime sins by the wayward jurist, but the gesture of his communist interrogator who lets him go free (presumably to take a government job) although he refuses to shake hands with him. In practice even this symbolic act of censure was dispensed with. Many hands were shaken vigorously although they were not too clean.

There can be no doubt that in the early postwar period Poland under communism was working out a style of its own, with a prominent admixture of native grandiloquence and insouciance. But this very fact that Polish communism was not grim enough, that life in Poland, even in ruined Warsaw, could be found to be almost pleasant by many Western visitors, that many of the new élite were known for the habit of making anti-regime jokes,—all this was a very dubious recommendation from the point of view of the Soviet Union. By 1947 the people in the Kremlin had diagnosed acute bipolarization in the world and had initiated a program of vigorous integration within their sphere. This meant the conversion of the communist parties of the "orbit" into Bolshevik, not merely Marxist, parties. In the case of the Polish party, this meant a purge of elements to whom the "Polish way" continued to be genuinely attractive, not merely tactically useful; the elimination of people and groups imbued with notions of a peculiar mission which Poland, a red Poland, was allegedly called upon to fulfill; above all, the change meant the imposition of a more serious, even grim, and certainly less easy-going (*niefrasobliwy*) style on Polish public life. The United Workers' Party (PZPR), which emerged from the fusion with the socialists, was not to be a synthesis of the two currents in Polish socialism; it was to be a party of the "higher type," a Bolshevik party, bent on doing away with the "glorification of noxious and false traditions" or, as one regime writer put it, a party "made of ideally pure metal, without any nationalistic-opportunist admixtures."

Bolshevized Polish communism is rapidly becoming "Leninist in content, Polish in form." The party is energetically rewriting its own childhood history, stressing with pride its direct descent from the KPP, a fact earlier not mentioned at all or referred to with embarrassment. New national heroes are being offered to the Polish people, after a period of vigorous exploitation of long deceased kings who appeared to have agreed to the Curzon Line many centuries before it was drawn. It is symbolic for the new period in Polish communism that monuments are now being erected not only to the Russian army (the latter took no chances and erected them for itself as it advanced through Poland), but to Julian Marchlewski, premier-designate of the government which was to be installed in Poland by the Red Army in 1920; to Feliks Dzierzynski, whose title to fame is based on his activities as head of the Cheka, forerunner of the GPU and MVD, rather than on his earlier connection with Polish socialism; even to lesser communists, Hibner, Rutkowski, Botwin—convicted and executed for high treason in the interwar period.

The purge of Gomulka and other actual or potential "nationalists" left enough Polish communists of apparently unquestionable loyalty to Moscow's version of "internationalism"—Bierut, Berman, Zawadzki, Radkiewicz—in charge of the transition from the "Polish way" to a Polish Bolshevism. Yet the Kremlin was not taking chances in Poland, main avenue to the west, main gate of possible attack from the west. A Soviet marshal, whose name indicates Polish origin (but whose official biography giving Warsaw as his birthplace may be apocryphal), was "loaned" to Poland, placed in supreme command of the Polish army, and included in the Politburo of the PZPR. By sending Konstantin Rokossowski to Poland, Stalin acted in line with his traditional distrust of foreign communists; he also acted in the tradition of Russian distrust of Poles, including "collaborating" ones.

State and Church. The elimination of political parties and the reduction of mass organizations to the role of "transmission

belts" has left in existence one center of independent spiritual—
and potentially political—influence: the Church. It was inevitable
that the regime should sooner or later try to curb the activities of
the Church.

To say that "the Poles are ardent Catholics" is to offer a plati-
tude conveying little information about the political power of the
Church. Most Poles are indeed deeply religious and Poland is
now—after the changes in borders and population—more homogeneously Catholic than ever before. Yet the intensity of religious
feeling among the people does not necessarily mean that they are
traditionally inclined to follow the lead of the Church in political matters. During the nineteenth century, when Polish independence was in abeyance, the Church frequently acted as a national symbol and some elements of the clergy have provided political leadership. In restored Poland, during the interwar period,
priests were active in political parties, mainly the right-wing National Democratic party, but the Church as such was never clearly
identified with any one particular group. It was ready, as W. J.
Rose puts it, to "support loyally whatever government was accepted by the majority of the people," provided, of course, that
the government respected the position of the Church. Such an
attitude was in perfect harmony with the traditional policies of
the Church; it was also a necessity in view of the pulverization of
political groups in Poland, most of whom consisted of equally
good Catholics. The Church in Poland had neither strikingly
large land holdings that would give it independent economic
power, nor control of public education to the same extent as, for
instance, in Hungary. In spite of the attachment of the people to
their religion, there was in Poland at all times a deep anticlerical
current dating back at least to the period of the Reformation and
the writings of Mikolaj Rey. That such tendencies reflected some
authentic feelings of the peasant masses may be seen from the
fact that the more radical peasant parties ("Wyzwolenie" and
others) had an actively anticlerical program.

As to relations between Poland and the Vatican, the filial loyalty of the Poles to Rome was on some occasions put to hard tests
by moves which the Church had to undertake in furtherance of
its own interests, but which did not always run parallel to those

of Poland. Much bitterness was engendered by the attitude of the Vatican toward the Polish uprising of 1830–31; many Poles were dismayed by the promptness with which the Holy See negotiated a *modus vivendi* with the Russian oppressors of the Poles in the interests of preserving Catholicism.

Relations between the reborn Polish state and the Vatican were not too smooth, in spite of the Concordat of 1925. Colonel Beck noted in his memoirs that there was a basic difference between the views of the Vatican and those of successive Polish governments concerning the "Uniate" church. To the Vatican that church, which combines allegiance to Rome with a Byzantinic-Slavonic liturgy, was a desirable bridge between Rome and the Orthodox schism, a symbol of the perennial hope that the schism might be one day eliminated. Polish statesmen, however, saw in the Uniate church an instrument of Ukrainian nationalism and supported the more or less forcible Latinization of the Uniates, frowned upon by the Vatican. In the crisis of 1939 the Polish government resented the suggestions emanating from the Vatican, including one made on the authority of the Pope late in August, that Poland cede territory to Germany in order to save the peace.[11] When the Polish government was forced to abandon Warsaw and the diplomatic corps faithfully followed it on the aimless trek from one temporary residence to another, the papal nuncio suddenly announced that he was returning to Warsaw. This caused Beck to express the fear that such an attitude "might lead to serious misunderstandings concerning the attitude of the Holy See toward the consequences of the invasion of Poland by the Germans."[12]

During World War II relations between the Polish government-in-exile and the Vatican were rather cool because of the Pope's readiness to confirm the appointment of German clergy as administrators of dioceses in Polish territory incorporated by Hitler. There is no doubt resentment now among some Polish elements in exile because the Church has reached a *modus vivendi* with the present regime of Poland whose leaders otherwise may be considered eligible for excommunication.

[11] Beck, *Dernier Rapport*, p. 213.
[12] Beck, p. 235.

From the point of view of the present regime the Church constitutes a danger because of its claim to the spiritual allegiance
of the faithful which competes with the tendency of the government to control the citizenry totally. Of course, the Polish communists have learned not to be identified with aggressive "god-
lessness" as the Bolshevik regime was in the early post-revolution-
ary period. Consequently, the practice of religion is not interfered with directly. The regime displayed conspicuous zeal in
helping to restore destroyed church buildings. A Catholic press,
independent of the government, was tolerated longer than other
opposition organs. But the government made it clear that it
would oppose the crystallization of a center of political opposition around the Church. Spectacular trials were staged to reveal
the connection of some priests with subversive organizations.
However, the main line of attack by the government, and one
rather adroitly chosen, was directed not so much against the
Church in Poland, as against the Vatican.

After the failure of early negotiations between representatives
of the regime (Grabski, Pruszynski, both good Catholics, the first
of them chief negotiator of the Concordat of 1925) and the Vatican, the Polish government began to attack the position of Rome
in the matter of the "recovered territories" that are so dear to the
heart of every Pole. Much was made, in 1948, of a statement of
the Pope to German Catholics which was presented as encouragement of German revisionism. A law promulgated in 1949 for the
purpose of "defending freedom of conscience" ominously prescribed heavy penalties for the "misuse of religious freedom to
pursue aims hostile to the structure of the Polish republic." Attempts to stir religious feelings following a report of a miracle
were squarely opposed by the government. Charitable organizations with international connections were subjected to government control. Church lands, other than those under places of
worship and religious institutions, were subjected to the law on
land reform (although small holdings necessary for the maintenance of parish priests were exempted). The position of the
Church was undermined indirectly by legislation which was, objectively speaking, long overdue: the introduction of secular mar-
riages and divorces. As to the latter, they were a necessity in the

postwar conditions of Poland, with the stability of literally millions of families broken up.[13]

The Polish Episcopate opposed the encroachments of the government with skill and determination, while at the same time realistically refraining from seeking martyrdom. The agreement finally reached between the government and the bishops—the form of agreement left the Vatican not involved directly—and signed on April 14, 1950, recognized the religious, dogmatic, and liturgical demands of the Church and, to some extent, its rights in the educational and cultural sphere (including the continued operation of the Catholic University of Lublin). The bishops made concessions on social matters which were of great value to the regime, as they could be interpreted as a lack of opposition, if not a direct blessing, to the collectivization of agriculture. The government also secured agreement on two other matters of importance. The bishops undertook to "request the Apostolic See to transform church administrations enjoying the rights of residential bishoprics into permanent episcopal ordinariates." This would mean the recognition of the permanent title of Poland to the "recovered territories." The bishops also agreed to "support all endeavors toward a permanent peace" and to oppose "all efforts to bring about a war." This last point was soon thereafter used by the government to demand that the leading dignitaries of the Church sign the Stockholm Peace Appeal. The refusal of Primate Wyszynski, Cardinal Sapieha, and other bishops to sign the appeal was followed by an attack of the government press, accusing the leaders of the Church in Poland of violating the *modus vivendi*. Finally, a statement was issued in the name of the Episocopate, lending support to the action of collecting signatures under the Stockholm Peace Appeal and condemning, in vague terms, the use of atomic energy for purposes of annihilation rather than as a contribution to the happiness of mankind.

[13] For a period of three years divorce was permitted by mutual agreement and without particular motives. It is interesting to note that in some cases this divorce procedure was used by couples actually separated for as much as forty years. Current legislation tends to preserve the stability of marriage, and divorces are to be granted only when the courts ascertain the actual and permanent disruption of the marriage. The courts may refuse to grant divorce if the interest of children requires continuation of the marriage.

In the fall of 1950 the Polish government presented the Episcopate with an "ultimatum" demanding the liquidation of the provisional status of the church administration in the "recovered
territories." How well the subject of attack was chosen may be
seen from the following evaluation by an analyst of the National
Committee for a Free Europe, an organization engaged in promoting resistance to the present communist regimes, with headquarters in this country and with a considerable degree of official
American support:

The battleground was carefully chosen. Polish society—in its entirety
—stands guard over the Western Territories, and does not understand
the reasons for the prolongation of the "provisorium." The Vatican, on
the other hand, with its customary caution in such matters, is not in a
hurry to reach a final decision, but (is) waiting for a complete peaceful, political regulation of territorial problems. This stand of the Apostolic See has aroused bitterness among the Poles. It has allowed the
Communists to play easily upon the patriotic sentiments of the people
and popularizes the idea of separation from Rome.[14]

The Vatican seems to have drawn its conclusions from the general feelings of the Poles on the subject. Rather than give the
communist government of Poland a chance to capitalize on the
opposition of the Holy See to the stabilization of a Polish church
administration in "recovered territory," Rome gave Primate
Wyszynski a free hand to deal with the situation as local conditions required. The primate called upon the vicars appointed by
the government to submit to his authority, thus indirectly recognizing the validity of the appointments and the legality of ousting
German priests.

In the inevitable conflict between a communist state and the
Catholic Church both sides in Poland are moving with a caution
that shows mutual recognition of and respect for the strength
and determination of the adversary. On the surface there seems
to be little change. The churches are open and more crowded
than ever. ("Poles will go to church just to spite the government.") The government announced early in 1951 that religious
orders were in charge of 300 kindergartens for 15 thousand chil-

---

[14] *Poland in the Year 1950: Review of Events.* (Mimeo.) National Committee for a Free Europe (New York, undated), p. 16.

dren, 600 elementary schools with 22 thousand children, 44 intermediary schools with some 9 thousand pupils. These figures, presumably correct, in themselves provide no proof that the Church is free to operate as it would like. In the long run peaceful coexistence between a communist government and a church organization may be impossible, especially if the latter is determined to maintain its international connection with the capital of Catholicism. The regime seems to be preparing the ground for the creation of a "national church" which would satisfy the demand for religious rites but would owe no allegiance to Rome. The lower clergy, financially and otherwise dependent on the government, is being drawn into various "patriotic organizations"; there is also some subtle play on the ambitions of individual Church dignitaries, so far without spectacular success. On the ideological level the government makes use of a Catholic Social Group of unknown strength, led by a former "national radical" politician with totalitarian leanings.

Apparently determined not to be exposed to attack for siding with "enemies of progress," the Polish bishops issued on May 13, 1951 (significantly, after a long visit of the primate to Rome), a striking episcopal letter calling upon the clergy to respect the existing laws and authorities. The letter expressed admiration for the achievements of the nation in the field of reconstruction, and pointed out the need of further sacrifices to secure "well-being for all groups of the population." The clergy was warned to stay away from political quarrels and "to refrain from evaluating people from the point of view of their political orientation." Nor should adherence to this or that political party serve as reason for refusing religious rites—a clear departure from the general Vatican policy. Priests were reminded by the bishops that "no one has appointed us the distributors of temporal goods . . . Priests serve the Fatherland best not when they fight with arms, but when they unite it in Christ."

In spite of this conciliatory gesture of the bishops, the Church continued to be under pressure, although rumors of drastic measures were slow in materializing. In Catholic circles abroad there was growing concern over what has been described in a magazine article as the "battle fatigue" noticeable among the clergy behind the so-called Iron Curtain. There can be no doubt that the position of the Church there is extremely delicate and the long-range prospects of a *modus vivendi* rather dubious, since both the Church and the regime have essentially conflicting claims to the loyalties of the citizenry. In this contest the government controls the apparatus of organized compulsion, while the Church has to rely on amorphous loyalties exposed to very serious pressures.

Early in 1953, the uneasy truce was broken. Several priests connected with the Cracow Metropolitan Curia were convicted together with Catholic laymen, of espionage on behalf of the United States; some of those convicted were sentenced to death. The London *Economist,* while discounting the more lurid details of the staged trial, commented (on February 7) : "It would be idle to deny that a steady stream of information about Poland does leak out through clerical channels; in Communist eyes, such leakages are intolerable. The root of the trouble lies in the failure of the Church–State agreement of 1950 to cut the Polish Church's ties with the West and turn it into a subservient instrument of the Communist state. On the whole, the bulk of the hierarchy has made little effort to make the agreement work . . . It is . . . possible that (the trial) was a grand and perhaps final warning that it must toe the line . . ."

The Government and the People.   Even the most detailed account of the progress made by the communist regime of Poland in liquidating articulate political opposition does not provide a satisfactory key to the attitudes and feelings of the majority of the Polish people, those millions who cannot "choose freedom" but have to adapt themselves to realities, such as they are.

There can be no doubt that since the early post-liberation days, when the authority of the regime was openly defied by Underground groups operating from forest hide-outs, the government has achieved an impressive degree of consolidation. It may continue to be regarded as alien, as imposed by the Russians, and surviving because of Russian protection, yet there it is and it has to be accepted. Acceptance does not mean enthusiasm, merely a realistic recognition of the present stability of a regime to which there is no discernible alternative on the horizon short of a major upheaval (about which many Poles have at best mixed feelings). Stern police measures have no doubt helped to implant in the minds of many people that mixture of fear and respect which keeps essentially unpopular groups in power. But there are other factors, too. Many Poles seem to have convinced themselves that the present solution is the only possible one or that, at any rate, the alternatives are too elusive.

In the immediate post-liberation period many non-communist Poles worked out more or less plausible theories rationalizing the inevitable. To some a "Russian" orientation was by no means necessarily dishonorable; there had been in the past respectable Polish leaders who for one reason or another advocated coöperation with Russia. Hopes that Stalin would be more Russian than communist or that he would permit Poland to go her own way helped to bolster these rationalizations. In this atmosphere Stanislaw Grabski—attracted by what looked like a modernized Pan-Slavism—praised the advantages of Poland's "new historical road." Ksawery Pruszynski, a talented writer of aristocratic descent (who fought during the war in the West and acquired an aversion to it), in a remarkable pamphlet revised traditional Polish views on Aleksander Wielopolski, the pro-Russian "collaborationist" of the nineteenth century. The amateur historian Bochenski produced a disturbing volume called *The History of Stupidity in Poland,* which summarily condemned much of Poland's history and almost all of history-writing as "stupidity," and at least implicitly advocated as "wise" a pro-Russian orientation.[15] Some Poles liked the regime's anti-German attitude; others, the national homogeneity of the state within its postwar borders. Members of the technical intelligentsia perceived great opportunities in the dynamic approach of the regime to problems of reconstruction; in this group some reasoned that the new government was not really communist but "managerial." Even many of those essentially opposed to the new order had to make peace with it, because of economic necessity and still more because of an understandable craving for stabilization of any kind

[15] The Polish author would probably be less scornful of Polish "stupidity" had he read Harold G. Nicolson's statement in *Peacemaking 1919* (Boston: Houghton Mifflin, 1933): "The factor of stupidity is inseparable from all human affairs. It is too often disregarded as an inevitable concomitant of human behavior . . ."

after years of abnormal existence under German occupation and in the initial post-liberation period.

Accounts of the war years usually stress the material destruction in Poland, but skip somewhat lightly over the moral effects of the occupation in the country that, according to an accepted cliché, produced no Quisling. Civic morality was never very high in Poland and the war situation, in which normal social relations were upset and evasion of the law was elevated to the dignity of a national duty, deeply affected moral standards. One of the major contributing factors was, in my opinion, the extermination of practically the entire Jewish population by the Germans. The Poles as a nation did not participate in this systematic slaughter; there were individual cases of active assistance to hiding Jews, but to many Poles offering shelter to a candidate for extermination became a source of extortionist income. The liquidation of the Jewish population also left heirless property, not all of which was taken away by the Germans. The disappearance of the traditional group of small traders opened new vistas in "commerce," and a new middle class—described in Poland and elsewhere in Europe as *lumpen-bourgeoisie*—came into existence. To some extent the acquisition of property and commercial positions in the towns was repeated in the last phase of the war at the expense of the Germans expelled from Poland: an army of looters descended upon the "recovered territories" like the locust. Consequently, many of the staunchest defenders of "private initiative" in postwar Poland were people whose property status was of very recent date and frequently of not too clean origin. The "furrow of immorality" was as deep in Poland as elsewhere in Europe and, in some respects, even deeper, because of the unprecedented experience of legalized lawlessness. Where thousands of people have made a living as "dentists," by pulling golden crowns from the mouths of the dead found under the ruins or in mass graves, the effect on the nation as a whole must be deep.

The Germans have not left us with twenty million democrats [writes Adolf Rudnicki in a remarkable short story, "Major Hubert of the Anders Army," essentially a plea for the return to Poland of all those interested in rebuilding the country]. On the contrary, they left us with a few million people who have lost the habit of work and become used to easy and high earnings, whose cynical immorality we try to explain away by the war. But whatever the explanation, there is in the country a lot of moral dirt that keeps piling up and must be cleaned out. Polish man has suffered enormously and has deteriorated through sufferings. Hitlerism has penetrated deeply into his soul.

One need not accept fully this description nor believe the sincerity of the communists in posing as the champions of morality. It may be argued that, in the first post-liberation period, the communists in Poland and elsewhere in eastern Europe rather encouraged immorality by offering easy protection to shady operators in the form of the party card, the all-powerful *legitymacja* of eastern Europe. For reasons of expediency the government was even ready to legitimize the proceeds of activities in the "economic Underground"; no questions were to be asked if capital was invested in socially useful enterprises. Many new dignitaries were affected by the intoxication of newly won power and the possibility of acquiring new riches, even only relative riches. However, as time went by, the government, in the interest of its own survival, had to offer some degree of order and stability at least for those not engaged in active political opposition. Stabilization of conditions, a reasonable predictability of things (including even unpleasant things), neutralizes popular dissatisfaction. Active opposition withers away when it cannot be nourished by immediate expectations of success. "One of the most difficult things to bear is to be in a state of permanent opposition, a state of constant negation in the face of reality—and this for the past eleven years." [16]

It is generally admitted that the regime has achieved a considerable degree of success in winning over the younger generation. The means used are roughly those habitually employed by totalitarian groups. Some young people may adapt themselves superficially, as "a means of keeping afloat," others are genuinely impressed by educational opportunities and careers offered by the government. An exile source, highly critical of the present regime, estimated early in 1951 the active pro-communist element among young people in Poland at 20 per cent, as against 8 to 10 per

[16] From a letter by a student who escaped from Poland in September 1950. Quoted in the publication of the National Committee for a Free Europe, *Poland in the Year 1950*, p. 21.

cent among the older generation. To quote a young man who escaped from Poland in 1950:

> The communist slavery is hard to bear, but the German was worse. The Communists are solicitous about young people and let them study. Under such conditions it is better to arrive at a compromise, to pretend that you believe in communism and to take advantage of an educational opportunity because later on it will be easy to wash it all away . . .[17]

The brave young man may be too optimistic about the possibility of "washing it all away." He escaped from Poland, but millions have to stay behind. They are constantly exposed to a thorough, systematic indoctrination process which may, as the influence of the older generation fades, penetrate below the surface of what is now, in many instances, only opportunistic adaptation.

The opening of educational facilities to a larger number of young people than was the case in the interwar period is no doubt a point of great attraction in a country like Poland where, to quote the sociologist Alexander Hertz, "the school diploma is regarded as a mark of social distinction and superiority." Because of the Nazi policy of cutting off the Poles from higher education there was, in the initial postwar period, a pent-up demand for schooling. The government was also in urgent need of a new intelligentsia loyal to its ideas, since a considerable part of the prewar bureaucracy either boycotted the regime or was in exile.

At first there was little direct interference with the established universities, where the surviving prewar teachers continued to offer their courses with little regard for the new realities of Poland. The government created a number of new schools parallel to the existing universities, where admission was by party card rather than by scholastic record. The curricula of these schools were trimmed to bare essentials and a new crop of communist judges, public prosecutors, and lawyers filled vacancies in the government apparatus. With the acceleration of planned economic development, there emerged the need for a new technical intelligentsia. In this field, too, admission standards were lowered, workers from the bench obtained the possibility of earning a pseudo-academic title with a minimum of theoretical training.

[17] *Poland in the Year 1950.*

The process is not unlike what happened in the Soviet Union in the period of the first Five-Year Plan.

It is therefore safe to predict that the present liberal policy of admission and emphasis on speedy training will be followed before long by upward revision of standards and presumably a more restrictive admission policy. For the time being, however, the belief seems to be widespread that education, that coveted key to social status in eastern Europe, is wide open to the sons and daughters of workers and peasants. The government is currently identified with the negative policy of "improving the social composition of the student body"—by 1955 the percentage of students of working-class and peasant origin is to reach 70—but also with a positive policy of liberal scholarships and grants in aid which in 1950 embraced over 30 per cent of all students and in 1951, according to official figures, 63 per cent. Unlike the governments of interwar Poland, it need not fear, at least for some time, that the market will be glutted with unemployable holders of diplomas. Not only are there wider possibilities in the sprawling bureaucracy of a regime determined to control all aspects of social life, but—what is infinitely more important—the possibilities of absorption of the new intelligentsia by the expanding economy of the country are greater than before. The current Six-Year Plan, for instance, calls for the absorption of over 54,000 graduates of engineering schools, 8000 agricultural specialists with higher education, over 20,000 economists, and so forth.

Needless to say, in spite of the wide publicity given the program of "improving the class composition" of the student body, only a fraction of the youths of college age will actually receive a higher education. There were 48,000 college students in 1939 and 116,000 in 1950 (unofficial figures for 1952 were 134,000); the increase, on a per capita basis, is impressive, but it certainly does not mean that all or most graduates of secondary schools are continuing their education. However, the mere myth of opportunity, when cleverly manipulated, can be—and appears to be widely accepted.

A careful examination of the official statistics reveals that there is still much to be done in Poland in the field of education, and not only at the higher level. The *Statistical Yearbook* for 1949 estimated that out of some 5 million children of school age (7 to 17) about 3.8 million attended school. The percentages vary with the age groups:

Age	Per Cent
7–10	98.9
11–13	92.0
14–17	40.3

This was an improvement over the prewar situation when in 1937–38 the percentages for the corresponding age groups were 94, 84, and 13.5. But there was still a discrepancy between town and countryside. It was estimated that in the towns all children between the ages of 7 and 13 and 76 per cent of those between 14 and 17 received schooling, whereas figures for the countryside were as follows:

Age	Per Cent
7–10	97.1
11–13	87.2
14–17	25.7

This would indicate that almost three out of four peasant children received no schooling after reaching the age of 14, while three out of four children in the urban population continued to attend school between 14 and 17 years of age. The situation has presumably improved since 1948–49, and considerable funds are earmarked for schools in the current Plan, but the inequality of educational opportunities between urban and rural areas is a basic problem which will no doubt continue for some time.

The quality and content of education in present-day Poland is a different problem from the mere quantitative spread of literacy and schooling. As the emphasis shifted from vague "democracy" to the open identification of the regime with "dictatorship of the proletariat," the schools, and especially the universities could not be left alone, nor could the regime wait patiently for the process of attrition to facilitate the capture of the universities by ideologically reliable elements, even if more than 30 per cent of university professors in 1950 were over 60 years of age. The teachers of the nation have been subjected to increasing demands in the ideological field; the various bodies concerned with higher education have been reorganized so as to make government control over them more effective. Polish scholars are given advice by their Soviet colleagues. In the case of historians a special conference called for this purpose produced a barrage of criticism of "incorrect" methods used by the Polish scholars, including some who had thought that they already had mastered their Marx.

In a purely quantitative way, the arts and sciences are blossoming in Poland. Writers belong to the privileged group and are being pampered provided they master the tricks of "socialist realism." An example of "socialist realism" is to see the beauty of the Tatra mountains as stemming primarily from the fact that Lenin spent some days in a resort there (Poronin, near Poland's "winter capital" Zakopane). Learned societies seem to have ample funds for the publication of serious material, provided they tolerate the as yet not too excessive admixture of ideologically "sound" stuff, such as articles on "Cosmopolitanism in Veterinary Medicine." [18]

The difficulties experienced by some creative artists of the older generation in the process of adaptation to the requirements of "socialist realism" were expressed in a remarkable confession by the famous poet Jaroslaw Iwaszkiewicz, under the title "A Letter to President Bierut":

> When you, my President, knew so well
> Which path to take and how to lead us,
> I believed too well in old-fashioned truths,
> Feeding my tired eyes on the landscape's beauty
> And rainbow's color; and failed to see
> A simple man burdened with dark slavery.
> I know now, now I understand much
> And try to forget that which was,
> And not to turn to it; but I regret a little
> The sunset's hue and roses and the marble.
> And—you see—it is hard for me,
> I am no longer young and one must march so quickly . . .*

Other writers, unable to produce poster-like poetry (the term, as now used in Poland, is not one of derision), have simply

[18] An article under that name was published in *Medycyna Weterynaryjna*, No. 7, 1950. (Cf. M. L. Danilewicz, "Periodical and Non-Periodical publications," in *The Pattern of Life in Poland*, VIII, Paris, June 1952.)

* Quoted from translation published in *News from Behind the Iron Curtain* (New York, April 1953), p. 38.

stopped creating, apparently preferring to be accused of the lesser offense of nonparticipation than of the deadly sin of "formalism."

Economic and Social Transformation. There is much room for conflicting evaluations of Poland's present economic and social system. The source of conflict is frequently a basic difference of views on what is "good" and what is "bad." However, there is at the same time a considerable area of agreement between friendly and unfriendly sources. For instance, it is generally accepted that Politburo member Hilary Minc, who has presided over Poland's economic destinies since the beginning of the postwar period, is an able economist and a good administrator. On occasions the praise lavished on Minc is of a kind he might not necessarily appreciate. It has been said, for instance, that he has been quite adroit at giving lip service to Soviet ideas on the direction of Poland's economy, while at the same time being mindful that in practice different policies should be followed or, at least, a slower pace adopted if the initial successes of the postwar reconstruction period are to be preserved. There is no way of telling how appropriate the praise is or even how much of the credit is due to other individuals or to the government as a whole. Critical observers, while admitting that Poland has made remarkable progress in the short period since the end of World War II, are inclined to give full credit to the energy and vitality of the Polish people, their determination to work hard for Poland, not for communism. A Polish saying, roughly translated, "The abbey outlasts the abbot," is frequently used as an explanation, excuse, or rationalization of the participation of the noncommunist majority of the nation in the economic effort directed by the government. Needless to say, communist sources ascribe all successes in the economic field to the introduction of the new political system. More recently, there has been much emphasis on the blessed results of "learning from the Soviet Union."

The secret of whatever success Poland has achieved in the years since 1945 should probably be explained in terms that do not give all the credit either to the talents of Mr. Minc or to the reconstruction urge of the Polish nation (two admittedly important but not easily measurable factors).

Postwar Poland started out with an economic windfall: the acquisition of the former German lands, the so-called "recovered territories." There are conflicting estimates of the exact "value" of the acquisition, but all sources are agreed that within her new frontiers, and assuming their retention, Poland has increased her productive potential considerably. Doreen Warriner has estimated that by the addition of the former German lands Poland has increased her capacity in heavy industry by "about fifty per cent"; the newly acquired coal mines "double potential production," while iron and steel capacity have been increased by about 30 per cent, and the electrical power is 30 to 50 per cent higher.[19] Hilary Minc stated on September 21, 1946 that Poland had come into possession "of a great apparatus for manufacturing means of production, an apparatus that requires not construction from the very beginning but reconstruction only, which is much less expensive." He listed some of the major industrial objects of the "recovered territories," such as the mining basins of Walbrzych (Waldenburg) and Opolian Silesia, metallurgic factories, including well-equipped works for the manufacture of locomotives and railway cars, foundries, optical glass factories, etc. He might also have mentioned the textile industries of Lower Silesia, were he not interested in stressing heavy industry only. The recovered territories offer to the economic development of postwar Poland: natural resources, a well-developed network of transportation lines, much superior to that of central Poland, and a wide system of power plants. From the point of view of planners, the recovered territories, emptied of their German population by spontaneous flight and deliberate expulsion, offered an ideal terrain for the absorption of people transferred as a result of territorial cession to Russia in the east, and also for a partial decongestion of the overpopulated countryside in central Poland. The movement of population into the empty western territories was not too well organized nor was it as rapid as the Polish government would have desired for reasons of prestige and in order to refute claims of German propaganda that the "recovered territories" could not be properly settled by Poland. However, findings to the effect that "nothing but thistles" grow in the new Polish West are by now obsolete. The "recovered territories" are inhabited by some

[19] *Revolution in Eastern Europe* (London Turnstile Press, 1950) , pp. 87–88.

six million Poles. The former German lands play a vital role in the economic life of the country and their integration is all but completed.

To the advantages gained by Poland by the acquisition of the "recovered territories," one must add the considerable amount of UNRRA assistance (about half a billion dollars) and, as official propaganda insisted, "fraternal aid from the USSR." This last item is not easily measurable in the absence of any but vague figures. While there can be no question that Poland obtained some assistance from the Soviet Union, mainly in the form of raw materials which permitted her to put some industries into motion, this aid was clearly not given on a "fraternal" basis and was rather the result of hard bargaining. The Soviet Union also engaged in the initial postwar period in some spectacular "takings," both in the form of removal of plant and in negotiating deliveries of considerable amounts of Polish coal at a nominal price at a time when this important commodity could be sold at very high prices in Scandinavia and in western Europe.[20] That the Soviet Union put her own rehabilitation needs ahead of every other consideration is neither surprising nor particularly shocking; that the Russians felt they "gave" Poland her new frontier in the West and were therefore entitled to some form of "payment" for this handsome gift, is also understandable. But that all this should go under the

[20] Here are some details of the coal story as recorded in a survey published under the auspices of the Royal Institute of International Affairs in London: In 1945 the Soviet Union took 5,128,000 tons of Polish coal (of a total output, from May to December, of about 20 million tons). Of this, 3,720,000 tons were repayment for coal lent to Poland before the Silesian mines were freed. The remainder was paid for at $10 a ton . . . By the Soviet-Polish Frontier and Reparations Agreement of August 16, 1945, the Soviet Union was to get 8 million tons of coal from Poland in 1946, 13 million tons each year from 1947 to 1950, and thereafter 12 million tons a year as long as Germany was occupied. The "special price" laid down in the agreement for these amounts—$1.30 a ton, at a time when the official export price of Polish coal was fixed at $8 a ton, and some western countries were offering as much as $12 and more—was explained as a return for the Soviet Union's waiving her rights to former German mines as "war booty." The amount of this "reparation coal" was halved by agreement in March 1947, and the agreement of January 1948 again fixed Poland's coal export to the Soviet Union at 6,500,000 tons. (R. R. Betts, ed., *Central and South East Europe 1945–1948*, Royal Institute of International Affairs, London and New York, 1950, p. 152.)

heading of "fraternal assistance," is a manifestation of a perverse sense of humor or of an equally perverse sense of righteousness. The Polish people reacted quite early to these claims of brotherly assistance by coining the saying that "in exchange for our coal the Russians agreed to take our sugar."

The Legal Framework. The social and economic transformation of Poland was carried out piecemeal, along lines similar to the evolution of the political system from a vaguely democratic coalition to a near-monopoly of power in the hands of the communists. The first enactments in the field of social and economic legislation followed the promises of the so-called July Manifesto of 1944 which pledged the Polish Committee of National Liberation to proceed immediately with an agrarian reform. The decree on land reform (dated September 6, 1944) abolished the economic foundations of the landlord class by ordering the expropriation of all real property exceeding 100 hectares (roughly 250 acres) or comprising more than 50 hectares of arable land. In addition, all land belonging to German nationals or to collaborationists was to be confiscated and added to the land pool created ostensibly for the purpose of distribution to peasants. Only part of the expropriated land was transferred to individual peasants, while a considerable part thereof was retained under state control. This was hardly surprising in view of the basic objection of the communists to the creation of a peasant middle class. However, acting in accordance with the tactical teachings of Lenin and Stalin, the regime at first played up the distribution of land to peasants, against its basic convictions but in the belief that in this way the mass of the peasantry could be politically neutralized if not won over to enthusiastic support.

Another basic reform was the nationalization of key industries, a measure hardly likely to cause much opposition in view of the structure of industrial ownership in Poland. As was pointed out earlier, basic industries had been either in the hands of the government, or were owned by foreign capital or, in some instances, by Jews. The all but complete extermination of the Jewish population by the Germans created a pool of heirless property which was simply "inherited" by the government. The nationalization of industries in its initial phase was a moderate measure, affecting adversely very few Poles and likely to be rather popular. The law of January 3, 1946 declared as state property certain branches of the national economy by reason of their key importance (thus creating a new legal framework for a situation which to some extent had existed before the war), and in addition ordered the nationalization of industrial enterprises with a capacity of more than fifty workers per shift. All industrial enterprises owned by German physical or legal persons were confiscated. Credit institutions were also nationalized. The principle of compensation was written into the law (with the exception of German property for which no compensation was foreseen), but in practice no compensation was paid or else token payments were made whenever the claims of expropriated companies were supported by foreign governments with whom Poland tried to maintain commercial relations in the postwar period. It was characteristic for the "stage of historical development" reached by Poland at the time that the law on nationalization was enacted together with a companion measure called "Law for the encouragement of private enterprise." [21]

The general impression created by the measures enacted by the Polish government was that, far from following the Soviet example, the new rulers of Poland were building a specific halfway type of social and economic order. Deliberate communist propaganda and wishful thinking by others who saw in the establishment of such an order the best way to a fruitful synthesis between capitalism and socialism, had brought about the general acceptance of the "triple decker" pattern. It was stated that the new social and economic structure of Poland consisted of three sectors, a socialized sector (which in the beginning consisted only of public enterprises but later, in accordance with a significant change in doctrine, was to include also coöperatives), a capitalist sector (in branches of industry and smaller enterprises not subject to nationalization, and in trade, at the time not affected by nationalization), and a small or petty production sector (made up of the individual peasant holdings, artisans' shops, and petty

[21] Details of the Polish nationalization law will be found in Samuel L. Sharp, *Nationalization of Key Industries in Eastern Europe* (Washington, D. C., 1946).

trade). In 1948 the distribution of the total labor forces among the three sectors was as follows:

	Per Cent
Nationalized sector	24
Capitalist sector	14
Small production	62
	100

To the careful reader the reservations made by the communists about the new economic order were clear from the very beginning. There was nothing static and lastingly harmonious in this three-sector economy. On the contrary, the communists (and the socialists, too) were pledged to a "march towards socialism" from the very beginning. Some people were inclined to ascribe undue importance to the formula frequently used by the communists that socialism was to be achieved "in a specific, Polish way." This was usually interpreted as an indication that the Soviet pattern would not be followed. It was questionable from the very beginning if other methods than those used in the Soviet Union could accomplish what the communists were after, but this was conveniently overlooked or deliberately blurred. By mid-1948 the tone of official comments on the nature of the economic order changed. In a publication dated August 1948 it is said of the three-sector economy:

These characteristics, based on the present conditions, shall in course of time lose their actuality. *Our regime is not stable:* by means of various carefully prepared reforms we shall proceed from the present transitional regime toward socialism. (Italics supplied.) [22]

The reforms were to come sooner than many expected, possibly sooner than some leading Polish communists wanted them. The reason for the acceleration of the tempo of transformation must be sought in the radical change in the international situation that occurred in late 1947. After the proclamation of the Marshall Plan and especially after the "Tito episode," the Soviet Union considered it necessary to proceed with a more energetic political and economic consolidation of the "satellite" area. As part of this change, the "satellite" regimes were to identify themselves more

[22] *Polish Planned Economy* (Warsaw, 1948), pp. 25-26.

openly with the aims and methods of Bolshevism; the earlier virtue of not following the Soviet way was transformed into a mortal
sin.

In his lengthy speech on the "Ideological foundations of the
Polish United Workers Party" on December 15, 1948, President
Bierut denounced as deviationists those who "defined the People's
Democracy in Poland as a peculiar Polish way leading to socialism" and who

> often understood by this peculiarity some particular process the result
> of which cannot be foreseen. Some people imagined that the result of
> this process would be a synthesis of a special kind between capitalism
> and socialism, a peculiar social and political regime in which socialist
> and capitalist elements co-exist on the basis of mutual recognition . . .
> Others wanted to perpetuate the new form of People's Democracy as a
> happy golden mean, as a peculiar bridge between the capitalist West
> and the socialist East.

He made it clear that

> there can be no question of any "freezing" of the existing economic
> relations, no question of the inviolability of the parallel positions of the
> various economic sectors . . . The working class must carry out a ruth
> less struggle against capitalist elements, must aim at the complete elimi
> nation of all forms and sources of economic exploitation . . . People's
> Democracy is not a synthesis or durable form of the joint existence of
> two different social systems, but is a form which gradually squeezes out
> and eliminates capitalist elements.

This speech by Bierut was given wide publicity throughout the
"satellite" area as a significant contribution to the revised theory
of People's Democracy. In terms of Polish realities it pointed the
road which the regime intended, or was forced, to take. In a way,
the issue was now stated more honestly than in the tactical doubletalk of the earlier period.[23]

The Two Plans. The tasks facing Poland in 1945 were such
that it was clear that the government would have to play a lead-

---

[23] The result of the efforts to extend the "socialized sector," i.e., state-
owned and coöperative enterprises, may be seen from the following table
illustrating the growth of that sector:

	In Percentages of Total Volume				
	1946	*1949*	*1950*	*1951*	*1955* (planned)
Industry and Handicrafts	79	89	94	96	99
Retail Trade	22	55	80	. .	99

ing role in the process of rehabilitation and reconstruction of the national economy. Private enterprise was permitted to concentrate on the revival of trade, repair and rebuilding of housing, and secondary industrial production. Overall planning was reserved to the government and was made possible by the assumption of control of the "commanding heights" of the economy.

In the first postwar period the government played, so to say, by ear, and it played quite successfully. Considerable immediate advantages were obtained from the campaign to speed up the rehabilitation of the coal mines and to export as much coal as was available after payment of the "coal tribute" to the Soviet Union, in order to obtain in exchange hard currency and machinery from the West. By the end of 1946 the period of improvisation came to an end and the country was presented with the first National Plan, known as the Three Year Plan and embracing the years 1947 through 1949. The ostensible motivation of the Plan was to raise the standard of living of the population by a speedy reconstruction of Poland's expanded productive facilities.

Characteristically absent from the list of goals pursued by the government in this period was the problem of strengthening Poland's defense potential. The official line even stressed deliberately that as a result of her new relationship with the Soviet Union Poland was now relieved of excessive preoccupation with military security and could therefore devote more of her resources to constructive purposes. This line was changed when the second or Six Year Plan was presented to the *Sejm,* in a radically different international climate. There the need to develop a local armament industry and in general to strengthen Poland's industrial and military potential is prominently stressed in the preamble.

The Three Year Plan aimed at reconstruction of industry which was to result, by 1949, in a level of production higher than that of 1938; targets for agriculture were much more modest and production was expected to reach about 80 per cent of the prewar level by the end of the plan period. This favoring of industry over agriculture was reflected in the investment figures, which earmarked 39 per cent of the total sum of $1950 million for mining and manufacture, 24 per cent for transportation, 13 per cent for agriculture, 9 per cent for housing, 11 per cent for social services, and 4 per cent for miscellaneous items. Some Western sources argued that larger funds should have been devoted to the reconstruction of agriculture and that Poland could industrialize best by restoring and developing her export of agricultural products and thus obtain the means for the purchase of industrial equipment from the West. Whatever the merits of this approach —and there are some debatable points in it—the communists were certainly not going to accept it. From their point of view the basis for industrialization is the rapid development of industry, and especially of the capital goods sector. As a result of the fulfillment of the Three Year Plan, the national income in 1949 was expected to be double that of 1946 (when it was, for obvious reasons, very low) and almost 14 per cent higher than that of the last prewar year (estimated at some 17 billion *zlotys* in 1938). According to independent sources the national income of Poland in 1949 actually reached the figure of 22.5 billion *zlotys* in terms of 1937 prices. Even more significant than this general increase (which, as we pointed out, was in part due to the fact that postwar Poland was a different, more generously equipped country) was the shifting relationship between the contribution of industry and agriculture to the formation of the national income. Official Polish sources pointed out that whereas in 1938 the share of industry in the formation of the national income was 35 per cent, it was 49 per cent in 1949; on the other hand, the share of agriculture and forestry was 42 per cent in 1938 and 22 in 1949. These figures must not be quite precise; early in 1953 Stefan Jedrychowski, head of the Planning Office, gave the following figures which are repeated here without attempting to evaluate their accuracy:

National income in 1952	28.8 billion zlotys (in terms of "constant" prices)
Share of industry and handicraft	52 per cent
Share of agriculture and forestry	25 per cent
Share of socialized sector in the formation of national income	75 per cent

Source: *For a Lasting Peace* . . . (Bucharest, May 1, 1953), and *Zycie Gospodarcze* (Warsaw, February 8, 1953).

According to Plan figures available at present, the share of industry is to be 58 and that of agriculture 16 by the end of the Plan period, in 1955. With an increase in total volume, this would mean that Poland would become a substantially industrialized country while retaining her agricultural self-sufficiency.

The Six Year Plan, first presented in outline in late 1948 and finally adopted in the summer of 1950, differs in many respects from its modest forerunner. It is called officially "Six Year Plan of Economic Development and Building the Foundations of Socialism." It lists the achievement of political and social purposes alongside purely economic ones. "Elimination of capitalist elements" and "voluntary transformation of small and medium peasant holdings into collective holdings" figure prominently as official aims of the Plan, with increase in living standard listed rather modestly at the very end. The financing of the Plan is to be based on closer relations with the Soviet Union (a series of investment agreements has already been negotiated, to run even beyond the current plan period, to 1958). The difference between the original version of the Plan and its final form, adopted as a law in July 1950, is striking. The final version set considerably higher production targets, including an increase of 160 per cent in industrial production over 1949 (instead of 90 in the first version) and an increase of 50 per cent in agricultural production (as against 40 per cent in the original version). This revision of targets necessitated an entirely new approach to the problem of planning, which Minc characterized as a break with the tendency toward "careful planning" and the adoption of "the Soviet Union's Bolshevik methods of planning." Those familiar with the history of the struggle over theories of planning which took place in the Soviet Union in the late twenties will easily recognize in the statements by Mr. Minc an echo of the controversy between the advocates of "genetic" planning as against "teleology." [24] The leader of Poland's economy was scornful of those planners who claimed that with the end of the period of reconstruction a slower rate of increase would have to be adopted in the Six Year Plan. The same argument, about the "descending

[24] Cf. Maurice Dobb, *Soviet Economic Development since 1917* (London, 1948), pp. 328 ff.

curve of the rate of economic development," was used, in the twenties, by Bazarov and other Soviet economists, whose views were condemned as bourgeois opportunism. On reading Mr. Minc's statements one wonders whether there was actually a similar difference of opinion between various trends in planning among Polish economists, or whether Mr. Minc was merely engaged in a very loud refutation of views which may have been his own and on which he was advised to change his mind.

In practical terms, the current Plan in its stepped-up version means the maximum utilization of "dormant" reserves in raw materials and in manpower. The success of the Plan depends above all on savings obtained from the introduction of better technical methods, more careful utilization of materials, and a considerably improved productivity of labor. The planners propose to obtain these goals by introducing in Poland Soviet methods of production, Soviet principles of management (including the "socialist" principle of one-man management currently translated into Polish as *jedynowladztwo,* meaning "autocracy") , labor discipline, and socialist emulation.[25]

It is no doubt easy to sneer at the suggestion that Poland might "learn from Soviet experience." The point has been made that in spite of the loss of various freedoms the nations of eastern Europe seem to have preserved intact the freedom of looking down on their neighbors as culturally backward. In the minds of many Poles the stereotype of the backward Muscovite is deeply embedded. Many Poles went through the vast expanses of Russia during the war and saw its worst features at the worst possible time. Yet it is by no means certain that the Polish worker and engineer has nothing to learn from the Soviet experience. It may be argued that they could learn much more from American experience, but this is not available at present, nor would it be

---

[25] There was some awareness in prewar Poland of the importance of raising the productivity of labor. The conservative economist, Wladyslaw Grabski, who served in the interwar period as premier and finance minister, once stated that in terms of output "one Pole equals one half and at times even a smaller fraction of an American, German or Czech." (As quoted in Andrzej Brzoza, *O powolaniu naszego pokolenia* ["On the mission of our generation"] published in Italy, 1945, p. 27.) The pamphlet, by a Polish economist in exile, stresses the importance of a new approach to the problem of productivity of labor in Poland.

fully applicable even if available. The Soviet Union has gone through an impressive experience of rapid industrialization under conditions of almost complete isolation from the outside world and consequently with the maximum utilization of local resources. There is a repulsive element of Byzantinic adulation involved in the current praise of Soviet methods in the official press of Poland, but any country embarked on a program of rapid industrialization can no doubt learn from the Soviet experience. This does not mean that Soviet methods of organization and of labor discipline are unobjectionable; they certainly pose the important problem of human cost involved in the production effort.

A serious obstacle to the introduction of these methods in Poland is the psychological attitude of the individual worker who tends to resent higher norms and tighter labor discipline especially if promises of improvements in the standard of living are not realized. After a period of substantial improvement, especially by comparison with the immediate postwar situation, serious difficulties and shortages have developed in the flow of consumer goods. This is probably the combined result of the drastic increase in investment, strategic stockpiling, and the breakdown of the channels of exchange between town and countryside. It has been made clear to the Polish workers that they could not expect any substantial improvement in wages without a spectacular effort to raise productivity. Minc frankly stated in a speech before the Central Committee of the Workers' (Communist) Party on February 22, 1951 that productivity must increase at a quicker pace than wages, if the basic assumptions of the Plan in the field of savings and investment are to be realized. The Central Council of the Trade Unions which, following the Soviet pattern, has been transformed into an organization to goad on the workers to higher production, came out in support of "a dynamic development of norms" and for the use of the wage system as "one of the chief levers in the struggle for efficiency." Of course, enforcement of labor discipline and a "socialist attitude toward work" is declared to be one of the main tasks of the Trade Unions under the new conditions.

The Polish government apparently believes that it will obtain the coöperation of the people not only by measures of compulsion

—the stick—combined judiciously with privileges and benefits for those working hard and well—the carrot— [26] but also by enlisting the enthusiasm of the people for the non-material aspects of the process of industrialization, by appealing to their pride of achievement and their new, "socialist patriotism." The dynamic force of such appeals should not be underestimated. It is recognized as an important factor by more thoughtful Western observers, including intelligent Poles in exile:

> It would be erroneous, and perhaps even dangerous, for the West to under-rate the powerful appeal of industrial creation for the new generation of intellectuals in the captive part of Europe. Many of the young people sincerely believe that, at the cost of immense efforts and privations, they are laying foundations for the future prosperity of their countries.[27]

Of course, propagandistic presentations of the achievements and goals of the Six Year Plan are marked by reckless juggling of statistics and by vague statements that are attractive but mean little. Take, for instance, the statement by Mr. Minc that Poland will have covered, by 1955, "half of the distance separating us from the United States in terms of industrialization." This statement was supported by the following calculation: Before the war the value of Poland's industrial production was ten times less than that of American output. As a result of the Three Year Plan and the Six Year Plan the value of industrial production in Poland will increase fivefold. This would mean that "half of the distance" between the levels of production of both countries will

---

[26] The "carrot" includes a substantial extension of social security benefits. Here are a few facts and figures: The prewar system of insurance against accidents and sickness has been preserved with increased benefits. A new type of insurance introduced family allocations, payable to employees with children below the age of 16. If the children continue to study after reaching 16, the allocations are paid until they are 21 years old and, in the case of university students, until the age of 24. There is also an allowance for a dependent wife who is bringing up minor children or is an invalid.

The number of insured against sickness was (in October 1950) over 5 million and together with family members a total of 12,373,000 people were listed as entitled to medical care. This means 49.6 per cent of the population (as against some 24 per cent before the war). The quality of the medical care offered is, of course, another problem.

[27] Jan Wszelaki, "The Rise of Industrial Middle Europe," *Foreign Affairs* (October 1951), p. 133.

INDUSTRIAL PRODUCTION IN POLAND, 1938 AND 1952

	1938	*1952*
Pig Iron	0.9 million tons	1.8 million tons
Crude Steel	1.5	3.2
Rolled Products	1.1	2.1
Iron Ore	0.87	1.0
Coal	38.1	84.5
Coke	2.3	7.3
Crude Oil	0.5	0.2
Electric Energy	4.0 billion kwh	12.8 billion kwh

NOTE: The figures for each year are for Poland within the state boundaries at the time. The figures for 1938 were extracted from statistical tables in *Pologne 1919-1939*, II. Vie Economique (Neuchatel: Editions de la Baconnière, n.d.). Estimates for 1952 are based on official Polish data, translated into absolute figures in *Wiadomosci o Polsce*, IV, 4, April 1953, p. 21 (New York, National Committee for a Free Europe).

have been covered by Poland. Of all the things that are wrong with this calculation the most obvious one is the comparison of prewar American production with Polish production expected in 1955, as if the level of American production remained static all these years, just waiting for Poland to catch up.

In spite of such foolish statements, there can be no doubt that the regime is engaged, with grim determination, in a process of rapid industrialization of the country which, along with other measures, will change radically the social and economic structure of Poland.

The industrialization program is expected within a very short time to change the nature of the manpower problem in Poland. Whereas before the war the issue—and seemingly a hopeless issue—was that of the redundant millions of the countryside, rapid industrialization is likely to create a shortage of manpower, both in absolute figures and especially in the field of skilled workers. This poses for the Polish government and planners the problem of tapping hitherto unused, but fortunately available, manpower reserves. Official statements to the effect that rural poverty is already "disappearing" are a gross exaggeration, but a move is no doubt under way to shake the countryside out of its stagnant poverty by transferring rural manpower to industrial centers. The distribution of Poland's total population between town and countryside already showed a drop of rural population from 61 per cent of the total in 1931 to about 45 per cent in 1950. This is in part due to territorial changes, but also to a movement of population to urban and industrial centers.

Within the drive to secure manpower for the realization of the Six Year Plan, there is a tendency to draw a larger number of women into employment. The current Plan calls for an increase in the number of employed women by over one million; this increase would account for almost half of the total planned increase in employment in the socialized sector (from 3,600,000 in 1949 to 5,700,000 in 1955). Employment of women, especially of family members of workers already established in industrial centers, would relieve the government of the need to provide housing for newcomers to the cities, which would have existed if the entire addition to industrial labor had come from the villages. The pooling of earnings of family members makes it possible to meet the high cost of living.

Propaganda directed to women makes the most of the new status of the woman under socialism. When presented from this angle even dubious benefits can be depicted as achievements. When a bill was passed by the *Sejm* to authorize the employment of women in night work and in jobs traditionally considered undesirable, such as mining, this was hailed as a victory of Polish womanhood and the achievement of equality denied women under the capitalist system. Relief from the drudgery of housework by the development of a network of government cafeterias will probably mean more to many Polish women than the acquisition of equal rights to work in mines, not exactly an important point in usual feminist programs. According to the Plan by 1955 women are to make up 33.5 per cent of the total labor force in Poland.

Land Reform and After. The expropriation of large landholdings and the distribution of land to peasants was an important part of the communist program in the initial postwar period. The reasons were of a social and political nature. In the "old territories" of Poland, some 3,183,000 hectares were expropriated but only 1,198,000 were distributed to peasants (47.7 per cent to former farm workers, 17.7 to landless peasants; the remainder went to increase existing dwarf, small, and medium-sized farms). In addition, about 623,000 families were settled in the "recovered territories" either on individual holdings or in settlers' coöperatives. If one assumes that the economic aim of land reform is to improve the system of tenure so as to maximize production, little or nothing was achieved by this move. One may agree with the findings of the FAO Mission to Poland that "this kind of parceling . . . merely converted the land from one uneconomic, socially undesirable form of administration to another equally undesirable." The former farm hands were left with holdings too small to provide a living. The addition of some land to former dwarf holdings accomplished little; the size of these farms remained economically inadequate. It cannot be said that the new rulers of Poland were unaware of this; they did all they could to retard the process of parceling the land, by withholding the issuance of title deeds to the new owners and by keeping out of the parceling scheme considerable amounts of land, converted mostly into state farms. In economic terms, the issue was as clear to the communists as it was to the FAO Mission; they differed on the solution. The Mission, with blissful disregard of the political realities of Poland, recommended "the creation of the greatest possible number of farms that are large enough to furnish an acceptable living to the farm family and provide the maximum marketable production per hectare over and above the requirements of the people who work the land." The communists were basically in agreement that the way to increase production was to create larger holdings, but they had no political interest in the establishment of what is usually known as a "healthy peasant middle class," a concept connected in the history of agriculture in Russia with the reforms attempted by Stolypin early in the twentieth century. The communist solution is to create large holdings by the amalgamation of individual plots in collective farms. However, in the early postwar period the very word "kolkhoz" was never pronounced in Poland and it was heresy to argue that collectives would have to be established some day.

A radical change in the situation came in 1948, after the break with Tito. Taking his cue from the resolution condemning Tito's farm policy, the alert Mr. Minc announced the desire of the Polish government to collectivize agriculture in Poland. It was to be a slow process and an entirely voluntary one. The Polish peasants were to be given the choice of three (later, four) types of producers' coöperatives involving various degrees of pooling of resources, from a loose association for the joint use of machinery to a form of collective whose members pool all their land and equipment. The term "voluntary" should, of course, be understood in the way it was used in Bolshevik practice in the Soviet Union. It means that the life of the individual peasant should be made sufficiently miserable through administrative and social pressure so that he would be glad to join the collective "voluntarily." Statements made by Polish communist leaders leave no doubt as to the methods used to demonstrate to the peasants the advantages of joining the new system. State ownership of machinery depots (POM), on which the peasants are made dependent, state control over the flow of supplies to the village stores—those are only some of the tools in the hands of the regime. A differential taxation policy administered on a "class basis" serves to undermine the position of the well-to-do peasants. Roman Zambrowski, a member of the Politburo in charge of the agricultural program, stated in an article published in the Cominform journal *For a Lasting Peace* on September 14, 1951 that "the land tax paid by poor peasants in our country accounts for 3.5 per cent of their cash income, while 378,000 kulaks and the wealthiest middle peasant households pay taxes amounting to 27.6 per cent of their cash income."

With all this, the progress of collectivization of agriculture in Poland has thus far been rather slow. The census of December 1950 listed a total of 3,249,000 individually owned farms, almost exactly the same number as in 1931 on the substantially larger area of interwar Poland. On the other hand, the agricultural producers' "coöperatives" of various types united probably no more than 50,000 peasant families on July 1, 1951, when the total number of collectives was reported to be 3054. A year later President Bierut admitted that the number of "coöperatives" was "more or less at a standstill," with only 308 collectives added during the year. Only about 2000 of the total number of the "coöperatives" were of the "highest" type which is similar to the Soviet *kolkhoz*. Another revealing aspect of the collectivization picture is the fact that 57 per cent of the collectives were in the so called recovered territories where new settlers were more dependent on government guidance and assistance than the peasants in the "old" part of Poland. In June 1952 Bierut reminded a gathering of communist leaders: "We must not for a single moment forget that the individual economy of the millions of peasant masses is the central problem for the economic bonds between town and countryside now and for a long time to come." [28] Has the government run into such resistance that it could not carry out its program? Were the Polish communists merely paying lip service to "the Soviet example" and actually preserving a system more popular with the peasant? One must not draw too hasty conclusions from the relatively slow tempo of collectivization in Poland. For a while it was not much quicker in Russia either, but suddenly the government pounced upon the peasantry, then retreated, and a few months later all but completed the drive and wiped out individual holdings. There are signs of considerable caution in the handling of the problem by the Polish government. In order to foster the myth of the benevolent central authority whose "correct" orders are being distorted by officials on the working level—a technique used by Stalin in his famous "Dizziness with Success" article in 1930—the Polish leaders ostentatiously punished a communist committee in a county near Stettin for being too zealous in carrying out the orders of the government and the party leadership. In this way the top of the party is being shown to the people as solicitous of their interests, while a few men on the working level are being made to take the blame.

In this presentation of the goals of the current Plan, Mr. Minc, who is otherwise so generous with figures, offered no statistics concerning the extent to which collectivization of agriculture is expected to have been accomplished by 1955. He spoke merely of a "considerable" advance. This left the way open to the government for opportunistic adaptation to concrete conditions,

[28] Report to the Seventh Plenum of the Central Committee, PUWP. (Quoted from text published in *For a Lasting Peace,* June 27, 1952, p. 2.)

such as the extent of peasant resistance and developments in the international situation. There has been, for instance, a return to the slogan of a "national front" (technically speaking, this is not a return but the first instance when the term is used in Poland; the original postwar coalition was never described as a "national front"). The government has obviously become interested in uniting the people in what is known as a "national front from below" in the name of defending the integrity of Polish territory against the "Anglo-American imperialists," presented as allies of revived German militarism. This new policy was expected by some to slow down the drive to force collectivization on the peasants. On the other hand, it is well to remember that the industrialization program, if it is to be carried out along Soviet lines, must be accompanied by a reorganization of agriculture which would permit the government to control the flow of food to the growing urban population on terms less favorable to the peasantry than those the producers could obtain if the rules of the free market were to prevail. At one point —with the proper moment chosen according to findings of the leaders who boast of being in possession of a "scientifically" accurate way of gauging those things—the Polish government will be forced to make a big jump. There is no alternative, certainly not in the long run.

By the spring of 1953 there were indications of a substantial acceleration in the tempo of collectivization. Whereas by the end of 1952 the total number of "coöperatives" was 4900, comprising an area of about a million hectares, on April 1, 1953 the total rose to 7034, covering an area of 1.4 million hectares and including 146,000 peasant households. The socialized sector in agriculture, i.e., state farms and "coöperatives," jointly account for some 20 per cent of Poland's arable land. Various new measures were enacted in the field of agriculture with the aim of encouraging collectivization. A decree published on February 9, 1953 gave the state the right to take over forcibly "improperly cared for land." This may turn into an instrument for the expropriation of larger peasant holdings under the pretext that they are not properly utilized. An owner of property so marked is under obligation to surrender it to the state (against indemnification); should he fail to do so, he is liable to punishment and, significantly, to forcible removal from the area of his residence for a period of two to five years. The "big jump" may well be under way.

Having rejected the notion of a "specific Polish way," the present leaders of Poland are steering in a direction of eventual identification with the Soviet system. In a widely publicized article, Mr. Minc stated that Poland's political and economic development was not to continue to be merely parallel to that of the Soviet Union ("Parallel lines intersect only in infinity.") This significant statement still leaves the way open to a variety of solutions, ranging from incorporation pure and simple into the Soviet Union, constitutionally a club with open membership, to some residual form of nominal independence along, say, the lines of the Mongolian People's Republic.

Until Poland's relationship with the Soviet Union crystallizes in its "final" form, economic ties between the two countries will grow closer as a result of the process of "integration" and building of something usually described as an Eastern Economic Bloc. It suits the needs of propaganda to present the relationship as that of one-sided exploitation or "bleeding white" of Poland by the senior partner. The situation seems to be more complicated than any simple formula would imply. From all evidence the Russians were rather slow in setting up machinery for systematic area-wide economic planning. It was in the interest of the Soviet Union to permit the "satellite" countries as much economic contact with the West as would help their reconstruction programs. In the sphere of trade, for instance, Poland maintained, and still does, lively export-import relations with an impressive number of countries all over the world. The current decrease in exchanges with western Europe is by no means due exclusively to Soviet interference. It is by now a matter of openly declared policy of the United States to discourage the shipment of strategic materials behind the "Iron Curtain." Since the term is rather broadly interpreted, East-West trade must suffer, especially since Poland and other eastern European countries are not in a position to buy nonessential goods.

In the summer of 1947 the Polish government, always eager to consider offers of economic and financial assistance, at first ac-

cepted the invitation to join in the Marshall Plan. The Soviet
Union nullified this intention by a direct intervention (although in less dramatic form than in the case of Czechoslovakia),
no doubt because of the clear political implications of the
American proposal. But having prevented the two major "satellites" from joining the Marshall Plan, the Soviet Union assumed
responsibilities for the direction of their economic development.
These responsibilities were further increased by the current stress
on defense measures. The Soviet Union obviously tried to get
the "satellite" countries to step up their own efforts by the adoption of "Bolshevik methods"; but if the current plans were to
succeed, the Russians had to provide, from their own limited
resources, raw materials and even capital equipment. While the
output of new steel mills, currently being erected in Poland
with Soviet assistance in materials and know-how, may be turned
to the benefit of the Soviet Union (or of the area as a whole,
which appears more likely), the acquisition of such a mill is a
lasting gain for Poland. Miss Warriner, in her cited work on
eastern Europe, concludes that "certainly Russia is putting more
into eastern Europe than it is taking out." [29] We certainly do not
have enough reliable information to accept this statement. There
is good reason, however, to reject the oversimplified picture of
one-sided exploitation.

An evaluation of developments in the Polish economy since
1945 on strictly economic merits is difficult. Too many factors
of a noneconomic nature enter the picture. Objectively, attempts
to change the economic structure of Poland in the direction of
industrialization are a desirable step to anyone but those imbued
with peculiar ideas about the charms of rural poverty. Objectively, there was a crying need for change in the structure of
Poland's agriculture and it was generally admitted that effective
change would require drastic measures. It is no use pretending,
however, that we are in a mood to consider the objective merits
of the situation. Poland does not industrialize in a vacuum; success of her current Plan means strengthening of the industrial
potential of the "Soviet bloc." This is almost automatically con-

[29] Doreen Warriner, *Revolution in Eastern Europe* (London, 1950), p. 166.

sidered undesirable under present circumstances. And the more successful—the more undesirable.

From a long-range point of view, if we look beyond the present period of tension and, hypothetically, toward a resumption of freer contacts between Poland and the West, it may be useful to realize that most of the changes being made at present, regardless of their merits, are of an *indefeasible* nature. Those who consider it their duty to plan for the future would be well advised to divest themselves of notions of bringing back the past.

As a result of circumstances not of its choice the area of eastern Europe is being incorporated in a huge producing and trading bloc. Under the "integrating" pressure of the Soviet Union, Poland, along with other countries of the area, is moving toward a basic transformation of her social and economic structure. It may be fortunate for Poland that the imperialist interests of the Soviet Union coincided with Poland's essential need to break out of the stagnation of an overpopulated, underindustrialized country. Whatever the future may bring, there is little chance of undoing Poland's current revolution.

"People's Republic." On July 22, 1952, anniversary of the "July Manifesto" of 1944, the *Sejm* adopted a new constitution. Its draft had been in circulation for a number of months and "discussed" at mass meetings. In accordance with Stalinist constitutional doctrine, a constitution is mainly a document summing up what a regime has already achieved (or what it claims to have achieved). Poland is now officially "The Polish People's Republic" where the power belongs to "the working people of town and country." The laws of the land are to express the interests and will of the working people. Further expansion of socialized ownership of industry is proclaimed as a constitutional principle. Individually owned farms of working farmers are to be protected by the state, but special support and encouragement is to be accorded to coöperative farms set up on the basis of "voluntary membership." The *Sejm*, a unicameral assembly, is proclaimed to be "the highest organ of State authority," but the actual business of legislating and bindingly interpreting the law is to be done by the Council of State, a body elected by the *Sejm*

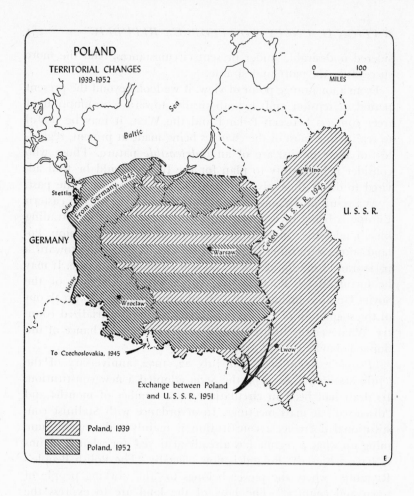

POLAND
TERRITORIAL CHANGES
1939-1952

0   100
MILES

Baltic Sea

From Germany, 1945

Stettin
Oder

GERMANY

Neisse

Wilno

Ceded to U. S. S. R., 1945

U. S. S. R.

Warsaw

Wroclaw

Lwow

To Czechoslovakia, 1945

Exchange between Poland
and U. S. S. R., 1951

Poland, 1939

Poland, 1952

and composed of a chairman, four deputies, a secretary, and nine members. Those familiar with the Stalin Constitution of 1936 will easily recognize in the Council of State a copy of the Presidium of the Supreme Soviet. The Presidency of the Republic was abolished and, in accordance with the Soviet model, its duties will be performed collectively by the Council of State.

The new Polish constitution pays semantic respect to Polish parliamentary tradition by using the historical term "Sejm" for the national assembly, "Marszalek" for Speaker, and the neutral "Council of State" for what is the equivalent of the Soviet-type

Presidium. The white eagle on a red field continues to be the national emblem.

In other respects the new constitution reflects both the degree of proximity to the Soviet model which present-day Poland has reached, and the temporary differences, resulting from the continued existence of private ownership of the land and other vestigial forms of private enterprise. There is the usual chapter on so-called "fundamental" rights of citizens, which are no more fundamental than they ever were. In interwar Poland the courts were expressly prohibited from questioning the constitutionality of duly promulgated laws. This is still the case now, although there is no specific article of the constitution spelling it out. The philosophy behind the Bill of "Rights" is that enforcement is guaranteed not by the possibility of court action, but by the actual adoption of measures which make the "rights" a living reality. The framers of the new Polish constitution were sufficiently honest not to claim that all necessary measures had actually been taken; they use the expression "on an increasing scale" with reference to measures in the fields of health care, social security, and educational standards. From the point of view of the communist authors of Poland's new constitution the country is under way to the degree of perfection under socialism allegedly achieved by the Soviet Union. Yet by Stalinist standards, Poland is a more "backward" country than, say, Rumania, whose new constitution was promulgated at about the same time as the Polish document. While in Rumania the (Communist) Workers' Party has a constitutionally recognized monopoly of power, Poland for the time being continues to recognize the formal existence of additional political parties acting as spokesmen for the peasantry and the middle class. In the elections which were held on October 26, 1952, the communists and their "front" associates operated under the label of a National Front whose ticket, unopposed, "won." It was officially reported that more than 95 per cent of all eligible voters cast their ballot in the elections. In only one of Poland's 67 electoral districts was the percentage of voters below 90 per cent.

Following the elections, the government was reshuffled to conform to the new constitutional structure. The communist Aleksander Zawadzki was elected to the largely representative position of Chairman of the Council of State, while Boleslaw Bierut, former holder of the now abolished Presidency of the Republic, became Chairman of the Council of Ministers (Premier). The ex-socialist Cyrankiewicz relinquished the premiership and became a deputy premier; the eight deputy premiers, together with Bierut and *eminence grise* Berman seem to comprise the super-cabinet while other members of the government are mere executors of policies and chief administrators of various branches of the nationalized economy.

From the point of view of the outside world the formal changes and reshuffle of personnel within the Polish government are rapidly losing significance because of preoccupation with the basic fact of Poland's "captivity" within the system erected by the Soviet Union in eastern and central Europe. (For an evaluation of the methods and results of the integration process, see Samuel L. Sharp, "Political and Economic Aspects of the Eastern European Communist Bloc," in *The World Influence of Communism* [Proceedings of 28th Institute, Harris Memorial Foundation in International Relations], University of Chicago, 1953, pp. 89–100.)

V. American–Polish Relations: The Record

Early History. The United States was born when the old Polish Commonwealth was about to die. Because of the lack of genuine points of contact between the United States and Poland as independent nations, the early history of Polish-American relations is necessarily reduced to disjointed episodes, including some of anecdotal and some of clearly apocryphal value, unearthed by apologists and reluctantly buried by historians.

The coincidence in time of the American Revolution and the last phase of the liquidation of Old Poland by its neighbors has produced the conclusion, repeated by many Polish writers, that Poland "covered with her body the birth of a republic in the New World." While there is some plausibility to the argument that Russia and Prussia, the chief despoilers of Poland, were prevented from intervening in America because they were tied up in Europe (although it is by no means certain that it was in their interest to support England), this circumstance adds no specific item to America's "debt of gratitude." More than once in the period of its growth and consolidation the United States was to profit—and with no visible pangs of conscience—from the fact that European Powers were busy elsewhere. This is in the very nature of international politics.

Kosciuszko and Pulaski. The fame acquired by Kosciuszko and Pulaski has reached proportions somewhat beyond the importance of their contributions to the military success of the American Revolutionary War. It is the composite result of deliberate cultivation on the part of Polish Americans, catering by politicians, and the inclination of some historians and writers to inject romantic episodes into the history of this essentially unromantic nation. In the case of Kosciuszko we witness the projection of the fame which he earned in 1794 as leader of an uprising in Poland on the background of his earlier American experience in 1776–1784. As a result of this not uncommon process of chronological distortion, he becomes "the first prominent foreigner to come to the help of the American revolution." In 1776, when he arrived in America, Tadeusz Bonawentura Kosciuszko was actually a penniless captain of engineers with a good education acquired in French military schools, for which there was no use in the armed forces of the crumbling Polish fatherland. An unhappy love affair clinched his determination to leave Poland. He intended to offer his services to Saxony but finally went to France, probably attracted by rumors that American agents were recruiting officers; he was hired together with a group of French engineers. A stubborn legend insisted for almost a century that Kosciuszko appeared at Washington's headquarters immediately on arrival, was asked, "What can you do?", answered resolutely, "Try me," and was forthwith appointed aide-de-camp to the General. Actually, it took Washington more than a year to discover Kosciuszko's existence and to start learning how to pronounce and spell his name, something that generations of Americans after him have never quite mastered. The little Toledo, Ohio schoolgirl who more than a hundred years later wrote in a contest essay that "Kosciuszko soon won Washington's heart and he was like a little brother to whom Washington told all his plans," was as ill-informed as hundreds of older writers who continued to stick to the aide-de-camp legend. Washington on various occasions recommended Kosciuszko as "a gentleman of science and merit," but there was never any warmth in their relations. This was partly because of Kosciuszko's reputation as somewhat of a radical.

There appears to have been a genuine friendship between Kosciuszko and Thomas Jefferson. In a touching document, Kosciuszko appointed Jefferson executor of his will and directed him to use the estate to liberate Negro slaves. Jefferson asked to be released from his duties because of advanced age, but some of Kosciuszko's money was used to establish a school for Negro children in New Jersey.

When his military service came to an end, Kosciuszko was included in the automatic and collective promotion from colonel to brigadier general voted by Congress, but he was not satisfied and insisted that as a foreigner who intended to return to Europe he needed an individual brevet as documentary proof of his rank. This was granted by Congress after Washington supported the request. In a voluminous correspondence Kosciuszko advanced various financial claims arising from his service and was finally accorded $12,280 in back pay. This sum was sent to a bank in Leipzig but never reached Kosciuszko who, upon his return to this country in 1797, had to start his claims all over again. With a bare majority, Congress voted to recognize the debt, finally funded at $18,940.25, including interest.

When Kosciuszko returned to America, he was no longer the obscure engineer of 1776; he had in the meantime acquired international fame as leader of the Polish uprising in 1794. He had spent some time in a Russian prison from which he was released with honors by Tsar Paul, after signing a declaration of loyalty. Kosciuszko's arrival, after the Third Partition of Poland had attracted international attention, started a mild flurry of sympathy for "noble Poland." The expressions of sympathy were limited to toasts, speeches, and the figurative dropping of tears over the sorrows of the unfortunate victim of rapacious European monarchies. George Washington wrote in a letter to Kosciuszko (who politely but firmly refused to visit Mount Vernon) that he "sincerely wished, during your arduous struggle in the cause of liberty and your country, that it might be crowned with success," but added philosophically that "the ways of Providence are inscrutable and mortals must submit." For more than a century the United States, by reason of its international position, was unable to offer Poland more than prayers and good wishes.

Kazimierz Pulaski's name is even more popular in this country than that of Tadeusz Kosciuszko, possibly because it is easier to pronounce and probably because he was killed in battle. Banned from Poland as participant in the ill-fated "Bar Confederation" of 1768, young Pulaski tried to influence Turkey to declare war on Russia. He finally went to France, "penniless and almost starving," but convinced of his great military talents (which other Poles questioned). For a while he hesitated between suicide and engaging in commerce, a fate worse than death for a Polish nobleman. He finally was put in touch with Silas

Deane and Benjamin Franklin, not without the discreet blessing of the French police, eager to see the troublesome "Count de
Pulaski" out of the country. Immediately upon his arrival in
America, recommended by Franklin as one of the best officers
in Europe, Pulaski asked for a commission "by which I may not
stand unter any other command as onter General Washinkton,"
preferably as commander of a "corps of vallentears." George
Washington, rather favorably impressed by Pulaski's voluntary
exploits in the Battle of Brandywine, suggested to Congress that
he be given "the command of the Horse," since "the principal
attention in Poland has been for some time past paid to the
cavalry and it is to be presumed this gentleman is not unac-
quainted with it." Appointed to the command of the beginnings
of American cavalry, the fiery Pulaski found it rather difficult
to get along with the slow-moving Americans. He was constantly
complaining of inaction, and working out fantastic schemes, including one of sending an expedition to Madagascar, in order,
as he explained, to rid the country of undesirable foreigners! A
source of difficulties was his inability to present accurate accounts of expenditures; he considered the request for accounts
a personal insult and complained of "ungenerous treatment."
He boasted of being an officer "who in Europe is by rank superior to all that are in your service" and on one occasion expressed the belief that "enthusiasm for liberty is not the predominant virtue in America." He was permitted to organize what
amounted to a foreign legion, composed mainly of deserters and
prisoners from the Hessian contingents, some French officers,
and almost no Americans, whose military talents Pulaski openly
questioned. In a spectacular but militarily unwise sortie of his
detachment, during the defense of Savannah, Pulaski was mor-
tally wounded. His glorious death, so one American biographer
concludes, "covered many unpleasant episodes" of the short but
turbulent career of the impatient warrior whom Lafayette is supposed to have referred to as a general with the brain of a lieu-
tenant.

In spite of the many controversial points in the history of
Pulaski's participation in the American Revolutionary War,
there was enough in it to foster the early growth of a myth and

a cult. In 1825 Longfellow wrote his poem "Hymn of the Moravian Nuns of Bethlehem—at the Consecration of Pulaski's Banner." It referred to the ceremony of handing a crimson banner to Pulaski by the Moravian Sisters of Bethlehem. No amount of deflating of this episode (which, according to conscientious research, seems to have been a commercial transaction) can now harm the Pulaski myth; neither can the fact that the behavior of his troops in Pennsylvania, which caused an unknown poet to describe him as a "devilish figure," hardly warranted acts of gratitude of the population. It is not even important, for the life of the legend, that according to Pulaski's Polish biographer, Konopczynski, his initial interest in America was that of a young man harassed by his creditors and searching for "an eldorado of easy money," no less than for an occasion to defend liberty. The Pulaski myth has outgrown the man; it has become the property of a nation. In addition to the efforts of Polish groups in this country to perpetuate and romanticize the memory of Pulaski, some contribution was made by the South, where, particularly after the Civil War, on many occasions his attachment to the ideals of freedom was likened to the struggle of the South against "oppression."

Polish Propaganda—Nineteenth-Century Style. Throughout most of the nineteenth century the United States was busily consolidating its international position and devoting its energies to a jealous defense of its rights against European intervention. Meanwhile Poland had ceased to be a state. From time to time groups of Americans felt an urge to embrace, rather platonically, various worthy causes while the government was steering clear of European involvements. The Polish revolt in 1830–31 was followed with interest in America and committees were created in response to an appeal made by Lafayette. The tsarist government intervened in Washington in connection with strong anti-Russian editorial comments by the American press. The collapse of the uprising brought to the shores of America the first group of Poles who preferred to call themselves "pilgrims" or exiles rather than immigrants. Congress made, in 1834, an extensive land grant to a group of Polish exiles, but the administration rejected the suggestions of compact colonization "under the

Polish flag" which were advanced by Polish emigré leaders in Paris and elsewhere. Some of the "pilgrims" wrote books, pamphlets, and letters to the editors explaining the intricacies of Polish politics, thus marking the beginning of a habit that has continued ever since.

One of the "pilgrims," Major Gaspard Tochman, spoke at seventy-two public meetings between 1840 and 1844, including sessions of State Legislatures, which passed resolutions in favor of the Polish Cause. In the legislature of Vermont one member raised the objection that expressions of sympathy for Poland were not an appropriate subject for debate and legislation, but the majority decided that, "technical parliamentary rule" notwithstanding, the people of Vermont had the right to consider the case of Poland, "as one of such peculiar interest to all friends of freedom as to justify this declaration of our sentiments." Tochman must be considered the first modern Polish propagandist in this country. He started his tour apparently in answer to a series of articles in the *National Intelligencer* wherein an anonymous author had stated that "to expect the resuscitation of Poland is to expect the tide of human affairs to roll backward, and about as rational as to hope for the resurrection of the Roman Empire."

Tochman's arguments combined deftly a presentation of Poland as "the morning star of conscience and toleration" with a description of what would nowadays be referred to as the Iron Curtain, the spying system, and passport difficulties encountered by citizen and foreigner alike in Russia. On a more practical level he pointed out that the existence of an independent Poland would be beneficial to "the interests and welfare of the commercial communities of England, France, and your own country," which, according to him, "is already feeling the pressure of Russia's anti-commercial policy" that stands in the way of free trade and access to the immense riches of the East "on which the prosperity of all commercial nations essentially depends." Tochman's immediate purpose apparently was to counteract a strong current of pro-Russian sentiment which was spreading in this country. He was ahead of many Americans in understanding that "the ocean is no longer a barrier" and that "steam power and the pursuits of commerce have brought you so near to Europe, that you are no longer inhabitants of a new world." [1]

Seward and the Polish Uprising. Sporadic expressions of American sympathies for the Polish Cause continued throughout the nineteenth century, gaining in intensity whenever the international situation seemed to warrant the expectation of a violent change in the system which had eliminated the name of Poland from the map of Europe.

In 1863, the American government was asked by Napoleon III to join in an intervention at the court of St. Petersburg, "with a view to the exercise of a moral influence" with the tsar in connection with the uprising in Poland. In a note approved by Abraham Lincoln, Secretary of State Seward politely refused and ingratiated himself with the Russians by permitting the publication of his reply. The note stated, almost apologetically, that because the institutions of this country were based on respect of the rights of man, "the builders of our republic came all at once to be regarded as political reformers and it soon became manifest that the revolutionists in every country hailed them in that character and looked to the United States for effective sympathy, if not for active support and patronage." Seward listed many instances when this country had resisted "seductions to a departure from what, superficially viewed, seemed a course of isolation and indifference" but actually was the result of a traditional policy which "could not be abandoned without the most urgent occasion amounting to a manifest necessity."

In order to evaluate properly the Seward note, it must be re-

---

[1] Tochman settled down to practice law in Washington and later became involved in the Civil War on the side of the South. He advanced claims against the Confederacy arising from the organization of "Polish regiments" for the South. Tochman undertook recruiting activities among Poles and other eastern Europeans settled in New Orleans. The Confederacy, as Jefferson Davis explained in a letter to Tochman, had expected him to bring volunteers from the North . . .

If Tochman was a nuisance to the Confederacy, the North also had at that time a troublesome self-appointed adviser of Polish origin, the eccentric Count Adam Gurowski, considered by some a Russian agent. Walt Whitman described Gurowski as "very sane and very crazy." Abraham Lincoln took his fiery letters very seriously and thought that "he might try to take my life." (Cf. LeRoy H. Fischer, "Lincoln's Gadfly—Adam Gurowski," *The Mississippi Valley Historical Review* (December 1949), pp. 415–434.)

membered that the American government had a Civil War on its hands and that the attitude of the Russians appeared helpful in staving off the threat of European intervention. This determined the choice between "our historical sympathy with the Poles and our ancient friendship with Russia." Nor was this sober attitude limited to the government alone. A study of American editorial opinion during the January 1863 Uprising, made by Professor A. P. Coleman, reveals that there was general satisfaction over the outbreak of the Uprising "as a potential source of diversion from American affairs of the attention of the Powers" and "an interposition of fate in behalf of the northern cause." Russia was called "Our Great Natural Ally" and people enthusiastically greeted the Russian fleet when it appeared in New York. Scattered and lukewarm expressions of sympathy for the Poles were lost in the happy chorus of rejoicing over the fact that "Napoleon will be so engaged in European developments that he would have little time for intervention in the American Continent."

So indiscreet was American satisfaction over the diversion provided by the Polish uprising that it elicited comments overseas. Lord Salisbury wrote in his essay on Poland:

> Our quarrelsome cousins upon the other side of the Atlantic are fully justified in the hope with which they solace themselves that Poland will prove a safe conductor for the inconvenient solicitude which European nations have hitherto bestowed upon the American Civil War.

Between the collapse of the January Uprising of 1863 and the outbreak of the first World War, the Polish problem passed through a relatively dormant period. America was meanwhile acquiring a Polish problem of its own, with the influx of great masses of Polish peasant immigrants. There was some inevitable friction in the process of adjustment, and there were early moves to restrict immigration. Slowly and painfully the mass of immigrants, organized by priests and a thin group of the intelligentsia, developed into an articulate body. Around the turn of the century Polish organizations began to send memoranda to the Congress of the United States. In 1898 they protested against restrictions on immigration suggested in the Lodge Bill. In 1904, during the Russo-Japanese war, which stirred the hopes of Poles all over the world, a Polish National Committee in the United States adopted a resolution expressing its admiration for the valiant Japanese nation, "this youngest son of the American civilization," and condemning Russia. In 1910, a Polish Congress was held in Washington, D. C. Its proceedings reflected the growing expectation of a world conflict from which an independent Poland might emerge. In all actions which they took, the Polish Americans were careful to point out that they were acting as American citizens and in harmony with the interests of this country. This attitude was carried over into the first period of World War I when Polish aspirations had to be adapted, at least on the surface, to the exigencies of American neutrality.

Wilson and Poland. The outbreak of the war found Poles everywhere divided over the problem of a proper "orientation." There were millions of Polish sons in the armies of Russia and of the Central Powers; there were political groups which staked the future of their cause on the victory of one side or the other. Repercussions of this conflict reached the United States where rival Polish groups, within the limits of American neutrality, favored either Russia or the Central Powers (particularly Austria, where the political situation of the Poles had been much better than in the other parts of divided Poland). In the first phase of the war, and until Wilson's open endorsement of an independent Poland, the main emphasis of Polish action in this country was on problems of relief, no doubt played up in the expectation that propaganda based on the sufferings of the Poles in war-devastated areas would help to increase sympathies for their political aspirations. Official American support for the relief schemes was easily obtained in the election year 1916 when the political parties became very attentive to the demands of what they considered important segments of the electorate. Woodrow Wilson proclaimed January 1, 1916 as donation day for the Polish people. Diplomatic support was put behind Hoover's futile attempts to ship relief supplies to Poland with the agreement of both belligerent camps.

In his "peace without victory" message of January 22, 1917, Woodrow Wilson declared that "statesmen everywhere agreed that there should be a united, independent and autonomous Poland." Historians are now agreed that never was a factually more incorrect statement made. "Statesmen everywhere" cared very little about Polish independence, but with Poland one of the chief theaters of the war and a relatively untapped source of manpower, the erstwhile despoilers had to make half-hearted promises to the Poles, in order to enlist support for their side and to undermine morale on the other side of the front. As a result there was the somewhat vague promise of autonomy to Poland, made by the Russian commander-in-chief early in the war (in the hope of enlarging Russian rule over Polish territories wrested from Austria and Germany) and the manifesto of the Central Powers, of November 5, 1916, setting up a rump Kingdom of Poland (mainly in the hope of carrying out a large-scale mobilization of Polish labor and military manpower). The Western Powers were at best indifferent on the Polish issue and had no freedom of movement because of relations with their ally, Russia. Even after the collapse of the tsarist regime they hoped that Russia would stay in the war and were careful not to offend her. But to Woodrow Wilson the statements on record were apparently a sufficient proof of the existence of points of agreement which could serve as an opening wedge for peace negotiations.

Wilson's adviser, Colonel House, was favorably inclined towards Polish aspirations, mainly through the influence of Ignacy Paderewski who had given up the piano for political activity in behalf of the Polish National Committee. Immediately after the entry of the United States into the war, House justified the hope expressed in a flattering letter by Paderewski who called him "the providential man for my country." He advocated in his conferences with Arthur Balfour the creation of a "restored and rejuvenated Poland, a Poland big enough and powerful enough to serve as a buffer state between Germany and Russia." When the British statesman objected that the creation of an independent Poland might weaken the position of France who would not be able to count on her Russian ally in the case of a new German aggression, House made the remarkable statement that "we had to take into consideration the Russia of fifty years from now rather than the Russia of today. While we might hope it would continue democratic and cease to be aggressive, yet if the contrary happened Russia would be a menace to Europe and not Germany." Balfour was the author of a secret memorandum written in 1916, in which he expressed fear that a reborn Poland, "far from promoting the cause of European peace, would be a perpetual occasion of European strife," and concluded that an autonomous Poland should remain "an integral part of the Russian Empire" because "the more Russia is made a European rather than an Asiatic Power, the better for everybody." He was naturally not convinced by Colonel House's arguments.

Nevertheless, American sponsorship of the Polish cause eventually forced the Allies to take a more pronounced stand on the issue. This was soon made easier by the outbreak of the Bolshevik Revolution in November 1917, which changed the calculations of the West on Russia and eventually brought to life the idea of a "strong" Poland serving as bulwark against the menace of Bolshevism.

Wilson's statement on Poland, repeated later with more emphasis in the thirteenth of his Fourteen Points, clearly constituted a departure from the established tradition of nonintervention in areas of no immediate concern to the United States. It reflected the shift in the position of the United States as a World Power.

Polish politicians, who began to flock to Washington to influence the mapping out of Poland's future frontiers, were elated by American advocacy of Polish independence, but somewhat worried by Wilson's tendency to "simplify difficult and complicated matters and a predilection for operating with abstract principles where real interests were involved." [2] At the same time, according to the testimony of Roman Dmowski, chief delegate of the Polish National Committee in Paris, the Poles based great hopes on the fact that "the American politician does not forget his constituents for a moment," an important asset in view of what was believed to be "a not inconsiderable electoral force" of Polish Americans. On many occasions it was made more or less

[2] All quotations in this paragraph are from Roman Dmowski, *Polish Policy and the Reconstruction of the State* (in Polish), 2nd ed. (Warsaw, 1926).

clear to Wilson that his reëlection was somehow decided by Polish votes. When the President voiced objections to Polish territorial demands in the West, Dmowski told him that "the majority of Polish-American leaders hail from parts of Poland taken by Prussia. If we should not get a proper frontier with Germany . . . they will never understand what has happened." Essentially, the Polish nationalist leader, Dmowski, had little respect for Wilson's "doctrinaire liberalism." He noted in his memoirs that Wilson did not understand the details of the Polish problem, had no feeling for European politics, was unduly devoted to the idea that everything could be settled on the basis of international law. Dmowski had been warned even before embarking for the United States "not to talk to Wilson about international politics in the language we are accustomed to" and particularly "not to mention the word European balance, which he detests." He recorded with a certain degree of amusement that Wilson brushed away strategic considerations, which he had presented to him, by saying that "nobody after this war will talk about strategic considerations. We will have a League of Nations."

This attitude of the Polish leader was characteristic of the general mood of European politicians who were exasperated by some aspects of Wilson's approach. Elements of this attitude survive in Poland and elsewhere in Europe where some people are still not sure that American leaders are able to grasp concrete issues as distinguished from generalities, especially in areas where American interests are involved in a not too tangible way.

The Thirteenth Point. The penultimate of the Fourteen Points proclaimed by Wilson on January 8, 1918 advocated the creation of "an independent Poland . . . which should include the territories inhabited by indisputably Polish populations, which should be assured a free and secure access to the sea and whose political and economic independence and territorial integrity should be guaranteed by international covenants." The Fourteen Points were essentially—though not necessarily consciously in Wilson's mind—a psychological warfare statement aimed at creating disaffection in the enemy camp and especially among the Poles of Galicia and other Slav nationalities in the crumbling Austro-Hungarian empire.[3] Another aim was to offer the small nations of Europe a more attractive program than the luring slogans spread by the Bolshevik revolution.

The Polish leader, Roman Dmowski, was according to his own memoirs only moderately impressed by the Thirteenth Point and worried about the insertion of the words "indisputably Polish" which he ascribed to "Jewish intrigues." In the light of his own account Dmowski appears to have been obsessed by the idea that Wilson was surrounded by Jewish agents working to save the Central Powers and especially the Austro-Hungarian empire. Yet we know from Colonel House's papers that it was he and the President who had decided that the demands of the Polish National Committee "could not be included in full" although they tried to make it "come as near to it as was wise and expedient." Polish efforts in Washington at that time were also directed against the conclusion of a "premature peace" before the situation became sufficiently favorable for Polish demands. Groups of Polish Americans organized meetings which passed resolutions asking for all of Silesia, Danzig, and considerable parts of Prussia. Secretary Lansing was asked to insist that the armistice with the Germans include a provision obligating the German army *not* to withdraw from Poland until ordered by the Allies, a measure designed to prevent the advance of the Bolsheviks until a Polish army could be organized.

In the haggling over frontiers which followed the armistice, Wilson's ideas were of limited help. The formula of national self-determination, so simple on paper, proved difficult of realization in an area where nationality lines have been blurred through centuries of intermingling, confusion of religion and nationality, military conquests, and deliberate policies, and where statistics were notoriously "dynamic." For a while the President believed that the issue of Poland's frontiers could be settled if only he were provided by his experts with a good map explaining "everything." Some American experts were considered fanatically pro-Polish; others came to the conclusion that there was no such

---

[3] "The Fourteen Points were designed as a statement of war aims and as an instrument of propaganda, both at home and abroad." (Thomas A. Bailey, *A Diplomatic History of the American People,* 3rd ed., Crofts, 1947, p. 649.)

thing as "indisputably Polish" territory. In Paris, Wilson was constantly lectured by Clemenceau that Poland was being restored not only (and not primarily) to set right the injustice of the Partitions but to provide a bulwark against Bolshevik Russia and an ally against nationalist Germany. Wilson slowly discovered that France was "interested in Poland only to the extent of weakening Germany." Meanwhile the Poles were pressing territorial demands supported by strategic and economic considerations, which Wilson at times felt to be in conflict with the principle of national self-determination. A series of compromises was worked out, including the creation of the Free City of Danzig and the plebiscites in a number of disputed regions, including the industrial region of Upper Silesia.

In these final arrangements Wilson, repudiated by the Senate on the issue of the Peace Treaty and the League of Nations, and a very sick man, had no voice. Poles in this country and elsewhere believed that the President's illness was the main reason for the passive attitude which the American government seemed to have adopted in the matter of Poland's outstanding territorial problems. Throughout the critical months of 1920 there were repeated attempts to break through with petitions directly to the President, from whom Secretary Colby and Mrs. Wilson tried to keep controversial material. On one occasion Paderewski, now a private citizen living in Paris, but used by the Poles to endorse appeals on matters pertaining to Poland's interests, wrote a long letter to the President, dated October 13, 1920, in which he complained about the injustice of the settlement of frontier issues between Poland and Germany under the supervision of England and France. Aware that some papers were being withheld from the President, Paderewski apparently sent his message through several channels. One of the copies, transmitted through the American Embassy in Paris to the Department of State, was promptly filed without any action.[4] But another copy, unsigned, reached Wilson through his daughter Margaret. The President then sent the message, whose author he did not identify, to Secretary Colby, with a passionate note on behalf of Poland, no doubt the last statement by Woodrow Wilson as President of the

4 National Archives, 86oc.01/333.

United States on the subject of Poland. This letter, too, was filed away without action.

In his letter Wilson accused those responsible for the management of European affairs of "most gross bad faith" and endorsed, without reservation, the Polish claims:

Poland not only deserves our friendship and such assistance as we can give her, but the injustice done her is certain to lead to international disturbances of the gravest character . . .[5]

There is a touch of tragedy in this letter, when one considers the date on which it was written: November 8, 1920, six days after Warren G. Harding and "normalcy" defeated formally James M. Cox, but actually Woodrow Wilson and internationalism. The date also explains the lack of reaction on the part of the Department of State to the passionate message of the President.

Woodrow Wilson is frequently described as the "greatest friend of the Poles" who has rendered to Poland such services "that his name will ever be gratefully remembered in the annals of Polish history." The Poles would probably have had more reason to be grateful if Wilsonian principles, as applied in their favor, had been carried out to the end. Collective security was the logical corollary of the creation of a number of small countries which were not viable in a military sense. When presenting the Peace Treaty to the Senate, Wilson made specifically the point that an independent Poland would be abandoned to the mercy of strong and hostile neighbors, if no effective system of collective security were set up. We know that no such system was created, not the least because the United States, the only country which emerged from the war with greatly enhanced strength and importance, was unwilling to assume the logical consequences of its attempts to influence the fate of remote parts of the world.

The reborn Poland did not turn out to be exactly what the late Lord Keynes caustically and with considerable exaggeration called "an economic impossibility with no industry but Jew-baiting, erected between the ashes of Russia and the ruin of Germany," but without an effective system of collective security

[5] National Archives, 86oc.01/333.

independence was a dubious blessing. Independent Poland was part of a postwar world which did not do away with the principles and practices of power politics and merely complicated international relations by building up the illusory sovereignty of states whose life expectancy was based on the irrational assumption that neither Russia nor Germany would rise from the ashes and ruins.

The Bulwark. America and the Polish-Soviet War. In the final settlement of Poland's frontiers the United States participated only indirectly. As a result of the Senate's refusal to ratify the Peace Treaty, there were no official American representatives on the inter-Allied bodies which had to deal with the disputes between the quarrelsome offspring of Versailles. American interest in Poland manifested itself mainly in the relief action directed by Herbert Hoover which, in addition to its humanitarian reasons, was motivated by the necessity of strengthening the new Bulwark against Bolshevism. There were discreet American interventions in disputes between Poland and her neighbors. When transports of munitions for Poland were held up in Czechoslovakia, the American minister in Prague was instructed to tell foreign minister Benes that "any attitude which he now adopts toward Poland in this great crisis will be likely to affect the sympathy which has been felt for his country." Hampered by the rising tide of isolationism at home and no doubt confused by the reports of American representatives in the field who were either completely sold on whatever the Poles told them or looked upon Poland as a militaristic outpost of France, the Department of State had no consistent policy.

In the half-hearted attempts of the Western Powers to intervene in the Russian civil war, Poland at first figured rather prominently. In October 1919, Brigadier General Edgar Jadwin reported to the American peace mission in Paris that "if the armies of Yudenich, Poland, Kolchak, Denikin, Petlura, and others all worked together under a common plan, the Bolsheviks can be eliminated." It was perhaps unfair to sandwich in Poland between the various "white" Russian and Ukrainian hopes of the West. From a Polish point of view a victory of Russian nationalists was no less dangerous than their defeat by the

Bolsheviks. None of the Russian generals and admirals was willing to agree to recognize Poland more than "in principle"; they refused to "give up Russia's gains of the last two hundred years" and to sacrifice the patrimony of Peter the Great, even for the price of winning an ally against the Bolsheviks. Consequently, there was poor coördination, in spite of the constant urging and pressure from Allied agents active at various points, from Archangel to Constantinople. The Poles played a lonely game and expected to obtain definite commitments and effective assistance from the West by stressing alternately their "desire to act in accordance with the views of the Allies" and the necessity to come to terms with the Bolsheviks if no aid were forthcoming. In this drive to obtain from their sponsors in the West more than empty compliments for their role as defenders of civilization, the Poles had the faithful support of the American minister to Warsaw, Hugh Gibson, who, throughout most of 1919 and half of 1920 was trying to pin down the Department of State to a definite policy.

In a lengthy dispatch cabled on January 30, 1920, Gibson asked the Secretary of State to provide answers to the following questions:

Does our Government desire (a) that Poland resist intention of Bolshevist invasion by force of arms, or (b) that the Poles make peace with the Bolshevists?

If the former, does our Government favor material and financial support to Poland and is there early prospect of some action being taken in this regard by us? What is our policy toward inducing the other great powers to assume some share of the burden?

If we inform Poland that she can expect no material support or if we encourage her to conclude peace she will undoubtedly do so on the best terms she can secure. In that event what measures does our Government consider desirable to prevent the spread of Bolshevist doctrines to more western countries?

To this quest for explicit instructions Secretary Lansing answered merely that the American Government was in no position to adopt a specific policy but offered, for the Minister's "private information," the view that "it would be most unfortunate if the Polish Government should conclude from the silence of this Government in the matter that there is implied

such military and economic assistance as might determine the
Polish Government in refusing to enter into armistice negotiations with Bolshevist Russia." Gibson insisted that the American
Government had built up Polish hopes of continued support and
had thus contributed "in some degree to bring about the present
situation"; he assured the Department that "the governing motive of the Polish Government agents at present is to do what
the Powers desire." But the Department of State continued to
maneuver between counsels of moderation to the Poles and discreet interventions on their behalf, motivated by a desire to
keep the record of aloofness from European matters as clean
as possible and yet somehow express American disapproval of
Bolshevism.

In August 1920, when the Red Army was practically at the
gates of Warsaw, Ambassador John W. Davis transmitted from
London a Polish scheme to obtain military manpower from
Great Britain and to pay for this assistance by taking over part
of the British war debt to the United States. He personally held
little hope that the American Government would accept the
proposal. Secretary Colby indeed answered, "Your assumption is
entirely correct . . . We do not see what aid can be given . . ."
On the issue of shipping arms to Poland through Germany the
Department showed great concern over the possible violation of
German neutrality. An American diplomatic representative even
voiced the opinion that a defeat of Poland by the Russians might
in a way be desirable from a European point of view because
harsh peace terms for Poland would have a sobering effect on
Germany where radical and anti-western sentiments prevailed.[6]

On August 10, 1920, an official American statement, in the
form of a note to the Italian ambassador in Washington, came
out in support of Poland's threatened independence and advanced the thesis that one should not negotiate with "the Bolsheviki." It was clearly directed against Lloyd George's attempts
to call an international conference to discuss things with the
Bolsheviks. When the opposition of leftist German workers in
Danzig rendered the unloading of munitions for Poland impossible and the Allies sent their warships to the harbor, the

[6] Dispatch by Dresel, American commissioner in Berlin, August 9, 1920.

American cruiser *Pittsburgh* also appeared there. It was explained at the time that the cruiser was dispatched for the sole purpose of protecting "a large number of Americans there" and not to intervene in the defense of Polish rights in Danzig, since this country was not a party to the Versailles treaty. This primitive alibi was destroyed by the Polish Minister to Washington, Lubomirski, who stated that the presence of the American cruiser "was very instrumental in pacifying the local population."

The Poles who, as their friend Gibson observed, easily swung "to the extremes of hopefulness and despair," quickly regained their composure after the miraculous victory over the Red Army in mid-August. It is rather amusing to see how the Polish Minister to Washington in two statements, separated by an interval of two days, expressed gratitude for the American note of August 10 as a source of uplift for the hard-pressed Poles, and voiced dissatisfaction with the views expressed by the Department of State on August 21, when the Poles were urged to stop their military advance on the Curzon Line. Riding on the crest of a miracle, the Poles were able to point out that the amount of gratuitously proffered advice was entirely out of proportion to the halfhearted aid given by the West. "Notwithstanding the sympathetic attitude of our Allies, said the Polish Minister to Washington, "the Polish nation had to face the danger alone." Poland was going to settle matters in accordance with her best interests. From Warsaw, Gibson opposed the imposition of the Curzon Line on the Poles as "disastrous from a military point of view." The Curzon Line, he explained, was advantageous to the Bolsheviks, not to the Poles. He transmitted to Washington the feeling of some Poles that the American Government was either misguided or angling for the good will of the Russians and using the Polish situation "for trading purposes."

In the military operations against the Red Army many Polish Americans who had fought in France under the command of General Jozef Haller participated. There also was in action an air squadron composed of former American air force members. In the words of the Polish Minister in Washington this "more than repaid the debt of Kosciuszko and Pulaski."

When the tide of war turned in favor of the Poles after the

near-disaster at the very gates of Warsaw in August 1920, the Department of State, which had earlier expressed the opinion that one should not negotiate with the Bolsheviks, reversed itself; while applauding the steadfast gallantry of the Polish army in its defense of Warsaw and declaring itself "sympathetic with all measures which Poland may take to preserve its political and territorial integrity," it urged moderation upon the Poles and stated that it could not approve the adoption of an offensive war program against Russia by the Polish government:

> The American government is of the opinion that the Polish advance into Russia tended to create a national sentiment in that country, which ignored the tyranny and oppression from which the people suffered and afforded an undeserved support to the Bolshevik regime, which enabled its leaders to embark upon the invasion of Polish territory.

The Polish government was advised to state that its policy "is not directed against the restoration of a strong and united Russia" and that Poland will temporarily remain within the boundary indicated by the Peace Conference, in other words, roughly within the Curzon Line. The Poles were also urged not to occupy Wilno. On another occasion the Poles were warned not to move eastward under the guise of strategic considerations.

The American notes reflect a certain degree of annoyance with what was interpreted as Polish "imperialism," as well as the beginning of a revised evaluation of the stability of the Soviet regime (the term was soon to be substituted for "Bolsheviki"). This attitude was also gradually adopted by the Western Allies with the recession of the interventionist tide. The Polish foreign minister, apparently mindful of earlier encouragements and blessings given to the war against the Russians, was still worried as to whether making peace with the Soviets would not be viewed "as desertion of the cause of the Allies," but he was not expressing the mood of his country, where there was universal desire for peace. The American government once more stated that it "cannot promise to render Poland material assistance if she should continue the struggle."

Enthusiasm for a continuation of the war against the retreating Bolsheviks was rapidly waning in Poland. Some military groups were still pressing for a realization of Pilsudski's early plans to push back Russia as far to the east as possible; they were looking for a new sign of encouragement in the West where the victories of General Wrangel in the south of Russia were likely to kindle a last white hope. Yet the Polish nation was exhausted and the politicians were not interested in granting Pilsudski a chance to rebuild his military reputation, shaken in the near-disaster of the Ukrainian campaign and only partly restored by propaganda attempts to give him exclusive credit for the "miracle of the Vistula." The Poles engaged in direct negotiations with the Bolsheviks; the armistice of Riga put an end to the fighting and the Peace of Riga settled the issue of the frontier, outside the framework of Allied tutelage and against the provisions of Article 87 of the Treaty of Versailles which had reserved for the victorious Powers the right to deal with the matter. The line established by the Treaty of Riga was not recognized by the Allies (or by the United States) until 1923. Immediately after the conclusion of the armistice, the Department of State was treated by Bakhmeteff, "Russian ambassador" to Washington representing a defunct regime, to a protest note which is worth quoting as true expression of an attitude toward Poland's eastern frontier which is authentically Russian, no matter who resides in the Kremlin:

Restored Russia [said Bakhmeteff in a note delivered on October 14, 1920], will never approve of a treaty of dismemberment forcibly imposed in times of adversity; nor will the peasant population, predominantly Orthodox, of the western provinces of Russia acquiesce to the domination of Polish Catholic landlordism. The Riga treaty is thus an act pregnant with disturbance and conflict; a menace to future world peace. It is in particular a flagrant violation of the principles announced by the United States as guiding its policy toward Russia.

In spite of America's withdrawal from active participation in the political affairs of post-Versailles Europe, this country wielded considerable influence in Poland because of the extensive relief program and the expectation of American loans.[7] When reports

---

[7] Practically the first document published by the Polish Legation in Washington was a mimeographed booklet describing Poland as a land of opportunities for American investment.

of pogroms against the Jews stirred public opinion here, Hoover used his influence with Paderewski, then Prime Minister of Poland, to have the Polish government agree to an American investigating commission. Henry Morgenthau, Sr., who headed the commission, concluded in his report that the excesses, which took the lives of some 280 Jews, were "apparently not premeditated" and resulted from widespread anti-Semitic prejudice which fed on the belief that the Jews were hostile to the Polish state and were in favor of the Bolsheviks. The Jews in Poland were not too happy with Morgenthau's findings which they considered a whitewash of the government; they believed that the authorities had not acted with sufficient vigor to suppress mob action.

Relief and Business. The recognition of Poland's sovereignty restored independence to an area which was in a state of chaos and destruction, resulting from four years of warfare, looting, and requisitions by various armies, depletion of agricultural manpower, and shutdown of industries deprived of machinery by the Germans and in many cases cut off from their prewar markets. Capital was practically nonexistent; countless dwellings were destroyed. The fluid frontier situation and continued fighting with Ukrainians and Russians, skirmishes with the Czechs, and economic and political wrangling with the Germans contributed little to stabilization of conditions. In this initial period of her new existence, Poland was largely dependent on American and Allied help. Herbert Hoover, whose efforts on behalf of feeding Poland during the war were thwarted, early in 1918 drew Wilson's attention to the fact that the "social structure of Europe" could be preserved from succumbing to the threat of Bolshevism only by an extensive relief program. The idea was also accepted by the Allies; the supplies and the credits were as a matter of course to come largely from the United States.

After the emergency "revictualment" action by Hoover who, on his own responsibility, dispatched flour shipments to Poland, Congress was asked to appropriate funds for relief of populations in various European countries. It did so, although reluctantly, and the Act, signed by President Wilson on February 24, 1919, provided for repayment by the governments and people concerned "so far as possible." The negotiators who were sent to

Poland obviously took this task of securing repayment too seriously, because they spent much time in trying to arrange conditions with a government which had neither cash nor any other resources. In addition to the shipment of foodstuffs in 1919 (a total of 260,202 tons valued at some $52,000,000), the Liquidation Board of the American Expeditionary Force was authorized to sell Poland various items from its surplus stocks.[8] Some $60,000,000 worth of surplus, rather overpriced according to the admission of the head of the Liquidation Board, was purchased by the eager Poles. A feeding program was established, which at one time included more than a million children. The credits extended to Poland for the purchase of food, surplus equipment, and sanitary units for delousing used to combat typhus, added to a total of $159,000,000, consolidated and funded as of November 14, 1924 at $176,560,000, including unpaid interest at 4.5 per cent. The fate of this Polish debt was the same as that of all other Allied debts, with the well-known exception of Finland. It probably would have been wiser to make this assistance available as an outright gift rather than to insist on making profit while being charitable. Under the surface of the messages of gratitude sent by official Polish personalities there was an undercurrent of resentment, caused by the poor quality of some of the goods received and the high prices charged.[9]

Herbert Hoover offered to Paderewski various suggestions, including one advocating the stimulation of foreign trade through a commission of businessmen, endowed with capital by the government, but devoted to the encouragement of private enterprise. After a closer observation of the Polish scene he dropped temporarily this remedy for economic difficulties and suggested a new plan taking into consideration "the predominant part which, under the existing conditions, the government and its various

[8] The figures and other details of the American relief activities are based on H. H. Fisher, *America and the New Poland*. (New York: The Macmillan Company, 1928).

[9] It was inevitable that these long-forgotten—and secondary—details should be unearthed by communist propaganda when relations between the United States and the postwar regime of Poland became openly unpleasant. In a speech made on February 15, 1951, President Bierut played up all the negative elements in the record of American attitude toward Poland in the early twenties.

agencies would have to play both in foreign and domestic economic problems."

At Hoover's suggestion, two American advisers were appointed by the Polish government, E. C. Durand and Colonel A. B. Barber. The latter stayed in Poland until August 1922, and his advice to the Polish government, aside from valuable assistance in problems of transportation, was mainly directed toward making Poland safe for the investment ventures of what he called "desirable capital." He suggested the "liberation of the building industry from the stifling influence of legally controlled rents," abolition of price controls, removal of export restriction. No Polish government, no matter what its social composition, could put these recommendations for normalcy into effect under the conditions then prevailing in Poland. Barber made some sound remarks about the excessive reliance of the Poles on foreign loans which they expected to be available "on more or less sentimental grounds"; he suggested that they "set about the unpleasant and politically difficult task of balancing the budget by taxation" and other internal efforts.

In later years credits were obtained in this country by the Polish government through banking concerns at an exorbitant rate of interest justified from the investors' point of view by the fact that Poland was, in spite of her apparent political stabilization, a poor risk—not a bad guess, as it turned out. Financial advisers, first Edwin Kemmerer and then Charles E. Dewey, were sent to the Polish government on the occasion of granting Poland bank loans.

Throughout most of the period between the two World Wars, the Department of State limited its efforts in Poland mainly to representations in the defense of American commercial interests. The published diplomatic papers for the period deal almost exclusively with complaints about "discrimination and injustice" to American business interests. In March 1920 the American government threatened to revise the attitude of "sympathetic responsiveness of the American government and its people" unless the Poles changed their "hostile attitude" toward American businessmen desirous of establishing "mutually profitable relations." An uproar was caused in this country by the closing of

American banks in Warsaw in connection with government efforts to introduce control of foreign exchange and an attempt to organize a monopoly for the handling of dollar remittances from the United States. In 1927 there was American diplomatic intervention in connection with the restrictions on the import of American automobiles. The Polish Minister of Foreign Affairs (August Zaleski, at present president of the Polish government-in-exile, still in existence in London) replied that the policy of regulating imports "was dictated by superior interests of national economy, to which, I should say, exporters in search of markets in Poland cannot be indifferent." The American government, clinging tenaciously to the provisions of the agreement with Poland of 1925 which guaranteed the United States the most-favored-nation status, insisted that the quota for American cars and tires be increased. A slight increase was eventually granted for a short period. Similar representations in which the hope was invariably expressed that "American competitors will receive the same consideration as that accorded to nationals of any other country" were made in the case of American manufacturers of machine guns and other business concerns.

This type of activity all but exhausted American diplomatic action in Poland until the eve of World War II, thus reflecting the prevailing trend of thought about the range of legitimate American interest in Europe.

On the political plane the only major action of the United States was the prompt recognition of the Pilsudski *coup d'état* of 1926, generally hailed in this country as the beginning of an era of more stabilized government. The suppression of parliamentary democracy was considered more or less inevitable. One American scholar, H. H. Fisher, assured the reading public that it was Pilsudski's purpose to "organize, not destroy, the Polish democracy by utilizing American methods adapted to conditions of Polish life." This may be a correct evaluation of Pilsudski's initial aims. As early as January 1919 he had stated in a speech that closer relations with the United States were bound "to facilitate the adoption of models of American administration in Poland." But whatever Pilsudski's intentions may have been, his lieutenants drew inspiration from other methods closer to home and, in the thirties, more than once voiced their lack of respect for "rotten" American democracy.

The U. S. and German Revisionism.   In the early thirties the American policy of aloofness in Europe manifested itself in an attitude of strict neutrality in the conflicts between Poland and the Free City of Danzig. In April 1931, when tension was particularly high and the High Commissioner of the League of Nations invited the American consul to join an investigating committee, Secretary of State Stimson instructed that official to refuse the invitation: "In general the Department desires that you carefully avoid becoming involved in any way in controversies arising between Polish and Danzig authorities."

The Polish government and Polish public opinion were at that time seriously alarmed over the increasing success of German revisionist propaganda in the West, particularly in Great Britain and in the United States. In spite of patient explanations by Ambassador Willys that the American government was neither responsible for what some American newspapers chose to print nor in a position to stop them from taking an anti-Polish position, high officials of the Polish foreign ministry insisted that the Department of State use its influence "to abate this disturbing publicity." Polish experts had it all figured out. In the words of Mr. Willys in his report to the Department of State on October 20, 1931:

> The belief obtains in Poland that the United States is so concerned over the security of its financial commitments in Germany that American influence is being aligned on the side of the Reich against Poland.

There were indeed insistent press dispatches from America reporting conferences at which President Hoover allegedly discussed the "Corridor" with Secretary Stimson and influential members of the Senate known for pro-German sympathies. The Polish government was determined to dispel the impression that the United States favored the revisionist claims of the Germans; Polish diplomacy went about it energetically even if somewhat crudely. In addition to exercising pressure on Ambassador Willys in Warsaw, the Pilsudski government instructed its ambassador in Washington, Filipowicz, to bring to Hoover's attention the fact that "there is at almost any moment the danger of the invasion of Polish territory by German irregular troops" and that the Poles were determined to counter by marching into Germany "to settle the thing once and for all" regardless "of any action of the League of Nations or anyone else." The Polish representations caused Secretary of State Stimson to state at a press conference that "the question of Polish-German frontiers was a purely European problem in which the American Government had no direct interest." This was followed by a terse communiqué issued by the White House on October 25, 1931:

A press statement that the President has proposed any revision of the Polish Corridor is absolutely without foundation. The President has made no suggestion of any such character.

The episode is significant not only as an indication that in times of tension and crisis the Polish government was by no means certain of the "traditional friendship" of the United States, and had rather grim apprehensions; it also offers an illustration of Pilsudski's ideas about what constituted effective diplomacy. The blustering statement about Poland's determination to march into Germany, which Pilsudski ordered his ambassador in Washington to bring to President Hoover's attention, was subjected to a masterly analysis by John C. Wiley, then American chargé d'affaires in Warsaw, in a dispatch dated December 2, 1931. The step was clearly designed as something forceful which, the Polish government apparently decided, was necessary in order to silence the revisionist campaign in the United States. "The Marshal . . . may have thought that by alarming the American government with the danger of war, it would, out of anxiety for the security of things in Germany, take effective steps to put an end to Corridor discussions in the United States." In spite of this interpretation of Pilsudski's step, Mr. Wiley nevertheless admitted the possibility that the threat of a Polish attack on Germany was "probably not an empty one" even if such a drastic step might not serve the best interest of Poland. The dispatch closes with a quotation from Pilsudski to the effect that a human being worthy of that name must show by actions his sure convictions "without regard for the consequences." This, one might say, reveals a line of thinking which is the exact opposite of that conducive to valid decisions in the field of politics.

In general, small matters rather than big problems seem to have formed the basis of Polish-American relations in the thirties.

The published State Department material for the period contains a series of dispatches concerning negotiations with the Polish government for indemnity to be paid one Justyn Fedoryszyn, an American citizen visiting his Ukrainian relatives in Eastern Galicia, who was caught in the "pacification" action of the Polish authorities [10] and, as a Ukrainian, "brutally beaten by uniformed soldiers of the Polish army." When Fedoryszyn insisted that he was an American, the officer in charge of the punitive expedition said: "We will give it to you *po amerykansku,* the American way." The lengthy negotiations ended with the expression of regrets by the Polish government and the payment of a sum of $4000. The American government also received the thanks of the Poles for not giving the matter any publicity.

Shortly before the outbreak of the war in 1939, American diplomacy showed a more active interest in the affairs of eastern Europe, but still limited itself to exploratory actions and sporadic offers of advice. It was by no means as instrumental in determin-

[10] See p. 89. In earlier years the Department of State, periodically flooded with telegrams and resolutions from Ukrainians residing in this country and various Ukrainian "missions" abroad, developed a considerable immunity to the entire problem by describing the protests as "certainly partly Bolshevist in origin." In 1922 Charles Evans Hughes, then Secretary of State, requested detailed information on the subject and was told in a memo by the Division of Western (*sic*) European Affairs, dated June 1, 1922, that "reports from Americans who have recently been in the region (Eastern Galicia) are that the Poles are, on the whole, carrying on a decent and efficient administration." In addition to Bolshevist inspiration the memo offered, tentatively and not quite consistently, another explanation for the Ukrainian propaganda on behalf of the independence of East Galicia. The "government of the Western Ukraine" residing in Vienna "has granted to a British syndicate, in which Lloyd George and others are said to be financially interested, a concession for the development of practically all the natural resources of East Galicia." There was therefore, in the opinion of the author of the memo, "some faint foundation of truth" in the suggestion that the British are "behind the independence movement, because they think they can get more oil concessions from an independent government than from the Poles." (National Archives, 760 I.C. 60 E 116/36; 760c 60 E 15/1.) At any rate the conclusion was that "the United States obviously cannot and will not interfere with whatever settlement may be made in East Galicia."

ing the attitude of Great Britain and France, and consequently the opposition of Poland to German demands, as Nazi propaganda claimed. The captured Polish diplomatic documents, released by the German Foreign Office and publicized by some isolationist elements in this country, offer at best fragmentary evidence to the effect that Ambassador Bullitt in the spring of 1939 promised the Polish envoy in Paris that he would "instruct" Ambassador Kennedy in London to have the British government adopt positive measures in support of its attitude toward Poland. The Polish ambassador in Paris, Lukasiewicz, expected Mr. Bullitt to "exaggerate somewhat" the importance of the statement which his colleague in London was to make; however, he explained to the Polish Foreign Minister that in the difficult and complicated situation in which Poland had found herself it might be useful to obtain Mr. Bullitt's coöperation.

Ambassador Kennedy denied having told Neville Chamberlain that "American sympathies for England in case of a conflict would depend to a great extent upon the determination with which England would take care of European states threatened by Germany." The Polish document quoted by the German White Book as proof of the Kennedy intervention merely repeats persistent "rumors circulating among journalists." That Mr. Kennedy was far from feeling that such determined action could be undertaken by the United States would appear indirectly from another dispatch published by the Germans. As late as June 1939, Mr. Kennedy pointed out in a conversation with a Polish diplomat, Jan Wszelaki, that he attached great importance to the impending return to the United States of his two sons from a European tour. "My eldest boy," the American ambassador is quoted as having told the Polish diplomat, "has the ear of the President." Upon which the diligent Polish diplomat decided to meet the younger Kennedy. Apparently the degree of Roosevelt's alleged diabolic wire-pulling was not too serious if in June 1939 it was considered vital to brief a young man who had the President's ear!

All this does not mean that the American government was indifferent to what was happening in Europe and to what was going to happen to Poland. The period which followed Munich quite naturally directed attention to Poland, generally considered next

on Hitler's agenda of conquest. But, as Mr. Bullitt told the
Polish ambassador in Paris in February 1939 (again according to
the "revealing" German documents) , there as yet was no "foreign
policy of the United States which endeavors to take part in the
development of affairs in Europe . . . It would not be endorsed
by public opinion which has not changed its isolationist attitude
in this respect." A good illustration of the limited influence that
the United States, hampered by the prevailing mood of isolationism, could exercise, is given by the findings of an otherwise
astute American observer who as late as the spring of 1939 had
nothing else to suggest in order to keep Poland out of the totalitarian camp than the general improvement of trade relations between the two countries and, specifically, a revision of American
tariffs affecting the export of Polish hams.[11]

The limited part played by this country in the early stages of
World War II was shown in the American attitude in the Polish-
German conflict. After making appeals to Hitler (which admittedly were not dictated by hope that they might succeed) , President Roosevelt formally limited the actions of this country to a
neutrality benevolent towards Poland, futile attempts to prevent
the bombing of civilians, interventions on behalf of ex-President
Moscicki, prompt recognition of the government-in-exile, and
frequent statements against German atrocities. Attempts of the
Polish diplomatic representative in Washington to obtain action
from the American government resulted only in expressions of
sympathy for the victims. As Langer and Gleason point out, "of
material support for Poland there could be no thought." The
proposal of the Polish ambassador that Poland be taken off the
list of belligerents subject to the neutrality law was rejected as
"academic." When Russian troops entered Polish territory on
September 17, 1939, the United States refused to protest against

[11] I am referring to the book by the late Raymond Leslie Buell, *Poland—
Key to Europe* (New York: Alfred A. Knopf, 1939) , no doubt the best work
on Poland published in America in the interwar period. The quoted passage
is from the first edition of the book. Subsequent editions, after the fall of
Poland, dropped this simple and obsolete suggestion. The preface to the third
edition, written in October 1939, contains the clear-cut conclusion: "Should
Germany or Russia conceivably win this war . . . *Poland cannot look to any
future.*" (Italics supplied.)

the Soviet move as an act of aggression. "It seemed ill-advised to antagonize the Soviets when there was no prospect of saving Poland.[12] On the other hand, the United States refused to act as channel for German peace feelers which implied the partial reconstitution of Poland and possibly Czechoslovakia as "independent" states, to be followed by the "ejection" of the Soviet Union from Europe. The British government was apparently more inclined to accept the idea that a settlement with Germany would mean that "Danzig and German Poland might go to Germany," as Sumner Welles was told by Neville Chamberlain during his exploratory mission to Europe.

"Inspiration" or "Intolerable Headache"? The period of the "phony war" in western Europe which followed the lightning defeat of Poland was, in the words of Robert Sherwood, one of "terrible, stultifying vacuum" in Roosevelt's political career. The President was caught between the conviction that the United States would have to join the war and the difficulty of maneuvering an unprepared public into facing the necessity. The case of Poland and the publicity given accounts of German atrocities stirred public opinion here. President Roosevelt encouraged the visits and public appearances of Polish leaders and made frequent statements expressing American sympathy with the struggle and suffering of the Poles. One such statement contained the phrase that Poland was the "inspiration of the world"; it was quoted back at Franklin D. Roosevelt many times afterwards as if it were a political commitment rather than a friendly gesture.

The German invasion of Russia and the Japanese bombardment of Pearl Harbor were bound to diminish the relative importance of the Polish issue in the eyes of American policy-makers. Russia's participation in the war—even if expected in the beginning to be only short-lived—was of incomparably greater military value to hard-pressed Great Britain than the somewhat romanticized contributions of the various Underground organizations in occupied Europe. The Japanese attack lessened the need for appeals to the idealistic indignation of Americans over remote happenings; Axis aggression acquired a very direct and painfully

---

[12] *The Challenge to Isolation*, p. 245, quoting the record of a conversation between Ambassador Potocki and James C. Dunn of the Department of State.

tangible meaning. Before long the importance of the Russian front as the main battlefield on land, the slow preparations for a second front and the resulting "guilt feeling" of the West, and the long-range ideas of Big Power leadership of the postwar world developed by Roosevelt and his entourage caused a further devaluation of Polish stock in official Washington. The cause of Poland, as represented by the Polish government-in-exile, was acquiring the embarrassing quality of a stumbling block on the way to friendship with Russia which at the time, for reasons considered sufficiently valid from the point of view of American interests, was given high priority. A moment would come when the Polish problem would be bluntly described by at least one high State Department official as "an intolerable headache." [13]

This development, from the "inspiration of the world" to the "intolerable headache" stage, was rather slow, uneven, and incomplete. The exigencies of domestic politics, the plans for a fourth term, the hope that things could always be somehow patched up at the conference table or, at least, be made to appear compatible with high principles prevented President Roosevelt from acting as directly as Churchill did in disowning the cause of the Poles in exile. However, for practical purposes, Roosevelt's evasiveness had the same effect as Churchill's bullying and threats. If the "London Poles" nevertheless clung to the hope of American support longer than the situation warranted, this was due in part to the lack of acceptable alternatives, to the ease with which soothing, though ineffectual, declarations of sympathy could be obtained in this country, and to the importance of the financial support which the regime in exile was receiving.

When General Wladyslaw Sikorski, then premier of the Polish government-in-exile, visited Washington in March 1941, he not only obtained permission to raise volunteer forces for the Polish army in then neutral America (the drive yielded no impressive results) [14] and a promise of Poland's inclusion in Lend-Lease

---

[13] Jan Ciechanowski, *Defeat in Victory*, p. 384.

[14] In the words of an old friend of the Poles: "General Sikorski overestimated the probable response of the younger Americans of Polish ancestry. These young men were perfectly willing to fight, but in the American army." (Paul Super, *Twenty-Five Years with the Poles*, New York: Paul Super Memorial Fund, 1951, p. 327.)

operations; he also found, in Mr. Roosevelt, a willing listener to his postwar plans for a European federation to be initiated by a confederation between Poland and Czechoslovakia. This confederation was to be joined by other countries of the area, including the Baltic republics, formally component parts of the Soviet Union but not recognized as such by the United States. In the early spring of 1941 the chancelleries of the regimes in exile and many private organizations were engaged in this type of postwar planning. Germany was going to be defeated by the West; Russia, compromised by the Ribbentrop-Molotov deal of 1939 and by her war against Finland, would not count. The Poles were in a special situation with regard to the Soviet Union. Although officially at war only with Germany, they were at the time not on speaking terms with Russia, a co-partitioner of their country. Victory to the Poles in exile meant not only the achievement of their aims against Germany, but of their peace aims against both Germany and Russia. It seemed both possible and advisable to make plans for the postwar period which envisaged for Poland a privileged status as "organizer" of the Middle Zone between a defeated Germany and an ostracized Russia. Although shorn of the blustering style which Beck had lent it, Polish foreign policy was still very optimistic. Anthony Eden described General Sikorski, a moderate by Polish standards, as "very difficult" and "unrealistic."

The Poles in exile were not the only ones to plan for the future without regard to the possible influence of Russia. The Atlantic Charter, drawn up a few months after Russia's entrance into the war, was another expression of the belief that the future of the world would be shaped exclusively or predominantly by the English-speaking Powers. "Federation" or "confederation" in eastern Europe sounded attractive to Americans who had developed serious doubts concerning the advocacy, a generation earlier, of separate national units and were now in favor of "integrated" and therefore more defensible groupings. The traditionally anti-Russian edge of such plans when applied to eastern Europe seemed to matter little. In occupied Poland, a former Underground leader notes in his memoirs, President Roosevelt was generally considered to be the author of postwar federation schemes. General

Sikorski told the *Times* of London (April 14, 1942): "President Roosevelt, indeed the American people as a whole . . . fully realize the part which Poland can play after the war as a crystallizing center for a federal grouping of Europe to guarantee a durable peace." [15]

Two years after General Sikorski received Roosevelt's blessing for the idea of a confederation with Czechoslovakia, Undersecretary of State Sumner Welles expressed, in a conversation with the Polish ambassador to Washington, the conviction that "Russia could not easily be persuaded to change her views on the subject." While continuing to be personally sympathetic to the idea of federation, the American official was expressing the changed evaluation of Russia's future role in eastern European matters.

Pressured by the British into renewing diplomatic relations with the Soviet Union after Hitler's attack on Russia, the Poles tried to obtain Stalin's pledge of a return to the prewar frontier. In the face of Soviet refusal and British insistence, the government-in-exile sought diplomatic support in the United States where public opinion was not as unqualifiedly enthusiastic about the Russian entrance into the war as it was then in England. The American government, not yet engaged in the war but holding the keys to the arsenal of democracy, could afford to voice its adherence to principles much more easily than the hard-pressed Mr. Churchill. An official American statement published at the time of the renewal of Polish-Soviet relations, although couched in careful diplomatic terms, implied an interpretation of the agreement concluded between General Sikorski and the Soviet ambassador to London, Maisky, as meaning Soviet recognition of Poland's prewar eastern frontier. It was an expression of American wishes rather than a correct interpretation of the actual situation. Some Poles interpreted the statement as an American "guarantee" of Poland's prewar frontier in the east.

[15] The former Polish diplomat Michal Sokolnicki writes, in a review of Sherwood's *Roosevelt and Hopkins:* "In the last months of his life General Sikorski was quite aware of the . . . uncertainty of Washington's support." Sokolnicki made this statement "on the basis of a personal conversation with General Sikorski in June 1943, in Beirut." (*Kultura*, Paris, No. 6/44, June 1951.)

The Poles were, of course, after more tangible forms of support. It seemed to them that the impending negotiations for Lend-Lease assistance to the Soviet Union offered a perfect opportunity for American intervention on Poland's behalf. Refusal to use this weapon of pressure throughout the war years was to become later one of the pivotal points of accusations of appeasement hurled at the Roosevelt administration by Poles and non-Poles alike. Apologists, on the other hand, argued and still argue that it would have been unfair to attach strings to Lend-Lease aid at the time when Russia was hard-pressed or, more realistically, that Stalin would have been less likely to keep agreements made under pressure than those negotiated in a spirit of friendly accommodation.

Poland was declared eligible for Lend-Lease assistance and was to draw a sum of $12,500,000 annually as "special credit" for Underground activities and for the maintenance of Polish diplomatic missions. Roosevelt showed sympathetic interest in the Polish army which was being raised in Russia after the renewal of diplomatic relations. He quite early realized the extent of disagreement between the Russians and the Poles over the size, training, equipment, and disposition of the Polish forces in Russia and he advocated their removal to the Middle East "for equipment and training." Needless to say, this so-called Anders army never returned to Russia to fight there. As part of the British forces in the Mediterranean, the Poles saw action in the desert campaign in Africa and in the invasion of Italy. They fought valiantly, and distinguished themselves particularly in storming Monte Cassino. Many of them still have not reached Poland. Some have become naturalized British citizens.

While the United States, after Pearl Harbor, was busy getting its war machine into gear, the Russians, having stopped the German onslaught, became more outspoken and insistent in their demands. The British, frightened by the prospect of a separate peace between Hitler and Stalin, were quite ready to make the territorial concessions insisted upon by Russia ("to placate Russia by paying her at other peoples' expense," as Harry Hopkins put it). Winston Churchill was pressing the President to agree to the Russian demands and to join the British alliance with Russia.

Officially, the United States opposed this demand. The President threatened to come out publicly against the British-Soviet alliance, should it contain territorial clauses, open or secret. This was a temporary diplomatic triumph for the Poles in exile. General Sikorski, alarmed by British pressure, came again to seek Roosevelt's support, and was reassured by the President that he had not forgotten the Atlantic Charter. At the same time, however, the change in the international situation was beginning to influence the thinking of official Washington. A visiting cabinet member of the Polish government-in-exile was told by Assistant Secretary of State Berle that the demands of victorious Big Powers would be difficult or impossible to resist in the postwar period, the sovereignty of small states notwithstanding.[16] Utterances of this kind were still isolated and the Poles in exile felt that American policy was still favorable to their cause, or, as they preferred to express it, still "true to its principles and traditions."

The attitude of official Washington indeed underwent a significant change during the year 1942, in the direction of avoiding anything that might contribute to the deterioration of interallied relations. These efforts were directed to secondary issues, mainly because on the major issue—that of the second front—assurances given to Molotov during his visit to Washington were not going to be kept; there would be no second front in 1942 and none in 1943. The time was therefore not considered propitious for American interventions on behalf of the Poles who were complaining of the difficulties piling up because of the treatment of their soldiers, officials, and civilians in Russia. President Roosevelt began to avoid the discussion of problems considered essential by the Poles.

The passive attitude of the American government, its unwillingness to face any issues except those connected with the immediate conduct of the war, created among the Poles in exile the feeling that the United States was "drifting away from attachment to principles" in the direction of appeasing Russia. At the same time Stalin felt neither appeased nor satisfied; on the contrary, he had the impression that the West was stalling in the matter of the second front and nursing anti-Soviet schemes. The

[16] Ciechanowski, *Defeat in Victory*, p. 94.

Russians were beginning to show defiance and determination in settling certain vital issues on their own.

Early in 1943 the Polish ambassador to Washington was asked by the Undersecretary of State "whether the Polish Government was of the opinion that American support would have explicitly to include the entire territory of prewar Poland, and if it meant that the Polish Government rejected the possibility of making any territorial concessions whatsoever to Soviet demands." This was a very tentative question, by an official essentially friendly to the Poles, and it was coupled with firm assurances of continued American support in the face of what was beginning to look like a Soviet attempt to break relations with the London Poles. But in the months to come, Roosevelt refused to intervene in Moscow, admitting frankly that the time was not propitious (it was after the Russian victory at Stalingrad and during a difficult phase of the North African operation which, in any case, Stalin refused to accept as a proper substitute for a second front). In view of what President Roosevelt's feelings and preoccupations were, suggestions made by the Poles in exile that Stalin be "solemnly warned" not to violate the principles of the United Nations Declaration of January 1, 1942 were, to say the least, untimely, although reflecting the mounting anxieties of the Poles in exile. While allied unity, meaning above all unity between the major participants in the war, was becoming paramount in Roosevelt's mind, the theory of two enemies, harbored by the Poles in exile, began to break the bonds of discretion imposed by the Western Allies. The wartime Polish ambassador to Washington records that, in a conversation with President Roosevelt on February 16, 1943, he pointed out that the German *Drang nach Osten* was likely to be followed by a Soviet *Drang nach Westen* unless Russia were checked "at this time, when her need of Allied assistance was so great." Roosevelt merely advised the Poles to "keep their shirt on." The necessity of remaining calm was impressed upon them in the following months, while the United States government adopted in the entire matter the attitude that it was primarily a British concern ("because the Polish government was located in London," as Mr. Hull explains it).

Katyn. The advice to avoid open scandal was officially given to the Poles by the American and British leaders when the Germans announced the discovery, in the forest of Katyn near Smolensk, of several thousand bodies of Polish army officers who had been shot in the back of the head and thrown into a mass grave. The problem of the missing officers had been worrying the Polish authorities ever since the re-establishment of relations with the Soviet Union. When pressed for an explanation, the Russians gave evasive or obviously unserious answers. The German discovery confirmed the suspicions of many Poles that their colleagues had been murdered, apparently by the NKVD. The government-in-exile could not remain silent after the announcement by the Nazis, but what steps was it to take? When apprised of the facts, Churchill told the Polish prime minister: "If they are dead nothing you can do will bring them back." [17] In the same vein, President Roosevelt urged "common sense" on the Poles, in an attempt to prevent a break between the Soviet government and the Polish government-in-exile. But Sikorski was unable to take the advice given him for the sake of "allied unity." The Poles asked for an investigation of the case by the International Red Cross. This demand was seized upon by Moscow as a pretext to break the diplomatic relations re-established in 1941 after laborious British intervention. The break had been maturing slowly and was becoming inevitable. The Russians had demonstrated their defiance in various ways on several occasions; one of the more gruesome manifestations was the disclosure of the execution of two Jewish labor leaders from Poland, Henryk Ehrlich and Wiktor Alter. Refugees and deportees from Poland were arbitrarily declared to be Soviet citizens. The plans to organize a Polish army to fight alongside the Red Army failed. It is therefore naive to assume that, impolitic as the Polish reaction to Katyn was, it constituted the real reason for the break. Of course, tolerable international relations are based on the art of forgetting rather than nursing incidents of the past, even of the most recent past. The perseverance with which some Polish officers have gone about gathering evidence of the gruesome Katyn story and bringing it to the attention of the world is, humanly speaking, quite touching. It is nevertheless impossible to overlook a certain ele-

[17] *The Hinge of Fate* (Boston: Houghton Mifflin Co., 1950) , p. 759.

ment of selectiveness in the way in which this crime is being kept alive. Poland has lost millions of citizens and the death of a few thousand more, barbaric and senseless as it was, would not deserve so much attention as it has received, were it not, among other reasons, for the clumsy self-righteousness with which the Russians denied the facts. Among various interpretations of what happened at Katyn (including planned genocide), some Polish sources offered one that was relatively charitable to the Russians; the crime, they said, was due to the misunderstanding of a telephoned order from the Kremlin to "liquidate" the camp. Instead of liquidating, that is, dissolving the camp, the officer who received the order "liquidated" its inmates. Yet the Soviet government never had the courage to admit that a terrible mistake had been made; it preferred to react with invectives against the Poles, with not too seriously staged investigations which put the blame on the Germans, and with a silly attempt to have the Katyn crime charged to the Nazis in the Nürnberg indictment. This last attempt certainly failed to produce the result hoped for by the Soviet government; one looks in vain in the judgment rendered by the Tribunal for an evaluation of the Katyn episode one way or another. Thus the inability of the Poles to forget and the inability of the Russians to admit guilt or even a mistake have jointly contributed another bitter chapter to the history of Polish-Russian relations.[18]

Roosevelt and the Underground. Aware of the weakness of their diplomatic position, the Poles in exile tried to awaken Roosevelt's interest in their fate by impressing him with the importance of the military contribution which their Underground could make to the allied war effort. These representations stressed the value of the intelligence services rendered by the Polish Underground network to the West. Another approach

---

[18] The issue of Katyn has recently reappeared as an item in American domestic politics. A special congressional committee dealt with various aspects of the problem: the circumstances of the massacre itself, the guilt of the Soviet government, and the alleged suppression of evidence contained in the affidavit of an American colonel who, as prisoner of war, was taken by the Germans to Katyn. The investigators, as well as some of the witnesses who appeared before the committee, at no point tried to evaluate the attitude of President Roosevelt and other American officials against the circumstances of 1943; it was all in the spirit of 1952.

was tried later, when it became clear that the Soviet armies and not the Anglo-American forces were going to be in Poland: the London-controlled Underground was declared ready and willing to coöperate militarily with the Russians, if only the latter would renew diplomatic relations with the government-in-exile, broken off in April 1943. At that time, however, the Russians had achieved the agreement in principle of the major allies to their territorial demands and they considered assistance of the Underground of militarily limited and politically questionable value. The President of the United States was always interested in possible contributions to the war effort against the Nazis, but the flow of material to the Polish Underground was not consistently maintained. An early decision to provide arms for the Underground was rather abruptly reversed by the Combined Chiefs of Staff in the autumn of 1943; to change this decision later, when the Russians were already on Polish territory, seemed rather awkward. The Poles continued to insist on the shipment of arms, but they could not obtain a clear decision in Washington, in spite of dramatic stunts, for example, the arrival of special envoys of the Underground, with detailed maps and operation plans. Mr. Roosevelt listened with fascination to tales of the "secret state," but he took no decisions satisfactory to the London Poles.

At the Moscow conference of Foreign Ministers, in October 1943, Mr. Hull made no effort to bring up the Polish issue beyond seconding Anthony Eden's tentative approach to Molotov. On his return to Washington the Secretary of State was chagrined to find that the Polish-American press was critical of his failure to intervene on behalf of Poland. Mr. Hull argued later in his memoirs that he had gone to Moscow to patch up things between the United States and Russia—and there was much to patch up—not between Russia and the Poles in exile. To the Polish ambassador in Washington he explained patiently that "one can insist, and even press, if one has the means to do so. We have no such means for the time being." The Poles, and some of their friends in this country, continued to believe that the United States had the means and that it was advisable to use them on behalf of the Polish cause.

Teheran.   The Big Three conference at Teheran was the next major step in American acceptance of Russian demands. President Roosevelt agreed there, "in principle," to Stalin's demand that the Curzon Line should be the future frontier between Poland and the Soviet Union. From the Hopkins papers it would appear that Roosevelt had even earlier, during Anthony Eden's visit to Washington in March 1943, acquiesced in this settlement; he merely wanted to keep it secret as long as possible.[19] It is important for an understanding of Roosevelt's motives to remember that at the Quebec conference, in August 1943, a high-level American military estimate of Russia's postwar possibilities was presented, in which it was suggested that no effort be spared to win the friendship of the Russians and to secure Soviet assistance in the war against Japan. The President was no doubt familiar with the contents of this top level estimate. The final decision concerning the Polish frontiers, taken at Yalta in February 1945, also seems to have been largely influenced by military estimates of the need for Soviet aid in the Far East. Concessions at the expense of Poland—or, for that matter, China—appeared justified in the light of such estimates.

The initiative in bringing up the matter of Poland's postwar frontiers at Teheran belonged to Mr. Churchill. He was eager to demonstrate to Stalin that the British government was inclined to accept the extension of Russia's frontier roughly to the Curzon Line, but was looking for a formula which would make the shift reasonable from the point of view of the Poles. He expressed the idea that "Poland might move westward, like soldiers taking two steps 'left close.' " He repeatedly demonstrated, with the help of three matches, the westward shift of Russia and Poland at the expense of Germany. This, Mr. Churchill noted in his memoirs, "pleased Stalin." The idea also pleased Churchill who stated at one point that he "would say to the Poles that if they did not accept it they would be foolish and I would remind them that but

---

[19] According to the Hopkins papers, Eden described the Poles in exile as "being very difficult" and as harboring ambitious postwar designs based on the expectation that "Russia will be so weakened and Germany crushed that Poland will emerge as the most powerful state in that part of the world." Roosevelt said that he "did not intend to go to the peace conference and bargain with Poland . . . The important thing is to set it (Poland) up in a way that will help maintain the peace of the world."

for the Red Army they would have been utterly destroyed. I would point out to them that they had been given a fine place to live in, more than three hundred miles each way." [20] He assured Stalin that he was "not going to break my heart about this cession of part of Germany to Poland" nor was he prepared "to make a great squawk about Lvov." He nevertheless knew that "nothing would satisfy the Poles." Churchill stressed the point that he was speaking only for the British and not for Roosevelt who "had many Poles in the United States." In the light of Churchill's account, the President seems to have said very little at the conference, about Poland; he tentatively expressed the hope that relations would be resumed between the Soviet government and the "London" Poles, so that the latter might accept whatever decisions were reached by the Big Three. The suggestion was rejected by Stalin. Roosevelt remained silent when Churchill, after suggesting to Stalin the compensation deal for Poland, stated that he did not think "we were very far apart in principle." [21] The President merely asked Stalin whether a transfer of populations would be possible, presumably between Poland and Russia as well as between Poland and Germany.

The fact that Roosevelt agreed in Teheran—at least tacitly and "in principle"—to the Soviet acquisition of eastern Poland, was not revealed officially in the United States; it would have been awkward to break the news in election year 1944. However, the Polish government-in-exile was soon told that

The basic position of the United States Government that general discussions of the many European frontier questions during the period of active hostilities will run the risk of creating confusion . . . does not preclude the possibility of any two countries having mutual territorial problems from seeking a direct settlement by mutual accord. This Government recognizes that recent developments present certain complex

[20] Churchill, *Closing the Ring* (Boston: Houghton Mifflin Co., 1952) , p. 396.
[21] At the third plenary meeting of the Yalta conference Roosevelt stated, according to Stettinius, that "he had said at Teheran that the American people were inclined to accept the Curzon Line as the eastern frontier of Poland." Sumner Welles, in *Seven Decisions that Shaped History* (New York: Harper and Brothers, 1951) , describes the Curzon Line as "in fact a settlement voluntarily offered by Churchill and Roosevelt at the Teheran Conference" (p. 142) .

and vital considerations which may render it desirable for the Polish Government to endeavor to reach a solution with regard to its territory without delay . . .

The statement also contained an offer of American good offices in re-establishing relations between the London Poles and the Soviet Union, although it clearly rejected any American guarantee of specific frontier arrangements. The President, preoccupied with the forthcoming elections and long determined to let Mr. Churchill take the initiative in forcing the London Poles to accept Stalin's conditions, tried to keep out of further involvement in the embarrassing Polish issue. In a long cable to Stalin the President very cautiously suggested that Mikolajczyk—premier of the Polish government-in-exile since General Sikorski's death —should be given a chance to reorganize the Polish government in accordance with Stalin's wishes but in a manner *which would make it appear* that no external pressure was being applied. Otherwise the President was trying, in Mr. Hull's words, "to refrain from stretching the United States on a bed of nettles." Mikolajczyk's planned visit to Washington was being discouraged in order to avoid the impression that the United States had embraced Poland's position versus Russia.

In June 1944, the President finally received the Polish prime minister, charmed him with his best smile, but made it quite clear that the Poles should agree to the Russian territorial demands and also to the new conditions advanced by Moscow— the removal of certain personalities from the government-in-exile. He assured Mikolajczyk that he himself would "unhesitatingly agree to make concessions" which were inevitable. "There are five times more Russians than Poles, and you cannot risk war with Russia. What alternative remains? Only to reach agreement."

While these statements were being made in private, the President counted on the loyalty of the London Poles not to spoil his election chances by indiscretion; delegations of Polish Americans were received and given vague but warm assurances of American support for the Polish cause. Unable to find more tangible reasons for optimism, some Poles ascribed special importance to the fact that during the reception of a Polish American delegation Mr. Roosevelt was sitting against the background of a map of

Poland showing the prewar, Riga frontier and bearing no markings along the Curzon Line.

Another encouraging gesture made shortly before the elections was the appointment of Arthur Bliss Lane to be ambassador to the Polish government-in-exile and thus fill the vacancy caused by the resignation of Anthony Drexel Biddle. It was clear that Mr. Lane was not going to assume his post in London and be accredited to a government marked for extinction. He eventually went to Warsaw, for a short and turbulent career as ambassador to the postwar government of Poland.

On the whole, the United States remained inactive while Mr. Churchill was trying to bring Mikolajczyk and his government to accept the Soviet demands. A few days after his re-election, the President again told Mikolajczyk that any settlement reached between the British, the Poles, and the Soviet Union would meet with no objection on his part. He tried to encourage the Poles to accept compensation in the form of German territory for the loss of the eastern half of their prewar territory, by offering American assistance in whatever transfer of populations might be necessary, and by aid for Poland's postwar economic reconstruction. Representations made by Poles and non-Poles at that time would meet with Mr. Roosevelt's impatient retort: *"Do you want me to go to war with Russia?"* He expressed, in a conversation with Arthur Bliss Lane, the feeling that Stalin was justified in trying to build a *cordon sanitaire* of "friendly" states around Russia. In the atmosphere of good will towards Russia, the State Department issued passports for a visit to Stalin by two American citizens of Polish origin, the obscure parish priest Orlemanski and the economist Oscar Lange, a distinguished scholar with an urge to engage in politics. Both returned from Moscow "convinced" of Stalin's best intentions toward Poland. The testimony of President Benes of Czechoslovakia about Stalin's intentions was also given wide publicity.

In the diplomatic game around the Polish issue, the United States was a passive observer of the disintegration of the "London" regime, much to the annoyance of the British who, as Hopkins was told in London, were indignant over the "somewhat sanctimonious, holier-than-thou attitude which the United States was assuming toward a situation in which it was undoubtedly concerned but for the solution of which it was taking no responsibility." American interest would flare up occasionally, as at the time of the ill-fated Warsaw uprising in August 1944. To most Americans the human side of the uprising, the hardships of the population subjected to constant bombardment by the Nazis and the studied indifference of the Soviet government overshadowed its political aims. Indignation was high, but it was not followed by determined action. Of course, there were statements praising the heroism of the Poles, and a warning to the Germans to adhere to the rules of international law in the treatment of captured Polish fighters; there were approaches to the Soviet government for military aid to the uprising, but actual support from the West was slow in materializing. Polish sources claimed that the Warsaw uprising was "in accordance with plans . . . disclosed (by a special envoy of the Underground) at the White House and discussed with the President and the British and American staffs," [22] but there is no indication that the exact timing of the uprising had actually been discussed and agreed upon.

While Warsaw was being burned down by the Germans, Mikolajczyk, under British pressure, was negotiating in Moscow. During the conferences which took place there, the American representative, Averell W. Harriman, limited his role to that of an observer. He neither confirmed nor denied Molotov's statements that Roosevelt had agreed to the Curzon Line at Teheran. After his return from Moscow, Mikolajczyk received, in November, a long letter from the President which convinced him that the United States was not prepared to support the stand that the Polish government-in-exile, citing "instructions" from the Underground, was taking. Consequently Mikolajczyk resigned and a new Polish government was formed. It was practically ignored by the British and, to a large extent, also by the American government. Mikolajczyk, now a private citizen, became the favorite of Anglo-American diplomacy.

[22] This is apparently a reference to the visit to Washington, in 1944, of General Tatar (who at the time used the pseudonym "Tabor"). In 1951 the general, who after the war returned to Poland, was sentenced to life imprisonment for alleged espionage.

Poland at Yalta.   On the way to the Yalta conference President Roosevelt was, according to the accounts of those who accompanied him, preoccupied with the problems of the war in the Pacific. Secretary of War Stimson revealed later that he had been informed by the military that an invasion of the Japanese home islands "might be expected to cost over a million casualties to American forces alone." The military memorandum presented at the Quebec conference had already stressed the point that "the most important factor the United States has to consider in relations to Russia is the prosecution of the war in the Pacific." When he met Mr. Churchill on the island of Malta on the way to the conference with Stalin, the President expressed concern that the Japanese war "might continue until 1947." Even in Europe the end of the war was not clearly in sight, and the possibility of a German comeback was dramatically demonstrated by the Battle of the Bulge. Although the Polish problem developed, at the Yalta conference, into an issue which consumed more time than any other subject, the haggling over Poland at the conference table was, at least in part, a form of shadow-boxing while the negotiations for Russian participation in the invasion of Japan were being conducted in deep secrecy. A Polish writer in exile stated a few years later: "Had Japan surrendered earlier, there would have been no Iron Curtain in Europe."

It cannot be said that the Department of State had neglected the study of the Polish frontier issue. A "problem paper" dated March 26, 1943, and made public by the Department as a sample of its wartime studies of postwar problems, contains a learned description of no less than ten alternative boundaries between Poland and the Soviet Union, none of them identical with the prewar frontier. This was followed by a "policy summary paper" of May 19, 1943, which summarized the discussions of various alternatives by two subcommittees of the Department. On the whole, the summary stated, there was "a general willingness to accept the Curzon Line if it proved impossible to secure a boundary more favorable to Poland." It was realized that the situation in the area at the close of formal hostilities might be such that even the Ribbentrop-Molotov Line, least favorable to Poland, "would have to be accepted." [23] American diplomatic efforts on the whole followed, though without much insistence, the basic recommendation of the quoted paper to retain within Poland the city of Lwow, the oil fields, and the line of the Carpathians. The policy-makers may have accepted the argument of the Political Subcommittee of the study group that "the extension of Soviet territory to the Carpathians would represent an insuperable obstacle to the creation of an East European federation."

The American delegation at Yalta came to the conference equipped with policy recommendations following the lines of the studies made earlier by the Department of State. Other recommendations opposed the idea of extending the Polish frontier in the west to the Oder-Neisse line and suggested instead a more limited acquisition of German territory in East Prussia, Silesia, and Pomerania.

At Yalta the President made a weak attempt to suggest that Lwow and the oil fields be left with Poland, by invoking the "salutary effect [of such a concession] on American opinion," but he made it clear that this was "merely a suggestion" on which he would not insist. In a letter to Stalin between meetings Roosevelt offered to examine the conditions under which the American government would be ready to dissociate itself from the London government to which, as he said on another occasion during the conference, he attached no importance whatsoever "since he felt that for some years there had been in reality no Polish government." The American formula quite early in the negotiations dropped the demand for Lwow and the oil fields and expressed agreement with larger acquisitions of German territory (although questioning the extension of the Polish frontier to the Neisse). At one point the American delegation suggested the creation of a Presidential Committee of three: the "Lublin" leader Bierut, the "reasonable" London Pole Grabski, and Archbishop Sapieha. This idea, too, was abandoned. The President joined forces with Mr. Churchill in insisting that an "entirely new" government be created in Poland instead of merely enlarging the "Lublin" body,

[23] *Postwar Foreign Policy Preparation 1939–1945* (Washington, 1949), pp. 510 ff.

already installed and functioning in the country. "It would be
much easier . . . to abandon the London government" if a new
start were made, argued Mr. Eden; the "impact of the Polish issue
on American public opinion" was stressed by Mr. Stettinius. The
President at one point said that it was "extremely important that
some recognition of the Polish Americans' desire for free elections be in the final agreement." Stalin understood how to counter
with the same kind of arguments; he impressed the President with
the troubles he would have with "his Ukrainians."

The final formula adopted by the conference stated that "the
provisional government now functioning in Poland should . . .
be reorganized on a broader democratic basis with the inclusion
of democratic leaders from Poland itself and from Poles abroad.
This new Government should then be called the Polish Provisional Government of National Unity." It is clear from an examination of the various formulae suggested during the conference that the final text was an attempt to reconcile, by using
vague and even contradictory terms, the positions taken by East
and West respectively. Immediately after the conference Mr.
Molotov could claim that the text of the agreement meant an
enlargement of the existing "Lublin" government, while the
British and the Americans insisted that it meant the creation of
an entirely new government.

The agreement, as Stettinius admitted, was not clear cut. There
was, if one wanted to be technical, room for both interpretations
—a real diplomat's delight—although it was not unimportant
that the "Lublin" government was mentioned as a body while
the "other Poles" were to be invited to participate in the "new"
government on an individual basis. Molotov was not the only one
to interpret the Yalta agreement on Poland as meaning that a
few non-communists would be added to the existing and functioning "Lublin" government; the Polish ambassador to Washington, Jan Ciechanowski, pointed out to Mr. Stettinius that "the
wording of the Yalta agreement . . . implied that a compromise
government, dominated by the Lublin communists, had been accepted." If both East and West quickly became disappointed in
the way the other side was interpreting Yalta this was apparently
due to the fact that Roosevelt and Churchill had expected Stalin

to be more coöperative in form, if not in essence, on the Polish issue, while Stalin felt that he had offered the West a face-saving formula, which was all it was "legitimately" entitled to in his view, and he disliked the attempts of Anglo-American diplomacy to overstep these limits of Yalta by insisting on actual influence on the shaping of the government of Poland.[24]

Concerning Roosevelt's stand at Yalta various interpretations have been offered, ranging from suggestions that the President was not in full control of his physical and mental faculties at the time of the conference, to claims that Yalta was actually a diplomatic victory for the American side or that "we gave nothing to the Russians that they were not holding already." Another theory is that the Yalta agreement on Poland was a very good agreement indeed but unfortunately the Russians did not keep it. Roosevelt himself was not quite sure that it was a "good" agreement. He called it, in his report to a joint session of Congress, "under the circumstances—the most hopeful agreement possible for a free, independent and prosperous Polish State." The "best possible" was not necessarily good, certainly not good enough from the point of view of the London Poles. Did the President accept the thesis to which Churchill seemed to adhere that for the price of territorial concessions one could obtain Stalin's agreement to a "truly independent" Poland or, more realistically speaking, to the inclusion of Poland in an area of "joint concern"? The validity of this theory has been questioned; while seeming to exonerate the Western leaders by making them Stalin's dupes, it actually would be an insult to their intelligence; Mr. Churchill, for one, is probably the last person willing to admit that he was naive.[25]

[24] On April 6, 1945, when difficulties had developed over the interpretation of the Yalta decisions concerning Poland, Ambassador Harriman cabled from Moscow: "It may be difficult for us to believe, but it still may be true that Stalin and Molotov considered at Yalta that by our willingness to accept a general wording of the declaration on Poland and liberated Europe, by our recognition of the need of the Red Army for security behind its lines, and of the predominant interest of Russia in Poland as a friendly neighbor and as a corridor to Germany, we understood and were ready to accept Soviet policies already known to us." (Walter Millis, ed., *The Forrestal Diaries,* New York: Viking Press, Inc., 1951, p. 40.)

[25] A former Polish diplomat who was connected with Polish government-in-exile and is now teaching in this country offered me the information that "Churchill told the Polish representatives in London after his return from

Some still consider Yalta a success because it provided Western diplomacy with leverage against the Soviet Union when relations deteriorated over issues much more fundamental than that of "free and unfettered elections" in Poland. Still others argue that the actual "surrender" of eastern Europe to Stalin happened not at Yalta, but much later, in the fall of 1945, when Secretary Byrnes accepted a deal concerning the "democratization" of the Rumanian government, "apparently not realizing the significance of what he was conceding." [26]

The weakness of the West in the matter of Poland was a result of the military situation in February 1945—or of its distorted evaluation by some of Roosevelt's top level advisers—but also of the secondary importance of the issue to the West while Stalin, voicing a traditional Russian view, looked upon it as a problem of a primary and vital nature.

In the last weeks of his life, President Roosevelt's attitude on the Polish issue stiffened considerably. He was dismayed by Stalin's unaccommodating attitude on the matter of forming a "new" Polish government. On April 1, 1945, he sent a message to Stalin in which he stated that "any . . . solution which would result in a thinly disguised continuation of the present government would be entirely unacceptable, and would cause our people to regard the Yalta agreement as a failure." The San Francisco conference was approaching and the President wanted to avoid anything that would influence adversely American public opinion, large segments of which were dubious about the prospects of building the peace together with Russia. The Polish

---

Teheran that they must accept the uncomfortable position of political dependence on the Soviet Union as though they were actually defeated in a war by Russia." Stettinius noted in *Roosevelt and the Russians* (Garden City, L. I.: Doubleday & Co., 1949) that on the way to Yalta Anthony Eden said that "to ask the Russians to give assurances . . . of *really* free elections in Poland, would be asking rather a lot."

[26] Sumner Welles, "What's the matter with our Foreign Policy?" *Saturday Evening Post* (March 31, 1951), p. 19. Early in 1952 President Truman stated that "at Potsdam we were by circumstances almost (*sic!*) forced to agree to Russian occupation of Eastern Poland and the occupation of that part of Germany east of the Oder river by Poland." Former Secretary of State Byrnes denied that. See "Byrnes Answers Truman," *Collier's* (April 26, 1952), p. 66.

issue was picked as a symbol of the feasibility of peacetime co-operation. In view of the strong military position of the Soviet armies and the determined attitude which Stalin had shown on the subject, it may have been ill-advised to choose as a test case an issue traditionally considered vital by Russia and admittedly viewed as secondary though "symbolic" by Western leaders.

This essential difference in the approach of East and West to the Polish problem was demonstrated in the talks which Harry Hopkins had with Stalin in May 1945. Dispatched to Moscow by President Truman, Hopkins stated that

the question of Poland *per se* was not so important as the fact that it had become a symbol of our ability to work out problems with the Soviet Union . . . We had no special interest in Poland and no special desire to see any particular kind of government . . . Poland had become a symbol in the sense that it bore a direct relation to the willingness of the United States to participate in international affairs . . . There were certain fundamental rights which, when impinged upon or denied, caused concern in the United States . . . Friends of international collaboration were wondering how it would be possible to work things out with the Soviet Union if we could not agree on the Polish question.

During another talk with Stalin, Hopkins, according to his own account, "made it clear again to Stalin that Poland was only a symbol . . ." While Hopkins no doubt presented the American case for Poland quite forcefully, there was inherent weakness in the attitude that Poland was "only a symbol."

Stalin, who had meanwhile made his stand clear by ordering the arrest of sixteen Polish leaders lured out of the Underground by an invitation to a conference in Moscow, was not looking upon the Polish problem as merely a symbol. Not entirely convinced of the good will of his Western Allies and especially suspicious of what he described as British "attempts to manage affairs in Poland," he was determined to settle matters in Poland entirely to his own satisfaction. Poland had been in the past

a corridor for German attacks on Russia . . .[27] Poland had been regarded as a part of the *cordon sanitaire* around the Soviet Union . . . Previous European policy had been that Polish governments must be

hostile to Russia . . . It is therefore in Russia's vital interest that
Poland should be strong and friendly.

In spite of his polite assurances that he "fully recognized the
right of the United States as a world power to participate in the
Polish question," Stalin made it quite clear that the negotiations
should be narrowed down to the problem of how many "other
Poles" should be included in the "reorganized" Polish government, in which the "Lublin" group was to retain a controlling
majority. After a series of strong public statements and diplomatic representations made by the American government during
the stalemate at the time of the San Francisco conference—its
successful opposition made the admission of the "Lublin" government to the founding conference of the United Nations impossible—the negotiations of the Moscow Commission consisting
of Mr. Molotov and the ambassadors of Great Britain and the
United States were nevertheless resumed and an agreement was
reached along the lines originally suggested by the Soviet side.
The "new" government of Poland was to be formed by a coalition in which the "Lublin" Poles would keep two-thirds of the
cabinet posts with the remainder going to Mikolajczyk's Peasant
Party and to Jan Stanczyk, a trade union leader who broke away
from the "London" government.

Why did the American government accept this arrangement
after spending months defending its own interpretation of the
Yalta agreement? A proper answer must again be sought outside the Polish issue. It was after V–E Day and the all-important
problem of defeated Germany, on which no specific agreements
had been reached in advance, made a new Big Three meeting
necessary. The Polish issue, while *per se* unimportant, had developed into an "intolerable headache" in relations with the
Soviet Union. And, last but not least, there was still the war
against Japan. Face-saving and leverage were provided by the
pledge that the new Polish government would hold "free and unfettered elections"; an additional alibi was the acceptance by
Mikolajczyk, a "reasonable Pole," of a cabinet post in the gov-

[27] As Arthur Bliss Lane pointed out in *I Saw Poland Betrayed,* Stalin's
words were an exact repetition of phrases used by Roosevelt in his report
to Congress on Yalta.

Yalta Stalin had agreed to the formula on "free and unfettered elections" but in his view it was not intended to be more than a face-saver for the West; any doubts on the subject were dispelled at Potsdam where Stalin—according to an account published by Philip Mosely of the American delegation—stated that he "could not afford" free elections in eastern Europe. Nevertheless, the American government undertook *démarches* and issued a number of diplomatic notes protesting against the manner in which the elections were being prepared and especially against the violence and restrictions applied to Mikolajczyk's party during the pre-election campaign. These protests could not possibly alter the situation; why then were they made? The London *Economist* at the time described analogous British efforts as "political demonstrations, condemned to ineffectiveness, in areas where Russia's legitimate interests are greater than ours." The West, having made what looked like a cold-blooded power-political deal with Stalin, was now recoiling from its consequences. Admittedly the protests accomplished "nothing positive," but, "they put on the official record the United States government's strong disapproval of the cynical disregard of international commitments by the Soviet Union," as Mr. Lane claimed. This is in itself an achievement if one considers the building up of such a record important. There is, however, always the danger that the record will have to be forgotten when the situation calls for a new rapprochement, as the case of Tito demonstrated so forcefully. Many Americans, conditioned to accept the record at face value, are understandably confused on such occasions; thrown off the high horse of principles, they tend to become too cynical.

The attitude of the American government during the period under scrutiny was not even uniformly and consistently "tough." While the American ambassador to Poland was assuming open championship of and identification with Mikolajczyk's cause—thus endangering United States prestige in the case of Mikolajczyk's failure—somewhere in Washington there were lingering hopes of weaning away the Polish regime from Russian influence by economic assistance. From his post in Warsaw the American ambassador was warning against the granting of credits to the Polish government, supporting his intervention with the opinions of "independent political leaders and businessmen" who had suggested that American refusal of assistance would be "appreciated as a mark of sympathy for the people's plight." Although the Poles were frustrated in their attempts to obtain a loan of half a billion dollars, they were nevertheless able to receive minor credits, for the price of agreement "in principle" to compensation for nationalized American property, which was for practical purposes rather meaningless. To Mr. Lane's despair, frozen Polish assets in this country were released by the State Department practically on the eve of the elections, even while the West's diplomatic offensive in regard to the elections was being stepped up. Immediately after the elections, which an official American statement condemned as not having fulfilled the provisions of the Yalta and Potsdam agreement, Arthur Bliss Lane, considering his mission a failure, asked to be relieved from his post as ambassador to Warsaw.[31]

As relations between the United States and Poland deteriorated, President Truman departed from custom at the ceremony of receiving the credentials of the new Polish ambassador to Washington, Winiewicz, by making a speech that, instead of the usual polite phrases, contained an expression of "deep concern . . . that the Polish Government has failed to fulfill that pledge (of free elections)." The President added that the United States will continue to be interested in "the welfare of the Polish people." His statement has set the pattern for official relations between the United States and Poland; their climate is a true reflection of the "cold war."

Minor irritations and profuse name-calling exhaust at present the tenor of official attitudes between the two countries. The *Voice of America* considered its mission to be to drive a wedge between the Polish people and their government, or between that government and the Soviet Union, or both, with little regard for the inconsistencies resulting from such an approach. All this is apparently to be accomplished by explaining to the Poles sev-

---

[31] Mr. Lane's successor, Stanton Griffis, in all seriousness suggested to some leading Polish communists that they mediate between the United States and the Soviet Union. It is difficult to imagine a more profound lack of understanding of Poland's subordinate status.

eral times a day things most of them know anyway. The "voice of Poland," echoing that of Moscow, is given to primitive vituperations against "Wall Street imperialism." Americans are blamed not only for supporting the revival of the wrong kind of Germany, but are also made responsible for occasional poor potato crops ("Colorado beetle") and the alleged spying activities of local Jehovah's Witnesses. Official propaganda works hard to superimpose in the minds of the Poles the image of the bloodthirsty American germ warfarer on the more traditional vision of a distant land of miraculous possibilities, peculiar in many respects, but somehow very human and generous, and certainly full of generous relatives, the source of welcome remittances.

VI. *America and the Future of Poland*

With respect to Poland and the Polish problem, the United States is bound to face all the difficulties which have beset relations between Poland and the West in the past. Unwilling to lean on one or another of their strong neighbors, because this would have meant acceptance of satellite status, the Poles have tried to perform a truly acrobatic act of keeping the balance between the two neighbors, a balance based not on true neutrality but rather on simultaneous hostility. Daring exploits by Polish leadership along these perilous lines were either based on the heroic assumption that where there is a will there is a way, on a naive and wishful reading of the facts of political life, or—most frequently—on the belief that Poland was essentially needed by distant Powers interested in keeping in check the growth of one or both of Poland's immediate neighbors. As early as the sixteenth century one of Poland's kings tried to enlist England in an effort to contain Muscovy. After the fall of Poland efforts to revive the defunct state were largely connected with the hope that this or that Power would recognize the need for some kind of Poland, but preferably a big Poland. In 1795, the year of the last Partition, a pamphlet appeared under the title *Remarks on the Connection between the Interests of Poland and the Political Interests of Other European Powers*. The arguments used in this little booklet by Waleryan Dzieduszycki have since served as the basis for similar pleas by authors and statesmen who may have never heard of its existence.

How did the West react to such pleas? The need for some kind of Poland was frequently recognized and on occasions advocated with zeal, but never pursued with sufficient determination and consistency as a matter of practical policy. Why? Because Poland may have appeared important, but rarely "that" important. It was unfortunate for Poland that what was for the

Poles a matter of life and death was never seen by the West as an item of the highest priority. Because of sheer distance and occasional other considerations, the West could never match its interest in Poland with that of Poland's immediate neighbors to whom it was a first-class issue. And it is well known that in diplomatic contests compromises can be achieved only at the price of subordinating secondary issues to vital ones. There is no objective test for what are and what are not national interests; the conclusions are reached by humans, who are, of course, fallible. On the record, Poland was never considered a first-rate issue by the West, in spite of appearances to the contrary. Poland has been at best, to borrow an excellent word from Arnold Wolfers, an object of "non-disinterestedness."

Western interest in the existence of an independent Poland has been formulated in various ways, but in essence it can be reduced to recognition of the fact that a Poland not dependent on its immediate neighbors could serve as a barrier to the expansion of a Power considered undesirable or uncomfortable by the West. Some past statements on the subject were formulated with admirable precision. In a memorandum to Napoleon, Duroc described the Poles as "the most useful auxiliaries in diminishing the power of Russia." In 1879 Lord Salisbury stated that "Poland was followed by the sympathies and exertions of liberal Europe for half a century, not for her own merits, but because she was a bulwark against the advance of a Power that was feared." In a similar vein Clemenceau, who had little love for the Poles, thought of them as a barrier against communism. The views of another westerner, Karl Marx, assigned Poland the role of a barrier a generation earlier. Marx saw in an independent Poland a barrier against the counterrevolutionary influence of tsarist Russia. In absolute terms, his views were identical with those of Clemenceau.[1]

[1] Marx and Engels tended to overrate the democratic aspects of the Polish national uprisings of the nineteenth century. On at least one occasion Engels expressed his very low esteem of the Poles. He described them in a letter to Marx, dated May 23, 1951, as a "nation fondue" to be used "als ein Mittel" until Russia should become revolutionary. After that, he wrote, an independent Poland would have "absolut keine raison d'etre mehr." This statement differed so much from the public utterances by Marx and Engels

The practical result of political efforts on behalf of Poland was no more impressive than that of flamboyant resolutions of helpless well-wishers, or what the German romantic writer Herwegh called the sympathetic despair of poets. Physical remoteness from Poland, a low priority in the hierarchy of commitments, and gnawing doubts concerning the actual possibilities of erecting or maintaining the barrier tended to limit the extent of Western exertions for Poland. If an independent Poland could be had somehow, this would be a welcome development. Beyond that it was considered unwise or impossible to go.

A very important obstacle was the recurrent shift in views concerning Russia. While the basic mistrust of a growing Russia never really disappeared, concrete situations called for a rapprochement with Russia. On such occasions Russian support and good will would be considered infinitely more valuable than anything Poland had to offer. Interest in Poland would then be subordinated, at times quite brutally, on other occasions with the accompaniment of soothing rationalizations, to the passing but urgent interest in Russian friendship. In essence, this pattern was followed by French diplomacy in the eighteenth century as well as by the representatives of the West during World War II. Teheran, Yalta, and Potsdam fall into this pattern. About French policy toward Poland in the second half of the eighteenth century it was said that "it suited the French cabinet to sacrifice Poland, but to sacrifice that unhappy country, since it could no longer be defended, noiselessly; and, so to speak, without making it or letting it cry." [2] This description is not wholly inapplicable to Western attitudes in our times.

But all this is the past, and while the past is interesting and in many ways instructive, it is the future that matters. Unless we believe in the tyranny of predetermined development, one must assume that the pattern, no matter how persistent, can conceiv-

---

on the Polish question that one student of the problem was prompted to ascribe it to an outbreak of ill temper on the part of Engels as a result of some exasperating contacts with Poles in exile. (Cf. N. Rjasanoff, "Karl Marx und Friedrich Engels ueber die Polenfrage," in *Archiv fuer die Geschichte des Sozialismus und der Arbeiterbewegung*, Leipzig, 1916, pp. 175–221.)

[2] The Duc de Broglie, *The King's Secret* (New York, 1879) , I, 248.

ably be broken by human action. What then is America's current Polish Problem? Is there still such a Problem in existence or has it become submerged in much larger issues? What can America do for the future of Poland?

Those most vocal on the subject advocate the "repudiation of Yalta," as if the agreement made there were more than a formalized recognition of a situation of fact, possibly an unnecessary recognition, but not one that made the facts. What would be the practical effect of such a repudiation? In the opinion of Arthur Bliss Lane this would prove that we have "reverted to the principles of international morality." How is this going to help Poland? Quite significantly, the most violent attacks on the recent past offer only the vaguest suggestions for the future. The following is picked at random from literally millions of words on the subject that can be found in the *Congressional Record:*

> We should immediately proclaim that the Yalta agreement no longer forms any part of our foreign policy and *pray* that the international situation will improve sufficiently so that the glorious nation of Poland will be freed from its present terrible fate . . . (Italics supplied.)

Most unfortunately, the combination of repudiation and prayers is not a substitute for a practical policy to be pursued by the most important World Power. The problem now is neither the repudiation of Yalta nor the legalistic harping on its violation by the Soviet Union. The issue, reduced to what matters, is: How does this country *now* view the fact of Soviet control over Poland? What is it going to do about it? Or—is it going to do anything about it?

The answer to the first question is quite easy. This country does not like the fact of exclusive Soviet control over Poland. Why? Simply because we would rather see Russia within her "legitimate" borders than witness the extension of her territorial and political domain into the heart of Europe.

What does this country propose to do about it? The Truman administration was more or less officially committed to the policy of containment which in essence amounted to holding the present line in the hope that Soviet power, frustrated in its expansionist ambitions, will begin to wither away, especially in areas outside the "legitimate" borders of Russia. Meanwhile the "captive" nations of eastern Europe are to be confirmed in the belief that they have not been forgotten. How? Presumably by the broadcasts of the official Voice of America and through other less official media. At the same time it was generally agreed that while the "captives" should be encouraged to implacable resistance, nothing should be done to provoke a premature uprising or acts of open rebellion against the local communist regimes or the Soviet Union, because liberation is not yet around the corner. This meant keeping the spirit of the Poles up while keeping their hopes down—an undertaking described by *The Economist* as "steering between the Scylla of enthusiasm and the Charybdis of despair."

Not everyone, of course, agrees that the Poles should be discouraged from trying to liberate themselves by their own efforts. Occasionally, a glib specialist in psychological warfare calls upon some eastern European nation to liberate itself, or suggests that American propaganda should take the line that no outside intervention is necessary to bring about the change. A militant Pole in exile had this to say in answer to such a suggestion:

Suppose that I am living in Warsaw. Suppose that I am a clerk. I have to be in my office at 8 A.M. and work among my fellow workers whose livelihood depends on these jobs. I can read only Communist papers. I have a son who is a member of the Communist Youth and for whom the state provides everything, while I can provide nothing. My wife works in a factory where political meetings are held daily . . . In our apartment block there are several official political officers and a number of unofficial ones. At night I have to attend political meetings also. Around 5 A.M. we have to stand in line to get our food. We see hardly anybody for fear of saying a word which could be interpreted as anti-Communist. We fear nights as one fears arrests. And only occasionally, with curtains drawn, we listen to the western radio. Suppose that I suddenly hear what Mr. Kellen suggests? It is up to me, I hear, to overthrow the regime. What can I do? . . .[3]

[3] Zygmunt Nagorski, Jr., in a letter to the editor, *The Reporter*, August 5, 1952. Professor D. W. Brogan, a sympathetic student of American affairs, concluded that some exhortations to resistance or revolt addressed to Poles and other eastern Europeans were aimed at causing the Russians discomfort and thus forcing them to relieve pressure in Korea and elsewhere in Asia. "The Poles are not even promised liberation; merely the satisfaction of

Here is, with tragic simplicity, an authentic Polish reaction to suggestions that the Poles "liberate themselves." Some Americans, who refuse to take into account the factors which under modern conditions permit an unpopular government to keep itself in power, conclude that since the Poles do not like the present setup, it cannot last and must be overthrown by the Poles themselves. This is a mistaken equation of latent dissatisfaction with the possibility to act on it. One of this country's leading specialists on psychological warfare has described such an attitude as a democratic fallacy. Inarticulate feelings of unorganized people are "either hidden and inconsequential or betrayed and disastrous to the dissenters." [4]

Whatever issues divide the Poles in exile, and they are many, there seems to be general agreement on this point: the people inside "captive" Poland should not attempt to overthrow their present regime. In a New Year's message to Poland, August Zaleski, who still clings to his position as President of a generally unrecognized government-in-exile, had this to say:

The order of the day for our compatriots in Poland is to refrain from arms. Their one task is to preserve the faith of their fathers and the Polish way of life. It is a difficult and hard task. It would be a crime to make this task still more trying by exhorting the people to an armed rising. Any action by them which may aim at organized sabotage and help (to) foreign intelligence services, can only multiply the futile sacrifices so often made by the best sons of Poland. (Quoted from *Free Poland Bulletin*, No. 7, London, March 1953, p. 3.)

The problem of the liberation of Poland is thus thrown back into our lap. And it is up to the United States to take one of several conceivable courses of action: Wait for the long-range effects of containment; engage in what has been described as "containment plus"; undertake positive action to roll back Russian power; or acquiesce, graciously or ungraciously, in the existing situation. To what extent does the advent of a new administration change the outlook for Poland? During the elec-

---

annoying the Russians and relieving the Americans." ("The Illusion of American Omnipotence," in *Harper's Magazine*, December 1952, p. 27.)

[4] Hans Speier, "International Political Communication: Elite vs. Mass," *World Politics* (April 1952).

toral campaign of 1952 the issue of the liberation of Poland and other eastern European countries for a while achieved considerable prominence, when statements by General Eisenhower and by John Foster Dulles were interpreted by leading Democratic spokesmen as exhortation to the peoples of eastern Europe to stage hopeless uprisings or as advocating the involvement of the United States and western Europe in a war for the liberation of the "satellites." The Republican side hastened to correct this impression by stressing that the restoration to the captive nations of Europe (and Asia) of their independence was to be achieved by peaceful means. These statements were addressed not only to the American voters but also to European public opinion where considerable uneasiness had developed as a result of what was cynically seen as "Mr. Dulles' readiness to use the threat of the hydrogen bomb in order to get votes in Hamtramck, Michigan." Of course, if the issue were limited only to campaign promises, there would be no reason to worry unduly about what was going to happen after the elections. In the words of a scholar actively associated with the Stevenson campaign: "Our allies should be relieved to know that there is no reason to suppose that Mr. Dulles always believes what he says." [5]

The student of the problem cannot prescribe any one course of action nor even predict which way the United States will move. To base such predictions on mere logic would be most misleading in view of the way democracies operate. One can only analyze the implications of certain current American attitudes and register some significant Polish reactions to such attitudes. On closer examination, the difference between the policies of containment and liberation "by peaceful means" is not very substantial, even if it is not, as Arthur Schlesinger, Jr. put it, "phony." Both policies express unwillingness to recognize the present situation combined with determination not to do anything drastic to bring about a change. The advocates of containment, burdened with the responsibility of office, had to be more discreet about the means short of war which they were planning to employ or were actually employing; their critics capitalized on the psychologically annoying implications of

[5] Arthur Schlesinger, Jr. in *New York Post*, November 30, 1952.

what appeared to be a static and not sufficiently bold policy.

Before the issue flared up in the elections of 1952, the idea of watchful containment, combined with aggressive psychological warfare ("containment plus") and based on the hope of a reasonable settlement once Soviet power has become sufficiently frustrated, appeared quite attractive to many Americans, but was understandably repugnant to groups connected with eastern European liberation movements. They believe that time is running short behind the Iron Curtain, that it is the will to resist that is being exposed to frustration rather than Soviet power in the area, that the younger generation in particular is being subjected to potent indoctrination or "erosion of the soul" to a point that may make it unreceptive to ideas coming from the West. On January 22, 1951 the *New York Times* made an incidental editorial comment to the effect that "no one in authority, for example, is planning a war to make Russia take her hands off Poland or Czechoslovakia or liberate the Baltic states. The most democracy can do at this stage of history is *to hold the ground it now occupies.*" (Italics supplied.) To many Americans this might have sounded reasonable enough, but to the Polish American Congress (which on occasions describes itself as the authorized spokesman for millions of Polish Americans) this was the expression of a "tragic policy" based on "subscribing to the crimes of the past and building the future on such foundations." There was, in the opinion of some militant Polish groups, the ever-present threat of a "deal" with the Soviet Union that would be made once more at the expense of Poland and other eastern European countries. The very idea of a "reasonable settlement," sound as it may appear to be from an American point of view, is repugnant to many Poles. In fact they consider a settlement impossible short of another "surrender" or "betrayal." The policy of containment was on one occasion branded by a frustrated political exile—incidentally, not a Pole—as "Machiavellian Liberalism." [6]

Does the change of administration in Washington put an end to the fear of a "deal"? General Eisenhower has stated in a

[6] Bogdan Raditsa, "Beyond Containment to Liberation," *Commentary* (September 1951).

campaign speech that the conscience of America can never rest
at ease until the captive nations had been restored to their
freedom; but former President Truman made similar statements and his administration made it clear that one of the
preconditions for a "reasonable settlement" would be the withdrawal of the Soviet Union from eastern Europe. Are such statements an indication of a precise course of action or, as has been
explained by some commentators, merely the kind of uplifting
affirmation of noble intentions which Americans in high office
believe they have to make? It would be rash to assume that a
basic identity of concrete political aims has finally been established between the United States and Poland, that identity which
generations of Poles have in vain hoped to see accepted by the
West.

Americans may be surprised to find that among various shades
of Polish political opinion in exile there is represented also a
"neutralist" tendency. This "neutralist" view is held not only
by those who believe that America will undertake nothing
against the present territorial extent of Soviet power, but also
by some of those who assume that sooner or later this country
will go to war against the Soviet Union. This brings to the
surface another problem that has weighed heavily on relations
between Poland and the West. Whenever Western thought
veered around to an anti-Russian attitude, it would become pro-
German—or at least, appear so to Poles.

Polish thought in exile may not be too important, but with
the Poles in Poland unable to express their feelings, one must
look upon the exiles as more or less authentic spokesmen. Some
Polish groups cling to the shibboleth of "legality" and insist on
the restitution of official status to the Polish government-in-exile
which continues to lead a shadow existence in a totally unrealistic setting. There are others who hopefully interpret American policies as a sign of awakening to the dangers of communism, an awakening that cannot fail to turn in favor of the
kind of Poland they would like to see re-established. These hopes
are based on the assumption that, as American military strength
grows and integration of western Europe progresses, this country
will pass to a more active policy of reducing the present sphere

of Soviet control in Europe. They hope that the Europe re-established under American auspices will not end on the Oder or on the Bug (the famous Curzon Line, which so many Americans and Mr. Churchill still consider a "good" line).

Those Poles who are most sanguine in their interpretation of current and future American policies argue that the intervention of the United States in European affairs will finally put an end to the tragic dilemma of Poland and to the limitations of Western policies which moved between "betrayal" in favor of Russia and "betrayal" in favor of Germany. It is argued that by submerging—or diluting—the delicate issue of Polish-German relations in the broader issue of a United Europe, it is possible to eliminate the old dilemma. In other words, there simply is not going to be any Polish-German issue in the new and better Europe which will be established under American guidance once Russia is defeated or rolled back. True, "in a united Europe there will be no room for a fully independent Polish foreign policy, nor for a specifically Polish defense policy nor for a balanced Polish account of international payments," [7] but the same would presumably apply to the Germans, too, who after accepting the "European" solution would find other things to do than to quibble with Poland over frontier lines. Meanwhile, "Whoever fights Moscow is our ally . . . whether or not he is prepared to guarantee our frontiers on the Oder-Neisse." [8]

Yet such views are not necessarily shared by all Poles. In answer to the cited declaration of confidence in American aims, the writer Jan Winczakiewicz expressed the opinion that "the Americans will quickly give up their ambitions to organize the world and the Germans will again reach for the Western lands. Russia, meanwhile, will refuse to give up Lwow and Wilno . . . A few years later Warsaw, too, will become the victim of our neighbors' appetites, and America won't even budge . . ." [9] Suggestions from some Polish quarters calling for a revived Polish army in exile were met with statements to the effect that "if a revived Polish army should in the future become an embarrassing

[7] J. Mieroszewski, in *Kultura*, Paris, March 1951.
[8] *Ibid.*
[9] *Wiadomosci Polskie*, London, No. 16 (264), 1951.

'asset' in the hands of the Allies, the Anglosaxons will put the 'asset' into a new Szczypiorno." Szczypiorno was the name of the internment camp to which the Austrians sent Pilsudski's legionnaires during World War I when they refused a loyalty oath. One former Polish officer wrote: "We have filled enough Katyn graves in trying to build a rampart of Christianity with our cracked skulls." The author of the original suggestion for recreating the Polish army as part of the European army (no one has, as yet, invited the Poles) revealed that no less than 40 per cent of those who reacted with letters to his suggestion expressed the view that the Poles should not participate at all in the "forthcoming conflict," and many of the remaining 60 per cent put forward all kinds of conditions or reservations. Some doubts were expressed in the political wisdom of America or in the ability of this country to solve "effectively" the Russian problem which, from the point of view of many Poles, means the creation of a Russia shorn of her border possessions and conveniently separated from Poland by an independent Ukraine, an independent Byelorussia, and independent Baltic states.

The cited views, though not necessarily representative of the opinions of the majority, either in Poland or abroad, reflect traditional distrust of the West strengthened by the "betrayal" of World War II. To what extent are these voices unreasonable expressions of despair? To what extent do they register awareness of the limitations of America's Polish Problem? This brings us back to the original question: To what extent is the "liberation of Poland" part of America's current policy, an object, that is, not of good wishes but of determination to act? It may be argued that our definition of foreign policy is too narrow; there are, it will be said, certain objectives which a country is ready to pursue though not to the point of going to war. Such objectives are not "vital interests." They are merely desirable items in the "shopping list" of foreign policy aims. On the other hand, there is no reason to believe that the traditional Russian position on Poland has undergone a miraculous change. Many interesting and surprising things have happened in the Soviet Union since Stalin's death, but nothing seems to indicate that his successors look upon Poland as a less vital issue in Russia's diplomacy than Stalin did.

The persistent nature of the problem was illustrated in a remark once made by Professor Waldemar Gurian to the effect that the emergence of "a Christian Russian government" would make the problem of Poland only more complicated for the West. Until something truly sensational happens behind the Kremlin walls, it is still safe to assume that the Soviet Union is unlikely to relinquish control over Poland unless defeated in war. It is true that this country has listed the evacuation by the Soviet Union of the satellite countries as a precondition for settlement. Should America be in a position to force Russia's withdrawal from Poland, it would then, as Max Beloff has pointed out, be able to do "much more." Short of that, one must be prepared to view Poland as the position which the Soviet Union is the least likely to abandon. Unhappy Poles in exile and some, although not too many, Poles in Poland, may be praying in the words of the romantic poet Adam Mickiewicz for a "war of the nations" as the only way to liberation. But war is apparently not accepted by Americans as either inevitable or necessary. A favorable position for negotiating with the Soviet Union, it is hoped, can be established short of war; but negotiating means inevitably bargaining, and on the issue of Poland the bargaining position of Russia is infinitely stronger than that of the United States. Not because Russia's position is morally superior but because Poland is a vital Russian interest and only incidentally or secondarily an object of American interests, unless, of course, this country should submit to what George F. Kennan calls "the tyranny of grandiose, unrealistic or even meaningless phrases."

The storm caused by some recent scholarly attempts to introduce precision into the formulation of American foreign policy aims is in itself no indication that Americans reject realism; they merely reject realistic terminology. The habit of making pronouncements broader in scope than the action contemplated dies slowly. However, it is safe to predict that as America's international importance grows we will witness a seemingly paradoxical yet probably inevitable development: a tendency toward greater caution in the formulation of American aims, a certain parsimony in subscribing to causes, a growing judiciousness in making commitments. This is understandably shocking to sensitive exiles as a manifestation of "Machiavellian liberalism" because it reveals the truth that American foreign policy aims are not automatically identical with or unconditionally benevolent to their own goals.

Poland may derivatively profit or suffer from American policies. Poland may yet be free again as we choose to understand the term, but by no means necessarily so. On many occasions in the past the Poles have been told by their allies that they must make sacrifices for the sake of European or world peace. The Poles do not see it that way, and they have never quite succeeded in converting their allies fully to the Polish point of view.

We have narrowed down the choices before the United States to containment, aggressive revindication of eastern Europe, or abandonment of the area to its present fate. To the operating diplomat the problem does not necessarily present itself in the same either-or terms. A high official of the Department of State said in a 1952 debate on the future of eastern Europe that in the conduct of diplomacy it is at times necessary to "turn on the bright light of obscurity" on certain matters. He spoke of the valuable technique of "fuzzing up" things and avoiding what he called —without contempt, I hope—classroom logic. This may well be the case. But if a mere student of the problem may be permitted to offer some advice, he would suggest that in the case of the Poles no great enthusiasm be expected for the subtle game of fuzziness. At the same time maximum care should be taken not to raise hopes that cannot be fulfilled. Any other course of action will only hasten the day when the resources of Polish attachment to the West, lavishly drawn upon for centuries, will become completely exhausted.

INDEX

Agrarian reform. *See* Collectivization, Land reform, Peasants
Agriculture, production, 102, 237
Alexis, Tsar, 37; Alexander I, 49, 51; Alexander II, 59
Allied Supreme Council (World War I), 117, 121, 127
Alter, Wiktor, 292
American-Polish relations. *See* United States
America and the New Poland, 277 n.
Anders, Wladyslaw, 163, 175, 188, 189, 192–194, 289
Andrussov, treaty of, 37
Anti-Semitism, 82, 90, 92, 276; *see also* Jews
Arciszewski, Tomasz, 193
AK, *Armia Krajowa. See* Underground
Army, 72, 93–94, 108–110, 153; organized in USSR, 289; under command of Rokossowski, 215; call for revival in exile, 323; *see also* Anders, Berling, Underground
Arts and sciences, 229–230
Askenazy, Szymon, quoted, 129
Atlantic Charter, 290
Augustus (The Strong) of Saxony, King, 39
Augustus III of Saxony, King, 40
Austria, 38, 39, 42, 43, 47, 49, 73–74; *see also* Central Powers, Habsburgs
Austrian orientation, 64, 71
Austrian Poland, 15, 52

Back Door to War, 142, 150
Bailey, Thomas A., quoted 11, 267 n.
Bakhmeteff, Boris, 275
Balance, Polish policy of, 132, 139, 148, 150, 314

Balance of power, 46, 123, 138
Baltic Sea, 16, 17, 21, 24, 30; Polish interest in area, 140, 324
Banks, nationalization of, 234
Bar, Confederation of, 42, 257
Barrier race, 50
Barthou, Jean-Louis, 130
Battle of Britain, Poles in, 183
BBWR. *See* Non-partisan Bloc
Bakunin, Mikhail A., 60
Balfour, Arthur James, 264–265
Batory. *See* Stefan Batory
Beck, Jozef, 92, 125, 131, 132 ff., 139, 145, 146–151, 217, 287
Belgium, 53, 54
Beloff, Max, 325
Benes, Edvard, 141, 270, 298
Berle, Adolf A., Jr., 290
Berling, Zygmunt, 175, 183, 189; Berling army, 183, 189
Berman, Jakub, 215, 254
Beseler, Hans Hartwig von, 73
Betts, R. R., quoted, 232 n.
Biddle, Anthony Drexel, 142, 298
Bierut, Boleslaw, 190, 191, 215, 235, 246–247, 254, 301
Big Three, 294, 295, 306; *see also* Potsdam, Teheran, Yalta
Bismarck, Otto von, 48, 59, 148
Bobrzynski, Michal, 19, 45, 80
Bochenski, Aleksander, 223
Bohemia, 20, 22, 27
Boleslaw the Brave, 19
Bolsheviks, 74, 117, 118, 123, 270, 276
Bona, Queen, 28
Bor-Komorowski, Tadeusz, 167, 172, 173–178, 184
Brest-Litovsk, treaty of, 74
Brest, Union of, 35; *see also* Uniate Church
Briand, Aristide, 4